PASCAL

Problem Solving and Program Design

THIRD EDITION

518.5

PASCAL

Problem Solving and Program Design

ADDISON-WESLEY PUBLISHING COMPANY
Reading, Massachusetts   Menlo Park, California   New York
Don Mills, Ontario   Wokingham, England   Amsterdam   Bonn
Sydney   Singapore   Tokyo   Madrid   San Juan

3RD EDITION

ELLIOT B. KOFFMAN

Temple University

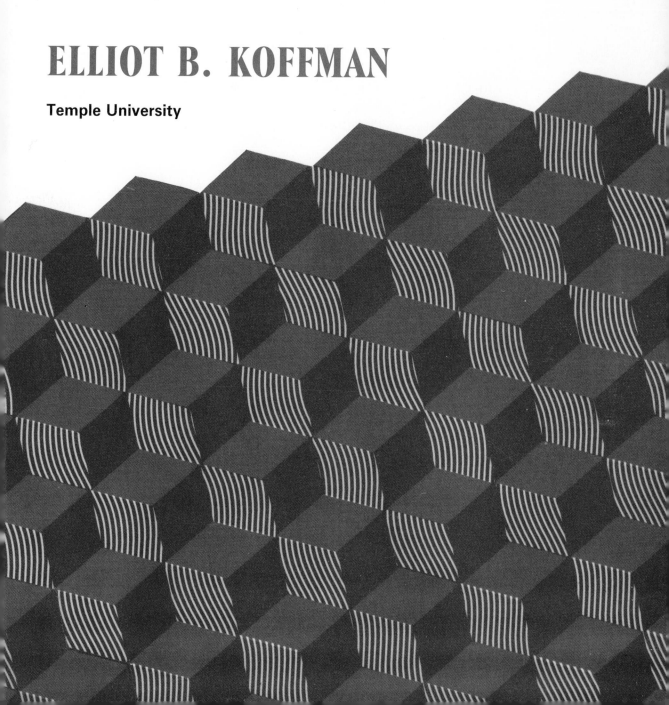

Keith Wollman, Sponsoring Editor
Bette J. Aaronson, Production Supervisor
Nancy Benjamin, Production Editor
Joyce Cameron Weston, Text Design
Hugh Crawford, Manufacturing Supervisor
Marshall Henrichs, Cover Design

Library of Congress Cataloging-in-Publication Data

Koffman, Elliot B.
  Pascal : problem solving and program design / by Elliot B.
Koffman.
    p. cm
  Rev. ed. of: Problem solving and structured programming in
Pascal.
2nd ed. ©1985.
  Includes index.
  ISBN 0-201-11834-3
  1. Pascal (Computer program language) I. Koffman, Elliot B.
Problem solving and structured programming in Pascal. II. Title.
QA76.73.P2K624 1989
005.13'3—dc19   88-13085
                                               CIP

Reprinted with corrections May, 1989

CDEFGHIJ-MU-89

To those who have filled my life with love—

My wife, Caryn; my children, Richard, Deborah, and Robin; my father, Edward; and my mother-in-law, Enid Jackson

In loving memory of my mother, Leah, and my father-in-law, Mitchell Jackson

Preface

I have been very fortunate in that previous editions of this book have consistently been among the top two or three textbooks used in the introductory programming course in Pascal. These books were successful because they filled a need of computer science educators. When the first edition was published in 1981, there were few textbooks available on Pascal. At that time, computer science faculty looked forward with great anticipation to the arrival of each new textbook on programming in Pascal. (Obviously, that is not the case today!) I believe the success of the first edition was due to its sound pedagogy and the abundance and variety of examples it provided.

While working on the second edition, I served as chairman of a Task Force sponsored by the ACM Curriculum Committee, whose purpose was to update the curricula for CS1 [1] and CS2 [2]. The second edition of this book, published in 1985, was the first book that followed the recommendations and philosophy expressed in the Task Force's final report for course CS1. The most significant difference between the second edition and its predecessor was the early introduction of procedures and the emphasis on procedural abstraction right from the start.

Prior to my starting this revision, Addison-Wesley's market research department contacted many loyal users of the previous editions to find out what they wanted to see in a new edition. Also around that time, the new ACM Curriculum Committee began to report on their work to define a computer science core and to develop an introductory course sequence in computer science with a programming course as a prerequisite [3]. The feedback I received from users of previous editions was that they wanted to retain the early introduction to procedures, but they also wanted to introduce the important concepts of software engineering and data abstraction in their initial programming course. Like the ACM Curriculum Committee, they wanted to see more

---

1. Koffman, E., Miller, P., and Wardle, C., Recommended Curriculum for CS1, Communications of the ACM 27, 10 (Oct. 1984), 998-1001.

2. Koffman, E., Stemple D., and Wardle, C., Recommended Curriculum for CS2, Communications of the ACM 28, 8 (Aug. 1985), 815-818.

3. Denning, P.J. et al, Draft Report of the ACM Task Force on the Core of Computer Science (Feb. 1988).

emphasis on theoretical aspects of computer science. They also wanted additional coverage of CS2 topics. Finally, they wanted all this packaged in smaller, more digestible chapters.

My goal for this revision was to accomplish all these objectives so that the new edition would continue to meet the changing needs of computer science faculty. This book can be used as a text for both CS1 and CS2, or for the prerequisite course to the introductory sequence in computer science proposed by the ACM Curriculum Committee.

Procedures

Like its predecessor, this edition provides an early introduction to the use of procedures. Procedures without parameters are introduced in Chapter 3 as a problem-solving tool to facilitate writing modular programs. This chapter shows how to utilize procedures to display messages and instructions to program users. In this way, students become familiar with procedures without the burden of passing parameters and without picking up bad habits such as referencing global variables from within a procedure.

Procedure parameters are introduced in Chapter 6. This material has been extensively revised and simplified. Value parameters are now introduced first, followed by variable parameters.

Software Engineering

As recommended by the ACM Task Force reports [1, 2], this edition introduces students to the fundamentals of software engineering as they begin their formal study of programming. The change in title from *Problem Solving and Structured Programming in Pascal* to *Pascal: Problem Solving and Program Design* reflects the increased emphasis on software engineering.

There is a new chapter on Programming in the Large (Chapter 8), which introduces the software life cycle. The important concepts of data abstraction and abstract data types are introduced in this chapter and carried throughout the rest of the book. We introduce enumerated types in this chapter and implement an abstract data type for days of the week.

The important software engineering topics of program style, documentation, and verification also receive increased emphasis. Loop invariants and assertions are introduced as a tool for documenting and designing loops in Chapter 5 and preconditions and postconditions are used to document procedures starting in Chapter 6.

Organization

Another major goal of this edition was to make the material in the book more accessible to a variety of students. To this end, we made a number of important changes. We reorganized the material so that each chapter would be shorter and introduce fewer new concepts. As an example of this, there are now separate chapters on the if statement (Chapter 4), on while loops (Chapter 5), and on procedure parameters (Chapter 6). In the previous edition, these topics were covered in a single chapter on control structures.

Another organizational change was to introduce the basics of text files earlier than before. Text files are first introduced in an optional section in Chapter 2 so that students' programs can read data files prepared by their instructors. This material is reviewed in Chapter 8, which discusses the use of text files for input/output in larger programs. Finally, complete coverage of binary files, including a discussion of direct access files, appears in Chapter 14.

Pedagogical Features

To facilitate our goal of making the book more useful as a learning tool, we also added several new pedagogical features which are discussed below.

End of Section Exercises: Following most sections there are two kinds of exercises, self-check and programming. The answers to selected self-check exercises appear at the end of the book; the answers to the programming exercises are provided in the instructor's manual.

End of Chapter Exercises: Each chapter ends with a set of quick-check exercises with answers. There are also chapter review exercises and a set of programming projects whose solutions appear in the instructor's manual.

Examples and Case Studies: The book contains a large number and variety of programming examples. Whenever possible, examples contain small, complete programs or procedures rather than incomplete program fragments. There are also substantial case studies that help a student integrate and apply concepts studied over several chapters.

Syntax Display Boxes: The syntax display boxes describe the syntax and semantics of each new Pascal feature. The syntax displays in this edition include examples.

Program Style Displays: The program style displays discuss issues of good programming style.

Error Discussions and Chapter Review: Each chapter ends with a section that discusses common programming errors and a review section that includes a table of new Pascal constructs.

CS2 Coverage

The coverage of advanced topics has been expanded to include most of the recommended topics in the ACM Task Force's final report for course CS2. The inclusion of these CS2 topics provides added flexibility for instructors who wish to cover advanced material in CS1. It also allows the book to be used either as a reference by students going onto CS2 or as the primary textbook for CS2 in some courses. CS2 topics covered include:

sets and strings (Chapter 13)
files (Chapter 14)
recursion (Chapter 15)
stacks and queues (Chapter 16)
pointers and linked lists (Chapter 17)
trees (Chapter 18)
searching and sorting (Chapter 19)
analysis of algorithms (Chapters 18 and 19)

Appendices and Supplements

There are separate appendices which cover Pascal language elements, syntax diagrams, character codes, error messages, and additional Pascal features not described in the main body of the book.

A new computerized test bank is available for this edition. Other supplements include an instructor's manual, transparency masters, and a program disk with all the programs that appear in the book. Use the reference numbers below to order these supplements from your Addison-Wesley sales representative.

Computerized Test Bank: 0-201-19477-5
Instructor's Manual: 0-201-18396-X
Transparency Masters: 0-201-18397-8
Program Disk: 0-201-18398-6

I am very grateful to Keith Pierce at the University of Minnesota for his work on producing the instructor's manual.

Acknowledgments

Many people participated in the development of this book. The principal reviewers were most essential in suggesting improvements and finding errors. They include: Robert B. Anderson, University of Houston; Robert Christiansen, University of Iowa; Denis Conrady, North Texas State University; Donald H. Cooley, Utah State University; Ed Deaton, San Diego State University; Paul L. Emerick, De Anza College; Dale Grosvenor, Iowa State University of Science and Technology; Bill Kraynek, Florida International University; Cary Laxer, Rose-Hulman Institute of Technology; Larry Neal, East Tennessee State University; Jacquelyn W. Palmer, Wright State University; Theresa M. Phinney, Texas A & M University; Keith Pierce, University of Minnesota; Howard D. Pyron, University of Missouri; Dennis E. Ray, Old Dominion University; Winifred J. Rex, Bowling Green State University; Gordon E. Stokes, Brigham Young University; Nai-Kuan Tsao, Wayne State University; R. Kenneth Walter, Weber State College.

When we were planning this revision, a group of experienced teachers provided their comments and suggestions for changes to a proposed table of contents in a series of focus group meetings. The faculty who contributed in this way included: John Buck, Indiana University, Bloomington; Philip East,

University of Northern Iowa; Donald Greenwell, Eastern Kentucky University; William J. Joel, Marist College; Larry Kotman, Grand Valley State College; Masoud Milani, Florida International University; Scott Owen, Georgia State University; Terry Seethoff, Northern Michigan University; and Dawn Wilkins, Illinois College.

We are also grateful to the hundreds of teachers who participated in telephone interviews or completed course surveys organized by Addison-Wesley's market research department. The information this research provided helped to shape the book's organization and pedagogy.

I would also like to acknowledge the contribution of Armando Picciotto, who wrote an excellent instructor's manual for high school teachers based on the second edition of this book. Several examples and exercises from this manual appear in the book.

The personnel at Addison-Wesley responsible for the production of this book worked diligently to meet a very demanding schedule. My editor, Keith Wollman, was closely involved in all phases of this project, starting with the initial market research. He did an excellent job of coordinating the writing and reviewing process and trying to keep me on schedule. He was also a very valuable sounding board in helping me to resolve questions raised by the reviewers. Debbie Lafferty, his assistant, was very effective in contacting reviewers and keeping the review process on schedule. Darlene Bordwell, the developmental editor, helped to improve the clarity of the presentation. Bette Aaronson supervised the design and production of the book, while Nancy Benjamin coordinated the conversion of the manuscript to a finished book.

Finally, I would like to thank a senior computer science student at Temple University, Alison Mosley, who did an excellent job of entering, editing, and testing all of the programs in the book. Alison also helped with the solutions to review questions and self-check exercises and made many valuable suggestions for improvements. I would also like to acknowledge the support given me by Temple University, as much of the book was written while I was on study leave from Temple.

Philadelphia, PA   E.B.K

Brief Contents

Contents

Introduction to Computers and Programming

1

From the 1940s until today—a period of only 50 years—the computer's development has spurred the growth of technology into realms only dreamed of at the turn of the century. It has also changed the way we live and how we do business. Today, we depend on computers to process our paychecks, send rockets into space, build cars and machines of all types, and help us do our shopping and banking. The computer program's role in this technology is essential; without a list of instructions to follow, the computer is virtually useless. Programming languages allow us to write those programs, and thus to communicate with computers.

You are about to begin the study of computer science using one of the most versatile programming languages available today: the Pascal language. This chapter introduces you to the computer and its components and to the major categories of programming languages.

1.1 Electronic Computers Then and Now

Computers were not always so pervasive in our society. Just a short time ago, computers were fairly mysterious devices that only a small percentage of the population knew much about. Computer know-how spread when advances in *solid-state electronics* led to cuts in the size and the cost of electronic computers. In the mid-1970s, a computer with the computational power of one of today's personal computers would have filled a nine-by-twelve-foot room and cost $100,000. Today, an equivalent personal computer (see Fig. 1.1) costs less than $3,000 and sits on a desktop.

If we take the literal definition for *computer* as "a device for counting or computing," then we could consider the abacus to be the first computer. The first electronic digital computer was designed in the late 1930s by Dr. John Atanasoff at Iowa State University. Atanasoff designed his computer to perform mathematical computations for graduate students.

The first large-scale, general-purpose electronic digital computer, called the ENIAC, was built in 1946 at the University of Pennsylvania. Its design was funded by the U.S. Army, and it was used to compute ballistics tables, predict the weather, and make atomic energy calculations. The ENIAC weighed 30 tons and occupied a thirty-by-fifty-foot space (see Fig. 1.2).

Although we are often led to believe otherwise, computers cannot reason as we do. Basically, computers are devices that perform computations at incredible speeds (more than one million operations per second) and with great accuracy. However, to accomplish anything useful, a computer must be *programmed*, that is, given a sequence of explicit instructions (a *program*) to perform.

To program the ENIAC, engineers had to connect hundreds of wires and arrange thousands of switches in a certain way. In 1946, Dr. John von Neumann, of Princeton University, proposed the concept of a *stored-program computer*: a program stored in computer memory rather than set by wires and switches. Von Neumann knew programmers could easily change the contents of computer memory, so he reasoned that the stored-program concept would greatly simplify

Figure 1.1 IBM Personal Computer

reprogramming the ENIAC. Von Neumann's design was a success and is the basis of the digital computer as we know it today.

 # 1.2   Components of a Computer

Despite large variations in cost, size, and capabilities, modern computers are remarkably similar to each other in a number of ways. Basically, a computer consists of the five components shown in Fig. 1.3: an *input device*, an *output device*, a *secondary storage device*, *memory*, and a *central processor unit (CPU)* (the arrows connecting the components show the direction of information flow). These computer components are called the *hardware*.

Most of you have seen or used a personal computer. The memory, the CPU, and the secondary storage devices are usually housed in a single cabinet. The input device is a keyboard, and the output device is a television-like monitor. These components and their interaction are described in more detail in the following sections.

Figure 1.2 The ENIAC Computer (Photo courtesy of Unisys Corporation)

Computer Memory

A computer's main memory (also called primary or core memory) stores information of all types: instructions, numbers, names, lists, even pictures. Picture a computer's memory as an ordered sequence of storage locations called *memory cells*. To be able to store and then *retrieve*, or access, information, we must have some way to identify the individual memory cells. Each memory cell has a unique *address* associated with it. The address indicates the cell's relative position in memory. The sample computer memory in Fig. 1.4 consists of 1,000 memory cells, with addresses 0 through 999. (Some large-scale computers have memories that consist of millions of individual cells.)

The information stored in a memory cell is called its *contents*. Every memory cell always contains some information, although we may have no idea what that information is. Whenever new information is placed in a memory cell, any information already there is destroyed and cannot be retrieved. In Fig. 1.4, the contents of memory cell 3 is the number -26, and the contents of memory cell 4 is the letter H.

The memory cells shown in Fig. 1.4 are actually aggregates, or collections, of smaller units called *bytes*. A byte is the amount of storage required to store a single character. The number of bytes in a memory cell varies from computer to computer. A byte is an aggregate of even smaller units of storage called *bits*, which are single binary digits (0 or 1). There are generally eight bits to a byte.

To store a value, the computer sets each bit of a selected memory cell to 0 or 1, thereby destroying what was previously in that bit. Each value is repre-

Figure 1.3 Components of a Computer

5

1.2 Components of a
Computer

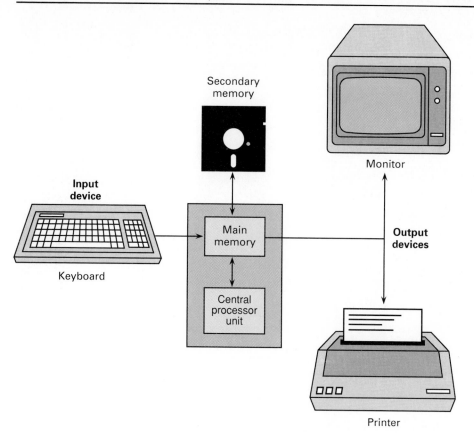

sented by a particular pattern of zeroes and ones. To retrieve a value from a memory cell, the computer copies the pattern of zeroes and ones stored in that cell to another storage area, the *memory buffer register*, where the bit pattern can be processed. The copy operation does not destroy the bit pattern currently in the memory cell.

The process just described is the same regardless of the kind of information—character, number, or program instruction—stored in a memory cell.

Central Processor Unit

The *central processor unit* (CPU) performs the actual processing and manipulation of information stored in memory. The CPU also retrieves information from memory. This information can be data or instructions for manipulating data. The CPU can also store the results of those manipulations back in memory for later use.

The *control unit* within the CPU coordinates all activities of the computer by determining which operations should be carried out and in what order. The

Figure 1.4 A Computer Memory with 1,000 Cells

control unit then transmits coordinating control signals to the computer components.

Also found within the CPU are the *arithmetic-logic unit* (ALU) and special storage locations called *registers*. The ALU consists of electronic circuitry to perform arithmetic operations (that is, addition, subtraction, multiplication, and division) and to make comparisons. The control unit copies the next program instruction from memory into the instruction register in the CPU. The ALU then performs the operation specified by the next instruction on data that are copied from memory into registers, and the computational results are copied to memory. The ALU can perform each arithmetic operation in about a millionth of a second. The ALU can also compare data stored in its registers (for example, Which value is larger? Are the values equal?); the operations that are performed next depend on the comparison results.

Input and Output Devices

Input and output (I/O) devices enable us to communicate with the computer. Specifically, I/O devices provide us with the means to enter data for a computation and to observe the results of that computation.

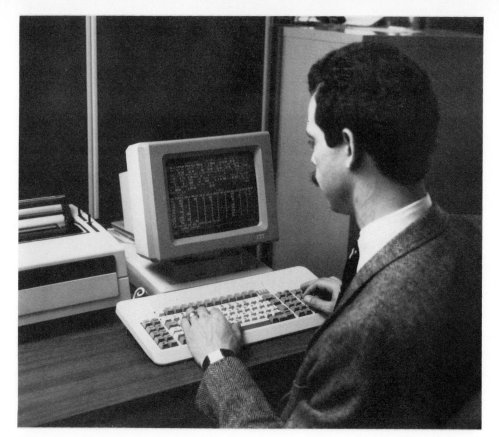

Figure 1.5 A Computer Terminal

Many of you will be using a *computer terminal* (see Fig. 1.5) as both an input and an output device. A terminal consists of a *keyboard* (used for entering information) and a *monitor* (used for displaying information). A terminal keyboard is similar to a typewriter keyboard except that it has some extra keys for special functions. A monitor is similar to a television screen. If you are using a personal computer, the keyboard and the monitor may be separate devices connected to the computer by cables or they may be built into the computer.

Some terminals are equipped with *graphics capability* (see Fig. 1.6), which enables the output to be displayed as a two-dimensional graph or picture. The user can communicate with some computers by using an input device called a *mouse* to move an electronic pointer.

The only problem with using a monitor as an output device is that it leaves no written record of the computation. Once the image disappears from the monitor screen, it is lost. If you want *hard-copy output*, you have to send your computational results to an output device called a *printer* (see Fig. 1.7) or use a hard-copy terminal.

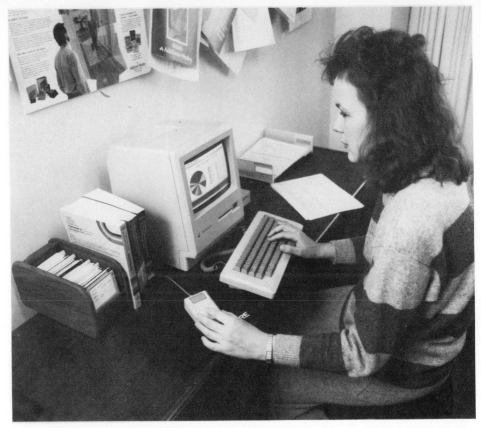

Figure 1.6 Macintosh Computer with Mouse

Secondary Storage

Most computers have only a limited amount of main memory. Consequently, *secondary storage* provides additional data storage capability on most computer systems. For example, a *disk drive*, which stores data on a disk, is a common secondary storage device for today's personal computers (Fig. 1.8).

There are two kinds of disks: *hard disks* and *floppy disks*, and a computer may have one or more drives of each kind. A hard disk normally cannot be removed from its drive, so the storage area on a hard disk is often shared by all the users of a computer. However, each computer user may have his or her own floppy disks that can be inserted into a disk drive as needed. Hard disks can store much more data than can floppy disks and operate much more quickly, but they are also much more expensive.

Information stored on a disk is organized into aggregates called *files*. The data for a program can be stored in a *data file* beforehand rather than being entered at the keyboard while the program is executing. Results generated by the computer can be saved as *output files* on disk. Most of the programs that you write will be saved as *program files* on disk.

Figure 1.7 Printer

Comparison of Main Memory and Secondary Memory

Main memory is much faster and more expensive than secondary memory. You must transfer data from secondary memory to main memory before it can be processed. Data in main memory is *volatile* and disappears when you switch off the computer. Data stored in secondary memory is *permanent* and does not disappear when the computer is switched off.

Exercises for Section 1.2

Self-Check

1. What are the contents of memory cells 0 and 999 in Fig. 1.4? What memory cells contain the letter X and the fraction 0.005?
2. Explain the purpose of the arithmetic-logic unit, memory, the central processor, and the disk drive and disk. What input and output devices do you use with your computer?

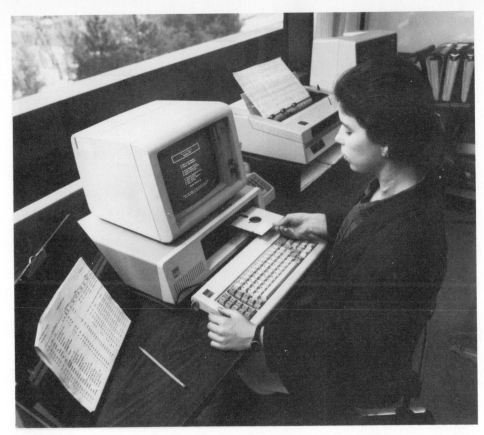

Figure 1.8   Inserting a Floppy Disk into a Disk Drive

 1.3   Problem Solving and Programming

We mentioned earlier that a computer cannot think; therefore, to get it to do any useful work, a computer must be provided with a *program*, that is, a list of instructions. Programming a computer is a lot more involved than simply writing a list of instructions. Problem solving is a crucial component of programming. Before we can write a program to solve a particular problem, we must consider carefully all aspects of the problem and then develop and organize its solution.

Like most programming students, at first you will probably spend a great deal of time in the computer laboratory entering your programs. You will spend more time later removing the errors that inevitably will crop up in your programs.

It is tempting to rush to the computer laboratory and start entering your program as soon as you have some idea of how to write it. Resist this temptation. Instead, think carefully about the problem and its solution before you write any program instructions. When you have a potential solution in mind, plan it out on paper and modify it if necessary before you write the program.

Once you have written the program on paper, *desk check* your solution by carefully performing each instruction much as the computer would. To desk check a program, simulate the result of each program instruction using sample data that is easy to manipulate (for example, small whole numbers). Compare these results with the expected results and make any necessary corrections to your program. Only then should you go to the computer laboratory and enter your program. A few extra minutes spent evaluating the proposed solution using the process summarized in Fig. 1.9 often saves hours of frustration later.

In this text, we stress a methodology for problem solving that has proved useful in helping students learn to program. This technique, called *structured programming*, should enable you to write programs that are relatively easy to read and understand and that contain fewer initial errors.

1.4   Programming Languages

Languages used for writing computer programs, called *programming languages*, fall into three broad categories: machine, assembly, and high-level languages.

High-level languages are more popular with programmers than the other two language categories. One reason for their popularity is that they are much easier to use than machine and assembly languages. Another reason is that a

Figure 1.9   Programming Strategy

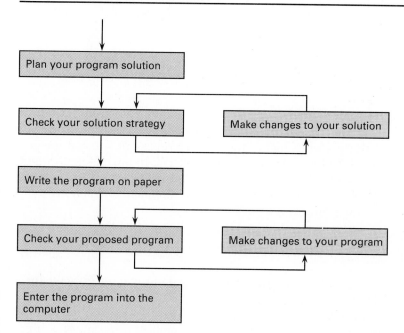

high-level language program is *portable*, which means that it can be used without modification on many different types of computers. An assembly language or a machine-language program, on the other hand, can be used on only one type of computer.

Some common high-level languages are FORTRAN, BASIC, COBOL, and Pascal. Each language was designed with a specific purpose in mind. FORTRAN is an acronym for FORmula TRANslation, and its principal users are engineers and scientists. BASIC (Beginners All-purpose Symbolic Instructional Code) was designed to be easily learned and used by students. COBOL (COmmon Business Oriented Language) is used primarily for business data-processing operations. Pascal was designed for teaching structured programming.

Each of these high-level languages has a *language standard* that describes the grammatical form (*syntax*) of the language. Every high-level language instruction must conform to the syntax rules specified in the language standard. These rules are very precise—no allowances are made for instructions that are *almost* correct.

An important feature of high-level languages is that they allow us to write program instructions that resemble English. We can reference data stored in memory using easily understood descriptive names, like Name and Rate, rather than the numeric memory cell addresses discussed in Section 1.2. We can also use familiar symbols to describe operations that we want performed. For example, in several high-level languages the instruction

```
Z := X + Y
```

means add X to Y and store the result in Z.

In *assembly language*, we can also use descriptive names to reference data; however, we must specify the operations to be performed on the data more explicitly. The high-level language instruction above might be written as

```
LOAD X
ADD Y
STORE Z
```

in an assembly language.

Machine language is the native tongue of a computer. Each instruction in machine language is a *binary string* (a string of zeroes and ones). Some of you may be familiar with the use of binary numbers to represent decimal integers (for example, binary 11011 corresponds to decimal 27). In an analogous way, a binary string can be used to indicate an operation to be performed and the memory cell or cells that are involved. The assembly language instructions above could be written in a machine language as

```
0010 0000 0000 0100
0100 0000 0000 0101
0011 0000 0000 0110
```

Obviously, what is easiest for a computer to understand is most difficult for a person to understand and vice versa.

A computer can understand only programs that are written in machine language. Consequently, each instruction in an assembler program or a high-level language program must first be translated into machine language. The next section discusses the steps required to process a high-level language program.

Exercises for Section 1.4

Self-Check

1. What do you think these high-level language statements mean?

    ```
    X := A + B + C      X := Y/Z      D := C - B + A
    ```

2. Which high-level language was designed for teaching programming? Which was designed for business applications? Which was designed for translating scientific formulas?
3. Which type of language has instructions such as ADD X? Which type has instructions that are binary numbers?

 # 1.5 Processing a High-Level Language Program

Before the computer can process a high-level language program, the programmer must enter it at the terminal. The program is stored on disk as a file called the program file or *source file* (see Fig. 1.10). The programmer uses an editor program to enter the program and to save it as a source file.

Once the source file is saved, it can be translated into machine language. A *compiler* program processes the source file and attempts to translate each statement.

One or more statements in the source file may contain a *syntax error*, which means that the statement does not correspond exactly to the syntax of the high-level language. In that case, the compiler causes an error message to be displayed on your monitor screen and no object file is created. Syntax errors are discussed in more detail in Section 2.8.

At this point, you can make changes to your source file and have the compiler process it again. If there are no more errors, the compiler creates an *object file*, which is your program translated into machine language. The object file and any additional object files (for example, programs for input and output operations) that may be needed by your program are combined into a *load file* by the *linker* program. Finally, the *loader* program places the load file into memory, ready for execution. The editor, compiler, linker, and loader programs are part of your computer system. This process is shown in Fig. 1.10.

Executing a Program

To execute a program, the CPU must examine each program instruction in memory and send out the command signals required to carry out the instruction. Normally, the instructions are executed in sequence; however, as we will discuss

Figure 1.10 Preparing a Program for Execution

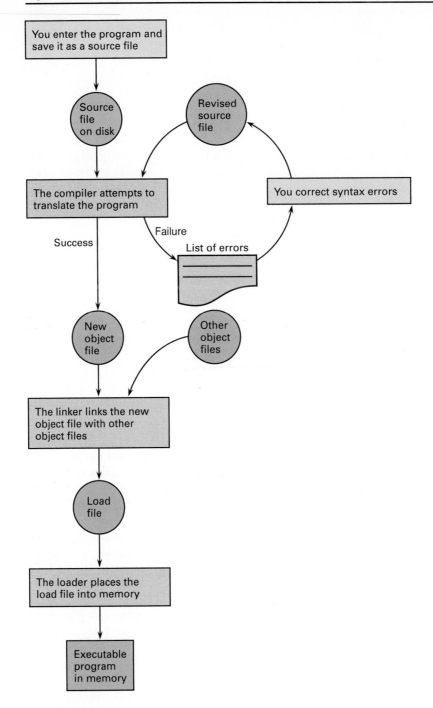

later, it is possible to have the CPU skip over some instructions or execute some instructions more than once.

During execution, data can be entered into memory and manipulated in some specified way. There are program instructions that are used for entering or reading a program's data (called *input data*) into memory. After the input data is processed, instructions for displaying or printing values in memory can be executed to display the program results. The lines displayed by a program are called the *program output*.

Let's use the situation illustrated in Fig. 1.11—executing a payroll program stored in memory—as an example. The first step of the program enters data into memory that describe the employee's hours and pay rate. In step 2, the program manipulates the employee data and stores the results of the computations in memory. In the final step, the computational results are displayed as payroll reports or employee payroll checks. The next chapter takes a closer look at a program that does this.

Exercises for Section 1.5

Self-Check

1. What is the role of a compiler? What is a syntax error? In which file would a syntax error be found?

Figure 1.11   Flow of Information during Program Execution

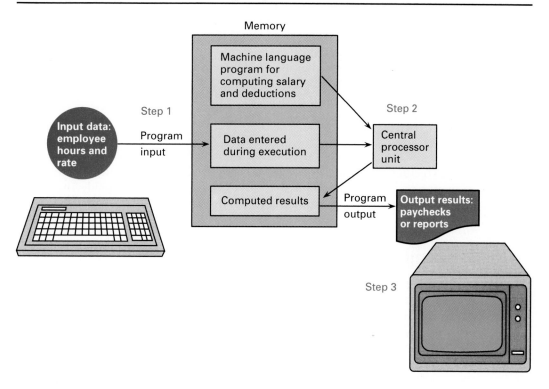

2. What is the source file? An object file? A load file? Which do you create and which does the compiler create? Which does the linker create and which is processed by the loader? What do the compiler, linker, and loader programs do?

 ## 1.6 Using the Computer

The mechanics of entering a program as a source file and translating and executing it differ from system to system. Although we cannot give specific details for a particular computer system, we describe the general process in this section.

Operating Systems

Some of you will be using a *timeshared computer*. Universities often use timeshared computers for instructional purposes. In a timeshare environment, many users are connected by terminals to one central computer, and all users share the central facilities.

Many of you will be using a personal computer, which is a smaller, desktop computer used by one individual at a time. Regardless of what type of computer you use, you will need to interact with a supervisory program, called the *operating system*, within the computer. In timeshared computers, the operating system allocates the central resources among many users. Some operating system tasks are as follows:

1. Validating user identification and account number.
2. Making the editor, compiler, or linker programs available to users.
3. Allocating memory and processor time.
4. Providing input and output facilities.
5. Retrieving needed files.
6. Saving new files.

The operating system for a personal computer performs tasks 2 through 6.

Each computer has its own special *control language* for communicating with its operating system. Although space does not allow us to provide the details here, we will discuss the general process. Your instructor will provide the specific commands for your system.

Creating a Program or File

Before you can use a personal computer, you first need to boot up the computer. *Booting* a personal computer involves inserting the operating system disk into the appropriate disk drive and switching on the computer. The operating system may prompt you for the date and time. Once booted, the operating system displays a prompt (for example, A>) to indicate that it is ready to accept commands. Fig. 1.12 demonstrates booting an IBM Personal Computer using MS-DOS (the Microsoft™ operating system); the computer user enters the characters that are in color; the other characters are those that the operating system displays.

Figure 1.12   Booting a Personal Computer

```
MS-DOS Version 3.0

Current date is Tue 1-01-1980
Enter new date: 4-05-89

Current time is 0:01:43.53
Enter new time: 10:30

A>
```

Before you can use a timeshared computer, you must *log on*, or *connect*, to the computer. To log on, you enter your account name and password (given to you by your instructor). For security reasons, your password is not displayed. Fig. 1.13 demonstrates this process for the Digital Equipment Corporation™ VAX computer. The computer user enters the characters that are in color; the other characters are those that the operating system displays. The timeshared operating system shown (named VMS Version 4.5) displays the symbol $ as a prompt.

Figure 1.13   Logging on to a Computer

```
Username: Koffman
Password: Madaket

                CIS Department Vax-11/780 VMS V4.5

       Last interactive login on Friday, 29-April-1989 10:20

$
```

Once you have booted your personal computer or logged on to a timeshared computer, you can begin to create your program. In most cases, you will use a special program called an *editor* to enter your Pascal program. After accessing the editor, you can start to enter a new Pascal program. If you want a record of the program once it is entered, you must save it as a permanent file on disk; otherwise, your program disappears when your session with the editor is over. Follow these steps to create and save a program file:

1. Log on to a timeshared computer or boot up a personal computer.
2. Access the editor program.
3. Indicate that you are creating a new file.
4. Enter each line of the program file.
5. Name your program file (if not named in step 3) and save it as a permanent file in secondary memory.
6. Exit from the editor.

Once you have created your program and you are satisfied that each line is entered correctly, you can attempt to compile, link, and execute it. On some systems you must give three separate commands; on other systems one command, such as RUN, initiates this sequence of operations.

If your program will not compile because it contains syntax errors, you must edit, or correct, the program. Follow these steps to correct and reexecute a program file:

1. Reaccess the editor program.
2. Access your program file.
3. Correct the statements containing syntax errors.
4. Save your edited program file.
5. Compile, link, and execute the new program file.

 # Chapter Review

This chapter described the basic components of a computer: main and secondary memory, the CPU, and input and output devices. Remember these important facts about computers:

1. A memory cell is never empty, but its initial contents may be meaningless to your program.
2. The current contents of a memory cell are destroyed whenever new information is placed in that cell.
3. Programs must be copied into the memory of the computer before they can be executed.
4. Data cannot be manipulated by the computer until they are first read into memory.
5. A computer cannot think for itself; you must use a programming language to instruct it in a precise and unambiguous manner to perform a task.
6. Programming a computer can be fun—if you are patient, organized, and careful.

✓ *Quick-Check Exercises*

1. The _____ translates a _____ language program into _____.
2. After a program is executed, all program results are automatically displayed. True or false?
3. Specify the correct order for these four operations: execution, linking, translation, loading.
4. A high-level language program is saved on disk as a _____ file or a _____ file.
5. The _____ finds syntax errors in the _____ file.
6. A machine language program is saved on disk as an _____ file.
7. The _____ program is used to create and save the source file.
8. The _____ creates the load file.
9. The _____ program is used to place the _____ file into memory.

10. Computers are becoming (more/less) expensive and (bigger/smaller) in size.
11. The first large-scale, general-purpose electronic computer was called the _____.
    It (was/was not) a stored-program computer.

Answers to Quick-Check Exercises

1. compiler, high-level, machine language
2. false
3. translation, linking, loading, execution
4. source, program
5. compiler, source
6. object
7. editor
8. linker
9. loader, load
10. less, smaller
11. ENIAC, was not

Review Questions

1. List at least three kinds of information stored in a computer.
2. List two functions of the CPU.
3. List two input/output devices and two secondary storage devices.
4. A computer can think. True or false?
5. List the three categories of programming languages.
6. Give three advantages of programming in a high-level language such as Pascal.
7. What processes are needed to transform a Pascal program to a machine-language program that is ready for execution?
8. What are three characteristics of a structured program?

Introduction to Pascal

2

This chapter introduces the programming language Pascal, which is a high-level, general-purpose language developed in 1971 by Professor Nicklaus Wirth of Zurich, Switzerland. (A general-purpose language is one that can be put to many different applications.) Pascal is the most popular programming language for teaching programming concepts because its syntax is relatively easy to learn. Pascal also facilitates writing structured programs—programs that are relatively easy to read, understand, and keep in good working order—which is now accepted as standard programming practice. For those reasons and the fact that Pascal compilers are relatively easy to write, Pascal is also widely used in industry.

A *language standard*, which describes all Pascal language constructs and specifies their syntax, ensures that a Pascal program written on one computer will execute on another computer. This text follows the recognized standard for Pascal.

This chapter describes Pascal statements for performing computations and statements for entering data and displaying results. Besides introducing Pascal, the chapter describes how to run Pascal programs interactively and in batch mode. In *interactive programming*, the program user enters data during program execution; in *batch mode*, the program user must prepare a data file before program execution begins. The use of data files is discussed in Section 2.5.

 ## 2.1 Overview of Pascal Programs

Before beginning our formal study of Pascal, we will examine two short programs. Don't worry about understanding the details of these programs yet; for now, concentrate on the look and the language of each program. Later we'll study them more closely.

■ Example 2.1

Figure 2.1 contains a Pascal program and a sample execution of that program (the last four lines of the figure). For easy identification the first and last lines of the program are in color, as are the input data typed in by the program user in the sample execution.

Figure 2.1 Printing a Welcoming Message

```
program Hello (Input, Output);

   var
      Letterl, Letter2, Letter3 : Char;

begin
  WriteLn ('Enter a 3 letter nickname and press return>');
  ReadLn (Letterl, Letter2, Letter3);
  WriteLn ('Hello ', Letterl, Letter2, Letter3, '.');
  WriteLn ('We hope you enjoy studying Pascal!')
end.
```

```
Enter a 3 letter nickname and press return>
Bob
Hello Bob.
We hope you enjoy studying Pascal!
```

The program line var and the line immediately below it identify the names
of the three memory cells (Letter1, Letter2, Letter3) that will store each
letter of the nickname. The part of the program that is translated into machine
language for execution follows the line begin.

Each program line that starts with the word WriteLn causes a line of
program output to be displayed. The first such line

```
WriteLn ('Enter a 3 letter nickname and press return>');
```

displays the first output line in the sample execution, which asks the program
user to enter three letters.

The program instruction

```
ReadLn (Letter1, Letter2, Letter3);
```

reads the three letters Bob (typed by the program user) into the three memory
cells listed, one letter per cell. The next line

```
WriteLn ('Hello ', Letter1, Letter2, Letter3, '.');
```

displays Bob after the message string 'Hello '. The string '.' causes a period
to be printed after the third letter. Finally, the next-to-last program line displays
the last line shown in the sample execution. ■

Some punctuation symbols appear in Fig. 2.1. The comma separates items
in a list, and the semicolon appears at the end of several lines. We will give
guidelines for the use of these symbols later.

■ Example 2.2

Suppose you are measuring shelves for a bookcase, and you want to convert
inches to centimeters. You might create a program like the one shown in Fig.
2.2. The program instruction

```
ReadLn (Inches);
```

reads the number of inches to be converted (30.0 in the sample execution) into
the memory cell Inches. The program instruction

```
Cent := CentPerInch * Inches;
```

computes the equivalent length in centimeters by multiplying the length in
inches by 2.54 (the number of centimeters per inch); the product is stored in
memory cell Cent.

Finally, the program instruction

```
WriteLn ('That equals ', Cent, ' centimeters.')
```

displays a message string, the value of Cent, and a second message string. The instruction displays the value of Cent as a real number in Pascal scientific notation (7.620000E+01). The value printed is equivalent to 7.62 x 10 or 76.2, as will be explained later. ∎

Figure 2.2 Converting Inches to Centimeters

```
program InchToCent (Input, Output);

  const
    CentPerInch = 2.54;

  var
    Inches, Cent : Real;
begin
  WriteLn ('Enter a length in inches>');
  ReadLn (Inches);
  Cent := CentPerInch * Inches;
  WriteLn ('That equals ', Cent, ' centimeters.')
end.


Enter a length in inches>
30.0
That equals              7.620000E+01 centimeters.
```

One of the nicest things about Pascal is that it lets us write programs that resemble English. At this point, you probably can read and understand the sample programs, even though you do not know how to write your own programs. In the following sections, you will learn more details about the Pascal programs we have looked at so far.

Reserved Words and Identifiers

All of the lines in the two preceding programs satisfy the syntax rules for the Pascal language. The programs contain several different elements, such as reserved words, standard identifiers, special symbols, and names for memory cells. Let's look at the first three categories. The reserved words all appear in lowercase; they have special meanings in Pascal and cannot be used for other purposes. The reserved words in Fig. 2.1 and Fig. 2.2 are

```
program, const, var, begin, end
```

The standard identifiers also have special meanings, but they can be used for other purposes (however, we don't recommend this practice). The standard identifiers in Fig. 2.1 and Fig. 2.2 are

```
Real, Char, ReadLn, WriteLn, Input, Output
```

Some symbols (for example, =, *, :=) have special meanings in Pascal. Appendix A contains a complete list of reserved words, standard identifiers, and special symbols.

What is the difference between reserved words and standard identifiers? You cannot use a reserved word as the name of a memory cell, but you can use a standard identifier. However, once you use a standard identifier to name a memory cell, the Pascal compiler no longer associates any special meaning with that identifier. For example, you could use WriteLn as the name of a memory cell, but then you would not be able to use WriteLn for its normal purpose (to display program output). Thus, standard identifiers lose a valuable purpose.

The other identifiers appearing in the programs in Fig. 2.1 and Fig. 2.2 are described in more detail in the next sections.

Use of Uppercase and Lowercase

Throughout the text, issues of good programming style are discussed in displays such as this one. Programming style displays provide guidelines for improving the appearance and the readability of your programs. Most programs are examined, studied, or used by someone other than the programmer. A program that follows consistent style conventions is easier to read and understand than one that is sloppy or inconsistent. And, although conventions make it easier for humans to understand programs, they have no effect whatsoever on the computer.

In this text, reserved words always appear in lowercase; identifiers are in mixed uppercase and lowercase. The first letter of each identifier is always capitalized. If an identifier consists of two or more words pushed together (for example, ReadLn is an abbreviation for Read Line), the first letter of each "word" is capitalized. We recommend that you follow this convention in your programs, so that it will be easy to distinguish reserved words from other identifiers.

The compiler does not really differentiate between uppercase and lowercase. That means you could write the reserved word const as CONST or the standard identifier ReadLn as READLN. However, const and ReadLn are preferable, according to our convention.

Because you should not redefine a standard identifier, many computer scientists emphasize this by writing standard identifiers the same as reserved words (that is, all lowercase). If your instructor prefers that you adopt this convention, you should write the standard identifier ReadLn as readln.

Exercise for Section 2.1

Self-Check

1. Why should you not use standard identifiers as names of memory cells in a program? Can you use reserved words instead?

2.2 Declarations in Pascal Programs

How do we tell the Pascal compiler what identifiers will be used in a program? One way is the *program heading*, as shown next:

```
program Hello (Input, Output);
```

The program heading, which begins with the reserved word program, identifies the name (Hello) of the program and tells the compiler where the input data will come from (file Input) and where output data will be written to (file Output). Input and Output are standard identifiers that represent the normal input and output devices for your computer system. For most of you, Input represents the keyboard and Output represents the monitor screen.

We tell the Pascal compiler the names of memory cells used in a program through constant and variable declarations. The *constant declaration*

```
const
    CentPerInch = 2.54;
```

specifies that the identifier CentPerInch will be used as the name of the memory cell that contains the number 2.54; the identifier CentPerInch is called a *constant*. Only data values that never change (for example, the number of centimeters per inch is always 2.54) should be associated with an identifier that is a constant. Instructions that attempt to change the value of a constant cannot appear in a Pascal program.

The *variable declaration*

```
var
    Letter1, Letter2, Letter3 : Char;
```

in Fig. 2.1 gives the names of three memory cells that will be used for storing individual characters. The variable declaration

```
var
    Inches, Cent : Real;
```

in Fig. 2.2 gives the names of two memory cells that will be used to store real numbers (for example, 30.0, 562.57). All the names listed in the preceding declarations are considered identifiers.

Identifiers listed on the left of the symbol : in a variable declaration are called *variables*. Variables are names of memory cells used in a program for storing input data and computational results. The identifier (for example, Real, Integer, Char) that appears to the right of the symbol : tells the Pascal compiler the *data type* (for example, a real number, an integer, or a character) of the information stored in a particular variable. A variable that is used for storing an integer value (a number without a decimal point) has data type Integer. Data types are discussed in more detail in Section 2.7.

You have quite a bit of freedom in selecting the identifiers that you use in a program. The syntactic rules are as follows:

1. An identifier must always begin with a letter.
2. An identifier must consist only of letters and/or digits.
3. You cannot use a Pascal reserved word as an identifier.

Some valid and invalid identifiers follow.

Valid identifiers:

```
Letter1, Letter2, Inches, Cent, CentPerInch, Hello
```

Invalid identifiers:

```
1Letter, const, var, Two*Four, Cent_Per_Inch, Joe's
```

Although the syntactic rules do not place a limit on the length of an identifier, some Pascal compilers use only a portion of each identifier (say, the first eight characters). Such compilers would consider the identifiers `Consonant1` and `Consonant2` to be the same identifier (`Consonan`); consequently, you could not declare those identifiers together in a program translated by such a compiler.

The identifier `Cent_Per_Inch` is invalid according to the Pascal language standard. However, many Pascal compilers allow the underscore symbol (_) to appear in an identifier and would consider this identifier to be valid. Even if this is so on your computer, we strongly recommend that you avoid the use of the underscore symbol. Pascal requires a declaration for every identifier used in a program unless that identifier is a standard identifier. Identifiers that are not standard identifiers are called *user-defined identifiers*. The reserved words and identifiers used in Fig. 2.1 and Fig. 2.2 are shown in Table 2.1 under their appropriate categories.

Table 2.1 Reserved Words and Identifiers in Figures 2.1 and 2.2

Reserved Words	Standard Identifiers	User-Defined Identifiers
program	Input	Hello
var	Output	Letter1
const	Char	Letter2
begin	Real	Letter3
end	ReadLn	InchToCent
	WriteLn	CentPerInch
		Inches
		Cent

This section introduced the program heading, constant declarations, and variable declarations; the syntactic form of each Pascal language construct is summarized in the following syntax displays. Each display describes the syntactic form of a language construct and provides an example.

Program Heading

Form: program *pname* (Input, Output);
Example: program Hello (Input, Output);
Interpretation: The name of the program is indicated by *pname*. The input data will be read from data file Input; the output results will be written to data file Output.

Constant Declaration

Form: const *constant* = *value*;
Example: const Pi = 3.14159;
Interpretation: The specified *value* is associated with the identifier *constant*. The *value* associated with *constant* cannot be changed. More than one constant declaration may follow the word const. A semicolon appears at the end of each constant declaration.
Note: The constant declarations immediately follow the program heading in a Pascal program.

Variable Declaration

Form: var *variable list* : *type*;
Example: var
              X, Y   : Real;
              Me, You : Integer;
Interpretation: A memory cell is allocated for each variable (an identifier) in the *variable list*. The *type* of data (Real, Integer) to be stored in each variable is specified between the colon and semicolon. Commas separate the identifiers in the *variable list*. More than one list of variables can be declared after the word var. The variable declarations immediately follow the constant declarations.

Choosing Identifier Names

It is important to pick meaningful names for identifiers to make it easier to understand their use. For example, the identifier Salary would be a good name for a variable used to store a person's salary; the identifiers S or Bagel would be bad choices.

As we mentioned earlier, Pascal places no restriction on the length of an identifier. However, it is difficult to form meaningful names with fewer than three letters. On the other hand, typing errors are more likely when identifiers are too long. As a reasonable rule of thumb, use names that are between three and ten characters in length.

> If you mistype an identifier, the compiler will usually detect this as a syntax error and display an *undefined identifier* error message during program translation. Sometimes mistyped identifiers resemble other identifiers, so avoid picking names that are similar to each other. Make sure you do not choose two names that are identical except for their use of case, because the compiler will not be able to distinguish between them.

Exercises for Section 2.2

Self-Check

1. Should the value of Pi (3.14159) be stored in a constant or a variable?
2. Which comes first, the constant declarations or the variable declarations?
3. Which of the following are valid Pascal identifiers?

   MyProgram   prog2   Prog#2   2NDone   Program   'MaxScores'

4. Which of the following identifiers are Pascal reserved words, standard identifiers, identifiers, and invalid identifiers?

end	ReadLn	Bill	program	Sue's
Rate	Operate	Start	begin	const
XYZ123	123XYZ	ThisIsALongOne		Y=Z

Programming

1. Write a program heading for a program named Mine that has declarations for variables Radius, Area, and Circumf (all type Real) and the constant Pi (3.14159).

2.3 Executable Statements in Pascal Programs

One of the main functions of a computer is to perform arithmetic computations and to display the results of those computations. Such operations are specified by the *executable statements* that appear in the program body (following the reserved word begin). Each executable statement is translated by the Pascal compiler into one or more machine language instructions, which are copied to the object file and later executed. Declarations, on the other hand, describe the meaning and the purpose of each user-defined identifier to the Pascal compiler; they are not translated into machine language instructions and do not appear in the object file.

Assignment Statements

The *assignment statement* is used in Pascal to perform computations. The assignment statement

Figure 2.3 Effect of Cent := CentPerInch * Inches;

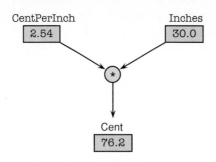

```
Cent := CentPerInch * Inches;
```

in Fig. 2.2 assigns a value to the variable Cent. In this case, Cent is assigned the result of the multiplication (* means multiply) of the constant CentPerInch by the variable Inches. Valid information must be stored in both CentPerInch and Inches before the assignment statement is executed. As shown in Fig. 2.3, only the value of Cent is affected by the assignment statement; CentPerInch and Inches retain their original values.

The symbol := is the *assignment operator* in Pascal and should be read as "becomes," "gets," or "takes the value of" rather than "equals." The : and the = must be adjacent characters with no intervening space. The general form of the assignment statement is shown in the next display.

SYNTAX
DISPLAY

Assignment Statement (Arithmetic)

Form: *result* := *expression*

Example: X := Y + Z + 2.0

Interpretation: The variable specified by *result* is assigned the value of *expression*. The previous value of *result* is destroyed. The *expression* can be a single variable or a single constant or involve variables, constants, and the arithmetic operators listed in Table 2.2. The *expression* must be assignment compatible (described next) with the variable specified by *result*.

Table 2.2 Some Arithmetic Operators

Arithmetic Operator	Meaning
+	Addition
−	Subtraction
*	Multiplication
/	Real division

The real division operator (/) always yields a real number as its result. Chapter 7 introduces a division operator that yields an integer as its result.

An *expression* is *assignment compatible* with a *result* variable if both are the same data type. This means that a type Real expression should be assigned to a type Real variable, and a type Integer expression should be assigned to a type Integer variable. We will have more to say about assignment compatible types in Chapter 7.

■ Example 2.3

In Pascal, you can write assignment statements of the form

```
Sum := Sum + Item
```

where the variable Sum is used on both sides of the assignment operator. Obviously this is not an algebraic equation, but it illustrates a common programming practice. This statement instructs the computer to add the current value of the variable Sum to the value of Item; the result is saved temporarily and then stored back into Sum. The previous value of Sum is destroyed in the process, as illustrated in Fig. 2.4; however, the value of Item is unchanged. ■

■ Example 2.4

In Pascal, you can also write assignment statements with an expression part that consists of a single variable or value. The statement

```
NewX := X
```

instructs the computer to copy the value of X into NewX. The statement

```
NewX := -X
```

instructs the computer to get the value of X, negate this value, and store the result in NewX. For example, if X is 3.5, NewX is -3.5. Neither assignment statement changes the value of X. ■

Input/Output Operations

Data can be stored in memory in three different ways: associated with a constant, assigned to a variable, or read into a variable. We have already discussed the first two methods. The third method, reading data into a variable, is necessary

Figure 2.4 Effect of Sum := Sum + Item

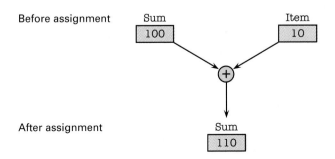

if you want the program to manipulate different data each time it executes. Reading data into memory is called an *input operation*.

As it executes, a program performs computations and assigns new values to variables. These program results can be displayed to the program user by an *output operation*.

All input/output operations in Pascal are performed by executing special program units called *input/output procedures*. The input/output procedures are supplied as part of the Pascal compiler and their names are standard identifiers. The next two sections discuss how to use the input procedure named ReadLn and the output procedure named WriteLn.

Using the ReadLn Procedure

In Pascal, a *procedure call statement* calls, or activates, a procedure. Calling a procedure is analogous to asking a friend to perform an urgent task. You tell your friend what to do (but not how to do it) and wait for your friend to report back that he or she is finished. After hearing from your friend, you can go on and do something else.

In Fig. 2.2, the procedure call statement

```
ReadLn (Inches);
```

calls procedure ReadLn to read data into the variable Inches. Where does procedure ReadLn get the data that it stores in variable Inches? It reads it from the standard input device (Input). In most cases, the standard input device is the keyboard. Consequently, the computer attempts to store in Inches whatever information is typed at the keyboard by the program user. Since Inches is declared as type Real, the input operation proceeds without error only if the program user types in a real number. The program user should press the Return or Enter key after typing the number. The effect of the ReadLn operation is shown in Fig. 2.5.

The program in Fig. 2.1 reads a person's nickname. Each person using the program may have a different nickname, so the procedure call statement

```
ReadLn (Letter1, Letter2, Letter3);
```

calls the ReadLn procedure to enter data into each of the three variables. Because these variables are declared as type Char, one character is stored in each variable. The next three characters entered at the keyboard are stored in these variables. Again, the program user should press the Return key after typing in three

Figure 2.5 Effect of ReadLn (Inches);

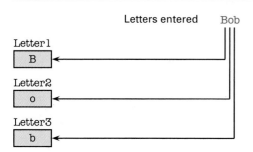

characters. Figure 2.6 shows the effect of this statement when the letters Bob are entered.

The number of characters read by the ReadLn procedure depends on the type of the variable in which the data will be stored. Only one character is read for a type Char variable; for a type Real variable, Pascal continues to read characters until it reaches a blank character or the Return key is pressed.

How do we know when to enter the input data and what data to enter? Your program should print a prompting message that informs you what data to enter and when. (Prompting messages are discussed in more detail in the next section.) Each character entered by the program user is *echoed* on the screen and is also processed by procedure ReadLn.

The ReadLn Procedure

Form: ReadLn (*input list*)
Example: ReadLn (Age, FirstInitial)
Interpretation: The ReadLn procedure reads data the program user types at the keyboard into memory during program execution. The program user must enter one data item for each variable specified in the *input list*. Commas are used to separate the variable names in the *input list*.

The order of the data must correspond to the order of the variables in the *input list*. Insert one or more blank characters between numeric data items. If a character data item is being read after a number, insert only one blank character between the number and the character. Do not insert any blanks between consecutive character data items unless the blank character is one of the data items being read. Press the Return key after you have entered all data items.

The WriteLn Procedure

To see the results of a program execution, we must have some way of specifying what variable values should be displayed. In Fig. 2.2, the procedure call statement

```
WriteLn ('That equals ', Cent, ' centimeters.')
```

calls the WriteLn procedure to display three items: the string literal 'That equals ', the value of Cent, and the string literal ' centimeters.'. A *string literal* (or *string*) is a sequence of characters enclosed in single quotation marks or apostrophes; the characters inside the quotation marks are printed but the marks are not. The WriteLn procedure displays the line

```
That equals          7.620000E+01 centimeters.
```

Unless directed otherwise, most Pascal compilers use Pascal scientific notation to display a real value. The number 7.620000E+01 is 76.2 expressed in Pascal scientific notation. In normal scientific notation, 7.62×10^1 means "multiply 7.62 by 10," or move the decimal point right one digit. Because you cannot enter or display superscripts with Pascal, the letter E indicates scientific notation (sometimes called *floating-point notation*).

In Fig. 2.1, the procedure call statement

```
WriteLn ('Hello ', Letter1, Letter2, Letter3, '.');
```

displays the line

```
Hello Bob.
```

In this case, three variable values are printed between the strings 'Hello ' and '.'.

Finally, the statements

```
WriteLn ('Enter a 3 letter nickname and press return>');
WriteLn ('Enter a length in inches>');
```

display prompts or prompting messages in Figs. 2.1 and 2.2, respectively. Always display a prompting message just before a call to procedure ReadLn to remind the program user to enter data. The prompt can also describe the format of the expected data. It is important to precede each ReadLn operation with a WriteLn that prints a prompt; otherwise, the program user may have no idea that the program is waiting for data or what data to enter.

The *cursor* is a moving place marker that indicates the next position on the screen where information will be displayed. After the WriteLn procedure is executed, the cursor advances to the start of the next line on the screen.

SYNTAX
DISPLAY

The WriteLn Procedure

Form: WriteLn (*output list*)

Interpretation: The WriteLn procedure displays the value of each variable or constant in the order in which it appears in *output list*. A string is printed without the quotation marks. The cursor advances to the start of the next line after the entire output line is displayed.

Self-Check

1. Write the following numbers in normal decimal notation.

   103E−4   1.2345E+6   123.45E+3

2. Correct the syntax errors in the following program and rewrite it so that it follows our style conventions. What does each statement of your corrected program do? What values are printed?

   ```
   program SMALL (INPUT, output) VAR X, Y, X , real:
   BEGIN Y = 15.0,
   Z:= -Y + 3.5; Y + z =: x;
   writeln (x; Y; z); end;
   ```

3. Show the output displayed by the following program lines when the data entered are 5 and 7.

   ```
   WriteLn ('Enter two integers>');
   ReadLn (M, N);
   M := M + 5;
   N := 3 * N;
   WriteLn ('M = ', M);
   WriteLn ('N = ', N);
   ```

Programming

1. Write statements that ask the user to type three numbers and that read the user's responses into First, Second, and Third.
2. Write a statement that displays the value of X in the following format:

   The value of X is _____

3. Write a program that asks the user to enter the radius of a circle and then computes and displays the circle's area and circumference. Use the formulas

   $area = \pi \times radius \times radius$
   $circumference = 2 \times \pi \times radius$

where π is the constant 3.14159.

 # 2.4   General Form of Pascal Programs

To summarize what we have discussed so far, the programs shown earlier have the general form described in Fig. 2.7. Each program begins with a program heading that identifies the name of the program.

Every identifier used in a program must be declared exactly once in the declaration part of a program unless it is a standard identifier. The reserved words const and var can appear no more than once and must be in the order shown. All constant declarations come after const and all variable declarations after var. More than one constant may be declared, and there may be more than one variable list. Commas separate identifiers in a variable list; the semicolon terminates each declaration.

The reserved word `begin` signals the start of the program body. The program body contains the statements that are translated into machine language and eventually executed. The statements we have looked at so far consist of statements that perform computations and input/output operations. The last line in a program is

```
end.
```

Figure 2.7 General Form of a Pascal Program

```
program Name (Input, Output);
  const
    constant = value;
          .
          .
          .
    constant = value;                 Declaration part
  var
    variable list : type;
          .
          .
          .
    variable list : type;
begin
  statement;
          .                           Program body
          .
          .
  statement
end.
```

Semicolons separate Pascal statements and must be inserted between statements in a program body. A semicolon is not needed before the first statement in a sequence nor after the last statement. Consequently, a semicolon should not appear after the reserved word `begin`. Most Pascal compilers allow a semicolon after the last statement in a program, but we do not recommend this practice. When present, this semicolon has the effect of inserting an "empty statement" between the last actual statement and the program terminator `end`.

As shown in Fig. 2.1, a Pascal statement can extend over more than one line. The variable and constant declarations start on one line and finish on the next. A statement that extends over more than one line cannot be split in the middle of an identifier, a reserved word, a number, or a string.

We can also write more than one statement on a line, although we recommend that you place only one statement on a line. For example, the line

```
WriteLn ('Enter two letters> '); ReadLn (Letter1,Letter2)
```

contains a statement that displays a prompt message and a statement that reads the data requested. A semicolon separates the two statements; you would insert another semicolon at the end of the line if another statement were to follow.

Use of Blank Space

The consistent and careful use of blank spaces can significantly enhance the style of a program. A blank space is required between words in a program line (for instance, between `program` and `Hello` in Fig. 2.1).

The compiler ignores extra blanks between words and symbols. You can insert spaces to improve the style and the appearance of a program. Always leave a blank space after a comma and before and after arithmetic operators such as `*`, `-`, `:=`. Remember to indent each line of the program except for the first and last lines and the line `begin`, and to write the reserved words `const`, `var`, and `begin` by themselves on a line so that they stand out. Indent all lines except for the first and last lines of the program and the line `begin` two or more spaces. Finally, use blank lines between sections of the program.

All these measures have the sole purpose of improving the style—and hence the clarity—of your programs. Stylistic issues have no effect whatever on the meaning of the program as far as the computer is concerned; however, they can make it easier for people to read and understand your program.

Be careful not to insert blank spaces where they do not belong. For example, there cannot be a space between the characters `:` and `=` when they form the assignment operator `:=`, nor can the identifier `StartSalary` be written as `Start Salary`.

Programs in Memory

Let's look at a new sample program and see what happens to memory when this program is loaded and executed.

■ Example 2.5

Figure 2.8 shows a payroll program that computes an employee's gross pay and net pay using the algebraic formulas

$gross\ pay\ =\ hours\ worked\ \times\ hourly\ rate$

$net\ pay\ =\ gross\ pay\ -\ tax\ amount$

These formulas are written as the Pascal assignment statements

```
Gross := Hours * Rate;
Net := Gross - Tax;
```

in the payroll program shown in Fig. 2.8. New values of Hours and Rate are read each time the program is executed; a constant Tax of $25.00 is always deducted.

Figure 2.8   A Payroll Program

```
program Payroll (Input, Output);

   const
     Tax = 25.00;

   var
     Hours, Rate, Gross, Net : Real;
begin
   WriteLn ('Enter hours worked>');
   ReadLn (Hours);
   WriteLn ('Enter hourly rate>');
   ReadLn (Rate);
   Gross := Hours * Rate;
   Net := Gross - Tax;
   WriteLn ('Gross pay is $', Gross);
   WriteLn ('Net   pay is $', Net)
end.


Enter hours worked>
40.0
Enter hourly rate>
4.50
Gross pay is $          1.800000E+02
Net   pay is $          1.550000E+02
```

The program first reads the data that represent the hours worked and the hourly rate and then computes gross pay as their product. Next, it computes net pay by deducting a constant tax amount of $25.00. Finally, it displays the computed values of gross pay and net pay.

Figure 2.9a shows the payroll program loaded into memory and the program memory area before execution of the program body. The question marks in memory cells Hours, Rate, Gross, and Net indicate that these variables are undefined (value unknown) before program execution begins. During program execution, the data values 40.0 and 4.50 are read into the variables Hours and Rate, respectively. After the assignment statements shown earlier are used to compute values for Gross and Net, all variables are defined, as shown in Fig. 2.9b. ∎

Exercise for Section 2.4

Self-Check

1. Show the contents of memory before and after execution of the program in Fig. 2.2.

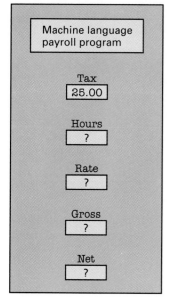

A. Memory before execution   B. Memory after execution

2.5 Interactive Mode, Batch Mode, and Data Files

There are two basic modes of computer operation: batch and interactive. The programs we have written so far are intended to be run in *interactive mode*. In that mode, the program user can interact with the program and enter data while the program is executing.

In *batch mode*, all data must be supplied beforehand—the program user cannot interact with the program while it is executing. Batch mode is an option on most time-shared or personal computers.

If you use batch mode, you must prepare a batch data file before you execute your program. On a time-shared or personal computer, a batch data file is created and saved in the same way as a program or source file. Creating a data file will be discussed later.

Because a batch mode program cannot interact with its user, it makes no sense to provide prompts. Each ReadLn operation reads data items from a previously prepared data file. A WriteLn operation is used after each ReadLn operation to echo the data values just read into memory; otherwise, there will be no record of the data being processed.

Figure 2.10 shows the payroll program rewritten as a batch program. The file Input is associated with a batch data file instead of with the keyboard. The first four statements in the program body read and echo print the data. The statement

```
ReadLn (Hours);
```

reads the value of Hours from the first line of the batch data file; the next statement

```
WriteLn ('Hours worked are ', Hours);
```

echo prints the value read into Hours.

Figure 2.10 Payroll Program as a Batch Program

```
program PayrollBatch (Input, Output);

   const
     Tax = 25.00;

   var
     Hours, Rate, Gross, Net : Real;
begin
   ReadLn (Hours);
   WriteLn ('Hours worked are ', Hours);
   ReadLn (Rate);
   WriteLn ('Hourly rate   is ', Rate);
   Gross := Hours * Rate;
   Net := Gross - Tax;
   WriteLn ('Gross pay is $', Gross);
   WriteLn ('Net   pay is $', Net)
end.


Hours worked are      4.000000E+01
Hourly rate   is      4.500000E+00
Gross pay is $        1.800000E+02
Net   pay is $        1.550000E+02
```

Preview of Data Files (Optional)

This section previews the use of text files as data files in Pascal. A complete treatment of this topic is discussed in Section 8.7. Skip this section if you will not be using data files until then.

A batch program reads its data from a data file that you create and save beforehand using an editor program. The process used to create a data file is the same as that used to create a program file (steps 2 through 6 on page 17). The payroll program in Fig. 2.11 reads its data from data file InData instead of system file Input.

```
program PayrollFile (InData, Output);

   const
     Tax = 25.00;

   var
     InData : Text;
     Hours, Rate, Gross, Net : Real;

begin
   Reset (InData);
   ReadLn (InData, Hours);
   WriteLn ('Hours worked are ', Hours);
   ReadLn (InData, Rate);
   WriteLn ('Hourly rate is ', Rate);
   Gross := Hours * Rate;
   Net := Gross - Tax;
   WriteLn ('Gross pay is $', Gross);
   WriteLn ('Net   pay is $', Net)
end.


Hours worked are        4.000000E+01
Hourly rate    is       4.500000E+00
Gross pay is $          1.800000E+02
Net    pay is $         1.550000E+02
```

In Fig. 2.11, the program heading

```
program PayrollFile (InData, Output);
```

identifies InData as the name of the data file instead of system file Input. The declaration

```
var
   InData : Text;
```

indicates that InData has data type Text (a standard identifier) and is, therefore, a text file. The statement

```
Reset (InData);
```

prepares file InData so that it can be read. Finally, each of the statements

```
ReadLn (InData, Hours);
ReadLn (InData, Rate);
```

reads one real value from a line of file InData. The sample output shown in Fig. 2.11 is generated when file InData contains the two lines

```
40.0
4.50
```

The program in Fig. 2.11 uses InData as the name of the data file being processed. The data file can be stored under a different name on disk (its *directory name*). The Pascal system does not know the file's directory name unless you specify it. Your instructor will tell you how to do this, because the process is system-dependent.

Exercises for Section 2.5

Self-Check

1. Explain the difference in placement of WriteLn statements used to display prompts and WriteLn statements used to echo data. Which are used in interactive programs and which are used in batch programs?

Programming

1. Rewrite the program in Fig. 2.2 as a batch program. Assume data are read from file InData.

 ## 2.6 Formatting Program Output

In the sample program output shown so far, all real numbers were printed in Pascal scientific notation. Consequently, we had little control over the appearance, or format, of each output line. This section shows you how to specify the format of an output item.

Formatting Integer Values

It is fairly easy to format program output in Pascal. This is illustrated in the next example for an integer value. An integer value in Pascal is a number without a decimal point.

■ Example 2.6

The program in Fig. 2.12 determines the value of a small collection of coins (nickels and pennies only) you receive as change for a purchase. The variables are declared to be type Integer, since it is impossible to have 2.5 coins. Only integer values can be stored in type Integer variables. The assignment statement

```
Cents := 5 * Nickels + Pennies;
```

computes the value in cents of the collection of coins in the obvious way (each nickel is worth five pennies).

The statement

```
WriteLn ('You have ', Coins :3, ' coins.')
```

causes an integer value to be printed between the two strings. The symbols :3 after the variable Coins specify the *field width* (3) of the *output field* that contains the value of Coins. A field width of 3 indicates that we expect the output value to be 3 digits or less. If the value of Coins is less than 100, it will be displayed *right justified* in its field, preceded by one or more blank spaces. This means that a single blank space will precede a two-digit number in the output field for Coins, or that two blank spaces will precede a one-digit number. In the output shown, there are actually three blank spaces before the digit 5 (value of Coins), because the string 'You have ' ends with a blank. ■

Figure 2.12 Formatting an Integer Value

```
program CountCoins (Input, Output);

  var
    Nickels, Pennies, Coins, Cents : Integer;

begin
  Write ('How many nickels do you have? ');
  ReadLn (Nickels);
  Write ('How many pennies do you have? ');
  ReadLn (Pennies);
  Coins := Nickels + Pennies;
  Cents := 5 * Nickels + Pennies;
  WriteLn ('You have ', Coins :3, ' coins.');
  WriteLn ('Their value is ', Cents :4, ' cents.')
end.



How many nickels do you have? 3
How many pennies do you have? 2
You have   5 coins.
Their value is   17 cents.
```

Table 2.3 shows how two integer values are printed using different format specifications. The symbol □ represents a blank character. The next to last line shows that the width specification can be a variable (Len) or even an expression that has an integer value. The last line shows that when a width of 1 is used, the number is printed with no blanks preceding it, and the number of print columns actually filled varies with the size of the number (that is, the field expands as needed).

Table 2.3 Printing Integer Values Using Formats

Value	Format	Printed Output
234	:4	□234
234	:5	□□234
234	:6	□□□234
−234	:4	−234
−234	:5	□−234
−234	:6	□□−234
234	:Len	□□□234 (if Len is 6)
234	:1	234

The Write Procedure

You may have noticed that the program body in Fig. 2.12 begins with two calls to an unfamiliar procedure, Write, that displays prompts. If you run the program in Fig. 2.12, you will see that the cursor remains positioned on the same line as the ? after each prompt is displayed. This is because the word Write is used instead of WriteLn in the statements that print the prompting messages. Whenever we call Write, the cursor remains positioned after the last character displayed (a space in Fig. 2.12). In contrast, whenever we call WriteLn, the cursor advances to the next line after the output is displayed. (On some compilers, it may not be possible to use ReadLn immediately after Write. If this is true for your compiler, continue to use WriteLn instead of Write.)

The three procedure call statements

```
Write ('You have ');
Write (Coins :3);
WriteLn (' coins.')
```

would cause the same line of output to be displayed as the single procedure call statement

```
WriteLn ('You have ', Coins :3, ' coins.')
```

It is generally more convenient to use the latter form.

> ### The Write Procedure
>
> **Form:** Write (*output list*);
> **Interpretation:** The value of each variable or constant in the *output list* is printed. Any string in the *output list* is printed without the quotation marks. The cursor does not advance to the next line after the output is displayed.

Formatting Real Values

Suppose you want to calculate your average speed on a trip and your gas mileage. You could do so with the program shown in Fig. 2.13, which uses the two formulas

$$speed = distance / time$$
$$mileage = distance / gallons$$

The input data consist of the trip distance, the trip time, and the number of gallons of gasoline you used.

Figure 2.13 Formatting Real Values

```
program Trip (Input, Output);

    var
        Speed, Time, Distance, Mileage, Gallons : Real;
```

```
begin
  Write ('Enter distance in miles> ');
  ReadLn (Distance);
  Write ('Enter time of trip in hours> ');
  ReadLn (Time);
  Speed := Distance / Time;
  WriteLn ('Average speed in MPH was ', Speed :5:1);
  WriteLn;

  Write ('Enter gallons used> ');
  ReadLn (Gallons);
  Mileage := Distance / Gallons;
  WriteLn ('Miles per gallon was ', Mileage :5:1)
end.
```

```
Enter distance in miles> 100
Enter time of trip in hours> 1.5
Average speed in MPH was   66.7

Enter gallons used> 25
Miles per gallon was    4.0
```

The two statements

```
WriteLn ('Average speed in MPH was ', Speed :5:1);
WriteLn ('Miles per gallon was ', Mileage :5:1)
```

each display a string followed by a real number. The symbols :5:1 specify that the real number should be displayed in five print positions and that there should be one digit after the decimal point. The output value displayed will be rounded to one decimal place; the decimal point accounts for one position in the field width.

The output line printed by the first call to WriteLn would have the form

```
Average speed in MPH was XXX.X
```

where XXX.X indicates the format of the real number (three digits, a decimal point, and a digit). A value less than or equal to 99.9 would be printed with extra blanks preceding the first digit so that the decimal point remains in the fourth print position. If the value is greater than 999.9, the field expands as needed but only one decimal digit will follow the decimal point.

Table 2.4 shows some real values that were printed using different format specifications. As shown in the table, it is possible to use a format specification of the form :n, where n is an integer expression. In this case, the real value is printed in scientific notation using a total of n print positions.

Table 2.4 Printing Real Values Using Formats

Value	Format	Printed Output	
3.14159	:5:2	□3.14	
3.14159	:4:2	3.14	
3.14159	:3:2	3.14	
3.14159	:5:1	□□3.1	
3.14159	:5:3	3.142	*(continued)*

Table 2.4 Printing Real Values Using Formats, *continued*

Value	Format	Printed Output
3.14159	:8:5	□3.14159
3.14159	:9	3.142E+00
0.1234	:4:2	0.12
−0.006	:4:2	−0.01
−0.006	:9	−6.00E−03
−0.006	:8:5	−0.00600
−0.006	:8:3	□□−0.006

PROGRAM
STYLE

Eliminating Leading Blanks

As shown in Tables 2.3 and 2.4, a number that requires fewer print positions than specified by the format is displayed with leading blanks. To eliminate extra leading blanks, choose a format that will display the smallest value expected without leading blanks. If the actual value requires more print positions, the field width will expand to accommodate it. A format of :1 displays any integer value without leading blanks. A format of :4:2 displays any real number accurate to two decimal places without leading blanks; similarly, a format of :5:3 displays any real number accurate to three decimal places without leading blanks.

Using WriteLn without an Output List

In Fig. 2.13, the call to procedure WriteLn

```
WriteLn;
```

has no output list and causes a blank line in the middle of the program output. Execution of a WriteLn always causes the cursor to be advanced to the next line. If nothing is printed on the current line, a blank line appears in the program output.

SYNTAX
DISPLAY

WriteLn Procedure (without an Output List)

Form: WriteLn
Interpretation: Executing the WriteLn procedure advances the cursor to the first column of the next line.

Formatting Strings

A string value is always printed right-justified in its field. Therefore, blank spaces precede a string if the field in which it is printed is bigger than the string. If *field width* is too small to accommodate a string value, only the first *field width* characters are displayed. Table 2.5 illustrates these points.

Table 2.5 Printing String Values Using Formats

String	Format	Printed Output
'*'	:1	*
'*'	:2	□*
'*'	:3	□□*
'ACES'	:1	A
'ACES'	:2	AC
'ACES'	:3	ACE
'ACES'	:4	ACES
'ACES'	:5	□ACES

Exercises for Section 2.6

Self-Check

1. What is the primary difference between Write and WriteLn? When would you use WriteLn without an output list?
2. Correct the following statement:

   ```
   WriteLn ("His salary is", Salary :2:10)
   ```

3. Show how the value −15.564 (stored in X) would be printed using the following formats

   ```
   X :8:4, X :8:3, X :8:2, X :8:1, X :8:0, X :8
   ```

4. Assuming X (type Real) is 12.335 and that I (type Integer) is 100, show the output lines for the following statements. For clarity, use the symbol □ to denote a blank.

   ```
   WriteLn ('X is ' :10, X :6:2, 'I is ', :4, I :5);
   Write ('I is ' :10, I :1);
   WriteLn ('X is ' :10, X :2:1);
   ```

Programming

1. If the variables A, B, and C are 504, 302.558, and −12.31, respectively, write a statement that will display the following line (for clarity, a □ denotes a space).

   ```
   □504□□□□□302.56□□□□−12.3
   ```

2. Extend the program in Fig. 2.12 to handle dimes and quarters as well as nickels and pennies.

 ## 2.7 Overview of Data Types

Before we go any further, let's clarify exactly what is meant by a data type in a programming language. A *data type* is a set of values and a set of operations on those values. The data type of the object stored in a particular memory cell determines how the bit pattern in that cell is interpreted. For example, a bit pattern that represents a type Integer object is different from a bit pattern that represents a type Char object or a program instruction.

A *standard data type* is a data type that is predefined in the programming language (for example, Real, Integer, Char). Besides using standard data types, programmers can define their own data types in Pascal.

In Pascal, the standard data types represent familiar objects. For example, the data type Real is the set of real numbers (in the mathematical sense) that can be processed in Pascal. Every type Real object in Pascal is a real number; however, not all real numbers can be represented. Some real numbers are too large or too small, and some real numbers cannot be precisely represented because of the finite size of a memory cell (more on this in Chapter 7).

The normal arithmetic operations (+, −, *, /) for real numbers and the assignment operation (:=) can be performed on type Real objects in Pascal. Input/output operations are performed using procedures Read (described later), ReadLn, Write, and WriteLn.

The other standard data type that represents numbers is type Integer. Type Integer objects in Pascal correspond to the integers in mathematics (for example, −77, 0, 999, +999). However, because of the finite size of a memory cell, not all integers can be represented.

The standard identifier MaxInt is a constant that represents the largest integer that can be represented in each Pascal system. Use the statement

```
WriteLn (MaxInt);
```

to display that value.

The arithmetic, assignment, and input/output operations listed for type Real objects can also be performed on type Integer objects. Chapter 7 discusses the integer division operators div and mod; Appendix A lists the Pascal operators.

Real and Integer data types differ in one basic way: real objects can store a number with a decimal point and a fractional part, whereas integer variables can store only a whole number. For this reason, type Integer objects are more restricted in their use. We often use them to represent a count of items (for example, our count of coins), because a count must always be a whole number.

Objects of a data type may be variables, constants, or literals; a *literal* is a value that appears directly in a program. A type Real literal is a number that begins with a digit and contains a decimal point followed by at least one digit (for example, 0.112, 456.0, 123.456). A type Real literal may have a *scale factor*, which is the capital letter E followed by an optional sign and an integer (for example, 0.112E3, 456.0E−2). The scale factor may also follow a string of digits without a decimal point (for example, 123E6 and 123.0E6 are equivalent Real literals). A scale factor means "multiply the number before the letter E by 10 raised to the power appearing after the letter E" (for example, 0.112E3 is 112.0, 456.0E−2 is 4.56). A Real literal may be preceded by a plus or a minus sign when it appears in a program. Table 2.6 shows examples of valid and invalid Real literals.

Valid Real Literals	Invalid Real Literals
3.14159	150 (no decimal point)
0.005	.12345 (no digit before the decimal point)
12345.0	16. (no digit after the decimal point)
15.0E-04 (value is 0.0015)	-15E-0.3 (0.3 is an invalid power)
2.345E2 (value is 234.5)	12.5E.3 (.3 is an invalid power)
12E+6 (value is 12000000)	.123E3 (.123 is an invalid real)
1.15E-3 (value is 0.00115)	

The last valid literal in the table, 1.15E-3, has the same value as 1.15×10^{-3} in normal scientific notation, where the exponent $^{-3}$ causes the decimal point to be moved left three digits. A positive exponent causes the decimal point to be moved to the right; the plus sign can be omitted when the exponent is positive.

The third standard data type is type Char. You have already seen (Fig. 2.1) that type Char variables can be used to store any single character value. A type Char literal must be enclosed in single apostrophes (for example, 'A'); however, you don't use apostrophes when you enter character data at a terminal. When the ReadLn procedure reads character data into a type Char variable, the next character you enter at the terminal is stored in that variable. Enter the blank character by pressing the space bar; a blank is written in a program as the literal ' '.

■ Example 2.7

The program in Fig. 2.14 first reads and echos three characters entered at the keyboard. Next, it prints them in reverse order and enclosed in asterisks. Each character is stored in a variable of type Char; the character value '*' is associated with the constant Border.
The line

```
WriteLn (Border, Third, Second, First, Border);
```

displays the three characters in reverse order. As shown in the program output, each character value is printed in a single print position. The second character read in the sample run of Fig. 2.14 is a blank.

Figure 2.14 Program for Example 2.7

```
program Reverse (Input, Output);

  const
    Border = '*';

  var
    First, Second, Third : Char;
```

```
begin
   Write ('Enter 3 characters> ');
   ReadLn (First, Second, Third);
   WriteLn (Border, Third, Second, First, Border)
end.
```

```
Enter 3 characters> E K
*K E*
```

In Fig. 2.14, the string literal 'Enter 3 characters> ' is displayed as a prompt. As in this case, strings are often used as prompts and to clarify program output. Strings cannot, however, be stored in type Char variables. (You will see how to process strings later in the text.) ■

The fourth standard data type is type Boolean (named after the mathematician George Boole). True and False are the only values associated with this data type. You will see examples of Boolean expressions (expressions that evaluate to True or False) in Chapter 3.

Exercises for Section 2.7

Self-Check

1. Which of the following values are valid? Which are invalid? Identify the data types of the valid values.

   ```
   15 'XYZ' '*' $ 25.123 15. −999 .123 'x' "x"
   '9' '−5' True 'True'
   ```

Programming

1. Write a program that stores the values 'X', '0', 1.345E10, and True in separate memory cells. Your program should read the first three values as data items; use an assignment statement to store the last value.

 ## 2.8 Common Programming Errors

One of the first things you will discover in writing programs is that a program rarely runs correctly the first time it is submitted. Murphy's Law, "If something can go wrong, it will," seems to be written with computer programming in mind. In fact, errors are so common that they have their own special name—*bugs*—and the process of correcting them is called *debugging a program*. To alert you to potential problems, a section on common errors appears near the end of each chapter.

When the compiler detects an error, the computer displays an *error message*, which indicates that you have made a mistake and what the cause of the error might be. Unfortunately, error messages are often difficult to interpret and are sometimes misleading. As you gain some experience, however, you will become more proficient at understanding them.

There are two basic categories of error messages: syntax error messages and run-time error messages. *Syntax errors* are detected and displayed by the compiler as it attempts to translate your program. If a statement has a syntax error, it cannot be translated and your program will not be executed.

Run-time errors are detected by the computer and are displayed during execution of a program. A run-time error occurs when the user directs the computer to perform an illegal operation, such as dividing a number by zero or manipulating undefined or invalid data. When a run-time error occurs, the computer stops executing your program and prints a diagnostic message that indicates the line where the error occurred. Sometimes, the computer prints the values of all variables as well.

Syntax Errors

Figure 2.15 shows a *compiler listing* of the payroll program. A compiler listing is printed by the compiler during program translation and shows each line of the source program (preceded by a line number) and also displays any syntax errors detected by the compiler. The errors are indicated by five asterisks and are summarized at the bottom of the compiler listing. The program contains the following syntax errors:

- missing semicolon after the program heading (line 1)
- use of : instead of = in the constant declaration (line 4)
- missing semicolon after the `WriteLn` statement (line 12)
- assignment statement with transposed variable and expression part (line 14)
- missing declaration for variable `Net` (lines 15 and 17)

Figure 2.15 Compiler Listing of a Program with Syntax Errors

```
     1 program Payroll (Input, Output)
     2
     3 const
*****       ^14
     4    Tax : 25.0;
*****          ^16,50
     5
     6 var
     7    Hours, Rate, Gross : Real;
     8
     9 begin
    10    WriteLn ('Enter hours worked');
    11    ReadLn (Hours);
    12    WriteLn ('Enter hourly rate')
    13    ReadLn (Rate);
*****           ^6
    14    Hours * Rate := Gross;
*****             ^59
    15    Net := Gross - Tax;
*****           ^104
    16    WriteLn ('Gross pay is $', Gross);
```

```
    17   WriteLn ('Net   pay is $', Net)
*****                                   ^104
    18 end.
```

```
  6: ILLEGAL SYMBOL
 14: ";" expected
 16: "=" expected
 50: error in constant
 59: error in variable
104  identifier not declared
```

The actual format of the listing and error messages produced by your compiler may differ from Fig. 2.15. In this listing, whenever an error is detected, the compiler prints a line starting with five asterisks, a caret symbol (^), and a list of numbers. The caret points to the position in the preceding line where the error was detected. Each number is a preassigned code for the error; the codes and their meanings follow the program.

To see how a compiler listing works, look at the first error in the program, which was detected after the reserved word const was processed by the compiler. At this point, the compiler recognized that a semicolon is missing (after the program heading) and indicated this by printing error code 14 (";" expected). In this case, the position of the caret is misleading, because the compiler could not detect the error until it started to process the constant declaration. There is also a missing semicolon in line 12; this time, however, the compiler prints error code 6 (illegal symbol) after processing the standard identifier ReadLn in line 13.

Two error codes are printed after line 4 to indicate an incorrect symbol (: instead of =). The transposed assignment statement in line 14 is printed as error code 59 (error in variable); the compiler was looking for the variable in the assignment statement and detected an error when it reached the asterisk.

An identifier not declared syntax error occurs if the compiler cannot find the declaration for an identifier referred to in the program body. This can happen because the programmer forgot the declaration or mistyped the name of the identifier. Omitting the declaration for variable Net caused the display of error code 104 (identifier not declared) after lines 15 and 17.

One syntax error often leads to the generation of multiple error messages. For example, forgetting to declare variable Net will cause an error message to be printed each time Net is used in the program. For this reason, it is often a good idea initially to concentrate on correcting the errors in the declaration part of a program and then recompile rather than attempt to fix all the errors at once. Many later errors disappear once the declarations are correct.

Syntax errors are often caused by the improper use of apostrophes with strings. Make sure you always use single quotation marks or apostrophes to begin and end a string; double quotation marks cannot be used to begin and end a string.

Another common syntax error is a missing or extra apostrophe in a string. If the apostrophe at the end is missing, the compiler assumes that whatever follows is part of the string. A string must begin and end on the same line. The following string contains an extra apostrophe:

```
WriteLn ('Enter Joe's nickname:');
```

The compiler will assume that the apostrophe used to indicate possession (Joe's) terminates the string. This string must be entered as

```
WriteLn ('Enter Joe''s nickname:');
```

The two consecutive apostrophes indicate a single apostrophe inside a string. Appendix C provides a list of errors and error numbers.

Run-Time Errors

Figure 2.16 is an example of a run-time error. The program compiles successfully but contains no statement assigning a value to variable X before the assignment statement

```
Z := X + Y;
```

is executed. The error messages shown after the program listing indicate the cause of the error (undefined variable), the location (line 8), and the values of all the variables in the program at the time of the error (X and Z are undefined).

Figure 2.16   A Program with a Run-Time Error

```
1 program TestError (Input, Output);
2
3    var
4       X, Y, Z : Real;
5
6 begin
7    Y := 5.0;
8    Z := X + Y;
9    WriteLn (X, Y, Z)
10 end.


Program terminated at line 8 in program TestError
Undefined variable in expression

                -- TestError ---

X = UNDEF                        Y = 5.000000E+00
Z = UNDEF
```

Another common run-time error is division by zero, which occurs if the program attempts to divide one variable by another that has a value of zero. Another common error, arithmetic overflow, occurs when a program attempts to store a number that is too large in a variable.

As indicated earlier, debugging a program can be time-consuming. The best approach is to plan your programs carefully and desk check them to eliminate bugs before you run the program. If you are not sure of the syntax for a particular statement, look it up in this text or in the glossary. By following this approach, you will save yourself much time and trouble.

 # Chapter Review

You have seen how to use the Pascal programming language to perform some fundamental operations. You have learned how to instruct the computer to read information into memory, perform some simple computations, and print the results of those computations. All of this was done using symbols (punctuation marks, variable names, and special operators such as *, −, and +) that are familiar, easy to remember, and easy to use. You do not have to know very much about your computer to understand and use Pascal.

The remainder of this text introduces more features of the Pascal language and provides rules for using those features. You must remember throughout that, unlike the rules of English, the rules of Pascal are precise and allow no exceptions. The compiler cannot translate Pascal instructions that violate these rules. Remember to declare every identifier used as a variable or a constant and to separate program statements with semicolons.

New Pascal Constructs

Table 2.7 describes the new Pascal constructs introduced in this chapter.

Table 2.7   Summary of New Pascal Constructs

Construct	Effect
Program Heading program Payroll (Input, Output);	Identifies Payroll as the name of the program and Input and Output as names of data files.

Constant Declaration
const
  Tax = 25.00;
  Star = '*';
	Associates the constant Tax with the real value 25.00 and the constant Star with the type Char value '*'.

Variable Declaration
var
  X, Y, Z : Real;
  Me, It : Integer;
	Allocates memory cells named X, Y, and Z for storage of real numbers and Me and It for storage of integers.

Assignment Statement Distance := Speed * Time	Assigns the product of Speed and Time as the value of Distance.
ReadLn Procedure ReadLn (Hours, Rate)	Enters data into the variables Hours and Rate.

Table 2.7 Summary of New Pascal Constructs, *continued*

Construct	Effect
Write Procedure `Write ('Net = ', Net :4:2)`	Displays the string `'Net = '` followed by the value of `Net` printed in a field of four columns and rounded to two decimal places.
WriteLn Procedure `WriteLn (X, Y)`	Prints the values of `X` and `Y` and advances the cursor to the next line.
Reset Procedure (Optional) `Reset (InData)`	Prepares file `InData` for reading.
ReadLn with File (Optional) `ReadLn (InData, X, Y)`	Reads values of `X` and `Y` from a line of file `InData`.

✓ *Quick-Check Exercises*

1. What value is assigned to X by the following statement?

   `X := 25.0 * 3.0 / 2.5`

2. What value is assigned to X by the following statement, assuming X is 10.0?

   `X := X - 20.0`

3. Show the exact form of the output line displayed when X is 3.456.

   `WriteLn ('Three values of X are ', X :4:1, '*', X :5:2, '*', X: 6:3);`

4. Show the exact form of the output line when N is 345.

   `WriteLn ('Three values of N are ', N :4, '*', N :5, '*', N :1);`

5. What data type would you use to represent the following items: number of children at school, a letter grade on an exam, the average number of school days students are absent each year?

6. When data are entered into an interactive program, which procedure is called first, `ReadLn` or `WriteLn`?

7. When data is entered into a batch program, which procedure is called first, `ReadLn` or `WriteLn`?

8. If procedure `ReadLn` is reading two numbers, what character is typed after the first number? What is typed after the second number?

9. If procedure `ReadLn` is reading two characters, what character is typed after the first character? What is typed after the second character?

10. How does the computer determine how many data values to enter when a `ReadLn` operation is performed?

11. How does a program user determine how many data values to enter when a ReadLn operation is performed?
12. What kind of errors does a compiler listing show?

Answers to Quick-Check Exercises
1. 30.0
2. −10.0
3. Three values of X are 3.5* 3.46* 3.456
4. Three values of N are 345* 345*345
5. Integer, Character, Real
6. WriteLn, to display a prompt
7. ReadLn, to get the data
8. a blank, the Return key
9. the second character, the Return key
10. It depends on the number of variables in the input list.
11. from reading the prompt
12. syntax errors

Review Questions

1. Are double or single quotation marks used as string delimiters?
2. Which of the following variables are syntactically correct?

```
Income      Two Fold
1time       C3PO
const       Income#1
Tom's       item
```

3. What is illegal about the following declarations and statement?

```
const
  Pi = 3.14159;
var
  C, R : Real;

begin
  Pi := C / (2 * R * R);
```

4. What computer action is required by the following statement?

```
var Cell : Real;
```

5. Write a program to read a five-character name and print the name out backward.
6. If the average size of a family is 2.8 and this value is stored in the variable FamilySize, provide a Pascal statement to display this fact in a readable way (leave the cursor on the same line).
7. List the four standard data types of Pascal.
8. Convert the following program statements to read and echo data in batch mode.

```
Write ('Enter three numbers separated by spaces> ');
ReadLn (X, Y, Z);
WriteLn ('Enter two characters> ');
ReadLn (Ch1, Ch2);
```

9. Write a program that reads in an integer value, doubles it, subtracts 10, and displays the result.

Programming Projects

1. Write a program to convert a temperature in degrees Fahrenheit to degrees Celsius. Use the formula

    Celsius = (5/9) × (*Fahrenheit* − 32)

2. Write a program that reads three data items into variables X, Y, and Z and then finds and prints their product and sum.

3. Write a program that reads in the weight (in pounds) of an object and then computes and prints its weight in kilograms and grams. (Hint: 1 pound equals 0.453592 kilogram and 453.59237 grams.)

4. Write a program that prints your first initial as a block letter. (Hint: Use a 6-by-6 grid for the letter and print six strings. Each string should consist of asterisks interspersed with blanks.)

5. If a human heart beats on the average of once a second for 78 years, how many times does it beat in a lifetime? (Use 365.25 for days in a year.) Rerun your program for a heart rate of 75 beats per minute.

Problem Solving and Procedures

3

All your life, you have been solving problems using your own intuitive strategies. Problem solving on a computer requires that you follow a more formal approach. This chapter will help you learn how to analyze a problem and devise an *algorithm*, or list of steps, to describe a possible solution. You will also learn how to verify that a proposed algorithm solves its intended problem.

In this chapter, we show you how to solve a problem by breaking it up into smaller, more manageable subproblems. We also introduce an important Pascal construct, the procedure. Procedures allow us to write each subproblem's solution as a separate group of Pascal statements.

3.1   Representing and Refining Algorithms

Divide and Conquer

One of the most fundamental methods of problem solving is to break a large problem into several smaller *subproblems*. In this way, we can solve a large problem one step at a time, rather than attempt to provide the entire solution at once. This technique is often called *divide and conquer*.

As an example, let's look forward to the year 2000. Our household robot, Robbie, helps us with some simple chores. Each morning, we would like Robbie to serve us breakfast. Unfortunately, Robbie is an early production model, and to get him to perform even the simplest task, we must provide him with a detailed list of instructions. In this case, the problem to be solved is getting Robbie to serve breakfast.

Case Study: Robbie Serving Breakfast

Problem
In Fig. 3.1, Robbie is at point R (for Robbie). We want Robbie to retrieve our favorite box of cereal (at point C) and bring it to the table (at point T) in the next room.

Design Overview
We can accomplish our goal by instructing Robbie to perform the following four steps, or subproblems.

1. Move from point R to point C.
2. Retrieve the cereal box at point C.
3. Move from point C to point T.
4. Place the cereal box on the table at point T.

Solving these four subproblems will give us the solution to the original problem.

We can attack each subproblem independently. To solve any of these problems, however, we must know which basic operations Robbie can perform.

Assume that Robbie can rotate or turn to face any direction, move straight ahead, and grasp and release specified objects. Given this information, subproblems 2 and 4 are basic operations, provided Robbie is in the correct position. First, we will concentrate on moving Robbie (subproblems 1 and 3).

In solving the first subproblem,

1. Move from point R to point C

we must allow for the fact that Robbie can move in only one direction at a time, and that direction is straight ahead. Consequently, the steps required to solve subproblem 1 are

1.1 Turn to face point C.
1.2 Move from point R to point C.

Subproblem 3 can be solved in a similar way. However, since Robbie cannot walk through walls, the steps for solving subproblem 3 might be

3.1 Turn to face the doorway (point D) between the rooms.
3.2 Move from point C to point D.
3.3 Turn to face point T.
3.4 Move from point D to point T.

To summarize the process so far, we divided the original problem into four subproblems, all of which can be solved independently. We then broke up two of those subproblems into even smaller subproblems.

Now look at the complete list of the steps required to solve our problem. A list of steps to solve a problem is called an *algorithm*. The process of adding detail to a solution algorithm (for example, rewriting step 1 as steps 1.1 and 1.2) is called *stepwise refinement*.

Algorithm

1. Move from point R to point C.
   1.1 Turn to face point C.
   1.2 Move from point R to point C.
2. Retrieve the cereal box at point C.

Figure 3.1 Robbie Serving Breakfast

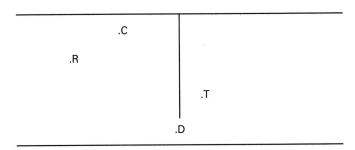

3. Move from point C to point T.
   3.1 Turn to face the doorway (point D) between the rooms.
   3.2 Move from point C to point D.
   3.3 Turn to face point T.
   3.4 Move from point D to point T.
4. Place the cereal box on the table at point T.

Algorithms in Everyday Life

Algorithms are not unique to the study of robots or computer programming. You have probably used algorithms to solve problems without being aware of it. Let's look at an everyday problem for which we can create an algorithm.

Case Study: Changing a Flat Tire

Problem
You are driving a car with two friends and suddenly get a flat tire. Fortunately, you have a spare tire and a jack in the trunk.

Design Overview
After pulling over to the side of the road, you might decide to divide the problem of changing a tire into the subproblems below.

Algorithm

1. Get the jack and jack up the car.
2. Loosen the lug nuts from the flat tire and remove it.
3. Get the spare tire, place it on the wheel, and tighten the lug nuts.
4. Lower the car.
5. Secure the jack and the flat tire in the trunk.

   Since these steps are relatively independent, you might decide to assign subproblem 1 to friend A, subproblem 2 to friend B, subproblem 3 to yourself, and so on. If friend A has used a jack before, then the whole process should proceed smoothly; however, if friend A does not know how to use a jack, you need to refine step 1 further.

   Step 1 Refinement
   1.1 Get the jack from the trunk.
   1.2 Place the jack under the car near the flat tire.
   1.3 Insert the jack handle in the jack.
   1.4 Place a block of wood under the car to keep it from rolling.
   1.5 Jack up the car until there is enough room for the spare tire.

Step 1.4 requires a bit of decision making on your friend's part. Because the actual placement of the block of wood depends on whether the car is facing uphill or downhill, friend A needs to refine step 1.4.

Step 1.4 Refinement
1.4.1 If the car is facing uphill, place the block of wood in back of a tire that is not flat; if the car is facing downhill, place the block of wood in front of a tire that is not flat.

Finally, step 1.5 involves a repetitive action: moving the jack handle until there is sufficient room to put on the spare tire. It may take a few attempts to complete step 1.5.

Step 1.5 Refinement
1.5.1 Move the jack handle repeatedly until the car is high enough off the ground that the spare tire can be put on the wheel.

Sequential Execution, Conditional Execution, and Repetition

The algorithm for changing a flat tire has three categories of action: sequential execution, conditional execution, and repetition. *Sequential execution* simply means to carry out steps 1.1 through 1.5 in the sequence listed. Step 1.4.1 illustrates *conditional execution* in that the placement of the block of wood depends on the angle of inclination of the car. Step 1.5.1 illustrates *repetition*.

These three categories of action must be possible in a computer program as well. A program carries out its executable statements in sequence. A program also may contain *control statements* that cause conditional execution and repetition. Chapter 4 describes one Pascal statement for specifying conditional execution, and Chapter 5 describes one Pascal statement for specifying repetition.

Understanding the Problem

An important skill in human communication is the ability to listen carefully. Often we are too busy thinking about our response to really hear what the other person is saying, which can lead to a lack of understanding between the speaker and listener.

Many of us suffer from a similar difficulty when we attempt to solve problems that are presented either verbally or in writing. We do not pay close enough attention to the problem statement to determine exactly what is being asked. Consequently, either we are unable to solve the stated problem or our problem solution is incorrect because it solves the wrong problem.

This text is concerned with improving your problem-solving skills, and presents hints and techniques for problem solving. To successfully solve a problem, you must analyze the problem statement carefully before you attempt to solve it. You may need to read each problem statement two or three times. The first time, get a general idea of what is being asked. The second time, try to answer these questions:

What information should the solution provide?
What data do I have to work with?

The answer to the first question will tell you the desired results, or the *problem outputs*. The answer to the second question will tell you the data provided, or the *problem inputs*. It may be helpful to underline the phrases in the problem statement that identify the inputs and the outputs, as in the problem statement discussed in the next section.

Exercise for Section 3.1

Self-Check

1. Write an algorithm for preparing and warming a baby's formula. Make sure your algorithm prevents you from feeding the baby if the formula is too cold or too hot.

 ## 3.2   Problem Solving Illustrated

In this section we apply the problem-solving principles discussed earlier. We begin with the problem statement and finish with a computer program that solves the problem.

● Case Study: Finding the Area and Circumference of a Circle

Problem
Read in the <u>radius of a circle</u> and compute and print its <u>area</u> and <u>circumference</u>.

Design Overview
After identifying the problem inputs and outputs, we must determine the amount and type of memory required to store those data. Clearly, one memory cell is required for the input data and two memory cells are required for the output information. All memory cells should be type Real because the inputs and outputs can contain fractional parts. You must also choose meaningful variable names for those cells.

Data Requirements

Problem Inputs
the radius of a circle (Radius : Real)

Problem Outputs
the area of the circle (`Area : Real`)
the circumference of the circle (`Circum : Real`)

Once you know the problem inputs and outputs, you should list the steps necessary to solve the problem. It is important that you pay close attention to the order of the steps. The initial algorithm follows.

Initial Algorithm

1. Read the value of `Radius`.
2. Find the area.
3. Find the circumference.
4. Print the values of the area and the circumference.

Algorithm Refinements
Next, refine any steps that do not have an obvious solution (for instance, steps 2 and 3).

Step 2 Refinement
2.1 Multiply the radius squared by the value of pi (3.14159).

Step 3 Refinement
3.1 Compute the product of 2, pi, and `Radius`.

Coding
Next, you must implement the algorithm as a program by first writing the declarations for the program using the problem input and output descriptions. You must also declare any additional variables or constants introduced in the algorithm. For example, pi was not mentioned as a problem input or output and should be declared as a constant (value is 3.14159). Next, write the algorithm steps in Pascal, implementing refined steps where applicable.

Following this procedure gives the program shown in Fig. 3.2. Algorithm steps 1, 2.1, 3.1, and 4 are implemented in the program body following the type declarations. The purpose of the curly braces is discussed in the next section.

Figure 3.2 Finding the Area and the Circumference of a Circle

```
program AreaAndCircum (Input, Output);
```
{Finds and prints the area and circumference of a circle}

```
    const
      Pi = 3.14159;

    var
      Radius,             {input - radius of a circle}
      Area,               {output - area of a circle}
```

```
        Circum : Real;       {output - circumference of a circle}

begin {AreaAndCircum}
  {Read the value of the radius}
  Write ('Enter radius> ');
  ReadLn (Radius);

  {Find the area}
  Area := Pi * Radius * Radius;

  {Find the circumference}
  Circum := 2.0 * Pi * Radius;

  {Print the values of Area and Circum}
  WriteLn ('The area is ', Area :4:2);
  WriteLn ('The circumference is ', Circum :4:2)
end. {AreaAndCircum}


Enter radius> 5.0
The area is 78.54
The circumference is 31.42
```

Exercises for Section 3.2

Self-Check

1. Describe the problem inputs and outputs and the algorithm for computing an employee's gross salary given the hours worked and the hourly rate.
2. Describe the problem inputs and outputs and the algorithm for the following problem: Read in a pair of numbers and determine the sum and average of the two numbers.

Programming

1. Write a program for question 2 in the self-check exercises.

 # 3.3 Comments and Documentation

The program in Fig. 3.2 contains some English phrases enclosed in curly braces. Programmers use such phrases, called *comments*, to make the program easier to understand by describing the purpose of the program (see the first comment line), the use of identifiers (see the comments in the variable declarations), and the purpose of each program step (see the comments in the program body). Comments are an important part of the *documentation* of a program because they help others read and understand the program. The compiler, however, ignores comments, and they are not translated into machine language.

As shown in Fig. 3.2, a comment can appear by itself on a program line, at the end of a line after a statement, or embedded in a statement. The comment at the end of the second line

```
var
    Radius,          {input - radius of a circle}
```

is embedded within the variable declaration, which is continued following the comment. This text documents the use of most variables in that way. The next two displays describe the syntax and use of comments.

Comment

Form: {comment}
Example: {This is a comment}
         (* and so is this *)
Interpretation: A left curly brace indicates the start of a comment; a right curly brace indicates the end of a comment. Alternately, (* and *) can mark the beginning and the end, respectively, of a comment. Comments are listed with the program but are otherwise ignored by the Pascal compiler.
Note: You cannot place one comment inside another.

Using Comments

Comments make a program more readable because they describe the purpose of the program and the use of each identifier. For example, the comment in the declaration

```
var
    Radius,          {input - radius of a circle}
```

describes the use of variable Radius.

Place comments within the program body to describe the purpose of each section of the program. Generally, you should include one comment in the program body for each major algorithm step. Make sure a comment within the program body describes what the step does rather than simply restate the step in English. For example, the comment

```
{Find the area}
Area := Pi * Radius * Radius
```

is more descriptive than and, hence, preferable to

```
{Multiply the Radius by itself and Pi}
Area := Pi * Radius * Radius
```

Begin each program with a header section that consists of a series of comments specifying

- the programmer's name
- the date of the current version
- a brief description of what the program does

If you write the program for a class assignment, you should also list the class identification and your instructor's name.

Exercise for Section 3.3

Self-Check

1. Explain what is wrong with the following comments:

```
(This is a comment? *)
(* How about this one {it seems like a comment} doesn't it *)
```

 ## 3.4 Subproblems and Procedures

The Structure Chart

As mentioned earlier, one of the most fundamental ideas in problem solving is dividing a problem into subproblems and solving each subproblem independently of the others. In the simple problem of finding the area and the circumference of a circle, this was not a difficult task. Only two subproblems required refinement, and that was not extensive. In many situations, one or more subproblems may require significant refinement, as you will see in the next problem.

● Case Study: Printing a Mother's Day Message

Problem
You would like to do something special for your mother on Mother's Day. You decide to write a Pascal program to print the message HI MOM in large capital letters.

Design Overview
You can interpret this problem in more than one way. You could simply print HI MOM as it appears here, but that would not be too impressive. It would be more unusual to use large block letters, as shown in Fig. 3.3. Because program output tends to run from the top of the screen downward, it is easier and more interesting to print the letters in a vertical column rather than across the screen.

Figure 3.3 Mother's Day Message

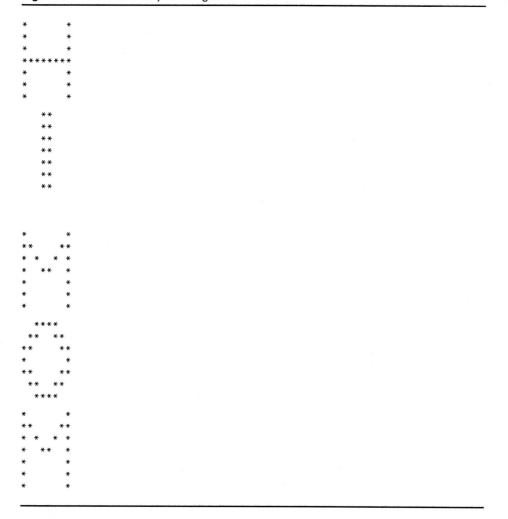

Initial Algorithm

1. Print the word HI in block letters.
2. Print three blank lines.
3. Print the word MOM in block letters.

Algorithm Refinements

The obvious refinements for each step are shown next.

Step 1 Refinement
1.1 Print the letter H.
1.2 Print the letter I.

Case Study: Printing a Mother's Day Message, continued

Step 3 Refinement
3.1 Print the letter M.
3.2 Print the letter O.
3.3 Print the letter M.

We can illustrate the steps in the problem-solving process with a diagram that shows the algorithm subproblems and their interdependencies. An example of such a diagram, called a *structure chart*, is shown in Fig. 3.4.

As we trace down this diagram, we go from an abstract problem to a more detailed subproblem. The original problem is shown at the top, or level 0, of the structure chart. The major subproblems appear at level 1. The different subproblems that result from the refinement of each level-1 step are shown at level 2 and are connected to their respective level-1 subproblems. The right side of the structure chart shows that the subproblem *Print MOM* (level 1) depends on the solutions to the subproblems *Print M* and *Print O* (level 2). Since the subproblem *Print 3 blank lines* is not refined further, no level-2 subproblems are connected to it.

Structure charts are intended to show the structural relationship between subproblems. The algorithm (not the structure chart) shows the order in which you must carry out each step to solve the problem.

Exercises for Section 3.4

Self-Check

1. Draw the structure chart for the case study in section 3.2.
2. Why was it all right to show the step *Print M* only once in the structure chart?

Figure 3.4 Structure Chart for Mother's Day Message

3.5 Procedures

The structure chart proceeds from the original problem at the top level down to its detailed subproblems at the bottom level. It would be convenient to follow this *top-down* approach when we code a program, and the procedure construct in Pascal enables us to do so.

A Pascal *procedure* is a grouping of program statements into a single program unit. Just like ReadLn and WriteLn, each Pascal procedure that we write can be activated through the execution of a procedure call statement. If we assume that we have procedures available that implement each of the level-2 subproblems in Fig. 3.4, we can use the following code fragment to implement the level-1 subproblem *Print HI*.

```
{Print HI.}
PrintH;
PrintI;
```

This code fragment contains two procedure call statements. During program execution, the procedure call statement

```
PrintH;
```

causes the statements contained in the body of procedure PrintH to be executed. The next section describes how to write procedure PrintH.

Figure 3.5 shows the body of the Mother's Day program, with the solution to each subproblem at level 2 in Fig. 3.4 implemented as a separate procedure. The program body (called the *main program*) implements the original algorithm. The program body begins with the code for step 1 (*Print HI*), which consists of the two procedure call statements previously listed. The code for step 2 (*Print three blank lines*) consists of three calls to procedure WriteLn. In the code for step 3 (*Print MOM*), the procedure call statement

```
PrintM
```

appears twice because the letter M must be printed twice.

Figure 3.5 Main Program Body for the Mother's Day Problem

```
begin {Mother}
  {Print HI}
  PrintH;
  PrintI;

  {Print three blank lines}
  WriteLn;
  WriteLn;
  WriteLn;

  {Print MOM}
  PrintM;
  PrintO;
  PrintM
end. {Mother}
```

Declaring Procedures

Just like other identifiers in Pascal, a procedure must be declared before it can be referenced in a program body. Figure 3.6 shows the declaration for procedure PrintM.

Figure 3.6 Procedure PrintM

```
procedure PrintM;

{Prints M.}

begin {PrintM}
   WriteLn ('*        *');
   WriteLn ('**      **');
   WriteLn ('* *    * *');
   WriteLn ('*   **   *');
   WriteLn ('*        *');
   WriteLn ('*        *');
   WriteLn ('*        *');
   WriteLn
end; {PrintM}
```

A procedure declaration begins with a *procedure heading*, which consists of the word procedure followed by the procedure name (an identifier) and a semicolon. A comment describing the purpose of the procedure comes next, followed by the *procedure body*. The procedure body always starts with begin and ends with end;. In Fig. 3.6, the procedure body contains the seven WriteLn statements that cause the computer to print the block letter M, followed by an additional WriteLn statement that displays a blank line. The procedure call statement

```
PrintM
```

causes these WriteLn statements to execute.

In this text, the begin and end that bracket a procedure body are followed by a comment that identifies the procedure's name. The comment is added for clarity and is not required by Pascal. Pascal does, however, require the semicolon following end.

Each procedure declaration may contain declarations for its own constants, variables, and even for other procedures. These identifiers are considered *local* to the procedure; in other words, they can be referenced only within the procedure (more on this later).

Procedure Declaration

Form:
```
       procedure pname;
           local declarations
       begin
           procedure body
       end;
```

Example:
```
       procedure SkipThree;
           {Skips three lines.}
       begin {SkipThree}
          WriteLn;
          WriteLn;
          WriteLn
       end; {SkipThree}
```

Interpretation: The procedure *pname* is declared. Any identifiers that are declared in the *local declarations* are defined only during the execution of the procedure and can be referenced only within the procedure. The procedure body describes the data manipulation to be performed by the procedure.

Placement of Procedure Declarations in a Program

The four procedures called in Fig. 3.5 must appear in the declaration part of the program, just before the program body. It makes no difference which procedure is declared first; their order of execution is determined by the order of procedure call statements in the program body. Figure 3.7 shows the program thus far; complete the remaining procedure declarations as an exercise.

Figure 3.7 Partially Completed Mother's Day Program

```
program Mother (Output);

{Prints a mother's day welcoming message.}

  procedure PrintM;

  {Prints M.}

  begin {PrintM}
    WriteLn ('*        *');
    WriteLn ('**      **');
    WriteLn ('* *    * *');
```

```
      WriteLn ('*   **  *');
      WriteLn ('*       *');
      WriteLn ('*       *');
      WriteLn ('*       *');
      WriteLn
   end; {PrintM}


   procedure PrintH;

   {Prints H.}

   begin {PrintH}
      {body of procedure PrintH goes here}
   end; {PrintH}

   procedure PrintI;

   {Prints I.}

   begin {PrintI}
      {body of procedure PrintI goes here}
   end; {PrintI}


   procedure PrintO;

   {Prints O.}

   begin {PrintO}
      {body of procedure PrintO goes here}
   end; {PrintO}


begin {Mother}
   {Print HI}
   PrintH;
   PrintI;

   {Print three blank lines}
   WriteLn;
   WriteLn;
   WriteLn;

   {Print MOM}
   PrintM;
   PrintO;
   PrintM
end. {Mother}
```

Notice that it is not necessary to include file Input in the program heading. This is because the program does not read any input data.

Use of Comments in a Program with Procedures

Figure 3.7 includes several comments. Each procedure begins with a comment that describes its purpose. The begin and the end that bracket each procedure body and the main program body are followed by a comment that identifies that procedure or program. The first and the last line of each procedure declaration is in color throughout this text to help you locate each procedure in the program listing.

Relative Order of Execution of Procedures and the Main Program

In the Mother's Day message problem, we wrote the main program body as a sequence of procedure call statements before we specified the details of all procedures. The next step is to provide the missing procedure declarations.

When we actually put the separate procedures and the main program body together, the procedures appear in the declaration part of the program just before the program body. The compiler must translate the procedure declarations before it translates the main program body. When it reaches the end of each procedure body, the compiler inserts a statement that causes a *transfer of control* back from the procedure to the calling statement. In the main program body, the compiler translates a procedure call statement as a transfer of control to the procedure.

Figure 3.8 shows the main program body and procedure PrintH of the Mother's Day program in separate areas of memory. Although the Pascal statements are shown in Fig. 3.8, the object code corresponding to each statement is actually stored in memory.

When the program is run, the first statement in the main program body is the first statement executed (the call to PrintH in Fig. 3.8). When the computer executes a procedure call statement, it transfers control to the procedure that is referenced (indicated by the colored line in Fig. 3.8). The computer allocates any memory that may be needed for the procedure's local data and then performs the statements in the procedure body. After the last statement in the

Figure 3.8 Flow of Control Between Main Program and Procedure

procedure body is executed, control returns to the main program (indicated by
the black line in Fig. 3.8), and the computer releases any memory that was
allocated to the procedure. After the return to the main program, the next
statement is executed (the call to `PrintI` in Fig. 3.8).

Advantages of Using Procedures

Pascal procedures are convenient because they allow us to delay the detailed
implementation of a complicated subproblem until a later stage. For example,
we can write procedures `PrintH`, `PrintI`, and `PrintO` of the program `Mother`
later. In fact, we are trying to accomplish the same goal when we divide a
problem into subproblems and add details of the solution through stepwise
refinement. The use of procedures enables us to implement our program in
logically independent sections in the same way that we develop the solution
algorithm.

Another advantage is that procedures can be executed more than once.
For example, procedure `PrintM` is called twice in Fig. 3.7. Each time `PrintM` is
called, the list of output statements shown in Fig. 3.6 is executed, and the letter
M is printed. If we did not use procedures, those eight output statements would
have to be listed twice in the program body, thereby increasing the program's
length and the chance of error.

Finally, once you have written and tested a procedure, you can use it in
other programs. For example, the procedures created for the program `Mother`
could easily be used to write programs that display the message OH HIM or
HI HO.

Exercises for Section 3.5

Self-Check

1. Assume you have procedures `PrintH`, `PrintI`, `PrintM`, and `PrintO`. What is
   the effect of executing the following main program body?

   ```
   begin {main}
     PrintO;
     PrintH;
     WriteLn; WriteLn; WriteLn;
     PrintH;
     PrintI;
     PrintM
   end. {main}
   ```

Programming

1. Write a procedure named `Skip3` that skips three blank lines. Explain how
   this procedure could be used in the main program for the Mother's Day
   message problem.
2. Write a program to print HI HO in block letters. But first, provide a structure
   chart for this problem.
3. Provide procedures `PrintH`, `PrintI`, and `PrintO` for the Mother's Day message problem.

3.6 Displaying User Instructions

Your use of procedures is limited for the time being because you do not yet know how to pass information into or out of a procedure that you declare. (Chapter 6 describes how to use procedure parameters for that purpose.) Until you can do that, we will use procedures only to display information or instructions to a program user.

■ Example 3.1

The procedure in Fig. 3.9 displays instructions to a user of the program that computes the area and the circumference of a circle (see Fig. 3.2). If procedure Instruct is placed in the declaration part of the original program, the new program body can begin with the procedure call statement

```
Instruct;
```

The rest of the program body consists of the executable statements shown earlier. Figure 3.10 shows the output lines displayed by calling procedure Instruct. The rest of the program output will be the same as the output shown in Fig. 3.2.

Figure 3.9 Procedure Instruct

```
procedure Instruct;

{Displays instructions to a user of program AreaAndCircum.}

begin {Instruct}
  WriteLn ('This program computes the area');
  WriteLn ('and circumference of a circle.');
  WriteLn;
  WriteLn ('To use this program, enter the radius of');
  WriteLn ('the circle after the prompt: Enter radius>');
  WriteLn;
  WriteLn ('The circumference will be computed in the');
  WriteLn ('same units of measurement as the radius. The');
  WriteLn ('area will be computed in the same units squared.');
  WriteLn
end; {Instruct}
```

Figure 3.10 Output Lines Displayed by Procedure Instruct

```
This program computes the area
and circumference of a circle.

To use this program, enter the radius of the
circle after the prompt: Enter radius>

The circumference will be computed in the
same units of measurement as the radius. The
area will be computed in the same units squared.
```

Exercises for Section 3.6

Programming

1. Show the revised program `AreaAndCircum`.
2. Write a procedure similar to `Instruct` for the program shown in Fig. 2.8.

 ## 3.7 Common Programming Errors

When using comments, you must be very careful to insert the curly braces or the combinations of parentheses and asterisks where required. If the opening { or (* is missing, the compiler will not recognize the beginning of the comment and will attempt to process the comment as a Pascal statement, causing a syntax error. If the closing } or *) is missing, the comment will simply be extended to include the program statements that follow it. If the comment is not terminated, the rest of the program will be included in the comment, and a syntax error such as `incomplete program` will be printed.

Remember to declare each procedure used in a program. The procedure declaration must precede the procedure call and is found in the declaration part of a program.

 ## Chapter Review

The first part of this chapter outlined a method for solving problems on the computer. This method stresses six points:

1. Understand the problem.
2. Identify the input data and the output data for the problem as well as other relevant data.
3. Formulate a precise statement of the problem.
4. Develop a list of steps for solving the problem (an algorithm).
5. Refine the algorithm.
6. Implement the algorithm in Pascal.

We showed you how to divide a problem into subproblems and how to use a structure chart to indicate the relationship between subproblems. We then introduced the procedure as a means of implementing subproblems as separate program units.

By now you have absorbed several guidelines for using program comments. Well-placed and carefully worded comments and a structure chart can provide all the documentation necessary for a program.

New Pascal Constructs in Chapter 3

The new Pascal constructs introduced in this chapter are described in Table 3.1.

Table 3.1 Summary of New Pascal Constructs **79**

Chapter Review

Construct	Effect

Comment
`{This is a comment}`
`(* So is this! *)`
	Comments document the use of variables and statements in a program. They are ignored by the compiler.

Procedure Declaration
`procedure Display;`
 	
`{Prints 3 lines}`
 	
`  const`
`    Star = '*';`
 	
`begin {Display}`
`  WriteLn (Star);`
`  WriteLn (Star);`
`  WriteLn (Star)`
`end; {Display}`
	Procedure `Display` is declared and can be called to print three lines of asterisks. The local constant `Star` is defined only when `Display` is executing.

Procedure Call Statement `Display`	Calls procedure `Display` and causes it to begin execution.

✓ Quick-Check Exercises

1. Does a compiler translate comments?
2. Each statement in a program should have a comment. True or false?
3. What are two ways to denote comments?
4. Each procedure is executed in the order in which it is declared in the main program. True or false?
5. How is a procedure executed in a program?
6. List the order of the declarations in a program.
7. What is a local declaration?
8. What is a structure chart?
9. Explain how a structure chart differs from an algorithm.
10. What does the following procedure do?

    ```
    procedure Nonsense;
    begin {Nonsense}
      WriteLn ('*****');
      WriteLn ('*   *');
      WriteLn ('*****')
    end; {Nonsense}
    ```

11. What does the following program body do?

    ```
    begin
      Nonsense;
      Nonsense;
      Nonsense
    end.
    ```

Answers to Quick-Check Exercises

1. no
2. false
3. using curly braces or a combination of parentheses and asterisks
4. false
5. It is called into execution by a procedure call statement.
6. constants, variables, procedures
7. It is an identifier declared in the declaration part of a procedure.
8. A structure chart is a diagram used to show an algorithm's subproblems and their interdependence.
9. A structure chart shows the relationship between subproblems; an algorithm lists the sequence in which subproblems are performed.
10. It displays a rectangle.
11. It displays three rectangles on top of each other.

Review Questions

1. Discuss the strategy of divide and conquer.
2. Provide guidelines for the use of comments.
3. Briefly describe the steps you would take to derive an algorithm for a given problem.
4. The diagram that shows the algorithm steps and their interdependencies is called a _____.
5. What are three advantages of using procedures?
6. Where in the final program is the main program body found and why?
7. When is a procedure executed? Where must it appear in the main program?
8. Is the use of procedures a more efficient use of the programmer's time or the computer's time? Explain.
9. Write a program that draws a rectangle made up of asterisks. Draw a structure chart for the problem. Use two procedures: DrawSides and DrawLine.

Programming Projects

1. Write three procedures: one that displays a circle, one that displays a triangle, and one that displays a rectangle. Use these procedures in a program that displays the stick figure of a woman.
2. Write procedures that display each of your initials in block letter form. Use these procedures to display your initials.
3. Write a procedure that displays a triangle. Use this procedure to display three triangles on top of each other.
4. Four track stars enter the mile race at the Penn Relays. Write a program that will read in the race time in minutes (Minutes) and seconds (Seconds) for a runner and compute and print the speed in feet per second (FPS) and in meters per second (MPS). (Hint: There are 5,280 feet in one mile and 3,282 feet in one kilometer.) Test your program on each of the times below.

Minutes	Seconds
3	52.83
3	59.83
4	00.03
4	16.22

Write and call a procedure that displays instructions to the program user.

5. A cyclist coasting on a level road goes from an initial velocity to a slower velocity in a certain time interval. Assuming a constant rate of deceleration, write a computer program that calculates the cyclist's rate of deceleration and determines how long it will take the cyclist to come to rest. (Hint: Use the equation

$$a = (v_f - v_i)/t$$

where a is acceleration, t is time interval, v_i is initial velocity, and v_f is the final velocity.) Write and call a procedure that displays instructions to the program user.

6. When shopping for a new house, you must consider several factors. In this problem, the initial cost of the house, the estimated annual fuel costs, and the annual tax rate are available. Write a program that will determine the total cost after a five-year period for each set of data below. Your program output should help you determine the "best buy."

Initial House Cost	Annual Fuel Cost	Tax Rate
$67,000	$2,300	0.025
$62,000	$2,500	0.025
$75,000	$1,850	0.020

To calculate the house cost, add the initial cost to the fuel cost for five years, then add the taxes for five years. Taxes for one year are computed by multiplying the tax rate by the initial cost. Write and call a procedure that displays instructions to the program user.

Decisions and the if Statement

4

T his chapter shows you how to represent decisions in algorithms by writing steps with two or more alternative courses of action. You will see how to implement conditional execution in Pascal by using Boolean expressions and the Pascal `if` statement. This chapter provides many examples of program fragments containing `if` statements. It also introduces syntax diagrams and shows you how to use them to check the syntax of a Pascal construct.

We discuss two more problem-solving stategies: extending an existing solution and solution by analogy. We also show how to desk-check, or hand-trace, the execution of an algorithm or a program.

4.1 Boolean Expressions and the if Statement

In all the algorithms thus far, we executed each algorithm step exactly once in the order in which it appeared. However, we are often faced with situations in which we must provide alternative steps that may or may not be executed, depending on the input data. For example, in the simple payroll problem discussed in Chapter 2, we deducted a tax of $25 regardless of the employee's salary. It would be fairer to base the amount deducted on the employee's gross salary. For example, we might want the program to deduct a tax only if an employee's salary exceeds $100. Carrying this one step further, we might want the program to deduct one tax percentage for salaries between $100 and $300 and a higher percentage for salaries greater than $300.

Boolean Expressions and Conditions

To achieve this goal, the computer must be able to answer questions such as "Is gross salary greater than $100?" In Pascal, this is accomplished by evaluating a Boolean expression. Assuming that the employee's salary is stored in the type real variable Gross, the Boolean expression corresponding to that question is

```
Gross > 100.00
```

There are only two possible values for a Boolean expression: True or False. If Gross is greater than 100.00, the preceding Boolean expression evaluates to True; if Gross is not greater than 100.00, the expression evaluates to False. Chapter 7 examines the operators that can be used with Boolean expressions. For now, we will concentrate on learning how to write and use simple Boolean expressions called conditions.

Most conditions that we use will have one of the following forms:

variable   *relational operator*   *variable*
variable   *relational operator*   *constant*

Relational operators are the familiar symbols < (less than), <= (less than or equal to), > (greater than), >= (greater than or equal to), = (equal to), or <> (not equal to).

■ Example 4.1

Table 4.1 shows the relational operators and some sample conditions. Each condition is evaluated assuming the following variable values.

X	Power	MaxPow	Y	Item	MinItem	MomOrDad	Num	Sentinel
-5	1024	1024	7	1.5	-999.0	'M'	999	999

Table 4.1 Pascal Relational Operators and Sample Conditions

Operator	Condition	English Meaning	Boolean Value
<=	X <= 0	X less than or equal to 0	True
<	Power < MaxPow	Power less than MaxPow	False
>=	X >= Y	X greater than or equal to Y	False
>	Item > MinItem	Item greater than MinItem	True
=	MomOrDad = 'M'	MomOrDad equal to 'M'	True
<>	Num <> Sentinel	Num not equal to Sentinel	False

The if Statement

A Pascal programmer can use the `if` statement to select among several alternatives. An `if` statement always contains a Boolean expression. For example, the `if` statement

```
if Gross > 100.00 then
   Net := Gross - Tax
else
   Net := Gross
```

Selects one of the two assignment statements listed. It selects the statement following `then` if the Boolean expresssion is true (that is, `Gross` is greater than `100.00`); it selects the statement following `else` if the Boolean expression is false (that is, `Gross` is not greater than `100.00`).

Figure 4.1 is a graphic description, called a *flow chart*, of the preceding `if`

Figure 4.1 Flow Chart of if Statement with Two Alternatives

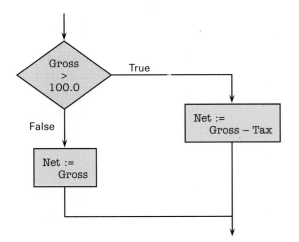

Figure 4.2 Flow Chart of if Statement with One Alternative

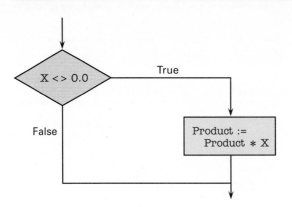

statement. Figure 4.1 shows that the condition enclosed in the diamond-shaped box (Gross > 100.00) is evaluated first. If the condition is true, the arrow labeled *True* is followed, and the assignment statement in the rectangle on the right is executed. If the condition is false, the arrow labeled *False* is followed, and the assignment statement in the rectangle on the left is executed.

More if Statement Examples

The preceding if statement has two alternatives, but only one will be executed for a given value of Gross. Example 4.2 illustrates that an if statement can also have a single alternative that is executed only when the condition is true.

■ Example 4.2
The following if statement has one alternative that is executed only when X is not equal to zero. It causes Product to be multiplied by X; the new value is then saved in Product, replacing the old value. If X is equal to zero, the multiplication is not performed. Figure 4.2 is a flow chart of this if statement.

```
{Multiply Product by a nonzero X only}
if X <> 0.0 then
   Product := Product * X
```
■

■ Example 4.3
The if statement below has two alternatives. It displays either Hi Mom or Hi Dad depending on the character stored in variable MomOrDad (type Char).

```
if MomOrDad = 'M' then
   WriteLn ('Hi Mom')
else
   WriteLn ('Hi Dad')
```
■

■ Example 4.4
The following if statement has one alternative; it displays the message Hi Mom only when MomOrDad has the value 'M'. Regardless of whether or not Hi Mom

is displayed, the message Hi Dad is always displayed. The semicolon terminates the if statement and is needed to separate the if statement from the second call to procedure WriteLn.

```
if MomOrDad = 'M' then
   WriteLn ('Hi Mom');
WriteLn ('Hi Dad')
```

The if statement that follows is incorrect because the semicolon appears before the line else. The compiler will detect a syntax error when it reaches the line else because the semicolon terminates the if statement, and a new statement cannot begin with else.

```
if MomOrDad = 'M' then
   WriteLn ('Hi Mom');
else                    {error - new statement}
   WriteLn ('Hi Dad')
```

The following displays summarize the forms of the if statement we have used so far. The next section illustrates the use of if statements and decision steps in solving problems. ■

SYNTAX
DISPLAY

---

if Statement (Two Alternatives)

Form: if *condition* then
         statement$_T$
    else
         statement$_F$

Example: if X >= 0.0 then
        Write ('Positive')
    else
        Write ('Negative')

Interpretation: If the *condition* evaluates to true, then *statement*$_T$ executes; otherwise, *statement*$_F$ executes.

SYNTAX
DISPLAY

---

if Statement (One Alternative)

Form: if *condition* then
         statement$_T$

Example: if X > 0.0 then
        PosProd := PosProd * X

Interpretation: If the *condition* evaluates to true, then *statement*$_T$ executes; otherwise, it does not execute.

Format of the if Statement

In all the if statement examples, *statement*$_T$ and *statement*$_F$ are indented. If you use the word else, enter it on a separate line, aligned with the word if. The format of the if statement makes its meaning apparent. Again we do this solely to improve program readability; the format used makes no difference to the compiler.

Exercises for Section 4.1

Self-Check

1. Assuming X is 15.0 and Y is 25.0, what are the values of the following conditions?

```
X <> Y    X < X    X >= (Y - X)    X = (Y + X - Y)
```

2. What do the following statements display?

```
a. if X < X then
      WriteLn ('Never')
   else
      WriteLn ('Always')

b. Var1 := 15.0;
   Var2 := 25.12;
   if Var2 <= (2 * Var1) then
      WriteLn ('O.K.')
   else
      WriteLn ('Not O.K.')
```

 4.2   Decision Steps in Algorithms

In the problem that follows, you will see how to improve the payroll program.

● Case Study: Modified Payroll Problem

Problem

Modify the simple payroll program to deduct a $25 tax only if an employee earns more than $100; otherwise, deduct no tax.

Design Overview

We will analyze this problem using the tools developed in the last chapter. We begin by listing the data requirements and the initial algorithm.

Data Requirements

Problem Constants
maximum salary without a tax deduction (TaxBracket = 100.00)
amount of tax deducted (Tax = 25.00)

Problem Inputs
hours worked (Hours : Real)
hourly rate (Rate : Real)

Problem Outputs
gross pay (Gross : Real)
net pay (Net : Real)

Unlike problem inputs, whose values may vary, problem constants have the same values for each run of the program. Each constant value is associated with an identifier (Tax and TaxBracket). The program style display following this problem describes the reason for this association.

Initial Algorithm

1. Display user instructions.
2. Enter hours worked and hourly rate.
3. Compute gross pay.
4. Compute net pay.
5. Print gross pay and net pay.

Algorithm Refinements
Figure 4.3 shows the structure chart for this algorithm. Now let's write the refinement of algorithm step 4 as a *decision step*.

Step 4 Refinement
```
4.1 if Gross > TaxBracket then
        Deduct a tax of $25
    else
        Deduct no tax
```

The decision step is expressed in *pseudocode*, which is a mixture of English and Pascal used to describe algorithm steps.

Coding
The modified payroll program is shown in Fig. 4.4. It begins with a multiple-line comment explaining the program purpose. Rather than surround each line of that comment with curly braces, we use the style convention of beginning and ending the comment block with an open curly brace and a close curly brace, respectively, on separate lines.

Case Study: Modified Payroll Problem, continued

Figure 4.3 Structure Chart for Modified Payroll Problem

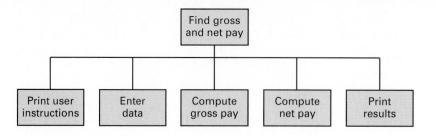

Figure 4.4 Program for Modified Payroll Problem

```
program ModPay (Input, Output);
{
 Computes and prints gross pay and net pay given an hourly
 rate and number of hours worked. Deducts a tax of $25 if
 gross salary exceeds $100; otherwise, deducts no tax.
}
   const
      TaxBracket = 100.00;      {maximum salary for no deduction}
      Tax = 25.00;             {tax amount}

   var
      Hours, Rate,             {inputs - hours worked, hourly rate}
      Gross, Net : Real;       {outputs - gross pay, net pay}

   procedure InstructModPay;

   {Displays user instructions.}

   begin {InstructModPay}
      WriteLn ('This program computes gross and net salary.');
      WriteLn ('A tax amount of $', Tax :4:2, ' is deducted');
      WriteLn ('for an employee who earns more than $', TaxBracket :4:2);
      WriteLn;
      WriteLn ('Enter hours worked and hourly rate');
      WriteLn ('on separate lines after the prompts.');
      WriteLn ('Press <return> after typing each number.');
      WriteLn
   end; {InstructModPay}

begin {ModPay}
   InstructModPay;                  {Display user instructions}

   {Enter Hours and Rate}
   Write ('Hours worked> ');
   ReadLn (Hours);
   Write ('Hourly rate> ');
   ReadLn (Rate);

   {Compute gross salary}
   Gross := Hours * Rate;

   {Compute net salary}
   if Gross > TaxBracket then
```

```
    Net := Gross - Tax     {Deduct a tax amount}
  else
    Net := Gross;          {Deduct no tax}

  {Print Gross and Net}
  WriteLn ('Gross salary is $', Gross :4:2);
  WriteLn ('Net salary is $', Net :4:2)
end. {ModPay}
```

```
This program computes gross and net salary.
A tax amount of $ 25.00 is deducted
for an employee who earns more than $100.00

Enter hours worked and hourly rate
on separate lines after the prompts.
Press <return> after typing each number.

Hours worked> 40.0
Hourly rate> 5.0
Gross salary is $200.00
Net salary is $175.00
```

The program begins by calling procedure InstructModPay to display the user instructions (the first six lines of program output). After the input data are read, the if statement

```
  if Gross > TaxBracket then
     Net := Gross - Tax     {Deduct a tax amount}
  else
     Net := Gross;          {Deduct no tax}
```

implements the decision step (step 4). The comments on the right are embedded in the if statement. The semicolon in the last line separates the if statement from the output statements that follow.

Testing

To test this program, run it with at least two sets of data. One data set should yield a gross salary greater than $100.00, and the other should yield a gross salary less than $100.00. You should also test the program with a data set that yields a gross salary that is exactly $100.00.

PROGRAM
STYLE

Use of Constants

The constants TaxBracket and Tax appear in the preceding if statement and in Fig. 4.4. We could just as easily place the constant values (100.00 and 25.00) directly in the if statement.

The result then would be

```
if Gross > 100.00 then
   Net := Gross - 25.00      {Deduct a tax amount}
else
   Net := Gross;            {Deduct no tax}
```

However, use of constants rather than constant values provides two advantages. First, the original if statement is easier to understand because it uses the descriptive names TaxBracket and Tax rather than numbers, which have no intrinsic meaning. Second, a program written with constants is easier to modify than one written with constant values. For example, to use different constant values in the ModPay program in Fig. 4.4, we need to change only the constant declaration. If, however, we had inserted constant values directly into the if statement, we would have to change the if statement and any other statements that manipulate the constant values.

Notice that the constants also appear in two WriteLn statements in procedure InstructModPay. It is perfectly all right to reference program constants in a procedure body.

Case Study: Finding the First Letter

Problem
Read three letters and find and print the one that comes first in the alphabet.

Design Overview
From your prior experience with conditions and decision steps, you know how to compare two numbers to see which is smaller using the relational operator <. We can also use this operator in Pascal to determine whether one letter precedes another in the alphabet. For example, the condition 'A' < 'F' is true because A precedes F in the alphabet.

Data Requirements

Problem Inputs
three letters (Ch1, Ch2, Ch3 : Char)

Problem Outputs
the alphabetically first letter (AlphaFirst : Char)

Initial Algorithm

1. Read three letters into Ch1, Ch2, and Ch3.
2. Save the alphabetically first of Ch1, Ch2, and Ch3 in AlphaFirst.
3. Print the alphabetically first letter.

Figure 4.5   Structure Chart for Finding Alphabetically First Letter

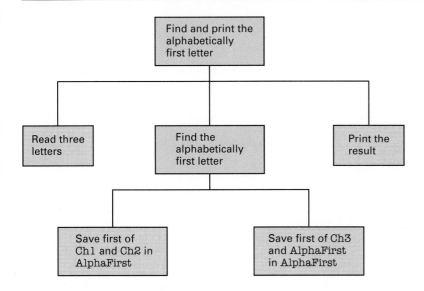

Algorithm Refinements

You can perform step 2 by first comparing Ch1 and Ch2 and saving the alphabetically first letter in AlphaFirst; the result can then be compared to Ch3. The refinement of step 2 follows.

Step 2 Refinement
2.1 Save the alphabetically first of Ch1 and Ch2 in AlphaFirst.
2.2 Save the alphabetically first of Ch3 and AlphaFirst in AlphaFirst.

Figure 4.5 shows the structure chart that corresponds to the algorithm.

Coding

Program FirstLetter is shown in Fig. 4.6. The if statement with two alternatives saves either Ch1 or Ch2 in AlphaFirst. The if statement with one alternative stores Ch3 in AlphaFirst if Ch3 precedes the value already in AlphaFirst. Later in this chapter, you will see that if statements with more than two alternatives are also possible in Pascal.

Figure 4.6   Finding the Alphabetically First Letter

```
program FirstLetter (Input, Output);

{Finds and prints the alphabetically first letter.}

   var
      Ch1, Ch2, Ch3,           {three letters read}
      AlphaFirst    : Char;    {alphabetically first letter}
```

```
begin  {FirstLetter}
  {Read three letters}
  Write ('Enter any three letters> ');
  ReadLn (Ch1, Ch2, Ch3);

  {Store the alphabetically first of Ch1 and Ch2 in AlphaFirst}
  if Ch1 < Ch2 then
    AlphaFirst := Ch1         {Ch1 comes before Ch2}
  else
    AlphaFirst := Ch2;        {Ch2 comes before Ch1}

  {Store the alphabetically first of Ch3 and AlphaFirst}
  if Ch3 < AlphaFirst then
    AlphaFirst := Ch3;        {Ch3 comes before AlphaFirst}

  {Print result}
  WriteLn (AlphaFirst, ' is the first letter alphabetically')
end. {FirstLetter}


Enter any three letters> EBK
B is the first letter alphabetically
```

Testing

To test this program, make sure it works when the smallest letter is in any of the three positions. Section 4.3 describes the four cases that should be tested. You should also see what happens when one of the letters is repeated, and when one or more of the letters is in lowercase.

Exercises for Section 4.2

Self-Check

1. What value is assigned to X for each of the following segments given that Y is 15.0?

    a.
    ```
    X := 25.0;
    if Y <> (X - 10.0) then
      X := X - 10.0
    else
      X := X / 2.0;
    ```
    b.
    ```
    if Y < 15.0 then
      X := 5 * Y
    else
      X := 2 * Y;
    ```

Programming

1. Write Pascal statements to carry out the following steps:

    a. If Item is nonzero, then multiply Product by Item and save the result in Product; otherwise, skip the multiplication. In either case, print the value of Product.

   b. Store the absolute difference of X and Y in Z, where the absolute difference
      is (X − Y) or (Y − X), whichever is positive.
   c. If X is zero, add 1 to ZeroCount. If X is negative, add X to MinusSum. If
      X is greater than zero, add X to PlusSum.

2. Modify the structure chart and program for the first-letter problem to find
   the first of four letters.
3. Write a structure chart and program to find the alphabetically last of three
   letters.

 ## 4.3   Tracing a Program or an Algorithm

A critical step in the design of an algorithm or a program is to make sure it is
correct before you spend a lot of time entering or debugging it. Often a few
extra minutes spent verifying the correctness of an algorithm saves hours of
testing time later.

   One important technique, a desk-check (also called a hand-trace) consists
of a careful, step-by-step simulation on paper of how the computer would
execute the algorithm or program. By using data that are relatively easy to
process by hand, you should be able to simulate the effect of each step's execution.

   Table 4.2 shows a trace of the program in Fig. 4.6 for the data string THE.
Each program step is listed at the left in order of its execution. The values of
variables referenced by a program step are shown after the step. If a program
step changes the value of a variable, the table shows the new value. The effect
of each step is described at the far right. For example, the table shows that the
statement

```
ReadLn (Ch1, Ch2, Ch3);
```

stores the letters T, H, and E in the variables Ch1, Ch2, and Ch3.

Table 4.2   Trace of Program in Figure 4.6

Program Statement	Ch1	Ch2	Ch3	AlphaFirst	Effect
	?	?	?	?	
Write ('Enter any three...')					Prints a prompt.
ReadLn (Ch1, Ch2, Ch3)	T	H	E		Reads the data.
if Ch1 < Ch2 then					Is 'T' < 'H'?
					Value is false.
AlphaFirst := Ch2				H	'H' is first so far.
if Ch3 < AlphaFirst...					Is 'E' < 'H'?
					Value is true.
AlphaFirst := Ch3				E	'E' is first.
WriteLn (AlphaFirst...					Prints E is the
					first letter...

The trace in Table 4.2 clearly shows that the alphabetically first letter, E, of the input string is stored in AlphaFirst and printed. To verify that the program is correct, you would need to select other data that cause the two conditions to evaluate to different combinations of their values. Because there are two conditions and each has two possible values (true or false), there are two times two, or four, different combinations that you should try. (What are they?) An exhaustive desk-check of the program would show that it works for all of these combinations.

Besides those four cases, you should verify that the program works correctly for unusual data. For example, what would happen if two or more of the letters were the same? Would the program still provide the correct result? To complete the desk-check, you would need to show that the program handles these special situations properly.

When tracing a case, you must be careful to execute the program exactly as the computer would execute it. A desk-check in which you assume that a particular step will be executed in a certain way without explicitly testing each condition and tracing each program step is of little value.

Exercises for Section 4.3

Self-Check

1. Provide sample data and traces for the remaining three cases of the alphabetically first-letter problem. Test the special cases where two letters are the same and where all three letters are the same. What is the value of the conditions in the latter case?
2. Trace the program in Fig. 4.4 when Hours is 30.0 and Rate is 5.00. Perform the trace when Hours is 20.0 and Rate is 4.00.

 ## 4.4 More Problem-Solving Strategies

Often what appears to be a new problem turns out to be a variation of one you have already solved. Consequently, an important skill in problem solving is the ability to recognize that a problem is similar to one solved earlier. As you progress through this course, you will start to build up a *library* of programs and procedures. Whenever possible, try to adapt or reuse parts of successful programs.

Extending a Problem Solution

An experienced programmer usually writes programs that can be easily changed or modified to fit other situations. One reason for this is that programmers (and program users) often want to make slight improvements to a program after they have used it. If the original program is designed carefully from the beginning, the programmer can accommodate changing specifications with a minimum of effort. In the next problem, it is possible to insert a new decision step rather than rewrite the entire program.

◼ Case Study: Computing Overtime Pay

Problem

You decide to modify the payroll program so that employees who work more than 40 hours a week are paid double for all overtime hours.

Design Overview

This problem is an extension of the modified payroll problem solved in Fig. 4.4. In this case, overtime pay must be added for eligible employees. We can solve this problem by adding a new step (step 3a) after step 3 in the original algorithm.

Data Requirements

Problem Constants
maximum salary for no tax deduction (TaxBracket = 100.00)
amount of tax deducted (Tax = 25.00)
maximum hours without overtime pay (MaxHours = 40.0)

Problem Inputs
hours worked (Hours : Real)
hourly rate (Rate : Real)

Problem Outputs
gross pay (Gross : Real)
net pay (Net : Real)

Initial Algorithm

1. Display user instructions.
2. Enter hours worked and hourly rate.
3. Compute gross salary.
3a. Add any overtime pay to gross salary.
4. Compute net salary.
5. Print gross salary and net salary.

Algorithm Refinements

The new step, step 3a, is refined next.

Step 3a Refinement
3a.1 if Hours > MaxHours then
    3a.2 Add extra pay for hours over 40 to Gross.

Coding

As shown in the following code segment, the if statement that implements step 3a should come after the statement in Fig. 4.4 that computes gross salary.

```
Gross := Hours * Rate;      {Compute gross salary}
```

```
{Add any overtime pay to gross salary}
if Hours > MaxHours then
   Gross := Gross + ((Hours - MaxHours) * Rate);
```

The assignment statement for step 3a.2 involves three arithmetic operators: +, –, and *. Chapter 7 discusses how Pascal evaluates arithmetic expressions with multiple operators. For the time being, however, you need to know that the parentheses cause the operators in the segment to be evaluated in the order of subtraction first, multiplication next, and addition last. Consequently, the overtime hours (Hours – MaxHours) will be multiplied by Rate and added to the value of Gross computed earlier; the result will be the new value of Gross.

Solution by Analogy

Sometimes a new problem is simply an old one presented in a new guise. Each time you face a problem, try to determine if you have solved a similar problem before; if you have, adapt the earlier solution. This problem-solving strategy requires a careful reading of the problem statement to detect requirements similar to those of earlier problems but worded differently.

Case Study: Computing Insurance Dividends

Problem

Each year an insurance company sends out dividend checks to its policyholders. The dividend amount is a fixed percentage (4.5%) of the policyholder's paid premium. If the policyholder has made no claims, the dividend rate for the policy is increased by 0.5%. Write a program to compute dividends.

Design Overview

This problem is similar to the overtime pay problem. You can determine the dividend amount by first computing the basic dividend, then adding the bonus dividend when applicable. (In the overtime pay problem, we followed a similar algorithm by first computing gross pay, then adding in overtime pay when earned.)

Data Requirements

Problem Constants
the fixed dividend rate of 4.5% (FixedRate = 0.045)
the bonus dividend rate of 0.5% (BonusRate = 0.005)

Figure 4.7 Structure Chart for Insurance Dividend Problem

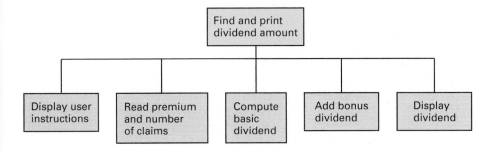

Problem Inputs
premium amount (`Premium : Real`)
number of claims (`NumClaims : Integer`)

Problem Outputs
dividend amount (`Dividend : Real`)

Initial Algorithm

1. Display user instructions.
2. Enter premium amount and number of claims.
3. Compute basic dividend.
4. Add any bonus dividend to basic dividend.
5. Print total dividend.

Algorithm Refinements

The refinement of step 4 in this problem is similar to the refinement of step 3a in the overtime pay problem. We'll look closer at this refinement next.

Step 4 Refinement
4.1 if NumClaims = 0 then
4.2 Add bonus dividend to `Dividend`

Coding

The complete insurance dividend program is shown in Fig. 4.8. Because Pascal possesses no % operator, decimal fractions are required. Thus, the dividend rate, 4.5%, is written as the decimal fraction `0.045` and the bonus rate, 0.5%, is written as the decimal fraction `0.005`. Also, all real numbers must begin with a digit; therefore, a zero before the decimal point is required for a real value less than 1.0.

Case Study: Computing Insurance Dividends, continued

Figure 4.8   Insurance Company Dividend Program

```
program CompDividend (Input, Output);

{Finds and prints the insurance dividend.}

  const
    FixedRate = 0.045;         {basic dividend rate 4.5%}
    BonusRate = 0.005;         {bonus dividend rate 0.5%}

  var
    NumClaims : Integer;       {input - number of claims}
    Premium,                   {input - premium amount}
    Dividend : Real;           {output - dividend amount}

  procedure InstructDividend;

  {Displays user instructions.}

  begin {InstructDividend}
    WriteLn ('This program displays an insurance policy dividend.');
    WriteLn ('The basic dividend is ',
             FixedRate :5:3, ' times the premium.');
    WriteLn ('A bonus dividend of ',
             BonusRate :5:3, ' times the premium is paid');
    WriteLn ('for policies with no claims against them.');
    WriteLn
  end; {InstructDividend}


begin {CompDividend}
  InstructDividend;                          {Display user instructions}

  {Enter Premium and NumClaims}
  Write ('Premium amount> $');
  ReadLn (Premium);
  Write ('Number of claims> ');
  ReadLn (NumClaims);

  {Compute basic dividend}
  Dividend := Premium * FixedRate;

  {Add any bonus dividend to basic dividend}
  if NumClaims = 0 then
    Dividend := Dividend + (Premium * BonusRate);

  {Print total dividend}
  WriteLn ('Total dividend is $', Dividend :4:2)
end. {CompDividend}


This program displays an insurance policy dividend.
The basic dividend is 0.045 times the premium.
A bonus dividend of 0.005 times the premium is paid
for policies with no claims against them.

Premium amount> $1200.00
Number of claims> 0
Total dividend is $60.00
```

Self-Check

1. Rewrite the algorithm for the overtime pay problem so that the computation of gross salary is performed in one step rather than in two (in other words, combine steps 3 and 3a). Use an `if` statement with two alternatives.
2. In Fig. 4.8, use an `if` statement with two alternatives to combine the two steps that compute `Dividend` into one step.

Programming

1. Provide the complete program for the overtime pay problem.

 4.5 Syntax Diagrams

We can use a syntax diagram to describe the syntax of any Pascal language construct. The syntax diagram in Fig. 4.9 describes a Pascal *identifier*. This syntax diagram references two other syntactical elements of Pascal: *letter* (A-Z, a-z) and *digit* (0-9). You will recall that an identifier is a sequence of letters and digits starting with a letter.

To use a syntax diagram, trace through the diagram following the arrows. Start at the arrow tail on the left and finish at the arrowhead on the right. The shortest path through the diagram in Fig. 4.9 is from left to right and passing through only the top box, labeled *letter*. This means that a Pascal identifier can be any single letter (for example, A, B, c, z).

There are many other paths through this diagram. Instead of exiting at the right after passing through the top box, you can follow either path leading down and to the left. These paths go through a box labeled *digit* or another box labeled *letter*. If you then exit the diagram, the identifier formed consists of two characters (for example, it, ME, R2, D2).

Because there is a closed cycle, or loop, in the diagram, you can pass through the lower box labeled *letter* and the box labeled *digit* several times before exiting the diagram. Each time, a symbol from the box passed through

Figure 4.9 Syntax Diagram Describing a Pascal Identifier

Identifier

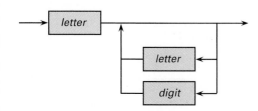

(*letter* or *digit*) is added to the identifier being formed. Some identifiers formed this way are A, ABC, and A23b4cd5. It is impossible to trace a path that establishes 123 or 12ABC as valid identifiers.

You can use syntax diagrams to verify that a program statement is correct before you enter it. If a syntax error occurs during debugging, you can refer to the appropriate syntax diagram to determine the correct form of the element that is incorrect. Appendix B contains all Pascal syntax diagrams.

Exercise for Section 4.5

Self-Check

1. Which of the identifiers

   Ace   R2D2   R245   A23B   A1c   B34d5c   A23cd

   satisfy the following syntax diagram?

 ## 4.6   The if Statement Revisited

The syntax diagram for an `if` statement is shown in Fig. 4.10. Two kinds of boxes are in this diagram: rounded boxes (ovals) and rectangular boxes. The contents of a rounded box are taken literally, whereas, the name in a rectangular box is the label of another syntax diagram (*expression, statement*).

The reserved words (`if`, `then`, `else`) are enclosed in ovals rather than rectangular boxes. When you pass through one of these ovals, the word inside is inserted in the `if` statement being formed.

An `if` statement is completed by exiting at either arrowhead at the far right of the diagram. If the top path is followed, the `if` statement consists of only one alternative (following `then`); there is no `else` part. If the path leading

Figure 4.10   Syntax Diagram for an if Statement

if statement

down and to the left (through else) is followed instead, the if statement consists of two alternatives.

The *statement* following the word then or else can be a single executable statement or a compound statement (described next). Some of the statements that can be used are assignment statements, procedure call statements, and other if statements.

More if Statement Examples

This section provides examples of if statements with compound statements as *statement*$_T$ or *statement*$_F$. A compound statement consists of a sequence of statements bracketed by begin and end. The body of a program or procedure is a compound statement.

■ Example 4.5

Suppose you are the manager of a clothing boutique and are planning a spring sale. You could use the following if statement to compute the discounted price of an item. The statement first determines the discount by multiplying the item price and the discount rate (a fraction); next, it deducts the discount. The compound statement is not executed when the discount rate is zero.

```
if DiscRate <> 0.0 then
   begin
      Discount := Price * DiscRate;    {Compute discount amount}
      Price := Price - Discount        {Deduct discount from price}
   end {if}                                                       ■
```

■ Example 4.6

In later chapters, you will see that it is useful to be able to order a pair of data values in memory so that the smaller value is stored in one variable (say, X) and the larger value in another (say, Y). The if statement in Fig. 4.11 rearranges any two values stored in X and Y so that the smaller number will always be in X and the larger number will always be in Y. If the two numbers are already in the proper order, the compound statement will not be executed.

Figure 4.11   if Statement to Order X and Y

```
if X > Y then
   begin {switch X and Y}
      Temp := X;            {Store old X in Temp}
      X := Y;               {Store old Y in X}
      Y := Temp             {Store old X in Y}
   end {if}
```

The variables X, Y, and Temp all should be the same data type. Although the values of X and Y are being switched, an additional variable, Temp, is needed for storage of a copy of one of those values. Table 4.3 illustrates the need for Temp, assuming X and Y have original values of 12.5 and 5.0, respectively.   ■

Table 4.3 Trace of if Statement to Order X and Y

Statement Part	X	Y	Temp	Effect
	12.5	5.0	?	
if X > Y then				12.5 > 5.0 is true
Temp := X;			12.5	Store old X in Temp
X := Y;		5.0		Store old Y in X
Y := Temp		12.5		Store old X in Y

■ Example 4.7

As the manager of a clothing boutique, you want to keep records of your bank transactions. You could use the following if statement to process a transaction (TransAmount) that represents a payment for goods received (in which case, TransType is 'C') or a cash deposit. In either case, an appropriate message is printed and the account balance (Balance) is updated. Both the true and the false statements are compound statements.

```
if TransType = 'C' then
  begin {check}
    Write ('Check for $', TransAmount :4:2);
    Balance := Balance – TransAmount    {Deduct check amount}
  end  {check}
else
  begin {deposit}
    Write ('Deposit of $', TransAmount :4:2);
    Balance := Balance + TransAmount    {Add deposit amount}
  end {deposit and if}
```

The semicolons in the preceding if statement separate the individual statements in each alternative. A common error would be to insert a semicolon after the first end (end; {check}). That would terminate the if statement prematurely. An *unexpected symbol* error message would be displayed when the compiler then tried to translate the rest of the if statement (beginning with else). ■

Writing if Statements with Compound True or False Statements

Each if statement in this section contains at least one compound statement bracketed by begin and end. Each compound statement is indented. The purpose of the indentation is to improve our ability to read and understand the if statement; indentation is ignored by the Pascal compiler.

The comment after each end helps to associate the end with its corresponding begin. The comments are not required, but they also improve program readability.

Semicolons are required between the individual statements within a compound statement. Semicolons should not be used before or after the reserved words then, else, or begin. A semicolon is needed, however, after the last end when another statement follows the if statement.

Exercises for Section 4.6

105

4.7 Nested if
Statements and
Multiple-Alternative
Decisions

Self-Check

1. Insert any necessary semicolons in the following segment and indicate how many spaces each line should be indented to improve readability.

```
if X > Y then
begin
X := X + 10.0
WriteLn ('X Bigger')
end
else
WriteLn ('X Smaller')
WriteLn ('Y is ', Y)
```

2. What would be the effect of removing the bracketing begin and end in the preceding segment?
3. What would be the effect of bracketing the last two lines in the preceding segment with begin and end?
4. Correct the following if statement:

```
if Num1 < 0 then
  begin
    Product := Num1 * Num2 * Num3;
    WriteLn ('Product is ', Product : 1)
  end;
else
  Sum := Num1 + Num2 + Num3;
  WriteLn ('Sum is ', Sum :1);
```

5. What syntax diagrams would you use to validate the following if statement? Provide the label of every syntax diagram that describes an element of this statement.

```
if X > 0 then
  begin
    X := 25.0;
    WriteLn ('Positive')
  end;
```

Programming

1. Write an if statement that assigns the larger of X and Y to Larger and the smaller to Smaller. Your statement should print 'X LARGER' or 'Y LARGER', depending on the situation.
2. Do the same as in programming exercise 1 but print the smaller value followed by the larger value.

4.7 Nested if Statements and Multiple-Alternative Decisions

Until now, we used if statements to implement decisions involving two alternatives. In this section, you will see how the if statement can be used to implement decisions involving several alternatives.

A *nested* if statement occurs when the true or false statement of an if statement is itself an if statement. A nested if statement can be used to implement decisions with several alternatives, as shown in the following examples.

■ Example 4.8

The following nested if statement has three alternatives. It causes one of three variables (NumPos, NumNeg, or NumZero) to be increased by one depending on whether X is greater than zero, less than zero, or equal to zero, respectively.

```
{increment NumPos, NumNeg, or NumZero depending on X}
if X > 0 then
  NumPos := NumPos + 1
else
  if X < 0 then
    NumNeg := NumNeg + 1
  else  {X = 0}
    NumZero := NumZero + 1
```

The execution of this if statement proceeds as follows: the first condition (X > 0) is tested; if it is true, NumPos is incremented by one and the rest of the if statement is skipped. If the first condition is false, the second condition (X < 0) is tested; if the second condition is true, NumNeg is incremented by one; otherwise, NumZero is incremented. It is important to realize that the second condition is tested only if the first condition is false.

Figure 4.12 charts the execution of this statement. Each condition is shown in a diamond-shaped box. If a condition is true, its arrow labeled True is followed. If a condition is false, its arrow labeled False is followed. The diagram shows that one and only one of the statement sequences in a rectangular box will be executed. Table 4.4 traces the execution of this statement when X is −7. ■

Table 4.4   Trace of if Statement in Example 4.8 for X = −7

Statement Part	Effect
If X > 0 then	−7 > 0 is false
else if X < 0 then	−7 < 0 is true
NumNeg := NumNeg + 1	Add 1 to NumNeg

PROGRAM
STYLE

Multiple-Alternative Decisions

Nested if statements can become quite complex. If there are more than three alternatives and the indentation is not consistent, you may find it difficult to determine the if to which a given else belongs. (In Pascal, this is always the closest if without an else.) It is easier to write the nested if statement in Example 4.8 as the following *multiple-alternative decision*.

```
{increment NumPos, NumNeg, or NumZero depending on X}
if X > 0 then
  NumPos := NumPos + 1
```

Figure 4.12 Flow Chart of Nested if Statement in Example 4.8

107

4.7 Nested if
Statements and
Multiple-Alternative
Decisions

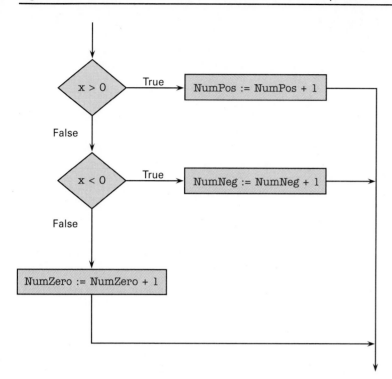

```
else if X < 0 then
   NumNeg := NumNeg + 1
else {X = 0}
   NumZero := NumZero + 1
```

In this format, the word else and the next condition appear on the same line. All the words else align, and each *dependent statement* is indented under the condition that controls its execution. The general form follows:

```
if condition₁ then
   statement₁
else if condition₂ then
   statement₂
. . .
else if conditionₙ then
   statementₙ
else
   statementₑ
```

The conditions in a multiple-alternative decision are evaluated in sequence until a true condition is reached. If a condition is true, the statement following it is executed and the rest of the multiple-alternative decision is skipped. If a condition is false, the statement following it is skipped and the next condition is tested. If all conditions are false, then *statement*ₑ following the last else is executed.

Order of Conditions

Often, the conditions in a multiple-alternative decision are not *mutually exclusive*; in other words, more than one condition may be true for a given data value. If this is the case, the order of the conditions becomes important because only the statement sequence following the first true condition is executed.

■ Example 4.9

Suppose you want to match exam scores to letter grades for a large class of students. The assignment of grades is based on the exam scores, as follows:

Exam Score	Grade Assigned
90 and above	A
80-89	B
70-79	C
60-69	D
below 60	F

The following multiple-alternative decision prints the letter grade assigned according to the exam score. For an exam score of 85, even though the last three conditions are true, a grade of B would be assigned because the *first* true condition is Score >= 80.

```
{correct grade assignment}
if Score >= 90 then
   Write ('A')
else if Score >= 80 then
   Write ('B')
else if Score >= 70 then
   Write ('C')
else if Score >= 60 then
   Write ('D')
else
   Write ('F')
```

The order of conditions can also affect program efficiency. If low exam scores are more likely than high scores, it would be more efficient to test first for scores below 60, next for scores between 60 and 69, and so on (see programming exercise 1 at the end of this section). It would, however, be incorrect to write the decision as follows. *All* passing exam scores (60 or above) would be incorrectly categorized as a grade of D, because the first condition would be true and the rest would be skipped.

```
{incorrect grade assignment}
if Score >= 60 then
   Write ('D')
else if Score >= 70 then
   Write ('C')
else if Score >= 80 then
   Write ('B')
else if Score >= 90 then
   Write ('A')
else
   Write ('F')
```

■

Example 4.10

109

4.7 Nested if
Statements and
Multiple-Alternative
Decisions

You can use a multiple-alternative if statement to implement a *decision table* that describes several alternatives. Let's say you are an accountant setting up a payroll system for a small firm. Each line of Table 4.5 indicates an employee's salary range and a corresponding base tax amount and tax percentage. Given a salary, you can calculate the tax by adding the *base tax* for that salary range to the product of the percent of excess and the amount of salary over the minimum salary for that range.

For example, the second line of the table specifies that the tax due on a salary of $2000.00 is $225.00 plus 16 percent of the excess salary over $1500.00 (that is, 16 percent of $500.00, or $80.00). Therefore, the total tax due is $225.00 plus $80.00, or $305.00.

Table 4.5 Decision Table for Example 4.10

Range	Salary	Base Tax	Percent of Excess
1	0.00-1,499.99	0.00	15
2	1,500.00-2,999.99	225.00	16
3	3,000.00-4,999.99	465.00	18
4	5,000.00-7,999.99	825.00	20
5	8,000.00-15,000.00	1425.00	25

The if statement in Fig. 4.13 implements the tax table. If the value of Salary is within the table range (0.00 to 15,000.00), exactly one of the statements assigning a value to Tax will be executed. A trace of the if statement for Salary = 2000.00 is shown in Table 4.6. You can see that the value assigned to Tax, 305.00, is correct. ■

Figure 4.13 if Statement for Table 4.5

```
if Salary < 0.0 then
   WriteLn ('Error! Negative salary $', Salary :10:2)
else if Salary < 1500.00 then            {first range}
   Tax := 0.15 * Salary
else if Salary < 3000.00 then            {second range}
   Tax := (Salary - 1500.00) * 0.16 + 225.00
else if Salary < 5000.00 then            {third range}
   Tax := (Salary - 3000.00) * 0.18 + 465.00
else if Salary < 8000.00 then            {fourth range}
   Tax := (Salary - 5000.00) * 0.20 + 825.00
else if Salary <= 15000.00 then          {fifth range}
   Tax := (Salary - 8000.00) * 0.25 + 1425.00
else
   WriteLn ('Error! Too large salary $', Salary :10:2)
```

Table 4.6 Trace of if Statement in Figure 4.13 for Salary = $2000.00

Statement Part	Salary	Tax	Effect
	2000.00	?	
if Salary < 0.0			2000.0 < 0.0 is false
else if Salary < 1500.00			2000.0 < 1500.0 is false
else if Salary < 3000.00			2000.0 < 3000.0 is true
Tax := (Salary – 1500.00)			Evaluates to 500.00
* 0.16			Evaluates to 80.00
+ 225.00		305.00	Evaluates to 305.00

PROGRAM
STYLE

Validating the Value of Variables

It is important to validate the value of a variable before you perform computations using invalid or meaningless data. Instead of computing an incorrect tax amount, the if statement in Fig. 4.13 prints an error message if the value of Salary is outside the range covered by the table (0.0 to 15,000.00). The first condition detects negative salaries; an error message is printed if Salary is less than zero. All conditions evaluate to False if Salary is greater than 15,000.00, so the alternative following else displays an error message.

Nested if Statements with More than One Variable

The nested if statements so far have all involved testing the value of a single variable; consequently, we were able to write each nested if statement as a multiple-alternative decision. This is not always so easy to do.

■ Example 4.11

You have just had a meeting with your parents to discuss your alternatives for next year. Your parents told you that you can apply to an Ivy League school if you can get your SAT scores above 1350 *and* earn more than $2,000 over the summer. If your SAT scores are not over 1350 but you still earn over $2,000, then you can apply to a state university and live at the dorm. If you cannot earn the necessary $2,000, you have to commute to a local community college. The following nested if statement summarizes the decision process you should follow; the flow chart in Fig. 4.14 diagrams it.

```
if Earnings > 2000 then
  if SAT > 1350 then
    WriteLn ('Apply to Ivy League')
  else
    WriteLn ('Apply to State University')
else
  WriteLn ('Apply to Community College')
```

Figure 4.14   Flow Chart of Nested if Statement

111

4.7 Nested if
Statements and
Multiple-Alternative
Decisions

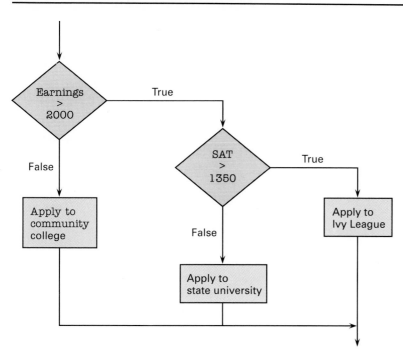

To verify that the nested if statement in Fig. 4.14 is correct, it is necessary to trace its execution for all possible combinations of SAT scores and summer earnings. It is clear that the rightmost rectangle is entered only when both conditions are true. The leftmost rectangle is always entered when the condition involving earnings is false. The rectangle in the middle is entered when the condition involving earnings is true, but the condition involving SAT scores is false. ■

Exercises for Section 4.7

Self-Check

1. Trace the execution of the nested if statement in Fig. 4.13 for Salary = 13500.00.
2. What would be the effect of reversing the order of the first two conditions in the if statement in Fig. 4.13?

Programming

1. Rewrite the if statement for Example 4.9 using only the relational operator < in all conditions.
2. Implement the following decision table using a nested if statement. Assume that the grade point average is within the range 0.0 through 4.0.

Grade Point Average	Transcript Message
0.0-0.99	Failed semester—registration suspended
1.0-1.99	On probation for next semester
2.0-2.99	(no message)
3.0-3.49	Dean's list for semester
3.5-4.0	Highest honors for semester

 ## 4.8   Common Programming Errors

Be careful with your use of semicolons inside an if statement. Use semicolons only to separate the statements of a compound statement within an if statement. A semicolon is needed after the if statement when more statements follow. Do not use semicolons before or after the reserved words then or else in an if statement.

When you are writing a nested if statement, try to select the conditions so that you can use the multiple-alternative format. If the conditions are not mutually exclusive (that is, more than one condition may be true), the most restrictive condition should come first.

 # Chapter Review

This chapter discussed how to use pseudocode to represent decision steps in an algorithm. We showed you how to implement decisions with several alternatives in Pascal programs using the if statement.

You learned to use traces to verify that an algorithm or a program is correct. You can discover errors in logic by carefully tracing an algorithm or a program. Tracing an algorithm or a program before entering the program in the computer saves you time in the long run.

You can also use syntax diagrams to help prevent syntax errors. Refer to the syntax diagrams in Appendix B if you are unsure of the syntax of a statement. If the compiler detects a syntax error that you do not understand, refer to the syntax diagram to determine the cause of the error.

New Pascal Constructs in Chapter 4

The new Pascal constructs introduced in this chapter are described in Table 4.7.

Table 4.7 Summary of New Pascal Constructs

113

Chapter Review

Construct	Effect
if Statement	
One Alternative	
`if X <> 0.0 then` `  Product := Product * X`	Multiplies `Product` by X only if X is non-zero.
Two Alternatives	

`if X >= 0.0 then`
`  WriteLn (X :4:2, ' is positive')`
`else`
`  WriteLn (X :4:2, ' is negative')`
	If X is greater than or equal to 0.0, display is positive; otherwise, display the message is negative.

Multiple Alternatives	

`if X < 0.0 then`
`  begin`
`    WriteLn ('negative');`
`    AbsX := -X`
`  end`
`else if X = 0.0 then`
`  begin`
`    WriteLn ('zero');`
`    AbsX := 0.0`
`  end`
`else`
`  begin`
`    WriteLn ('positive');`
`    AbsX := X`
`  end`
	One of three messages is printed depending on whether X is negative, positive, or zero. AbsX is set to represent the absolute value or magnitude of X.

✓ *Quick-Check Exercises*

1. An `if` statement implements _____ execution.
2. What is a compound statement?
3. What is pseudocode?
4. What values can a Boolean expression have?
5. The relational operator `<>` means _____.
6. A _____ is used to verify that an algorithm is correct.
7. A _____ is used to verify that a program statement is grammatically correct.
8. Correct the following syntax errors:

```
if X > 25.0 then
  begin
      Y := X;
    else
      Y := Z
    end;
```

9. What value is assigned to Fee by the following `if` statement when `Speed` is 75?

```
if Speed > 35 then
    Fee := 20.00
else if Speed > 50 then
    Fee := 40.00
else if Speed > 75 then
    Fee := 60.00
```

10. Answer question 9 for the following `if` statement. Which `if` statement is correct?

```
if Speed > 75 then
    Fee := 60.00
else if Speed > 50 then
    Fee := 40.00
else if Speed > 35 then
    Fee := 20.00
```

11. What output line(s) are displayed by the following statements when X is 5.53? When X is 9.95?

```
if X >= 7.5 then
    begin
        X := 90.0;
        WriteLn ('X is ', X :4:2)
    end
else
    X := 25.0;
    WriteLn ('X is ', X :3:1);
```

12. Explain the difference between the statements on the left and the statements on the right. For each, what is the final value of X if the initial value of X is 1?

```
if X >= 0 then              if X >= 0 then
    X := X + 1                  X := X + 1;
else if X >= 1 then        if X >= 1 then
    X := X + 2;                X := X + 2;
```

Answers to Quick-Check Exercises

1. conditional
2. a statement bracketed by begin and end.
3. a mixture of English and Pascal used to describe algorithm steps
4. True and False
5. not equal
6. hand-trace or desk check
7. syntax diagram
8. Remove begin, end, and the first semicolon.
9. 20.00 first condition is met
10. 40.00, the one in 10
11. when X is originally 5.53:
    ```
    X is 25.0
    ```
    when X is originally 9.95:
    ```
    X is 90.00
    X is 90.0
    ```
12. A nested `if` statement is on the left; a sequence of `if` statements is on the right. X becomes 2 on the left; X becomes 4 on the right.

Review Questions

1. A decision in Pascal is actually an evaluation of a(n) _____ expression.
2. List the six relational operators discussed in this chapter.
3. What should a programmer do after writing the algorithm but before entering the program?
4. Trace the following program fragment and indicate which procedure will be called if a data value of 27.34 is entered.

```
WriteLn ('Enter a temperature> ');
ReadLn (Temp);
if Temp > 32.0 then
   NotFreezing
else
   IceForming
```

5. Write the appropriate if statement to compute GrossPay, given that the hourly rate is stored in the variable Rate and the total hours worked is stored in the variable Hours. Pay time-and-a-half for more than 40 hours worked.
6. How can syntax diagrams help a new user become comfortable with an unfamiliar programming language?
7. Given the following syntax diagram, circle the words under the diagram that are valid.

Syntax diagram for words

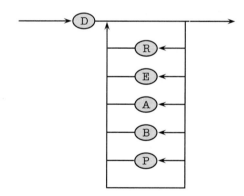

PEAR   BREAD   DREAR   DEADEN   DAD   DRAB

Programming Projects

1. Write a program that displays a message that consists of three block letters, where each letter is an X or an 0. The program user's data determines whether a particular letter will be an X or an 0. For example, if the user enters the three letters X0X, the block letters X, 0, and X will be displayed.
2. Write a program to simulate a state police radar gun. The program should read an automobile speed and print the message SPEEDING if the speed exceeds 55 mph.
3. You need a program that will read a character value and a number. Depending on

what is read, certain information will be printed. The character should be either an
S or a T. If an S is read and the number is 100.50, the program will print

    Send money! I need $100.50.

If a T is read and the number is 100.50, the program will print

    The temperature last night was 100.50 degrees.

4. Write a program that reads in a room number, the room's capacity, and the size of
the class enrolled so far and prints an output line showing the classroom number,
the capacity, number of seats filled, number of seats available, and whether the class
is filled. Call a procedure to display the heading below before the output line.

    Room   Capacity   Enrollment   Empty seats   Filled/Not Filled

Display each part of the output line under the appropriate column heading. Test
your program with the following classroom data:

Room	Capacity	Enrollment
426	25	25
327	18	14
420	20	15
317	100	90

5. Write a program that determines the additional state tax owed by an employee. The
state charges a 4-percent tax on net income. Determine net income by subtracting a
$500 allowance for each dependent from gross income. Your program should read
gross income, number of dependents, and tax amount already deducted. It should
then compute the actual tax owed and print the difference between tax owed and
tax deducted followed by the message SEND CHECK or REFUND, depending on whether
the difference is positive or negative.

6. The New Telephone Company has the following rate structure for long-distance
calls:

1. Any call started after 6:00 p.m. (1800 hours) but before 8:00 a.m. (0800 hours) is
discounted 50 percent.
2. Any call started after 8:00 a.m. (0800 hours) but before 6:00 p.m. (1800 hours) is
charged full price.
3. All calls are subject to a 4-percent Federal tax.
4. The regular rate for a call is $0.40 per minute.
5. Any call longer than 60 minutes receives a 15-percent discount (after any other
discount is subtracted and before tax is added).

Write a program that reads the start time for a call based on a twenty-four-hour
clock and the length of the call. The gross cost (before any discounts or tax) should
be printed followed by the net cost (after discounts are deducted and tax is added).
Use a procedure to print instructions to the program user.

Repetition and the while Statement

Chapters 3 and 4 introduced you to two Pascal control statements: the procedure call statement and the if statement. The control statements of a programming language enable a programmer to control the sequence and the frequency of execution of program segments. Control statements call procedures into execution and implement decisions and repetition in programs.

In this chapter, you will see how to specify the repetition of a group of program statements (called a *loop*) using the while statement. You will study how to design loops in Pascal programs. This chapter describes how to verify that a loop is correct and how to use special comments, called *assertions* and *loop invariants*, that are helpful in loop design and verification.

5.1 Repetition in Programs: The while Statement

Just as the ability to make decisions is an important programming tool, so is the ability to specify repetition of a group of operations. For example, a company that has seven employees will want to repeat the gross pay and net pay computations in its payroll program seven times, once for each employee.

The repetition of steps in a program is called a *loop*. The *loop body* contains the steps to be repeated. Pascal provides three control statements for specifying repetition. This chapter examines the while statement and previews the for statement. The for statement and the third loop form, the repeat statement, are examined in Chapter 9.

The while Statement

The program shown in Fig. 5.1 computes and displays gross pay for seven employees. The loop body (steps that are repeated) is the compound statement starting on the third line. The loop body reads an employee's payroll data and computes and displays that employee's salary. After seven salaries are displayed, the last statement in Fig. 5.1 calls procedure WriteLn to display the message All employees processed.

Figure 5.1 Loop to Process Seven Employees

```
CountEmp := 0;                        {no employees processed yet}
while CountEmp < 7 do                 {test value of CountEmp}
  begin
    Write ('Hours> ');
    ReadLn (Hours);
    Write ('Rate > $');
    ReadLn (Rate);
    Salary := Hours * Rate;
    WriteLn ('Salary is $', Salary :4:2);
    CountEmp := CountEmp + 1        {increment CountEmp}
  end; {while}

WriteLn ('All employees processed');
```

The three lines in color in Fig. 5.1 control the looping process. The first statement

```
CountEmp := 0;              {no employees processed yet}
```

stores an initial value of 0 in the variable CountEmp, which represents the count of employees processed so far. The next line evaluates the Boolean expression CountEmp < 7. If the expression is true, the compound statement representing the loop body is executed, causing a new pair of data values to be read and a new salary to be computed and displayed. The last statement in the loop body

```
CountEmp := CountEmp + 1      {increment CountEmp}
```

adds 1 to the value of CountEmp. After executing the last step in the loop body, control returns to the line beginning with while, and the Boolean expression is reevaluated for the next value of CountEmp.

The loop body is executed once for each value of CountEmp from 0 to 6. Eventually CountEmp becomes 7, and the Boolean expression evaluates to false. When that happens, the loop body is not executed, and control passes to the display statement that follows the loop body.

The Boolean expression following the reserved word while is called the *loop repetition condition*. The loop is repeated when this condition is true. We say that the *loop is exited* when this condition is false.

Figure 5.2 is a flow chart of the while loop. It summarizes what we have explained so far about while loops. In the flow chart, the Boolean expression in the diamond-shaped box is evaluated first. If that expression is true, the loop body is executed, and the process is repeated. The while loop is exited when the expression becomes false.

Make sure you understand the difference between the while statement in Fig. 5.1 and the following if statement:

```
if CountEmp < 7 then
  begin
    ...
  end; {if}
```

The compound statement after the reserved word then executes at most one time. In a while statement, the compound statement after the reserved word do can execute more than once.

Syntax of the while Statement

In Fig. 5.1, variable CountEmp is called the *loop control variable* because its value determines whether the loop body is repeated. Three critical steps involve the loop control variable CountEmp:

1. CountEmp is set to an initial value of 0 (*initialized to 0*) before the while statement is reached.
2. CountEmp is tested before the start of each loop repetition (called an *iteration* or a *pass*).
3. CountEmp is updated (its value increases by 1) during each iteration.

Figure 5.2 Flow Chart of a while Loop

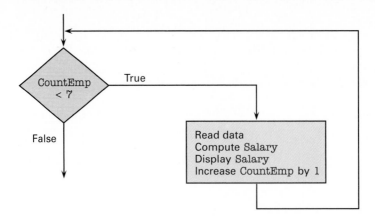

Steps similar to these three steps (initialization, test, and update) must be performed for every while loop. If the first step is missing, the initial test of CountEmp will be meaningless. The last step ensures that we progress toward the final goal (CountEmp >= 7) during each repetition of the loop. If the last step is missing, the value of CountEmp cannot change, so the loop will execute "forever" (an *infinite loop*). The syntax diagram for the while statement follows; it is described in the next display.

while statement

while Statement

Form: while *expression* do
                  statement

Example: {Display N asterisks.}
             CountStar := 0;
             while CountStar < N do
               begin
                  Write ('*');
                  CountStar := CountStar + 1
               end {while}

Interpretation: The *expression* (a condition to control the loop process) is tested and if it is true, the *statement* is executed and the *expression* is retested. The *statement* is repeated as long as (while) the *expression* is true. When the *expression* is tested and found to be false, the while loop is exited and the next program statement after the while statement is executed.

Note: If the *expression* evaluates to false the first time it is tested, the *statement* is not executed.

Exercises for Section 5.1

Self-Check

1. How many times is the following loop body repeated? What is printed during each repetition of the loop body?

```
X := 3;
Count := 0;
while Count < 3 do
   begin
      X := X * X;
      WriteLn (X);
      Count := Count + 1
   end {while}
```

2. Answer self-check exercise 1 if the last statement in the loop is

```
Count := Count + 2
```

3. Answer self-check exercise 1 if the last statement in the loop body is omitted.

Programming

1. Write a while loop that displays each integer from 1 through 5 on a separate line together with its square.

 # 5.2 Accumulating a Sum or a Product in a Loop

Often we use loops to accumulate a sum or a product by repeating an addition or multiplication operation. The next example uses a loop to accumulate a sum.

■ Example 5.1

The program in Fig. 5.3 has a while loop similar to the loop in Fig. 5.1. Besides displaying each employee's salary, it accumulates the total payroll (TotalPay) for a company. The assignment statement

```
TotalPay := TotalPay + Salary;      {add next salary}
```

adds the current value of Salary to the sum being accumulated in TotalPay. Fig. 5.4 traces the effect of repeating this statement for the three values of Salary shown in the sample run.

Figure 5.3 Computing Company Payroll

```
program CompanyPayroll (Input, Output);

{Computes the payroll for a company.}

   var
      NumberEmp,                  {number of employees}
      CountEmp : Integer;         {current employee}
      Hours,                      {hours worked}
      Rate,                       {hourly rate}
      Salary,                     {salary}
      TotalPay : Real;            {company payroll}

begin
   {Enter number of employees.}
   Write ('Enter number of employees >');
   ReadLn (NumberEmp);

   {Compute each employee's salary and add it to the payroll.}
   TotalPay := 0.0;
   CountEmp := 0;                 {start with first employee}
   while CountEmp < NumberEmp do
      begin
         Write ('Hours> ');
         ReadLn (Hours);
         Write ('Rate > $');
         ReadLn (Rate);
         Salary := Hours * Rate;
         WriteLn ('Salary is $', Salary :4:2);
         WriteLn;
         TotalPay := TotalPay + Salary;     {add next salary}
         CountEmp := CountEmp + 1
      end; {while}

   WriteLn; WriteLn ('All employees processed');
   WriteLn ('Total payroll is ', TotalPay :4:2)
end. {CompanyPayroll}

Enter number of employees> 3
Hours> 5
Rate > $4.00
Salary is $20.00

Hours> 6
Rate > $5.00
Salary is $30.00

Hours> 1.5
Rate > $10.00
Salary is $15.00

All employees processed
Total payroll is $65.00
```

Prior to loop execution, the statement

```
TotalPay := 0.0;
```

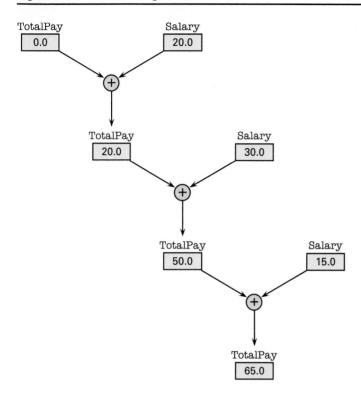

initializes the value of TotalPay to zero. This step is critical; if it is omitted, the final sum will be off by whatever value happens to be stored in TotalPay when the program begins execution. ∎

Generalizing a Loop

The first loop shown in Fig. 5.1 has a serious deficiency: it can only be used when the number of employees is exactly seven. The loop in Fig. 5.3 is much better because it can be used for any number of employees. This program begins by reading the total number of employees into variable NumberEmp. Before each execution of the loop body, the loop repetition condition compares the number of employees processed so far (CountEmp) to NumberEmp.

Accumulating Partial Products

In a similar way, we can use a loop to accumulate a product as shown in the next example.

■ Example 5.2

The loop below computes and displays all products of its data items that are less than 10000. It computes each new partial product by repeated execution of the statement

```
Product := Product * Item   {Compute next product}
```

Figure 5.5 traces the change in the value of Product with each execution of the above statement. If the data items are 10, 500, and 3, the partial products 1 (initial value of Product), 10, and 5000 are displayed.

```
{Display partial products less than 10000}
Product := 1;
while Product < 10000 do
  begin
    WriteLn (Product);             {Display partial product}
    Write ('Enter next item> ');
    ReadLn (Item);
    Product := Product * Item   {Compute next product}
  end {while}
```

Loop exit occurs when the value of Product is greater than or equal to 10000. Consequently, the last value assigned to Product (15000 in Fig. 5.5) is not displayed.   ■

The loop in Fig. 5.5 differs from the other loops in this section. Its repetition condition involves a test of the variable Product. Besides controlling loop repetition, the variable Product also stores the result of the computation being performed in the loop. The other loops involve a test of a variable, CountEmp, that represents the count of loop repetitions. CountEmp is not directly involved in the computation being performed in the loop. We will discuss these differences further in the next section.

Exercises for Section 5.2

Self-Check

1. What is the purpose of the statement

```
WriteLn;
```

in the loop body of Fig. 5.3?
2. What output values are displayed by the following while loop for a data value of 5?

```
WriteLn ('Enter an integer> ');
ReadLn (X);
Product := X;
Count := 0;
while Count < 4 do
  begin
    WriteLn (Product);
    Product := Product * X;
    Count := Count + 1
  end; {while}
```

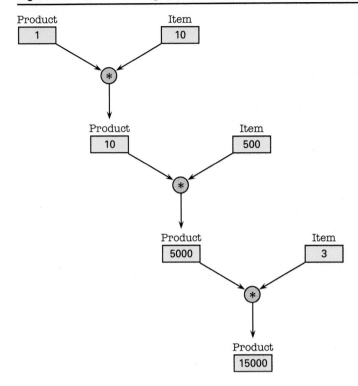

3. What values are displayed if the call to WriteLn comes at the end of the loop instead of the beginning?
4. What does the following segment display? Insert begin and end where needed and correct the errors. The corrected segment should read five numbers and display their sum.

```
Count := 0;
while Count <= 5 do
Count := Count + 1;
Write ('Next number> ');
ReadLn (NextNum);
NextNum := Sum + NextNum;
WriteLn (Count :1, 'numbers were added;');
WriteLn ('their sum is ', Sum:4:2)
```

Programming

1. Write a program segment that computes $1 + 2 + 3 + \ldots + (N - 1) + N$, where N is a data value. Follow the loop body with an if statement that compares this value to $(N * (N + 1)) / 2$ and displays a message that indicates whether the values are the same or different. What message do you think will be displayed?

5.3 Counting Loops and Conditional Loops

The while loop shown in Fig. 5.3 is called a *counter-controlled loop* (or *counting loop*) because its repetition is controlled by a variable whose value represents a count. A counter-controlled loop follows this general format described in pseudocode.

> Set *counter variable* to an initial value of 0
> while *counter variable* < *final value* do
>   begin
>
>   ...
>
>   *increase counter variable* by 1
>   end

We use a counter-controlled loop when we can determine prior to loop execution exactly how many loop repetitions will be needed to solve the problem. This number should appear as the *final value* in the while condition.

Preview of the for Statement

Pascal provides the for statement as another loop form for implementing counting loops. The for statement is the loop form most commonly used in the BASIC programming language and may be familiar to you if you have had some prior programming experience. The for statement implementation of the loop in Fig. 5.3 is shown in Fig. 5.6.

Figure 5.6 Using a for Statement in a Counting Loop

```
{Process each employee starting with the first.}
TotalPay := 0.0;
for CountEmp := 1 to NumberEmp do
  begin
    Write ('Hours> ');
    ReadLn (Hours);
    Write ('Rate > $');
    ReadLn (Rate);
    Salary := Hours * Rate;
    WriteLn ('Salary is $', Salary :4:2);
    WriteLn;
    TotalPay := TotalPay + Salary
  end; {for}

WriteLn ('All employees processed');
```

The for statement heading

```
for CountEmp := 1 to NumberEmp do
```

contains all the control information for the loop. It specifies that the loop body will execute for each value of CountEmp from 1 through NumberEmp and combines the three loop control steps of initialization, update, and testing in one place. Consequently, separate steps to initialize and update CountEmp must not appear in Fig. 5.6. Note that the counter variable, CountEmp, is initialized to 1 (not 0) in the for statement heading.

Although the for statement implementation of a counting loop is shorter and simpler than that of the while statement, the for statement is not as versatile as the while statement and can be used only to implement counting loops. For that reason, we will continue our study of loops using the while statement; we will cover the for statement in Chapter 9.

Conditional Loops

In many programming situations, you will not be able to determine the exact number of loop repetitions before loop execution begins. The number of repetitions may depend on some aspect of the data that is not known before the loop is entered, but that usually can be stated by a condition. For example, you may want to continue writing checks as long as your bank balance is positive, as indicated by the following pseudocode description:

while the balance is still positive do
    begin
        Read in the next transaction
        Update and print the balance
    end

The actual number of loop repetitions performed depends on the type of each transaction (deposit or withdrawal) and its amount.

■ Example 5.3

The program in Fig. 5.7 traces the progress of a hungry worm approaching an apple. Each time it moves, the worm cuts the distance between itself and the apple in half until the worm is close enough to enter the apple. A while loop is the correct looping structure to use because we have no idea beforehand how many moves the worm will need to reach the apple.

Figure 5.7 Worm Bites Apple

```
program WormAndApple (Input, Output);
{
  Prints distances between a worm and an apple.
  The worm keeps cutting the distance in half
  until it is close enough to enter the apple.
}
  const
    Close = 0.5;        {maximum distance for entry to apple}

  var
    InitialDist,        {starting distance of worm from apple}
    Distance : Real;    {distance between worm and apple}

begin {WormAndApple}
  Write ('Enter initial distance between worm and apple> ');
  ReadLn (InitialDist);
```

```
{
  Cut the distance between the worm and the apple in half
  until the worm is close enough to enter the apple.
}
Distance := InitialDist;
while Distance > Close do
  begin
    WriteLn ('The distance is ', Distance :4:2);
    Distance := Distance / 2.0          {cut Distance in half}
  end; {while}

{Print final distance before entering the apple.}
WriteLn;
WriteLn ('Final distance between the worm and apple is ',
         Distance :4:2);
WriteLn ('The worm enters the apple.')
end. {WormAndApple}


Enter initial distance between worm and apple> 2.8
The distance is 2.80
The distance is 1.40
The distance is 0.70

Final distance between the worm and apple is 0.35
The worm enters the apple.
```

Let's take a closer look at the while loop in Fig. 5.7. The assignment statement just before the loop initializes the variable Distance to the starting distance (2.8), which was previously read into InitialDist. Next, the loop header is reached and the *loop repetition condition* (or while condition)

```
Distance > Close
```

is evaluated. Since this condition is true, the loop body (through end) is executed. The loop body displays the value of Distance and the statement

```
Distance := Distance / 2.0       {cut Distance in half}
```

halves the value of Distance, thereby bringing the worm closer to the apple. The loop repetition condition is retested with the new value of Distance (1.4); since 1.4 > 0.5 is true, the loop body displays Distance again, and Distance becomes 0.7. The loop repetition condition is tested a third time; since 0.7 > 0.5 is true, the loop body displays Distance again, and Distance becomes 0.35. The loop repetition condition is tested again; since 0.35 > 0.5 is false, loop exit occurs, and the statements following the loop end are executed.

It is important to realize that the loop is not exited at the exact instant that Distance becomes 0.35. If more statements appeared in the loop body after the assignment to Distance, they would be executed. Loop exit does not occur until the loop repetition condition is retested at the top of the loop and found to be false. ■

Just as in the counting loop shown earlier, there are three critical steps in Fig. 5.7 that involve the loop control variable Distance.

1. Distance is initialized to InitialDist before the loop header is reached.

2. `Distance` is tested before each execution of the loop body.
3. `Distance` is updated (divided by `2.0`) during each iteration.

Remember that steps similar to these must appear in every loop you write.

Exercises for Section 5.3

Self-Check

1. What is the least number of times that the body of a `while` loop can be executed?
2. What is displayed by the following segment? Correct it so that it prints all multiples of 5 from 0 through 100.

```
Sum := 0;
while Sum < 100 do
Sum := Sum + 5;
WriteLn (Sum : 1);
```

3. What values are displayed if the data value in the sample run of the program in Fig. 5.7 is `9.45`? Answer this question if the order of the statements in the loop body is reversed.
4. How would you modify the loop in Fig. 5.7 so that it also determines the number of moves (`CountMoves`) made by the worm before entering the apple? Which is the loop control variable, `Distance` or `CountMoves`?

Programming

1. There are 9,870 people in a town whose population increases by 10 percent each year. Write a loop that determines how many years (`CountYears`) it will take for the population to go over 30,000.

 ## 5.4 Loop Design

It is one thing to be able to analyze the operation of a loop and another to design your own loops. Let's consider the latter problem. The comment just before the loop in Fig. 5.7

```
{
  Cut the distance between the worm and the apple in half
  until the worm is close enough to enter the apple
}
```

summarizes the purpose of the loop. To accomplish that purpose, we must concern ourselves with loop control and loop processing. Loop control involves making sure that loop exit occurs when it is supposed to; loop processing involves making sure the loop body performs the required operations.

To help us formulate the necessary loop control and loop processing steps, it is useful to list what we know about the loop. In the worm and apple problem, if `Distance` is the distance of the worm from the apple, we can make the following observations.

1. `Distance` must be equal to `InitialDist` just before the loop begins.

2. `Distance` during pass i must be half the value of `Distance` during pass $i-1$ (for $i > 1$).

3. `Distance` must be between `Close/2.0` and `Close` just after loop exit.

Statement 1 simply indicates that `InitialDist` is the starting distance of the worm from the apple. Statement 2 says that the distance of the worm from the apple must be cut in half during each iteration. Statement 3 derives from the fact that the worm enters the apple when `Distance <= Close`. `Distance` cannot be `<= Close/2.0` after loop exit; if it is, the loop should have been exited at the end of an earlier pass.

Statement 1 by itself tells us what initialization must be performed. Statement 2 tells us how to process `Distance` within the loop body (that is, divide it by 2.0). Finally, statement 3 tells us when to exit the loop. Because `Distance` is decreasing, loop exit should occur when `Distance <= Close` is true. These considerations give us the following outline, which is the basis for the `while` loop shown in Fig. 5.7. The loop repetition condition, `Distance > Close`, is the opposite of the exit condition, `Distance <= Close`.

1. Initialize `Distance` to `InitialDist`
2. while `Distance > Close` do
   ```
       begin
   ```
   3. Display `Distance`
   4. Divide `Distance` by 2.0
   ```
       end {while}
   ```

While Loops with Zero Iterations

The body of a `while` loop is not executed if the loop repetition test fails (evaluates to false) when it is first reached. To verify that you have the initialization steps correct, make sure that the program still generates the correct results for zero iterations of the loop body. For example, if `Close` is greater than or equal to the value read into `InitialDist` (say, 0.4), the loop body in Fig. 5.7 would not execute and the following lines would be correctly displayed.

```
Enter initial distance between worm and apple > 0.4

Final distance between the worm and apple is 0.40
The worm enters the apple.
```

Displaying a Table of Values

The next example shows you how to use a loop to display a table of values.

■ Example 5.4

Your physics professor wants you to write a program that displays the effect of gravity on a free-falling object. Your instructor would like a table that shows the height of an object dropped from a tower for every second that it is falling.

Assuming that t is the time of free fall, we can make the following observations about the height of an object dropped from a tower.

1. At $t = 0.0$, the object height is the same as the tower height.
2. While the object is falling, its height is the tower height minus the distance that the object has traveled.
3. Free fall ends when the object height is $<= 0.0$.

These considerations form the basis for the while loop shown in Fig. 5.8. The object height (Height) is initialized to the tower height (Tower). The while condition

```
Height > 0.0
```

ensures that loop exit occurs when the object hits the ground. Within the loop body, the assignment statement

```
Height := Tower - 0.5 * g * t * t
```

computes the object height where distance travelled is represented by the formula

$$distance = \tfrac{1}{2} gt^2$$

and g is the gravitational constant.

The number of lines in the table depends on the time interval between lines (DeltaT) and the tower height (Tower), both of which are data values. During each loop iteration, the current elapsed time, t, and the current object height, Height, are displayed and new values assigned to these variables. The message following the table is displayed when the object hits the ground. ■

Figure 5.8 Dropping an Object from a Tower

```
program FreeFall (Input, Output);
{
   Displays the height of an object dropped
   from a tower until it hits the ground.
}

   const
     g = 9.80665;        {gravitational constant for metric units}

   var
     Height,            {height of object}
     Tower,             {height of tower}
     t,                 {elapsed time}
     DeltaT : Real;     {time interval}

begin
   {Enter tower height and time interval.}
   Write ('Tower height in meters> ');
   ReadLn (Tower);
   Write ('Time in seconds between table lines> ');
   ReadLn (DeltaT); WriteLn;

   {Display object height until it hits the ground.}
   WriteLn ('Time' :10, 'Height' :10);
   t := 0.0;
   Height := Tower;
```

```
    while Height > 0.0 do
       begin
          WriteLn (t :10:2, Height :10:2);
          t := t + DeltaT;
          Height := Tower - 0.5 * g * t * t
       end; {while}

    {Object hits the ground.}
    WriteLn;
    WriteLn ('SPLATT!!!'); WriteLn
 end. {FreeFall}


Tower height in meters> 100.0
Time in seconds between table lines> 1.0

    Time      Height
    0.00      100.00
    1.00       95.10
    2.00       80.39
    3.00       55.87
    4.00       21.55

SPLATT!!!
```

Displaying a Table

The program in Fig. 5.8 displays a table of output values. Before the loop is reached, the statement

```
    WriteLn ('Time' :10, 'Height' :10);
```

displays the two strings that appear in the table heading. A string is printed right-justified in its field, so the rightmost character of the first string appears in column 10, and the rightmost character of the second string appears in column 20 (10 + 10).

Within the loop body, the statement

```
    WriteLn (t :10:2, Height :10:2);
```

displays a pair of output values each time it is executed. The rightmost digit of the first number appears in column 10, and the rightmost digit of the second number appears in column 20. Therefore, a table consisting of two columns of numbers is displayed, and each column is right-aligned with its respective heading. Make sure that the field width (10, in this case) is large enough to accommodate the largest value that will be printed.

Working Backward to Determine Loop Initialization

It is not always so easy to come up with the initialization steps for a loop. In some cases, you will have to work backward from the results that you know are required in the first pass to determine what initial values will produce those results.

■ Example 5.5

Your little cousin is learning the binary number system and has asked you to write a program that displays all powers of 2 that are less than a certain value (say, 10000). Assuming that each power of 2 is stored in the variable Power, you can make the following observations about the loop.

1. Power during pass i is 2 times Power during pass $i-1$ (for $i > 1$).
2. Power must be between 10000 and 20000 just after loop exit.

Statement 1 derives from the fact that the powers of 2 are all multiples of 2, and statement 2 from the fact that only powers less than 10000 are displayed. From statement 1, you know that Power must be multiplied by 2 in the loop body. From statement 2 you know that the loop exit condition is Power >= 10000, so the loop repetition condition is Power < 10000. These considerations lead us to the outline below.

1. Initialize Power to _____
2. while Power < 10000 do
    begin
        3. Display Power
        4. Multiply Power by 2
    end

One way to complete step 1 is to ask what value should be displayed during the first loop repetition. The value of N raised to the power zero is one for any number N. Therefore, if we initialize Power to 1, the value displayed during the first loop repetition will be correct.

1. Initialize Power to 1   ■

Sentinel-Controlled Loops

Frequently, you will not know exactly how many data items a program will process before it begins execution. This may happen because there are too many data items to count beforehand or because the number of data items provided depends on how the computation proceeds.

One way to handle this situation is to instruct the user to enter a unique data value, called a *sentinel value*, when finished. The program then tests each data item and terminates when the sentinel value is read. You must choose the sentinel value carefully; it must be a value that could not normally occur as data.

■ Example 5.6

The following statements must be true for a sentinel-controlled loop that accumulates the sum (in Sum) of a collection of exam scores, where each score is read into the variable Score. The sentinel score must not be included in the sum.

1. Sum is the sum of all scores read so far.
2. Score contains the sentinel value just after loop exit.

From statement 1 we know that we must add each score to Sum in the loop body, and that Sum must initially be zero for its final value to be correct. From statement 2 we know that loop exit must occur after the sentinel value is read into Score. These considerations lead to the following trial loop form.

Incorrect Sentinel-Controlled Loop

1. Initialize Sum to zero
2. while Score is not the sentinel do
   begin
       3. Read the next score into Score
       4. Add Score to Sum
   end

Because Score has not been given an initial value, the while condition in step 2 cannot be evaluated when the loop is first reached. Another problem is that after step 3 reads the sentinel value, step 4 adds the sentinel to Sum before loop exit occurs. The solution to these problems is to read the first score as the initial value of Score before the loop is reached and to switch the order of the read and add steps in the loop body. The outline for this solution is as follows:

Correct Sentinel-Controlled Loop

1. Initialize Sum to zero
2. Read the first score into Score
3. while Score is not the sentinel do
   begin
       4. Add Score to Sum
       5. Read the next score into Score
   end

Step 2 reads in the first score, and step 4 adds this score to Sum (initial value of zero). Step 5 reads all remaining scores, including the sentinel. Step 4 adds all scores except the sentinel to Sum.

The initial read (step 2) is often called the *priming read*, because it is analogous to the priming of a pump, in which a cup of water must first be poured into a pump before it can begin to pump water out of a well. The Pascal implementation shown in Fig. 5.9 uses −1 (value of Sentinel) as the sentinel because all exam scores should be nonnegative.

Figure 5.9 A Sentinel-Controlled Loop

```
Sum := 0;
WriteLn ('When done, enter -1 to stop.');
WriteString ('Enter the first score> ');
ReadLn (Score);
while Score <> Sentinel do
  begin
    Sum := Sum + Score;
    WriteLn ('Enter the next score> ');
    ReadLn (Score)
  end; {while}
```

```
WriteLn;
WriteLn ('Sum of exam scores is ', Sum :1)
```

Although it may look strange at first to see the statement

```
ReadLn (Score);
```

at two different points in the program, this is a perfectly good programming practice and causes no problems. The following sample dialogue would be used to enter the scores 55, 33, and 77.

```
When done, enter -1 to stop.
Enter the first score> 55
Enter the next score> 33
Enter the next score> 77
Enter the next score> -1

Sum of exam scores is 165
```

It is usually instructive (and often necessary) to question what happens when there are no data items to process. In this case, the sentinel value should be entered as the "first score." Loop exit would occur right after the first (and only) test of the loop repetition condition, so the loop body would not be executed (in other words, it is a loop with zero iterations). Sum would retain its initial value of zero, which would be correct. ∎

Exercises for Section 5.4

Self-Check

1. Write statements similar to the ones shown in this section that summarize the properties of the loop in Fig. 5.3.
2. Why would it be incorrect to move the assignment statement in the loop of Fig. 5.9 to the end of the loop body?

Programming

1. Modify the loop in Fig. 5.3 so that it is a sentinel-controlled loop. Use a negative value of Hours as the sentinel. Read the value of Hours before loop repetition and at the end of the loop body.
2. Write a program segment that allows the user to enter values and prints out the number of positive and negative values entered. Use 0 as the sentinel value.
3. Write the while loop for a program that prints all powers of an integer, N, less than a specified value, MaxPower. On each line of a table, show the exponent (0, 1, 2, ...) and the value of the integer N raised to that exponent.
4. Write a loop that prints a table of equivalent Fahrenheit and Celsius temperature values. Use the formula

   Fahrenheit = 1.8 × *Celsius* + 32.0

   to convert from degrees Celsius to Fahrenheit. Assume that the initial and final Celsius values are available in InitCel and FinalCel (type Real), respectively, and that the change in Celsius values between table entries is given by StepCel.

 ## 5.5 Assertions and Loop Invariants

Once a loop is designed, you should verify that it works properly. One verification method is to trace the loop's execution for a variety of different sets of data, making sure that the loop always terminates and that it produces the correct results, even when zero iterations are performed.

Exhaustive testing of a loop can be time-consuming. For this reason, computer scientists have devised techniques for quickly proving that a loop is correct. Detailed analysis of that process is beyond the scope of the text, but we will introduce some principles of loop verification that will help you design loops.

A critical part of loop verification is documentation of the loop with a special comment called an *assertion*—a logical statement that is always true. An assertion should be placed just before the loop body and just after the loop end. The assertion that precedes the loop body is called the *loop invariant*. Like the while condition, the loop invariant is evaluated just before each repetition of the loop body. The execution of the loop body may change the value of the while condition from true to false; however, the value of the loop invariant must remain true. The loop in Fig. 5.7 is rewritten in Fig. 5.10 using assertions. Remember that assertions, like all comments, are ignored by the compiler.

Figure 5.10 Worm and Apple Loop with Assertions

```
{
 Cut the distance between the worm and the apple in half
 until the worm is close enough to enter the apple
}
Distance := InitialDist;
while Distance > Close do
  {invariant:
      Distance <= InitialDist and
      Distance > Close / 2.0 and
      Distance in pass i is half Distance in pass i-1 (for i > 1)
  }
  begin
    WriteLn ('The distance is ', Distance :4:2);
    Distance := Distance / 2.0          {cut Distance in half}
  end; {while}

{assert: Distance <= Close}
```

The invariant summarizes all we know about the loop and is similar to our earlier observations:

1. Distance must be equal to InitialDist just before the loop begins.
2. Distance during pass i must be half the value of Distance during pass $i-1$ (for $i > 1$).
3. Distance must be between Close/2.0 and Close just after loop exit.

Example 5.7

137

5.5 Assertions and
Loop Invariants

Example 5.7

The sentinel-controlled loop (see Fig. 5.9) is rewritten in Fig. 5.11 using assertions. Compare the loop invariant with the following statements that summarize the loop properties.

1. Sum is the sum of all scores read so far.
2. Score is the sentinel just after loop exit. ■

Figure 5.11   Sentinel-Controlled Loop with Assertions

```
Sum := 0;
WriteLn ('When done, enter -1 to stop.');
WriteLn ('Enter the first score> ');
ReadLn (Score);
while Score <> Sentinel do
  {invariant:
      Sum is the sum of all scores read and
      no prior score was the sentinel
  }
  begin
    Sum := Sum + Score;
    WriteLn ('Enter the next score> ');
    ReadLn (Score)
  end; {while}

{assert: Score is Sentinel and Sum is the sum of all scores}
```

Some computer scientists use loop invariants for loop design as well as for loop verification. By first writing the loop invariant as a comment inside the loop, they can discern from the invariant what initialization, testing, and processing steps are required.

Remembering the Last Data Value in a Loop

In a number of situations, your program may need to remember the data value processed during the last iteration of a loop. For example, some keyboards are "bouncy" and cause multiple occurrences of the same character when you press a key. Some faculty are forgetful and may enter the same exam score two times in succession. We can avoid errors like those by using an if statement nested inside a loop to check whether the current data value is the same as the last data value.

Example 5.8

The program in Fig. 5.12 finds the product of a collection of data values. If there are consecutive multiple occurrences of the same data value, only the first occurrence is included in the product. For example, the product of the numbers 10, 5, 5, 5, and 10 is $10 \times 5 \times 10$, or 500. Assuming that a new data value is read into NextNum during each loop iteration, we can make the following observations:

1. Product in pass i is the same as Product in pass $i-1$ if NextNum in pass i is NextNum in pass $i-1$; otherwise, Product during pass i is NextNum times Product in pass $i-1$ (for $i > 1$).
2. NextNum is the sentinel just after loop exit.

Statement 1 requires the loop to "remember" the value read into NextNum during the previous iteration. We will introduce a new program variable, LastNum, for that purpose. The current value of NextNum should be incorporated in the product only if it is different from the previous value of NextNum (saved in LastNum). A trial loop form follows.

Initial Loop Form

1. Initialize Product to _____
2. Initialize LastNum to _____
3. Read the first number into NextNum
4. while NextNum is not the sentinel do
   begin
       5. if NextNum is not equal to LastNum then
           6. Multiply Product by NextNum
       7. Set LastNum to NextNum
       8. Read the next number into NextNum
   end

For Product to be correct during the first pass, it must be initialized to 1 (step 1). We must also initialize LastNum so that the condition in step 5 can be evaluated. To ensure that the first number read into NextNum is incorporated in the product, we must pick a value for LastNum that is different from the initial data value. If we initialize LastNum to the sentinel, we know that LastNum will be different from the initial data value unless there are no actual data. These considerations lead to the revised loop form that follows:

Revised Loop Form

1. Initialize Product to 1
2. Initialize LastNum to the sentinel
3. Read the first number into NextNum
4. while NextNum is not the sentinel do
   begin
       5. if NextNum is not equal to LastNum then
           6. Multiply Product by NextNum
       7. Set LastNum to NextNum
       8. Read the next number into NextNum
   end

Within the loop, steps 7 and 8 prepare for the next iteration by saving the previous value of NextNum in LastNum before reading the next data value. What would happen if the order of those two steps was reversed? ∎

```pascal
program Multiply (Input, Output);
{
 Finds the product of a collection of nonzero integers. If there
 are multiple consecutive occurrences of the same value, only the   first
 value is included in the product.
}
 const
   Sentinel = 0;                    {sentinel value}

 var
   NextNum,                         {input — new data item}
   LastNum,                         {last data item}
   Product : Integer;               {output — product of data}


 procedure Instruct;

 begin {Instruct}
   WriteLn ('This program computes the product of a collection');
   WriteLn ('of integer data values. If consecutive numbers');
   WriteLn ('are the same, only the first number is used.');
   WriteLn ('Enter 0 as a data value to stop the program.');
   WriteLn
 end; {Instruct}


begin {Multiply}
   Instruct;                        {Display user instructions}

   {Compute product of nonzero, nonrepeating data items.}
   Product := 1;
   LastNum := Sentinel;
   Write ('Enter first number> ');
   ReadLn (NextNum);                          {read first item}
   while NextNum <> Sentinel do
     {invariant:
         No prior value of NextNum is the sentinel and
         Product in pass i is Product in pass i-1 if NextNum is
         LastNum; otherwise, Product in pass i is NextNum * Product
         in pass i-1 (for i > 1)
     }
     begin
       if NextNum <> LastNum then
         Product := Product * NextNum;    {compute next product}
       LastNum := NextNum;                {remember last item}
       Write ('Enter next number> ');
       ReadLn (NextNum)                   {read next item}
     end; {while}

   {assert:
      NextNum is the sentinel and Product is the product of
      every value of NextNum such that NextNum <> LastNum
   }
   WriteLn ('The product is ', Product :1)
end. {Multiply}
```

This program computes the product of a collection
of integer data values. If consecutive numbers

```
are the same, only the first number is used.
Enter 0 as a data value to stop the program.

Enter first number> 10
Enter next  number> 5
Enter next  number> 5
Enter next  number> 5
Enter next  number> 10
Enter next  number> 0
The product is 500
```

The program in Fig. 5.12 illustrates the proper form of a sentinel-controlled loop. The constant `Sentinel` has the value zero, since it is meaningless to include zero in a collection of numbers being multiplied. To determine whether or not to execute the loop, each value read into `NextNum` must be compared to `Sentinel`. For this test to make sense in the beginning, the first data value must be read before the `while` loop is reached. The next value must be read at the end of the loop so that it can be tested before starting another iteration. This general pattern is illustrated as follows:

Read the first data item
while current data item is not the sentinel do
  begin
    Process current data item
    Read the next data item
  end

Remember, in a sentinel-controlled loop, the read operation appears twice: before the `while` header (the priming read) and at the end of the loop body.

Exercises for Section 5.5

Self-Check

1. Write the loop invariant for the loop in Fig. 5.8 and the assertion following the loop.
2. What is the product computed by the program in Fig. 5.12 if only one data value besides the sentinel is supplied? What product would be computed if steps 7 and 8 of the revised algorithm were reversed and several data items were provided?

 ## 5.6 Displaying a Table in an Interactive Program

The next problem applies the ideas developed in this chapter to display a table of interest values. The tabular output is set off from the prompts and data values that also appear on the screen.

Problem

Now that you are finally graduating, your parents want to invest some money for you, and they are interested in finding out the best investment strategy. They ask you to write a program that shows how the value of a certificate of deposit increases annually. They want to use your program for fixed-rate or variable-rate certificates in which the interest rate changes at the beginning of each year. Whenever it is run, your program should display a table that shows the investment year, the annual interest, and the certificate balance at the end of each year until the balance has passed a target amount.

Design Overview

What is needed is a program that computes annual interest and new balance using the formulas

  *interest = balance * rate*
  new balance = old balance + interest

The program should display these values while the new balance is less than the target balance. You can use a single variable (`Balance`) to represent the old and the new balances, where the initial value of `Balance` is the deposit amount (`Deposit`).

Data Requirements

Problem Inputs
the deposit amount (`Deposit : Real`)
the target balance (`TargetBal : Real`)
the annual interest rate as a fraction (`Rate : Real`)
an indicator of whether the interest rate is fixed or variable
  (`FixedOrVar : Char`)

Problem Outputs
the current investment year (`Year : Integer`)
the annual balance (`Balance : Real`)
the annual interest earned (`Interest : Real`)

The type `Char` variable `FixedOrVar` indicates whether the annual interest rate is fixed (value is `'F'`) or varying (value is `'V'`).

Initial Algorithm

1. Enter the deposit amount, the value of `FixedOrVar`, and the interest rate for a fixed-rate certificate.
2. Print a table showing the year, interest earned, and account balance as long as the balance has not passed the target balance. If the interest rate is variable,

Case Study: Computing Interest, continued

read in the new rate at the start of each year before computing the annual
interest.

Algorithm Refinements

Step 2 requires a loop. Since you don't know how many iterations are needed,
use a while loop with the following properties:

1. Year is the number of loop iterations performed so far.
2. Balance is the sum of Deposit plus all prior values of Interest.
3. Balance is between TargetBal and TargetBal + Interest just after loop
   exit.

The preceding statements suggest the following refinement for step 2 of the
algorithm.

> *Step 2 Refinement*
> 2.1 Initialize Year to zero
> 2.2 Initialize Balance to Deposit
> 2.3 while Balance < TargetBal do
>   begin
>   2.4 Increment Year by 1
>   2.5 if the interest rate is variable then
>   2.6 Read this year's rate
>   2.7 Compute the interest for this year
>   2.8 Compute the new value of Balance
>   2.9 Display the table line for the current year
>   end

Coding

The program and a sample run are shown in Fig. 5.13. The sample run uses a
variable interest rate. Using a fixed rate would eliminate the lines needed to
read each annual rate.

Figure 5.13 Increasing Your Money

```
program GrowMoney (Input, Output);
{
  Prints a table of interest earned and account balance for each
  investment year for fixed or varying rate certificates.
}
  const
    Fixed = 'F';
    Variable = 'V';
    Pad = '                         ';

  var
    FixedOrVar : Char;      {input - indicates fixed or varying rate}
```

```pascal
      Deposit,              {input - initial amount of deposit}
      Rate,                 {input - annual rate of interest}
      TargetBal,            {input - the target certificate amount}
      Balance,              {output - current certificate amount}
      Interest : Real;      {output - amount of annual interest}
      Year : Integer;       {output - year of investment}

begin {GrowMoney}
  Write ('Enter the deposit amount $');
  ReadLn (Deposit);
  Write ('Enter the desired final balance $');
  ReadLn (TargetBal);
  Write ('Is the interest rate fixed (F) or variable (V)? ');
  ReadLn (FixedOrVar);
  if FixedOrVar = Fixed then
    begin
      Write ('Enter the interest rate as a decimal fraction>');
      ReadLn (Rate)
    end
  else
    begin
      WriteLn ('Enter the interest rate as a decimal fraction');
      WriteLn ('after each prompt in the table below.')
    end; {if}

  {Display table heading}
  WriteLn;  Write (Pad);
  WriteLn ('Year' :10, 'Interest' :15, 'Balance' :15);

  {Display the certificate balance for each year.}
  Year := 0;
  Balance := Deposit;
  while Balance < TargetBal do
    {invariant:
        Balance < TargetBal + last value of Interest and
        Balance is the sum of Deposit and all values of Interest
    }
    begin
      Year := Year + 1;
      if FixedOrVar = Variable then
        begin
          Write ('Enter rate for year ', Year :2, '> ');
          ReadLn (Rate)
        end; {if}

      Interest := Balance * Rate;
      Balance := Balance + Interest;

      Write (Pad);                          {print table line}
      WriteLn (Year :10, Interest :15:2, Balance :15:2)
    end; {while}

  {assert: Balance >= TargetBal and
      Balance is the sum of Deposit and all values of Interest
  }
  WriteLn;
  Write ('Certificate amount reaches target after ');
  WriteLn (Year :1, ' years');
  WriteLn ('Final balance is $', Balance :4:2)
end. {GrowMoney}
```

Case Study: Computing Interest, continued

```
Enter the deposit amount $100.00
Enter the desired final balance $200.00
Is the interest rate fixed (F) or variable (V)? V
Enter the interest rate as a decimal fraction
after each prompt in the table below.
```

		Year	Interest	Balance
Enter rate for year	1> 0.075			
		1	7.50	107.50
Enter rate for year	2> 0.080			
		2	8.60	116.10
Enter rate for year	3> 0.085			
		3	9.87	125.97
Enter rate for year	4> 0.090			
		4	11.34	137.31
Enter rate for year	5> 0.095			
		5	13.04	150.35
Enter rate for year	6> 0.100			
		6	15.03	165.38
Enter rate for year	7> 0.150			
		7	24.81	190.19
Enter rate for year	8> 0.200			
		8	38.04	228.23

```
Certificate amount reaches target after 8 years
Final balance is $228.23
```

In the program output of Fig. 5.13, the lines used for data entry appear on the left, and the lines showing interest and certificate values appear on the right. This separation makes it easier to read the output table. The statement

```
Write (Pad);
```

accomplishes this separation by displaying a string of thirty blanks before each table line. The cursor remains positioned on the current output line after the blanks are displayed.

Testing

Test the program with a variable and a fixed interest rate. Use 10 percent to make it easy to check the table values. What happens if the character read into FixedOrVar is not F or V? You should also verify that the program works properly when the target balance is less than the initial deposit. In that case, the program should display the deposit amount as the final balance.

Suggestions for Improvement

Unfortunately, the program will not work properly if the user enters a lowercase f or v as the value of FixedOrVar. One solution to that problem is to insert the following multiple-alternative statement after the statement that reads the value of FixedOrVar. This statement changes a lowercase f or v to uppercase.

```
if FixedOrVar = 'f' then
   FixedOrVar := Fixed
else if FixedOrVar = 'v' then
   FixedOrVar := Variable;
```

Self-Check

1. What happens in the program of Fig. 5.13 if the program user enters a letter other than F or V? Explain how a while loop could be used to correct this problem.

5.7 Debugging and Testing Programs

Section 2.8 described the general categories of error messages that you are likely to see: syntax errors and run-time errors. It is possible for a program to execute without generating any error messages, but still produce incorrect results. Sometimes the cause of a run-time error or the origin of incorrect results is apparent and the error can be fixed easily. Often, however, the error is not obvious and may require considerable effort to locate.

The first step in attempting to find a hidden error is to try to determine what part of the program is generating incorrect results. Then insert extra WriteLn statements in your program to provide a trace of its execution. For example, if the loop in Fig. 5.9 is not computing the correct sum, you could insert an extra diagnostic WriteLn statement, as shown by the line in color in the following loop:

```
ReadLn (Score);
while Score <> Sentinel do
  begin
    Sum := Sum + Score;
    WriteLn ('***** score is ', Score, 'sum is ', Sum);
    WriteLn ('Enter the next  score> ');
    ReadLn (Score)
  end; {while}
```

The diagnostic WriteLn statement displays each partial sum that is accumulated and the current value of Score. This WriteLn statement displays a string of asterisks at the beginning of its output line. The asterisks make it easier to identify diagnostic output in the debugging runs and to locate the diagnostic WriteLn statements in the source program.

Be careful when you insert extra diagnostic WriteLn statements—they themselves can be a source of syntax errors. Sometimes it is necessary to add a begin...end pair if a single statement inside an if or while statement becomes a compound statement when a diagnostic WriteLn is added. If you insert a WriteLn statement after the last statement in the loop body, don't forget to separate the two statements with a semicolon.

Once it appears that you have located an error, take out the extra diagnostic statements. As a temporary measure, it is sometimes advisable to make the diagnostic statements comments by enclosing them in curly braces. If errors crop up again in later testing, it is easier to remove the braces than to retype the diagnostic statements.

Using Debugger Programs

Many computer systems have *debugger programs* available to help you debug a Pascal program. The debugger program lets you execute your program one statement at a time so you can see the effect of each statement. Besides printing a diagnostic when a run-time error occurs, the debugger indicates the statement that caused the error and allows you to display the values of selected variables at the time of the error. You can also request the debugger program to trace the values of selected variables during program execution so you can observe how those variables change as the program executes. Finally, you can request the debugger to halt execution when certain statements (*breakpoints*) are reached during program execution. You can then inspect the values of selected variables to determine if they are correct.

Testing

After you have corrected all errors and the program appears to execute as expected, test the program thoroughly to make sure that it works. Earlier, we discussed tracing an algorithm and suggested that you provide enough sets of test data to ensure that all possible paths are traced. The same is true for the completed program. Make enough test runs to verify that the program works properly for representative samples of all possible data combinations.

 5.8   Common Programming Errors

Beginners sometimes confuse `if` and `while` statements because both statements contain a condition. Make sure that you use an `if` statement to implement a decision step and a `while` statement to implement a conditional loop.

Be careful when you use tests for inequality to control the repetition of a `while` loop. For instance, the following loop is intended to process all transactions for a bank account while the balance is positive.

```
while Balance <> 0.0 do
   UpDate (Balance)
```

If the bank balance goes from a positive to a negative amount without being exactly 0.0, the loop does not terminate; it becomes an infinite loop. The next loop below would be safer:

```
while Balance > 0.0 do
   UpDate (Balance)
```

You should verify that the repetition condition for a `while` loop will eventually become false. If you use a sentinel-controlled loop, remember to provide a prompt that tells the program user what value to enter as the sentinel. Make sure that the sentinel value cannot be confused with a normal data item.

If the loop body contains more than one statement, remember to bracket it with `begin` and `end`. Otherwise, only the first statement will be repeated, and the remaining statements will be executed when and if the loop is exited. The following loop will not terminate because the step that updates the loop control variable is not considered part of the loop body. The program will continue to print the initial value of Power until it either exceeds its time limit or you instruct the computer to terminate its execution.

```
while Power <= 10000 do
  WriteLn ('Next power of N is ', Power :6);
  Power := Power * N;
```

The same situation exists for if statements with a compound statement as the True task or False task. If the bracketing begin and end are missing, only the first statement will be considered part of the task, which can lead to a syntax error. In the following example, the begin and end bracket around the True task is missing. The compiler assumes that the semicolon at the end of the assignment statement terminates the if statement, so it will be unable to translate the lines that follow. This may lead to syntax errors of ; expected (at the end of the first WriteLn statement) and unexpected symbol (the reserved word else).

```
if X > 0 then
  Sum := Sum + X;
  WriteLn ('Greater than zero')
else
  WriteLn ('Less than zero');
```

Finally, be sure to initialize to zero a variable used for accumulating a sum by repeated addition, and to initialize to one a variable used for accumulating a product by repeated multiplication. Omitting this step will lead to results that are inaccurate.

 # Chapter Review

This chapter examined the while statement and used it to repeat steps in a program. You learned how to implement counter-controlled loops, or loops where the number of repetitions required can be determined before the loop is entered. You also learned that the while statement is useful when you do not know the exact number of repetitions required before the loop begins.

In designing a while loop, you must consider both the loop control and the loop-processing operations that must be performed. Separate Pascal statements are needed to initialize and update the loop control variable, which is tested in the loop repetition condition.

In this chapter, you also discovered a common technique for controlling the repetition of a while loop: using a special sentinel value to indicate that all required data has been processed. In this case, an input variable must appear in the loop repetition condition. This variable is initialized when the first data value is read (the priming read), and it is updated at the end of the loop when the next new data value is read. Loop repetition terminates when the sentinel value is read.

The chapter discussed the importance of using assertions and loop invariants in loop verification and loop design. Throughout this text, we use loop invariants to document the processing performed by the loop body.

New Pascal Constructs

The new Pascal constructs introduced in this chapter are described in Table 5.1.

Table 5.1 Summary of New Pascal Constructs

Construct	Effect

while Statement
`Sum := 0;`
`while Sum <= MaxSum do`
`  begin`
`    Write ('Next integer> ');`
`    readln (Next);`
`    Sum ; = Sum + Next`
`  end`
	A collection of input data items is read and their sum is accumulated in `Sum`. This process stops when the accumulated sum exceeds `MaxSum`.

for Statement (Optional)
`for Count := 1 to 9 do`
`  WriteLn (Count, Count * Count)`
	Displays each of the digits from 1 through 9 inclusive on an output line together with its square.

✓ *Quick-Check Exercises*

1. A while loop is called a _____ loop.
2. A while loop is (always, sometimes, never) used for counting.
3. The priming step for a while loop is what kind of statement? When is it used?
4. The sentinel value is always the last value added to a sum being accumulated in a sentinel-controlled loop. True or false?
5. It is an error if a while loop body never executes. True or false?
6. What does the following segment display?

   ```
   Product := 1;
   Counter := 2;
   while Counter <= 5 do
     Product := Product * Counter;
     Counter := Counter + 1;
   WriteLn (Product)
   ```

7. What does the segment in exercise 6 display if the bracketing begin and end are inserted where intended?
8. Write the loop invariant of the segment in exercise 6.
9. Which of these may be false: loop invariant, while condition, assertion?
10. The use of loop invariants is useful for which of the following: loop control, loop design, loop verification?

1. conditional
2. sometimes
3. an input operation, used in a sentinel-controlled loop
4. false—the sentinel should not be processed.
5. false
6. nothing—the loop executes "forever"
7. The value of 1 * 2 * 3 * 4 * 5, or 120.
8. {invariant:
       Counter <= 6 and Product is the product of all
       integers < Counter
   }
9. while condition
10. loop design, loop verification

Review Questions

1. Define a sentinel value.
2. For a sentinel value to be used properly when data are being read, where should the input statements appear?
3. Write a program called Sum to add and print a collection of payroll amounts entered at the terminal until a sentinel value of −1 is entered.
4. Hand-trace the following program, given the following data:

```
4 2 8 4     1 4 2 1     9 3 3 1     −22 10 8 2     3 3 4 5

program Slopes (Input, Output);

   const
     Sentinel = 0.0;

   var
     Slope, y2, y1, x2, x1 : real;

begin {Slopes}
   WriteLn ('Enter four numbers separated by spaces');
   WriteLn ('The last two numbers cannot be the same, but');
   WriteLn ('The program terminates if the first two are.');
   WriteLn ('Enter four numbers> ');
   ReadLn (y2, y1, x2, x1);
   Slope := (y2 − y1) / (x2 − x1);
   while Slope <> Sentinel do
     begin
        WriteLn ('Slope is ', Slope :5:2);
        WriteLn ('Enter four more numbers> ');
        ReadLn (y2, y1, x2, x1);
        Slope := (y2 − y1) / (x2 − x1)
     end {while}
end. {Slopes}
```

5. Explain when it is appropriate to use semicolons within
   a. the variable declaration statement
   b. the constant declaration statement
   c. the program body

    d. an if statement

    e. a while statement

6. Which of the following statements is incorrect?
   a. Loop invariants are used in loop verification.
   b. Loop invariants are used in loop design.
   c. A loop invariant is always an assertion.
   d. An assertion is always a loop invariant.

Programming Projects

1. Write a program that finds the product of a collection of data values. Your program should ignore any negative data and should terminate when a zero value is read.

2. Write a program to read in an integer N and compute $Slow = \sum_{i=1}^{N} i = 1 + 2 + 3 + \dots$ + N (the sum of all integers from 1 to N). Then compute $Fast = (N * (N + 1)) / 2$ and compare Fast and Slow. Your program should print both Fast and Slow and indicate whether they are equal. (You will need a loop to compute Slow.) Which computation method is preferable?

3. Write a program to read a collection of integer data items and find and print the index of the first occurrence and the last occurrence of the number 12. Your program should print index values of 0 if the number 12 is not found. The index is the sequence number of the data item 12. For example, if the eighth data item is the only 12, then the index value 8 should be printed for the first and last occurrence.

4. Write a program to read in a collection of exam scores ranging in value from 1 to 100. Your program should count and print the number of outstanding scores (90-100), the number of satisfactory scores (60-89), and the number of unsatisfactory scores (1-59). It should also display the category of each score. Test your program on the following data:

63	75	72	72	78	67	80	63	75
90	89	43	59	99	82	12	100	55

   Modify your program to display the average exam score (a real number) at the end of the run.

5. Write a program to process weekly employee time cards for all employees of an organization. Each employee has three data items, which indicate an identification number, the hourly wage rate, and the number of hours worked during a given week. Each employee is paid time-and-a-half for all hours worked over 40. A tax amount of 3.625 percent of gross salary is deducted. The program output should show the employee's number and net pay. Display the total payroll and the average amount paid at the end of the run.

6. Suppose you own a beer distributorship that sells Piels (ID number 1), Coors (ID number 2), Bud (ID number 3), and Iron City (ID number 4) by the case. Write a program to (a) read in the case inventory for each brand for the start of the week; (b) process all weekly sales and purchase records for each brand; and (c) print out the final inventory. Each transaction consists of two data items. The first item is the brand identification number (an integer); the second is the amount purchased (a positive integer value) or the amount sold (a negative integer value). The weekly

inventory for each brand (for the start of the week) also consists of two items: the identification number and the initial inventory for that brand. For now, you can assume that you always have sufficient foresight to prevent depletion of your inventory for any brand. (Hint: Your data entry should begin with eight values that represent the case inventory. These should be followed by the transaction values.)

7. Write a program to find the largest, smallest, and average value in a collection of N numbers, where the value of N is the first data item read.

Procedure Parameters

6

Chapter 3 introduced you to procedures; you learned how to use them to write separate program units corresponding to the individual steps in a problem solution. We have not used procedures extensively because we have not yet discussed how to pass information between individual procedures or between procedures and the main program. So far, our procedures can only manipulate data that are stored locally.

This chapter introduces an important concept in programming: the use of procedure parameters. In this chapter, you will see that parameters provide a convenient way to pass information between a main program and a procedure. Parameters also make procedures more versatile because they enable a procedure to manipulate different data each time it is called. For example, WriteLn (M) displays the value of M, whereas WriteLn (N) displays the value of N.

 ## 6.1   Introduction to Parameter Lists

We can make an analogy between a carefully designed program that uses procedures and a stereo system. Each stereo component is an independent device that performs a specific function. The tuner and the amplifier may contain similar electronic parts, but each component uses its own internal circuitry to perform its required function. Information in the form of electronic signals is passed back and forth between components over wires. If you look at the rear of a stereo amplifier, you will find that some plugs are marked input and others are marked output. The wires attached to the plugs marked input carry electronic signals into the amplifier, where they are processed. (These signals may come from a cassette deck, a tuner, or a compact disc player.) New electronic signals are generated. Those signals come out of the amplifier from the plugs marked output and go to the speakers or back to the tape deck for recording.

Right now, you know how to design the separate components (procedures) of a programming system, but you don't yet know how to pass data between the main program and a procedure that you write. In this chapter, you will learn how to use *parameter lists* to provide communication paths between the main program and its procedures (or between two procedures).

Actual Parameter Lists

Each procedure call statement has two parts: a procedure name and an actual parameter list. In the procedure call statement

```
WriteLn (X, Y);
```

the *actual parameter list* is (X, Y), so there are two *actual parameters*, X and Y, whose values are passed into procedure WriteLn. We know that procedure WriteLn displays the values of X and Y.

In the procedure call statement

```
ReadLn (V, W);
```

the actual parameters are V and W. In this case, the procedure reads data values into these variables. The data type of each variable determines what kind of value is read.

The actual parameters are treated differently in these two procedure call statements. In the first call statement, the values of X and Y are passed into procedure WriteLn, and the procedure displays the values. Because the procedure does not change the values of X and Y, they are considered *procedure inputs*. In the second call statement, the execution of procedure ReadLn changes the contents of V and W. Because ReadLn sends values back to the calling program, V and W are considered *procedure outputs*.

Formal Parameter Lists

The system procedures WriteLn and ReadLn differ from procedures that you write in two important respects. The number of actual parameters may vary from one call to the next, and the data type of a particular actual parameter (say, the first) may also vary from one call to the next. For each procedure that you write, the number of actual parameters must be the same each time the procedure is called, and the data type of a particular parameter must be the same.

How do we tell the Pascal compiler the number of procedure parameters and the type of each parameter? The answer is through the formal parameter list.

Procedure ReportSumAve in Fig. 6.1 computes and displays the sum and average of two type Real values that are passed into the procedure as procedure inputs. The *formal parameter list*

```
(Numl, Num2 {input} : Real)
```

tells the Pascal compiler the number of parameters being processed (two), the data type of each parameter (both type Real), and the names that we will use in place of the actual parameter names in the procedure body (Numl for the first parameter and Num2 for the second). We use the *formal parameters*, Numl and Num2, in the procedure body to describe what we want done to the actual parameters. The actual parameters are not known when the procedure is written but are determined when the procedure call statement executes. The comment {input} identifies Numl and Num2 as procedure inputs.

Figure 6.1   Procedure to Display Sum and Average

```
procedure ReportSumAve (Numl, Num2 {input} : Real);
{
   Displays the sum and average of Numl and Num2.
   Pre : Numl and Num2 are assigned values.
   Post: The sum and average value of Numl and Num2 are displayed.
}
   var
     Sum,                     {sum of Numl, Num2}
     Average : Real;          {average of Numl, Num2}
```

```
begin {ReportSumAve}
  Sum := Num1 + Num2;
  Average := Sum / 2.0;
  WriteLn ('The sum is ', Sum :4:2);
  WriteLn ('The average is ', Average :4:2)
end; {ReportAverage}
```

Preconditions and Postconditions as Comments

The declaration for procedure ReportSumAve begins with a lengthy comment that describes the procedure's operations. We use the following commenting style:

```
{
    ... comments ...
}
```

for comments that extend over multiple lines.

The comment line

```
Pre : Num1 and Num2 are assigned values.
```

describes the condition that must be true before the procedure is called; this condition is known as the *precondition*. The line

```
Post: The sum and average value of Num1 and Num2 are displayed.
```

describes the condition that must be true after the procedure execution is completed; this condition is called the *postcondition*. The use of explicit preconditions and postconditions provides valuable documentation to other programmers who might want to use the procedure. It also aids in verifying the correctness of a program that calls this procedure.

Parameter Correspondence

The body of procedure ReportSumAve begins by adding together the two values stored in its parameters Num1 and Num2 and then finds their average. For the procedure call statement

```
ReportSumAve (6.5, 3.5)
```

the formal parameter Num1 is passed the value 6.5, and the formal parameter Num2 is passed the value 3.5. The value assigned to Sum is 10.0, and the value assigned to Average is 5.0. These two values are displayed. The correspondence between the actual and the formal parameters is shown next:

Actual Parameter	Formal Parameter
6.5	Num1
3.5	Num2

For the procedure call statement

```
ReportSumAve (X, Y)
```

the value of X is passed to formal parameter Num1, and the value of Y is passed to formal parameter Num2. The data type of each actual parameter must be assignment compatible (see Section 2.3) with the data type of its corresponding formal parameter; otherwise, an `illegal parameter substitution` syntax error occurs.

Procedure ReportSumAve finds the sum and the average of its two parameter values at the time of the procedure call. Figure 6.2 shows the main program data area and the procedure data area after the procedure call statement

```
ReportSumAve (X, Y)
```

executes. The values 8.0 and 10.0 are passed into the actual parameters Num1 and Num2, respectively. The local procedure variables Sum and Average are undefined initially; the execution of the procedure body changes the values of these variables to 18.0 and 9.0, respectively.

Procedure ReportSumAve can compute and display the sum and the average of any pair of type Real numbers. We can get the procedure to operate on a different pair of numbers simply by changing the parameter list. The procedure call statement

```
ReportSumAve (Y, X)
```

would generate the same results as the previous procedure call statement; in this case, however, formal parameter Num1 corresponds to actual parameter Y and formal parameter Num2 corresponds to actual parameter X.

Figure 6.2 Data Areas at Call of ReportSumAve

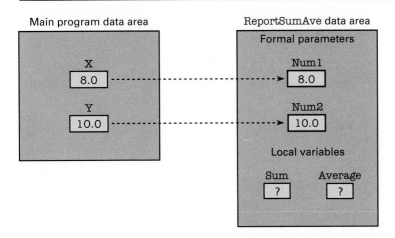

Choosing Formal Parameter Names

We have stated that the names used for formal parameters are arbitrary. Nonetheless, you should continue to follow the convention of picking names that help to document the use of the formal parameter. If a procedure is written for use in a particular program and is called only once in that program, it is reasonable to use the same name for both the formal parameter and its corresponding actual parameter. Remember that the correspondence between an actual and a formal parameter is determined solely by their position in the parameter lists, regardless of what names are used.

The Procedure Data Area

Each time a procedure call statement is executed, an area of memory is allocated for storage of that procedure's data. Included in the procedure data area are storage cells for any local variables or constants that may be declared in the procedure. The procedure data area is always erased when the procedure terminates; it is re-created empty (all values undefined) when the procedure is called again.

Exercises for Section 6.1

Self-Check

1. What is the primary purpose of procedure parameters?
2. For procedure Cube, which follows, what is displayed when the procedure call statement

   ```
   Cube (3)
   ```

   executes?

   ```
   procedure Cube (N : Integer);
   begin {Cube}
     Write (N :1, ' cubed is ');
     N := N * N * N;
     WriteLn (N :1)
   end; {Cube}
   ```

3. If M is 5, what happens when the procedure call statement

   ```
   Cube (M)
   ```

   executes? What is the value of the actual parameter M after the procedure executes? Where should M be declared and what should its data type be?

Programming

1. Write a procedure that displays the positive difference of its two formal parameters, X and Y (that is, if X is larger, the positive difference is X − Y; if Y is larger, the positive difference is Y − X.)

6.2 Value Parameters and Variable Parameters

By studying procedure ReportSumAve you learned how to pass inputs into a procedure. When a call to ReportSumAve is reached, the computer allocates memory space in the procedure data area for each formal parameter. The value of each actual parameter is stored in the memory cell(s) allocated to its corresponding formal parameter. The procedure body can manipulate this value. Next, we discuss how a procedure returns outputs to the program (or procedure) that calls it.

Procedure ComputeSumAve in Fig. 6.3 is similar to ReportSumAve. The differences are that ComputeSumAve has four parameters: two for input (Num1 and Num2) and two for output (Sum and Average). Procedure ComputeSumAve computes the sum and the average of its inputs but does not display them. Instead, those values are assigned to formal parameters Sum and Average and returned as procedure results to the calling program.

Figure 6.3 Procedure to Compute Sum and Average

```
procedure ComputeSumAve (Num1, Num2 {input} : Real;
                         var Sum, Average {output} : Real);
{
  Computes the sum and average of Num1 and Num2.
  Pre : Num1 and Num2 are assigned values.
  Post: The sum and average of Num1 and Num2 are computed
        and returned.
}

begin {ComputeSumAve}
  Sum := Num1 + Num2;
  Average := Sum / 2.0
end; {ComputeSumAve}
```

To see how this works, assume that the main program declares X, Y, Sum, and Mean as type Real variables. The procedure call statement

```
ComputeSumAve (X, Y, Sum, Mean)
```

sets up the parameter correspondence below.

Actual Parameter	Formal Parameter
X	Num1
Y	Num2
Sum	Sum
Mean	Average

The values of X and Y are passed into the procedure when the procedure is first called. These values are associated with formal parameters Num1 and Num2. The statement

```
Sum := Num1 + Num2;
```

stores the sum of the procedure inputs in the main program variable Sum (the third actual parameter). The statement

```
Average := Sum / 2.0
```

takes half of the value stored in the main program variable Sum and stores it in the main program variable Mean (the fourth actual parameter). The procedure execution shown in Fig. 6.4 changes the values of main program variables Sum and Mean to 18.0 and 9.0, respectively.

In Fig. 6.3, the reserved word var precedes the declaration of formal parameters Sum and Average. This tells the compiler to treat them as *variable parameters*. The compiler stores the memory address of the actual variable that corresponds to each variable parameter in the procedure data area. Through this address, the procedure can access the actual variable in the calling program and change its value or use its value in a computation. In Fig. 6.4, this relationship is shown by using a double-headed arrow to connect each variable parameter with its corresponding actual parameter. Notice that the reserved word var appears only in the formal parameter list, not in the actual parameter list.

Protection Afforded by Value Parameters

Figure 6.4 points out an important difference between formal parameters that are used as procedure inputs and those used as procedure outputs. Because they are not preceded by the reserved word var, formal parameters Num1 and Num2 are considered *value parameters*. As such, they have their own local storage cells in the procedure data area. The value passed into formal parameter Num1 is stored in the procedure data area at the time of the procedure call, and there is no further connection between formal parameter Num1 and its corresponding actual parameter. This is indicated by the dashed line in Fig. 6.4.

Figure 6.4 Data Areas after Execution of ComputeSumAve

The value of formal parameter `Num1` or `Num2` can be used in computations or even changed by the procedure body without affecting the corresponding actual parameter. For example, if we add the statement

```
Num1 := -5.0
```

to the end of procedure `ComputeSumAve`, the value of formal parameter `Num1` is changed to `-5.0`, but the value stored in the actual parameter `X` is still `8.0`.

By making an input parameter a value parameter, we protect its value and prevent it from being changed by the procedure's execution. If we forget to declare an output parameter as a variable formal parameter, its value (not its address) will be stored locally, and any change to its value will not be returned to the calling program. This is a common source of error.

Writing Formal Parameter Lists

In Fig. 6.3, the formal parameter list

```
(Num1, Num2 {input} : Real;
 var Sum, Average {output} : Real);
```

is written on two lines to improve program readability. The value parameters are written on the first line with the comment `{input}` inserted to document their use as procedure inputs. The variable parameters are written on the second line with the comment `{output}`.

Generally, this text follows the convention shown here in writing formal parameter lists. Input parameters are listed first and any output parameters are listed last. The order of the actual parameters in the procedure call must correspond to the order of the formal parameters.

Passing Information Between Procedures

So far you saw two similar procedures, `ReportSumAve` and `ComputeSumAve`, and you learned how to pass information between a main program and a procedure. Sometimes we need to pass information between procedures. For example, we might want to pass the results returned by `ComputeSumAve` to another procedure, say `Correlate`, for further processing.

Let's assume that the main program variables `X` and `Y` are passed into procedure `ComputeSumAve`. We can declare two more main program variables, say `TempSum` and `TempAve`, to hold the procedure results. The following procedure call statements

```
ComputeSumAve (X, Y, TempSum, TempAve);
Correlate (TempSum, TempAve)
```

pass the outputs of `ComputeSumAve` (`TempSum` and `TempAve`) to `Correlate` for further processing. Frequently, we will use main program variables to facilitate the exchange of information between procedures.

When to Use a Variable Parameter or a Value Parameter

You may be wondering how to decide when to use a variable parameter and when to use a value parameter. Some rules of thumb follow:

- If information is to be passed into a procedure and does not have to be returned or passed out of the procedure, the formal parameter representing that information can be a value parameter (for example, `Num1` and `Num2` in Fig. 6.1 and Fig. 6.3).
- If information is to be returned to the calling program from a procedure, the formal parameter representing that information must be a variable parameter (for example, `Sum` and `Average` in Fig. 6.3).
- If information is to be passed into a procedure, perhaps modified, and a new value returned, the formal parameter representing that information must be a variable parameter. We call such a parameter an *input/output* parameter.

You can use an assignment-compatible expression (or variable or constant) as an actual parameter corresponding to a value parameter. For example, the procedure call statement

```
ComputeSumAve (X + Y, 10.5, MySum, MyAve);
```

calls `ComputeSumAve` to compute the sum (returned in `MySum`) and the average (returned in `MyAve`) of the expression `X + Y` and the number `10.5`. Remember, only variables can correspond to variable parameters, so `MySum` and `MyAve` must be declared as type `Real` variables in the calling program. This restriction is imposed because an actual parameter corresponding to a variable parameter may be modified when the procedure executes; it is illogical to allow a procedure to change the value of either a constant or an expression.

Exercises for Section 6.2

Self-Check

1. Show the output displayed by the following program in the form of a table of values for X, Y, and Z.

```
program Show (Output);

  var
    X, Y, Z : Integer;


  procedure Sum (Num1, Num2 : Integer;
                   var Num3 : Integer);
  begin {Sum}
    Num3 := Num1 + Num2
  end; {Sum}

begin
  X := 5; Y := 3; Z := 7;
  WriteLn ('   X    Y    Z');
  Sum (X, Y, Z);
```

```
            WriteLn (X :4, Y :4, Z :4);
            Sum (Y, X, Z);
            WriteLn (X :4, Y :4, Z :4);
            Sum (Z, Y, X);
            WriteLn (X :4, Y :4, Z :4);
            Sum (Z, Z, X);
            WriteLn (X :4, Y :4, Z :4);
            Sum (Y, Y, Y);
            WriteLn (X :4, Y :4, Z :4)
         end.
```

Programming

1. Write a procedure that returns through its third parameter the positive difference of its first two parameters.
2. Write a procedure that raises its first parameter (type Real) to the power indicated by its second parameter (a positive integer). Use repeated multiplication. Return the result through the third parameter.

 ## 6.3 Syntax Rules for Parameter Lists

This section formally presents the syntax rules for procedure declarations and procedure call statements with parameters. The displays that follow summarize these rules.

SYNTAX
DISPLAY

Procedure Declaration (Procedure with Parameters)

Form: procedure *pname* (*formal parameters*);
                 declaration section
               begin
                 procedure body
               end;

Example: procedure Highlight (Ch {input} : Char
                              var NumStars {output} : Integer);
             {
                Displays Ch between two asterisks and returns the
                numbers of asterisks printed.
                Pre : Ch is defined.
                Post: Returns 3 in NumStars if Ch = Border; otherwise,
                      returns 2 in NumStars.
             }
                const
                  Border = '*';

             begin {Highlight}
                Write (Border); Write (Ch); Write (Border);
                if Ch = Border then
                  NumStars := 3
                else
                  NumStars := 2
             end; {Highlight}

Interpretation: The procedure *pname* is declared. The *formal parameters* are enclosed in parentheses. The identifiers that are declared in the *declaration section* are local to the procedure and are defined only during the execution of the procedure. A formal parameter cannot be declared as a local identifier in the *declaration section*.

The *procedure body* describes the data manipulation to be performed by the procedure using the formal parameter names in the description. For a variable parameter, the procedure manipulates the corresponding actual parameter; for a value parameter, a local memory cell is initialized to the actual parameter's value, and the procedure manipulates the local copy without altering the actual parameter.

SYNTAX
DISPLAY

Procedure Call Statement (Procedure with Parameters)

Form:　　*pname* (*actual parameters*)
Example: Highlight ('A', NumAsterisks)
Interpretation: The *actual parameters* are enclosed in parentheses. When procedure *pname* is called into execution, the first actual parameter is associated with the first formal parameter, the second actual parameter with the second formal parameter, and so on. For a value parameter, the actual parameter's value is saved in the procedure. For a variable parameter, the actual parameter's address is saved in the procedure.
Note: The actual parameters must satisfy the rules for parameter list correspondence, discussed later in this section.

When writing parameter lists, you must follow certain rules, as illustrated by this syntax diagram for a formal parameter list:

formal parameter list

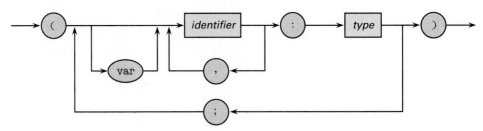

This diagram shows that a formal parameter list is always enclosed in parentheses. It consists of one or more lists of identifiers. Each list may be preceded by var. Identifiers are separated by commas, lists of identifiers are separated by semicolons, and each list must end with a colon followed by a data type name (for example, Real, Char, and so on).

■ Example 6.1

Two formal parameter lists follow. Each list is printed on two or more lines to improve readability.

```
(Ch3 : Char;              (M, N, O : Integer;
   var X, Y, Z : Real)       A, B, C : Real;
                             var X, Y, Z : Real)
```

In both lists, X, Y, Z are declared to be type Real variable parameters; Ch3, on the left, is a type Char value parameter; A, B, C, on the right, are type Real value parameters; M, N, O, on the right, are type Integer value parameters. ■

The formal parameter list also determines the form of any actual parameter list that may be used to call the procedure. This form is determined during the translation of the program when the compiler processes the procedure declaration.

Later, when it reaches a procedure call statement, the compiler checks the actual parameter list for consistency with the formal parameter list. An actual parameter list can be a list of expressions, variables, or constants separated by commas. The actual parameter list must satisfy the following rules.

1. Correspondence between actual and formal parameters is determined by position in their respective parameter lists. The lists must be the same size. The names of corresponding actual and formal parameters can be different.
2. For variable parameters, the types of corresponding actual and formal parameters must be identical. For value parameters, the types of corresponding actual and formal parameters must be assignment compatible (see Section 7.8).
3. For variable parameters, an actual parameter must be a variable. For value parameters, an actual parameter can be a variable, a constant, or an expression.

■ Example 6.2

The main program contains the following declarations:

```
var
   X, Y : Real;
   M : Integer;
   Next : Char;


procedure Test (A, B : Integer;
                 var C, D : Real;
                 var E : Char);
```

where only the heading for procedure Test is shown. Procedure Test has two value parameters (A and B) and three variable parameters (C, D, and E). Any of the following procedure call statements would be syntactically correct in the main program.

```
Test (M + 3, 10, X, Y, Next);
Test (M, MaxInt, Y, X, Next);
Test (35, M * 10, Y, X, Next);
```

The correspondence specified by the first parameter list is shown in Table 6.1.

Table 6.1 Parameter Correspondence for Test (M + 3, 10, X, Y, Next)

Actual Parameter	Formal Parameter	Description
M + 3	A	Integer, value
10	B	Integer, value
X	C	Real, variable
Y	D	Real, variable
Next	E	Char, variable

The third column in Table 6.1 describes each formal parameter. The table shows that an expression (M + 3) or a constant (10) can be associated with a value parameter. The procedure call statements in Table 6.2 contain syntax errors as indicated.

Table 6.2 Invalid Procedure Call Statements

Procedure Call Statement	Error
Test (30, 10, M, X, Next)	Type of M is not Real.
Test (M, 19, X, Y)	Not enough actual parameters.
Test (M, 10, 35, Y, 'E')	Constants 35 and 'E' cannot correspond to variable parameters.
Test (M, 3.0, X, Y, Next)	Type of 3.0 is not Integer.
Test (30, 10, X, X + Y, Next)	Expression X + Y cannot correspond to a variable parameter.
Test (30, 10, C, D, E)	C, D, and E are not declared in the main program.

The last procedure call statement in Table 6.2 points out an error that programmers often make in using procedures. The actual parameter names (C, D, E) are the same as their corresponding formal parameter names. However, since these names are not declared in the main program, they cannot appear in an actual parameter list used in the main program. ∎

When writing relatively long parameter lists such as the ones in Table 6.2, you must be careful not to transpose two actual parameters; that will result in a syntax error if it causes a violation of a parameter correspondence rule. Even if no syntax is violated, the procedure execution will probably generate incorrect results.

Self-Check

1. Provide a table similar to Table 6.1 for the other correct parameter lists shown in Example 6.2.
2. Correct the syntax errors in the following formal parameter lists:

```
(var A, B : Integer, C : Real)
(value M : Integer; var Next : Char)
(var Account, Real; X + Y , Real)
```

3. Assuming the declarations

```
const
  MaxInt = 32767;

var
  X, Y, Z : Real;
  M, N : Integer;

procedure Massage (var A, B : Real;
                      X : Integer);
```

what is wrong with each incorrect procedure call statement?

a. Massage (X, Y, Z);
b. Massage (X, Y, 8);
c. Massage (Y, X, N);
d. Massage (M, Y, N);
e. Massage (25.0, 15, X);
f. Massage (X, Y, M+N);
g. Massage (A, B, X);
h. Massage (Y, Z, M);
i. Massage (Y+Z, Y−Z, M);
j. Massage (Z, Y, X);
k. Massage (X, Y, M, 10);
l. Massage (Z, Y, MaxInt);

Programming

1. Redo programming exercise 2 for section 6.2 assuming that the second parameter can be any integer value.

6.4 More Procedure Examples

This section provides more examples of procedures with parameter lists.

■ Example 6.3

Procedure PrintStars in Fig. 6.5 prints a row of asterisks. In the procedure heading

```
procedure PrintStars (NumStars {input} : Integer);
```

NumStars is declared to be a formal parameter of type Integer; NumStars is a value parameter (indicated by the absence of the word var).

Figure 6.5 Procedure PrintStars

```
procedure PrintStars (NumStars : Integer);
{
  Prints a row of asterisks. The number of
  asterisks printed is determined by NumStars.
  Pre : NumStars is assigned a value.
  Post: A row of asterisks is displayed.
}
  const
    Star = '*';                  {symbol being printed}

  var
    CountStars : Integer;    {loop control for PrintStars}

begin {PrintStars}
  {Print a row of asterisks}
  CountStars := 1;
  while CountStars <= NumStars do
    begin
      Write (Star);
      CountStars := CountStars + 1
    end; {while}
  WriteLn
end; {PrintStars}
```

Parameter NumStars determines how many asterisks are printed. Its initial value is passed into procedure PrintStars when the procedure is called. Since there is no need for the procedure to change its parameter value, NumStars is declared to be a value parameter. The three procedure call statements

```
PrintStars (5);
PrintStars (3);
PrintStars (1)
```

would cause the following three lines to be printed:

```
*****
***
*
```

An integer value (5, 3, or 1) is assigned to NumStars when each procedure call statement is executed.

■ Example 6.4

Procedure Triangle in Fig. 6.6 uses procedure PrintStars to draw a triangle. This example shows that a procedure can be declared locally in another procedure and called by that procedure. In this case, the calling procedure (Triangle) passes information into procedure PrintStars each time it calls PrintStars.

Figure 6.6 Procedure Triangle

169

6.4 More Procedure
Examples

```
procedure Triangle (NumRows {input} : Integer);
{
   Prints a triangle by displaying lines of increasing length.
   The number of lines is determined by NumRows.
   Pre : NumRows is assigned a value.
   Post: A triangle is displayed.
   Requirements: Calls procedure PrintStars to display each line.
}
   var
     Row : Integer;          {loop control for Triangle}


   procedure PrintStars (NumStars : Integer);
   {
      Prints a row of asterisks. The number of
      asterisks printed is determined by NumStars.
      Pre : NumStars is assigned a value.
      Post: A row of asterisks is displayed.
   }

      const
        Star = '*';                 {symbol being printed}

      var
        CountStars : Integer;       {loop control for PrintStars}
   begin {PrintStars}
     {Print a row of asterisks}
     CountStars := 1;
     while CountStars <= NumStars do
       begin
         Write (Star);
         CountStars := CountStars + 1
       end; {while}
     WriteLn
   end; {PrintStars}


begin {Triangle}
  {Print lines of increasing length}
  Row := 1;
  while Row <= NumRows do
    begin
      PrintStars (Row);
      Row := Row + 1
    end {while}
end; {Triangle}
```

The while loop in the body of procedure Triangle repeatedly executes
the procedure call statement

```
PrintStars (Row)
```

Each time PrintStars is called, the current value of Row (1 to NumRows) determines how many asterisks will be displayed.

The parameter NumRows determines the number of lines in the triangle. The procedure call statement

```
Triangle (5)
```

assigns a value of 5 to NumRows and causes the following triangle to be drawn:

```
*
**
***
****
*****
```

Because procedure PrintStars is declared within procedure Triangle, PrintStars is considered a local identifier in Triangle, and PrintStars can be called only by Triangle (or by PrintStars itself). This *scope of identifiers* is discussed in detail in section 6.6. ∎

■ Example 6.5

Your accountant uses the tax table shown in Table 4.5 to determine the income tax due for a particular salary. Because this table appears in many different programs, your accountant has decided to place it in procedure FindTax (see Fig. 6.7). A value is passed into input parameter Salary when the procedure is called. If Salary is within the range of the table, the tax owed is computed and assigned to output parameter Tax by the procedure execution; otherwise, –1.0 is assigned to Tax. The value assigned to Tax is returned to the calling program.

Figure 6.7 Driver Program with Procedure FindTax

```
program Driver (Input, Output);

{Tests procedure FindTax.}

  var
    MySalary,                      {input - salary}
    MyTax     : Real;              {output - tax}

  procedure FindTax (Salary {input} : Real;
                     var Tax {output} : Real);
  {
    Computes tax amount (Tax) owed for a
    salary (Salary) < $15000.
    Pre : Salary is assigned a value.
    Post: If Salary is within range, the tax owed is returned
          in Tax; otherwise, -1.0 is returned.
  }
    const
      MaxSalary = 15000.00;        {Maximum salary for table}
      OutOfRange = -1.0;           {"Tax" for an out-of-range salary}

  begin {FindTax}
    if Salary < 0.0 then
      Tax := OutOfRange                   {Salary too small}
    else if Salary < 1500.00 then         {first range}
      Tax := 0.15 * Salary
```

```
    else if Salary < 3000.00 then              {second range}
        Tax := (Salary - 1500.00) * 0.16 + 225.00
    else if Salary < 5000.00 then              {third range}
        Tax := (Salary - 3000.00) * 0.18 + 465.00
    else if Salary < 8000.00 then              {fourth range}
        Tax := (Salary - 5000.00) * 0.20 + 865.00
    else if Salary <= MaxSalary then           {fifth range}
        Tax := (Salary - 8000.00) * 0.25 + 1425.00
    else
        Tax := OutOfRange                      {Salary too large}
  end; {FindTax}

begin {Driver}
  Write ('Enter a salary less than or equal to $15000.00> $');
  ReadLn (MySalary);
  FindTax (MySalary, MyTax);
  if MyTax >= 0.0 then
    WriteLn ('The tax on $', MySalary :4:2, ' is $', MyTax :4:2)
  else
    WriteLn ('Salary $', Salary :4:2, ' is out of table range')
end. {Driver}


Enter a salary less than or equal to $15000.00> $6000.00
The tax on $6000.00 is $1065.00
```

In Fig. 6.7, the statement

```
FindTax (MySalary, MyTax);
```

calls procedure FindTax. The parameter correspondence specified by this procedure call is shown in Fig. 6.8. Assuming a data value of 6000.00 was read into MySalary before FindTax was called, the value 1065.00 would be assigned to MyTax during the execution of procedure FindTax. ∎

Figure 6.8 Parameter Correspondence for FindTax (MySalary, MyTax)

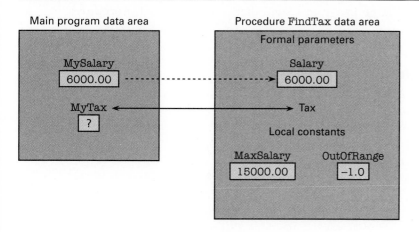

Validating Input Parameters

The `if` statement in procedure `FindTax` tests for an invalid value of the input parameter `Salary` before performing the tax computation. Make sure that all procedures validate their input parameters; there are no guarantees that the values passed to an input parameter will be meaningful.

Cohesive Procedures

Procedure `FindTax` is concerned only with the tax computation. It neither reads in a value for `Salary` nor displays the computed result. The result is returned to the calling program, which may display it or pass it on to another procedure that prints results. Notice that `FindTax` does not display an error message in the event that the value passed to `Salary` is out of range. It simply returns a special value (−1.0) to indicate this, and the calling program displays the error message.

Procedures that perform a single operation are called *cohesive procedures*. It is good programming style to write cohesive procedures, which helps to keep each procedure relatively compact and easy to read, write, and debug.

Writing Driver Programs to Test Procedures

The main program body in Fig. 6.7 consists of a statement for data entry, a procedure call statement, and an `if` statement to display the procedure result. Its sole purpose is to test procedure `FindTax`. Such a program is called a *driver program*.

Experienced programmers often use driver programs to pretest procedures. Generally, the small investment in time and effort required to write a short driver program pays off by reducing the total time spent debugging a large program system that contains several procedures.

Exercises for Section 6.4

Self-Check

1. Why is the `if` statement currently in `FindTax` better than the one that follows?

```
if Salary < 0.0 then
   WriteLn (Salary :4:2, ' is out of range') {Salary too small}
   . . .
else
   WriteLn (Salary :4:2, ' is out of range') {Salary too large}
```

Programming

1. Write a driver program that tests procedure FindTax for all values of Salary from -100.00 to 15100.00 in increments of 500.00.

 # 6.5 Stepwise Design with Procedures

Now that you can pass data into and out of procedures, you can make more use of procedures in your programming. Many of the level-one subproblems shown in a structure chart will be implemented as separate procedures. In this text, if the solution to a subproblem cannot be written easily using just a few Pascal statements, it is coded as a procedure.

In this section, you will see how to add *data flow* information to a structure chart and how to practice *stepwise* design of programs.

Case Study: General Sum-and-Average Problem

Problem
Procedure ReportSumAve in Fig. 6.1 was used to find the sum and the average of a pair of data items. In this section, we will solve the general case of this problem by writing a program that finds and prints the sum and the average of a list of data items.

Design Overview
Figure 5.3 shows a loop that computes the total payroll for a company. We can adapt this approach to compute the sum and the average of a collection of data values.

Data Requirements

Problem Inputs
Number of data items to be summed (NumItems : Integer)
Each data item (Item : Real)

Problem Outputs
Sum of data items (Sum : Real)
Average of data (Average : Real);

Initial Algorithm
1. Read the number of items (NumItems).
2. Compute the sum of the data.
3. Compute the average of the data.
4. Print the sum and the average.

Algorithm Refinements

Steps 2 and 3 are the only steps that need refinement. To perform step 3, we can divide the result of step 2 by the number of data items. The average is undefined if `NumItems` is not positive. The refinement of step 3 follows.

> ### Step 3 Refinement
> 3.1 if NumItems > 0 then
>   3.2 Divide Sum by NumItems.

Rather than refine step 2 now, let's assume we have a procedure, `FindSum`, that performs this step. (We will consider how to implement `FindSum` later.)

The structure chart in Fig. 6.9 documents the data flow between subproblems. Downward-pointing arrows indicate inputs to a subproblem; upward-pointing arrows indicate outputs from a subproblem. The variables involved in the data transfer are listed inside the arrow. A label under a step contains the name of the procedure that implements the step.

Because the step "Read the number of data items" defines the value of the variable `NumItems`, `NumItems` is an output of this step. Procedure `FindSum` needs this value to know how many data items to read; consequently, `NumItems` is an input to procedure `FindSum`. The procedure result, `Sum`, is an output of `FindSum`. `Sum` must be provided as an input to the steps that compute the average (step 3) and display the program results (step 4). The main program variable `Average` is an output of step 3 and an input to step 4. For reasons that are discussed later, we will implement step 4 as procedure `PrintSumAve`.

Coding the Main Program

Once the data flow information has been added to the structure chart, the main program can be written even if the details of the procedures are not yet known.

Figure 6.9   Structure Chart with Data Flow Information

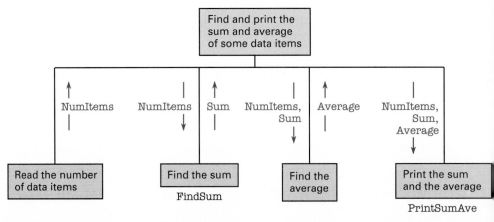

For example, we know from the data flow information in Fig. 6.9 that the procedure call statement

    FindSum (NumItems, Sum)

can call FindSum. We also know that NumItems should correspond to a value parameter and Sum to a variable parameter. We also know that

    PrintSumAve (NumItems, Sum, Average)

can call PrintSumAve, where all three parameters are procedure inputs.

The program, except for procedure FindSum, is shown in Fig. 6.10. All the variables that appear in the structure chart are declared in the main program because they store data passed to a procedure or results returned from a procedure.

Figure 6.10   Main Program with a Stub for Procedure FindSum

```
program SumItems (Input, Output);

{Finds and prints the sum and average of a list of data items.}

   var
     NumItems : Integer;   {input - number of items to be added}
     Sum,                  {output - sum being accumulated}
     Average : Real;       {output - average of the data}


   procedure PrintSumAve (NumItems {input} : Integer;
                          Sum, Average {input} : Real);
   {
     Displays the sum and the average of NumItems data items.
     Pre : NumItems, Sum, and Average are defined.
     Post: Displays Sum and also Average if NumItems > 0.
   }
   begin {PrintSumAve}
     if NumItems > 0 then
       begin
         WriteLn ('The sum is ', Sum :4:2);
         WriteLn ('The average is ', Average :4:2)
       end
     else
       WriteLn ('Sum and average are not defined')
   end; {PrintSumAve}


   procedure FindSum (NumItems {input} : Integer;
                      var Sum {output} : Real);
   {
     Finds the sum of a list of data items.
     Pre : NumItems is assigned a value.
     Post: NumItems data items are read; their sum is stored in Sum.
   }
   begin {FindSum stub}
     WriteLn ('Procedure FindSum entered.');
     Sum := 0.0
   end; {FindSum stub}
```

```
begin {SumItems}
  {Read the number of items to be summed}
  Write ('How many items will be summed? ');
  ReadLn (NumItems);

  {Find the sum (Sum) of a list of data items}
  FindSum (NumItems, Sum);

  {Find the average (Average) of the data}
  if NumItems > 0 then
    Average := Sum / NumItems;

  {Print the sum and average}
  PrintSumAve (NumItems, Sum, Average)
end. {SumItems}
```

Coding Procedure FindSum

The declaration for procedure `FindSum` shown in Fig. 6.10 is called a *stub*. Including this declaration enables the main program to be compiled, checked for syntax errors, and even run before `FindSum` is written. However, the program will not yet generate meaningful results because the value returned by the stub for `FindSum` is always zero.

Section 5.2 discussed accumulating a sum in a loop. We emphasized the need to initialize the sum to zero prior to loop entry. The loop control steps must ensure that the correct number of items are included in the sum being accumulated. These considerations lead to the following data requirements and algorithm for procedure `FindSum`. The completed procedure, shown in Fig. 6.11, replaces the stub in Fig. 6.10.

Procedure Inputs
The number of data items to be summed (`NumItems : Integer`)

Procedure Outputs
The sum of the data (`Sum : Real`)

Local Procedure Variables
Each data item (`Item : Real`)
Count of data items summed (`Count : Integer`)

Algorithm for FindSum

1. Read in the number of items to be summed.
2. Initialize `Sum` to zero.
3. Initialize count of items summed to zero.
4. `while` count of items < number of items `do`
   ```
   begin
   ```
   5. Read in the next item.
   6. Add it to `Sum`.
   7. Increment count of items.
   ```
   end
   ```

Figure 6.11   Procedure FindSum

```
procedure FindSum (NumItems {input} : Integer;
                   var Sum {output} : Real);
{
  Finds the sum of a list of NumItems data items.
  Pre : NumItems is assigned a value.
  Post: NumItems data items are read; their sum is stored in Sum.
}

  var
    Count : Integer;      {count of items added so far}
    Item : Real;          {the next data item to be added}
begin {FindSum}
  {Read each data item and add it to Sum}
  Sum := 0.0;
  Count := 0;
  while Count < NumItems do
    {invariant:
        Count is <= NumItems and
        Sum is the accumulated sum of data items read
    }
    begin
      Write ('Next number to be summed> ');
      ReadLn (Item);
      Sum := Sum + Item;
      Count := Count + 1
    end {while}
end; {FindSum}
```

Because Count and Item are used only within procedure FindSum, they are declared as local variables in FindSum. Figure 6.12 shows the parameter correspondence specified by the procedure call statement

```
FindSum (NumItems, Sum);
```

assuming the value 10 is read into NumItems just before the procedure call.

The body of the procedure begins by initializing to zero the main program variable Sum, which corresponds to variable parameter Sum. The while loop reads each data item into the local variable Item and adds it to the main program variable Sum. The loop and procedure exit occur after ten items are added.

Testing

In testing SumItems, make sure that the program displays the sum and the average correctly when NumItems is positive and displays a diagnostic when NumItems is zero or negative. The main program can be tested before and after FindSum is written. If it is tested before FindSum is completed, the values displayed for Sum and Average should be zero.

Fig 6.12 Parameter Correspondence for FindSum (NumItems, Sum)

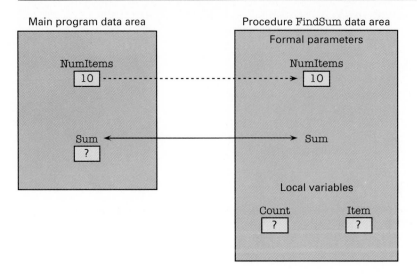

When to Use a Procedure in a Program System

The structure chart for the general sum-and-average program shown in Fig. 6.9 contains four steps, two of which are performed by procedures. We used a procedure for step 2 because its algorithm was relatively complicated, and we felt that its implementation would require several program statements. Even though it was easy to implement step 4, we used a procedure because its implementation was rather lengthy. It was obvious that the remaining steps could be implemented using just a few program statements; consequently, they were written directly in the main program. You should follow this line of reasoning in determining whether to implement a step as a separate procedure. In a large, complicated program, the main program body often consists of little more than procedure calls.

Program and Procedure Inputs and Outputs

An interesting aspect of the structure chart shown in Fig. 6.9 is that variables Sum and Average are considered problem outputs, yet they are shown as inputs to the display step (step 4). Further, they are listed as inputs in the heading for procedure PrintSumAve. Similarly, NumItems, which is a problem input, is shown as an output of step 1 in the structure chart.

Although this may seem puzzling at first, it is correct. The determination of whether a variable manipulated by a particular step is an input or an output depends solely on its usage in that step. It is permissible for a variable to be returned as an output from one step (for example, Sum in step 2) and passed as an input to another step (for example, Sum in step 4).

● Case Study: Simple Sorting Problem

Next, we will write a program that uses the same procedure to process a different pair of numbers each time it is called. You will see how procedure parameters make this possible.

Problem

In many real-life and programming situations, we want to arrange a set of data so that it follows some numerical or alphabetical sequence. In programming, this is called the sorting problem. You aren't able to solve this problem for large data sets yet; however, you can write a program that reads any three numbers into the variables Num1, Num2, Num3 and rearranges the data so that the smallest number is stored in Num1, the next smallest number in Num2, and the largest number in Num3.

Design Overview

This is a special case of a sorting problem: rearranging a collection of data items so that the values are in either increasing or decreasing order. Since we have only three items to be sorted, we will solve this special case now. The general sorting problem is a bit more complicated, so we will consider it later.

Data Requirements

Problem Inputs
Three numbers (Num1, Num2, Num3 : Real)

Problem Outputs
The three numbers stored in increasing order in Num1, Num2, Num3

Initial Algorithm

1. Read the three numbers into Num1, Num2, and Num3
2. Place the smallest number in Num1, the next smallest in Num2, and the largest number in Num3.
3. Print Num1, Num2, and Num3

Algorithm Refinements

Think of the three variables Num1, Num2, Num3 as representing a list of consecutive storage cells. To perform step 2, we can compare pairs of numbers, always

Case Study: Simple Sorting Problem, continued

moving the smaller number in the pair closer to the front of the list (Num1) and the larger number closer to the end of the list (Num3). It should take three comparisons to sort the numbers in the list; one possible sequence of comparisons follows.

Step 2 Refinement

2.1 Compare Num1 and Num2 and store the smaller number in Num1 and the larger number in Num2.

2.2 Compare Num1 and Num3 and store the smaller number in Num1 and the larger number in Num3.

2.3 Compare Num2 and Num3 and store the smaller number in Num2 and the larger number in Num3.

Table 6.3 traces this refinement for the input sequence 8.0, 10.0, 6.0. The final order is correct.

Table 6.3 Trace of Step 2 Refinement for Data 8.0, 10.0, 6.0

Algorithm Step	Num1	Num2	Num3	Effect
	8.0	10.0	6.0	
2.1	8.0	10.0		Num1, Num2 are in order.
2.2	6.0		8.0	8.0 > 6.0, switch Num1 and Num3.
2.3		8.0	10.0	10.0 > 8.0, switch Num2 and Num3.

The structure chart for step 2 of this algorithm is shown in Fig. 6.13. The data flow information for step 2.1 shows that Num1 and Num2 are used as both inputs and outputs. Since steps 2.1, 2.2, and 2.3 perform the same operation on different data, it would be a waste of time and effort to write a different procedure for each step. We will use one procedure, Order, to order any pair of numbers.

Coding

The procedure call statement

```
Order (Num1, Num2)
```

can be used to perform step 2.1 of the algorithm: store the smaller number in Num1 and the larger number in Num2. The complete program is shown in Fig. 6.14. The main program body contains three statements that call procedure Order:

```
Order (Num1, Num2);      {Order the data in Num1 and Num2}
Order (Num1, Num3);      {Order the data in Num1 and Num3}
Order (Num2, Num3);      {Order the data in Num2 and Num3}
```

Because each statement contains a different actual parameter list, a different pair of variables is manipulated each time the procedure is called.

Figure 6.13   Structure Chart for Step 2 of Sorting Problem

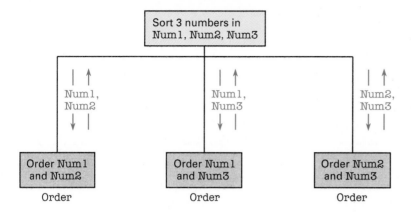

Figure 6.14   Program to Order Three Numbers

```
program Sort3Numbers (Input, Output);
{
   Reads three numbers and sorts them
   so that they are in increasing order.
}
   var
     Num1, Num2, Num3 : Real;        {a list of three cells}


   procedure Order (var X, Y {input/output} : Real);
   {
      Orders a pair of numbers represented by X and Y so that the
      smaller number is in X and the larger number is in Y.
      Pre : X and Y are assigned values.
      Post: X is the smaller of the pair and Y is the larger.
   }
      var
        Temp : Real;        {copy of number originally in X}

   begin {Order}
      if X > Y then
        begin {Switch the values of X and Y}
           Temp := X;                    {Store old X in Temp}
           X := Y;                       {Store old Y in X}
           Y := Temp                     {Store old X in Y}
        end {if}
   end; {Order}


begin {Sort3Numbers}
   WriteLn ('Enter 3 numbers to be sorted separated by spaces> ');
   ReadLn (Num1, Num2, Num3);

   {Sort the numbers}
   Order (Num1, Num2);        {Order the data in Num1 and Num2}
```

Case Study: Simple Sorting Problem, continued

```
Order (Num1, Num3);        {Order the data in Num1 and Num3}
Order (Num2, Num3);        {Order the data in Num2 and Num3}

   {Print the results}
   WriteLn ('The three numbers in order are:');
   WriteLn (Num1 :8:2, Num2 :8:2, Num3 :8:2)
end. {Sort3Numbers}


Enter 3 numbers to be sorted separated by spaces>
8.0  10.0  6.0
The three numbers in order are:
   6.00    8.00   10.00
```

The body of procedure Order consists of the if statement from Fig. 4.11. The procedure heading contains the formal parameter list

```
(var X, Y {input/output} : Real)
```

which identifies X and Y as the formal parameters. X and Y are classified as input/output parameters because the procedure uses the current actual parameter values as inputs and may return new values.

The sequence of the actual parameters is important. The first actual parameter is paired with the first formal parameter, the second actual parameter is paired with the second formal parameter, and so on. If the first procedure call statement in Fig. 6.14 were written as

```
Order (Num2, Num1)
```

the smaller number would be stored in Num2 and the larger number in Num1 instead of the other way around.

Exercises for Section 6.5

Self-Check

1. Add data flow information to the structure chart shown in Fig. 4.7. Implement each subproblem as a procedure with parameters.
2. How does adding data flow information to a structure chart help you determine where variables should be declared?
3. Trace the execution of the three procedure call statements

```
Order (Num3, Num2);
Order (Num3, Num1);
Order (Num2, Num1)
```

for the data sets 8.0, 10.0, 6.0 and 10.0, 8.0, 60.0. What does this sequence do?

1. A procedure has four formal parameters: W, X, Y, and Z (all type Real). The procedure execution stores the sum of W and X in Y and the product of W and X in Z. Which parameters are inputs and which are outputs? Write the procedure.

 # 6.6 Scope of Identifiers

Nested Procedures

In Fig. 6.10, procedures FindSum and PrintSumAve are nested or contained in program SumItems. It is also possible for one procedure to be nested within another. For example, procedure PrintStars is nested in procedure Triangle in Fig. 6.6. Nested procedures occur frequently in Pascal and are a natural consequence of the top-down design process.

Each procedure in a nest of procedures has its own declaration part and body; this is also true for the main program. A procedure's parameter list is included in its declaration part.

Figure 6.15 displays the organization of procedures in program Nested. Each box represents a procedure or program *block*. A block consists of the declaration part (including any parameter list) and the body of a program or procedure. The name of the block is indicated just above it.

Figure 6.15 shows procedures Outer and Too nested in the main program block. Procedure Inner is shown nested in the block for Outer.

Scope of Identifiers

The statements in each program or procedure body written so far manipulate only local identifiers. Although you have not done so yet, it is possible in Pascal to reference identifiers that are not declared locally.

The Pascal scope rules tell us where an identifier can be referenced.

Pascal Scope Rules

1. The scope of an identifier is the block in which it is declared. Therefore, an identifier declared in procedure P can be referenced in procedure P and in all procedures enclosed in procedure P.
2. If an identifier I declared in procedure P is redeclared in some inner procedure Q enclosed in P, then procedure Q and all its enclosed procedures are excluded from the scope of I declared in P.

According to rule 1, the *scope of an identifier* is the block in which it is declared. The scope of the parameter Letter and the constant Blank (in Fig. 6.15) is the block for procedure Too; therefore, Letter and Blank can be referenced only in procedure Too.

Figure 6.15   Procedure Nesting

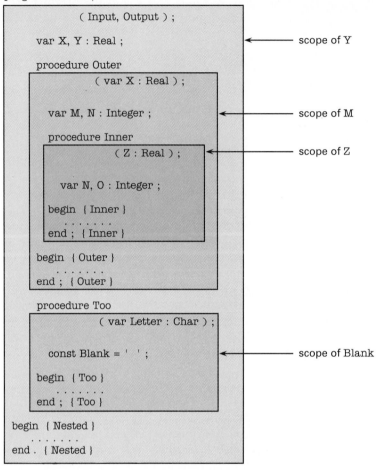

program Nested ;

(Input, Output) ;

var X, Y : Real ;   ◄────── scope of Y

procedure Outer

(var X : Real) ;

var M, N : Integer ;   ◄────── scope of M

procedure Inner

(Z : Real) ;   ◄────── scope of Z

var N, O : Integer ;

begin { Inner }
. . . .
end ; { Inner }

begin { Outer }
. . . .
end ; { Outer }

procedure Too

(var Letter : Char) ;

const Blank = ' ' ;   ◄────── scope of Blank

begin { Too }
. . . .
end ; { Too }

begin { Nested }
. . . .
end . { Nested }

Because procedure Inner is nested in procedure Outer, the scope of an identifier declared in procedure Outer includes the block for procedure Inner. Therefore, an identifier declared in Outer (for example, variable M) can be referenced in the body of either procedure.

Figure 6.15 shows the scope of formal parameter Z as the block for procedure Inner only. Formal parameter Z cannot be referenced in the body of procedure Outer or procedure Too or in the main program body.

Rule 2 takes effect when there are multiple declarations of the same identifier. We discuss rule 2 in the next section.

Because all procedures are nested in the main program block, an identifier declared in the main program can be referenced anywhere in the program system. For this reason, main program variables are called *global variables*.

Although global variables can be referenced in procedures, this is a dangerous practice. If a procedure references a global variable, it is possible for the value of that variable to change when the procedure is executed (a phenomenon called a *side effect*). Often, no documentation exists to indicate that the procedure manipulates a global variable; consequently, it may be difficult to find a statement in a procedure that is responsible for assigning an incorrect or unexpected value to a global variable. If the statement

```
Y := Y + 3.5;        {Example of a side effect}
```

appears in any procedure in Fig. 6.15, it will cause a side effect (adding 3.5 to global variable Y) whenever that procedure is called.

The formal parameter list and local declarations for a procedure explicitly document the data that will be manipulated. In this text, only identifiers (including parameters) that are declared locally in a procedure. The only exceptions are global constants and type identifiers (discussed in later chapters). It is permissible to reference a global constant in a procedure because Pascal does not allow the value of a constant to be changed. Hence, there cannot be a side effect when a global constant is referenced.

Multiple Declarations of Identifiers

An identifier can be declared only once in a given procedure; however, the same identifier can be declared in more than one procedure. In Fig. 6.15, for example, X is declared as a global variable in the main program and as a formal parameter in procedure Outer. Consequently, when X is referenced in the program system, some question may arise as to which declaration takes precedence.

According to scope rule 2, procedures Outer and Inner are excluded from the scope of global variable X, because X is declared as a formal parameter of Outer. Therefore, when X is referenced in the body of procedure Outer or Inner, formal parameter X is manipulated. When X is referenced anywhere else in the program system, global variable X is manipulated.

If an identifier is not declared locally, then scope rule 2 requires the compiler to use the closest declaration in an outer block that contains the point of reference. For example, if identifier N is referenced in procedure Inner or procedure Outer, the corresponding local declaration for identifier N is used. If identifier M is referenced in procedure Inner where it is not declared locally, the declaration for variable M in procedure Outer is used. A reference to identifier M in either the main program body or procedure Too would cause an identifier not declared syntax error.

Table 6.4 lists the meanings of the valid references to identifiers in the blocks of Fig. 6.15. Procedure names are included with other identifiers in this table; they are discussed shortly.

Illustrating the Scope Rules

Next, we will look at a program that illustrates bad programming practice, because the identifier names are not meaningful and are unnecessarily redundant. Studying this example should help you master the Pascal scope rules.

Table 6.4 Valid Identifier References for Figure 6.15

Block	Meaning of Each Identifier
Nested	Input, Output (parameters of Nested) X, Y (global variables) Outer, Too (procedures declared in Nested)
Outer	X (parameter of Outer) M, N (local variables) Inner (local procedure) Y (variable declared in Nested) Outer, Too (procedures declared in Nested)
Inner	Z (parameter of Inner) N, O (local variables) M (variable declared in Outer) X (parameter of Outer) Inner (procedure declared in Outer) Y (variable declared in Nested) Outer, Too (procedures declared in Nested)
Too	Letter (parameter of Too) Blank (local constant) X, Y (global variables) Outer, Too (procedures declared in Nested)

■ Example 6.6

Figure 6.16 shows a procedure declared in a main program. W is declared as a variable in both the procedure and the main program; X is declared as a variable in the main program and as a parameter in the procedure; Y is declared as a variable in the main program only.

Figure 6.16 Example of Scope Rules

```
program ScopeRules (Output);

    var
      W, X, Y : Real;


    procedure Change (var X {input/output} : Real);

      var
        W, Z : Real;

    begin {Change}
      W := 35.0;          {change local W}
      X := 6.0;           {change parameter X}
      Y := Y + 1.0;       {side effect - change global Y}
      Z := 3.0            {change local Z}
    end; {Change}
```

```
begin {ScopeRules}
  W := 5.5;               {change global W}
  X := 2.0;               {change global X}
  Y := 3.0;               {change global Y}
  Change (W);
  WriteLn ('W' :5, 'X' :5, 'Y' :5);
  WriteLn (W :5:2, X :5:2, Y :5:2)
end. {ScopeRules}


    W    X    Y
   6.0  2.0  4.0
```

The main program begins by initializing global variables W, X, and Y. The initial values of the three main program variables are

```
  W        X        Y
 5.5      2.0      3.0
```

The procedure call statement

```
Change (W);
```

calls procedure Change with main program variable W corresponding to parameter X. In Change, the assignment statement

```
X := 6.0;          {change parameter X}
```

stores 6.0 in the main program variable W, and the assignment statement

```
Y := Y + 1.0;      {side effect – change global Y}
```

increments main program variable Y (a side effect). The other two assignment statements in Change affect only its local variables W and Z. The main program variables after Change executes are as follows. Notice that main program variable X is unchanged and that the value of W is 6.0 (not 35.0).

```
  W        X        Y
 6.0      2.0      4.0
```

It is interesting to consider what happens if X or Y is used as the actual parameter instead of W. That question is left as an exercise. ∎

Procedure Calls

Because procedure names are identifiers, the Pascal scope rules specify where a procedure can be referenced or called. Procedures Outer and Too are global identifiers (declared in the main program), so they can be called anywhere. Procedure Inner is declared in procedure Outer, so it can be called only by procedure Outer or by Inner itself (called a *recursive procedure call*).

As things stand now, a call to Inner in the body of procedure Too or the main program body would cause an identifier is undeclared syntax error.

If we declare procedure Inner in the main program instead of inside procedure Outer, then both the main program and procedure Too will be able to call Inner.

The Forward Declaration

In the preceding section, we implied that procedures Outer and Inner can call procedure Too because Too is a global identifier. However, procedure Too is declared after procedure Outer, the Pascal compiler has no way of checking that a call to Too in procedure Outer (or Inner) is correct. Therefore, we must provide a *forward declaration* for procedure Too that includes the procedure heading if Too is called by a procedure declared before it. The first line that follows is a forward declaration:

```
procedure Too (var Letter : Char); Forward;

procedure Outer (var X : Real);
  . . . . . .
end; {Outer}

procedure Too;
  . . . . . .
end; {Too}
```

The heading for procedure Too comes first, followed by the complete declaration for procedures Outer and Too. The formal parameter list for procedure Too appears only in the forward declaration.

Exercises for Section 6.6

Self-Check

1. Explain why variable N declared in Outer cannot be referenced by the main program, procedure Inner, or procedure Too.
2. What would be the effect of executing the body of Inner as follows?

```
begin {Inner}
  X := 5.5;
  Y := 6.6;
  M := 2;
  N := 3;
  O := 4
end; {Inner}
```

3. If the preceding statement sequence was the body of Outer, Too, or Nested, then some of the assignment statements would be syntactically incorrect. Identify the incorrect statements and indicate the effect of executing all the others in each block.
4. What kind of error would occur if the assignment statement

```
Z := 15.0;
```

was inserted into the main program in Fig. 6.16?

5. Show the new values of W, X, and Y if X is the actual parameter in the procedure call statement of Fig. 6.16. What is the answer if Y is the actual parameter? What would be the effect of making the formal parameter a value parameter?

 # 6.7   Top-Down Design Illustrated

This section demonstrates the top-down design process in solving a problem. The program solution will be implemented in a stepwise manner starting at the top of the structure chart or with the main program. The problem solution makes extensive use of procedures with parameters.

● Case Study: Balancing a Checkbook

Problem
You have just received a new personal computer and you want to write a program to help balance your checkbook. The program should read your initial checkbook balance and each transaction (check or deposit). It should also print the new balance after each transaction and a warning message if the balance becomes negative. At the end of the session, the starting and final balance should be printed, along with a count of the number of checks and deposits processed.

Design Overview
After the starting balance is read, each transaction is read and processed separately. We can use a simple code ('C' and 'D') to distinguish between checks and deposits. The transaction amount will be a real number. The starting balance must be available at the end, so we will save it in variable StartBal and use a different variable (CurBal) to keep track of the current balance.

Data Requirements

Problem Inputs
Starting checkbook balance (StartBal : Real)
Transaction data
  type of transaction (TranType : Char)
  amount of transaction (Amount : Real)

Problem Outputs
Current balance after each transaction (CurBal : Real)
Number of checks (NumCheck : Integer)
Number of deposits (NumDep : Integer)

Case Study: Balancing a Checkbook, continued

Figure 6.17 Structure Chart (Levels 0 and 1) for Checkbook Problem

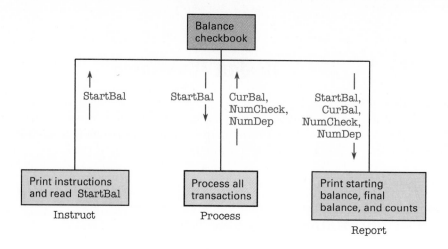

Initial Algorithm

1. Display the instructions and read the starting balance.
2. For each transaction read the transaction, update and print the current balance, and increment the count of checks or deposits.
3. Print the starting and final balance and the number of checks and deposits processed.

Figure 6.17 shows the structure chart for this algorithm. The level-1 subproblems will be written as procedures Instruct, Process, and Report. The data flow information shows that StartBal is read by Instruct and passed to Process. Procedure Process defines the program results (CurBal, NumCheck, NumDep); these results are passed to Report and printed.

The variables shown in the structure chart should be declared in the main program, because each variable must be declared at the highest level in which it appears in the structure chart. Variables that are passed between the main program and a level-1 procedure must be declared in the main program.

Coding the Main Program

The data flow information is used to write the parameter lists in the program shown in Fig. 6.18. Procedures Instruct and Report consist of input/output statements only, so we write them now. Because procedure Process requires further refinement, we write it as a stub.

Figure 6.18 Checkbook-Balancing Program with Stub for Process

```
program CheckBook (Input, Output);
{
  Reads the starting balance for a checking account and processes
  all transactions. Prints the new balance after each transaction
  is processed. Also prints a count of the total number of checks
  and deposits processed
}
  var
    StartBal,                  {input - starting balance}
    CurBal    : Real;          {output - current balance}
    NumCheck,                  {output - number of checks}
    NumDep    : Integer;       {output - number of deposits}


  procedure Instruct (var {output} StartBal : Real);
  {
    Displays the instructions and reads the starting balance.
    Pre : None
    Post: User instructions are displayed and StartBal is read in.
  }

  begin {Instruct}
    WriteLn ('Balance your checking account!');
    WriteLn;
    WriteLn ('Enter C (Check), D (Deposit), or Q (Quit)');
    WriteLn ('after prompt C, D, or Q> ');
    WriteLn;
    WriteLn ('Enter a positive number after prompt Amount $');
    WriteLn;
    Write ('Begin by entering your starting balance $');
    ReadLn (StartBal)
  end; {Instruct}


  procedure Process (StartBal {input} : Real;
                     var CurBal {output} : Real;
                     var NumCheck, NumDep {output} : Integer);

  begin {Process stub}
    WriteLn ('Procedure Process entered.');
    CurBal := 0.0;  NumCheck := 0;  NumDep := 0
  end; {Process}


  procedure Report (StartBal, CurBal {input} : Real;
                    NumCheck, NumDep {input} : Integer);
  {
    Prints the starting and final balances and the count of checks
    and deposits
    Pre : StartBal, CurBal, NumCheck, and NumDep are assigned values.
    Post: Program results are displayed.
  }

  begin {Report}
    WriteLn;
```

```
      WriteLn ('Starting balance was $', StartBal :10:2);
      WriteLn ('Final    balance  is $', CurBal :10:2);
      WriteLn ('Number of checks written: ', NumCheck :3);
      WriteLn ('Number of deposits made : ', NumDep :3)
   end; {Report}

begin {CheckBook}
   {Display user instructions and read StartBal}
   Instruct (StartBal);

   {Process each transaction}
   Process (StartBal, CurBal, NumCheck, NumDep);

   {Print starting and final balances and count of checks/deposits}
   Report (StartBal, CurBal, NumCheck, NumDep)
end. {CheckBook}
```

Coding the Procedures
Procedure Process performs step 2 of the algorithm, which is repeated below.

Algorithm for Process
2. For each transaction read the transaction, update and print the current balance, and increment the count of checks or deposits.

It is obvious that a while loop is needed. Assuming that we do not know how many transactions will occur, we can use a sentinel-controlled loop that compares the transaction code to a sentinel value. The loop properties follow:

1. CurBal is StartBal plus all transactions that are deposits and minus all transactions that are checks.
2. NumCheck is the count of checks so far.
3. NumDep is the count of deposits so far.
4. The transaction code is the sentinel just after loop exit.

These statements suggest the following refinement.

Algorithm for Process
1. Initialize NumCheck and NumDep to zero.
2. Initialize CurBal to StartBal.
3. Read the first transaction.
4. while the transaction code is not the sentinel do
  begin
    5. Update CurBal and increment NumCheck or NumDep.
    6. Display CurBal and the transaction.
    7. Read the next transaction.
  end

  The structure chart for Process is shown in Fig. 6.19. Procedure ReadTran performs steps 3 and 7 of the refined algorithm, UpDate performs step 5, and

Figure 6.19 Structure Chart for Procedure Process

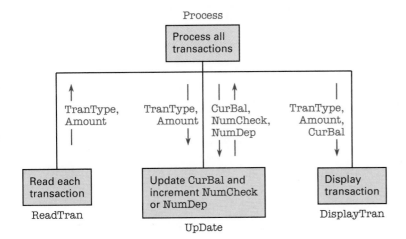

DisplayTran performs step 6. Two new variables, TranType and Amount, should be declared as local variables in procedure Process. Variables passed between a level-1 and a level-2 procedure should be declared in the level-1 procedure. The identifiers CurBal, NumCheck, and NumDep are declared already as formal parameters of Process.

Local Variables for Process
The transaction type (TranType : Char)
The transaction amount (Amount : Real)

The procedure nesting prescribed by this structure chart and the earlier one is summarized in Fig. 6.20. Each procedure that is subordinate to a higher-level procedure is nested in that higher-level procedure. Figure 6.20 shows that ReadTran, Update, and DisplayTran are nested in Process, which is nested in CheckBook. Procedures Instruct and Report are also nested in CheckBook.

Figure 6.20 Procedure Nesting for Checkbook Problem

```
program CheckBook
  procedure Instruct
  procedure Process
    procedure ReadTran
    procedure Update
    procedure DisplayTran
  procedure Report
```

Procedure UpDate will consist of an if statement that implements the decision table shown in Table 6.5. Procedure Process is shown in Fig. 6.21.

Case Study: Balancing a Checkbook, continued

Table 6.5 Decision Table for UpDate

Condition	Desired Action
TranType = 'D'	Increment NumDep, add Amount to CurBal
TranType = 'C'	Increment NumCheck, subtract Amount from CurBal

Figure 6.21 Procedure Process for Checkbook Balancing Program

```
procedure Process (StartBal {input} : Real;
                   var CurBal {output} : Real;
                   var NumCheck, NumDep {output} : Integer);
{
  Processes each transaction. Reads each transaction, updates and
  prints the current balance, and increments the count of checks or
  deposits.
  Pre : StartBal is assigned a value.
  Post: CurBal is StartBal plus deposits and minus withdrawals.
        NumCheck is the count of checks.
        NumDep is the count of deposits.
  Uses: ReadTran, Update, and DisplayTran
}

  const
    Sentinel = 'Q';          {sentinel value}
    Deposit = 'D';           {deposit code}
    Check = 'C';             {check code}

  var
    TranType : Char;         {transaction type (check or deposit)}
    Amount : Real;           {transaction amount}


  procedure ReadTran (var TranType {output} : Char;
                      var Amount {output} : Real);
  {
    Reads each transaction.
    Pre : None
    Post: TranType and Amount are read in.
  }

  begin {ReadTran}
    WriteLn;
    Write ('C, D, or Q: ');
    ReadLn (TranType);
    if TranType <> Sentinel then
      begin {Read amount}
        Write ('Amount $');
        ReadLn (Amount)
      end {if}
  end; {ReadTran}


  procedure UpDate (TranType {input} : Char;
                    Amount {input} : Real;
                    var CurBal {input/output} : Real;
                    var NumCheck, NumDep {input/output} : Integer);
```

```
   {
      Updates CurBal and increments NumCheck for a check or
      NumDep for a deposit.
      Pre : TranType, Amount, CurBal, NumCheck, and NumDep are defined.
      Post: CurBal is increased (deposit) or decreased (check) by
            Amount. NumCheck or NumDep is increased by one.
   }

   begin {Update}
      if TranType = Deposit then
         begin
            CurBal := CurBal + Amount;
            NumDep := NumDep + 1
         end {if}
      else if TranType = Check then
         begin
            CurBal := CurBal - Amount;
            NumCheck := NumCheck + 1
         end {if}
   end; {UpDate}


   procedure DisplayTran (TranType {input} : Char;
                          Amount,
                          CurBal {input} : Real);
   {
      Displays current transaction and balance.
      Pre : TranType, Amount, and Curbal are assigned values.
      Post: Transaction data are displayed.
   }
   begin {DisplayTran}
      if TranType = Deposit then
         begin
            Write ('Depositing $', Amount :8:2);
            WriteLn ('Balance of $', CurBal :12:2)
         end {Deposit}
      else if TranType = Check then
         begin
            Write ('Check for   $', Amount: 8:2);
            WriteLn ('   Balance of $', CurBal :12:2);
            if CurBal < 0.0 then
               WriteLn ('Warning! Your account is overdrawn.')
         end {Check}
      else {not check or deposit}
         begin
            Write ('Invalid transaction type ', TranType);
            WriteLn (' - transaction ignored.')
         end {if}
   end; {DisplayTran}


begin {Process}
   {Initialize counters to zero and CurBal to StartBal}
   NumCheck := 0;  NumDep := 0;  CurBal := StartBal;

   {Read first transaction}
   ReadTran (TranType, Amount);

   {Process each transaction until done}
   while TranType <> Sentinel do
```

Case Study: Balancing a Checkbook, continued

```
{invariant:
   CurBal is StartBal + all deposits, - minus all checks and
   NumDep is the number of deposits so far and
   NumCheck is the number of checks so far and
   no prior value of TranType was Sentinel
}
  begin
    UpDate (TranType, Amount, CurBal, NumCheck, NumDep);
    DisplayTran (TranType, Amount, CurBal);
    ReadTran (TranType, Amount)
  end {while}
end; {Process}
```

Procedure `Process` processes all transactions. `Process` calls `ReadTran` to read each transaction, `UpDate` to process the transaction just read, and `DisplayTran` to display the result. Because these three procedures are called by `Process` only, they are declared inside `Process`.

Procedure `DisplayTran` contains a nested `if` statement that differentiates between checks and deposits. When `TranType` is `'C'`, the inner `if` statement is executed and detects an overdrawn account (`CurBal` is negative).

Testing

A sample run of the checkbook balancing program is shown in Fig. 6.22. When you test this program, make sure you provide invalid as well as valid transaction types. Also make sure that invalid transaction types are not counted as either deposits or checks and that the amount associated with an invalid transaction type is ignored.

Figure 6.22 Sample Run of Checkbook Balancing Program

```
Balance your checking account!

Enter C (Check), D (Deposit), or Q (Quit)
after prompt C, D, or Q:

Enter a positive number after prompt Amount $

Begin by entering your starting balance   $1000.00

C, D, or Q > D
Amount $100.00
Depositing $  100.00        Balance of $    1100.00

C, D, or Q > C
Amount $1200.00
Check for  $ 1200.00        Balance of $     -100.00
Warning! Your account is overdrawn.

C, D, or Q > X
Amount $500.00
Invalid transaction type X - transaction ignored.
```

```
C, D, or Q > Q

Starting balance was $    1000.00
Final    balance  is $    -100.00
Number of checks written:    1
Number of deposits made :    1
```

PROGRAM
STYLE

Stepwise Design

The program system for the checkbook problem is a good illustration of the stepwise design process. It uses procedures to implement each of the subproblems shown in the structure chart. With the exception of procedure Process, each procedure is relatively short.

The main program at the bottom of Fig. 6.18 contains three procedure call statements. The second procedure call statement

```
Process (StartBal, CurBal, NumCheck, NumDep);
```

processes all transactions. Procedure Process calls procedures ReadTran, UpDate, and DisplayTran to perform the read, update, and display operations, respectively. These level-2 procedures are declared inside procedure Process.

The variables TranType and Amount are declared in Process, because they are used only by Process and the level-2 procedures. Similarly, the constants Sentinel, Check, and Deposit are declared in Process and are referenced as needed in the level-2 procedures.

Exercise for Section 6.7

Programming

1. Modify the checkbook program so that a penalty amount of $15.00 is deducted for each overdrawn check, and a count of overdrawn checks is maintained and printed next to each overdrawn check. Reset the count of overdrafts to zero whenever the balance becomes positive.

6.8 Debugging and Testing a Program System

Top-Down and Bottom-Up Debugging and Testing

As the number of statements in a program system grows, the possibility of error also increases. If we keep each procedure to a manageable size, the likelihood of error is less. It is also easier to read and test each procedure. Finally, the limited use of global variables minimizes the chance of harmful side effects, which are difficult to locate.

In some of the case studies in this chapter, we inserted stubs in the main program for procedures that were not yet written. This is a common practice when a team of programmers is working on a problem. Obviously not all procedures are ready at the same time. The use of stubs enables programmers to test and debug the main program flow and those procedures that are available.

Each stub displays an identification message and assigns values to its output parameters to prevent execution errors caused by undefined values. The messages provide a trace of procedure execution. This process is called *top-down testing*.

When a complicated procedure is completed, it can be tested separately with a short driver program. It is easier to locate and correct errors when dealing with a single procedure rather than with a complete program system. The driver program should (1) contain all necessary declarations and statements that assign values to all input and input/output parameters, (2) call the procedure, and (3) display the procedure results. Once we are confident that a procedure works properly, it can be substituted for its stub in the program system. The process of separately testing individual procedures before inserting them in a program system is called *bottom-up testing*.

By following a combination of top-down and bottom-up testing, a programming team can be fairly confident that the complete program system will be relatively free of errors when it is finally put together. Consequently, the final debugging sessions should proceed quickly and smoothly. A list of suggestions for debugging a program system follows.

Debugging Tips for Program Systems

1. Carefully document each procedure parameter and local identifier using comments as you write the code. Also describe the procedure operation using comments.
2. Leave a trace of execution by printing the procedure name as you enter it.
3. Print the values of all input and input/output parameters upon entry to a procedure. Check that these values make sense.
4. Print the values of all output parameters after returning from a procedure. Hand-check these values to verify that they are correct. Make sure that all input/output and output parameters are declared as variable parameters.
5. Make sure that a procedure stub assigns a value to each of its output parameters.

It is a good idea to plan for debugging as you write each procedure rather than afterward. Include the output statements required for debugging tips 2, 3, and 4 in the original Pascal code for the procedure. When you are satisfied that the procedure works, you can remove the debugging statements. One efficient way to remove the debugging statements is to change them to comments by enclosing them in curly braces. If you have a problem later, you can remove the braces, thereby changing the comments to executable statements. We describe another technique for controlling the display of debugging diagnostics in Section 7.4.

Figure 6.23 demonstrates these points for procedure `FindTax` and its driver program (first shown in Fig. 6.7).

Figure 6.23 Debugging Statements for a Procedure Call

```pascal
program Driver (Input, Output);

{Tests procedure FindTax.}

   var
     MySalary,                   {input - salary}
     MyTax      : Real;          {output - tax}


   procedure FindTax (Salary {input} : Real;
                          var Tax {output} : Real);

   begin {FindTax}
     WriteLn ('Procedure FindTax entered');
     WriteLn ('Value of Salay is ', Salary :4:2);
     ......
   end; {FindTax}


begin {Driver}
   .....
   FindTax (MySalary, MyTax);
   WriteLn ('Value returned from FindTax is ', MyTax :4:2)
   .....
end. {Driver}
```

 ## 6.9 Common Programming Errors

The Pascal scope rules determine where an identifier can be referenced. If an identifier is referenced outside its scope, an `identifier not declared` syntax error results.

There are many opportunities for error when you use procedures with parameter lists. The proper use of parameters is difficult for beginning programmers to master. One obvious pitfall occurs in ensuring that the actual parameter list has the same number of parameters as the formal parameter list. The syntax error `number of parameters does not agree with declaration` indicates this problem.

Each actual parameter must be assignment-compatible with its corresponding formal parameter (for a value parameter) or the same data type (for a variable parameter). An actual parameter that corresponds to a variable formal parameter must be a variable. Violation of either of these rules results in an `illegal parameter substitution` syntax error.

You should return a procedure result to the calling module by assigning a value to a variable parameter. Any value assigned to a value parameter will be stored locally in the procedure and will not be returned.

 # Chapter Review

This chapter focused on the use of procedure parameters for passing data to and from procedures. The parameter list provides a highly visible communication path between the procedure and the calling program. By using parameters, we can cause different data to be manipulated by a procedure each time we call it, making it easier to reuse the procedure in another program system.

There are two types of parameters: value and variable. A value parameter is used only for passing data into a procedure. A variable parameter is used to return results from a procedure. The actual parameter corresponding to a value parameter can be an expression or a constant; the actual parameter corresponding to a variable parameter must be a variable.

We also examined the scope of identifiers. An identifier can be referenced anywhere within the block that declares it. If one block is nested inside another and an identifier is declared in the outer block, then the identifier's meaning in the inner block is determined by its declaration in the outer block. If the identifer is declared in both blocks, its meaning in the inner block is determined by its declaration in the inner block.

A global variable is a variable that is declared in the main program; a local variable is declared in a procedure. A local variable is defined only during the execution of the procedure; its value is lost when the procedure is finished.

New Pascal Constructs

The new Pascal constructs introduced in this chapter are described in Table 6.6.

Table 6.6 Summary of New Pascal Constructs

Construct	Effect
| **Procedure with Parameters**<br>```pascal
procedure A (X : Real;
             Op : Char;
             var XTo3 : Real);

begin {A}
  if Op = '*' then
    XTo3 := X * X * X
  else if Op = '+' then
    XTo3 := X + X + X
  else
``` | Procedure A has two value parameters (X and Op) and one variable parameter (XTo3). If Op is '*', the value returned is X * X * X; if Op is '+', the value returned is X + X + X; otherwise, an error message is printed. A result is returned by assigning a new value to the actual parameter (a variable) that corresponds to parameter XTo3. |
```

```
      WriteLn ('Invalid')
  end; {A}
```

Procedure Call Statement

```
A (5.5, '+', Y)
```
Calls procedure A. 5.5 is passed
into X, '+' into Op, and the value
16.5 is stored in Y.

✓ Quick-Check Exercises

1. The _____ parameters appear in the procedure call and the _____ parameters appear in the procedure declaration.
2. Constants and expressions can correspond to formal parameters that are _____ parameters.
3. Formal parameters that are _____ parameters must have actual parameters that are _____.
4. Formal parameters that are _____ parameters must have actual parameters that are the _____ data type.
5. The data types of corresponding value parameters must be _____.
6. Which is used to test a procedure, a driver or a stub?
7. Which is used to test main program flow, a driver or a stub?
8. A side effect is a change to a _____ variable caused by execution of a procedure.
9. What are the values of main program variables X and Y after the following program executes?

```
program Nonsense;
  var X, Y : Real;

  procedure Silly (X : Real);
    var Y : Real;
  begin
    Y := 25.0;
    X := Y
  end; {Silly}

begin {Nonsense}
  Silly (X)
end. {Nonsense}
```

10. Answer exercise 9 if parameter X of Silly is a variable parameter.
11. Answer exercise 9 if parameter X of Silly is a variable parameter and the local declaration for Y is removed from Silly.
12. Answer exercise 9 if parameter X of Silly is a variable parameter, Y is a local variable in Silly, and the procedure call statement is changed to

```
Silly (Y)
```

13. Answer exercise 12 if the local declaration for Y is removed from Silly.

Answers to Quick-Check Exercises
  1. actual; formal
  2. value
  3. variable; variables

4. variable; same
5. assignment-compatible
6. driver
7. stub
8. nonlocal, or global
9. both undefined
10. X is 25.0, Y is undefined
11. both 25.0
12. X is undefined, Y is 25.0
13. X is undefined, Y is 25.0

Review Questions

1. Write the procedure heading for a procedure called Script that accepts three parameters passed to it. The first parameter is the number of spaces to print at the beginning of a line. The second parameter is the character to print after the spaces. The third parameter is the number of times to print the second parameter on the same line.
2. Write a procedure called LetterGrade that has one input parameter called Grade, and that prints out the corresponding letter grade using a straight scale (90-100 is an A, 80-89 is a B, and so on).
3. Explain the difference between a value parameter and a variable parameter with respect to the parameter's relationship to the variables in the calling program.
4. Explain the allocation of memory cells when a procedure is called.
5. Write the procedure heading for a procedure named Pass that passes two integer parameters. The first parameter should be a value parameter and the second a variable parameter.
6. Explain the use of a stub in refining an algorithm.
7. In the following chart, which procedures on the right can be referenced (called) by the corresponding procedure on the left? Which procedures are inaccessible?

```
program ProcScope;
    procedure A;
        procedure B;
            procedure C;
            .........
            end; {C}
            procedure D;
            .........
            end; {D}
        .........
        end; {B}
    .........
    end; {A}
.........
end. {ProcScope}
```

| | Callable Procedures | | | |
Calling Procedure	A	B	C	D
A	X			
B		X		
C			X	
D				X

Programming Projects

1. a. Write a program to process a collection of savings account transactions (deposits or withdrawals). Your program should begin by reading in the previous account

balance, then read and process each transaction. Enter a positive value for a deposit and a negative value for a withdrawal. For each transaction, print the message `Withdrawal` or `Deposit` and the new balance. Print an error message if a withdrawal would result in a negative balance and do not change the balance.

b. Compute and print the number of deposits, the number of withdrawals, the number of invalid withdrawals, and the total dollar amount for each type of transaction.

2. a. Write a program that computes and prints the fractional powers of two ($\frac{1}{2}$, $\frac{1}{4}$, $\frac{1}{8}$, and so on). The program should also print the decimal value of each fraction as shown below.

Power	Fraction	Decimal Value
1	$\frac{1}{2}$	0.5
2	$\frac{1}{4}$	0.25
3	$\frac{1}{8}$	0.125

Print all values through power equal to 10.

b. Add an extra output column that shows the sum of all decimal values so far. The first three sums are 0.5, 0.75, and 0.875.

3. a. The trustees of a small college are considering voting a pay raise for the twelve faculty members. They want to grant a 5.5 percent pay raise; however, before doing so, they want to know how much this will cost. Write a program that will print the pay raise for each faculty member and the total amount of the raises. Also, print the total faculty payroll before and after the raise. Test your program for the following salaries:

$12,500	$14,029.50	$16,000	$13,250
$15,500	$12,800	$20,000.50	$18,900
$13,780	$17,300	$14,120.25	$14,000

b. Redo the program assuming that faculty earning less than $14,000 receive a 4 percent raise, faculty earning more than $16,500 receive a 7 percent raise, and all others receive a 5.5 percent raise. For each faculty member, print the raise percentage as well as the amount.

4. The assessor in your town has estimated the market value of all fourteen properties and wants a program that determines the tax owed on each property and the total tax to be collected. The tax rate is 125 mils per dollar of assessed value. (A mil is 0.1 of a penny.) The assessed value of each property is 28 percent of its estimated market value. The market values are

$50,000	$48,000	$45,500	$67,000	$37,600	$47,100	$65,000
$53,350	$28,000	$58,000	$52,250	$48,000	$56,500	$43,700

5. Patients required to take many kinds of medication often find it difficult to remember when to take their medicine. Given the following set of medications, write a program that prints an hourly table indicating what medication to take at any given hour. Use a counter variable `Clock` to go through a twenty-four-hour day. Print the table based on the following prescriptions:

Medication	Frequency
Iron pill	0800, 1200, 1800
Antibiotic	Every 4 hours, starting at 0400
Vitamin	0800, 2100
Calcium	1100, 2000

6. A monthly magazine wants a program that will print out renewal notices to its subscribers and cancellation notices when appropriate. Using procedures when advisable, write a program that first reads in the current month number (1 through 12) and year. For each subscription processed, read in four data items: the account number, the month and the year the subscription started, and the number of years paid for the subscription.

   Read in each set of subscription information and print a renewal notice if the current month is either the month prior to expiration or the month of expiration. Print a cancellation notice if the current month comes after the expiration month.

   Sample input might be

10, 88	for a current month of October 1988
1364, 4, 85, 3	for account 1364 whose 3-year subscription began in April 1985

7. The square root of a number N can be approximated by repeated calculation using the formula

   $$NG = .5(LG + N / LG)$$

   where NG stands for next guess and LG stands for last guess. Write a procedure that implements this process. The first parameter will be a positive real number, the second will be an initial guess of the square root, and the third will be the computed result.

   The initial guess will be the starting value of LG. The procedure will compute a value for NG using the preceding formula. The difference between NG and LG is checked to see whether these two guesses are almost identical. If so, the procedure is exited and NG is the square root; otherwise, the new guess (NG) becomes the last guess (LG) and the process is repeated (that is, another value is computed for NG, the difference is checked, and so forth).

   For this program, the loop should be repeated until the magnitude of the difference is less than 0.005 (Delta). Use an initial guess of 1.0 and test the program for the numbers 4, 120.5, 88, 36.01, and 10,000.

Simple Data Types

7

S o far, you have used the four standard data types of Pascal: Integer, Real, Char, and Boolean (conditions in if and while statements). This chapter takes a closer look at these data types and introduces new operators and operations that you can perform on them. We describe the standard functions of Pascal and demonstrate how they can help you simplify computations.

You'll also learn how to declare new data types, called subrange types. All of the data types in this chapter are *simple* data types—that is, only a single value can be stored in each variable. Later chapters examine variables that can be used to store multiple values.

 ## 7.1 Constant Declarations

Let's begin by reexamining constants in Pascal. The syntax diagram of a constant declaration follows:

Constant declaration

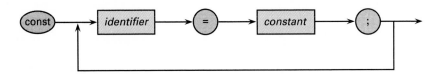

Each constant definition has the form

   identifier = *constant*

where *constant* is described in the next syntax diagram.

Constant

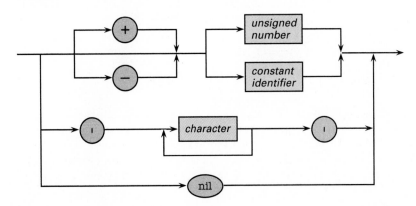

■ Example 7.1

A sample constant declaration follows.

```
const
  Max = 100;
  Min = -Max;
  SpeedOfLight = 2.998E+5;
  Debug = True;
  Name = 'Alice';
```

The constant declaration for `Min` uses the previously defined constant `Max`. Because `Max` has the value `100`, `Min` has the value `-100`. The constant `Speed-OfLight` is associated with a real value (`299800.0`) expressed in scientific notation. The Boolean constant `Debug` is associated with the `Boolean` value `True`. The constant `Name` is associated with the *string value* `'Alice'`. (String values are discussed further in Chapter 10 and Chapter 13. The constant value `nil` is discussed in Chapter 17.) ■

As mentioned earlier, there are two reasons for using constants. First, the name `SpeedOfLight` has more meaning to a reader of a program than the value `2.998E+5`. Second, if we change the declaration of a constant, we also change the value of that constant wherever it is referenced in the program.

Exercise for Section 7.1

Self-Check

1. Which of the following declared constants are valid and which are invalid?

```
const
  MinInt = -MaxInt;
  MaxLetter = 'Z';
  MinusZ = -MaxLetter;
  MaxSize = 50;
  MinSize = MaxSize - 10;
```

 ## 7.2 Numeric Data Types—Real and Integer

The data types `Integer` and `Real` represent numeric information. We used `Integer` variables as loop counters and to represent data, such as exam scores, that were whole numbers. In most other instances, we used type `Real` numeric data.

Differences Between Numeric Types

You may be wondering why it is necessary to have two numeric types. Can the data type Real be used for all numbers? The answer is yes, but on many computers, operations that involve integers are faster than those that involve real numbers. Less space is needed to store integers. Also, operations with integers are always precise, whereas there may be some loss of accuracy when you are dealing with real numbers.

These differences result from how real numbers and integers are represented internally in a computer's memory. All data are represented in memory as *binary strings*, that is, strings of zeros and ones. However, the binary string stored for the integer 13 is not the same as the binary string stored for the real number 13.0. The actual internal representation is computer-dependent; compare the integer format and the real format shown in Fig. 7.1.

Figure 7.1 shows that positive integers are represented by standard binary numbers. If you are familiar with the binary number system, you know that the integer 13 is represented as the binary number 01101.

Real format is analogous to scientific notation. The storage area occupied by a real number is divided into two sections: the *mantissa* and the *exponent*. The mantissa is a binary fraction between 0.5 and 1.0 (-0.5 and -1.0 for a negative number). The exponent is a power of two. The mantissa and the exponent are chosen so that the following formula is correct:

$$real\ number = mantissa \times 2^{exponent}$$

Because of the finite size of a memory cell, not all real numbers in the range of reals can be represented precisely. We will talk more about this later.

Besides the capability of storing fractions, the range of numbers that can be represented in real format is considerably larger than that for integer format. For example, on Control Data Corporation's Cyber series of computers, positive real numbers range in value from 10^{-294} (a very small fraction) to 10^{+322}, whereas the range of positive integers extends from 1 to approximately 10^{15}. In that series of computers, a real number requires twice the storage space that an integer does.

You can find the largest integer represented in your Pascal system by executing the statement

```
WriteLn ('Largest integer = ', MaxInt);
```

where MaxInt is a predefined constant. The range of integers represented must extend from –MaxInt through MaxInt, inclusive. (On many systems, the smallest integer is –(MaxInt + 1).)

Figure 7.1 Integer Format and Real Format

Integer format

Binary number

Real format

Mantissa	Exponent

Numeric Literals

A constant value that appears in an expression is called a *literal*. The data type of a numeric literal is determined in the following way. If the literal has a decimal point, it is considered type Real. A type Real literal can also have a decimal *scale factor*. For example, in the literal 2.998E+5, the scale factor is 10^5. A literal without a decimal point or a scale factor is considered type Integer.

Type of an Expression

The data type of an expression depends on the type of its operands. For example, the expression

    Ace + Bandage

is type Integer if both Ace and Bandage are type Integer; otherwise, it is type Real. The expression

    Ace / Bandage

is type Real because the Real division operator, /, always generates a type Real result.

All the arithmetic operators you have encountered so far (+, –, *, and /) can be used with either Integer or Real operands. Table 7.1 shows the data type of an expression with one arithmetic operator. The first two columns list the data type of the operands; the remaining columns show the data type of the expression for different operators. If one or both operands are type Real, the expression is always type Real; only when both operands are type Integer can the result be type Integer. If the operator is /, the result is type Real, even when both operands are type Integer.

Table 7.1 Data Type of an Arithmetic Expression

Operands		Operator		
Left	**Right**	**+, –, ***	**/**	**mod, div**
Real	Real	Real	Real	illegal
Real	Integer	Real	Real	illegal
Integer	Real	Real	Real	illegal
Integer	Integer	Integer	Real	Integer

Pascal does not allow a type Real expression to be assigned to a type Integer variable because the fractional part cannot be represented and will be lost. This means that the following assignment statements will generate syntax errors if Count is a type Integer variable. However, a type Real or type Integer expression can be assigned to a type Real variable.

```
Count := 3.5;          {illegal assignment of a real number to Integer}
Count := Count + 1.0;      {illegal; 1.0 is Real, so result is Real}
Count := Count / 2;          {illegal; result of division is Real}
```

Arithmetic Operators div and mod

In Table 7.1, two new operators—div and mod—can be used only with type Integer operands. The integer division operator, div, computes the integral part of the quotient that results when its first operand is divided by its second operand; the modulus operator, mod, computes the integer remainder.

The expression M div N (M and N both integers) is equal to the truncated quotient of M divided by N. For example, if M is 7 and N is 2, the value of M div N is the truncated quotient of 7 divided by 2, or 3. The result of M div N is always type Integer.

■ Example 7.2

Table 7.2 shows some examples of valid and invalid expressions involving the operator div. The result is always zero when the magnitude of the first operand is less than the magnitude of the second operand. The last example in the last column is invalid because the expression (4 / 2) is type Real.　■

Table 7.2　The div Operator

Expression	Result	Expression	Result	Expression	Result
3 div 15	0	3 div −15	0	15.0 div 3	invalid
15 div 3	5	15 div −3	−5	15.0 div 3.0	invalid
16 div 3	5	16 div −3	−5	15 div 3.0	invalid
17 div 3	5	−17 div 3	−5	15 div (4 / 2)	invalid
18 div 3	6	−18 div −3	6		

The modulus operator, mod, must also be used with integer operands. The expression M mod N (M and N both type Integer) is equal to the remainder of M divided by N. For example, 7 mod 2 is equal to the remainder of 7 divided by 2, or 1. The second operand of mod must always be greater than zero.

The formula

```
M = (M div N) * N + (M mod N)
```

defines the relationship between the operators div and mod. This relationship is also illustrated by the example

```
7 = (7 div 2) * 2 + (7 mod 2) = 3 * 2 + 1 = 7
```

In this example, M is 7 and N is 2, so the quotient is 3 (7 div 2) and the remainder is 1 (7 mod 2). The process of dividing 7 by 2 is shown in the following diagram.

```
7 div 2
     ↓
    3 R1  ← 7 mod 2
 2√ 7
    6
    1
```

Example 7.3

211

7.2 Numeric Data
Types—Real and
Integer

Example 7.3

Table 7.3 illustrates the `mod` operator. The magnitude of the result is always less than the second operand (the divisor). The `mod` operation is undefined when its second operand is zero or negative. By comparing the second and third columns, you can see that M `mod` N is the negation of –M `mod` N. ◢

Table 7.3 The mod Operator

Expression	Result	Expression	Result	Expression	Result
3 mod 5	3	5 mod 3	2	–5 mod 3	–2
4 mod 5	4	5 mod 4	1	–5 mod 4	–1
5 mod 5	0	15 mod 5	0	–15 mod 5	0
6 mod 5	1	15 mod 6	3	–15 mod 6	–3
7 mod 5	2	15 mod 7	1	–15 mod –7	undefined
8 mod 5	3	15 mod 8	7	15 mod 0	undefined

Operators div and mod

Form: operand$_1$ `div` operand$_2$
operand$_1$ `mod` operand$_2$
Interpretation: The operator `div` yields the integral part of the result of operand$_1$ divided by operand$_2$; any remainder is truncated. The operator `mod` yields the integer remainder of this division. Both operands must be integer constants, variables, or expressions with integer values.
Note: If operand$_2$ is 0, the result of the `div` or `mod` operation is undefined. If operand$_2$ is negative, the result of the `mod` operation is undefined.

According to the above display, the result of a `div` or `mod` operation is undefined if the second operand is negative. This means that the result is not defined by the Pascal standard, so it is system dependent and may not be the same for all compilers.

Example 7.4

Procedure `PrintDigits` in Fig. 7.2 prints each digit of its parameter `Decimal` in reverse order (e.g., if `Decimal` is 738, the digits printed are 8, 3, 7). This is accomplished by printing each remainder (0 through 9) of `Decimal` divided by 10; the integer quotient of `Decimal` divided by 10 becomes the new value of `Decimal`.

The parameter `Decimal` is the loop-control variable. Within the `while` loop, the `mod` operator assigns to `Digit` the rightmost digit of `Decimal`; the `div` operator assigns the rest of the number to `Decimal`. The loop is exited when `Decimal` becomes 0. Because `Decimal` is a value parameter, the actual parameter value is not changed by the procedure execution.

Figure 7.2   Printing Decimal Digits

```
procedure PrintDigits (Decimal {input} : Integer);
{
  Prints the digits of Decimal in reverse order.
  Pre : Decimal is assigned a value.
  Post: Each digit of Decimal is displayed, starting with the
        least significant one.
}
  const
    Base = 10;                           {number system base}

  var
    Digit : Integer;                     {each digit}

begin {PrintDigits}
  Decimal := Abs(Decimal);              {assert: Decimal is positive}
  {Find and print remainders of Decimal divided by Base}
  while Decimal <> 0 do
    {invariant:
       Digit in pass i is the rightmost digit of Decimal (for i >=1)
       and Decimal in pass i is Decimal in pass i-1 with its rightmost
       digit removed (for i > 1)
       and Decimal >= 0
    }
    begin
      Digit := Decimal mod Base;        {Get next digit}
      Write (Digit :1);
      Decimal := Decimal div Base       {Get next quotient}
    end; {while}

  {assert: Decimal is zero}
  WriteLn
end; {PrintDigits}
```

Table 7.4   Trace of Execution of PrintDigits(43)

Statement	Decimal 43	Digit	Effect
while Decimal <> 0 do			43 <> 0 is true.
Digit := Decimal mod Base		3	Next digit is 3.
Write (Digit :1)			Print 3.
Decimal := Decimal div Base	4		Quotient is 4.
while Decimal <> 0 do			4 <> 0 is true.
Digit := Decimal mod Base		4	Next digit is 4.
Write (Digit : 1)			Print 4.
Decimal := Decimal div Base	0		Quotient is 0.
while Decimal <> 0 do			0 <> 0 is false.
			Exit loop.

Table 7.4 shows a trace of the loop execution for an actual parameter of 43. The digits 3 and 4 are printed. (Section 7.3 discusses function Abs.)

Expressions with Multiple Operators

To write expressions that compute the desired results, you must know the Pascal rules for evaluating expressions. For example, in the expression A + B * C, is * performed before +, or vice versa? Is the expression X / Y * Z evaluated as (X / Y) * Z or as X / (Y * Z)?

Some expressions with multiple operators are

```
1.8 * Celsius + 32.0
(Salary - 5000.00) * 0.20 + 1425.00
```

In both these cases, the algebraic rule that multiplication or division is performed before addition or subtraction applies. The use of parentheses in the second expression ensures that subtraction is done first. The Pascal rules for expression evaluation are based on standard algebraic rules.

Rules for Expression Evaluation

a. All parenthesized subexpressions are evaluated first. Nested parenthesized subexpressions are evaluated inside out, with the innermost subexpression evaluated first.

b. *The operator precedence rule:* operators in the same subexpression are evaluated in the following order:

   *, /, div, mod   first

   +, −   last

c. *The left associative rule:* operators in the same subexpression and at the same precedence level (such as + and −) are evaluated left to right.

■ Example 7.5

The formula for the area of a circle

$$a = \pi r^2$$

can be written in Pascal as

```
Area := Pi * Radius * Radius
```

where Pi is the constant 3.14159. Figure 7.3 shows the *evaluation tree* for this formula. In the tree, the arrows connect each operand with its operator. The number to the left of each operator shows the order of operator evaluation; the letter to the right is that of the rule that applies. ■

Figure 7.3 Evaluation Tree for Area : = Pi * Radius * Radius

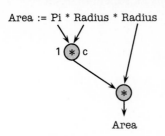

The next section discusses another way to specify Radius * Radius.

■ Example 7.6

The formula for the average velocity, v, of a particle traveling on a line between points p_1 and p_2 in time t_1 to t_2 is

$$v = \frac{p_2 - p_1}{t_2 - t_1}$$

This formula can be written and evaluated in Pascal as shown in Fig. 7.4.

Inserting parentheses in an expression affects the order of operator evaluation. Use parentheses freely to clarify the order of evaluation. ■

Figure 7.4 Evaluation Tree for V : = (P2 − P1) / (T2 − T1)

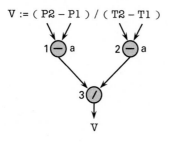

■ Example 7.7

Consider the expression

```
Z - (A + B div 2) + W * Y
```

containing integer variables only. The parenthesized subexpression (A + B div 2) is evaluated first (rule (a)) beginning with B div 2 (rule (b)). Once the value of B div 2 is determined, it can be added to A to obtain the value of (A + B div 2). Next, the multiplication operation is performed (rule (b) and the value for W * Y is determined. Then the value of (A + B div 2) is subtracted from Z (rule (c)). Finally, that result is added to W * Y. The evaluation tree for this expression is shown in Fig. 7.5. ■

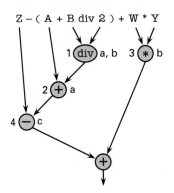

Writing Mathematical Formulas in Pascal

There are two problem areas in writing a mathematical formula in Pascal: one concerns multiplication and the other concerns division. You can imply multiplication in a mathematical formula by writing the two items to be multiplied next to each other, for example, $a = bc$. In Pascal, however, you must always use the * operator to indicate multiplication, as in

```
A := B * C
```

The other difficulty arises in formulas involving division. We normally write the numerator and the denominator on separate lines:

$$m = \frac{y - b}{x - a}$$

In Pascal, all assignment statements must be written in a linear form. Consequently, parentheses are often needed to separate the numerator from the denominator and to clearly indicate the order of evaluation of the operators in the expression. The preceding formula would be written in Pascal as

```
M := (Y - B) / (X - A)
```

■ Example 7.8

This example illustrates how several mathematical formulas can be written in Pascal.

Mathematical Formula	Pascal Expression
1. $b^2 - 4ac$	`B * B - 4 * A * C`
2. $a + b - c$	`A + B - C`
3. $\dfrac{a + b}{c + d}$	`(A + B) / (C + D)`
4. $\dfrac{1}{1 + x^2}$	`1 / (1 + X * X)`
5. $a\,x - (b + c)$	`A * (-(B + C))`

The points illustrated are as follows:

- Always specify multiplication explicitly by using the operator * where needed (example 1).
- Use parentheses when required to control the order of operator evaluation (examples 3 and 4).
- Never write two arithmetic operators in succession; they must be separated by an operand or an open parenthesis (example 5). ∎

Exercises for Section 7.2

Self-Check

1. What result is generated for `PrintDigits (23)` and `PrintDigits (64)` if Base is 2? If Base is 8?
2. Evaluate the following expressions with 7 and 22 as operands.

   ```
   22 div 7        7 div 22       22 mod 7       7 mod 22
   ```

   Repeat this exercise for the following pairs of integers:

   ```
   15, 16      3, 23      4, 16
   ```

3. Given the declarations

   ```
   const
     Pi = 3.14159;
     MaxI = 1000;

   var
     X, Y : Real;
     A, B, I : Integer;
   ```

   find the value of each of the following statements that are valid. Also indicate which are invalid and why. Assume that A is 3, B is 4, and Y is −1.0.

   a. I := A mod B
   b. I := (990 − MaxI) div A
   c. I := A mod Y
   d. X := Pi * Y
   e. I := A / B
   f. X := A / B
   g. X := A mod (A / B)
   h. I := B div 0
   i. I := A mod (990 − MaxI)
   j. I := (MaxI − 990) div A
   k. X := A / Y
   l. I := Pi * A
   m. X := Pi div Y
   n. X := A div B
   o. I := (MaxI − 990) mod A
   p. I := A mod 0
   q. I := A mod (MaxI − 990)

4. What values are assigned by the legal statements in exercise 3, assuming A is 5, B is 2, and Y is 2.0?
5. Assume that you have the following variable declarations:

   ```
   var
     Color, Lime, Straw, Yellow, Red, Orange : Integer;
     Black, White, Green, Blue, Purple, Crayon : Real;
   ```

Evaluate each of the following statements given these values: Color is 2, Black is 2.5, Crayon is −1.3, Straw is 1, Red is 3, and Purple is 0.3E1.

a. White := Color * 2.5 / Purple

b. Green := Color / Purple

c. Orange := Color div Red

d. Blue := (Color + Straw) / (Crayon + 0.3)

e. Lime : = Red div Color + Red mod Color

f. Purple : = Straw / Red * Color

6. Let A, B, C, and X be the names of four type Real variables and let I, J, and K be the names of three type Integer variables. Each of the following statements contains a violation of the rules for forming arithmetic expressions. Rewrite each statement so it is consistent with the rules.

a. X := 4.0 A * C

b. A := AC

c. I := 2 * −J

d. K := 3(I + J)

e. X := 5A / BC

f. I := 5J3

 ## 7.3 Mathematical Functions

This section describes the use of functions in expressions. Functions are Pascal features that are helpful in specifying numeric computations. Each function performs a different mathematical operation (square root, cosine, and the like) and returns a single value. Functions are referenced directly in an expression; the value computed by the function is then substituted for the function reference.

■ Example 7.9

Sqrt is the name of a function that computes the square root of a positive value. If the value of X is 20.0, the statement

```
Y := 5.7 + Sqrt(X + 5.0)
```

assigns a value of 10.7 to the type Real variable Y. The execution of this statement is as follows:

1. The expression argument (X + 5.0) is evaluated as 25.0.
2. The function returns the square root of 25.0, or 5.0.
3. The sum of 5.7 and the function result (5.0) is assigned to Y, so Y gets 10.7. ■

Pascal provides a number of standard mathematical functions, such as Sqrt, that programmers can use (see Table 7.5). The function name is always followed by its *argument* (an actual parameter) enclosed in parentheses, as shown in Example 7.9 (where the argument is X + 5.0). Any legal expression of the proper type can be an argument for these functions.

Table 7.5 Standard Functions

Function	Purpose	Argument	Result
Abs(X)	Returns the absolute value of its argument.	Real or Integer	Same as argument
Arctan(X)	Returns the angle y in radians, satisfying X = tan(y) where $-\pi/2$ <= y <= $\pi/2$.	Real or Integer	Real (radians)
Cos(X)	Returns the cosine of angle X.	Real or Integer	Real (radians)
Exp(X)	Returns e^x where $e = 2.71828. \ldots$	Real or Integer	Real
Ln(X)	Returns the natural logarithm of X for X > 0.0.	Real or Integer	Real
Odd(N)	Returns True if its argument is an odd integer; otherwise, returns False.	Integer	Boolean
Round(X)	Returns the closest integer value to its argument.	Real	Integer
Sin(X)	Returns the sine of angle X.	Real or Integer	Real (radians)
Sqr(X)	Returns the square of X.	Real or Integer	Same as argument
Sqrt(X)	Returns the positive square root of X for X >= 0.0.	Real or Integer	Real
Trunc(X)	Returns the integral part of its argument.	Real	Integer

Except for Abs, Sqr, Round, and Trunc, each of the functions listed in Table 7.5 returns (computes) a Real value regardless of its parameter type (Real or Integer). The type of the result computed by a reference to Abs or Sqr is the same as the type of its parameter.

The functions Round and Trunc require type Real parameters and always return integer values. These functions determine the integral part of a real-valued expression. Consequently, the expressions

```
Trunc(1.5 * Gross)
Round(TotalScore / NumStudents)
```

have integer values and can be assigned to type Integer variables. Trunc simply *truncates*, or removes, the fractional part of its parameter; function Round *rounds* its parameter to the nearest whole number. For example, Trunc(17.5) is 17, while Round(17.5) is 18; Trunc(-3.8) is -3, while Round(-3.8) is -4.

Most of the functions in Table 7.5 perform common mathematical computations. The arguments for Ln and Sqrt must be positive. The arguments for Sin and Cos must be expressed in radians, not degrees. Arctan expresses its result in radians.

One additional function, Odd, is used only with an integer parameter. Odd determines whether an integer variable or expression evaluates to an odd number. The function Odd returns the Boolean value True or False (for example, Odd(3) is True; Odd(4) is False).

■ Example 7.10

You could use the Pascal functions Sqr and Sqrt to compute the roots of a quadratic equation in X of the form

$$AX^2 + BX + C = 0$$

The two roots are defined as

$$Root_1 = \frac{-B + \sqrt{B^2 - 4AC}}{2A} \quad \text{and} \quad Root_2 = \frac{-B - \sqrt{B^2 - 4AC}}{2A}$$

The if statement in Fig. 7.6 assigns values to Root1 and Root2 when the *discriminant* $(B^2 - 4AC)$ is greater than or equal to zero.

Figure 7.6 Roots of a Quadratic Equation

```
Disc := Sqr(B) - 4 * A * C ;           {Define discriminant}
if Disc > 0.0 then
  begin
    Root1 := (-B + Sqrt(Disc)) / (2 * A);
    Root2 := (-B - Sqrt(Disc)) / (2 * A)
  end {Disc > 0.0}
else if Disc = 0.0 then
  begin
    Root1 := -B / (2 * A);
    Root2 := Root1              {roots are equal}
  end {Disc = 0.0}
else
  WriteLn ('Roots are imaginary and were not defined.')
```

■ Example 7.11

The program in Fig. 7.7 illustrates the use of several arithmetic functions. The function references are inserted in the output list of the WriteLn statement. The Abs function finds the absolute value of X before the Sqrt function is called, because the square root of a negative number is undefined.   ■

Figure 7.7 Using the Arithmetic Functions

```
program ArithFunc (Input, Output);

{Illustrates the arithmetic functions.}

  const
    Sentinel = 0.0;                        {sentinel value}

  var
    X : Real;                              {each data value}
```

```
begin  {ArithFunc}
   {Print the table heading}
   WriteLn ('After each line enter a real number or 0.0 to stop');
   WriteLn;
   WriteLn ('X', 'Trunc(X)' :16, 'Round(X)' :10, 'Abs(X)' :10,
            'Sqr(X)' :10, 'Sqrt(Abs(X))' :15);

   {Read and process each value of X}
   ReadLn (X);                                    {Get first number}
   while X <> Sentinel do
      begin
         WriteLn (Trunc(X) :17, Round(X) :10, Abs(X) :10:2,
                  Sqr(X) :10:2, Sqrt(Abs(X)) :10:2);
         ReadLn (X)                               {Get next number}
      end {while}
end. {ArithFunc}


After each line enter a real number or 0.0 to stop
X         Trunc(X)   Round(X)     Abs(X)     Sqr(X)   Sqrt(Abs(X))
4.3
                 4          4       4.30      18.49       2.07
-24.78
               -24        -25      24.78     614.05       4.98
0.0
```

Advanced Mathematical Functions (Optional)

This section and the problem that follows discuss more advanced concepts of mathematics, including logarithms, exponents, trigonometric functions, and series approximations. You may want to skip some of this material if you do not have the appropriate mathematical background. ·

■ Example 7.12

There is no exponentiation operator in Pascal. This means that it is not possible to write u^v directly when u and v are type Real. However, from the study of logarithms we know that

$$\ln(u^v) = v \times \ln(u)$$

and

$$z = e^{\ln(z)}$$

where e is 2.71828.... So we can derive that

$$u^v = e^{(v \times \ln(u))}$$

This formula can be implemented in Pascal as

```
UToPowerV := exp(v * ln(u))
```

■

■ Example 7.13

The program in Fig. 7.8 draws a sine curve. It uses the Pascal function Sin, which returns the trigonometric sine of its parameter, an angle expressed in radians.

Figure 7.8 Plotting a Sine Curve

221

7.3 Mathematical
Functions

```
program SineCurve (Output);

{Plots a sine curve.}

   const
     Pi = 3.14159;                      {constant Pi}
     Star = '*';                        {symbol being plotted}
     Scale = 20;                        {scale factor for plot}
     MinAngle = 0;                      {smallest angle}
     MaxAngle = 360;                    {largest angle}
     StepAngle = 18;                    {increment in degrees}

   var
     Theta,                             {angle in degrees}
     Indent : Integer;                  {column of each *}
     Radian : Real;                     {angle in radians}
     RadPerDegree : Real;               {radians per degree}


begin {SineCurve}
   RadPerDegree := Pi / 180.0;
   WriteLn ('Sine curve plot' :28);
   Theta := MinAngle;                   {initial value of Theta}
   while Theta <= MaxAngle do
     begin
       Radian := Theta * RadPerDegree;          {Compute radians}
       Indent := 1 + Round(Scale * (1.0 + Sin(Radian)));
       Write (Star :Indent);           {Plot * in column Indent}
       WriteLn (Sin(Radian) :20);              {Print sine value}
       Theta := Theta + StepAngle                 {Get next angle}
     end {while}
end. {SineCurve}
```

```
                Sine curve plot
                    *                   0
                        *           3.090168E-01
                          *           5.877849E-01
                            *           8.090166E-01
                              *           9.510562E-01
                              *           1.000000E+00
                              *           9.510570E-01
                            *           8.090180E-01
                          *           5.877869E-01
                        *           3.090194E-01
                      *           2.621549E-06
                   *           -3.090146E-01
                 *           -5.877830E-01
               *           -8.090152E-01
            *           -9.510555E-01
           *           -1.000000E+00
            *           -9.510579E-01
              *           -8.090194E-01
                *           -5.877893E-01
                   *           -3.090214E-01
                      *           -5.243099E-06
```

The while loop is executed for values of Theta equal to 0, 18, 36, ..., 360 degrees. For each Theta, the first assignment statement below

```
Radian := Theta * RadPerDegree;          {Compute radians}
Indent := 1 + Round(Scale * (1.0 + Sin(Radian)));
```

computes the number of radians corresponding to Theta. Then the variable Indent is assigned a value based on Sin(Radian). This value increases from 1 when Sin(Radian) is -1.0 to 41 (1 + Scale * 2.0) when Sin(Radian) is 1.0. Finally, the statement

```
Write (Star :Indent);       {Plot * in column Indent}
```

plots an asterisk somewhere in columns 1 through 41 as determined by the value of Indent. Remember, a string (or a character) is printed right-justified in its field; the value of Indent determines the size of the output field. ∎

PROGRAM
STYLE

Checking Boundary Values

The discussion for Example 7.13 states that the value of Indent ranges from 1 to 41 as the sine value goes from -1 to 1. It is a good idea to check the accuracy of those assumptions; you can usually do so by checking the boundaries of the range, as follows:

```
Sin(Radian) is -1.0, Indent := 1 + Round(Scale * (1.0 + (-1.0))
                     Indent := 1 + Round(20 * 0.0)
                     Indent := 1

Sin(Radian) is +1.0, Indent := 1 + Round(20 * (1.0 + 1.0))
                     Indent := 1 + Round(20 * 2.0)
                     Indent := 41
```

● Case Study: Approximating the Value of e (Optional)

Problem

A number of mathematical quantities can be represented using a series approximation where a series is represented by a summation of an infinite number of terms. For example, the base of the natural logarithms, e (value is 2.71828...), can be determined by evaluating the expression

$$1 + 1/1! + 1/2! + 1/3! + ... + 1/n! + ...$$

where $n!$ is the factorial of n, defined as follows:

$$0! = 1$$
$$n! = n \times (n-1)! \text{ (for } n > 1)$$

Design Overview

We can get an approximation to the value of e by summing the series for a finite value of n. Usually, the larger the value of n, the more accurate the computed result. This expression can be represented, using *summation notation*, as

$$\sum_{i=0}^{n} 1/i!$$

where the first term is obtained by substituting 0 for i (1/0! is 1/1), the second term is obtained by substituting 1 for i (1/1!), and so on. A counting loop can be used to easily implement the preceding formula.

Data Requirements

Problem Inputs
The number of terms, n, in the sum (n : Integer)

Problem Outputs
The approximate value of e (e : Real)

Program Variable
The ith term of the series (ithTerm : Real)
Loop-control variable (i : Integer)

Algorithm
1. Read in the value of n.
2. Initialize e to 1.0.
3. Initialize the ith term to 1.0.
4. for each i from 1 to n do
      begin
      5. Compute the ith term in the series
      6. Add the ith term to e
      end
7. Print the approximate value of e.

The program is shown in Fig. 7.9. Inside the loop, the statement

```
ithTerm := ithTerm / i;
```

computes the value of the ithTerm in the series by dividing the previous term by the loop-control variable i. The following formula shows that this division does indeed produce the next term in the series.

$$(1 / (i-1)!) / i = 1 / (i \times (i-1)!) = 1 / i!$$

Because 0! is 1, ithTerm must be initialized to 1.0. The statement

```
e := e + ithTerm
```

adds the new value of ithTerm to the sum being accumulated in e. Trace the execution of this loop to satisfy yourself that ithTerm takes on the values 1/1!, 1/2!, 1/3!, and so on, during successive loop iterations.

Figure 7.9   Series Approximation to e

```
program eSeries (Output);

{Computes the value of e by a series approximation.}

   var
     e,                     {the value being approximated}
     ithTerm : Real;        {ith term in series}
     n,                     {number of terms in series}
     i : Integer;           {loop control variable}
begin
  Write ('Enter the number of terms in the series> ');
  ReadLn (n);

  {Compute each term and add it to the accumulating sum.}
  e := 1.0;                {initial sum}
  ithTerm := 1.0;          {first term}
  i := 1;
  while i <= n do
    begin
      ithTerm := ithTerm / i;
      e := e + ithTerm;
      i := i + 1
    end; {while}

  {Print the result.}
  WriteLn ('The approximate value of e is ', e :20)
end. {eSeries}


Enter the number of terms in the series> 15
The approximate value of e is     2.7182818284E+00
```

Numerical Inaccuracies

One of the problems in processing real numbers is that sometimes an error occurs in the representation of real data. Just as certain numbers cannot be represented exactly in the decimal number system (for example, the fraction ⅓ is 0.333333...), so some numbers cannot be represented exactly in real format. The *representational error* depends on the number of binary digits (bits) used in the mantissa: the more bits, the smaller the error.

The number 0.1 is an example of a real number that has a representational error. The effect of a small error is often magnified through repeated computations. Therefore, because the result of adding 0.1 ten times is not exactly 1.0, the following loop may fail to terminate on some computers.

```
Trial := 0.0;
while Trial <> 1.0 do
  begin
    . . .

    Trial := Trial + 0.1
  end {while}
```

If the loop repetition test is changed to `Trial < 1.0`, the loop may execute ten times on one computer and eleven times on another. For this reason, it is best to use integer variables whenever possible in loop repetition tests.

Other problems occur during the manipulation of very large and very small real numbers. When a large number and a small number are added, the larger number may cancel out the smaller number, resulting in a *cancellation error*. If X is much larger than Y, then X + Y may have the same value as X (e.g., `1000.0 + 0.0001234` is equal to `1000.0` on some computers).

For this reason, you can sometimes obtain more accurate results by carefully selecting the order in which computations are performed. For example, in computing the value of e in the preceding case study, the terms of the series

$$1 + 1/1! + 1/2! + ... + 1/n!$$

were generated in left-to-right order and added to a sum being accumulated in e. When n is large, the value of `1/n!` is very small; thus, the effect of adding a very small term to a sum larger than `2.0` may be lost. If the terms are generated and summed in right-to-left order instead, the computation result might be more accurate.

If two very small numbers are multiplied and the result is too small to be represented accurately, it will be represented as zero. This phenomenon is called *arithmetic underflow*. Similarly, if two very large numbers are multiplied, the result may be too large to be represented. This phenomenon, called *arithmetic overflow*, is handled in different ways by Pascal compilers. (Arithmetic overflow can also occur when very large integer values are processed.)

For an illustration of the numerical inaccuracy that may result when real computations are performed, examine the sine value for angles of 180 and 360 degrees printed in Fig. 7.8. The actual sine should be zero; the sine value computed is quite small (approximately 10^{-6}) in both cases, but it is not zero. Because the value of the constant `Pi` is imprecise, the result of any computation involving `Pi` has a small numerical error.

Exercises for Section 7.3

Self-Check

1. Rewrite the following mathematical expressions using Pascal functions.
   a. $\sqrt{U + V} \times W^2$
   b. $\log_n (X^Y)$

    c. $\sqrt{(X - Y)^2}$

    d. $|XY - W/Z|$

2. Evaluate the following:
    a. `Trunc(-15.8)`
    b. `Round(-15.8)`
    c. `Round(6.8) * Sqr(3)`
    d. `Sqrt(Abs(Round(-15.8)))`

Programming

1. Write a procedure that computes

    $e^{a \times \ln(b)}$

    Call this procedure with several different values of a and b and display the results. Verify for yourself that the results are correct.

2. Using the Round function, write a Pascal statement to round any real value X to the nearest two decimal places. Hint: You have to multiply by `100.0` before rounding.

3. The value of e^x is represented by the series

    $1 + x + x^2/2! + x^3/3! + \ldots + x^n/n! + \ldots$

    Write a program to compute and print the value of this series for any x and any n. Compare the result to `exp(x)` and print a message `O.K.` or `Not O.K.`, depending on whether the difference between these results exceeds `0.001`.

7.4 Boolean Variables, Expressions, and Operators

Chapter 1 introduced the data type `Boolean`. Since then we have used Boolean expressions (expressions that evaluate to true or false) to control loop repetition and to select one of the alternatives in an `if` statement. Some examples of Boolean expressions follow:

```
Gross > TaxBrak
Item <> Sentinel
TranType = 'C'
```

The simplest Boolean expression is a Boolean variable or constant that can be set to either of the Boolean values, `True` or `False`. The statement

```
const
   Debug = True;
```

specifies that the Boolean constant `Debug` has the value `True`; the statement

```
var
   Switch, Flag : Boolean;
```

declares `Switch` and `Flag` to be Boolean variables—variables that can be assigned only the values `True` and `False`.

Boolean Operators

A Boolean variable or constant is the simplest form of a Boolean expression (for example, `Switch`). We have used the relational operators (`<`, `=`, `>`, and so on) with numeric data to form conditions or Boolean expressions (for example, `Salary < MinSal`).

There are three Boolean operators: `and`, `or`, and `not`. These operators work in conjunction with operands that are Boolean expressions, for example,

```
(Salary < MinSal) or (NumDepend > 5)
(Temp > 90.0) and (Humidity > 0.90)
WinningRecord and (not Probation)
```

The first Boolean expression determines whether an employee pays no income tax. It evaluates to true if either condition in parentheses is true. The second Boolean expression describes an unbearable summer day, with temperature and humidity both above 90. The expression evaluates to true only when both conditions are true. The third Boolean expression manipulates two Boolean variables (`WinningRecord`, `Probation`). A college team for which this expression is true may be eligible for the postseason tournament.

The Boolean operators, which can be used only with Boolean expressions, are described in Table 7.6, Table 7.7, and Table 7.8.

Table 7.6   and Operator

Operand1	Operand2	Operand1 and Operand2
True	True	True
True	False	False
False	True	False
False	False	False

Table 7.7   or Operator

Operand1	Operand2	Operand1 or Operand2
True	True	True
True	False	True
False	True	True
False	False	False

Table 7.8   not Operator

Operand1	not Operand1
True	False
False	True

Table 7.6 shows that the and operator yields a True result only when both its operands are true; Table 7.7 shows that the or operator yields a False result only when both its operands are False. The not operator has a single operand; Table 7.8 shows that the not operator yields the *logical complement*, or negation, of its operand.

The precedence of an operator determines its order of evaluation. Table 7.9 shows the precedence of all operators in Pascal, including the relational operators.

Table 7.9 Operator Precedence

Operator	Precedence
not	Highest (evaluated first)
*, /, div, mod, and	
+, −, or	
<, <=, =, <>, >=, >	Lowest (evaluated last)

As you can see, the not operator has the highest precedence, followed by the multiplicative operators (including and), the additive operators (including or), and, last, the relational operators. Because the relational operators have the lowest precedence, you should generally use them with parentheses to prevent syntax errors.

■ Example 7.14

The expression

        X < Y + Z

involving the real variables X, Y, and Z is interpreted correctly as

        X < (Y + Z)

because + has higher precedence than <. However, the expression

        X < Y or Z < Y

causes the syntax error invalid type of operands. It is interpreted as

        X < (Y or Z) < Y

because or has higher precedence than <. This is an error because the type Real variables Y and Z cannot be operands of the Boolean operator or.

This error is quite common; however, you can avoid it and similar errors by using parentheses freely. The following parentheses prevent a syntax error.

        (X < Y) or (Z < Y)   ■

■ Example 7.15

The following are all legal Boolean expressions if X, Y, and Z are type Real and Flag is type Boolean. The value of each expression, shown in brackets, assumes that X is 3.0, Y is 4.0, Z is 2.0, and Flag is False.

1. `(X > Z) and (Y > Z)`   [True]
2. `(X + Y / Z) <= 3.5`   [False]
3. `(Z > X) or (Z > Y)`   [False]
4. `not Flag`   [True]
5. `(X = 1.0) or (X = 3.0)`   [True]
6. `(0.0 < X) and (X < 3.5)`   [True]
7. `(X <= Y) and (Y <= Z)`   [False]
8. `not Flag or ((Y + Z) >= (X - Z))`   [True]
9. `not (Flag or ((Y + Z) >= (X - Z)))`   [False]

Expression 1 gives the Pascal form of the relationship "X and Y are greater than Z." You may be tempted to write expression 1 as

    X and Y > Z

However, that is an illegal Boolean expression because the real variable X cannot be an operand of the Boolean operator and. Similarly, expression 5 shows the correct way to express the relationship "X is equal to 1.0 or to 3.0."

F..pression 6 is the Pascal form of the relationship 0.0 < X < 3.5 (that is, "X is in the range 0.0 to 3.5"). Similarly, expression 7 shows the Pascal form of the relationship X <= Y <= Z (that is, "Y is in the range X to Z, inclusive").

Finally, expression 8 is evaluated in Fig. 7.10; the values given at the beginning of Example 7.15 are shown above the expression.

The expression in Fig. 7.10 is rewritten as follows with parentheses enclosing the term not Flag. Although the parentheses are not required, they do clarify the meaning of the expression.

    (not Flag) or ((Y + Z) >= (X - Z))

Figure 7.10 Evaluation Tree for not Flag or ((Y + Z) >= (X - Z))

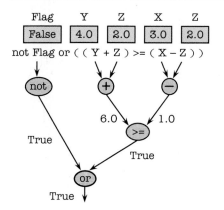

Short-Circuit Evaluation of Boolean Expressions

When evaluating Boolean expressions, we often employ a technique called *short-circuit evaluation*. This means that we can stop evaluating a Boolean expression as soon as its value can be determined. For example, if the value of `Flag` is `False`, then `not Flag` is `True`, so the expression in Fig. 7.10 must evaluate to `True` regardless of the value of the parenthesized expression following `or` (that is, `True or (...)` must always be `True`). Consequently, there is no need to evaluate the parenthesized expression following `or` when `not Flag` is `True`. By similar reasoning, we can show that `False and (...)` must always be `False`, so there is no need to evaluate the parenthesized expression following `and`.

Your Pascal compiler may not use short-circuit evaluation. This means that it may continue to evaluate a Boolean expression even after its value is determined. This can lead to execution errors, as shown next.

■ Example 7.16

If `X` is zero, the `if` condition

```
if (X <> 0.0) and (Y / X > 5.0) then
```

is `False`, because `(X <> 0.0)` is `False` so `False and (...)` must always be `False`. Consequently, there is no need to evaluate the subexpression `(Y / X > 5.0)` when `X` is zero. However, if this expression is evaluated, a `division by zero` run-time error occurs because the divisor `X` is zero.

Because of the possibility of error, the `if` condition should be split:

```
if (X <> 0.0) then
   if (Y / X > 5.0) then
```

The first condition *guards* the second condition and prevents the latter from being evaluated when `X` is zero. ■

Be wary of short-circuit evaluation and avoid writing Boolean expressions that rely on it. Even if your compiler happens to use short-circuit evaluation, a run-time error may result when the program is compiled and executed on another computer.

Boolean Assignment Statements

We can write assignment statements that assign a Boolean value to a Boolean variable. The statement

```
Same := X = Y
```

assigns the value `True` to the Boolean variable `Same` when `X` and `Y` are equal; otherwise, the value `False` is assigned. This assignment is more efficient than the `if` statement

```
if X = Y then
   Same := True
else
   Same := False
```

which has the same effect.

■ Example 7.17

Either of the following assignment statements assigns the value True to Even if N is an even number.

```
Even := not Odd(N)          |        Even := (N mod 2) = 0
```

The statement on the left assigns to Even the complement of the value returned by the Boolean function Odd; the one on the right assigns a value of True to Even when the remainder of N divided by 2 is 0. (All even numbers are divisible by 2.)   ■

Using Boolean Variables as Program Flags

Boolean variables are often used as *program flags*, which signal whether or not a special event occurs in a program. The fact that such an event occurs is important to the future execution of the program. A Boolean variable that is a program flag is initialized to one of its two possible values (True or False) and reset to the other as soon as the event being monitored occurs.

■ Example 7.18

Procedure ReadPos in Fig. 7.11 continues to read integer values until an integer greater than 0 is entered. The first value greater than 0 is returned as the procedure result.

The Boolean variable Positive acts as a program flag to signal whether the event data entry of a positive integer has occurred. Positive is initialized to False when the procedure is entered. Inside the while loop, the assignment statement

```
Positive := N > 0
```

resets Positive to True when an integer greater than 0 is entered. The loop is repeated as long as Positive is still False.   ■

Figure 7.11 Procedure ReadPos

```
procedure ReadPos (var N {output} : Integer);
{
  Reads a positive integer into N.
  Pre : None
  Post: Returns in N the next data value greater than 0.
}
  var
    Positive : Boolean;              {program flag - loop control}

begin {ReadPos}
  {Keep reading until a valid number is read}
  Positive := False;          {Assume valid number not read}
  while not Positive do
    {invariant:
       No prior value of N was greater than zero.
    }
    begin
      Write ('Enter an integer greater than 0> ');
```

```
      ReadLn (N);                  {Read next integer into N}
      Positive := N > 0            {Set Positive to True if N > 0}
   end  {while}
end; {ReadPos}
```

Reading and Writing Boolean Values

Procedure WriteLn displays Boolean values, but procedure ReadLn cannot be used to read a Boolean value. Procedure ReadLnBool (see Fig. 7.12) "reads" a Boolean value. It does this by assigning a Boolean value to output parameter BoolVal based on the next data character. The statement

```
      BoolVal := (NextChar = 'T') or (NextChar = 't');
```

assigns True to BoolVal if the data character read into NextChar is T or t; otherwise, it assigns False to BoolVal.

Figure 7.12   Procedure ReadLnBool

```
procedure ReadLnBool (var BoolVal {output} ,
                          Success {output} : Boolean);
{
  Reads a Boolean value (represented by T or F) into BoolVal and
  sets the flag Success.
  Pre : None
  Post: BoolVal is set to True if T or t is read; otherwise,
        BoolVal is set to False. Success is set to True only
        if one of the four characters T, t, F, or f is read.
}
  var
    NextCh : Char;               {a data character}

begin {ReadLnBool}
  ReadLn (NextCh);
  BoolVal := (NextCh = 'T') or (NextCh = 't');
  Success := BoolVal or (NextCh = 'F') or (NextCh = 'f')
end; {ReadLnBool}
```

Using a Boolean Parameter as a Flag

The second parameter of ReadLnBool is used as a flag to signal whether a valid data character was read. In ReadLnBool, the assignment statement

```
      Success := BoolVal or (NextCh = 'F') or (NextCh = 'f')
```

assigns True to Success if the character read was T, t, F, or f. If the value returned in Success is False, the calling program should call ReadLnBool again. Assuming the calling program contains the variable declarations

```
   var
     NextBool,                {input - next Boolean data value}
     ReadDone : Boolean;      {flag -- True if read succeeds; }
                              {                otherwise, False}
```

the following while loop could be used to read a Boolean value into NextBool.

```
ReadDone := False;          {no value read yet}
while not ReadDone Do
  begin
    Write ('Enter T or F> ');
    ReadLnBool (NextBool, ReadDone)
  end; {while}
```

The while loop body executes until procedure ReadLnBool sets ReadDone to True.

Using a Global Boolean Constant for Debugging

As mentioned earlier, a programmer should plan for debugging by including diagnostic print statements in the original code. One way to prevent the diagnostic print statements from executing during production runs is to declare a global Boolean constant (say Debug) whose value is True during debugging and False during production runs. The declaration part of the main module contains the constant declaration

```
const
  Debug = True;     {turn debugging diagnostics on}
```

during debugging runs and the constant declaration

```
const
  Debug = False;    {turn debugging diagnostics off}
```

during production runs. The following diagnostic print statements are executed only when Debug is True (that is, during debugging runs). Sections 5.7 and 6.8 discuss where to place diagnostic print statements.

```
if Debug then
  begin
    WriteLn ('Procedure ProcessGoods entered');
    WriteLn ('Input parameter Salary is ', Salary :12:2)
  end; {if}
```

Exercises for Section 7.4

Self-Check

1. Draw the evaluation tree for expression 9 of Example 7.15.
2. Write the following Boolean assignment statements:
   a. Assign a value of True to Between if the value of N lies between –K and +K, inclusive; otherwise, assign a value of False.
   b. Assign a value of True to UpCase if Ch is an uppercase letter; otherwise, assign a value of False.
   c. Assign a value of True to Divisor if M is a divisor of N; otherwise, assign a value of False.

Programming

1. Write a procedure that returns a Boolean flag indicating whether or not its first parameter is divisible by its second parameter.

7.5 Character Variables and Functions

Pascal provides a character data type that can store and manipulate the individual characters that make up a person's name, address, and other personal data. Character variables are declared using the data type Char in a declaration. A type Char literal consists of a single character (a letter, a digit, a punctuation mark, or the like) enclosed in apostrophes. A character value can be assigned to a character variable or associated with a constant identifier, as shown in the following examples:

```
const
  Star = '*';

var
  NextLetter : Char;

begin
  NextLetter := 'A'
```

The character variable NextLetter is assigned the character value 'A' by the assignment statement. A single character variable or value can appear on the right side of a character assignment statement. Character values can also be compared, read, and printed.

Using Relational Operators with Characters

Assuming Next and First are type Char, the Boolean expressions

```
Next = First
Next <> First
```

determine whether two character variables have the same or different values. Order comparisons can also be performed on character variables using the relational operators <, <=, >, >=.

To understand the result of an order comparison, you must know something about how characters are represented internally in your computer. Each character has its own unique numeric code; the binary form of this code is stored in a memory cell that has a character value. These binary numbers are compared by the relational operators in the normal way.

Three common character codes are shown in Appendix D. The digit characters are an increasing sequence of consecutive characters in all three codes. For example, the American Standard Code for Information Interchange (ASCII), the digit characters '0' through '9' have code values of 48 through 57 (decimal). The following order relationship holds for the digit characters (that is, '0' < '1', '1' < '2', and so on).

```
'0'<'1'<'2'<'3'<'4'<'5'<'6'<'7'<'8'<'9'
```

The uppercase letters are also an increasing sequence of characters, but they are not necessarily consecutive. In ASCII, the uppercase letters have the decimal code values 65 through 90. The following order relationship holds for uppercase letters.

    'A'<'B'<'C'< ... <'X'<'Y'<'Z'

If the lowercase letters are included in the character set, they are also an increasing, but not necessarily consecutive, sequence of characters. In ASCII, the lowercase letters have the decimal code values 97 through 122, and the following order relationship holds.

    'a'<'b'<'c'< ... <'x'<'y'<'z'

The examples and programs in this text assume that the lowercase letters are included and that the letters are consecutive characters.

In ASCII, the *printable characters* have codes from 32 (for a blank or a space) to 126 (for the symbol ~). The other codes represent nonprintable *control characters*. Sending a control character to an output device causes the device to perform a special operation, such as returning the cursor to column one, advancing the cursor to the next line, or ringing a bell.

The Ordinal Functions: Ord, Pred, and Succ

The data types Integer, Boolean, and Char are considered *ordinal types*. With ordinal data types, each value (except the first) has a unique predecessor; each value (except the last) has a unique successor. For example, the predecessor of 5 is 4; the successor of 5 is 6. The data type Real is not an ordinal type because a real number like 3.1415 does not have a unique successor. (Is its successor 3.1416 or 3.14151?)

The order or sequence of an ordinal data type is well defined. For example, −MaxInt (or −(MaxInt + 1) on some systems) is the smallest integer, and the positive integers follow the sequence 1, 2, 3, ..., MaxInt. The order of the Boolean values is False, True.

The Pascal function Ord determines the *ordinal number*, or relative position, of an ordinal value in its sequence of values. If the parameter of Ord is an integer, the ordinal number returned is the integer itself. For all other ordinal types, the ordinal number of the first value in the sequence is zero, the ordinal number of the second value is one, and so on. Thus, Ord(False) is zero and Ord(True) is one. If A and B belong to the same ordinal type and A < B is true, then Ord(A) < Ord(B) must also be true.

The Pascal function Pred returns the predecessor of its parameter, and the Pascal function Succ returns the successor. These functions, like Ord, can be used only with parameters that are ordinal types.

■ Example 7.19

Table 7.10 shows the results of using the Ord, Succ, and Pred functions with an integer or a Boolean parameter. As shown in Table 7.10, one value in each ordinal type does not have a successor (MaxInt, True). The Boolean value that does not have a predecessor is False. The integer value that does not have a predecessor is system dependent and is either $-$MaxInt or $-($MaxInt $+ 1)$.

Table 7.10 Results of Ord, Succ, and Pred

Parameter	Ord	Succ	Pred
15	15	16	14
0	0	1	-1
-30	-30	-29	-31
MaxInt	MaxInt	undefined	MaxInt-1
$-$MaxInt	$-$MaxInt	$-($MaxInt $- 1)$	undefined or $-($MaxInt $+ 1)$
False	0	True	undefined
True	1	undefined	False

Although you can use these functions with any of the ordinal types, they are most often used with type Char and the enumerated types discussed in Chapter 8. The ordinal number of a character is based on the character set code used by Pascal and, therefore, is computer dependent. ■

■ Example 7.20
The following table is for ASCII.

Table 7.11 Results of Ord, Succ, and Pred Functions for ASCII

Parameter	Ord	Succ	Pred
C	67	D	B
7	55	8	6
y	121	z	x
blank	32	!	nonprintable

Table 7.11 shows that the digit '7' has the ordinal number 55 in ASCII. Regardless of the character code used, the expression

```
Ord('7') - Ord('0') = 7
```

is always true because the digit characters must be in consecutive sequence.

Table 7.11 also shows that the character 'C' has the ordinal number 67 in ASCII. Because the character 'D' is the successor of the character 'C', it must have an ordinal number of 68. Because the letters are in consecutive sequence in ASCII, the Boolean expression

```
Ord('C') - Ord('A') = 2
```

is True. In ASCII, the lowercase letters follow the uppercase letters, and the difference in code values for both cases of the same letter is 32 (for example, Ord('a') - Ord('A') is 32). ■

The Function Chr

The function Chr returns a character as its result. The character returned is the one whose ordinal number is the function argument. Therefore, the result of the function reference Chr(67) is the character with ordinal number 67 (the letter C in the ASCII code).

If Ch is a type Char variable, the *nested function reference*

```
Chr(Ord(Ch))
```

has the same value as Ch. Therefore, the function Chr is the *inverse* of the Ord function for the characters.

■ Example 7.21

The following if statement sets LowCase to the lowercase form of a capital letter stored in NextChar, where NextChar and LowCase are both type Char. If NextChar does not contain a capital letter, LowCase is assigned the same value as NextChar.

```
if ('A' <= NextChar) and (NextChar <= 'Z') then
  LowCase := Chr(Ord(NextChar) - Ord('A') + Ord('a'))
else
  LowCase := NextChar
```

If NextChar has the value 'C', the Boolean expression is True and the assignment statement is evaluated as follows, assuming the letters are consecutive characters.

```
LowCase := Chr(Ord('C') - Ord('A') + Ord('a'))
           Chr(2 + Ord('a'))
           Chr(99) = 'c'
```

If the ASCII code is used, we can write the first assignment statement in the previous if statement as

```
LowCase := Chr(Ord(NextChar) + 32)
```

If NextChar is 'C', Ord(NextChar) is 67 so 'c' is assigned to LowCase. ■

■ Example 7.22

A *collating sequence* is a sequence of characters arranged by ordinal number. The program in Fig. 7.13 prints part of the Pascal collating sequence. It lists the characters with ordinal numbers 32 through 90, inclusive. The sequence shown is for the ASCII code; the first character printed is a blank (ordinal number 32). ■

Figure 7.13 Printing Part of a Collating Sequence

```
program Collate (Output);

{Prints part of the collating sequence.}

  const
    Min = 32;                      {smallest ordinal number}
    Max = 90;                      {largest ordinal number}

  var
   NextOrd : Integer;              {each ordinal number}
```

```
begin {Collate}
  {Print characters Chr(32) through Chr(90)}
  for NextOrd := Min to Max do
    Write (Chr(NextOrd));              {Print next character}
  WriteLn
end. {Collate}
```

```
 !"#$%&'()*+,-./0123456789:;<=>?-ABCDEFGHIJKLMNOPQRSTUVWXYZ
```

Table 7.12 summarizes the functions introduced in this section.

Table 7.12 Functions for Ordinal Types

Function	Purpose	Argument	Result
Chr(N)	Returns the character whose ordinal number is N.	Integer	Char
Ord(N)	Returns the ordinal number of its argument.	Any ordinal type	Integer
Pred(N)	Returns the predecessor of its argument.	Any ordinal type	Same as argument
Succ(N)	Returns the successor of its argument.	Any ordinal type	Same as argument

Exercises for Section 7.5

Self-Check

1. Evaluate the following:
   a. Ord(True)
   b. Pred(True)
   c. Succ(False)
   d. Ord(True) − Ord(False)

2. Evaluate the following; assume the letters are consecutive characters.
   a. Ord('D') − Ord('A')
   b. Ord('d') − Ord('a')
   c. Succ(Pred('a'))
   d. Chr(Ord('C'))
   e. Chr(Ord('C') − Ord('A') + Ord('a'))
   f. Ord('7') − Ord('6')
   g. Ord('9') − Ord('0')
   h. Succ(Succ(Succ('d')))
   i. Chr(Ord('A') + 5)

7.6 The Read Procedure

So far, we have used the ReadLn procedure to read data into a program. Pascal also provides the Read procedure for data entry. We often use Read in a loop to read a sequence of data characters into a single input variable, as shown next.

■ Example 7.23

The program in Fig. 7.14 reads a sentence ending in a period and counts the number of blanks in the sentence. Each character entered after the prompting message is read into the variable Next and tested to see if it is a blank.

The statement

```
Read (Next)
```

which appears twice in the program, reads one character at a time from the data line because Next is type Char. The while loop exit occurs after the sentinel character (.) is read. ■

Figure 7.14 Counting Blanks in a Sentence

```pascal
program BlankCount (Input, Output);

{Counts the number of blanks in a sentence.}

   const
     Blank = ' ';                    {character being counted}
     Sentinel = '.';                 {sentinel character}

   var
     Next   : Char;                  {next character in sentence}
     Count : Integer;                {number of blank characters}
begin   {BlankCount}
   Count := 0;                       {Initialize Count}
   WriteLn ('Enter a sentence ending with a "', Sentinel, '"');

   {Process each input character up to the sentinel}
   Read (Next);                      {Get first character}
   while Next <> Sentinel do
     {invariant:
         Count is the count of blanks so far and
         no prior value of Next is the sentinel
     }
     begin
       if Next = Blank then
         Count := Count + 1;         {Increment blank count}
       Read (Next)                   {Get next character}
     end;   {while}

   {assert: Count is the count of blanks and Next is the sentinel}
   WriteLn;
   WriteLn ('The number of blanks is ', Count :1)
end. {BlankCount}


Enter a sentence ending with a "."
There was an old woman who lived in a shoe.
The number of blanks is 9
```

The Read Procedure

The program in Fig. 7.14 uses the standard Pascal Read procedure to read individual characters from a data line. Like the ReadLn statement, the Read statement causes input data to be stored in the variables specified in its input list. Both statements

```
Read (Next)          |          ReadLn (Next)
```

cause one data character to be read into the character variable Next, but with one important difference. After the ReadLn statement is executed, the computer automatically skips past the end of the current data line (indicated when Return is pressed) to the start of the next data line; any additional characters entered on the current data line before the Return key is pressed are not processed. There is no skip to the next line after a Read statement is executed; therefore, any additional characters entered on the current line are processed by the next Read or ReadLn statement.

If ReadLn (Next) is substituted for Read (Next) in Fig. 7.14, the first data character (the letter T) is read into Next before loop entry; the remaining characters on the first data line are skipped. When the ReadLn statement in the loop body is executed, no characters are left to process, so the computer waits for more data to be entered. To process the same sentence using ReadLn instead of Read, it is necessary to enter each data character on a separate line. Section 8.7 further details the differences between procedures Read and ReadLn.

SYNTAX
DISPLAY

> ### Read Procedure
>
> **Form:**   Read (*input list*)
> **Example:** Read (Next, N, X);
> **Interpretation:** Data are entered into each variable specified in the *input list*. There must be one data item for each variable in the *input list*, and the order of the data must correspond to the order of the variables in the *input list*. Insert one or more blank characters between numeric data items. If a character data item is being read after a number, insert only one blank character between the number and the character. Do not insert any extra blanks between consecutive character data items. The first character that follows the last one read will be processed when the next Read or ReadLn statement is executed. Press the Return key after you have entered all data items.
>
> **Note:** Read is system dependent. On some systems, data characters are processed as they are typed in; on other systems, the data characters are not processed until after the Return key is pressed, so you can edit the data line (using the backspace key) before you press Return.

■ Example 7.24

It is sometimes desirable to read a number as a string of individual characters. This enables the program to detect and ignore data entry errors. For example, if the program user enters a letter instead of a number, the error is detected and the program prompts again for a data value. Similarly, if the program user types in $15,400 instead of the number 15400, the extra characters are ignored.

Procedure `ReadInt` in Fig. 7.15 reads in a string of characters ending with a sentinel (the character %) and ignores any character that is not a digit. It also computes the value of the number (an integer) formed by the digits only. For example, if the characters $15,43AB0% are entered, the value returned through `NumData` is 15430.

7.6 The Read Procedure

Figure 7.15 Reading a Number as a String of Characters

```
procedure ReadInt (var NumData {output} : Integer);
{
  Reads consecutive characters ending with the symbol %. Computes
  the integer value of the digit characters, ignoring nondigits.
  Pre : None
  Post: Returns in NumData the numeric value of the digit
        characters read.
}
  const
    Base = 10;                        {the number system base}
    Sentinel = '%';                   {the sentinel character}

  var
    Next : Char;                      {each character read}
    Digit : Integer;    {the value of each numeric character}

begin {ReadInt}
  {Accumulate the numeric value of the digits in NumData}
  NumData := 0;                       {initial value is zero}
  Read (Next);                        {Read first character}
  while Next<> Sentinel do
    {invariant:
        No prior value of Next is the sentinel and
        NumData is the accumulated numeric value of all prior digit
        characters read into Next
    }
    begin
      if ('0' <= Next) and (Next <= '9') then
        begin {digit}
          Digit := Ord(Next) - Ord('0');      {Get digit value}
          NumData := Base * NumData + Digit    {Add digit value}
        end;  {digit}
      Read (Next)                     {Read next character}
    end  {while}

  {assertion:
    Next is the sentinel and
    NumData is the number formed from the digit
    characters read as data
  }
end; {ReadInt}
```

In Fig. 7.15, the statements

```
Digit := Ord(Next) - Ord('0');      {Get digit value}
NumData := Base * NumData + Digit    {Add digit value}
```

assign to Digit an integer value between 0 (for character value '0') and 9 (for character value '9'). The number being accumulated in NumData is multiplied by 10, and the value of Digit is added to it. Table 7.13 traces the procedure execution for the input characters 3N5%; the value returned is 35. ∎

Table 7.13 Trace of Execution of Procedure ReadInt for Data 3N5%

Statement	Next	Digit	NumData	Effect
NumData := 0			0	Initialize NumData.
Read (Next)	3			Get character.
while Next <> Sentinel do				'3' <> '%' is true.
if ('0'<=Next) and (Next<='9')				'3' is a digit.
Digit := Ord(Next) − Ord ('0')		3		Digit value is 3.
NumData := Base*NumData+Digit			3	NumData gets 3.
Read (Next)	N			Get character.
while Next <> Sentinel do				'N' <> '%' is true.
if ('0'<=Next) and (Next<='9')				'N' is not a digit.
Read (Next)	5			Get character.
while Next <> Sentinel do				'5' <> '%' is true.
if ('0'<=Next) and (Next<='9')				'5' is a digit.
Digit := Ord(Next) − Ord ('0')		5		Digit value is 5.
NumData := Base*NumData+Digit			35	NumData gets 10 * 3 + 5.
Read (Next)	%			Get character.
while Next<> Sentinel do				'%' <> '%' is false.

7.7 Subrange Types

One of the most important features of Pascal is that it permits the declaration of new data types. Many of these data types are discussed in later chapters. This section focuses on new data types that are subranges of the ordinal types, where a *subrange* defines a subset of the values associated with a particular ordinal type (the *host type*). Subranges make a program more readable and enable Pascal to detect when a variable is given a value that is unreasonable in the problem environment.

■ Example 7.25

Type declarations begin with the reserved word type and are used to declare a new data type. The Pascal scope rules for identifiers apply to names of data types. Declarations of two subrange types and a variable of each new type follow.

```
type
  Letter = 'A'..'Z';
  DaysInMonth = 1..31;
```

```
var
  NextChar : Letter;
  InDay : DaysInMonth;
```

The first subrange, `Letter`, has the host type `Char`. Any character value from `'A'` to `'Z'`, inclusive, can be stored in a variable of type `Letter`. The computer displays an error message and stops program execution if an attempt is made to store any other character in a variable of type `Letter`. For example, the assignment statement

```
NextChar := 'a'
```

would cause the run-time error value `out of range` and stop program execution, because the character value `'a'` is not included in data type `Letter`. Some Pascal compilers detect this *range violation* as a syntax error during compilation.

`DaysInMonth` is a subrange with host type `Integer`. A variable of type `DaysInMonth` can be used to keep track of the current date, a value between 1 and 31, inclusive. The statement

```
ReadLn (InDay)
```

reads a data value into `InDay` (type `DaysInMonth`). A value `out of range` run-time error occurs if the data value is less than 1 or greater than 31. ∎

Subrange Type Declaration

Form: type *subrange type* = *minvalue* .. *maxvalue*;

Example: type LowCase = 'a' .. 'z';

Interpretation: A new data type named *subrange type* is defined. A variable of type *subrange type* can be assigned a value from *minvalue* through *maxvalue*, inclusive. The values *minvalue* and *maxvalue* must belong to the same ordinal type (called the host type), and Ord(*minvalue*) must be less than or equal to Ord(*maxvalue*). *minvalue* and *maxvalue* can be constant identifiers of the same data type.

The scope rules for a subrange-type identifier are the same as for other Pascal identifiers. The operations that can be performed on a variable whose type is a subrange are the same as for the host type of the subrange. The host type can be a standard ordinal type (`Integer`, `Char`, or `Boolean`) or any previously declared enumerated type (discussed in Section 8.4). The host type is determined by the pair of values that define the subrange; the ordinal number of the first value must be less than the ordinal number of the second value.

The `type` declarations come before the variable declarations in a Pascal block. The form of the declaration part is summarized as follows:

constant declarations
type declarations
variable declarations
procedure declarations

Motivation for Using Subranges

You may be wondering, "Why bother with subranges? They don't seem to provide any new capabilities." Subranges do, however, provide additional opportunity for your program to "bomb," because attempting to store an out-of-range value in a variable whose type is a subrange stops program execution. This should happen only as the result of an error by the programmer or program user and prevents the error from going undetected.

For example, if InDay is type Integer (instead of DaysInMonth), the program continues to execute regardless of what value is assigned to InDay. Assigning an overly large value (say, 1000) to InDay may cause a later statement to fail or the program to generate incorrect results. In the former case, the program user may have difficulty finding the statement that was actually at fault (that is, the statement that assigned the out-of-range value). In the latter case, the program user may not even be aware that an error has occurred if program execution is completed in a normal manner. The use of subranges ensures the immediate detection of an out-of-range value.

Exercise for Section 7.7

Self-Check

1. Identify which of the following subranges are illegal.

    a. `1..MaxInt`   f. `0..'9'`
    b. `'A'..'Z'`   g. `15..-15`
    c. `-15..15`   h. `'ACE'..'HAT'`
    d. `'A'..'z'`   i. `'a'..'Z'`
    e. `'c'..'c'`   j. `-MaxInt..-MaxInt + 5`

 ## 7.8   Type Compatibility and Assignment Compatibility

Two data types are considered *type compatible* if they are the same type, if one is a subrange of the other (for example, Letter and Char in Example 7.25), or if they are both subranges of the same host type. For example, the following data type, Characters, is considered the same type as Char, so Characters and Char are type compatible.

```
type
   Characters = Char;
   Letter = 'A'..'Z';
```

```
var
   NextCh : Characters;
```

Operands that are type compatible can be manipulated by the same operator. For example, the expression

```
NextCh <> '3'
```

is syntactically correct as long as `NextCh` is type `Char`, `Characters`, or `Letter`. On the other hand, the expression

```
NextCh <> 3
```

causes a syntax error because the integer 3 is not type compatible with `NextCh`.

The variable `InDay` declared in Example 7.25 can be manipulated like any type `Integer` variable. It can be used as an actual parameter that corresponds to a formal value parameter that is type `Integer`, type `DaysInMonth`, or any other subrange with host type `Integer`. However, the rules for correspondence of variable parameters are more restrictive (that is, corresponding variable parameters must be the same type), so `InDay` can correspond only to a formal variable parameter that is type `DaysInMonth`.

An expression is considered *assignment compatible* with a variable if their types are type compatible. Further, if the variable type is a subrange, the value of the expression must be within the allowable range. If an expression is assignment compatible with a variable, then the expression can be assigned to the variable without error.

Assuming the declarations

```
type
   Letter = 'A'..'Z';

var
   NextCh : Letter;
```

the assignment statement

```
NextCh := '3'
```

causes the syntax error `value to be assigned is out of bounds`, because the constant value `'3'` is not assignment compatible with the variable `NextCh` (type `Letter`). If `Ch` is type `Char`, the assignment statement

```
NextCh := Ch
```

compiles, but it may cause a `value out of range` run-time error. This error occurs if the character stored in `Ch` is not an uppercase letter.

There is one exception to the rule that a variable and an expression must be type compatible to be assignment compatible. A type `Integer` expression is assignment compatible with a type `Real` variable. This means that a type `Integer` expression can be assigned to a type `Real` variable or can correspond to a value parameter that is type `Real`.

Other issues of type compatibility and assignment compatibility are discussed in later chapters.

Exercise for Section 7.8

Self-Check

1. Assuming that I is type 0..10, J is type Integer, and K is type Real, indicate whether each expression below is assignment compatible with the variable on the left and whether any constraints are necessary to avoid an out of range error.

a. `K := 3 * I + J`
b. `I := 15`
c. `J := Trunc(K) + 2 * I`
d. `I := I div J`
e. `I := I / J`
f. `I := J mod 11`
g. `J := 2 * K + 3`

 # 7.9 Problem Solving Illustrated

The case study for Chapter 7 involves the manipulation of type Integer and Char data. It also illustrates the use of Boolean variables as program flags.

___

Case Study: Prime Numbers

Problem

A prime number is an integer that has no divisors other than 1 and itself. Examples of prime numbers are the integers 2, 3, 5, 7, and 11. Your mathematics professor wants you to write a program that tests a positive integer to determine whether or not it is a prime number.

Design Overview

A number cannot be prime if it has a divisor, other than itself, that is greater than 1. Even numbers cannot be prime because they have 2 as a divisor. To determine whether an odd number, say N, is prime, you must test whether it is divisible by any integer from 2 through $N - 1$. Your program should either print a message indicating that an integer is a prime number or print the smallest divisor of the number if it is not prime.

Data Requirements

> *Problem Inputs*
> The number to be tested for a prime number (N : Integer)

> *Problem Outputs*
> The smallest divisor if N is not prime (FirstDiv : Integer)

Initial Algorithm

1. Read in the number to be tested for a prime number.
2. Find the smallest divisor > 1 or determine that the number is prime.
3. Print a message that the number is prime or print its smallest divisor

Algorithm Refinements and Structure Chart

Use the Boolean variable Prime, described below, as a program flag to indicate whether N is prime. The structure chart is shown in Fig. 7.16.

Additional Program Variables

Program flag that will be set to True if N is prime and will be set to False if N is not prime (Prime : Boolean)

Step 2 of the algorithm is performed by procedure TestPrime which is described after the main program. TestPrime returns the value of Prime and FirstDiv.

Step 3 of the algorithm is relatively simple; it is included in the main program. The refinement for step 3 follows.

Step 3 Refinement

3.1 if N is prime then
        3.2 Print a message that N is prime
    else
        3.3 Print the first divisor of N

Coding the Main Program

The main program consists of calls to procedure EnterInt, which performs step 1, and procedure TestPrime, which performs step 2. A stub is provided

Figure 7.16   Structure Chart for Prime Number Problem

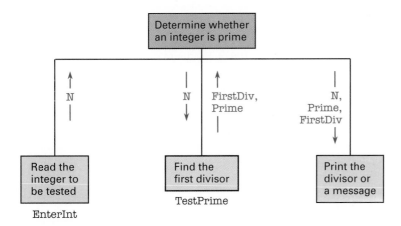

for TestPrime, but EnterInt is included with the main program shown in Fig. 7.17. Procedure EnterInt returns the first data value that lies between its two input parameter values. (EnterInt is used in other programming examples in this text.)

Figure 7.17   Main Program to Test for a Prime Number

```
program PrimeNumber (Input, Output);
{
  Prints the smallest divisor (other than 1) of the integer N if
  a divisor exists; otherwise, prints a message that N is prime.
}
  const
    Maximum = 1000;              {largest prime candidate}

  type
    SmallInt = 2..Maximum;   {range of values for N}

  var
    N : Integer;             {input - number being tested as a prime}
    FirstDiv : SmallInt;  {output - first divisor if found}
    Prime    : Boolean;   {flag - signals whether N is prime
                               (True) or not prime (False)          }


  procedure EnterInt (MinN, MaxN {input} : Integer;
                           var N {output} : Integer);
  {
    Reads an integer between MinN and MaxN into N.
    Pre : MinN and MaxN are assigned values.
    Post: Returns in N the first data value between MinN and MaxN
          if MinN <= MaxN is true; otherwise, N is not defined.
  }
    var
      InRange : Boolean;        {program flag - loop control}

  begin {EnterInt}
    if MinN <= MaxN then
      InRange := False          {no valid value in N as yet}
    else
      begin
        WriteLn ('Error - empty range for EnterInt');
        InRange := True                {skip data entry loop}
      end; {if}

    {Keep reading until a valid number is read into N.}
      while not InRange do
        {invariant:
           No prior value of N is in the range MinN through MaxN
        }
        begin
          Write ('Enter an integer between ');
          Write (MinN :1, ' and ', MaxN :1, '> ');
          ReadLn (N);
          InRange := (MinN <= N) and (N <= MaxN)
        end {while}
```

```
      {assert: N is in the range MinN to MaxN if MinN <= MaxN}
    end; {EnterInt}


    procedure TestPrime (N {input} : Integer;
                         var FirstDiv {output} : SmallInt;
                         var Prime {output} : Boolean);
    {
     Finds first divisor (FirstDiv) of N if it exists.
     Pre : N is assigned a value.
     Post: FirstDiv is the first divisor of N besides 1 and N.
           Prime is True if a divisor is not found; otherwise,
           Prime is False.
    }
    begin {TestPrime stub}
      WriteLn ('Procedure TestPrime entered');
      FirstDiv := 2;
      Prime := True
    end; {TestPrime stub}

begin {PrimeNumber}
  {Enter an integer to test for a prime number}
  WriteLn ('Enter a number that you think is a prime.');
  EnterInt (2, Maximum, N);

  {
   Find smallest divisor FirstDiv or determine that N is prime.
   Set Prime to indicate whether or not N is a prime number.
  }
  TestPrime (N, FirstDiv, Prime);

  {Print first divisor or a message that N is prime}
  if Prime then
    WriteLn (N :1, ' is a prime number')
  else
    WriteLn (FirstDiv :1, ' is the smallest divisor of ', N :1)
end. {PrimeNumber}
```

Coding the Procedures

EnterInt begins with an if statement that verifies that its two input parameters, MinN and MaxN, satisfy the condition MinN <= MaxN. If this condition is true, the program flag InRange is set to False and the while loop executes until a valid data value is read (InRange becomes True). If this condition is false, the program flag InRange is set to True and an error message is displayed. Setting InRange to True ensures that the while loop will be skipped. This is critical because the while loop will execute forever if it is entered when MinN is greater than MaxN.

It is unlikely that a caller of EnterInt will pass it two integer values that do not satisfy the condition MinN <= MaxN. However, it is a good idea to practice *defensive programming* and display an error message just in case the improbable occurs.

Procedure TestPrime determines whether N has any divisors other than 1 and itself. If N is an even integer, then it is divisible by 2. Therefore, 2 is the only even integer that can be prime, and 2 is the smallest divisor of all other even integers.

If N is an odd integer, its only possible divisors are the odd integers less than N. In fact, it can be proven that a number is prime if it is not divisible by any odd integer less than or equal to its square root. These considerations form the basis for the following algorithm.

Algorithm for Procedure TestPrime

```
1. if N = 2 then
        2. N is a prime number
   else if N is even then
        3. 2 is the smallest divisor and N is not prime
   else
        4. Test each odd integer between 3 and the square root
           of N to see whether it is a divisor of N
```

Step 4 must test each odd integer as a possible divisor of N until a divisor is found. We will write a separate procedure (TestOdd) to accomplish this. TestOdd should contain a while loop with the following loop invariant:

```
{invariant:
    FirstDiv during pass i is 1 + 2 * i (i.e., 3, 5, 7, ... ) and
    no prior value of FirstDiv is a divisor of N or
    is greater than the square root of N
}
```

This invariant suggests the while loop shown in the following algorithm; the structure chart for TestPrime and TestOdd is shown in Fig. 7.18.

Algorithm for TestOdd

1. Assume N is a prime number (i.e., set Prime to True).
2. Initialize FirstDiv to 3.

Figure 7.18   Structure Chart for TestPrime and TestOdd

3. while N is still prime and FirstDiv <= Sqrt(N) do
4. if FirstDiv is a divisor of N then
     5. Set Prime to False (N is not prime).
   else
     6. Set FirstDiv to the next odd number.

The nesting of procedures for the entire program system is shown in Fig. 7.19. Procedure TestPrime (with nested procedure TestOdd) is shown in Fig. 7.20.

Figure 7.19   Nesting of Procedures in Program PrimeNumber

```
program PrimeNumber
  procedure EnterInt
  procedure TestPrime
    procedure TestOdd
```

Figure 7.20   Procedure TestPrime with TestOdd

```
procedure TestPrime (N {input} : SmallInt;
                     var FirstDiv {output} : SmallInt;
                     var Prime {output} : Boolean);
{
 Finds first divisor (FirstDiv) of N if it exists.
 Pre : N is assigned a value.
 Post: FirstDiv is the first divisor of N besides 1 and N.
       Prime is True if a divisor is not found; otherwise,
       Prime is False.
}


  procedure TestOdd (N {input} : SmallInt;
                     var FirstDiv {output} : SmallInt;
                     var Prime {output} : Boolean);
  {
    Tests each odd integer from 3 to the square root of N as a
    divisor of N.
    Pre : N is odd.
    Post: FirstDiv is the smallest divisor if one is found.
          Prime is True if a divisor is not found; otherwise,
          Prime is False.
  }
    var
      MaxPossibleDiv : SmallInt; {largest possible divisor}

  begin {TestOdd}
    Prime := True;                  {Assume that N is prime}
    FirstDiv := 3;                            {Try 3 first}
    MaxPossibleDiv := Trunc(Sqrt(N));
    while Prime and (FirstDiv <= MaxPossibleDiv) do
      {invariant:
          FirstDiv during pass i is 1 + 2 * i (3, 5, 7, ... ) and
```

```
                         no prior value of FirstDiv is a divisor of N or
                         is greater than the square root of N
             }
           if (N mod FirstDiv) = 0 then
             Prime := False                        {N is not prime}
           else
             FirstDiv := FirstDiv + 2       {Try next odd number}

        {assertion:
           Prime is True and FirstDiv > Sqrt(N) or
           Prime is False and FirstDiv is the smallest divisor of N
         }
      end; {TestOdd}


  begin {TestPrime}
    if N = 2 then
      Prime := True                            {2 is a prime number}
    else if not Odd(N) then
      begin   {N is even}
        Prime := False;
        FirstDiv := 2                          {2 is first divisor}
      end {N is even}
    else   {N is odd}
      TestOdd (N, FirstDiv, Prime)             {Test for a divisor}
  end; {TestPrime}
```

The program flag `Prime` is set within `TestOdd` or `TestPrime` to indicate whether `N` is a prime number. In `TestOdd`, `Prime` is initialized to `True` before any candidate divisors are tested. If a divisor is found, `Prime` is reset to `False` and the `while` loop is exited. If no divisors are found, `Prime` remains `True` and the loop is exited when `FirstDiv` becomes greater than `Sqrt(N)`. The values of `Prime` and `FirstDiv` are returned to the main program.

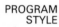

PROGRAM STYLE

Removing Unnecessary Computation from Loops

In procedure `TestOdd`, the local variable `MaxPossibleDiv` is used to hold the maximum possible divisor ($\sqrt{N}$) and is assigned its value by the statement

```
    MaxPossibleDiv := Trunc(Sqrt(N));
```

just before the `while` loop. The `Trunc` function returns the integral part of the square root of `N`.

If `MaxPossibleDiv` was not declared as a local variable, the preceding expression would be included in the `while` loop condition and would be reevaluated each time the loop was repeated. This is not necessary, since the expression value never changes. You should examine loops carefully and remove any computations that always generate the same results.

Planning for Reuse

The parameter N represents the prime number candidate in all procedures described earlier. N is declared as type Integer in the main program and procedure EnterInt and as type SmallInt (the subrange 2..Maximum) in TestPrime and TestOdd. This is permissible, because N is a value parameter in TestPrime and TestOdd and SmallInt is a subrange of type Integer.

There are two reasons why N cannot be declared type SmallInt in procedure EnterInt. First, if an out-of-range value is read into N, a run-time error might occur. Second, we are planning to reuse EnterInt in other program systems. Because N is a variable parameter, its data type must be the same as the data type of its corresponding actual parameter. It is easier to use the standard type Integer than to redefine type SmallInt in each program that calls EnterInt.

Testing

You should test the complete program for both small and large numbers that are prime numbers. You should be able to find a table of primes to help you select sample cases. Make sure you test nonprimes that are odd numbers and nonprimes that are even numbers. Also, test procedure EnterInt using data values that are not in range.

Several sample runs of the prime number program are shown in Fig. 7.21. The test values used for N were selected to exercise all parts of the program and to verify that the program works for prime numbers as well as nonprime numbers. The operation of the program at the boundaries (2 and 1000) was also checked, as well as the operation of the program for invalid data values (0 and 1001). A very large prime number (997) was used as a test case, as well as odd and even numbers that are not prime. Although many valid data values were not tested, the sample selected is representative and provides a fair indication that the program is correct.

Figure 7.21 Four Sample Runs of the Prime Number Program

```
Enter a number that you think is a prime.
Enter an integer between 2 and 1000> 1000
2 is the smallest divisor of 1000


Enter a number that you think is a prime.
Enter an integer between 2 and 1000> 997
997 is a prime number


Enter a number that you think is a prime.
Enter an integer between 2 and 1000> 35
5 is the smallest divisor of 35
```

```
Enter a number that you think is a prime.
Enter an integer between 2 and 1000> 0
Enter an integer between 2 and 1000> 1001
Enter an integer between 2 and 1000> 2
2 is a prime number
```

Use a similar strategy when you select test data to exercise your programs. Avoid choosing sample test data that are similar. Also, select test data that are at or near any boundary values.

Exercise for Section 7.9

Programming

1. Modify TestPrime to print all divisors of N where N may be any positive integer (odd or even). If N is prime, the only divisors printed should be 1 and N.

 ## 7.10   Common Programming Errors

A good deal of care is required when you work with complicated expressions. It is easy to inadvertently omit parentheses or operators. If an operator or a single parenthesis is omitted, a syntax error will be detected. If a pair of parentheses is omitted, the expression, although syntactically correct, will compute the wrong value.

Sometimes it is beneficial to break a complicated expression into subexpressions that are separately assigned to *temporary variables* and then to manipulate those temporary variables. For example, it is easier to write correctly the three assignment statements

```
Temp1 := Sqrt(X + Y);
Temp2 := 1 + Temp1;
Z := Temp1 / Temp2
```

than the single assignment statement

```
Z := Sqrt(X + Y) / (1 + Sqrt(X + Y))
```

which has the same effect. Using three assignment statements is also more efficient, because the square root operation is performed only once; it is performed twice in the single assignment statement.

Be careful that you use the correct type of operator with each operand. The arithmetic operators can be used only with type Integer or type Real operands. The operators div and mod can be used only with type Integer operands.

The only operators that you can use with type Char data are the relational operators. The Boolean expression

```
3 <> '3'
```

is invalid because one of its operands is an integer and the other is a character value.

You can use the Boolean operators, `and`, `or`, and `not`, only with Boolean expressions. In the expression

```
Flag and (X <= Y)
```

the variable `Flag` must be type `Boolean`. This statement would be invalid without the parentheses unless `X` and `Y` are type `Boolean`.

Syntax or run-time errors may occur when you use the built-in functions. The argument of the functions `Chr` and `Odd` must be type `Integer` or a subrange of `Integer`; the argument of the functions `Ord`, `Succ`, and `Pred` must be an ordinal type (not type `Real`).

If the argument of `Sqrt` or `Ln` is negative, an error will occur. The result of the functions `Succ`, `Pred`, and `Chr` will be undefined for certain arguments.

Subranges can help you detect erroneous computations or data. If a value being assigned is outside the subrange, an `out of range` error occurs. The operations that can be performed on a variable with a subrange type are determined by the host type for that subrange. However, a variable whose type is a subrange type cannot correspond to a formal variable parameter whose type is the host type for that subrange.

 # Chapter Review

This chapter described how to write arithmetic expressions involving several operators and the built-in functions of Pascal. It also discussed the manipulation of other simple data types, including the standard types—`Boolean` and `Char`—and programmer-defined subranges. Several new operators were introduced, including the operators `div` and `mod` for manipulating integer data and the operators `and`, `or`, and `not` for manipulating Boolean data.

This chapter also discussed the concept of an ordinal number and introduced the functions `Pred`, `Succ`, and `Ord` for the manipulation of ordinal data types. We used the function `Chr`, the inverse of `Ord`, to find the character corresponding to a given ordinal number.

New Pascal Constructs

Table 7.14 describes the new Pascal constructs introduced in this chapter.

Table 7.14 Summary of New Pascal Constructs

Construct	Effect
Arithmetic Assignment	
`I := J div K + (L + 5) mod N;`	Adds the result (an integer) of `J div K` to the result (an integer)

Table 7.14 *continued*

Construct	Effect
	of $(L + 5)$ mod N. J, K, L, and N must be type Integer.
Character Assignment `NextCh := 'A';`	Assigns the character value 'A' to NextCh.
Boolean Assignment `Even := not Odd(N);`	If N is an even number, assigns the value True to Even; otherwise, assigns the value False to Even.

Subrange Declaration
`type`
`  Digit = '0'..'9';`
	A subrange of the characters is declared. This subrange (named Digit) consists of the character values '0' though '9'.

✓ *Quick-Check Exercises*

1. The operator _____ means real division, the operator _____ means integer division, and the operator _____ yields the remainder of _____ division.
2. Complete the following formula for integers N and M.
   N = (N _____ M) _____ M + (N _____ M)
3. Write a condition that is True if N divides M.
4. Evaluate the Boolean expression

   `True and ((30 mod 10) = 0)`

   Is the outer pair of parentheses required? What about the inner pair?
5. Evaluate the Boolean expression

   `False and (((30 mod 10) div 0) = 0)`

   What error occurs when Pascal evaluates this expression? When would this error not be detected?
6. In ASCII, what is the value of `Chr(Ord('a'))`? Of `Chr(Ord('a') + 3)`? Of `Chr(Ord('z') - 26)`? `Chr(Ord('z') - 32)`?
7. What is the value of `Ord('9') - Ord('0')`? Is this answer the same for all Pascal compilers? What about `Ord('z') - Ord('a')`?
8. Can a variable whose type is a subrange type correspond to a formal variable parameter whose type is the host type? What if the formal parameter is a value parameter?
9. If two variables are type compatible, can one always be assigned to the other?
10. Under what condition can one variable be assigned to another when they are not type compatible?

1. /, div, mod, integer
2. N = (N div M) * M + (N mod M)
3. (M mod N) = 0
4. True, outer needed, inner not needed
5. False, attempted division by zero, not detected if compiler uses short-circuit evaluation
6. 'a', 'd', 'a', 'Z'
7. 9, yes, 26 on ASCII and CDC character sets but not on EBCDIC
8. No, yes
9. Yes, if they are the same type or the one getting a new value is the host type and the other is a subrange of that host. If the one getting a new value is a subrange type, the value of the variable being assigned must be in range.
10. A variable whose type is Integer or a subrange type whose host type is Integer can be assigned to a type Real variable.

Review Questions

1. What are the advantages of data type Integer over data type Real?
2. Given the following declarations, indicate the data type of the result of each expression below.

```
var
    X, Y : Real;
    A, B : Integer;
```

Type

X * Y	_____
A * B	_____
B / Y	_____
B div A	_____
X / Y	_____
A mod B	_____
X mod Y	_____

3. What is the answer to each of the following operations?

11 mod 2	_____	11 div 2	_____
12 mod -3	_____	12 div -3	_____
27 mod 4	_____	-25 div 4	_____
18 mod 6	_____	-18 div -5	_____

4. What is the result of the expression (3 + 4 / 2) + 8 - 15 mod 4?
5. Write an assignment statement that rounds a real variable Num1 to two digits after the decimal point, leaving the result in Num1.
6. Write a procedure called Change that has one real parameter C and four integer parameters Q, D, N, and P. C is a value parameter; the others are variable parameters. The procedure returns the number of quarters in Q, the number of dimes in D, the number of nickels in N, and the number of pennies in P to make change with the minimum number of coins. C (the change amount) is less than $1.00. Hint: Use the mod and div operators.

7. List and explain three computational errors that may occur in type `Real` expressions.

8. Write an `if` statement that writes out `True` or `False` according to the following conditions: either `Flag` is `True` or `Color` is `'R'`, or both `Money` is `'P'` and `Time` is 1230.

9. Write the statement to assign a value of `True` to the Boolean variable `OverTime` only if a worker's weekly `Hours` are greater than 40.

10. Write a Boolean expression using the `Ord` function that determines whether the ordinal value for `'a'` is greater than the ordinal value for `'Z'`. What is the value of this expression in ASCII?

11. Write the Pascal statements necessary to enter an integer between 0 and 9, inclusive, and convert it to an equivalent character value (for example, 0 to `'0'`, 1 to `'1'`) to be stored in a character variable `Num`.

Programming Projects

1. A company has ten employees, many of whom work overtime (more than forty hours) each week. The company accountant wants a payroll program that reads each employee's name, hourly rate (`rate`), and hours worked (`hours`). The program must compute the gross salary and net pay as follows:

$$gross = \begin{cases} hours \times rate \ (if \ hours \ \texttt{<=} \ 40) \\ 1.5 \times rate \times (hours - 40) + 40rate \ (if \ hours > 40) \end{cases}$$

$$net = \begin{cases} gross \ (if \ gross \ \texttt{<=} \ \$65) \\ gross - (15 + 0.45gross) \ (if \ gross > \$65) \end{cases}$$

The program should print each employee's gross salary and net pay. The total amount of the payroll, which can be computed by adding the gross salaries for all employees, should be printed at the end. Test your program on the following data:

Name	Rate	Hours
Ivory Hunter	6.50	35
Track Star	4.50	10
Smokey Bear	3.25	80
Oscar Grouch	6.00	10
Jane Jezebel	4.65	25
Fat Eddie	8.00	40
Pumpkin Pie	9.65	35
Sara Lee	5.00	40
Human Eraser	6.25	52

2. Write a program to read in a collection of integers and determine whether each is a prime number. Test your program with the four integers 7, 17, 35, and 96. All numbers should be processed in one run.

3. Let n be a positive integer consisting of up to ten digits, $d_{10}d_9...d_1$. Write a program to list in one column each of the digits in the number n. The rightmost digit, d_1, should be listed at the top of the column. Hint: If n = 3704, what is the value of `digit` as computed according to the following formula?

```
digit = n mod 10
```

Test your program for values of n equal to 6, 3704, and 17498.

4. An integer N is divisible by 9 if the sum of its digits is divisible by 9. Use the algorithm developed for project 3 to determine whether the following numbers are divisible by 9.

```
N = 154368
N = 621594
N = 123456
```

5. Redo project 4 by reading each digit of the number to be tested into the type Char variable Digit. Form the sum of the numeric values of the digits. Hint: The numeric value of Digit (type Char) is Ord(Digit) - Ord('0').

6. The interest paid on a savings account is compounded daily. This means that if you start with StartBal dollars in the bank, at the end of the first day you will have a balance of

```
StartBal * (1 + rate/365)
```

dollars, where rate is the annual interest rate (0.10 if the annual rate is 10 percent). At the end of the second day, you will have

```
StartBal * (1 + rate/365) * (1 + rate/365)
```

dollars, and at the end of N days you will have

$$\text{StartBal} * (1 + \text{rate}/365)^N$$

dollars. Write a program that processes values for StartBal, rate, and N, and computes the final account balance.

7. Compute the monthly payment and the total payment for a bank loan, given:
   a. the amount of the loan
   b. the duration of the loan in months
   c. the interest rate for the loan

   Your program should read in one loan at a time, perform the required computation, and print the values of the monthly payment and the total payment.
   Test your program with at least the following data (and more if you want).

Loan	Months	Rate
16000	300	12.50
24000	360	13.50
30000	300	15.50
42000	360	14.50
22000	300	15.50
300000	240	15.25

   Hints: The formula for computing monthly payment is

   $$\text{monthpay} = \frac{\text{ratem} \times \text{expm}^{\text{months}} \times \text{loan}}{\text{expm}^{\text{months}} - 1.0}$$

   where

   ```
   ratem = rate / 1200.0
   expm = (1.0 + ratem)
   ```

   and you will need a loop to multiply expm by itself months times.
   The formula for computing the total payment is

   $$\text{total} = \text{monthpay} \times \text{months}$$

Programming in the Large

8

U p to this point, this book has been primarily concerned with the writing of small, "throwaway" programs that solve particular programming problems, but that otherwise have little general use. In this chapter, you will begin to consider large-scale programming, called *programming in the large*. The discussion will focus on some principles of software engineering that have proved useful for designing large program systems. You will also learn more about abstraction and its use in programming.

To make large programs more readable, you can declare new data types whose values—which depend on the problem domain—you specify. You can then combine these data types with relevant operator procedures in library modules that you can reuse.

Finally, you will learn how to use files of data with your programs. You will be able to enter program data from data files and save program output on output files. Using data files frees you from having to continually reenter test data while debugging a program. Using output files enables you to save output on disk rather than simply view it on the screen.

 ## 8.1 The Software Life Cycle

Programming in college is somewhat different from programming in the real world. In college, you are generally given the problem specification by an instructor. Sometimes the problem specification is ambiguous or incomplete, and interaction between the instructor and the class is necessary so the students can pin down the details.

In the real world, the initial specification for a software product (a large program system) may also be incomplete. The specification is clarified through extensive interaction between the prospective users of the software and its designers (called *system analysts*). Through this interaction, the software designers determine precisely what the users want the proposed software to do, and the users determine what to expect from the software product. Although it may seem like common sense to proceed in this manner, very often a "final" software product does not perform as expected. The reason is usually a communication gap between those responsible for the product's design and its eventual users; generally, both parties are at fault when the software fails to meet expectations.

One cause of the communication gap is that software users often are not familiar enough with computers and their capabilities to know if their requests are reasonable or how to specify what they want. Software designers, on the other hand, often assume that they are the best judges of what the user really wants; they are quick to interpret a user's incomplete or unclear specification as a "blank check" to do what they think best. To avoid these problems, it is imperative that a complete, written description of the *requirements specification* for a new software product be generated at the beginning of the project and that both users and designers sign the document.

The design process begins as soon as the requirements specification is completed. A major part of the software design process is decomposing the complete software system into a set of subsystems. Each subsystem is further decomposed into a set of smaller programs and procedures. It is important to determine whether any procedures from existing systems can be reused in the new system.

Another critical part of the design process is determining the software's internal data representation. In college programming, the instructor often recommends or requires a particular data type or data structure. In the real world, the programmer must choose the internal representation that will lead to the most efficient and effective solution.

Once the design is complete, it is *coded*, that is, implemented as a program in a particular programming language. Some programmers may have been involved with the design; others, however, are new to the project. For this reason, it is critical that the software design be carefully documented in a report that contains structure charts and high-level pseudocode. Part of the coding task involves removing all apparent program bugs (debugging) and performing preliminary tests on each procedure, subsystem, and system. Once the bugs are removed, the coding and debugging phase is complete, and it is time to exhaustively test the software product.

In college programming, you design, code, debug, and test your programs. Testing a program in a college environment often consists of making several sample runs. Since you are the programmer and also do the testing and are responsible for correcting any bugs, the testing process often is not as complete as it should be. Once you are satisfied that the program is correct, you hand it in to the instructor and go on to something else.

In the real world, testing is a more rigorous process that is usually performed by a group other than the programmers; the users of the software product should be involved in the testing phase. It is important to identify all bugs early, because the software that controls a rocket or processes payroll checks must be absolutely free of errors before its first use. Also, a software product usually must continue to perform effectively over a long period, sometimes in a changing environment. This requirement may cause periodic updating, or *maintenance*, of the program to correct new errors or to incorporate changes, for example, revised tax laws.

The *software life cycle* described above consists of at least the following phases:

1. Requirements specification
2. Design
3. Coding and debugging
4. Testing
5. Operation and maintenance

This cycle is iterative. During the design phase, problems may arise that make it necessary to modify the requirements specification. Any such changes require approval of the users. Similarly, during coding it may become necessary to reconsider decisions made in the design phase. Again, any changes must be approved by the system designers and users.

Estimates vary as to the percentage of time spent in each phase. For example, a typical system may require a year to proceed through the first three phases, three months of testing, then four years of operation and maintenance. So you can see why it is important to design and document software in such a way that it can be easily understood and maintained by a variety of users.

You may be wondering what relevance all of this has to your current course. Those of you who are majoring in computer science will begin to participate in the design of large program systems in your next course. Consequently, a major goal of the Pascal course is to prepare you to work on increasingly larger and more complex problems. Some of the techniques may seem out of place or unnecessary to solve the simpler problems assigned in this class, but it is important that you learn and practice these techniques now so you will be able to apply them later.

Exercise for Section 8.1

Self-Check

1. Name the five phases of the software life cycle. Which phase is the longest?

 ## 8.2 Using Abstraction to Manage Complexity

Beginning programmers often find it difficult to get started on a problem. They are often reluctant to start writing the code for a program until they have worked out the solution to every detail. Of course, preplanning and concern for detail are commendable, but these normally positive work habits can be overdone to the extent that they block the problem-solving process. To make problem solving flow as smoothly as possible, use the strategy of "divide and conquer" to decompose a problem into more manageable subproblems.

Procedural Abstraction

Abstraction is a powerful technique that helps programmers deal with complex issues in a piecemeal fashion. The dictionary defines *abstraction* as the act or process of separating the inherent qualities or properties of something from the actual physical object to which they belong. An example of the use of abstraction is our description in Chapter 1 of a memory cell as a storage location for a data value. We are not concerned with the details of the physical structure of memory and memory cells; we don't need to know them to use a memory cell in programming.

So far, you have practiced *procedural abstraction*, which is the philosophy that procedure development should separate the concern of *what* is to be achieved by a procedure from the details of *how* it is to be achieved. In other words, you can specify what you expect a procedure to do, then use that procedure in the design of a problem solution before you know how to implement the procedure. You have even been able to perform a preliminary test of overall design by using procedure stubs. Of course, each procedure stub must be replaced by an actual procedure before you can execute the final program.

Programming Teams

Nowadays, it is rare for a large software project to be implemented by a single programmer. Most often, a large project is assigned to a team of programmers. It is important for team members to coordinate beforehand the overall organization of the project.

Each team member is responsible for a set of procedures, some of which are accessed by other team members. After the initial organization meeting, each team member provides the others with a specification for each procedure that he or she is implementing. The specification is similar to the documentation provided for each procedure in this text. It consists of a brief statement of the purpose of the procedure, its preconditions and postconditions, and its formal parameter list. This information is all that a potential user of the procedure needs to know to call it correctly.

Normally, one team member acts as "librarian" by assuming responsibility for determining the status of each procedure in the system. Initially, the *library of procedures* consists of a stub for each procedure. As a new procedure is completed and tested, its updated version replaces the version currently in the library. The librarian keeps track of the date that each new version of a procedure was inserted in the library and makes sure that all programmers are using the latest version of any procedure.

 # 8.3 Creating a Library of Procedures

As you progress through this course, you will write many Pascal programs and procedures. Try to keep each new procedure as general as possible so you can reuse it in other applications. You will eventually build up a sizable library of your own procedures. Reusing tried and tested procedures is always more efficient than starting from scratch; each new procedure that you write has to be thoroughly tested and debugged, which requires a lot of startup time in every case. The procedures in your personal library have already been tested, saving time as you use procedures over and over again.

For example, it would be useful to have a set of procedures available for performing some common data entry operations. Because procedure Read cannot be used to read Boolean values, it would be useful to have a procedure for this purpose. Procedure ReadLnBool, shown in Fig. 7.12, reads a character value and returns either True or False based on the data character. ReadLnBool should certainly be included in your programming library.

In many situations, you want a data value to lie within a specific subrange of values. For example, you might want to enter a character that is an uppercase letter or an integer in the range −10 to +10. Procedure EnterInt (see Fig. 7.17) accomplishes the latter operation. You can easily write similar procedures, called EnterChar and EnterReal, for the other standard data types of Pascal.

Although you don't know how to declare your own functions yet, it would be nice to have a function named Cap that returns the uppercase form of an argument that is a lowercase letter. Function Cap is used later in this chapter; you'll see how to implement it in the next chapter.

PROGRAM
STYLE

Validating a Library Procedure's Parameters

Procedure EnterInt begins by checking whether its user correctly entered its input parameters, MinN and MaxN. If the parameters define an empty range, an error message is displayed and the read operation is skipped. Make sure that you carefully validate input parameters for procedures that are candidates for inclusion in a library. Since library procedures can be reused many times and by many different programmers, this extra effort can pay valuable dividends.

Exercises for Section 8.3

Programming

1. Write procedure EnterChar that returns a data character that lies within a specified range of characters. Your procedure should display an error message if the specified range is invalid.
2. Redo exercise 1 for a procedure that reads a real data value between a specified range of real numbers.

 ## 8.4 Enumerated Types

This section introduces a feature of Pascal that improves the readability of large programs. In many programming situations, the standard data types and their values are inadequate. For example, in a budget program you might want to distinguish among the following categories of expenditures: entertainment, rent, utilities, food, clothing, automobile, insurance, miscellaneous. Pascal allows you to create *enumerated types*, each with its own set of values.

For example, the following enumerated type, Expenses, has eight possible values enclosed in parentheses.

```
type
  Expenses = (Entertainment, Rent, Utilities, Food,
              Clothing, Automobile, Insurance, Miscellaneous);

var
  ExpenseKind : Expenses;
```

The variable ExpenseKind (type Expenses) can contain any of the eight values. The following if statement tests the value stored in ExpenseKind.

```
if ExpenseKind = Entertainment then
  WriteLn ('Postpone until after your payday.')
```

```
      else if ExpenseKind = Rent then
         WriteLn ('Pay before the first of the month!')
      .....
```

■ **Example 8.1**

The following enumerated type Day has the values Sunday, Monday, and so on.

```
type
   Day = (Sunday, Monday, Tuesday, Wednesday,
          Thursday, Friday, Saturday);      {days of the week}
```

The values associated with an enumerated type must be identifiers; they cannot be numeric, character, or string literals (for example, 'Sunday' cannot be a value for an enumerated type).   ■

The scope rules for identifiers apply to enumerated types and their values. Each enumerated type value is treated as a constant identifier in the block containing the type-declaration statement. The type declaration must precede any variable declaration that references it.

Enumerated Type Declaration

Form: type *enumerated type* = (*identifier list*) ;
Example: type Class = (Freshman, Sophomore, Junior, Senior);
Interpretation: A new data type named *enumerated type* is declared. The values associated with this type are specified in the *identifier list*. Each value is defined as a constant identifier in the block containing the type declaration statement.
Note: A particular identifier can appear in only one *identifier list* in a given block.

An identifier cannot appear in more than one enumerated type declaration. If type Day is already declared, the type declaration

```
type
   TDay = (Tuesday, Thursday);
```

is invalid.

Enumerated Type Operators

Like the standard types Integer, Boolean, and Char, each enumerated type is considered an ordinal type, so the order relationship between its values is fixed when the enumerated type is declared. For type Day, the first value in its list (Sunday) has ordinal number 0, the next value (Monday) has ordinal number 1, and so on. The only operators that can accompany ordinal types are the relational and assignment operators. The following order relations are all true:

```
Sunday < Monday
Wednesday <> Tuesday
```

```
Wednesday = Wednesday
Wednesday >= Tuesday
Entertainment < Rent
```

The order relation

```
entertainment < Wednesday
```

would cause a syntax error, because the values shown are associated with two different enumerated types.

The assignment operator can define the value of a variable whose type is an enumerated type. The variable declaration

```
var
   Today,              {current day of the week}
   Tomorrow : Day;     {day after Today}
```

specifies that Today and Tomorrow are type Day; therefore, they can be assigned any of the values listed in the declaration for type Day. Consequently, the assignment statements

```
Today := Friday;
Tomorrow := Saturday;
```

assign the value Friday to variable Today and Saturday to variable Tomorrow. After the assignments, the following order relations are all true.

```
Today = Friday
Tomorrow = Saturday
Today < Tomorrow
Today <> Wednesday
Today >= Sunday
```

We can use functions Succ, Pred, and Ord (see Section 7.5) with enumerated types. Some examples follow, assuming that Today is Friday and Tomorrow is Saturday.

```
Ord(Today) is 5
Ord(Tomorrow) is 6
Succ(Today) is Saturday
Pred(Today) is Friday
Succ(Tomorrow) is undefined
Pred(Tomorrow) is Friday
```

The next-to-last example above is undefined because no value of type Day follows Saturday. Similarly, if Today is Sunday, the value of Pred(Sunday) is undefined. Succ or Pred operations leading to undefined results may cause a range error or overflow error during program execution.

■ Example 8.2

The following if statement reassigns the value of Today (type Day) to the next day of the week.

```
if Today = Saturday then
   Tomorrow := Sunday
```

```
else
   Tomorrow := Succ(Today)
```

Because the days of a week are cyclical, the `if` statement assumes that Sunday is the day after Saturday. The last value (`Saturday`) in the enumerated type `Day` is treated separately, because `Succ(Today)` is undefined when `Today` is `Saturday`. ∎

Subranges of Enumerated Types

We can declare subranges of enumerated types. The following declarations specify that `WeekDay` (values `Monday` through `Friday`) is a subrange of type `Day` and variable `SchoolDay` is type `WeekDay`.

```
type
   Day = (Sunday, Monday, Tuesday, Wednesday,
          Thursday, Friday, Saturday);    {days of the week}
   WeekDay = Monday..Friday;              {week days only}

var
   SchoolDay : WeekDay;
```

The assignment statement

```
SchoolDay := Monday;
```

is valid; however, the assignment statement

```
SchoolDay := Sunday;
```

causes a `constant out of range` syntax error.

Reading and Writing Enumerated Type Values

The programmer defines the enumerated types; thus, their values are not known in advance. The Pascal input/output procedures cannot read or write enumerated type values. However, you can write your own procedures for this purpose.

■ Example 8.3
Given the declarations

```
type
   Color = (Red, Green, Blue, Yellow);

var
   Eyes : Color;
```

the statement

```
Write (Ord(Eyes) :1)
```

can be used for diagnostic printing during debugging. It does not print the value of `Eyes`, but it does display the ordinal number of the value, that is, an integer from 0 (for `Red`) to 3 (for `Yellow`).

Procedure `WriteColor` in Fig. 8.1 prints a string that represents a value of type `Color`. If the value of `Eyes` is defined, the statement

    WriteColor (Eyes)

displays the value of `Eyes` as a string. Make sure you understand the difference between the string `'Blue'` and the constant identifier `Blue`. ∎

Figure 8.1   Procedure to Print a Value of Type Color

```
procedure WriteColor (InColor {input} : Color);
{
   Displays the value of InColor.
   Pre : InColor is assigned a value.
   Post: The value of InColor is displayed as a string.
}
begin {WriteColor}
  if InColor = Red then
     WriteLn ('Red')
  else if InColor = Green then
     WriteLn ('Green')
  else if InColor = Blue then
     WriteLn ('Blue')
  else if InColor = Yellow then
     WriteLn ('Yellow')
end; {WriteColor}
```

It is slightly more difficult to read the value of an enumerated type variable than it is to display it. The next example shows one method.

∎ Example 8.4

Procedure `ReadLnColor` in Fig. 8.2 returns one value of type `Color` and one of type `Boolean`. If `Eyes` is type `Color` and `ValidColor` is type `Boolean`, the procedure call statement

    ReadLnColor (Eyes, ValidColor)

attempts to read the value of `Eyes` and sets `ValidColor` to indicate the success (`ValidColor` is True) or failure (`ValidColor` is False) of this operation. `ReadLnColor` reads a single color value from each data line, ignoring all but the first letter on the line. If `Black` and `Brown` are added to the list of values for `Color`, it becomes necessary to read additional characters when the first letter read is B (see programming exercise 1 at the end of this section).

Figure 8.2   Procedure ReadLnColor

```
procedure ReadLnColor (var ItemColor  {output} : Color;
                       var ValidColor {output} : Boolean);
{
  Assigns a value to ItemColor based on an input character. Sets
  ValidColor to indicate whether the assignment was made.
  Pre : None
  Post: ItemColor is defined if the character read is 'R', 'G',
        'B', or 'Y'.
```

```
        ValidColor is set to True if ItemColor is defined;
        otherwise, ValidColor is set to False.
   Uses: Cap (see Fig. 9.19)
}
   var
     ColorChar : Char;              {first letter of color name}

begin  {ReadLnColor}
   Write ('Enter first letter of color> ');
   ReadLn (ColorChar);
   ColorChar := Cap(ColorChar);          {Convert to uppercase}

   {Assign the color value}
   ValidColor := True;                    {Assume valid color}
   if (ColorChar = 'R') then
     ItemColor := Red
   else if (ColorChar = 'G') then
     ItemColor := Green
   else if (ColorChar = 'B') then
     ItemColor := Blue
   else if (ColorChar = 'Y') then
     ItemColor := Yellow
   else
     ValidColor := False           {valid color was not read}
end; {ReadLnColor}
```

The last line in the documentation for procedure ReadLnColor is

```
   Uses: Cap (see Fig. 9.19)
```

This line indicates that ReadLnColor calls library function Cap, which is shown in Fig. 9.19. Cap returns the uppercase form of a lowercase letter. Function Cap must be inserted in the declaration section of any program that calls ReadLnColor. ■

Motivation for Using Enumerated Types

At this point you may have a legitimate concern: Is it worth using enumerated types, considering that it is so much trouble to read and write their values? Also, if we need to use a letter code to enter the value of an enumerated type variable, why not use that code throughout the program? The fact is that enumerated types in a program make that program considerably easier to read and understand.

■ Example 8.5
The if statement

```
   if DayNum = 1 then
     PayFactor = 2.0        {double pay for Sunday}
   else if DayNum = 7 then
     PayFactor := 1.5       {time and a half for Saturday}
   else
     PayFactor := 1.0       {regular pay}
```

might appear in a payroll program without enumerated types if Sunday and Saturday are "coded" as the integers 1 and 7, respectively. If we use the enumerated type Day and variable Today (type Day), we can write this statement as

```
if Today = Sunday then
   PayFactor := 2.0
else if Today = Saturday then
   PayFactor := 1.5
else
   PayFactor := 1.0
```

The latter form is obviously more readable because, instead of an obscure code, it uses values (Saturday and Sunday) that are meaningful to the problem. Consequently, the comments in the first statement are not needed. ■

In a lengthy program, the extra overhead required to implement procedures for reading and writing the values associated with an enumerated type are insignificant. If you place these procedures in your programming library, it is easy to reuse them.

Another advantage to using enumerated types is that the creation of an enumerated type automatically limits the range of values that can be assigned to a variable. With an integer code, any integer value can be assigned unless you take the trouble to declare a subrange type. When you declare an enumerated type, you explicitly declare the set of values that can be assigned to a variable of that type. In the preceding example, any integer value can be assigned to variable DayNum; however, only one of the seven values listed in the declaration for enumerated type Day can be assigned to variable Today.

Exercises for Section 8.4

Self-Check

1. Evaluate each of the following, assuming that Today (type Day) is Thursday.
   a. Ord(Monday)
   b. Ord(Today)
   c. Today < Tuesday
   d. Succ(Wednesday)
   e. Pred(Succ(Today))
   f. Succ(Today)
   g. Pred(Today)
   h. Today >= Thursday
   i. Pred(Sunday)
   j. Ord(Succ(Succ(Today)))

2. Which of the following type declarations are valid? Which are invalid? What is wrong with each invalid type declaration?
   a. type Letters = ('A', 'B', 'C');
   b. type Letters = (A, B, C);
        TwoLetters = (A..B);
   c. type Letters = ('A'..'Z');
   d. type Boolean = (True, False);
   e. type Day = (Sun, Mon, Tue, Wed, Thu, Fri, Sat);
        WeekDay = Mon..Fri;
        WeekEnd = Sat..Sun;
        TDay = (Tue, Thu);

3. Declare an enumerated type Month and rewrite the following if statement, assuming that CurMonth is type Month instead of type Integer.

```
if CurMonth = 1 then
   WriteLn ('Happy new year')
else if CurMonth = 6 then
   WriteLn ('Summer begins')
else if CurMonth = 9 then
   WriteLn ('Back to school')
else if CurMonth = 12 then
   WriteLn ('Happy Holidays');
```

Programming

1. Rewrite procedure ReadLnColor (see Fig. 8.2), assuming that Black and Brown are also values for enumerated type Color.
2. Write procedure WriteMonth for enumerated type Month in exercise 3.

8.5 Data Abstraction and Abstract Data Types

To analyze the solution to a case study, we first list its data requirements and the algorithm. Then, we use procedural abstraction to design and implement the algorithm. The next step is to analyze a problem's data requirements.

Data abstraction is a powerful programming tool. It is the conceptual approach of combining a data type with a set of operations on that data type. Furthermore, data abstraction is the philosophy that we can use such data types without knowing the details of the underlying computer system representation. Just as procedural abstraction enables us to focus on *what* a procedure does without worrying about *how* it does it, data abstraction enables us to consider the data objects needed and the operations that must be performed on those objects, without being concerned with unnecessary details.

You have already practiced data abstraction—you have used the Real data type to represent certain numbers, without knowing much about the internal representation of that data type on a computer. The specification for the Pascal data type Real is shown in the following display.

SYNTAX
DISPLAY

Specification for Data Type Real

Elements: The elements are real numbers whose range depends on the number of bits used for storage. For example, for Digital Equipment Corporation's VAX-11 computer, the range of positive real numbers is $0.29E-38$ to $1.70E38$. Because of the nature of the representation, not all real numbers in this range are included. Type Real literals may be written with an optional scale factor. There must be a decimal point and at least one digit before and after the decimal point in each Real literal.

> **Operators:** The arithmetic operators are +, –, *, and /. The relational operators are <=, <, =, <>, >, and >=. The assignment operator is :=. The functions Abs, Exp, Ln, Sqr, Sqrt, Round, Trunc, Arctan, Cos, and Sin can be used with type Real arguments. Also, procedures Read, ReadLn, Write, and WriteLn can be passed type Real parameters.

Abstract Data Types

The combination of a data type and its operators is called an *abstract data type* (ADT). Through its type declaration facility, Pascal enables you to create your own abstract data types. You can declare a new data type and write operators for that type in the form of procedures. You can encapsulate the data type and procedures (operators) together in a separate file. Whenever you want to use the data type in a program, you can copy that file into the declaration section of a program that you are writing.

Exercise for Section 8.5

Self-Check

1. Write the specifications for the data types Integer, Char, and Boolean.

 ## 8.6 Abstract Data Type Day

In many programming problems, you need to process information relating to the day of the week or the month of the year. To facilitate this processing, you can implement an ADT containing data type Day and operators for reading and writing the days of the week.

The ADT should contain declarations for the enumerated type Day and procedures ReadLnDay and WriteDay. The ADT shown in Fig. 8.3 is separated into two sections: an interface section and an implementation section. Programmers who want to use the ADT should read the *interface section* because it contains all the information they need to know. The first line of the interface section

    EXPORTS: Day, ReadLnDay, WriteDay

lists the names of the three identifiers that are *exported* to all programs that use ADT Day and that may, therefore, be referenced by a user of the abstract data type. The next line

    IMPORTS: Function Cap (See Fig. 9.19)

identifies the one function (Cap) declared elsewhere that is referenced in the abstract data type and must, therefore, be *imported* into the abstract data type.

The specification of the ADT begins with the type declaration for Day. Users of the ADT must know about data type Day, so its declaration appears in the interface section. Next comes a long comment that describes procedures ReadLnDay and WriteDay. The comment contains each procedure's heading and documentation. We have omitted the comments {input} and {output} normally found in a procedure heading because Pascal does not permit nested comments. For that reason, we have also omitted the curly braces that normally surround the procedure documentation.

Figure 8.3 Abstract Data Type Day

```
{
  Abstract data type Day: contains declarations for enumerated
  type Day and procedures for reading and displaying values of
  type Day.

INTERFACE SECTION —

  EXPORTS: Day, ReadLnDay, WriteDay

  IMPORTS: Function Cap (see Fig. 9.19)

  SPECIFICATION:
}

  type
    Day = (Sunday, Monday, Tuesday, Wednesday,
           Thursday, Friday, Saturday);

{
  procedure ReadLnDay (var OneDay   : Day;
                       var ValidDay : Boolean);
    Reads a value into OneDay.
    Pre : None
    Post: OneDay is assigned a value if the
          two characters read are SU, MO, TU, WE, TH, FR, or SA;
          otherwise, OneDay is undefined.
          ValidDay is set to True if OneDay is defined;
          otherwise, ValidDay is set to False.
    Uses: Cap (see Fig. 9.19)


  procedure WriteDay (OneDay : Day);
    Displays the value of OneDay.
    Pre : OneDay is defined.
    Post: Displays OneDay as a string.



IMPLEMENTATION SECTION —

  Insert function Cap here (see Fig. 9.19)
}

  procedure ReadLnDay (var OneDay   {output} : Day;
                       var ValidDay {output} : Boolean);
```

```
{See user interface for documentation.}
  var
    DayCh1,                        {input - first letter in day}
    DayCh2 : Char;                 {input - second letter in day}

begin {ReadLnDay}
  Write ('Enter first two letters of the day name> ');
  Read (DayCh1, DayCh2);
  {Convert to uppercase}
  DayCh1 := Cap(DayCh1);
  DayCh2 := Cap(DayCh2);

  {Convert to day of week}
  ValidDay := True;                        {Assume valid day}
  if (DayCh1 = 'S') and (DayCh2 = 'U') then
    OneDay := Sunday
  else if (DayCh1 = 'M') and (DayCh2 = 'O') then
    OneDay := Monday
  else if (DayCh1 = 'T') and (DayCh2 = 'U') then
    OneDay := Tuesday
  else if (DayCh1 = 'W') and (DayCh2 = 'E') then
    OneDay := Wednesday
  else if (DayCh1 = 'T') and (DayCh2 = 'H') then
    OneDay := Thursday
  else if (DayCh1 = 'F') and (DayCh2 = 'R') then
    OneDay := Friday
  else if (DayCh1 = 'S') and (DayCh2 = 'A') then
    OneDay := Saturday
  else
    ValidDay := False                      {day is not valid}
end; {ReadLnDay}


procedure WriteDay (OneDay {input} : Day);

{See user interface for documentation.}
begin {WriteDay}
  if OneDay = Sunday then
    Write ('Sunday')
  else if OneDay = Monday then
    Write ('Monday')
  else if OneDay = Tuesday then
    Write ('Tuesday')
  else if OneDay = Wednesday then
    Write ('Wednesday')
  else if OneDay = Thursday then
    Write ('Thursday')
  else if OneDay = Friday then
    Write ('Friday')
  else if OneDay = Saturday then
    Write ('Saturday')
end; {WriteDay}
```

Because users of ADT Day do not need to know the details of the procedure implementations, those details are provided in the *implementation section*, which follows the interface section. The procedure declarations are preceded by a comment that reminds users to insert the function Cap, which is called by procedure ReadLnDay. Because of space limitations, we have omitted the procedure documentation, which already appears in the interface section.

Using Abstract Type Day

You should save the complete ADT shown Fig. 8.3 as a file on disk. But first, make sure you insert function Cap where indicated in the implementation section. When you use ADT Day in a new program, this file can be read from disk and inserted in the declaration part of the new program. Place the declaration for type Day so that it appears with the other type declarations in the new program and precedes the declaration of any variable of type Day. The declarations for ReadLnDay and WriteDay should appear with the other procedure declarations. If your compiler allows procedures to be declared before variables, you can insert the entire abstract data type right after the last type declaration in the new program. This is nonstandard, however, and is not possible on all Pascal compilers.

Some Pascal compilers have *compiler directives*, which are special lines inserted into a program file that provide instructions to the compiler. Often, a compiler directive instructs the compiler to include a previously saved file into another file that is being compiled. For example, in VAX-Pascal (implemented on Digital Equipment Corporation VAX computers), the line

```
%Include 'Day.ADT'
```

instructs the compiler to include file Day.ADT at the point where this comment appears in the program being compiled. The lines in file Day.ADT are then inserted and translated and any syntax errors are displayed.

Alternatively, some compilers allow you to compile source files that are not complete Pascal programs. In that case, a file containing Pascal code similar to the one shown in Fig. 8.3 could be compiled as a separate program unit, resulting in an object file that would be saved on disk. You could then write a new program using ADT Day without including this code in your program. After compiling the new program and the file containing ADT Day, you could instruct the computer to link the two object files. The *link step* fills in missing parts of instructions in the new program that reference objects declared in the ADT. You could then load the file created by the link step into memory and run it.

For our purposes, assume that the exportable items in the disk file for ADT Day must be inserted directly into the source file of any new program that uses it. Comments such as

```
{Insert data type Day from ADT Day.}
{Insert procedures ReadLnDay and WriteDay from ADT Day.}
```

will remind you to do this; perform the insertion manually or use a compiler directive if one is available on your system.

■ Example 8.6

The program in Fig. 8.4 uses ADT Day. It reads and displays a day of the week and prints a message if that day is the first day of the week.

Figure 8.4 Testing ADT Day

```
program TestDay (Input, Output);
{
  Tests abstract data type Day.

  IMPORTS: Day, ReadLnDay, WriteDay from ADT Day (see Fig. 8.3)
}

  {Insert data type Day from ADT Day.}

  var
    Today : Day;              {input – day being read}
    GoodDay : Boolean;        {program flag}

  {Insert procedures ReadLnDay and WriteDay from ADT Day.}


begin {TestDay}
  WriteLn ('What day is today?');
  ReadLnDay (Today, GoodDay);
  WriteLn;
  if not GoodDay then
    WriteLn ('Error – no day read')
  else
    begin
      Write ('Today is ');
      WriteDay (Today);
      WriteLn;
      if Ord(Today) = 0 then
        WriteLn ('Today is the first day of the week')
    end {if}
end. {TestDay}


What day is today?
Enter first two letters of the day name> SU
Today is Sunday
Today is the first day of the week
```

The *module dependency diagram* in Fig. 8.5 summarizes the interaction between a program's components or *modules*. It shows that program TestDay uses ADT Day and that ADT Day uses function Cap. A module dependency diagram resembles a structure chart. The difference is that a structure chart shows control flow and data flow between the procedures of a single module or program system, whereas a module dependency diagram shows control flow between modules.

Exercise for Section 8.6

Programming

1. Write an abstract data type containing the declaration for type Color and procedures ReadLnColor and WriteColor (Example 8.3 and Example 8.4, respectively).

Figure 8.5 Module Dependency Diagram

279

8.7 Text Files

 ## 8.7   Text Files

Up to this point, we have written most programs as interactive programs; in other words, each program reads all input data from the keyboard and displays all outputs on the screen. This mode of operation is fine for small programs. However, as you begin to write larger programs, you will see that there are many advantages to using disk files for program input and output.

You can create a data file using a text editor in the same way you create a program file. Once the data file is entered in computer memory, you can carefully check and edit each line before you save it as a disk file. When you enter data interactively, you do not have the opportunity to examine and edit the data.

After the data file is saved on disk, you can instruct your program to read data from the data file rather than from the keyboard. Recall from Chapter 2 that this mode of program execution is called batch mode. Because the program data are supplied before execution begins, prompting messages are not required in batch programs. Instead, batch programs must contain display statements that echo print data values, thereby providing a record of the data that are read and processed in a particular run.

Besides giving you the opportunity to check for errors in your data, using data files has another advantage. Because a data file can be read many times, during debugging you can rerun the program as often as you need to, without retyping the test data each time.

You can also instruct your program to write its output to a disk file rather than display it on the screen. When output is written to the screen, it disappears after it scrolls off the screen and cannot be retrieved. However, if program output is written to a disk file, you can use an operating system command such as

TYPE *filename*

to display file *filename* as often as you wish. You can also get a hard copy of a disk file by sending it to the printer.

Finally, you can use the output file generated by one program as a data file for another program. For example, a payroll program may compute employee salaries and write each employee's name and salary to an output file. A second program that prints employee checks could use the output of the payroll program as its data file.

Text Files

This section shows you how to get a Pascal program to read from a data file and to write program results to an output file. In Pascal, these files are called text files.

The text file is the first data structure we will examine. A *data structure* is a collection of data stored in the computer under one name. A *text file* is a collection of characters stored under the same name in secondary memory (that is, on a disk). A text file has no fixed size. To mark the end of a text file, the computer places a special character, called the *end-of-file* character (denoted as <eof>), following the last character in a text file.

As you create a text file using an editor program, you press the Return key to separate the file into lines. Each time you press Return, another special character, called the *end-of-line* character (denoted as <eoln>), is placed in the file.

Figure 8.6 shows a text file that consists of two lines of letters, blank characters, an exclamation point, and a period. Each line ends with <eoln>, and <eof> follows the last <eoln> in the file. For convenience in scanning the file's contents, we have listed each line of the file as a separate line. In the actual file stored on disk, the characters are stored in consecutive storage locations, with each character occupying a single storage location. The first character of the second line (the letter I) occupies the next storage location following the first <eoln>.

Figure 8.6   A Text File

```
This is a text file!<eoln>
It has two lines.<eoln><eof>
```

A text file can also contain numeric data or mixed numeric and character data. Figure 8.7 shows a text file that consists of numeric data and blank characters. Each number is stored on disk as a sequence of digit characters; blank characters separate numbers on the same line.

Figure 8.7   A Text File of Numbers

```
1234 345<eoln>
999 −17<eoln><eof>
```

In interactive programming, Pascal treats data entered at the keyboard as if they were read from the system file Input. Pressing the Return key enters the <eoln> in this file. Normally in interactive mode, we use a sentinel value to indicate the end of data rather than attempt to enter <eof> in system file Input (<eof> could be used, however).

Similarly, displaying characters on the screen is equivalent to writing characters to system file Output. The WriteLn procedure places the <eoln> in this file, resulting in the cursor moving to the start of the next line of the screen. Both Input and Output are text files because their individual components are characters.

The EOLN and EOF Functions

<eoln> and <eof> are different from the other characters in a text file because they are not data characters. A program can read <eoln> into a type Char variable; however, the character value ' ' (blank or space) will be stored in that variable, and its value prints as a blank. If a program attempts to read <eof>, an attempt to read beyond end of file run-time error results.

If we can't read or write these characters in the normal way, how do we process them? Pascal provides two functions that enable us to determine whether the next character is <eoln> or <eof>. The function EOLN returns a value of True if the next character is <eoln>; the function EOF returns a value of True if the next character is <eof>. The algorithm in Fig. 8.8 uses the EOLN and EOF functions to control the processing of a data file.

Figure 8.8   Using EOF and EOLN to Process a File

```
while not EOF(data file) do
  begin
    while not EOLN(data file) do
      Process each data character in the current line;

    {assert: the next character is <eoln> }
    Process the <eoln> character
  end; {while}

{assert: the next character is <eof> }
```

If the data file is not empty, the initial call to EOF returns a value of False (not EOF is True), and the computer executes the inner while loop. This loop processes each character in a line up to (but not including) the <eoln>. For the data file shown in Fig. 8.6, the first execution of the while loop processes the first line of characters:

```
This is a text file!
```

When the next character is <eoln>, the EOLN function returns True, so the inner while loop is exited. The <eoln> is processed immediately after loop exit, and the outer while loop is repeated.

Each repetition of the outer while loop begins with a call to the EOF function to test whether the next character is the <eof> character. If it is, the EOF function returns True (not EOF is False), so the outer loop is exited. If the next character is not <eof>, the EOF function returns False (not EOF is True), so the inner loop executes again and processes the next line of data up to <eoln>. For the file in Fig. 8.6, the second execution of the inner while loop processes the second line of characters:

```
It has two lines.
```

After the second <eoln> is processed, the next character is <eof>, so the EOF function returns True, and the outer while loop is exited. We use this algorithm later in a program that duplicates a file by copying all its characters to another file.

EOLN Function (for Text Files)

Form: EOLN(*filename*)
Interpretation: The function result is True if the next character in file *filename* is <eoln>; otherwise, the function result is False.
Note: If *filename* is omitted, the file is assumed to be the system file Input. It is an error to call the EOLN function if EOF(*filename*) is True.

EOF Function (for Text Files)

Form: EOF(*filename*)
Interpretation: The function result is True if the next character in file *filename* is <eof>; otherwise, the function result is False.
Note: If *filename* is omitted, the file is assumed to be the system file Input. If a read operation is attempted when EOF (*filename*) is True, an attempt to read past the end of the input file error occurs and the program stops.

Declaring a Text File

Before we can reference a text file in a program, we must declare it just like any other data object. For example, the declaration

```
var
   InData, OutData : Text;
```

identifies InData and OutData as variables of type Text. Text is the predefined data type for a text file; therefore, InData and OutData are names of text files in any program that contains the preceding declaration.

In addition, the program heading must include the names of all disk files being processed. So, if program IODemo1 reads all its data from file InData and displays its output on the screen, you would use the program heading

```
program IODemo1 (InData, Output);
```

If program IODemo2 reads all its input data from file Indata and writes its output to file OutData, you would use the program heading

```
program IODemo2 (InData, OutData);
```

It is possible for a program to read data from more than one input file or to write results to more than one output file. You would use the program heading

```
program IODemo3 (Input, InData, Output, OutData);
```

if some input data came from the keyboard and some from file InData and if some output was displayed on the screen and some written to file OutData. The file names may appear in any order in the program heading.

If you did not need to retain file OutData on disk after program IODemo3 finishes execution, you would omit its name from the program heading. A file that exists only during the execution of a program is called a *temporary file*.

Directory Names for Files

To access a text file created by a Pascal program after a program finishes execution, we must know the file's *directory name*, or *external name*, which is the name used to identify it in the disk's directory. A disk's directory lists the names of all files stored on the disk. A file's directory name must follow whatever conventions apply on your particular computer system. For example, some systems limit you to a file name that consists of eight characters, a period, and a three-letter extension. Many programmers use the extension .DAT or .TXT to designate a text file.

You need to communicate to the operating system the directory names of any files you are using so that the system knows the correspondence between file variables and directory names. This process varies from computer to computer. Your instructor will give you the details for your particular system.

Preparing a File for Input or Output

Before a program can use a file, the file must be prepared for input or output. At any given time, a file can be used for either input or output, but not both simultaneously. If a file is being used for input, then its components can be read as data. If a file is being used for output, then new components can be written to the file.

The procedure call statement

```
Reset (InData)
```

prepares file `InData` for input by moving its file position pointer to the beginning of the file. The *file position pointer* selects the next character to be processed in the file. After the `Reset` operation is performed, the next character to be read is always the first character in the file. The `Reset` operation must be done before any characters are read from file `InData`. The `Reset` operation fails if file `InData` was not previously saved on disk.

The procedure call statement

```
Rewrite (OutData)
```

prepares file `OutData` for output. If no file `OutData` is saved on disk, a file that is initially empty (that is, `OutData` has no characters) is created. If a file `OutData` is already saved on disk, its file position pointer moves to the beginning of the file. Any program output replaces the old data associated with file `OutData` and all old data are lost. You do not have to prepare the system files `Input` or `Output` for processing.

To read and process a file a second time in the same program run, perform the `Reset` operation again. A program can also read and echo print (to the screen) an output file it creates by calling the `Reset` procedure with the newly created file as its parameter. The `Reset` operation prepares this file for input, and your program can then read data from that file and display it.

Reset Procedure

Form: `Reset` (*infile*)
Interpretation: File *infile* is prepared for input and the file position pointer for *infile* is moved to the first file component. The `Reset` operation is automatically performed on system file `Input`, so `Reset (Input)` is not required.

Rewrite Procedure

Form: `Rewrite` (*outfile*)
Interpretation: File *outfile* is prepared for output and *outfile* is initialized to an empty file. Any data previously associated with file *outfile* are lost. The `Rewrite` operation is automatically performed on system file `Output`, so `Rewrite (Output)` is not required.

Using Reset and Rewrite to Specify Directory Names

Some Pascal systems use the `Reset` and `Rewrite` procedures to associate a file name used in a Pascal program with that file's directory name. For example, the procedure call statements

```
Reset (InData, 'InData.DAT');
Rewrite (OutData, 'OutFile.DAT');
```

specify that file variable InData corresponds to disk file InData.DAT and that file variable OutData corresponds to disk file OutData.DAT. This use of Reset and Rewrite is nonstandard, however, and may not be supported on your system.

Reading and Writing a Text File

You've learned how to declare a text file and how to prepare one for processing. All that remains is to find out how to instruct the computer to read data from an input file or to write program results to an output file.

If NextCh is a type Char variable, we know that the procedure call statement

```
Read (NextCh)
```

reads the next data character typed at the keyboard into NextCh. This is really an abbreviation for the procedure call statement

```
Read (Input, NextCh)
```

which has the same effect. The first parameter for a Read (or ReadLn) operation should be a file name. However, the file name may be omitted if it is the file Input.

The statement

```
Read (InData, NextCh)
```

reads the next character from file InData into NextCh, where the next character is the one selected by the file position pointer. The computer automatically advances the file position pointer after each read operation. Remember to prepare InData for input using Reset before the first read operation.

In a similar manner, the procedure call statements

```
Write (Ch)          Write (Output, Ch)
```

display the value of Ch on the screen. The statement

```
Write (OutData, Ch)
```

writes the value of Ch to the end of file OutData. Remember to prepare OutData for output using Rewrite before the first call to procedure Write.

■ Example 8.7

It is a good idea to have a backup or duplicate copy of a file in case the original file data are lost. Even though many operating systems provide a command that copies a file, we will write our own Pascal program to do this. Program CopyFile in Fig. 8.9 copies each character in file InData to file OutData. The program heading lists the three text files that are processed, including file Output (the screen).

Figure 8.9 Program to Copy a File

```
program CopyFile (Output, InData, OutData);

{Copies file InData to file OutData.}

   var
      InData,                {data file}
      OutData : Text;        {output file}
      NextCh : Char;         {each data character}

begin {CopyFile}
   {Prepare the text files for input/output.}
   Reset (InData);
   Rewrite (OutData);

   {Copy each character from InData to OutData.}
   while not EOF(InData) do
      begin
         {Copy the next data line.}
         while not EOLN(InData) do
            begin
               Read (InData, NextCh);
               Write (OutData, NextCh)
            end; {inner while}

         {assertion: next character is <eoln> }
         ReadLn (InData);
         WriteLn (OutData)
      end; {outer while}

   {assertion: next character is <eof> }
   WriteLn (Output, 'File InData copied to file OutData.')
end. {CopyFile}


File InData copied to file OutData.
```

The nested while loops in Fig. 8.9 implement the algorithm first shown in Fig. 8.8. The data file, InData, is the argument in the calls to functions EOLN and EOF. As long as the next character is not <eoln>, the statements

```
Read (InData, NextCh);
Write (OutData, NextCh)
```

read the next character of file InData into NextCh, then write that character to file OutData.

If the next character is <eoln>, the inner while loop is exited and the statements

```
ReadLn (InData);
WriteLn (OutData)
```

are executed. The data file, InData, is the only parameter in the call to ReadLn. This is the first time we have used procedure ReadLn without a variable in its parameter list. In this case, the ReadLn procedure does not read any data, but simply advances the file position pointer for InData past the <eoln> to the first character of the next line. The second statement writes the <eoln> to file OutData. After the <eoln> is processed, function EOF is called again to test whether there are more data characters left to be copied.

Figure 8.10 shows the result of executing the preceding statement pair after the end of the first line of file InData. The next character in file InData is in color.

Figure 8.10   Effect of First ReadLn and WriteLn

```
        File InData                          File OutData
This is a text file!<eoln>          This is a text file!
It has two lines.<eoln><eof>
```

a) **Before** ReadLn **and** WriteLn

```
        File InData                          File OutData
This is a text file!<eoln>          This is a text file!<eoln>
It has two lines.<eoln><eof>
```

b) **After** ReadLn **and** WriteLn

It is interesting to contemplate the effect of omitting either of the preceding statements. If WriteLn (OutData) is deleted, the <eoln> will not be written to file OutData whenever the end of a line is reached in file InData. Consequently, OutData will contain all the characters in file InData, but on one line. If ReadLn (InData) is omitted, the file position pointer will not be advanced and the <eoln> will still be the next character. Consequently, EOLN (InData) will remain True, the inner loop is exited immediately, and another <eoln> is written to file OutData. This continues "forever," or until the program is terminated by its user, or until its time limit is exceeded.

Figure 8.11 shows the effect of executing the statement pair after the end of the second line of file InData. After the pair executes, the <eof> is the next character in file Indata, so the EOF function returns True and the outer loop is exited.

After loop exit, the statement

```
WriteLn (Output, 'File InData copied to file OutData.')
```

writes a message to file Output (the screen). (We have included the file parameter Output for the sake of consistency with the other calls to Pascal's input/output procedures.) After finishing program CopyFile, the computer automatically writes the <eof> at the end of file OutData.

Figure 8.11   Effect of Second ReadLn and WriteLn

```
        File InData                          File OutData
This is a text file!<eoln>          This is a text file!<eoln>
It has two lines.<eoln><eof>        It has two lines.
```

a) **Before** ReadLn **and** WriteLn

File InData

This is a text file!<eoln>
It has two lines.<eoln><eof>

File OutData

This is a text file!<eoln>
It has two lines.<eoln>

b) **After** ReadLn **and** WriteLn

Omitting the File Parameter in an Input/Output Operation

A common source of error is forgetting to use a file name with EOLN or EOF. In this case, the system uses file Input. A similar error is forgetting to use a file name with Read/ReadLn (file Input used) or Write/WriteLn (file Output used). Normally, no error diagnostic is displayed, so the cause of the error is not obvious.

Reading and Writing Numeric Data

When a value is being read into a type Char variable, only a single character is read, regardless of what that character might be (for example, a letter, a digit, a blank, or an <eoln>). Consequently, the file position pointer is advanced one character position. When a value is being read into a numeric variable (type Integer or type Real), a group of characters is read, and the file position pointer is advanced past all characters in the group.

When it reads a numeric value, the computer skips over any leading blanks or <eoln> characters until it encounters a character that is neither a blank nor an <eoln>. That character must be a sign or a digit; if it is not, an execution error such as non-digit found while reading number occurs, and the program stops. If the first character is valid, the computer continues reading characters until it encounters a terminating character. The terminating character must be a blank or an <eoln>. The file position pointer is then advanced to the terminating character.

Although you have not yet done so in interactive programming, it is possible to read more than one number at a time or a mixture of numeric and character data. If several variables are listed in the parameter list for Read or ReadLn, the computer reads data into each variable in the order in which it appears. The file position pointer advances after each value is entered. When procedure Read is used, the file position pointer advances to the first character that was not read. When ReadLn is used, the file position pointer advances past any characters at the end of the current data line to the start of the next data line (that is, past the next <eoln> character). Any characters skipped over in this way are not processed.

Table 8.1 shows several examples of Read and ReadLn statements and their effects. Assume that X is type Real, N is type Integer, C is type Char, and the first character processed is the first character in the file. The position of the file position pointer after each read operation is shown in color to the right. The symbol □ denotes a blank character.

Table 8.1 Effects of Read/ReadLn

289

8.7 Text Files

Statement and Effect	Next Character after Read
Read (InData, X, N, C) X is 1234.56, N is 789, C is ' '	1234.56□789□A345.67<eoln> W<eoln><eof>
ReadLn (InData, X, N, C) X is 1234.56, N is 789, C is ' '	1234.56□789□A345.67<eoln> W<eoln><eof>
Read (InData, X, C, N) X is 1234.56, C is ' ', N is 789	1234.56□789□A345.67<eoln> W<eoln><eof>
ReadLn (InData, X, C, N) X is 1234.56, C is ' ', N is 789	1234.56□789□A345.67<eoln> W<eoln><eof>
Read (InData, C, X, N) C is '1', X is 234.56, N is 789	1234.56□789□A345.67<eoln> W<eoln><eof>
ReadLn (InData, C, X, N) C is '1', X is 234.56, N is 789	1234.56□789□A345.67<eoln> W<eoln><eof>
ReadLn (InData, X, N); Read (InData, C); X is 1234.56, N is 789, C is 'W'	1234.56□789□A345.67<eoln> W<eoln><eof>
ReadLn (InData, X); ReadLn (InData, C); X is 1234.56, C is 'W'	1234.56□789□A345.67<eoln> W<eoln><eof>

Writing a numeric value to a file is similar to writing a numeric value to the screen. The computer writes the number as a sequence of digit characters. The character – precedes a negative number. The character . is inserted in a type Real value. You can specify the number of characters that represent a numeric value by using a format specification; otherwise, the Pascal system controls this specification.

■ Example 8.8

A friend has a text file that contains numeric data (all integers) and wants you to write a program that finds the sum and the average of all numbers in that file. Because your friend has not been very careful in preparing the data file, some lines contain more numbers than others. A sample file, InNumbers, follows:

```
20  50<eoln>
100<eoln>
80  42  60<eoln><eof>
```

Program SumFile in Fig. 8.12 computes the sum and the average requested and displays them on the screen. To simplify later processing of the data, it

also creates a new file, OutNumbers, that contains a single number per line. The
following output file corresponds to the preceding data file:

```
 20<eoln>
 50<eoln>
100<eoln>
 80<eoln>
 42<eoln>
 60<eoln><eof>
```

Figure 8.12 Adding Numbers in a Text File

```
program SumFile (Output, InNumbers, OutNumbers);
{
  Finds the sum of a file of integers and writes
  each integer on a separate line of the output file.
}
  var
    InNumbers,                   {input file}
    OutNumbers : Text;           {output file}
    NextNum,                     {input - each integer}
    Sum,                         {output - sum of integers}
    Count : Integer;             {output - count of integers}
    Average : Real;              {output - average of integers}

begin
  {Prepare files InNumbers and OutNumbers.}
  Reset (InNumbers);
  Rewrite (OutNumbers);

  {Accumulate sum of integers.}
  Sum := 0;
  Count := 0;
  while not EOF(InNumbers) do
    begin
      {Process each integer on the current line.}
      while not EOLN(InNumbers) do
        begin
          Read (InNumbers, NextNum);        {get the number}
          WriteLn (OutNumbers, NextNum);    {copy it to file}
          Sum := Sum + NextNum;
          Count := Count + 1
        end; {inner while}

      {assertion: next character is <eoln> }
      ReadLn (InNumbers)
    end; {outer while}

  {assertion:
    next character is <eof> and
    Sum is the sum of all integers read
  }
  if Count <> 0 then
    begin
      Average := Sum / Count;
      WriteLn (Output, 'The sum is ', Sum :1);
      WriteLn (Output, 'The average is ', Average :3:1)
    end
```

```
      else
         WriteLn (Output, 'Data file is empty')
      end. {SumFile}
```

```
The sum is 352
The average is 58.7
```

Within the inner while loop, the first statement below

```
Read (InNumbers, NextNum);                    {get the number}
WriteLn (OutNumbers, NextNum)                 {copy it to file}
```

reads the next number from file `InNumbers` into `NextNum`. The integer value corresponding to the string of digits read is stored in `NextNum`. The `WriteLn` procedure writes this value as a string of digit characters to `OutNumbers` and writes an `<eoln>` after each number. Each value of `NextNum` is also added to `Sum`.

The inner while loop is exited after the last number in a line is read because the next character is `<eoln>`. The statement

```
ReadLn (InNumbers)
```

advances the file position pointer for `InNumbers` to the start of the next line. After the last line of `InNumbers` is processed, the next character is the `<eof>`, so the outer while loop is exited and the program results are displayed on the screen.

SYNTAX
DISPLAY

Read, ReadLn Procedures (for Text Files)

Form: Read (*infile, input list*)
           ReadLn (*infile, input list*)

Example: Read (InData, X, Y, Z);
           ReadLn (InData, Ch1, Ch2)

Interpretation: A sequence of characters is read from file *infile* into the variables specified in *input list*. The type of each variable in *input list* must be `Char`, `Integer`, a subrange of `Char` or `Integer`, or `Real`. If the data type of a variable is `Char`, only a single character is read into that variable; if the data type of a variable is `Integer` or `Real`, a sequence of numeric characters is read, converted to a binary value, and stored in that variable. If Read is used, the file position pointer for *infile* is advanced past the last character read. If ReadLn is used, the file position pointer for *infile* is advanced to the start of the next line.

Notes: If *infile* is omitted, the file is assumed to be the system file Input. File *infile* must first be prepared for input with Reset (*infile*), except when *infile* is Input. An error results if EOF(*infile*) is true before the read operation.

Write, WriteLn Procedures (for Text files)

Form: Write (*outfile, output list*)
            WriteLn (*outfile, output list*)

Example: Write (MyResult, Salary);
            WriteLn (MyResult, Hours :3:1, ' $', Salary :4:2)

Interpretation: The characters specified by *output list* are written to the end of file *outfile*. The type of each expression in *output list* must be one of the standard data types (Boolean, Char, Integer, Real), a subrange of a standard data type, or a character string. If an expression is type Char, a single character is written to file *outfile*; otherwise, a sequence of characters may be written. If WriteLn is used, an <eoln> is written as the last character in *outfile*. The file position pointer for *outfile* is at the end of the file.

Notes: If *outfile* is omitted, the file is assumed to be the system file Output. File *outfile* must first be prepared for output with Rewrite (*outfile*) except when *outfile* is Output.

Exercises for Section 8.7

Self-Check

1. Let X be type Real, N type Integer, and C type Char. Indicate the contents of each variable after each read operation is performed, assuming that the file consists of the following lines and that the Reset operation occurs before each read.

```
123 3.145 XYZ<eoln>
35 Z<eoln>
```

  a. ReadLn (InData, N, X); Read (Indata, C)
  b. Read (InData, N, X, C);
  c. Read (InData, N, X, C, C);
  d. ReadLn (InData, N); Read (InData, C);
  e. ReadLn (InData, X); Read (InData, C, N);
  f. ReadLn (InData, C, N, X); Read (InData, C);
  g. ReadLn (InData, C, C, C, X); Read (InData, N);
  h. Read (InData, N, X, C, C, C, C, N);
  i. Read (InData, N, X, C, C, C, C);

2. What would be the effect, if any, of trailing blanks at the end of data lines in the data file for the program in Fig. 8.12? What would be the effect of blank lines?

If one program writes its output to a disk file rather than to the screen, a second program may use this output file as its own data file. In this way, the two programs communicate with each other through the disk file. This case study is an example of a program whose output file is intended for later use as an input data file.

Case Study: Preparing a Payroll File

Problem

Your company's accountant wants you to write two programs for processing the company's payroll. The first program will read a data file consisting of employee salary data. The data for each employee are stored on two consecutive lines: the first line is the employee's name, and the second line contains that employee's hours worked and hourly rate. A sample data file follows.

```
Peter Liacouras<eoln>
40.0  50.00<eoln>
Caryn Koffman<eoln>
20.0  10.00<eoln><eof>
```

The first program echoes each employee's name to an output file, followed by a line that contains the employee's computed gross salary. It also computes and displays the total payroll amount. The output file corresponding to the data file is shown next. The second line of the output file contains the product of the two values read from the second line of the data file.

```
Peter Liacouras<eoln>
2000.00<eoln>
Caryn Koffman<eoln>
200.00<eoln><eof>
```

The second program will read the output file and print payroll checks based on the contents of this file. For example, the first check issued should be a check for $2,000.00 made out to Peter Liacouras.

Design Overview

We will write the first program now and leave the second one as a programming project at the end of this chapter. The program must copy each employee's name to the output file. It must also compute each employee's salary, copy it to the output file, and add it to the payroll total.

Data Requirements

Problem Inputs (from Data File InEmp)
Each employee's name

Each employee's hours worked (Hours : Real)
Each employee's hourly rate (Rate : Real)

Problem Outputs (to Output File OutEmp)
Each employee's name
Each employee's salary (Salary : Real)

Problem Outputs (to System File Output)
The payroll total (Payroll : Real)

Initial Algorithm

1. Prepare files InEmp and OutEmp.
2. Initialize payroll total to 0.0.
3. while there are more employees do
   begin
       4. Read next employee's name from InEmp and
          write it to OutEmp.
       5. Read next employee's salary data.
       6. Compute next employee's salary.
       7. Write next employee's salary to OutEmp and
          add it to payroll total.
   end
8. Display payroll total on screen.

Algorithm Refinements

We will use procedure CopyLine to perform step 4. The algorithm for CopyLine
follows.

Algorithm for CopyLine

1. while the next character is not the <eoln> character do
       Copy the next character from InEmp to OutEmp.
2. Advance past the <eoln> in the input file.
3. Write the <eoln> to the output file.

Coding

The main program and procedure CopyLine are shown in Fig. 8.13. The
program uses three text files: Output, InEmp, and OutEmp.

Figure 8.13 Writing a Payroll File

```
program PreCheck (Output, InEmp, OutEmp);
{
  Writes each employee's name and gross salary to an
  output file and computes total payroll amount.
}
  var
    InEmp,              {data file}
    OutEmp : Text;      {output file}
    Hours,              {input - hours worked}
```

```
      Rate,                   {input - hourly rate}
      Salary,                 {output - gross salary}
      Payroll : Real;         {output - total payroll}


   procedure CopyLine (var InFile, {input file}
                           OutFile {output file} : Text);
   {
      Copies one line of file InFile to file OutFile.
      Pre : InFile and OutFile are prepared for input/output.
      Post: Next line of InFile is copied to OutFile.
   }
      var
         NextCh : Char;                    {each data character}
   begin {CopyLine}
      {Copy all data characters up to <eoln>}
      while not EOLN(InFile) do
         begin
            Read (InFile, NextCh);
            Write (OutFile, NextCh)
         end; {while}

      {assertion: next character is <eoln>}
      ReadLn (InFile);
      WriteLn (OutFile)
   end; {CopyLine}


begin {PreCheck}
   {Prepare InEmp and OutEmp}
   Reset (InEmp);
   Rewrite (OutEmp);

   {Compute each individual salary and total payroll amount.}
   Payroll := 0.0;
   while not EOF(InEmp) do
      begin
         CopyLine (InEmp, OutEmp);          {copy employee name}
         ReadLn (InEmp, Hours, Rate);       {get salary data}
         Salary := Hours * Rate;
         WriteLn (OutEmp, Salary :4:2);
         Payroll := Payroll + Salary
      end; {while}

   {assertion: at end of file}
   {Display result}
   WriteLn (Output, 'Total payroll is $', Payroll :4:2)
end. {PreCheck}


Total payroll is $2200.00
```

The while loop in the main program tests whether the next character is the <eof>. If it is not, procedure CopyLine copies an employee's name from its input file (InEmp) to its output file (OutEmp). CopyLine processes every other line of file InEmp, starting with the first line.

After `CopyLine` processes the `<eoln>` following an employee's name, the statement

```
ReadLn (InEmp, Hours, Rate);      {get salary data}
```

reads that employee's salary data from `InEmp` and advances the file position pointer to the first letter of the next employee's name. Next, the statement

```
WriteLn (OutEmp, Salary :4:2);
```

writes the salary for the current employee to file `OutEmp`. After the current employee's salary is added to the payroll total, the next employee is processed.

The Importance of Advancing Past the `<eoln>`

It is easy to make an error when you are reading character data mixed with numeric data. Many problems are caused by not advancing past the `<eoln>`. For example, consider what would happen if we attempt to use the statement

```
Read (InEmp, Hours, Rate);      {get salary data}
```

to read the first employee's salary data instead of the call to `ReadLn` shown in Fig. 8.13. The difficulty is that the `Read` procedure advances the file position pointer for file `InEmp` up to the `<eoln>`, but not past it.

```
40.0 50.00 <eoln>
```

When `CopyLine` is called to copy the second employee's name, the `while` loop exit occurs immediately, without reading the name, because the next character is the `<eoln>`. The `<eoln>` is processed just before `CopyLine` returns to the main program, and the next character is now the first letter of an employee's name. When

```
Read (InEmp, Hours, Rate);      {get salary data}
```

executes again, a non–digit found while reading number error occurs and the program stops.

File Parameters

Procedure `CopyLine` has two variable parameters, `InFile` and `OutFile`. It may seem strange to declare file parameter `InFile` as variable, since this parameter represents an input file. However, Pascal requires all file parameters to be variable because it is not possible to make a local copy of a complete file in memory.

Programming

1. Rewrite CopyFile (see Fig. 8.9) as a procedure where the input file and output file are parameters.

 ## 8.9 Common Programming Errors

When you are declaring enumerated types, remember that only identifiers can appear in the list of values for an enumerated type. Strings, characters, and numbers are not allowed. Make sure that the same constant identifier does not appear in more than one enumerated type declaration in a given block. It is permissible for a given constant identifier to appear in more than one subrange type declaration. Remember that there are no standard procedures available to read or write the values of an enumerated type.

File processing in any programming language tends to be difficult to master; Pascal is no exception. Remember to include in the program heading the name of each file you want to process. The name, which will be used as a file variable in the program, may differ from the actual directory name of the associated disk file. All file names must be declared as variables (type Text), except for system files Input and Output.

Do not forget to prepare a file for input or output using the Reset or Rewrite procedure (except for system files Input and Output). If you rewrite an existing file, the data on that file may be lost. Make sure you do not inadvertently place the Reset or Rewrite statement in a loop. If you do, a read operation in the loop will repeatedly read the first file component; a write operation in the loop will repeatedly write the first file component.

The Read/ReadLn procedure can be used only after a file has been prepared for input. Similarly, the Write/WriteLn procedure can be used only after a file has been prepared for output. Be sure to specify the file name as the first procedure parameter; otherwise, the system file Input or Output is assumed. An attempt to read beyond end of file error occurs if a read operation is performed when the file position pointer for a file is at the <eof>. Also, when you use function EOLN or EOF to control data entry, don't forget to include the data file name as the function argument.

 # Chapter Review

This chapter discussed programming in the large. It introduced many techniques that are useful in writing larger program systems, such as the use of procedure libraries, enumerated types, abstract data types, and text files for input and output.

You saw that there are many advantages to creating and using your own procedure libraries. Procedures are the building blocks of larger program systems. The use of procedures makes it easier to assign pieces of a large project to different members of a programming team. Once a procedure is completed and tested, it can be included in a library of procedures to simplify its reuse in other programs and by other programmers.

This chapter also described how to declare enumerated types with a list of values tailored to a particular application. The use of enumerated types makes large programs more readable. You saw how to encapsulate an enumerated type, together with its operators, as an abstract data type (ADT).

You learned how to instruct a program to read its data from a data file rather than from the keyboard and how to save the output generated by a program as a file on disk. Both features make it easier to debug large programs.

The file type Text is predefined as a file of characters. The <eoln> character breaks a text file into lines. The EOLN function can test for an <eoln>, and the WriteLn statement places one in a Text file. If an <eoln> is read into a type Char variable, it is stored as a blank character.

When Text files are processed, sequences of characters are transferred between main memory and disk storage. The data type of a variable used in an input list must be Char, Integer, a subrange of Char or Integer, or Real. The data type of an expression used in an output list must be Char, Integer, a subrange of Char or Integer, Boolean, Real, or a character string.

Use the Reset procedure to move the file position pointer for an input file to the first character in the file. Use the Rewrite procedure to prepare an output file before writing to it. While you are reading a file, the EOF function can test whether the end of the file has been reached.

New Pascal Constructs

Table 8.2 describes the new Pascal constructs introduced in this chapter.

Table 8.2 Summary of New Pascal Constructs

Construct	Effect
Enumerated Type Declaration ```type BColor = (Blue, Black, Brown)```	An enumerated type BColor is declared with values Blue, Black, and Brown.

File Declaration
``var
  MoreChars,
  MoreDigits : Text;
  I : Integer,
  NextCh : Char;```
	MoreChars and MoreDigits are text files.

Reset and Rewrite Procedures ```Reset (MoreDigits); Rewrite (MoreChars);```	MoreDigits is prepared for input, and MoreChars is prepared for output.

Table 8.2 *continued*

299

Chapter Review

Construct	Effect
Read and Write Procedures	
`Read (MoreDigits, I);`	The next integer is read from file
`WriteLn (MoreChars, 'number: ', I);`	`MoreDigits` into variable `I` (type Integer). The string `'number: '` is written to `MoreChars` followed by the value of `I`.
EOF Function	
`Reset (MoreDigits);`	File `MoreDigits` is prepared for input
`Rewrite (MoreChars);`	and file `MoreChars` for output. The first
`while not EOF(MoreDigits) do`	integer value on each line of file More-
`  begin`	Digits is written to a separate line of
`    ReadLn (MoreDigits, I);`	file `MoreChars`.
`    WriteLn (MoreChars, I)`	
`  end; {while}`	
EOLN Function	
`Reset (MoreDigits);`	File `MoreDigits` is prepared for input.
`while not EOLN(MoreDigits) do`	Each character on the first line is read
`  begin`	into `NextCh` and displayed on the termi-
`    Read (MoreDigits, NextCh);`	nal screen. The file position pointer for
`    Write (Output, NextCh)`	`MoreDigits` is advanced to the first
`  end;   {while}`	character of the second line.
`ReadLn (MoreDigits)`	

✓ *Quick-Check Exercises*

1. The five phases of the software life cycle follow, listed in arbitrary order. Place them in their correct order.

   testing, design, requirements specification, operation and maintenance, coding and debugging

2. In which phases are the users of a software product likely to be involved?
3. In which phases are the programmers and the analysts likely to be involved?
4. Which phase lasts the longest?
5. Explain the difference between a subrange type and an enumerated type.
6. Can you declare a subrange whose host type is an enumerated type?
7. What is wrong with the following enumerated type declaration?

   ```
   type Prime = (2, 3, 5, 7, 9, 11, 13);
   ```

8. Name the two sections of an abstract data type. Where is the data type declaration found? Where are the procedure declarations found?
9. The _____ operation prepares a file for input, and the _____ operation prepares it for output.

10. A _____ separates a _____ file into lines, and the _____ appears at the end of a file.
11. Correct the following segment:

```
Reset (Number);
while not EOF do
   Read (InFile, Number);
```

Answers to Quick-Check Exercises

1. Requirements specification, design, coding and debugging, testing, operation and maintenance
2. Requirements specification, testing, operation and maintenance
3. All phases
4. Operation and maintenance
5. A subrange type is a subset of values of a previously declared ordinal type; an enumerated type is an ordinal type whose values are identifiers not previously declared.
6. Yes
7. Integers cannot be used as enumerated type values.
8. Interface and implementation sections, interface, implementation
9. Reset, Rewrite
10. <eoln>, text, <eof>
11. Reset (InFile);
    while not EOF(InFile) do
       Read (InFile, Number);

Review Questions

1. Write an enumerated type declaration for `Fiscal` as the months from `July` through `June`. Declare the subrange `Winter` as `December` through `February`.
2. Write an abstract data type for the positions on a baseball team (pitcher, catcher, infield, outfield) and operators to read and write those positions.
3. List three advantages to using files for input and output as opposed to the standard input and output you have used thus far in this course.
4. Where are files stored?
5. Explain why a file may have two distinct names. What conventions are followed for choosing each name? Which name appears in the program heading? Which name appears in the file variable declaration? Which name appears in an operating system command?
6. Write a loop that reads up to 10 integer values from a data file and displays them on the screen. If there are not 10 integers in the file, the message `That's all, folks` should be displayed after the last number.
7. Define the terms *procedural abstraction* and *data abstraction*.
8. Which of the following are likely to occur in a programmer's library of procedures? Explain your answer.
   a. A procedure that raises a number to a specified power
   b. A procedure that writes the user instructions for a particular program
   c. A procedure that displays the message `HI MOM` in block letters
   d. A procedure that displays the block letter `M`

Programming Projects

1. Write an abstract data type that consists of data type MyColor and operators for reading and writing the colors (red, yellow, green, blue, black, and white).
2. Write a program to read in a collection of positive integers and print all divisors of each, except for 1 and the number itself. If the number has no divisors, print a message indicating that it is prime.
3. Each month, a bank customer deposits $50 into a savings account. The account earns 6.5 percent interest, calculated on a quarterly basis (one-fourth of 6.5 percent every three months). Write a program to compute the total investment, total amount in the account, and the interest accrued for each of the 120 months of a 10-year period. Assume that the rate is applied to all funds in the account at the end of a quarter, regardless of when the deposits were made.

    Print all values accurate to two decimal places. The table printed by your program should begin as follows:

MONTH	INVESTMENT	NEW AMOUNT	INTEREST	TOTAL SAVINGS
1	50.00	50.00	0.00	50.00
2	100.00	100.00	0.00	100.00
3	150.00	150.00	2.44	152.44
4	200.00	202.44	0.00	202.44
5	250.00	252.44	0.00	252.44
6	300.00	302.44	4.91	307.35
7	350.00	357.35	0.00	357.35

4. Read in a positive integer value and determine the following information about it.
    a. Is it a multiple of 7, 11, or 13?
    b. Is the sum of the digits odd or even?
    c. What is the square root value?
    d. Is it a prime number?
   You should have at least four procedures and label all output. Test your program with the following values:

       104 3773 13 121 77 3075

5. Write a program that reads several lines from a data file and prints each word of the file on a separate line of an output file, followed by a count of the number of letters in that word. After all lines are processed, the program should display the number of words processed. Assume that words are separated by one or more blanks. Include a procedure, SkipBlanks, that skips over a sequence of blanks between words. Modify your solution to display the number of data lines read.
6. Whatsamata U. offers a service to its faculty in computing grades at the end of each semester. A program processes three weighted test scores and calculates a student's average and letter grade (an A is 90-100, a B is 80-89, etc.). Read the student data from a file and write each student's ID number, test score, average, and grade to an output file.

    Write a program to provide this valuable service. The data will consist of the three test weights followed by three test scores and a student ID number (four digits) for each student. Calculate the weighted average for each student and the corresponding grade. This information should be printed along with the initial three test scores. The weighted average for each student is equal to:

       weight1 * grade1 + weight2 * grade2 + weight3 * grade3

For summary statistics, print the highest average, the lowest average, the average of
the averages, and the total number of students processed.

Sample data:

```
0.35  0.25  0.40        Test weights
100    76    88  1014   Test scores and id
```

7. An employee time card is represented as one long string of characters. Write a
   program that processes a collection of these strings stored on a data file and writes
   the results to an output file.

   a. Compute gross pay using the formula

   $$gross = regular\ hours \times rate + overtime\ hours \times 1.5 \times rate$$

   b. Compute net pay by subtracting the following deductions:

   $federal\ tax = .14 \times (gross - 13 \times dependents)$
   $Social\ Security = 0.052 \times gross$
   $city\ tax = 4\%$ of $gross$ if employee works in the city
   $union\ dues = 6.75\%$ of $gross$ for union member

   The data string for each employee takes up forty-two positions:

Positions	Data
1-10	Employee's last name
11-20	Employee's first name
21	C for city office or S for suburban office
22	U for union or N for nonunion
23-26	Employee's identification number
27	Blank
28-29	Number of regular hours (a whole number)
30	Blank
31-36	Hourly rate (dollars and cents)
37	Blank
38-39	Number of dependents
40	Blank
41-42	Number of overtime hours (a whole number)

More Control Statements

9

This chapter introduces more control statements. You are already familiar with how to use the `if` statement to implement decisions; the `case` statement is another way to select among several alternative tasks.

We also introduce two new loop forms: the `for` loop and the `repeat` loop. We discuss the relative advantages of each of the three loop forms (`while`, `for`, and `repeat`) and determine when it is best to use each form. We also reexamine nested control structures, especially nested loops, and demonstrate how to use them.

So far, you have used the standard Pascal functions to simplify computations. In this chapter, you will see how to declare and use your own functions.

9.1   The case Statement

The `case` statement is used in Pascal to select one of several alternatives. It is especially useful when the selection is based on the value of a single variable or a simple expression. This variable or expression must be an ordinal type.

■ Example 9.1

The `case` statement

```
case MomOrDad of
   'M', 'm' : WriteLn ('Hello Mom - Happy Mother''s Day');
   'D', 'd' : WriteLn ('Hello Dad - Happy Father''s Day')
end   {case}
```

behaves the same as the following `if` statement when the character stored in `MomOrDad` is one of the four letters listed (`M`, `m`, `D`, or `d`).

```
if (MomOrDad = 'M') or (MomOrDad = 'm') then
   WriteLn ('Hello Mom - Happy Mother''s Day')
else if (MomOrDad = 'D') or (MomOrDad = 'd') then
   WriteLn ('Hello Dad - Happy Father''s Day')
```

The message displayed by the `case` statement depends on the value of the *case selector* `MomOrDad` (type `Char`). If the case selector value is `'M'` or `'m'`, the first message is displayed. If the *case selector* value is `'D'` or `'d'`, the second message is displayed. The lists `'M'`, `'m'` and `'D'`, `'d'` are called *case labels*.   ■

■ Example 9.2

Procedure `WriteDay` in Fig. 9.1 uses a `case` statement to print a string that indicates the value of a variable whose type is the enumerated type `Day`. This procedure is more readable and efficient than the one shown in Fig. 8.3.

Figure 9.1   Procedure WriteDay

```
procedure WriteDay (OneDay {input} : Day);
{
  Displays the value of OneDay.
  Pre : OneDay is defined.
```

```
    Post: Displays OneDay as a string.
}
begin {WriteDay}
  case OneDay of
    Sunday    : WriteLn ('Sunday');
    Monday    : WriteLn ('Monday');
    Tuesday   : WriteLn ('Tuesday');
    Wednesday : WriteLn ('Wednesday');
    Thursday  : WriteLn ('Thursday');
    Friday    : WriteLn ('Friday');
    Saturday  : WriteLn ('Saturday')
  end {case}
end; {WriteDay}
```

Seven alternatives are shown in Fig. 9.1; the value of OneDay (type Day) is used to select one of those alternatives for execution. The seven possible values of OneDay are listed as case labels to the left of each colon; the task for that case label follows the colon. After the WriteLn statement selected is executed, the case statement and the procedure are exited. ∎

A common error is the use of a string such as 'Sunday' as a case label. This causes a syntax error such as identifier expected or illegal character in identifier. It is important to remember that only ordinal values (that is, characters or integers) or ordinal constants (that is, identifiers) may appear in case labels.

∎ Example 9.3

The following case statement could be used to compute the numeric value of the hexadecimal digit stored in HexDigit (type Char). In the hexadecimal number systems, the valid "digits" are the character values 0 through 9 and A through F. The character values 0 through 9 have the numeric values 0 through 9; the character values A through F have the numeric values 10 (for 'A') through 15 (for 'F').

```
case HexDigit of
    '0','1','2','3','4','5','6','7','8','9' :
              Decimal := Ord(HexDigit) - Ord('0');
    'A','B','C','D','E','F' :
              Decimal := Ord(HexDigit) - Ord('A') + 10
end {case}
```

This case statement causes the first assignment statement to be executed when HexDigit is one of the digits 0 through 9. The assignment statement

```
Decimal := Ord(HexDigit) - Ord('A') + 10
```

executes when HexDigit is one of the letters A through F. Assuming that the letters are consecutive characters (as in the ASCII character set), this statement assigns to Decimal a value from 10 (for A) to 15 (for F). If the value of HexDigit is not listed in either of the preceding case labels, a case expression out of range error occurs, and program execution stops. (You cannot abbreviate either case label list as a subrange; in other words, '0'..'9' and 'A'..'F' are invalid case labels.) ∎

■ **Example 9.4**

Your professor uses the case statement in Fig. 9.2 in a student transcript program that computes grade point average (GPA). For each case shown, the total points (Points) earned toward the GPA increase by an amount based on the letter grade (Grade); the total credits earned towards graduation (Grad- Credits) increase by one if the course is passed. Assuming that the letters are in consecutive order, the expression

```
Ord('A') - Ord(Grade) + 4
```

evaluates to 4 when Grade is A, 3 when Grade is B, etc.

Figure 9.2 case Statement for Student Transcript Program

```
case Grade of
  'A', 'B', 'C', 'D' :
      begin
         Points := Points + (Ord('A') - Ord(Grade) + 4);
         GradCredits := GradCredits + 1
      end;
  'P' : GradCredits := GradCredits + 1;
  'F', 'I', 'W' : {no points or credits}
end {case}
```

In Fig. 9.2, grades of A through D earn variable numbers of points (4 for an A, 3 for a B, etc.) and 1 graduation credit each. A grade of P (Pass) earns 1 graduation credit, and grades of F (Fail), I (Incomplete), or W (Withdrawal) earn no graduation credit and no points. The last case must be listed to prevent a case expression out of range error, even though no points or credits are earned when Grade has one of those values. ■

The case statement is described in the next display.

SYNTAX
DISPLAY

case Statement

Form: case *selector* of
                 label$_1$: *statement*$_1$;
                 label$_2$: *statement*$_2$;
                                 .

                                 .

                                 .

                 label$_n$: *statement*$_n$
              end

Example: case N of
                 1, 2 : WriteLn ('Buckle my shoe');
                 3, 4 : WriteLn ('Shut the door');
                 5, 6 : WriteLn ('Pick up sticks')
              end

Interpretation: The *selector* expression is evaluated and compared to each case label. Each *label*ᵢ is a list of one or more possible values for the *selector*, separated by commas. Only one *statement*ᵢ is executed; if the *selector* value is listed in *label*ᵢ, *statement*ᵢ is executed. Control is then passed to the first statement following end. Each *statement*ᵢ may be a single or a compound Pascal statement.

Note 1: If the value of the *selector* is not listed in any case label, an error message is printed and program execution stops.

Note 2: A particular *selector* value may appear in, at most, one case label.

Note 3: The type of each *selector* value must correspond to the type of the selector expression.

Note 4: Any ordinal data type is permitted as the *selector* type.

As indicated in note 1 of the case statement display, an error message is printed if the selector value does not match a case label. Consequently, all possible values of the selector must be listed in exactly one case label. If no action is to be performed for a particular case label, this is indicated by placing the semicolon, or end (for the last case), immediately following the colon.

Each *statement*ᵢ, except the last one, should be followed by a semicolon; the last statement is followed by the word end. There is no corresponding begin for a case statement.

As mentioned earlier, a case expression out of range error occurs when the case selector value is not present. You will learn how to protect against this error later.

Comparison of Nested if Statements and the case Statement

You can use nested if statements, more general than the case statement, to implement a multiple-alternative decision. The case statement, however, is more readable and should be used whenever practical. Case labels that contain type Real values or strings are not permitted.

You should use the case statement when each case label contains a list of values of reasonable size (ten or less). However, if the number of values in a case selector is large or there are large gaps in those values, use a nested if statement. You should also use a nested if statement when a case expression out of range error is possible because of a large number of values that require no action to be taken.

Exercises for Section 9.1

Self-Check

1. Write an if statement that corresponds to the following case statement:

```
case X > Y of
  True  : WriteLn ('X greater');
```

```
       False : WriteLn ('Y greater or equal')
     end
```

2. If type Color is described as the list of identifiers (Red, Green, Blue, Brown, Yellow), write a case statement that assigns a value to Eyes (type Color), given that the first two letters of the color name are stored in Letter1 and Letter2.

Programming

1. Rewrite the case statement in Fig. 9.1 as a nested if statement.
2. Write a case statement that prints a message indicating whether NextCh (type Char) is an operator symbol (+, −, *, =, <, >, /), a punctuation symbol (comma, semicolon, parenthesis, brace, or bracket), or a digit. Your statement should print the category selected. Write the equivalent if statement.

 # 9.2   Set Values in Decisions

Many of you have studied sets in a mathematics course. In mathematics, a *set* is represented by a list of *set elements* enclosed in curly braces. In Pascal, set elements are enclosed in square brackets. For example, the set of odd integers from 1 through 9 is written as {1, 3, 5, 7, 9} in mathematics and as [1, 3, 5, 7, 9] in Pascal. The order in which elements are listed in a set is immaterial; the Pascal set [9, 5, 7, 1, 3] is equivalent to [1, 3, 5, 7, 9].

■ Example 9.5

The case statement in Example 9.3 is rewritten as the following nested if statement:

```
if HexDigit in ['0'..'9'] then
   Decimal := Ord(HexDigit) − Ord('0')
else if HexDigit in ['A','B','C','D','E','F'] then
   Decimal := Ord(HexDigit) − Ord('A') + 10
else
   WriteLn (HexDigit, ' is an invalid Hexadecimal digit.')
```

This statement uses the set ['A','B','C','D','E','F'] to represent the letters A through F. The set membership operator in is used to test whether HexDigit is one of the elements of this set. The Boolean expression

```
HexDigit in ['A','B','C','D','E','F']
```

evaluates to True if HexDigit is one of the set elements listed; otherwise, the Boolean expression evaluates to False.

The Boolean expression

```
HexDigit in ['0'..'9']
```

uses subrange notation to describe a set whose elements are the digits '0' through '9'. The following set describes the set of characters that may appear in a real number (the digits and the characters +, −, E, and .).

```
['0'..'9', '+', '−', 'E', '.']
```
■

Set Values

Form: [*list of elements*]
Example: ['+', '-', '*', '/', '<', '>', '=']
Interpretation: A set is defined whose set elements are the *list of elements* enclosed in brackets. The elements of a set must belong to the same ordinal type or to compatible ordinal types. Commas separate elements in the *list of elements*. A group of consecutive elements may be specified using subrange notation [(that is, *minval . . maxval*, where *minval* and *maxval* are type-compatible expressions and Ord(*minval*) is less than or equal to Ord(*maxval*)].

Set Membership Operator in

Form: *element* in [*list of elements*]
Example: NextCh in ['+','-','*','/','<','>','=']
Interpretation: The set membership operator in describes a condition that evaluates to True when *element* is included in *list of elements*; otherwise, the condition evaluates to False. The data type of *element* must be compatible with the set elements.

Guarding a case Statement

The if statement in Example 9.5 has one advantage over the case statement in Fig. 9.2. In the case implementation, if the value of HexDigit is not one of the characters listed in the case labels, a case expression out of range error occurs and program execution stops. The if statement simply displays an error message if HexDigit is invalid, and program execution continues. Next, you will see how to *guard* a case statement to prevent a run-time error.

■ **Example 9.6**
The following if statement has a case statement as its True alternative.

```
if HexDigit in ['0'..'9', 'A'..'F'] then
  case HexDigit of
    '0','1','2','3','4','5','6','7','8','9' :
            Decimal := Ord(HexDigit) - Ord('0');
    'A','B','C','D','E','F' :
            Decimal := Ord(HexDigit) - Ord('A') + 10
  end {case}
else
  WriteLn (HexDigit, ' is an invalid Hexadecimal digit.')
```

The case statement executes only when HexDigit is valid; an error message is printed when HexDigit is invalid.   ■

Otherwise Clause (Nonstandard)

Some compilers provide the `otherwise` clause as a means of avoiding a `case` expression out of range error. The preceding statement is rewritten next using a `case` statement with an `otherwise` clause. If the value of `HexDigit` does not match any of the `case` labels, the `otherwise` clause executes and displays an error message. Because the `otherwise` clause is nonstandard, we do not recommend its use.

```
case HexDigit of
   '0','1','2','3','4','5','6','7','8','9' :
            Decimal := Ord(HexDigit) - Ord('0');
   'A','B','C','D','E','F' :
            Decimal := Ord(HexDigit) - Ord('A') + 10
otherwise
   WriteLn (HexDigit, ' is an invalid Hexadecimal digit.')
end {case}
```

Exercises for Section 9.2

Self-Check

1. Which of the following sets are valid and which are invalid? What are the elements of the valid sets?
   a. [1, 3, 1..5]
   b. ['1', '3', '1'..'5']
   c. [1, 3, '1'..'5']
   d. ['1', '3', 'A'..'C']

2. Write a set that consists of the special characters used for punctuation in Pascal or to denote operators.

Programming

1. Guard a `case` statement with an `if` statement so that the `case` statement displays the category of `NextCh` as a vowel, as a digit, or as a Pascal operator. Otherwise, the `else` clause of the `if` statement should print a message indicating that `NextCh` is not one of the characters being checked for.

 ## 9.3 Counter-Controlled Loops and the for Statement

So far, you have used the `while` statement to implement repetition in programs. Pascal provides another loop form, the `for` statement, that is more efficient for implementing counter-controlled loops. You will recall from Chapter 5 that a counter variable controls the repetition of a counter-controlled loop, and that a counter-controlled loop is of the following general format described in pseudocode:

Set *counter variable* to *initial value*

```
while counter variable <= final value do
   begin
      . . .
      increment counter variable to its next value
   end
```

The next pseudocode describes a `for` statement that has the same behavior as the preceding `while` statement.

```
for counter variable := initial value to final value do
   begin
      . . .
   end
```

All manipulation of the *counter variable* is specified in the `for` statement header. These three operations are

1. Initializing the *counter variable* to *initial value*
2. Testing if *counter variable* <= *final value*
3. Incrementing *counter variable* to its next value before each test

■ Example 9.7

The following statements behave in the same way.

```
{Print N blank lines}            {Print N blank lines}
Line := 1;                       for Line := 1 to N do
while Line <= N do                  WriteLn
   begin
      WriteLn;
      Line := Line + 1
   end {while}
```

If `Line` and `N` are type `Integer` variables, the `for` statement on the right causes the `WriteLn` operation to be performed `N` times. The `while` loop implementation shown on the left is longer because of the assignment statements

```
Line := 1;
Line := Line + 1
```

which are needed to initialize and update the counter variable.   ■

■ Example 9.8

The `for` statement in Fig. 9.3 reads salary data for seven employees and computes and displays each employee's gross salary. (Compare it with the `while` statement shown in Fig. 5.1.)

Figure 9.3 for Loop for Seven Employees
_____

```
for EmpNumber := 1 to 7 do
   begin
      Write ('Hours >');
      ReadLn (Hours);
      Write ('Rate  > $');
      ReadLn (Rate);
      Salary := Hours * Rate;
```

```
        WriteLn ('Salary is $', Salary :4:2);
        WriteLn
    end; {for}

WriteLn ('All employees processed')
```

Read the first line of Fig. 9.3 as "for each value of EmpNumber from 1 to 7 do." There is no need to provide additional Pascal statements to set EmpNumber to an initial value or to update the value of EmpNumber; these two operations are automatically performed in a for loop. ∎

∎ Example 9.9

We can write procedure PrintI for the Mother's Day problem in Fig. 3.7 using the for statement shown in Fig. 9.4. This procedure prints seven lines that contain asterisks in columns 4 and 5. A blank line is printed just before the return from the procedure.

Figure 9.4   Procedure PrintI

```
procedure PrintI;

{Prints the block letter I.}

    var
       NextLine : Integer;   {Loop control variable –
                                      from 1 to 7            }
begin {PrintI}
   for NextLine := 1 to 7 do
     WriteLn ('    **');
   WriteLn
end; {PrintI}
```

The for statement in Fig. 9.4 specifies that the counter variable NextLine should take on each of the values in the range 1 to 7 during successive loop repetitions. This means that the value of NextLine is 1 during the first loop repetition, 2 during the second loop repetition, and 7 during the last loop repetition. ∎

PROGRAM
STYLE

> ### Counter Variables as Local Variables
>
> In Fig. 9.4, the counter variable NextLine is declared as a local variable in procedure PrintI. All counter variables must be declared as local variables.

The counter variable can also be referenced in the loop body, but its value cannot be changed. The next example illustrates a for statement for which the counter variable is referenced in the loop body.

The program in Fig. 9.5 uses a for loop to print a list of integer values and their squares. During each repetition of the loop body, the statement

```
Square := Sqr(I);
```

calls function Sqr to compute the square of the counter variable I; then the value of I and Square are displayed. Table 9.1 traces the execution of the for loop.

Figure 9.5 Printing a Table of Integers and Their Squares

```
program Squares (Output);

{Displays a table of integers and their squares.}

  const
    MaxI = 4;            {largest integer in table}

  var
    I,                   {counter variable}
    Square : Integer;    {output - square of I}
begin {Squares}
  {Prints a list of integer values and their squares.}
  WriteLn ('I' :10, 'I * I' :10);
  for I := 1 to MaxI do
    begin
      Square := Sqr(I);
      WriteLn (I :10, Square :10)
    end {for}
end. {Squares}
```

```
         I        I * I
         1            1
         2            4
         3            9
         4           16
```

Table 9.1 Trace of Program in Figure 9.5

Statement	I	Square	Effect
	?	?	
for I := 1 to MaxI	1		Initialize I to 1.
Square := Sqr(I)		1	Assign 1 * 1 to Square.
WriteLn (I, Square)			Print 1, 1.
Increment and test I	2		2 <= 4 is True.
Square := I * I		4	Assign 2 * 2 to Square.
WriteLn (I, Square)			Print 2, 4.
Increment and test I	3		3 <= 4 is True.
Square := I * I		9	Assign 3 * 3 to Square.
WriteLn (I, Square)			Print 3, 9.

Table 9.1 *continued*

Statement	I	Square	Effect
Increment and test I	4		4 <= 4 is True.
Square := I * I		16	Assign 4 * 4 to Square.
WriteLn (I, Square)			Print 4, 16.
Increment and test I	?		Exit loop.

The trace in Table 9.1 shows that the counter variable I is initialized to 1 when the for loop is reached. After each loop repetition, I is incremented by one and tested to see whether its value is still less than or equal to MaxI (4). If the test result is True, the loop body is executed again, and the next values of I and Square are printed. If the test result is False, the loop is exited.

I is equal to MaxI during the last loop repetition. After this repetition, the value of I becomes undefined (indicated by ? in the last table line), and the loop is exited. You should not reference the variable I again until it is given a new value. ∎

Syntax of a for Statement

The syntax diagram for a for statement is shown next.

for Statement

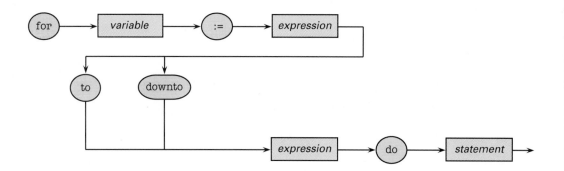

SYNTAX
DISPLAY

for Statement

Form: for *counter* := *initial* to *final* do
          statement

         for *counter* := *initial* downto *final* do
            statement

Example:
```
for I := 1 to 5 do
    begin
        ReadLn (Indata, NextNum);
        Sum := Sum + NextNum
    end;

for CountDown := 10 downto 0 do
    WriteLn (CountDown :2)
```

Interpretation: The statement that comprises the loop body is executed once for each value of *counter* between *initial* and *final*, inclusive. *initial* and *final* can be constants, variables, or expressions of the same ordinal type as *counter*.

Note 1: The value of *counter* cannot be modified in *statement*.

Note 2: The value of *final* is computed once, just before loop entry. If *final* is an expression, any change in the value of that expression has no effect on the number of iterations performed.

Note 3: After loop exit, the value of *counter* is considered undefined.

Note 4: *statement* is not executed if *initial* is greater than *final*. (In the downto form, *statement* is not executed if *initial* is less than *final*.)

More for Loop Examples

The for loop can be used with other ordinal types besides Integer. The examples that follow use counter variables of type Char and the enumerated type Day.

■ Example 9.11

The following for loop prints each uppercase letter and its ordinal number. The counter variable, Next, must be type Char.

```
for Next := 'A' to 'Z' do
    WriteLn (Next, Ord(Next))
```

■ Example 9.12

The for loop in Fig. 9.6 reads hours worked during each week day for an employee and accumulates the sum of the hours worked in WeekHours. Assuming that the counter variable Today is declared as the enumerated type Day (see Fig. 8.3), the loop executes for Today equal to Monday through Friday. During each iteration, the calls to Write, WriteDay (see Fig. 9.1), and WriteLn display a prompt such as

```
Enter hours for Monday>
```

where WriteDay fills in the day name. Next, each value read into DayHours is added to WeekHours. After loop exit, the final value of WeekHours is displayed. ■

Figure 9.6 Accumulating Hours Worked

```
WeekHours := 0.0;
for Today := Monday to Friday do
  begin
    Write ('Enter hours for ');
    WriteDay (Today);
    Write ('> ');
    ReadLn (DayHours);
    WeekHours := WeekHours + DayHours
  end; {for}

WriteLn ('Total weekly hours are ', WeekHours :4:2)
```

The examples so far use the reserved word to and increase the value of the counter variable after each loop repetition. If the reserved word downto is used instead, the value of the counter variable decreases after each loop repetition.

■ Example 9.13

A student wants a fast way to compute and print the Fahrenheit temperature that corresponds to each integer Celsius (C) temperature from 5 degrees C downto −10 degrees C. She could use the following for loop.

```
for Celsius := 5 downto -10 do
  begin
    Fahrenheit := 1.8 * Celsius + 32;
    WriteLn (Celsius :10, Fahrenheit :15:1)
  end {for}
```

Exercises for Section 9.3

Self-Check

1. Trace the following program segments.

    a. ```
    J := 10;
    for i := 1 to 5 do
      begin
        WriteLn (i, j);
        j := j - 2
      end; {for}
    ```

    b. ```
    for Ch := 'A' to 'Z' do
      WriteLn (Chr(Ord(Ch) + Ord('a') - Ord('A')), Ch)
    ```

2. Write for loop headers that process all value of Celsius (type Integer) in the following ranges:

    −10 through +10
    100 through 1
    15 through 50
    50 through −75

1. Write a for statement that prints each digit character and its ordinal number on a separate output line.
2. Write a for loop that computes the sum of the first N integers, where N is a data value. After loop exit, compare the sum with the value of the algebraic formula

$$\frac{N(N + 1)}{2}$$

and print a message indicating whether or not the sum equals this value.

 ## 9.4   The repeat Statement

The repeat statement specifies a conditional loop that is repeated until its condition becomes true. Such a loop is called a repeat-until loop.

■ Example 9.14

Both program segments in Fig. 9.7 print the powers of 2 whose values lie between 1 and 1000.

Figure 9.7   while and repeat Statements

```
Power := 1;                        Power := 1;
while Power < 1000 do              repeat
  begin                              Write (Power :5);
    Write (Power :5);                Power := Power * 2
    Power := Power * 2            until Power >= 1000
  end {while}
a) while statement               b) repeat statement
```

The test used in the repeat-until loop (Power >= 1000) is the *complement*, or opposite, of the test used in the while loop. The loop body is repeated until the value of Power is greater than or equal to 1000.   ■

Because loop repetition stops when the condition is True, the test is called a *loop-termination test* rather than a loop-repetition test. There is no need for a begin/end bracket around the loop body because the reserved words repeat and until perform that function.

Repeat Statement (repeat-until Loop)

Form: repeat
                  loop body
              until *termination condition*

Example: repeat
      Write ('Enter a digit: ');
      Read (Ch)
   until ('0' <= Ch) and (Ch <= '9')

Interpretation: After each execution of *loop body, termination condition* is evaluated. If *termination condition* is True, loop exit occurs and the next program statement is executed. If *termination condition* is False, *loop body* is repeated.

■ Example 9.15

You can use the repeat statement in a loop that attempts to read a valid data item from the keyboard. Procedure ReadBool in Fig. 9.8 is an improved version of a procedure that reads a Boolean value. ReadBool uses a repeat-until loop to read in a letter (T or F) that represents a Boolean value (True or False). Compare this to procedure ReadLnBool (see Fig. 7.12) which needed a second Boolean parameter to signal whether a valid data character was read. This parameter is not needed here because loop exit cannot occur unless a valid character is read.

Figure 9.8 Procedure ReadBool with repeat-until Loop

```
procedure ReadBool (var BoolVal {output} : Boolean);
{
  Reads a Boolean value (represented by T or F) into BoolVal.
  Pre : None
  Post: BoolVal is set to True if T or t is read, and to False
        if F or f is read.
}
  var
    NextCh : Char;              {a data character}

begin {ReadBool}
  repeat
    {invariant:
      No prior value of NextCh was 'T','t','F','f'.
    }
    Write ('Enter T or F> ');
    Read (NextCh)
  until NextCh in ['T','t','F','f'];

  {assertion:  NextCh is valid}
  BoolVal := (NextCh = 'T') or (NextCh = 't')
end; {ReadBool}
```

Figure 9.8 shows the loop invariant for a repeat-until loop as a comment following the word repeat. A set value is used to simplify the until condition. ■

Example 9.16

319

9.4 The repeat
Statement

To play the children's game Rock, Scissors, Paper, each player must enter the letter R (rock), S (scissors), or P (paper). In Fig. 9.9, if `PlayerNum` is 1, the repeat statement in procedure `EnterMove` continues to display the prompt

```
Player number 1, enter your move>
```

and to read a data character until a valid letter is entered. ∎

Figure 9.9 Procedure EnterMove for Rock, Scissors, Paper Game

```
procedure EnterMove (PlayerNum {input} : Integer;
                     var Move {output} : Char);
{
  Enters a valid move for the Rock, Scissors, Paper game.
  Pre : PlayerNum is the number (1 or 2) of the current player.
  Post: A valid move is returned through Move.
}
begin {EnterMove}
  repeat
    Write ('Player number ', PlayerNum :1);
    Write (', enter your move> ');
    ReadLn (Move)
  until Move in ['r', 'R', 's', 'S', 'p', 'P']
end; {EnterMove}
```

Example 9.17

A repeat statement is often used to control a *menu-driven program*, which prints a list of choices from which the program user selects a program operation. For example, procedure `DisplayMenu` might display the following menu for a statistics program.

```
1. Compute an average.
2. Compute a standard deviation.
3. Find the median.
4. Find the smallest and largest value.
5. Plot the data.
6. Exit the program.
```

The main control routine for such a program would follow the pseudocode

```
repeat
  Display the menu.
  Read the user's choice.
  Perform the user's choice.
until choice is exit
```

In the program fragment in Fig. 9.10, procedures `DisplayMenu`, `EnterInt` (see Fig. 7.17) and `DoChoice` are repeated until the value read into `Choice` is `ExitChoice` (a constant). Recall that `EnterInt` returns in its third parameter an integer value bounded by its first two parameters. ∎

Figure 9.10 Main Control Loop for Menu-Driven Program

```
repeat
  DisplayMenu;
  EnterInt (1, ExitChoice, Choice);
  DoChoice (Choice)
until Choice = ExitChoice
```

Complementing a Condition

Figure 9.7 showed a simple Boolean expression (Power < 1000) and its complement (Power >= 1000). To switch from one loop form to the other, we need to
know how to complement a condition.

We can complement a simple condition by changing the relational operator,
as follows:

Operator	Operator in Complement
<	>=
<=	>
>	<=
>=	<
=	<>
<>	=

For example, the complement of X <= Y is X > Y. If the expression begins with
not, remove the not (for example, the complement of not Flag is Flag).

DeMorgan's theorem explains how to complement a compound Boolean
expression: write the complement of each individual Boolean expression and
change each and to or and each or to and. Another way to complement a
Boolean expression is to precede the entire expression with not. Table 9.2
shows the complements of some Boolean expressions.

SYNTAX
DISPLAY

DeMorgan's Theorem

Form: not ($expression_1$ and $expression_2$) =
$$(\text{not } expression_1) \text{ or } (\text{not } expression_2)$$
not ($expression_1$ or $expression_2$) =
$$(\text{not } expression_1) \text{ and } (\text{not } expression_2)$$

In Table 9.2, Flag is a Boolean variable, Next is type Char, and X, Y, M,
and N are type Integer. In the complement of the expression on the first line,
the relational operators are reversed (for example, >= is changed to <) and the
operator and is changed to or. The last two lines show two complements of the
same expression. In the last line, the expression is complemented by simply

Expression	Complement
(X >= 1) and (X <= 5)	(X < 1) or (X > 5)
(not Flag) or (X <= Y)	Flag and (X > Y)
Flag and (not Switch)	(not Flag) or Switch
(N mod M = 0) and Flag	(N mod M <> 0) or (not Flag)
Next in ['A','B','C']	not (Next in ['A','B','C'])
(Next = 'A') or (Next = 'a')	(Next <> 'A') and (Next <> 'a')
(Next = 'A') or (Next = 'a')	not((Next = 'A') or (Next = 'a'))

inserting the Boolean operator not in front of the entire condition. Any Boolean expression can be complemented in this way.

Table 9.2 also shows how to form the complement of a test for set membership (third line from bottom). Programmers often make the common error of writing an expression of the form Next not in [...], which is invalid because it contains two consecutive operators (not in).

Review of for, while, and repeat Loops

Pascal contains three kinds of loops: for, while, and repeat. Use the for loop as a counting loop, a loop for which the number of iterations required can be determined at the beginning of loop execution. The counter variable of a for loop must belong to an ordinal type.

The while and repeat loops are both conditional loops; their numbers of iterations depend on whether the value of a condition is True or False. The while loop is repeated as long as its loop repetition condition is True; the repeat loop is repeated until its loop-termination condition becomes True. It is relatively easy to rewrite a repeat loop as a while loop by complementing the condition. Not all while loops can be written as repeat loops, however, because a repeat loop always executes at least once, whereas a while loop body may be skipped entirely. For this reason, a while loop is preferred over a repeat loop, unless you are certain that at least one loop iteration must always be performed.

Figure 9.11 illustrates, with a simple counting loop, the three loop forms. (The dotted lines represent the loop body.) The for loop is the best to use in this situation. The repeat loop must be nested in an if statement to prevent it from being executed when StartValue is greater than StopValue. For this reason, the repeat-until version of a counting loop is least desirable.

Figure 9.11 Comparison of Three Loop Forms

```
for Count := StartValue to StopValue do
   begin
      . . . . . .

   end   {for}
```

```
Count := StartValue
while Count <= StopValue do
  begin
     . . . . . .

     Count := Succ(Count)
  end  {while}


Count := StartValue;
if StartValue <= StopValue then
  repeat
     . . . . . .

     Count := Succ(Count)
  until Count > StopValue
```

In Fig. 9.11, Count, StartValue, and StopValue must be compatible ordinal types. The successor function (Succ) is used in both the while and the repeat loops to update the loop-control variable Count, although Count := Count + 1 can be used if Count is type Integer. Count is equal to Succ(StopValue) after the while or repeat loops are executed; Count is equal to StartValue if those loops are skipped. If an enumerated type is used and StopValue is the largest value of this type, the value of Succ(StopValue) is undefined. This could lead to a run-time error in the while and repeat versions. The value of Count is considered undefined after loop exit in the for loop version and must be redefined before its next use.

Exercises for Section 9.4

Self-Check

1. What are the complements of the following conditions?
   a. (X <= Y) and (X <> 15)
   b. (X <= Y) and (X <> 15) or (Z = 7.5)
   c. (X <> 15) or (Z = 7.5) and (X <= Y)
   d. Flag or (X <> 15.7)
   e. not Flag and (NextCh in ['A'..'H'])

2. What does the following while statement display? Rewrite it as a for statement and as a repeat statement.

   ```
   Num := 10;
   while Num <= 100 do
     begin
       WriteLn (Num);
       Num := Num + 10
     end {while}
   ```

3. What does the following for statement display? Rewrite it as a while statement and as a repeat statement.

```
for Ch := 'a' to 'z' do
   begin
      NumSpaces := Ord(Ch) - Ord('a') + 1;
      WriteLn ('*' :NumSpaces, Ch)
   end {for}
```

Programming

1. Write a procedure that reads the next character that is not a letter or a digit from a data line. Write two versions: one using `repeat` and one using `while`.

 ## 9.5 Nested Control Structures

This section examines nested control structures. You have seen examples of nested `if` statements in earlier programs. It is also possible to nest `case` statements, as shown next.

■ Example 9.18

Figure 9.9 shows a procedure that enters a valid move for the Rock, Scissors, Paper game. Assuming that the two players' moves are stored in Move1 and Move2, procedure CheckWin (see Fig. 9.12) displays the result for one play of the game. The value of Move1 determines which of the three inner `case` statements executes; the value of Move2 selects the message that is displayed. For example, if Move1 is 'r' and Move2 is 'p', the line in color executes and displays the message

```
Paper covers rock
```

which implies that player 2 (Move2 is 'p') wins this time.   ■

Figure 9.12   Procedure CheckWin

```
Procedure CheckWin (Move1, Move2 {input} : Char);
{
   Displays the result of one play of "Rock, Scissors, Paper".
   Pre : Move1 and Move2 contain valid moves.
   Post: Displays the result of the current play.
}
   begin {CheckWin}
      case Move1 of
         'r', 'R' : {Check second player's move}
                     case Move2 of
                        'r', 'R' : WriteLn ('Rock ties rock');
                        's', 'S' : WriteLn ('Rock crushes scissors');
                        'p', 'P' : WriteLn ('Paper covers rock')
                     end; {case Move2}
         's', 'S' : {Check second player's move}
                     case Move2 of
                        'r', 'R' : WriteLn ('Rock crushes scissors');
                        's', 'S' : WriteLn ('Scissors ties scissors');
                        'p', 'P' : WriteLn ('Scissors cuts paper')
                     end; {case Move2}
         'p', 'P' : {Check second player's move}
                     case Move2 of
```

```
                  'r', 'R' : WriteLn ('Paper covers rock');
                  's', 'S' : WriteLn ('Scissors cuts paper');
                  'p', 'P' : WriteLn ('Paper ties paper')
              end {case Move2}
      end {case Move1}
   end; {CheckWin}
```

Nested Loops

This section examines nested loops. You have seen examples of nested loops in earlier programs; however, the nesting was not apparent because the inner loop was contained in a procedure. Nested loops consist of an outer loop with one or more inner loops. Each time the outer loop is repeated, the inner loops are reentered, their loop control parameters reevaluated, and all required iterations performed.

■ Example 9.19

Figure 9.13 shows a sample run of a program with two nested for loops. The outer loop is repeated three times (for I equals 1, 2, and 3). Each time the outer loop is repeated, the statement

```
    WriteLn ('Outer' :5, I :7);
```

displays the string 'Outer' and the value of I (the outer loop-control variable). Next, the inner loop is entered, and its loop control variable J is reset to 1. The number of times the inner loop is repeated depends on the current value of I. Each time the inner loop is repeated, the statement

```
    WriteLn ('Inner' :7, J :10)
```

displays the string 'Inner' and the value of J.

Figure 9.13   Nested for Loop Program

```
program NestLoop (Output);
{Illustrates a pair of nested for loops.}

   type
     SmallInt = 1..3;

   var
     I, J : SmallInt;               {loop control variables}

begin  {NestLoop}
   WriteLn ('I' :12, 'J' :5);     {Print heading}
   for I := 1 to 3 do
     begin  {outer loop}
       WriteLn ('Outer' :5, I :7);
       for J := 1 to I do
         WriteLn ('Inner' :7, J :10)
     end  {outer loop}
end. {NestLoop}
```

```
             I    J
Outer        1
   Inner          1
Outer        2
   Inner          1
   Inner          2
Outer        3
   Inner          1
   Inner          2
   Inner          3
```

A compound statement executes each time the outer for loop is repeated. This statement displays the value of the outer loop-control variable and then executes the inner for loop. The body of the inner for loop is a single statement that displays the value of the inner loop-control variable. This statement executes I times, where I is the outer loop-control variable. ■

In Fig. 9.13, the outer loop-control variable I is the loop parameter that determines the number of repetitions of the inner loop. Although this is perfectly valid, you cannot use the same variable as the loop-control variable of both an outer and an inner for loop in the same nest.

■ Example 9.20

Program Triangle in Fig. 9.14 prints an isosceles triangle. The program contains an outer loop (loop-control variable Row) and two inner loops. Each time the outer loop is repeated, two inner loops are executed. The first inner loop prints the leading blank spaces; the second inner loop prints one or more asterisks.

Figure 9.14   Isosceles Triangle Program

```
program Triangle (Output);

{Draws an isosceles triangle.}

   const
      NumLines = 5;               {number of rows in triangle}
      Blank = ' ';  Star = '*';   {output characters}

   var
      Row,                         {loop control for outer loop}
      LeadBlanks,                  {loop control for first inner loop}
      CountStars : Integer;   {loop control for second inner loop}

begin {Triangle}
   for Row := 1 to NumLines do
      begin                                {Draw each row}
         for LeadBlanks := NumLines – Row downto 1 do
            Write (Blank);                {Print leading blanks}
         for CountStars := 1 to 2 * Row – 1 do
            Write (Star);                  {Print asterisks}
         WriteLn                           {Terminate line}
      end   {for Row}
end. {Triangle}
```

The outer loop is repeated five times; the number of repetitions performed by the inner loops is based on the value of Row. Table 9.3 lists the inner loop-control parameters for each value of Row. As shown in Table 9.3, four blanks and one asterisk are printed when Row is 1, three blanks and three asterisks are printed when Row is 2, and so on. When Row is 5, the first inner loop is skipped and nine (2 * 5 – 1) asterisks are printed. ∎

Table 9.3 Inner Loop-Control Parameters

Row	LeadBlanks	CountStars	**Effect**
1	4 downto 1	1 to 1	Displays 4 blanks and 1 star.
2	3 downto 1	1 to 3	Displays 3 blanks and 3 stars.
3	2 downto 1	1 to 5	Displays 2 blanks and 5 stars.
4	1 downto 1	1 to 7	Displays 1 blank and 7 stars.
5	0 downto 1	1 to 9	Displays 0 blanks and 9 stars.

∎ Example 9.21

The program in Fig. 9.15 prints the addition table for integer values between 0 and 9 (type SmallInt). For example, the table line beginning with the digit 9 shows the result of adding to 9 each of the digits 0 through 9. The initial for loop prints the table heading, which is the operator +, and the list of digits from 0 through 9.

The nested for loops are used to print the table body. The outer for loop (loop-control variable AddEnd1) first prints the current value of AddEnd1. In the inner for loop, each value of AddEnd2 (0 through 9) is added to AddEnd1 and the individual sums are printed. Each time the outer loop is repeated, 10 additions are performed; a total of 100 sums are printed. ∎

Figure 9.15 Printing an Addition Table

```
program AddTable (Output);
{Prints an addition table.}

   const
     Maxdigit = 9;                          {largest digit}

   type
     SmallInt = 0..Maxdigit;                {range of digits}

   var
     AddEnd1,                               {first addend}
     AddEnd2  : SmallInt;                   {second addend}
     Sum      : Integer;                    {sum of addends}
```

```
begin  {AddTable}
  {Print the table heading.}
  Write ('+');
  for AddEnd2 := 0 to Maxdigit do
    Write (AddEnd2: 3);              {Print each digit in heading}
  WriteLn;                                  {Terminate heading}

  {Print the table body.}
  for AddEnd1 := 0 to Maxdigit do
    begin                           {Print each row of the table}
      Write (AddEnd1 :1);              {Identify first addend}
      for AddEnd2 := 0 to Maxdigit do
        begin
          Sum := AddEnd1 + AddEnd2;
          Write (Sum :3)                {Print sum of addends}
        end;  {for AddEnd2}
      WriteLn                            {Terminate table row}
    end  {for AddEnd1}
end.  {AddTable}
```

```
+  0  1  2  3  4  5  6  7  8  9
0  0  1  2  3  4  5  6  7  8  9
1  1  2  3  4  5  6  7  8  9 10
2  2  3  4  5  6  7  8  9 10 11
3  3  4  5  6  7  8  9 10 11 12
4  4  5  6  7  8  9 10 11 12 13
5  5  6  7  8  9 10 11 12 13 14
6  6  7  8  9 10 11 12 13 14 15
7  7  8  9 10 11 12 13 14 15 16
8  8  9 10 11 12 13 14 15 16 17
9  9 10 11 12 13 14 15 16 17 18
```

■ Example 9.22

The program in Fig. 9.16 contains a pair of nested while loops that can be used to read and echo-print the data on an existing data file. The inner loop reads a line of the data file and displays it on the screen. The outer loop is repeated as long as there are more lines to read.

Figure 9.16 Reading and Echoing a File

```
program EchoText (InData, Output);

{Reads and echos an existing data file.}

  var
    NextChar : Char;             {each character in the file}
    InData : Text;               {input — the data file}

begin  {EchoText}
  Reset (InData);
  while not EOF(InData) do               {Echo each line}
    begin
      while not EOLN(InData) do           {Echo each character}
        begin
          Read (InData, NextChar);
          Write (NextChar)
        end;  {of line}
```

```
        ReadLn (InData);        {Skip <eoln> character}
        WriteLn                 {Terminate output line}
      end   {of file}
end.  {EchoText}
```

It is interesting to contemplate the effect of omitting the ReadLn statement. Exit from the inner loop occurs when the <eoln> at the end of the first line is the next character to be read (not EOLN is False). The outer loop is repeated because there are more data on the file (not EOF is True); however, the inner loop is then skipped because the next character is still the <eoln>. An endless loop results because the outer loop is repeated again and the inner loop skipped again, *ad infinitum*. If your program reads lines of character data, remember to use the ReadLn statement to skip over each <eoln>. ■

Exercises for Section 9.5

Self-Check

1. What is displayed by the following program segments assuming M is 3 and N is 5?

   a.
   ```
   for I := 1 to N do
      begin
        for J := 1 to I do
          Write ('*');
        WriteLn
      end; {for I}
   ```
   b.
   ```
   for I := 1 to N do
      begin
        for J := 1 to M do
          Write ('*');
        WriteLn
      end; {for I}
   ```

2. Show the output printed by the following nested loops:

   ```
   for I := 1 to 2 do
     begin
       WriteLn ('Outer' :5, I :5);
       for J := 1 to 3 do
         WriteLn ('Inner' :7, I :3, J :3);
       for K := 2 downto 1 do
         WriteLn ('Inner' :7, I :3, K :3)
     end; {for I}
   ```

Programming

1. Write a main program for playing the Rock, Scissors, Paper game. Use procedures EnterMove (see Fig. 9.9) and CheckWin (see Fig. 9.12).
2. Rewrite the nested case statement in CheckWin as a nest of multiple-alternative if statements.
3. Write a program that prints the multiplication table. Use separate procedures to print the table heading and the table body.

4. Write a nest of loops that causes the following output to be printed.

```
1
1 2
1 2 3
1 2 3 4
1 2 3
1 2
1
```

 ## 9.6 User-Defined Functions

Chapter 7 introduced some Pascal functions, such as Abs, Sqrt, and Ord. You can also declare your own functions in much the same way you declare procedures. Think of a function as a special type of procedure—a procedure that returns exactly one result. Generally, the parameters of a function are value parameters that cannot be modified by the function execution.

■ Example 9.23

Function Cube in Fig. 9.17 returns the cube of its argument. The function heading

```
function Cube (X : Real) : Real;
```

identifies the function name and its parameter list. The formal parameters for a function are generally input parameters, so we did not insert the comment {input} after X. A type identifier after the parameter list indicates the type of the result returned by the function. The result can be any previously defined simple data type, including Real, Integer, Boolean, Char, an enumerated type, or a subrange type.

Figure 9.17   Function Cube

```
function Cube (X : Real) : Real;
{
  Returns the cube of its argument.
  Pre : X is assigned a value.
  Post: X * X * X is returned.
}
begin {Cube}
  Cube := X * X * X
end; {Cube}
```

Unlike a procedure, which returns a result by modifying a variable parameter, a function result is defined by the assignment of a value to the function name. Within the function body, the statement

```
Cube := X * X * X
```

defines the function result.

A user-defined function is called in the same way as a standard Pascal function: by reference to it in an expression. If Y and Z are type Real variables in the main program, the assignment statement

```
Z := Cube(Y)
```

stores the value of Y cubed in Z. The *function designator* Cube(Y) calls function Cube with Y as its argument. The function result is assigned to Z. A function must always be called by including a function designator in an expression; a procedure call statement cannot be used to call a function. Notice that there is no space between the function name Cube and the parameter list (Y). ■

■ Example 9.24

Function Powers in Fig. 9.18 raises its first parameter, X, to the integer power indicated by its second parameter, N. This is accomplished by multiplying X by itself N times and accumulating the product in Product. The function designator Abs(N) ensures that the required number of multiplications are performed, even when N is negative.

Figure 9.18 Function Powers

```
function Powers (X : Real; N : Integer) : Real;
{
  Computes the value of X raised to the power N.
  Pre : X and N are assigned values.
  Post: Returns X raised to the power N.
}
  var
     Product : Real;              {the accumulated product}
     Count   : Integer;           {loop control variable}

begin {Powers}
  if X = 0.0 then
    Powers := 0.0
  else
    begin {X <> 0.0}
      Product := 1.0;                    {Initialize Product}
      for Count := 1 to Abs(N) do
        Product := Product * X; {Multiply X by itself N times}

      {Define function result}
      if N >= 0 then
        Powers := Product          {function result when N >= 0}
      else
        Powers := 1.0 / Product  {function result when N < 0}
    end {X <> 0.0}
end; {Powers}
```

If X is zero, the function result is 0.0. If X is nonzero, the for loop in function Powers multiplies X by itself N times, saving the partial products in local variable `Product`. The `for` loop limit expression, `Abs(N)`, ensures that the required number of multiplications are performed, even when `N` is negative.

After loop exit, the `if` statement defines the function result. If `N` is positive, the statement

```
Powers := Product
```

defines the function result as the last partial product; if `N` is negative, the statement

```
Powers := 1.0 / Product
```

defines the function result as a fraction. ∎

Be careful when you use a function name inside its function declaration. Normally, a function name should not appear in an expression inside the function. For example, the assignment statement

```
Powers := Powers * X
```

would be illegal inside function `Powers`. Later, in Chapter 15, we remove this restriction and see that the expression in the assignment statement

```
Powers := Powers(X, N-1) * X
```

contains a valid *recursive call* to function `Powers`.

Suppose you want to calculate the amount of money that accumulates in your savings account over a certain period of time. The following assignment statement computes the actual amount, `Amount`, in the savings account after `N` days have passed. `Deposit` is the initial amount deposited at a daily interest rate of `DailyRate`.

```
Amount := Deposit * Powers(1 + DailyRate, N)
```

This statement is derived from the formula

$$amount = deposit \times (1 + daily\ rate)^N$$

The function designator

```
Powers(1 + DailyRate, N)
```

calls function `Powers` to raise the expression `1 + DailyRate` to the power `N`. After execution of the function body, the function result replaces the function designator in the calling expression. That result is then multiplied by the value of `Deposit`, and the product is stored in `Amount`.

SYNTAX
DISPLAY

Function Declaration

Form: function *fname* (*formal parameters*) : *result type*;

        local declaration section

```
      begin
       function body
      end;
```
Example: `function Hypotenuse (A, B : Real) : Real;`
```
      begin {Hypotenuse}
        Hypotenuse := Sqrt(Sqr(A) + Sqr(B))
      end; {Hypotenuse}
```

Interpretation: The function *fname* is declared. The list of *formal parameters* is enclosed in parentheses. The data type of the function result is indicated by the identifier *result type*. Any identifiers declared in the *local declaration section* are defined only during the execution of the function.

function body describes the data manipulation to be performed by the function. At least one statement that gives a value to *fname* must be executed each time the function is called. The last value given to *fname* is returned as the function result upon completion of *function body*. This value replaces the function reference in the expression that calls the function.

Note 1: The identifier *result type* must be the name of a standard data type (`Boolean`, `Integer`, `Real`, or `Char`), a previously defined enumerated type, a subrange type, or a pointer type (described in Chapter 17).

Note 2: If there are no parameters, omit the *formal parameters* and the parentheses.

Function Designator

Form: *fname* (*actual parameters*)

Example: `Hypotenuse(X, Y)`

Interpretation: The function *fname* is executed, and its result replaces the function designator. During the function execution, the first actual parameter is associated with the first formal parameter, the second actual parameter with the second formal parameter, and so on.

Note: The *actual parameters* are separated by commas. The number of actual and formal parameters must be the same. Each actual parameter that is an expression is evaluated when *fname* is called; this value is assigned to the corresponding formal parameter. Each actual parameter must be assignment compatible with its corresponding formal parameter. If there are no formal parameters, omit the *actual parameters* and enclosing parentheses.

Checking Special Cases

What happens in function `Powers` if the value of `X` or `N` happens to be zero? If `X` is zero, the statement

```
    Powers := 0.0
```

executes and the function exit occurs. If N is zero, the statement

```
    Product := 1.0;
```

executes and the for loop is skipped. In this case, the if statement following the for loop correctly assigns a value of 1.0 as the function result.

Often a procedure or function fails for special cases such as these. It is important to identify special cases and verify that they are handled properly.

Functions with Nonnumeric Results

A function can return a value belonging to any of the standard types, an enumerated type, a subrange type, or a pointer type (discussed in Chapter 17). This section provides examples of functions with different result types.

■ Example 9.25

Function Cap (see Fig. 9.19) returns a result that is type Char. If its argument is a lowercase letter, it returns the corresponding uppercase letter; otherwise, it returns its argument.

Figure 9.19 Function Cap

```
function Cap (Ch : Char) : Char;
{
  Returns the uppercase letter corresponding to Ch.
  Pre : Ch is defined.
  Post: If Ch is lowercase, returns the corresponding uppercase
        letter; otherwise, returns Ch.
}
begin {Cap}
  if Ch in ['a'..'z'] then
    Cap := Chr(Ord(Ch) - Ord('a') + Ord('A'))
  else
    Cap := Ch
  end; {Cap}
```

If the argument passed to Cap is a lowercase letter, the assignment statement

```
Cap := Chr(Ord(Ch) - Ord('a') + Ord('A'))
```

executes. If Ch is 'c' and the letters are in consecutive order, then the argument of function Chr is 2 + Ord('A') and the value 'C' is assigned to Cap. If the ASCII code is used, we can write this statement as

```
Cap := Chr(Ord(Ch) - 32)
```

■ Example 9.26

Function `DayConvert` in Fig. 9.20 converts a number representing the day of the week (0 through 6) to a value of enumerated type `Day` (Sunday through Saturday). The `case` statement performs the conversion. In the event that `DayNum` is outside the range 0 through 6, the function displays an error message and returns to the calling expression without defining the function result. The fact that the function result is undefined may cause an execution error. ■

Figure 9.20 Function DayConvert

```
function DayConvert (DayNum : Integer) : Day;
{
  Converts a day number to a value of type Day.
  Pre : DayNum is assigned a value between 0 and 6.
  Post: Returns the corresponding value of type Day using
        0 for Sunday, 1 for Monday, etc.
}
begin {DayConvert}
  if (DayNum < 0) or (DayNum > 6) then
    WriteLn ('Invalid parameter for DayConvert')
  else
    case DayNum of
       0 : DayConvert := Sunday;
       1 : DayConvert := Monday;
       2 : DayConvert := Tuesday;
       3 : DayConvert := Wednesday;
       4 : DayConvert := Thursday;
       5 : DayConvert := Friday;
       6 : DayConvert := Saturday
    end {case}
end; {DayConvert}
```

■ Example 9.27

Janice and Guy are arguing about the number of days that will be in the month of February in year 1995. They could use the function in Fig. 9.21 to determine the number of days in any month of the twentieth century. The data types `Month`, `YearRange`, and `DayRange` are defined as follows.

Figure 9.21 Function DaysInMonth

```
type
   Month = (January, February, March, April, May, June, July,
            August, September, October, November, December);
   YearRange = 1900..1999;
   DayRange = 1..31;

function DaysInMonth (CurMonth : Month;
                      ThisYear : YearRange) : DayRange;
{
  Determines the number of days in a given month and year.
  Pre : CurMonth and ThisYear are assigned values.
  Post: Returns an integer between 28 and 31 representing
        the number of days in month CurMonth for year ThisYear.
}
   var
     LeapYear : Boolean;        {Is ThisYear a leap year?}
```

```
begin {DaysInMonth}
  case CurMonth of
    April, June, September, November :
                DaysInMonth := 30;
    January, March, May, July, August, October, December :
                DaysInMonth := 31;
    February : begin
                LeapYear := (ThisYear <> 1900) and
                            ((ThisYear mod 4) = 0);
                if LeapYear then
                   DaysInMonth := 29
                else
                   DaysInMonth := 28
              end {February}
  end {case}
end; {DaysInMonth}
```

If CurMonth is February, the Boolean variable LeapYear is set to indicate whether ThisYear is a leap year. The leap years in the twentieth century are 1904, 1908, 1912, and so on. If ThisYear is a leap year, DaysInMonth is set to 29; otherwise, DaysInMonth is set to 28. An example of a function designator that calls the function DaysInMonth is

```
DaysInMonth(May, 1942)
```

The value returned is 31. ∎

∎ Example 9.28

Boolean functions are often used to make Boolean expressions more readable. The Boolean function LowerCase in Fig. 9.22 determines whether its argument is a lowercase letter (returns True) or not (returns False). Function LowerCase is referenced in the following loop, which reads a sequence of lowercase letters and stops reading after a character that is not a lowercase letter is read.

```
Read (Ch);
while LowerCase(Ch) do
  Read (Ch);
```

A similar function called UpperCase is left as an exercise at the end of this section. ∎

Figure 9.22   Function LowerCase

```
function LowerCase (Ch : Char) : Boolean;
{
  Determines whether Ch is a lowercase letter.
  Pre : Ch is assigned a value.
  Post: Returns True if Ch is a lowercase letter;
        otherwise, returns False.
}
begin {LowerCase}
  LowerCase := Ch in ['a'..'z']
end; {LowerCase}
```

All the function examples in this section can transform one or more input values into a single output value. A variety of result types are illustrated: `Real`, `Char`, `Boolean`, enumerated type `Day`, and subrange type `DayRange`. Because a function should not return a result by modifying its parameters, all the function parameters were value parameters.

When to Use a Function Instead of a Procedure

Some of the procedures that we wrote earlier can also be implemented as functions. Any procedure that returns a single result can be rewritten as a function.

A general rule of thumb is to always use a procedure when more than one result is returned. If a single result is returned, use a function when a pure computation is performed that requires no data beyond what is provided through the parameter list.

If input or output operations are also performed, use a procedure instead of a function, even if only a single result is returned. The reason is that a function call can be inserted in an expression, and it is generally not useful to read or display information as part of an expression evaluation.

Unlike a procedure, a function should not return a result by modifying a parameter. When a function changes a parameter's value during execution, a *side effect* is said to have occurred. For now, make sure you protect all function parameters from modification by making them value parameters. (In later chapters, you will see that variable parameters can be used under certain circumstances.)

Exercises for Section 9.6

Self-Check

1. What does the following function do? Does it have any side effects? Remove any side effects and correct the errors in the function declaration.

```
function MyTest (var X, Y : Real;
                     var Result : Real) : Real;
{
  Returns the sum of the square roots of X and Y.
  Pre : X and Y defined.
  Post: Returns square root of X + square root of Y.
}
begin {MyTest}
  X := Abs(X);
  Y := Abs(Y);
  Result := Sqrt(X) + Sqrt(Y)
end;   {MyTest}
```

1. Write a function that computes the absolute difference of its two arguments, where the absolute difference of A and B is A – B if A is greater than B and B – A if B is greater than A.
2. Write a function that computes the tuition you owe for a specified number of credit hours at a university. Assume the charge per credit hour is $100 for up to twelve credit hours, and a flat fee of $1,200 is charged for twelve to sixteen credit hours. An additional fee of $100 is charged for each credit hour over sixteen.
3. Function Powers in Fig. 9.18 works perfectly well for an integer exponent; however, the exponent cannot be type Real. Write a new function that will handle type Real exponents. Hint: Use the Ln and Exp functions of Pascal.
4. Write a program that uses function Powers to compute and print a table showing the powers of 2.
5. Write function UpperCase.
6. Rewrite function Cap using function LowerCase.

9.7 Problem Solving Illustrated

This problem illustrates most of the concepts discussed in the last two chapters. The problem involves writing a file of payroll checks where the amount of each check is written in words.

Case Study: Writing a File of Payroll Checks

Problem

In the last chapter, we implemented a program that created a payroll file consisting of an employee's name and salary amount on consecutive lines of the file. Now, we will consider how to implement a program that processes this file, writing a new file of checks for each employee. For instance, if the first employee's name is Sam Johnson and his salary is $35.67, the lines

```
PAY TO THE ORDER OF: Sam Johnson
thirty-five dollars and sixty-seven cents       $35.67
```

should be written to the output file.

Design Overview

When you write a check, you indicate the amount in both figures and words. As part of a check writing program, we would need a procedure, WriteWords, that writes a check amount in words. Our program will read each employee's name and salary amount from file Payroll and write a check for each employee to an output file.

Data Requirements

Problem Inputs
The employee data file (Payroll : Text)
Each employee's name
Each employee's salary (Salary : Real)

Problem Outputs
A file of checks, one for each employee (Checks : Text)

Initial Algorithm

1. while there are more employees do
   begin
       2. Copy the next employee's name from file Payroll
          to file Checks.
       3. Write the next employee's salary in words.
       4. Write the next employee's salary.
   end

Coding the Main Program

We can use procedure CopyLine in Fig. 8.13 to perform step 2, and procedure WriteWords to perform step 3. The main program is shown in Fig. 9.23. Because we are reading and writing from text files, each call to an input/output procedure has a file name as its first parameter. The main program displays a message on the screen when it finishes writing file Checks.

Figure 9.23   Check Writing Program

```
program WriteChecks (Payroll, Output, Checks);

{Writes a check for each employee to file Checks.}

   var
      Salary : Real;              {input - current salary}
      Payroll,                    {input - file of employees}
      Checks   : Text;            {output - file of checks}

   {Insert procedures WriteWords and CopyLine (see Fig. 8.13)}

begin {WriteChecks}
   {Prepare text files.}
   Reset (Payroll);
   Rewrite (Checks);

   {Write each employee name and check amount to file Checks.}
   while not EOF(Payroll) do
      begin
         Write (Checks, 'PAY TO THE ORDER OF: ');
         CopyLine (Payroll, Checks);                  {Write name}
         WriteLn (Checks);
         ReadLn (Payroll, Salary);
```

```
        WriteWords (Checks, Salary);           {Write amount in words}
        WriteLn (Checks, '      $', Salary :4:2);
        WriteLn (Checks); WriteLn (Checks)          {Skip lines}
    end;   {while}

  WriteLn (Output, 'File of checks completed.')
end. {WriteChecks}
```

```
File of checks completed.
```

Procedure WriteWords

Next we focus on procedure `WriteWords`, which writes a check amount in words. Some examples of the desired procedure output follow.

Amount	*Amount in Words*
43.55	forty-three dollars and fifty-five cents
62.05	sixty-two dollars and five cents
15.20	fifteen dollars and twenty cents
0.95	zero dollars and ninety-five cents
35.00	thirty-five dollars and zero cents

`WriteWords` must separate the check amount into two integers, `Dollars` and `Cents`. Once this is done, `Dollars` can be written, followed by the string ' dollars and ', the value of `Cents`, and the string ' cents'. For the sake of simplicity, we restrict the check writing procedure to amounts less than $100.

Data Requirements for WriteWords

Procedure Inputs
The output file name (`Checks : Text`)
Check amount as a real number (`Amount : Real`)

Procedure Outputs
Description of check amount in words

Local Variables for WriteWords
Dollar amount (`Dollars : 0..99`)
Number of cents (`Cents : 0..99`)
Total check amount in pennies (`CheckPennies : Integer`)

Algorithm for WriteWords
1. `if` check amount is invalid `then`
    2. Print an error message
   `else`
   `begin`

Case Study: Writing a File of Payroll Checks, continued

Figure 9.24 Structure Chart for Procedure WriteWords

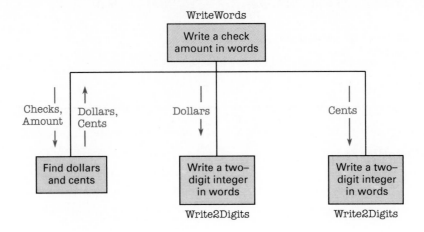

3. Separate check amount into Dollars and Cents.
4. Write Dollars in words.
5. Write ' dollars and '.
6. Write Cents in words.
7. Write ' cents'.

end

Coding Procedure WriteWords

The structure chart for procedure WriteWords is shown in Fig. 9.24. Procedure Write2Digits is called twice: first to write the value of Dollars in words (step 4), then to write the value of Cents in words (step 6). Because the operation of writing a two-digit number in words is fairly general and may be needed by other programs that we develop, we include procedure Write2Digits in our library. We place a reminder to insert Procedure Write2Digits in procedure WriteWords (see Fig. 9.25). For reasons that will become clear, we also need to insert procedure Write1Digit (a procedure that writes a single-digit number in words).

Figure 9.25 Procedure WriteWords

```
procedure WriteWords (var Checks {input} : Text;
                          Amount {input} : Real);
{
  Writes a check amount in words to file Checks.
  Pre : Amount is assigned a value between 0.0 and 99.99.
  Post: Writes the value of Check in words.
  Uses: Write2Digits and Write1Digit
}
  const
    MaxInteger = 99;       {Maximum dollar value of check}
    CentsPerDollar = 100;  {Number of cents in a dollar}
```

```
    type
      SmallInt = 0..MaxInteger;       {range of check amount}

    var
      Dollars,                        {the dollar amount}
      Cents     : SmallInt;           {the cents amount}
      CheckPennies : Integer;         {total check in pennies}

    {Insert procedures Write2Digits and Write1Digit here.}
begin {WriteWords}
  if (Amount <= 0.0) or (Trunc(Amount) > MaxInteger) then
    WriteLn (Output, 'Check amount ', Amount, ' is invalid.')
  else
    begin {valid amount}
      CheckPennies := Round(CentsPerDollar * Amount);
      Dollars := CheckPennies div CentsPerDollar;
      Cents := CheckPennies mod CentsPerDollar;
      Write2Digits (Checks, Dollars);    {Write dollar amount}
      Write (Checks, ' dollars and ');
      Write2Digits (Checks, Cents);      {Write cents amount}
      Write (Checks, ' cents')
    end {valid amount}
end; {WriteWords}
```

WriteWords displays an error message on the screen if the check amount
is invalid. Otherwise, the assignment statements

```
    CheckPennies := Round(CentsPerDollar * Amount);
    Dollars := CheckPennies div CentsPerDollar;
    Cents := CheckPennies mod CentsPerDollar;
```

determine the value of Dollars and Cents (for instance, if Amount is 95.63
then CheckPennies is 9563, Dollars is 95, and Cents is 63).

Coding Write2Digits and Write1Digit

Procedure Write2Digits writes in words an integer value less than 100. Its
parameter value is separated into a tens digit (stored in Tens) and a units digit
(stored in Units). Once this separation is performed, the two digits are written
in words. The data requirements and algorithm for Write2Digits follow.

Procedure Inputs
The output file name (OutFile : Text)
A number less than 100 (TwoDigitNum : Integer)

Procedure Outputs
A two-digit integer written in words

Local Variables for Write2Digits
The tens digit (Tens : 0..9)
The units digit (Units : 0..9)

Case Study: Writing a File of Payroll Checks, continued

Algorithm for Write2Digits

1. Separate TwoDigitNum into Tens and Units digits.
2. Write Tens digit and Units digit in words.

Step 2 of Write2Digits must be able to write integers that are less than 10 (Tens is 0), in the teens (Tens is 1), and above the teens (Tens >= 2). If Tens is 0, only the Units digit is written. If Tens is 1, then the string for a number between 10 ('ten') and 19 ('nineteen') is written. If Tens is between 2 and 9, then a string ('twenty' through 'ninety') representing the Tens digit is written, followed by a string for the Units digit, provided the latter is not 0. The refinement of step 2 follows.

Refinement of Step 2 of Write2Digits

```
2.1    case Tens of
          0 : Write the Units digit
          1 : Select and write a string based on the Units digit
          2 : Write 'twenty' and a nonzero Units digit
          3 : Write 'thirty' and a nonzero Units digit
          4 : Write 'forty' and a nonzero Units digit
          5 : Write 'fifty' and a nonzero Units digit
          8 : Write 'eighty' and a nonzero Units digit
          6, 7, 9 : Write the Tens digit followed by 'ty'
                    and a non-zero Units digit
       end
```

The preceding case alternatives are similar for values of Tens (the case selector) between 2 and 8. After a string is written, procedure Write1Digit is called to write the value of Units. If Tens is 6, 7, or 9, procedure Write1Digit is called once to write the value of Tens and a second time to write the value of Units. If Tens is 0, Write1Digit is called to display the value of Units only. Finally, if Tens is 1, a second case statement with selector Units is needed to determine which of the strings 'ten', 'eleven', 'twelve', and so on, is written. This case statement is shown in the code for procedure Write2Digits (see Fig. 9.26).

Figure 9.26   Procedures Write1Digit and Write2Digits

```
procedure Write1Digit (var OutFile {input} : Text;
                           InDigit {input} : Integer);
{
   Writes InDigit in words to OutFile.
   Pre : InDigit is assigned a value between 0 and 9.
   Post: InDigit is written in words.
}
begin {Write1Digit}
   if not (InDigit in [0..9]) then
      WriteLn (Output, 'error in Write1Digit parameter')
```

```
    else
      case InDigit of
        0 : Write (OutFile, 'zero');
        1 : Write (OutFile, 'one');
        2 : Write (OutFile, 'two');
        3 : Write (OutFile, 'three');
        4 : Write (OutFile, 'four');
        5 : Write (OutFile, 'five');
        6 : Write (OutFile, 'six');
        7 : Write (OutFile, 'seven');
        8 : Write (OutFile, 'eight');
        9 : Write (OutFile, 'nine')
      end {case}
end; {WritelDigit}


procedure Write2Digits (var OutFile {input} : Text;
                            TwoDigitNum {input} : Integer);
{
  Writes its two-digit parameter in words to OutFile.
  Pre : TwoDigitNum is assigned a value between 0 and 99.
  Post: TwoDigitNum is written in words.
  Uses: WritelDigit
}
  type
    Digit = 0..9;

  var
    Tens,                                {tens digit}
    Units : Digit;                       {units digit}


  procedure CalllDigit (var OutFile {input} : Text;
                            Units {input} : Digit);
  {
    Writes a dash to file OutFile and calls procedure
    WritelDigit if Units is not zero.
    Pre : Units is assigned a value between 0 and 9.
    Post: Calls WritelDigit if Units is not 0.
  }
  begin {CalllDigit}
    if Units <> 0 then
      begin
        Write (OutFile, '-');
        WritelDigit (OutFile, Units)
      end {if}
  end; {CalllDigit}


begin   {Write2Digits}
  Tens := TwoDigitNum div 10;
  Units := TwoDigitNum mod 10;
  if not (TwoDigitNum in [0..99]) then
    WriteLn (Output, 'invalid parameter for Write2Digits')
  else
    case Tens of
      0 : WritelDigit (OutFile, Units);    {Write units digit only}
      1 : case Units of            {Write the special case teens}
            0 : Write (OutFile, 'ten');
            1 : Write (OutFile, 'eleven');
```

```
                    2 : Write (OutFile, 'twelve');
                    3 : Write (OutFile, 'thirteen');
                    5 : Write (OutFile, 'fifteen');
                    8 : Write (OutFile, 'eighteen');
                    4, 6, 7, 9 : begin {Write ...teen}
                          WritelDigit (OutFile, Units);
                          Write (OutFile, 'teen')
                        end {Write ...teen}
                  end; {case Units}
              2 : begin                                    {Write twenty ... }
                    Write (OutFile, 'twenty');
                    CalllDigit (OutFile, Units)
                  end; {2}
              3 : begin                                    {Write thirty ... }
                    Write (OutFile, 'thirty');
                    CalllDigit (OutFile, Units)
                  end; {3}
              4 : begin                                    {Write forty ... }
                    Write (OutFile, 'forty');
                    CalllDigit (OutFile, Units)
                  end; {4}
              5 : begin                                    {Write fifty ... }
                    Write (OutFile, 'fifty');
                    CalllDigit (OutFile, Units)
                  end; {5}
              8 : begin                                    {Write eighty ... }
                    Write (OutFile, 'eighty');
                    CalllDigit (OutFile, Units)
                  end; {8}
              6, 7, 9 : begin                              {Write ...ty ...}
                          WritelDigit (OutFile, Tens);
                          Write (OutFile, 'ty');
                          CalllDigit (OutFile, Units)
                        end {6, 7, 8, 9}
          end  {case Tens}
end;  {Write2Digits}
```

Write2Digits introduces a new procedure, CalllDigit, whose purpose is
to "screen" calls to WritelDigit. CalllDigit is called when Tens is between 2
and 9; CalllDigit calls WritelDigit to write the value of Units only if Units
is nonzero. The reason for this is so that a number such as 80 (Tens is 8, Units
is 0) will be written as eighty rather than as eighty-zero.

The subrange Digit is declared in procedure Write2Digits and is used
as the data type of the formal parameter for CalllDigit. A common error in
using a programmer-defined data type is specifying the type declaration in the
procedure heading. The procedure heading

```
procedure CalllDigit (var OutFile {input} : Text;
                      Units {input} : 0..9);
```

causes a syntax error because the type of parameter Units must be an identifier,
not a subrange.

Validating Case Selectors

In procedure `Write2Digits`, an `if` statement tests the value of the case selector `Tens` before the `case` statement is executed. In a similar manner, an `if` statement in procedure `Write1Digit` tests the value of the case selector `InDigit`. Both conditions involve a test for membership in the set `[0..9]`.

Each `if` statement displays an error message on the screen if the case selector value is outside its expected range. Without these tests, an execution error occurs if the case selector value is out of range. Although this is unlikely, it is a good idea to include these tests as a precaution, particularly since both procedures are candidates for inclusion in a procedure library.

Exercises for Section 9.7

Self-Check

1. Show by example that the assignment statements in `Write2Digits` that assign values to `Tens` and `Units` are correct. Do the same for the assignment statements in `WriteWords` that assign values to `Dollars` and `Cents`.

Programming

1. A salary amount of $1.01 is written as `one dollars and one cents` to file `Checks`. How could this error be fixed? What procedure block should be changed?

 ## 9.8 Common Programming Errors

When you use a `case` statement, make sure the case selector and labels are of the same ordinal type. Remember that only lists of ordinal values can be used as case labels and that no value can appear in more than one case label. If the selector evaluates to a value not listed in any of the case labels, an error diagnostic occurs and your program stops. Be sure to insert the end `{case}`; there is no matching `begin`.

A repeat-until loop always executes at least once. Use a repeat statement only if you are certain that there is no possibility of zero loop iterations; otherwise, use a `while` loop.

Be sure to trace each nest of loops carefully, checking all loop parameter values. A loop-control variable for a `for` statement cannot be changed inside the loop body. It is also illegal to use the same loop-control variable for two `for` statements within the same nest.

When you are using functions, make sure that the function result is defined for all valid parameter values. Do not use the function name in an expression inside the function body. Avoid using variable parameters and returning a result by modifying a function parameter (a function side effect).

Chapter Review

This chapter introduced the case statement as a convenient means of implementing decisions with several alternatives. You saw how to use the case statement to implement decisions that are based on the value of a variable or a simple expression (the case selector). The case selector must have an ordinal data type.

We completed our discussion of loops by introducing the for statement (for loop) and repeat statement (repeat-until loop). We used the for statement to implement counting loops in which the exact number of loop iterations could be determined before loop repetition begins. The counter variable may increase in value (to form) or decrease in value (downto form) after each loop iteration.

We used the repeat statement to implement conditional loops. With the repeat statement, you can implement a loop that will always execute at least one time.

We also analyzed nested loops. Every inner loop of a nest is reentered and executed to completion each time an outer loop is repeated.

We used functions to implement modules that return a single result. The parameters of a function should be value parameters. Usually, you define a function result by assigning a value to the function name inside the function body. You call a function by using it in an expression in the calling program; the function name and actual parameters (function arguments) are inserted directly in the expression.

New Pascal Constructs

Table 9.4 shows the new Pascal constructs introduced in this chapter.

Table 9.4 Summary of New Pascal Constructs

Construct	Effect
case Statement	
``` case NextCh of 'A', 'a' : WriteLn ('Excellent'); 'B', 'b' : WriteLn ('Good'); 'C', 'c' : WriteLn ('O.K.'); 'D', 'd', 'F', 'f' : begin WriteLn ('Poor'); Probation (IDNum) end end {case} ```	Prints one of four messages based on the value of NextCh (type Char). If NextCh is 'D', 'd' or 'F', 'f', procedure Probation is also called with IDNum as an actual parameter.
Set Values and Operator in	
``` if CurMonth in [Dec, Jan, Feb] then WriteLn ('Winter storm watch') ```	The message 'Winter storm watch' is printed if the value of CurMonth is one of the three constants listed. CurMonth and the constants must belong to the same enumerated data type.

Table 9.4 *continued*

347

Chapter Review

Construct	Effect

for Statement
```for CurMonth := March to July do```
``` begin```
```   Read (MonthSales);```
```   YearSales := YearSales +```
```   MonthSales```
``` end {for}```
	The loop body is repeated for each value of CurMonth from March through July, inclusive. For each month, the value of MonthSales is read and added to YearSales.

Declaring a Function
```function Sign (X : Real) : Char;```
```begin {Sign}```
``` if X > 0.0 then```
```   Sign := '+'```
``` else```
```   Sign := '-'```
```end; {Sign}```
	Returns a character value that indicates the sign ('+' or '-') of its type Real argument.

✓ *Quick-Check Exercises*

1. A case statement is often used instead of _____.
2. Which of the following can appear in a case label? In a set value?

   a subrange of integers, a list of integers, a real value, a Boolean value, a type Char value, a string value, an enumerated type value

3. Explain how to use a set value to guard a case statement and prevent a case value out of range error.
4. Which loop form always executes at least one time? Which loop form is the most general? Which loop form should you use to implement a counting loop? Which loop form should you use in a menu-driven program?
5. How many times does the following Write statement execute? How many times does the WriteLn execute? What is the last value displayed?

```
for I := 1 to 10 do
  begin
    for J := 1 to I do
      Write (I * J);
    WriteLn
  end
```

6. How many times does the following Write statement execute? How many times does the WriteLn execute? What is the last value displayed?

```
for I := 1 to 10 do
  begin
    for J := 1 to 5 do
      Write (I * J);
    WriteLn
  end
```

7. How does a function return its value? How many values should be returned by a user-defined function?

8. A _____ occurs when a function assigns a value to one of its variable parameters.

9. The parameters of a function generally should be _____ parameters.

Answers to Quick-Check Exercises

1. Nested `if` statements or a multiple-alternative `if` statement

2. In a `case` label: a list of integers, a Boolean value, a `Char` value, an enumerated type value. In a set value: a list of integers, a Boolean value, a `Char` value, an enumerated type value, and a small subrange of integers.

3. A set value can be used in an `if` condition that permits the `case` statement to be executed only when the `case` selector matches one of the elements in the set. All `case` label values should appear in the set value.

4. repeat, while, for, repeat

5. $1 + 2 + 3 + \ldots + 9 + 10$, or 55, for `Write`, 10 for `WriteLn`, last value displayed is 100

6. 50 for `Write`, 10 for `WriteLn`, last value displayed is 50

7. Returns one value by assigning a value to the function name.

8. side effect

9. value

Review Questions

1. When should a nested `if` statement be used instead of a `case` statement?

2. Write a `case` statement to select an operation based on `Inventory`. Increment `TotalPaper` by `PaperOrder` if `Inventory` is `'B'` or `'C'`; increment `TotalRibbon` by `RibbonOrder` if `Inventory` is `'L'`, `'T'`, or `'D'`; increment `TotalLabel` by `LabelOrder` if `Inventory` is `'A'` or `'X'`. Do not take any action if `Inventory` is `'M'`.

3. Write the `for` statement that displays the character values of the ordinal numbers 32 through 126, inclusive. Use `OrdNum` as the loop control variable. What is the value of `OrdNum`, after completion of the loop?

4. Write a `repeat` statement that will accept only a valid response to a menu. A valid response would be any of the following: `'A'`, `'a'` or `'B'`, `'b'`.

5. Write the complement of each of the following Boolean expressions

   ```
   Flag and (I < 20)
   (Ord(NextCh) = 0) or EOLN(InData)
   not (Vowel and Consonant)
   (Round(N) = N) or (N < Sqr(M))
   ```

6. Write an `if` statement that tests to see if `Today` is a working day. Print either the message `'Workday'` or `'Weekend'`. Assume that `Today` is type `Day`, an enumerated type that has the days of the week as its values.

7. Write an equivalent `case` statement for exercise 6.

8. Write a `for` statement that runs from `'Z'` to `'A'` and prints only the consonants. Test each character against the set of vowels.

9. Write a nested loop that prints the first six letters of the alphabet on a line, the next five letters on the next line, the next four letters on the next line, and so on, down to and including one letter (the letter U) on the last line. Use either uppercase or lowercase letters.

10. Write a function called `FindNet` that computes a worker's weekly net pay given

Hours (an Integer) and Rate (a Real) as input parameters. Pay time-and-a-half for any hours worked over forty and subtract 30 percent for taxes. For thirty or more hours but less than forty, subtract 20 percent for taxes. For twenty or more hours but less than thirty, subtract 10 percent for taxes. Do not deduct any taxes for less than twenty hours. Be sure to check for a valid number of hours (0 <= Hours <= 168).

Programming Projects

1. Write a program that reads in a positive real number and finds and prints the number of digits to the left of the decimal point. Hint: Find the whole part and repeatedly divide by 10 until the number becomes less than 1. Test the program with the following data:

4703.62	0.01	0.47	5764	10.12	40000

2. Write a program that finds the largest value, the smallest value, and the sum of the input data. After all data are processed, call two functions to find the average value and the range of values in the data collection. Print the results.

3. Each year the state legislature rates the productivity of the faculty of each of the state-supported colleges and universities. The rating is based on reports submitted by the faculty members indicating the average number of hours worked per week during the school year. Each faculty member is ranked, and the university receives an overall rank.

   The faculty productivity ranks are computed as follows:

   a. Faculty members averaging over fifty-five hours per week are considered highly productive.

   b. Faculty members averaging between thirty-five and fifty-five hours a week, inclusive, are considered satisfactory.

   c. Faculty members averaging fewer than thirty-five hours a week are considered overpaid.

   The productivity rating of each school is determined by first computing the faculty average for the school, then comparing the faculty average to the category ranges.

   Write a program to rank the following faculty:

Name	*Hours*
Herm	63
Flo	37
Jake	20
Maureen	55
Saul	72
Tony	40
Al	12

   Your program should print a three-column table giving the name, hours, and productivity rank of each faculty member. It should also compute and print the school's overall productivity ranking.

4. Write a savings account transaction program that will process the following set of data:

```
Adam        1054.37 ⎤
W             25.00 ⎥
D            243.35 ⎬ group 1
W            254.55 ⎥
Z                   ⎦

Eve         2008.24 ⎤
W             15.55 ⎬ group 2
Z                   ⎦

Mary         128.24 ⎤
W             62.48 ⎥
D             13.42 ⎬ group 3
W             84.60 ⎥
Z                   ⎦

Sam            7.77 ⎤
Z                   ⎬ group 4

Joe           15.27 ⎤
W             16.12 ⎥
D             10.00 ⎬ group 5
Z                   ⎦

Beth       12900.00 ⎤
D           9270.00 ⎬ group 6
Z                   ⎦
```

The first record in each group (header) gives the name for an account and the starting balance in the account. All subsequent records show the amount of each withdrawal (W) and deposit (D) made for that account, followed by a sentinel value (Z). Print out the final balance for each account processed. If a balance is negative, print an appropriate message and take whatever corrective steps you deem proper. If there are no transactions for an account, print a message so indicating.

5. Write a program to print a table of the following form.

```
Home Loan Mortgage Interest Payments per $1000.00
Rate (Percent)      Duration (Years)     Monthly Payment      Total Payment
10.00               20                   _____       _____
10.00               25                   _____       _____
10.00               30                   _____       _____
10.25               20                   _____       _____
```

where the formula for monthly payment and total payment is given in programming project 7 of Chapter 7.

Your program should print a table that shows the monthly and total payments on a loan of $1,000 for interest rates from 10% to 14% with increments of 0.25%. The loan duration should be 20, 25, and 30 years. Your program should contain nested loops, some of which may be inside separate procedures, depending on your solution. Make sure you remove all redundant computations from inside your loops.

6. Write a program to read in a string of characters that represent a Roman numeral and then convert it to Arabic form (an integer). The character values for Roman numerals are as follows:

M	1000
D	500
C	100
L	50
X	10
V	5
I	1

Test your program on the following data: LXXXVII (87), CCXIX (219), MCCCLIV (1354), MMDCLXXIII (2673), MCDLXXVI (1476).

7. A problem often encountered in writing compilers or determining efficient means of storing data on disks is that of converting a name into a unique (or relatively unique) numeric value. This procedure is called *hashing*. Several algorithms are used to accomplish hashing.

   One of the simpler methods is to use the numeric representation of each letter in some type of equation. In this problem, you are to convert a word into a reproducible integer value between 0 and 500. To get this value, add each ordinal value of a letter times that letter's position within the word. This should generate a rather large number that may not be within the required range. To calculate a number within the range, determine the modulus of this large number and 500. For example, the number for ACE would be: 1 * 65 + 2 * 67 + 3 * 69, or 406.

   Test your program with several words read from a data file and print out the calculated value for each word.

8. Generate a graph that indicates the rainfall for the city of Bedrock and that can be used to compare the average rainfall with the previous year's rainfall. Assume a maximum monthly rainfall of 15 inches. In addition, provide some summary statistics that will indicate (1) annual rainfall for last year, (2) average annual rainfall, and (3) the difference between the two. The input data will consist of twelve pairs of numbers. The first number in each pair will be the average rainfall for a month, and the second number will be what fell the previous year. The first data pair will represent January, the second February, and so forth. The output should resemble the following:

```
January     !****************
            !##################
            !
February    !***********
            !########
            !          .
                       .
                       .
            !----1----2----3----4----5  . . .
```

```
* - average rainfall for a given month

# - previous year's rainfall for a given month
```

The data for the chart above begins with 3.2 4.0 (for January) 2.2 1.6 (for February).

Arrays

10

I n the programs we have written so far, each variable was associated with a single memory cell. These variables are called simple variables, and their data types are simple ones. The only exceptions were file variables, which were associated with a collection of characters stored on disk.

In this chapter, you will study *structured variables*, or data structures. A structured variable represents a grouping of related data items in main memory. The items in a structured variable can be processed individually, although some operations can be performed on the structure as a whole.

Pascal provides *type constructors*, which can be used to form new data types from simpler objects. The type constructor `array` is described in this chapter. The type constructors `record` and `set` are discussed in later chapters.

The *array* is a data structure in which we store a collection of data items of the same type (for example, all the exam scores for a class). By using an array, we can associate a single variable name (for example, `Scores`) with the entire collection of data. This association enables us to save the entire collection of data in main memory (one item per memory cell) and to reference individual items easily. To process an individual item, we specify the array name and indicate the array element being manipulated (for example, `Scores[3]` references the third item in the array `Scores`).

Because each score is saved in a separate cell in main memory, we can process the individual items more than once and in any order. In previous programs, we reused the same cell to store each exam score. Consequently, we could not access the third score after the fourth score was read.

The use of arrays of characters makes it easier to store character strings in memory. String variables or strings are introduced for that purpose, and you will see how to read textual data into strings.

 ## 10.1 The Array Data Type

This section illustrates the basic operations that can be performed on an array. We begin by showing how to allocate memory space for an array in Pascal.

Array Type Declaration

Normally, we first describe the structure of an array in an *array type declaration*. Then we can allocate storage for one or more arrays of that type. The array type `RealArray`, declared next, is followed by the declaration of array `X` of type `RealArray`.

```
type
  RealArray = array [1..8] of Real;

var
  X : RealArray;
```

Pascal associates eight memory cells with the name `X`. Each element of array `X` can contain a single real value. So a total of eight real values can be stored and referenced using the array name `X`.

Array X

X[1]	X[2]	X[3]	X[4]	X[5]	X[6]	X[7]	X[8]
16.0	12.0	6.0	8.0	2.5	12.0	14.0	– 54.5

First element   Second element   Third element   Eighth element

To process the data stored in an array, we must be able to reference each individual element. The *array subscript* differentiates among elements of the same array. For example, if X is the array with eight elements, we can refer to the elements of array X as shown in Fig. 10.1.

The *subscripted variable* X[1] (read as "X sub 1") references the first element of the array X, X[2] the second element, and X[8] the eighth element. The number enclosed in brackets is the array subscript. Later, you will see that the subscript can be an expression of any ordinal type.

■ Example 10.1

Let X be the array shown in Fig. 10.1. Some statements that manipulate this array are shown in Table 10.1.

Table 10.1 Statements that Manipulate Array X

Statement	Explanation
WriteLn (X[1])	Displays the value of X[1], or 16.0.
X[4] := 25.0	Stores the value 25.0 in X[4].
Sum := X[1] + X[2]	Stores the sum of X[1] and X[2], or 28.0, in the variable Sum.
Sum := Sum + X[3]	Adds X[3] to Sum. The new Sum is 34.0.
X[4] := X[4] + 1.0	Adds 1.0 to X[4]. The new X[4] is 26.0.
X[3] := X[1] + X[2]	Stores the sum of X[1] and X[2] in X[3]. The new X[3] is 28.0.

The contents of array X after execution of these statements are shown next. Notice that only X[3] and X[4] have changed. ■

Array X

X[1]	X[2]	X[3]	X[4]	X[5]	X[6]	X[7]	X[8]
16.0	12.0	28.0	26.0	2.5	12.0	14.0	– 54.5

First element   Second element   Third element   Eighth element

■ Example 10.2

The declaration section for a plant operations program is shown next. The type declaration declares two simple types, EmpRange and Day, and two array types, EmpArray and DayArray. Two arrays, Vacation and PlantHours, are declared in the variable declaration section.

```
const
   NumEmp = 10;                         {Number of employees}

type
   EmpRange = 1..NumEmp;                {subscript range}
   EmpArray = array [EmpRange] of Boolean;
   Day = (Sunday, Monday, Tuesday, Wednesday,
          Thursday, Friday, Saturday);
   DayArray = array [Day] of Real;

var
  Vacation : EmpArray;
  PlantHours : DayArray;
```

The array Vacation has ten elements (subscripts 1 through NumEmp); each element of array Vacation can store a Boolean value. The contents of this array could indicate which employees are on vacation (Vacation[i] is True if employee i is on vacation). If employees 1, 3, 5, 7, and 9 are on vacation, the array would have the values shown in Fig. 10.2.

The array PlantHours has seven elements (subscripts Sunday through Saturday). The array element PlantHours[Sunday] could indicate how many hours the plant was operating on Sunday of the past week. The array shown in Fig. 10.3 indicates that the plant was closed on the weekend and operated a single shift on Monday and Thursday, double shifts on Tuesday and Friday, and a triple shift on Wednesday.   ■

It is possible to eliminate the declarations for the constant NumEmp and data types EmpRange and EmpArray and just declare the array Vacation, as shown next.

```
var
   Vacation : array [1..10] of Boolean;
```

Figure 10.2 Array Vacation

Vacation[1]	True
Vacation[2]	False
Vacation[3]	True
Vacation[4]	False
Vacation[5]	True
Vacation[6]	False
Vacation[7]	True
Vacation[8]	False
Vacation[9]	True
Vacation[10]	False

Figure 10.3 Array PlantHours

357

10.1 The Array Data
Type

PlantHours[Sunday]	0.0
PlantHours[Monday]	8.0
PlantHours[Tuesday]	16.0
PlantHours[Wednesday]	24.0
PlantHours[Thursday]	8.0
PlantHours[Friday]	16.0
PlantHours[Saturday]	0.0

There are three advantages to the original set of declarations. First, it is easy to change the declared size of array `Vacation`. By simply redefining the constant `NumEmp`, we change the array size. Second, the data types `EmpArray` and `DayArray` can be used as type identifiers elsewhere in the program. And third, the constant `NumEmp` can be referenced in the program body.

Because a type identifier is not used in the revised declaration of array `Vacation`, its type is said to be *anonymous*. In general, you should avoid using anonymous types (unnamed types).

Array Type Declaration

Form: `type`
 array type = `array` [*subscript type*] `of` *element type*;

Example: `type`
 `SmallArray = array [1..5] of Char;`

Interpretation: The identifier *array type* describes a collection of array elements; each element can store an item of type *element type*. The *subscript type* can be either of the standard ordinal types `Boolean` or `Char`, an enumerated type, or a subrange type. There is one array element for each value in the *subscript type*.

The *element type* describes the type of each element in the array. All elements of an array are the same type.

Note 1: The standard types `Real` and `Integer` cannot be used as a *subscript type*; however, a subrange of the integers may be a *subscript type*.

Note 2: The *element type* can be any standard or user-defined type.

Note 1 in the preceding display states that the standard types `Integer` and `Real` cannot be used as subscript types. Type `Integer` is not allowed because an array of type `Integer` would have an excessive number of elements. Type `Real` is not allowed because it is not an ordinal type.

It is important to realize that an array type declaration does not require allocation of storage space in memory. The array type describes the structure of an array only. Only variables actually store information and require storage. Storage space is not allocated until a variable of this type is declared.

Abstract Array

We can summarize what we have discussed so far about arrays in the following specification for an abstract array.

Specification for Abstract Array

Structure: An array is a collection of elements of the same data type. For each array, an ordinal subscript type is specified. There is an array element that corresponds to each value in the ordinal type. The ordinal type Integer cannot be a subscript type; however, a subrange of type Integer can be a subscript type.

Operators: Two basic operations act on the elements of an array: *store* and *retrieve*. The store operation inserts a value into the array. If A is an array and C is a variable that is assignment compatible (defined in Section 7.8) with the element type of A, the statement

```
A[i] := C
```

stores the contents of C in element i of array A. If the element type of A is assignment compatible with the type of variable D, the statement

```
D := A[i]
```

retrieves element i of array A and copies its value into D. For both of these statements, the value of subscript i must be in the range of the array subscript type; otherwise, a run-time error occurs.

The assignment operator can also be used to copy the contents of one array to another of the same type. If arrays A and B are the same type, the statement

```
A := B
```

copies all values associated with array B to array A.

The preceding display summarizes all the information you need to know to use an array. You do not need to know how Pascal stores the elements of an array in memory or how it implements the retrieve and store operators.

Exercises for Section 10.1

Self-Check

1. What is the difference between the expressions X3 and X[3]?
2. For the following declarations, how many memory cells are reserved for data and what type of data can be stored there? When is the memory allocated: after the type declaration or after the variable declaration?

```
type
  AnArray = array [1..5] of Char;
```

```
var
    Grades : AnArray;
```

3. Write the variable and type declarations for the valid array descriptions that follow.
   a. subscript type `Boolean`, element type `Real`
   b. subscript type `'A'..'F'`, element type `Integer`
   c. subscript type `Char`, element type `Boolean`
   d. subscript type `Integer`, element type `Real`
   e. subscript type `Char`, element type `Real`
   f. subscript type `Real`, element type `Char`
   g. subscript type `Day` (enumerated type), element type `Real`

10.2 Selecting Array Elements for Processing

Using a Subscript as an Index to an Array

Each array reference includes the array name and a subscript enclosed in brackets; the subscript determines which array element is processed. The subscript (sometimes called an *index*) used in an array reference must be an expression that is assignment compatible with the *subscript type* specified in the array declaration. Very often, the *subscript type* is a subrange whose host type is `Integer`. In this case, the subscript must be an integer expression whose value is in the range specified by the *subscript type*. For the array `Vacation` declared in Example 10.2, the allowable subscript values are the integers 1 through 10.

■ Example 10.3

Table 10.2 shows some sample statements involving the array `X` shown in Fig. 10.1. `I` is assumed to be a type `Integer` variable with value 6. Make sure you understand each statement.

Table 10.2 Some Sample Statements for Array X in Figure 10.1

Statement	Effect
`Write (4, X[4])`	Displays 4 and 8.0 (value of `X[4]`).
`Write (I, X[I])`	Displays 6 and 12.0 (value of `X[6]`).
`Write (X[I] + 1)`	Displays 13.0 (value of 12.0 + 1).
`Write (X[I] + I)`	Displays 18.0 (value of 12.0 + 6).
`Write (X[I+1])`	Displays 14.0 (value of `X[7]`).
`Write (X[I+I])`	Illegal attempt to display `X[12]`.
`Write (X[2*I])`	Illegal attempt to display `X[12]`.
`Write (X[2*I-4])`	Displays −54.5 (value of `X[8]`).
`Write (X[Trunc(X[5])])`	Displays 12.0 (value of `X[2]`).
`X[I] := X[I+1]`	Assigns 14.0 (value of `X[7]`) to `X[6]`.
`X[I-1] := X[I]`	Assigns 14.0 (new value of `X[6]`) to `X[5]`.
`X[I] − 1 := X[I-1]`	Illegal assignment statement.

You can see two attempts to display element X[12], which is not in the array. These attempts result in an index expression out of bounds run-time error. This means there is no array element with the current subscript, or index, value.

The last Write statement in Table 10.2 uses Trunc(X[5]) as a subscript expression. Because this evaluates to 2, the value of X[2] (and not X[5]) is printed. If the value of Trunc(X[5]) is outside the range 1 through 8, a run-time error occurs.

Two different subscripts are used in the last three assignment statements in the table. The first assignment statement copies the value of X[7] to X[6] (subscripts I+1 and I); the second assignment statement copies the value of X[6] to X[5] (subscripts I and I−1). The last assignment statement causes a syntax error because there is an expression to the left of the assignment operator. ∎

Array Reference

Form: *name*[*subscript*]

Example: X[3 * I − 2]

Interpretation: The *subscript* must be an expression that is assignment compatible with the subscript type specified in the declaration for array *name*. If the expression is the wrong data type, the syntax error index type is not compatible with declaration is detected. If the expression value is not in range, the run-time error index expression out of bounds occurs.

Using for Loops with Arrays

Frequently, we want to process the elements of an array in sequence, starting with the first element, for example, entering data into the array or printing its contents. We can accomplish this sequential processing using a for loop whose loop-control variable (I) is also the array subscript (X[I]). Increasing the value of the loop-control variable by 1 causes the next array element to be processed.

∎ Example 10.4

The array Cube, declared as follows, stores the cubes of the first ten integers (for example, Cube[1] is 1, Cube[10] is 1000).

```
type
   IntArray = array [1..10] of Integer;

var
   Cube : IntArray;                  {array of cubes}
   I : Integer;                      {loop control variable}
```

The `for` statement

```
for I := 1 to 10 do
   Cube[I] := I * I * I
```

initializes this array as follows.   ■

Array Cube

[1]	[2]	[3]	[4]	[5]	[6]	[7]	[8]	[9]	[10]
1	8	27	64	125	216	343	512	729	1000

■ Example 10.5

For array `PlantHours` (see Ex mple 10.2), the enumerated type `Day` is the declared subscript type. The assignment statements

```
PlantHours[Sunday]    := 0.0;
PlantHours[Monday]    := 8.0;
PlantHours[Tuesday]   := 16.0;
PlantHours[Wednesday] := 24.0
```

assign the values shown in Fig. 10.3 to the first four elements of `PlantHours`. Assuming that `Today` is type `Day`, the following statements have the same effect.

```
PlantHours[Sunday] := 0.0;
for Today := Monday to Wednesday do
   PlantHours[Today] := PlantHours[Pred(Today)] + 8.0
```

The assignment statement in the `for` loop executes for three values of `Today` (Monday through Wednesday). Table 10.3 shows the effect of the assignment statement for each value of `Today`.   ■

Table 10.3   Assigning Values to Array PlantHours

Today	Pred(Today)	**Effect**
Monday	Sunday	Assigns 8.0 to PlantHours[Monday].
Tuesday	Monday	Assigns 16.0 to PlantHours[Tuesday].
Wednesday	Tuesday	Assigns 24.0 to PlantHours[Wednesday].

■ Example 10.6

In Fig. 10.4, the declarations

```
const
   MaxItems = 8;                        {number of data items}

type
   IndexRange = 1..MaxItems;
   RealArray = array [IndexRange] of Real;
```

```
var
  X : RealArray;                          {array of data}
  I : IndexRange;                         {loop-control variable}
```

allocate storage for an array X of Real elements with subscripts in the range
1..8. The program uses three for loops to process the array X. The loop-
control variable I ($1 <= I <= 8$) is also the array subscript in each loop. The
first for loop

```
for I := 1 to MaxItems do
  Read (X[I]);
```

reads one data value into each array element (the first item is stored in X[1],
the second item in X[2], and so on). The Read statement is repeated for each
value of I from 1 to 8; each repetition causes a new data value to be read and
stored in X[I]. The subscript I determines the array element that receives the
next data value. The data line shown in the sample run causes the array to be
initialized, as in Fig. 10.1.

The second for loop accumulates (in Sum) the sum of all values stored in
the array. (We trace this loop later.) The last for loop

```
for I := 1 to MaxItems do
  WriteLn (I :4, X[I] :8:2, X[I]-Average :14:2)
```

displays a table that shows each array element, X[I], and the difference between
that element and the average value, X[I]-Average.

Figure 10.4 Table of Differences

```
program ShowDiff (Input, Output);
{
  Computes the average value of an array of data and
  prints the difference between each value and the average.
}
  const
    MaxItems = 8;                         {number of data items}

  type
    IndexRange = 1..MaxItems;
    RealArray = array [IndexRange] of Real;

  var
    X : RealArray;                        {array of data}
    I : IndexRange;                       {loop-control variable}
    Average,                              {average value of data}
    Sum      : Real;                      {sum of the data}

begin   {ShowDiff}
  {Enter the data.}
  Write ('Enter ', MaxItems :1, ' numbers> ');
  for I := 1 to MaxItems do
    Read (X[I]);

  {Compute the average value.}
  Sum := 0.0;                                       {Initialize Sum}
  for I := 1 to MaxItems do
    Sum := Sum + X[I];                   {Add each element to Sum}
  Average := Sum / MaxItems;                {Get average value}
  WriteLn ('Average value is ', Average :3:1); WriteLn;
```

```
{Display the difference between each item and the average.}
WriteLn ('Table of differences between X[I] and the average');
WriteLn ('I' :4, 'X[I]' :8, 'Difference' : 14);
for I := 1 to MaxItems do
   WriteLn (I :4, X[I] :8:1, X[I]-Average :14:1)
end. {ShowDiff}
```

```
Enter 8 numbers> 16.0  12.0  6.0  8.0  2.5  12.0  14.0  -54.5
The average value is 2.0

Table of differences between X[I] and the average
   I    X[I]    Difference
   1    16.0        14.0
   2    12.0        10.0
   3     6.0         4.0
   4     8.0         6.0
   5     2.5         0.5
   6    12.0        10.0
   7    14.0        12.0
   8   -54.5       -56.5
```

The program fragment

```
Sum := 0.0;                        {Initialize Sum}
for I := 1 to MaxItems do
   Sum := Sum + X[I];        {Add each element to Sum}
```

accumulates the sum of all eight elements of array X in the variable Sum. Each time the for loop is repeated, the next element of array X is added to Sum. The execution of this program fragment is traced in Table 10.4 for the first three repetitions of the loop.

Table 10.4 Partial Trace of for Loop

Statement Part	I	X[I]	Sum	Effect
Sum:= 0.0;			0.0	Initializes Sum.

for I := 1 to MaxItems do
   Sum := Sum + X[I]
	1	16.0	
			16.0
				Initializes I to 1;
				   add X[1] to Sum.

increment and test I
   Sum := Sum + X[I]
	2	12.0	
			28.0
				2 <= 8 is True;
				   add X[2] to Sum.

increment and test I
   Sum := Sum + X[I]
	3	6.0	
			34.0
				3 <= 8 is True;
				   add X[3] to Sum.

In Fig. 10.4, the subscripted variable X[I] is an actual parameter for the standard Pascal Read or WriteLn procedure. You always have to read data into an array one element at a time, as shown in this example. In most instances, you also have to display one array element at time; however, Section 10.7 shows that this requirement may be waived when you are dealing with strings and packed arrays of characters.

Exercises for Section 10.2

Self-Check

1. If an array is declared to have ten elements, must the program use all ten of them?
2. The following sequence of statements changes the initial contents of array X displayed in Fig. 10.4. Describe what each statement does to the array and show the final contents of array X after all statements execute.

```
I := 3;
X[I] := X[I] + 10.0;
X[I - 1] := X[2 * I - 1];
X[I + 1] := X[2 * I] + X[2 * I + 1];
for I := 5 to 7 do
  X[I] := X[I + 1];
for I := 3 downto 1 do
  X[I + 1] := X[I]
```

3. Write program statements that will do the following to array X shown in Fig. 10.4.
   a. Replace the third element with 7.0.
   b. Copy the element in the fifth location into the first one.
   c. Subtract the first element from the fourth and store the result in the fifth element.
   d. Increase the sixth element by 2.
   e. Find the sum of the first five elements.
   f. Multiply each of the first six elements by 2 and place each product in an element of the array AnswerArray.
   g. Display all even-numbered elements on one line.

 10.3 Using Arrays

This section illustrates the use of an array. It demonstrates two different methods for array access: sequential access and random access. We discuss their differences after the case study.

● Case Study: Home Budget Problem

Problem

Your parents want a program that keeps track of their monthly expenses in each of several categories. The program should read each expense amount, add it to the appropriate category total, and print the total expenditure by category. The input data consist of the category and the amount of each purchase made during the past month.

Design Overview

Your parents have selected these budget categories: entertainment, food, clothing, rent, tuition, insurance, and miscellaneous. Seven separate totals must be accumulated; each total can be associated with a different element of a seven-element array. The program must read each expenditure, determine to which category it belongs, and then add that expenditure to the appropriate array element. When finished with all expenditures, the program should print a table that shows each category and its accumulated total. As in all programs that accumulate a sum, each total must be initialized to zero.

Data Requirements

We could simply use an array with subscripts 1 through 7; however, the program would be more readable if we declare a data type `BudgetCat` and use this data type as the array subscript type.

> *Data Type*
> ```
> BudgetCat = (Entertainment, Food, Clothing, Rent,
>              Tuition, Insurance, Miscellaneous);
> ```
>
> *Problem Inputs*
> Each expenditure and its category
>
> *Problem Outputs*
> The array of seven expenditure totals (`Budget`)

Initial Algorithm

1. Initialize all category totals to zero.
2. Read each expenditure and add it to the appropriate total.
3. Print the accumulated total for each category.

Structure Chart and Refinements

The structure chart in Fig. 10.5 shows the relationship between the three steps. The array `Budget` is manipulated by all three procedures in the program solution. Procedures `Initialize` and `Post` store information in this array; this information is displayed by procedure `Report`.

Coding the Main Program

Figure 10.6 shows the program. The main program contains declarations for the data type `BudgetCat` and the array `Budget`. The array `Budget` (type `BudgetArray`) appears in each parameter list and is passed between each procedure and the main program. When an entire array is passed, no subscript is used.

Case Study: Home Budget Problem, continued

Figure 10.5 Structure Chart for Home Budget Problem

Figure 10.6 Home Budget Program

```
program HomeBudget (Input, Output);

{Prints a summary of all expenses by budget category.}

  type
    BudgetCat = (Entertainment, Food, Clothing, Rent,
                 Tuition, Insurance, Miscellaneous);
    BudgetArray = array [BudgetCat] of Real;   {array type}

  var
    Budget : BudgetArray;              {output - array of totals}


  procedure Initialize (var Budget {output} : BudgetArray);
  {
    Initializes array Budget to all zeros.
    Pre : None
    Post: Each element of Budget is 0.0
  }
    var
      NextCat : BudgetCat;             {loop-control variable }
                                              array subscript}
  begin  {Initialize}
    for NextCat := Entertainment to Miscellaneous do
      Budget[NextCat] := 0.0
  end;  {Initialize}


  procedure Post (var Budget {input/output} : BudgetArray);
  {
    Reads each expenditure amount and adds it to the appropriate
    element of array Budget.
```

```
      Pre : Each array element Budget[i] is 0.0
      Post: Each array element Budget[i] is the sum of expense
            amounts for category i.
  }
  begin  {Poststub}
    WriteLn ('Procedure Post entered')
  end;  {Poststub}


  procedure Report (Budget {input} : BudgetArray);
  {
    Prints the expenditures in each budget category.}
    Pre : Array Budget is defined.
    Post: Displays each budget category name and amount.
  }
    var
      NextCat : BudgetCat;                    {loop control-variable }
                                              {  array subscript     }

    procedure PrintCat (NextCat {input} : BudgetCat);
    {
      Displays budget category.
      Pre : Nextcat is a budget category.
      Post: Displays NextCat as a string.
    }
    begin  {PrintCat}
      case NextCat of
        Entertainment : Write ('Entertainment' :15);
        Food          : Write ('Food          ' :15);
        Clothing      : Write ('Clothing      ' :15);
        Rent          : Write ('Rent          ' :15);
        Tuition       : Write ('Tuition       ' :15);
        Insurance     : Write ('Insurance     ' :15);
        Miscellaneous : Write ('Miscellaneous' :15)
      end  {case}
    end; {PrintCat}


  begin  {Report}
    WriteLn;
    WriteLn ('Category       ' :15,  'Expenses' :15:2);  {heading}
    {Print each category name and the total}
    for NextCat := Entertainment to Miscellaneous do
      begin
        PrintCat (NextCat);
        WriteLn (Budget[NextCat] :15:2)
      end {for}
  end;  {Report}

begin  {HomeBudget}
  {Initialize array Budget to all zeros.}
  Initialize (Budget);

  {Read and process each expenditure.}
  Post (Budget);

  {Print the expenditures in each category.}
  Report (Budget)
end. {HomeBudget}
```

The loop-control variable NextCat (type BudgetCat) is declared as a local variable in each procedure. In procedure Initialize, the assignment statement

```
Budget[NextCat] := 0.0
```

is repeated once for each value of NextCat and sets each element of Budget to zero. In procedure Report, the statements

```
PrintCat (NextCat);
WriteLn (Budget[NextCat] :15:2)
```

call PrintCat to display a budget category name and WriteLn to display the category total.

Procedure Post must read each expenditure and add it to the appropriate array element. The total of all entertainment expenditures is accumulated in Budget[Entertainment], all food expenditures are accumulated in Budget[Food], and so forth.

Coding Procedure Post

Procedure Post is shown in Fig. 10.7; it uses procedure EnterCat to read the budget category as an integer value and function ConvertCat to convert this value to type BudgetCat.

Figure 10.7 Procedure Post for Home Budget Problem

```
procedure Post (var Budget {input/output} : BudgetArray);
{
   Reads each expenditure amount and adds it to the appropriate
   element of array Budget.
   Pre : Each array element Budget[i] is 0.0
   Post: Each array element Budget[i] is the sum of expense
         amounts for category i.
}
   const
     Quit = 0;                        {sentinel category number}
     MaxCategory = 7;                 {number of budget categories}

   var
     Choice  : Integer;              {next category as an integer}
     NextCat : BudgetCat;            {next category as type BudgetCat}
     Expense : Real;                 {expenditure amount}


   procedure EnterCat (var Choice {output} : Integer);
   {
      Reads the budget category as an integer value.
      Pre : None
      Post: Choice is an integer from 0 to 7.
   }
   begin
     repeat
       WriteLn ('1 — Entertainment');
       WriteLn ('2 — Food');
       WriteLn ('3 — Clothing');
```

```
        WriteLn ('4 - Rent');
        WriteLn ('5 - Tuition');
        WriteLn ('6 - Insurance');
        WriteLn ('7 - Miscellaneous');
        WriteLn ('0 - Quit program');
        WriteLn ('Enter the category number> ');
        ReadLn (Choice)
    until Choice in [Quit..MaxCategory]
  end; {EnterCat}


  function ConvertCat (Choice : Integer) : BudgetCat;
  {
    Converts from an integer value to a value of type BudgetCat.
    Pre : Choice is between 1 and 7.
    Post: Returns a value from Entertainment to Miscellaneous.
  }
  begin {ConvertCat stub}
    ConvertCat := Rent
  end; {ConvertCat}


begin  {Post}
  {Read each budget category and expense and add it to Budget.}
  EnterCat (Choice);
  while Choice <> Quit do
    {invariant:
        no prior value of Choice is Quit
        and Budget[NextCat] is the sum of prior budget entries
        for category NextCat.
    }
    begin
      NextCat := ConvertCat(Choice);   {Convert to type BudgetCat}
      Write ('Enter the expenditure amount $');
      ReadLn (Expense); WriteLn;
      Budget[NextCat] := Budget[NextCat] + Expense;
      EnterCat (Choice)
    end {while }
end; {Post}
```

Procedure Post begins by calling EnterCat to read an integer representing the category into Choice. The while loop body is executed for each value of Choice that is not zero. Function ConvertCat assigns a value to NextCat (type BudgetCat) based on the value of Choice. The assignment statement

```
Budget[NextCat] := Budget[NextCat] + Expense;
```

adds the expense amount to whatever element of array Budget is selected by NextCat.

Testing

A sample run of the home budget program is shown in Fig. 10.8. For the sake of brevity, we display the list of categories just once. As indicated in this run, it is not necessary for the input data to be in order by category. You should verify that all budget categories without purchases remain zero. Also, verify that out-of-range category values do not cause the program to terminate prematurely.

Figure 10.8 Sample Run of Home Budget Program

```
1 - Entertainment
2 - Food
3 - Clothing
4 - Rent
5 - Tuition
6 - Insurance
7 - Miscellaneous
0 - Quit program
Enter the category number> 3
Enter the expenditure amount $25.00

Enter the category number> 7
Enter the expenditure amount $25.00

Enter the category number> 3
Enter the expenditure amount $15.00

Enter the category number> 1
Enter the expenditure amount $675.00

Enter the category number> 0

    Category      Expenses
    Entertainment  675.00
    Food             0.00
    Clothing        40.00
    Rent             0.00
    Tuition          0.00
    Insurance        0.00
    Miscellaneous   25.00
```

Sequential versus Random Access to Arrays

The home budget program illustrates two common ways of selecting array elements for processing. Often, we need to manipulate all elements of an array in some uniform manner (for instance, we might want to initialize them all to zero). In such situations, it makes sense to process the array elements in sequence (*sequential access*), starting with the first and ending with the last. In procedures Initialize and Report, we accomplish that by using a for loop whose loop-control variable is also the array subscript.

In procedure Post, the order in which the array elements are accessed depends completely on the order of the data. The value assigned to NextCat determines the element to be incremented. This approach is called *random access* because the order is not predictable.

Self-Check

1. What happens if the user of the budget program enters the category –1 by mistake?
2. Write function ConvertCat. Integer values from 1 to 7 should be converted to values of type BudgetCat from Entertainment to Miscellaneous. Use a case statement.

Programming

1. Write a procedure that copies each value stored in one array to the corresponding element of another array. (For example, if the arrays are InArray and OutArray, copy InArray[1] to OutArray[1], then copy InArray[2] to OutArray[2], and so on.)
2. Write a procedure that reverses the values stored in an array. If array X has N elements, then X[1] becomes X[N], X[2] becomes X[N–1], and so forth. Hint: Make a local copy of the array before you start to reverse the elements.

 ## 10.4 Arrays as Operands and Parameters

The Pascal operators (for example, <, =, >, +, and –) can manipulate only one array element at a time (provided the element type is an appropriate simple type). Consequently, an array name in an expression is generally followed by its subscript.

Copying an Array

One exception to the preceding rule is the *array copy* operation. It is possible to copy the contents of one array to another array, provided the arrays are the same array type. Given the declarations

```
const
  MaxSize = 100;

type
  Index = 1..MaxSize;
  TestArray = array [Index] of Real;

var
  W, X, Y : TestArray;
  Z : array [Index] of Real;
```

the assignment statements

```
X := Y                 {valid array copy}
W := Y                 {valid array copy}
```

copy each value in array Y to the corresponding element of arrays X and W (that is, Y[1] is copied to X[1] and W[1], Y[2] to X[2] and W[2], and so forth.

It is important to realize that the assignments

```
Z := Y;                    {invalid array copy}
X := Z                     {invalid array copy}
```

are invalid. Even though array Z has the same structure as arrays W, X, and Y, the type of array Z is anonymous and is not considered the same as the named type TestArray. Therefore, you must either declare array Z as type TestArray or use a loop to copy each element individually. This is another reason to avoid the use of anonymous or unnamed types (see Section 10.1).

Arrays as Parameters

If several elements of an array are being manipulated by a procedure, it is generally better to pass the entire array of data instead of individual array elements. In Fig. 10.6, the procedure call statements

```
Initialize (Budget);
Post (Budget);
Report (Budget)
```

pass the entire array Budget to each procedure. Budget is declared as a variable parameter in procedures Initialize and Post and as a value parameter in procedure Report.

In all three procedures, the formal parameter is declared as type BudgetArray. This is necessary because the formal and the actual parameter must be the same array type. The procedure heading

```
procedure Initialize (var Budget : array [BudgetCat] of Real);
```

is invalid because the parameter type must be an identifier.

When an array is used as a variable parameter, Pascal passes the address of the first actual array element into the procedure data area. Because the array elements are stored in adjacent memory cells, the entire array of data can be accessed. The procedure directly manipulates the actual array.

When an array is used as a value parameter, a local copy of the array is made when the procedure is called. The local array is initialized so that it contains the same values as the corresponding actual array. The procedure manipulates the local array, and any changes made to the local array are not reflected in the actual array.

The next two examples illustrate the use of arrays as parameters, assuming the following declarations.

```
const
  MaxSize = 5;

type
  IndexType = 1..MaxSize;
  TestArray = array [IndexType] of Real;

var
  X, Y, Z : TestArray;
```

Although it is possible to use a single assignment statement to copy one array to another, the assignment statement

```
Z := X + Y        {illegal addition of arrays}
```

is invalid because the operator + cannot have an array as an operand. You might use procedure AddArray (Fig. 10.9) to add two arrays of type TestArray.

Figure 10.9 Procedure AddArray

```
procedure AddArray (A, B  {input}  : TestArray;
                    var C {output} : TestArray);

{
  Stores the sum of A[i] and B[i] in C[i]. Array elements
  with subscripts 1..MaxSize are summed, element by element.
  Pre : A[i] and B[i] (1 <= i <= MaxSize) are assigned values
  Post: C[i] := A[i] + B[i] (1 <= i <= MaxSize).
}
  var
    I : IndexType;          {loop control and array subscript}

begin  {AddArray}
  {Add corresponding elements of each array}
  for I := 1 to MaxSize do
    C[I] := A[I] + B[I]
end;   {AddArray}
```

The parameter correspondence for arrays established by the procedure call statement

```
AddArray (X, Y, Z)
```

is shown in Fig. 10.10. Arrays A and B in the procedure data area are local copies of arrays X and Y. As indicated by the solid arrow, the address of the first element of array Z is stored in parameter C. The procedure results are stored directly in array Z. After execution of the procedure, Z[1] will contain the sum of X[1] and Y[1], or 3.5; Z[2] will contain 6.7; and so on. Arrays X and Y will be unchanged. ■

■ Example 10.8

Function SameArray in Fig. 10.11 determines whether two arrays (of type TestArray) are identical. Two arrays are considered identical if the first element of one is the same as the first element of the other, the second element of one is the same as the second element of the other, and so forth.

We can determine that the arrays are not identical by finding a single pair of unequal elements. Consequently, the while loop may be executed anywhere from one time (first elements unequal) to MaxSize − 1 times. Loop exit occurs when a pair of unequal elements is found or just before the last pair is tested.

Figure 10.10 Parameter Correspondence for AddArray (X, Y, Z)

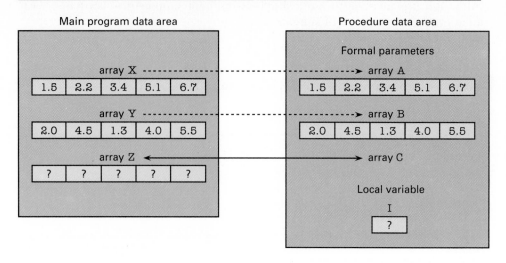

Figure 10.11 Function SameArray

```
function SameArray (A, B : TestArray) : Boolean;
{
  Returns a value of True if the arrays A, B are identical;
  otherwise, returns a value of False.
  Pre : A[i] and B[i] (1 <= i <= MaxSize) are assigned values.
  Post: Returns True if A[i] = B[i] for all i in range
          1..MaxSize; otherwise, returns False.
}
    var
      I : Integer;                    {Array subscript}

begin
    I := 1;                          {Start with first pair}

    {Test corresponding elements of arrays A and B.}
    while (I < MaxSize) and (A[I] = B[I]) do
      {invariant:
          1 <= I <= MaxSize and
          A[I] = B[I] for all prior values of I
      }
      I := I + 1;                    {Advance to next pair}

    {assert:
       an unequal pair was found or all but the
       last pair were compared
    }
    SameArray := A[I] = B[I]         {Define result}
end;   {SameArray}
```

After loop exit, the Boolean assignment statement

```
SameArray := A[I] = B[I]     {Define result}
```

defines the function result. If loop exit occurs because the pair of elements with subscript I is unequal, the function result is False. If loop exit occurs because the last pair of elements is reached, the function result is True if this pair is equal; otherwise, the function result is False.

As an example of how you might use function SameArray, the if statement

```
if SameArray(X, Y) then
   Z := X
else
   AddArray (X, Y, Z)
```

either copies array X to array Z (when X and Y are identical) or stores the sum of arrays X and Y in array Z (when X and Y are not identical).

Because the arrays have MaxSize elements, a common error is to use the condition

```
(I <= MaxSize) and (A[I] = B[I])
```

as the while condition in Fig. 10.11, which causes all element pairs to be tested by the while condition if the arrays are equal. When I is MaxSize + 1, the first part of this condition evaluates to False; however, the second part must still be evaluated unless short-circuit evaluation is used. This leads to an index expression out of bounds run-time error because array element A[MaxSize+1] does not exist.

PROGRAM
STYLE

Efficiency of Variable Parameters versus Protection of Value Parameters

Parameters A and B in Fig. 10.11 are declared as value parameters because they only store data passed into procedure AddArray and their values should not be changed by AddArray. Pascal must create a local copy of these two arrays each time procedure AddArray is called. This copying uses valuable computer time and memory space. If the arrays being copied are very large, the program may terminate with an error because all of its memory space has been used.

To conserve time and memory space, experienced programmers sometimes declare arrays that are used only for input as variable parameters rather than as value parameters. This means, however, that the corresponding actual array is directly manipulated by the procedure and is no longer protected from accidental modification by the procedure. Any changes (either by accident or by design) made to the actual array are an undesirable side effect of the function's execution. If an array corresponds to a value parameter, the changes are made to a local copy, and the actual array is unaffected.

Finding the Minimum or Maximum Value in an Array

A common operation is to determine the minimum or maximum value stored in an array. In Chapter 4, we wrote a program to find the smallest of three characters (see Fig. 4.6). The approach taken to finding the minimum or maximum value in an array is similar. The algorithm for finding the maximum value follows.

Algorithm for Finding the Maximum Value in an Array

1. Assume that the first element is the largest so far and save its subscript as the subscript of the largest so far.
2. for each array element do
      3. if the current element is > than the largest so far then
            4. Save the subscript of the current element as the subscript of the largest so far.

Function MaxBudget in Fig. 10.12 implements this algorithm for the array Budget displayed in Fig. 10.8. The function returns the subscript (type Category) of the largest value in array Budget.

Figure 10.12   Function MaxBudget

```
function MaxBudget (Budget {input} : BudgetArray) : BudgetCat;
{
  Returns the subscript of the largest element in array Budget.
  Pre : Array Budget is defined.
  Post: Budget[MaxIndex] is the largest value in the array.
}
  var
    MaxIndex,                   {Index of largest so far}
    NextIndex : BudgetCat;   {Index of current element}

begin {MaxBudget}
  MaxIndex := Entertainment;   {Assume first element is largest}
  for NextIndex := Entertainment to Miscellaneous do
    if Budget[NextIndex] > Budget[MaxIndex] then
      MaxIndex := NextIndex;

  {assertion:
    All elements are examined and
    MaxIndex is the index of the largest element
  }
  MaxBudget := MaxIndex               {Define result}
end; {MaxBudget}
```

It is important to realize that function MaxBudget returns the subscript (or index) or the largest value, not the largest value itself. Assuming NextCat is type BudgetCat, the following statements display the largest value.

```
NextCat := MaxBudget(Budget);
WriteLn ('The largest expenditure is $', Budget[NextCat] :4:2)
```

Although not as easy to read, the single statement that follows is equivalent; it uses the function designator as the subscript expression.

```
WriteLn ('The largest expenditure is $',
        Budget[MaxBudget(Budget)] :4:2)
```

Individual Array Elements as Parameters

It is acceptable practice to use a single array element as an actual parameter. For example, the expression

```
Round(Budget[5])
```

rounds the value stored in the fifth element of array `Budget`, where the subscripted variable `Budget[5]` is the actual parameter passed to function `Round`.

■ Example 10.9

Procedure `Exchange` in Fig. 10.13 exchanges the values of its two type `Real` parameters.

Figure 10.13 Procedure Exchange

```
procedure Exchange (var P, Q {input/output} : Real);
{
  Exchanges the values of P and Q.
  Pre : P and Q are assigned values.
  Post: P has the value passed into Q and vice-versa.
}
  var
    Temp : Real;              {temporary variable for the exchange}

begin {Exchange}
  Temp := P;   P := Q;   Q := Temp
end; {Exchange}
```

The procedure call statement

```
Exchange (X[2], X[1])
```

uses this procedure to exchange the contents of the first two elements (type `Real`) of array `X`. The identifier `X` is the name of an array in the calling program. The actual parameter `X[2]` corresponds to formal parameter `P`; the actual parameter `X[1]` corresponds to formal parameter `Q`. This correspondence is shown in Fig. 10.14 for a particular array `X`. ■

Figure 10.14 Parameter Correspondence for Exchange (X[2], X[1])

It is illegal to use a subscripted variable as a formal parameter. For example, the procedure declaration

```
procedure Exchange (var X[i], X[j] {input/output} : Real);
```

would cause a syntax error.

Exercises for Section 10.4

Self-Check

1. When is it better to pass an entire array of data to a procedure rather than individual elements?
2. When is a copy of an entire array made for an array that is a procedure parameter? What happens to the copy after the procedure executes?
3. In function SameArray, what will be the value of I when the statement

   ```
   SameArray := A[I] = B[I]
   ```

   executes if array A is equal to array B? If the third elements do not match?
4. Describe how to modify function MaxBudget to get a new function, Min-Budget, that returns the smallest array element.

Programming

1. Write a procedure that assigns a value of True to element I of the output array if element I of one input array has the same value as element I of the other input array; otherwise, assign a value of False. If the input arrays have subscript type IndexType, the output array should have the following type.

   ```
   type
      BoolArray = array [IndexType] of Boolean;
   ```

 ## 10.5   Reading Part of an Array

Usually, we don't know in advance exactly how many elements will be stored in an array. For example, if a professor is processing exam scores, there might be 150 students in one class, 200 in the next, and so on. In this situation, we should declare an array that can accommodate the largest class. Only part of this array will actually be processed for a smaller class.

■ Example 10.10

The array Scores, declared as follows, can accommodate a class of up to 250 students. Each array element can contain an integer value between 0 and 100.

```
const
   MaxSize = 250;
   MaxScore = 100;

type
   ClassIndex = 1..MaxSize;
   ScoreRange = 0..MaxScore;
```

```
  ScoreArray = array [ClassIndex] of ScoreRange;
  ClassRange = 0..MaxSize;

var
  Scores : ScoreArray;
  ClassSize : ClassRange;
```

Procedure ReadScores in Fig. 10.15 reads up to 250 exam scores and prints a warning message when the array is filled. The actual number of scores read is returned as the value of ClassSize. It calls EnterInt (see Fig. 7.17) to read each exam score.

Figure 10.15 Reading Part of an Array

```
procedure ReadScores (var Scores {output} : ScoreArray;
                      var ClassSize {output} : ClassRange);

{
  Reads an array of exam scores (Scores)
  for a class of up to MaxSize students.
  Pre : None
  Post: The data values are stored in array Scores.
        The number of values read is stored in
        ClassSize (0 <= ClassSize <= MaxSize).
  Uses: Procedure EnterInt (see Fig. 7.17)
}
  const
    Sentinel = -1;                    {Sentinel value}

  var
    TempScore : Integer;              {Temporary storage for a score}
begin
  Write ('Enter next score after the prompt or enter ');
  WriteLn (Sentinel :1, ' to stop.');

  {Read each array element until done.}
  ClassSize := 0;                            {initial class size}
  EnterInt (Sentinel, MaxScore, TempScore);
  while (TempScore <> Sentinel) and (ClassSize < MaxSize) do
    {invariant:
       No prior value of TempScore is Sentinel and
       ClassSize <= MaxSize
    }
    begin
      ClassSize := ClassSize + 1;            {Increment ClassSize}
      Scores[ClassSize] := TempScore;        {Save the score}
      EnterInt (Sentinel, MaxScore, TempScore);
    end;   {while}

  {Assert:  Sentinel was read or array is filled.}
  if ClassSize = MaxSize then
    WriteLn ('Array is filled.')
end;   {ReadScores}
```

In any subsequent processing of array Scores, use the variable ClassSize to limit the number of array elements processed. Only the subarray with subscripts 1..ClassSize contains meaningful data; consequently, array elements with subscripts larger than ClassSize should not be manipulated. ClassSize should be passed as a parameter to any procedure that processes the partially filled array.

Exercises for Section 10.5

Self-Check

1. In procedure ReadScores, what prevents the user from entering more than MaxSize scores?
2. What is the range of data values that can be entered? What is the range of data values that can be stored in the array?
3. Rewrite the while loop in ReadScores as a repeat-until loop. Why is the while loop better? Why can't we use a for loop?

 ## 10.6 More Examples of Array Processing

Many of the arrays processed so far had subscript types that were subranges of the integers. This, of course, is not required in Pascal, because a subscript type can be any ordinal type (except Integer). A number of different array types are described in Table 10.5.

Table 10.5 Some Array Types and Applications

Array Type	Application
type NameArray = array [1..10] of Char; var Name : NameArray;	Name[1] := 'A'; stores a person's name (up to 10 letters).
type Temperatures = array [-10..10] of Real; var Fahrenheit : Temperatures;	Fahrenheit[0] := 32.0; stores Fahrenheit temperatures corresponding to -10 through 10 degrees Celsius.
type Counters = array ['A'..'Z'] of Integer; var LetterCount : Counters;	LetterCount['A'] := 0; stores the number of times each uppercase letter occurs.
type Flags = array ['A'..'Z'] of Boolean; var LetterFound : Flags;	LetterFound['X'] := False; stores a set of flags indicating which letters occur and which do not.
type BoolCounts = array [Boolean] of Integer; var Answers : BoolCounts;	Answers[True] := 15; stores the number of True answers and False answers to a quiz.

The array Name has ten elements and can store the letters of a person's name. The array Fahrenheit, with twenty-one elements, can store the Fahrenheit temperature corresponding to each Celsius temperature in the range −10 through +10 degrees Celsius. For example, Fahrenheit[0] would be the Fahrenheit temperature, 32.0, corresponding to 0 degrees Celsius. Arrays LetterCount and LetterFound have the same subscript type (that is, the uppercase letters) and are discussed in the next section. The array Answers has only two elements, with subscript values True and False.

Arrays with Subscripts of Type Char

An array with subscript type Char (or a subrange of Char) is a useful data structure, as shown in the next example.

■ Example 10.11

The arrays LetterCount and LetterFound described in Table 10.5 have the subscript type ['A'..'Z']. Thus, there is an array element for each uppercase letter. The program in Fig. 10.16 displays the number of occurrences of each letter in a line of text. It uses LetterCount['A'] to store the number of occurrences of the letter 'A'. If the letter A occurs, LetterFound['A'] is True; otherwise, LetterFound['A'] is False. Function Cap (see Fig. 9.19) converts the case of each letter read into NextChar to uppercase so that both t and T cause the count for letter T to be incremented.

Figure 10.16   Counting Letters in a Line

```
program Concordance (Input, Output);
{
  Finds and prints the number of occurrences of each letter.
  The case of each letter is immaterial. Letters with counts
  of zero are not displayed.
}
  const
    Sentinel = '*';                  {sentinel character}

  type
    Letter = 'A'..'Z';
    CountArray = array [Letter] of Integer;
    FoundArray = array [Letter] of Boolean;

  var
    LetterCount : CountArray;        {output -- array of counts}
    LetterFound : FoundArray;        {array of flags}
    NextChar : Char;                 {input — each input character}

  {Insert function Cap (see Fig. 9.19) here.}

begin  {Concordance}
  {Initialize LetterCount and LetterFound.}
  for NextChar := 'A' to 'Z' do
    begin
      LetterCount[NextChar] := 0;      {Initialize counts}
      LetterFound[NextChar] := False   {Initialize flags}
    end; {for}
```

```
{Count the letters in a line.}
WriteLn ('Type in a line of text ending with ', Sentinel);
repeat
  Read (NextChar);              {Get next character}
  NextChar := Cap(NextChar);    {Convert to uppercase}
  if NextChar in ['A'..'Z'] then
    begin  {letter}
      LetterCount[NextChar] := LetterCount[NextChar] + 1;
      LetterFound[NextChar] := True      {Set letter flag}
    end  {letter}
until NextChar = Sentinel;

{Print counts of letters that are in the line.}
WriteLn;
WriteLn ('Letter', 'Occurrences' :16);
for NextChar := 'A' to 'Z' do
  if LetterFound[NextChar] then
    WriteLn (NextChar :6, LetterCount[NextChar] :16)
end. {Concordance}
```

```
Type in a line ending with *
This is it!*

Letter     Occurrences
    H            1
    I            3
    S            2
    T            2
```

In the last `if` statement, the condition

```
LetterFound[NextChar]
```

is true if there are one or more occurrences of the letter `NextChar`. This `if` statement ensures that only counts greater than zero are printed. This condition can also be written as

```
LetterCount[NextChar] > 0
```

Doing this is more efficient, because it allows us to eliminate the array `LetterFound`.

● Case Study: Cryptogram Generator Problem

Problem

Your local intelligence agency needs a program to encode messages. One approach is to use a program that generates cryptograms. A cryptogram is a coded message that is formed by substituting a code character for each letter of the original message. The substitution is performed uniformly throughout the original message—for instance, every A is replaced by an S, every B is replaced by a P, and so forth. All punctuation (including spaces between words) remains unchanged.

Design Overview

The program must examine each character in the message and replace each character that is a letter by its code symbol. We can store the code symbols in an array Code with subscript type 'A'..'Z' and element type Char. The character stored in Code['A'] will be the code symbol for the letter 'A'. This enables us to simply look up the code symbol for a letter by using that letter as an index to the array Code.

Data Requirements

Problem Inputs
The array of code symbols (Code : array ['A'..'Z'] of Char)
Each message character

Problem Outputs
Each character of the cryptogram

Initial Algorithm

1. Read in the code symbol for each letter.
2. Read each message character and display the cryptogram.

Algorithm Refinements and Structure Chart

As shown in the structure chart (see Fig. 10.17), procedure ReadCode performs step 1 and procedure Encrypt performs step 2. The data requirements and algorithms for these procedures follow the structure chart.

Local Variable for ReadCode
Loop control variable for accessing array Code
(NextLetter : ['A'..'Z'])

Figure 10.17   Structure Chart for Cryptogram Generator

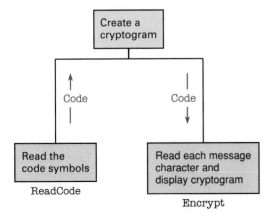

Algorithm for ReadCode
1. Display the alphabet.
2. for each letter do
> 3. Read in the code symbol and store it in array Code.

Local Constant for Encrypt
The sentinel character for the message (Sentinel = '#')

Local Variable for Encrypt
Each message character (NextChar : Char)

Algorithm for Encrypt
1. repeat
> 2. Read the next message character.
> 3. Display the message character or its code symbol.

until the message is complete

Coding

The program in Fig. 10.18 assumes that the uppercase letters are consecutive characters, as they are in the ASCII character set. This program must be modified slightly for computers that use the EBCDIC character set. The character set contains some special characters between the letters I and J and between the letters R and S. One possible modification would be to replace the for statement in procedure ReadCode with

```
for NextLetter := 'A' to 'Z' do
   if NextLetter in ['A'..'I', 'J'..'R', 'S'..'Z'] then
      Read (Code[NextLetter]);
```

The if statement causes the Read statement to be skipped when NextLetter is a special character.

Figure 10.18 Cryptogram Generator

```
program Cryptogram (Input, Output);

{Generates cryptograms corresponding to input messages.}

   type
     Letter = 'A'..'Z';
     CodeArray = array [Letter] of Char;

   var
     Code : CodeArray;              {input - array of code symbols}


   procedure ReadCode (var Code {output} : CodeArray);
   {
     Reads in the code symbol for each letter.
     Pre : None
     Post: 26 data values are read into array Code.
```

```
    }
    var
      NextLetter : Letter;                {each letter}

  begin {ReadCode}
    WriteLn ('First specify the code.');
    WriteLn ('Enter a code symbol under each letter.');
    WriteLn ('ABCDEFGHIJKLMNOPQRSTUVWXYZ');
    {Read each code symbol into array Code.}
    for NextLetter := 'A' to 'Z' do
      Read (Code[NextLetter]);
    ReadLn;                               {Terminate input line}
    WriteLn                               {Skip a line}
  end;   {ReadCode}


  procedure Encrypt (Code {input} : CodeArray);
  {
    Reads each character and prints it or its code symbol.
    Pre : Array Code is defined.
    Post: Each character read was printed or its code
          symbol was printed and the sentinel was just read.
    Uses: Cap (see Fig. 9.19)
  }
    const
      Sentinel = '#';                     {sentinel character}

    var
      NextChar : Char;        {input — each message character}

  begin   {Encrypt}
    WriteLn ('Enter each character of your message;');
    WriteLn ('terminate it with the symbol ', Sentinel);
    repeat
      Read (NextChar);
      NextChar := Cap(NextChar);    {convert to uppercase}
      if NextChar in ['A'..'Z'] then
        WriteLn (Code[NextChar] :5)          {Print code symbol}
      else
        WriteLn (NextChar :5)                {Print non—letter}
    until NextChar = Sentinel
  end;   {Encrypt}


begin   {Cryptogram}
  {Read in the code symbol for each letter.}
  ReadCode (Code);

  {Read each character and print it or its code symbol.}
  Encrypt (Code)
end. {Cryptogram}
```

```
First specify the code you wish to use.
Enter a code symbol under each letter.
ABCDEFGHIJKLMNOPQRSTUVWXYZ
BCDEFGHIJKLMNOPQRSTUVWXYZA

Enter each character of your message;
terminate it with the symbol #
A     B
```

```
t    U
i    J
n    O
y    Z

o    P
n    O
e    F
!    !
#    #
```

Testing

In the preceding sample run, the code symbol for each letter is entered directly beneath that letter and read by procedure ReadCode. The sample run ends with two output columns: the first contains the message; the second contains its cryptogram. For a simple test, try using each letter as its own code symbol. In that case, both columns should be the same. Make sure the program encodes lowercase letters as well as uppercase letters. Characters that are not letters should not be changed.

Exercises for Section 10.6

Self-Check

1. Describe the following array types:
   a. `array [1..20] of Char`
   b. `array ['0'..'9'] of Boolean`
   c. `array [-5..5] of Real`
   d. `array [Boolean] of Char`

2. Provide array type declarations for representing the following:
   a. A group of rooms (living room, dining room, kitchen, etc.) that have a given area.
   b. Elementary school grade levels with a given number of students per grade.
   c. A group of colors with letter values assigned according to the first letter of their name (for example, 'B' for blue).

3. Why is it that spaces and commas are not encoded in the cryptogram program?

Programming

1. Make changes to the cryptogram program to encode the blank character and the punctuation symbols , ; : ? ! . . Hint: Use subscript type Char.

10.7   Strings and Packed Arrays of Characters

Until now, our use of character data has been quite limited. We have used variables of type Char to hold single character values. This section discusses the manipulation of character arrays.

The variable declaration statement

```
const
  Size = 10;

type
  CharArray = array [1..Size] of Char;

var
  Name : CharArray;
  I : Integer;
```

declares a character array Name with ten elements; a single character can be stored in each array element.

The program in Fig. 10.19 first reads a sequence of characters into the array Name, then prints the characters stored in Name. For the data shown in Fig. 10.19, the array Name would be defined as shown below. Name[9] contains the blank character.

Array Name

	[1]	[2]	[3]	[4]	[5]	[6]	[7]	[8]	[9]	[10]
	J	o	n	a	t	h	a	n	□	B

Figure 10.19 Program StoreChars

```
program StoreChars (Input, Output);

{Reads a string of characters into an array.}

  const
    Size = 10;

  type
    CharArray = array [1..Size] of Char;

  var
    Name : CharArray;
    I : Integer;

begin {StoreChars}
  Write ('Enter your first name and an initial ');
  WriteLn ('using 10 characters> ');
  for i := 1 to Size do
    Read (Name[i]);
```

```
     WriteLn;
     Write ('Hello ');
     for i := 1 to Size do
       Write (Name[i]);
     WriteLn ('!')
end. {StoreChars}
```

```
Enter your first name and initial using 10 characters> Jonathan B
Hello Jonathan B!
```

As with any other array, a loop must be used to print all the data stored in a character array. The next section introduces a special type of array that simplifies operations on strings.

Declaring String Variables

You can use a *packed array* to facilitate the manipulation of character strings. When an array is *packed*, some compilers can store more than one character in each computer memory cell. This means that less storage space is required for storing a character string in a packed array. Another important benefit is that Pascal makes it easier for the programmer to manipulate character strings that are stored in packed arrays.

The declaration of two packed arrays, FirstName and LastName, follow.

```
const
  StringSize = 10;

type
  String10 = packed array [1..StringSize] of Char;

var
  FirstName, LastName : String10;
```

Variables FirstName and LastName are called *string variables*, or *strings*, of length 10 (value of StringSize), because they can each store a character string consisting of exactly ten characters.

The statement

```
FirstName := 'A.C. Jones';    {Assign a string to FirstName}
```

stores the string value 'A.C. Jones' in the string variable FirstName, as follows.

Array FirstName

[1]	[2]	[3]	[4]	[5]	[6]	[7]	[8]	[9]	[10]
A	.	C	.	□	J	o	n	e	s

If FirstName is not a string variable, this statement causes a syntax error. Because FirstName and LastName are both the same array type, the assignment statement

```
LastName := FirstName;          {copy FirstName to LastName}
```

copies the string value stored in `FirstName` to `LastName`.

Each string value stored in a string variable must have the same length as the string variable receiving it. The string assignments

```
FirstName := 'Jones';          {invalid — string too short}
FirstName := 'A.C. Johnson';   {invalid — string too long}
```

would cause a `type conflict of operands` syntax error because they violate this rule.

String Variable Declaration

Form: type *string type* = packed array [1.. *size*] of Char;
Example: type String10 = packed array [1..10] of Char;
Interpretation: The identifier *string type* denotes an array type that can store a string value consisting of *size* characters.
Note: The subscript type for *string type* must begin with 1.

Referencing Individual Characters in a String

For the most part, we can manipulate individual characters of a string just like any type `Char` variable. If `FirstName` contains the string `'A.C. Jones'`, the statements

```
FirstName[1] := 'D';
FirstName[6] := 'B';
```

change the value of `FirstName` to the string `'D.C. Bones'`. If `NextChar` is type `Char`, the statement

```
NextChar := FirstName[2];
```

stores a period in `NextChar`. Also, the following `if` condition is true when the value of `i` is 2 or 4.

```
if FirstName[i] = '.' then
   WriteLn ('Period at position ', i :1)
```

The only thing we can't do is pass an element of a string as a variable parameter to a procedure declared in a program system. However, it is permissible to read individual characters directly into a string variable. The statement

```
Read (FirstName[1])
```

replaces the first character in string `FirstName` with the next data character.

Displaying String Variables

The statements

```
Write ('Hello ', FirstName);
WriteLn ('. Good to see you.')
```

display the line

```
Hello D.C. Bones. Good to see you.
```

when `FirstName` contains the string `'D.C. Bones'`. As shown, a string variable can appear without a subscript as a parameter in a `Write` or `WriteLn` statement. When this is done, the variable's contents are printed as a single string.

A format specification can be used with a string variable. The statements

```
Write ('Hello ', FirstName :4);
WriteLn ('! Good to see you.')
```

display the line

```
Hello D.C.! Good to see you.
```

Because the field width 4 is less than the length (10) of string `FirstName`, only the first 4 characters of `FirstName` are displayed. If the field width is larger than the length of the string, leading blanks are displayed before the string value. Table 10.6 provides some examples.

Table 10.6 Displaying a Formatted String

Statement	Effect
Write (FirstName : 10)	D.C. Bones
Write (FirstName : 6)	D.C. B
Write (FirstName : 12)	D.C. Bones

Reading a Value into a String Variable

Unfortunately, standard Pascal provides no shortcut for reading a string value into a string variable. You must use a loop to read individual characters.

■ Example 10.12

Procedure `ReadLnString` in Fig. 10.20 reads a data string from the text file passed as its first parameter. The length (`StrLength`) of the string variable receiving the data is passed as the second parameter, and the string variable name is the third parameter. The number of characters actually read is returned through the fourth parameter and must be between 0 and `StrLength`. Assuming `StrLength` is declared as an `Integer` constant, the type declaration

```
type
   StringType = packed array [1..StrLength] of Char;
```

must precede the declaration of procedure `ReadLnString`.

```
procedure ReadLnString (var InFile {input} : Text;
                        StrLength {input} : Integer;
                        var InString {output} : StringType;
                        var CurLength {output} : Integer);
{
  Reads a data string into InString and returns the number of
  characters read through CurLength.
  Pre : StrLength is the length of a string
        variable of type StringType and file InFile
        is opened for input.
  Post: Reads up to StrLength characters from file InFile into
        InString and advances to the next data line.
        Stops reading characters if <eoln>
        is reached before InString is filled and pads
        the rest of the string with blanks. The
        number of characters read is saved in CurLength
        (0 <= CurLength <= StrLength).
}
  const
    Pad = ' ';                      {character used for padding}

  var
    I : Integer;                    {loop control character}

begin {ReadLnString}
  {Read each character and store it in the next array element.}
  CurLength := 0;                       {no characters read}
  while (not EOLN(InFile)) and (CurLength < StrLength) do
    {invariant: no prior read encountered <eoln> and
       0 <= CurLength <= StrLength and InString[1..CurLength]
       contains data characters read from file InFile
    }
    begin
      CurLength := CurLength + 1;          {Increment subscript}
      Read (InFile, InString[CurLength])   {Read next character}
    end;   {while}

  {assert: at end of line or string is filled}
  ReadLn (InFile);                       {Advance to next line}
  {Pad rest of string with blanks}
  for I := CurLength + 1 to StrLength do
    InString[I] := Pad
end;   {ReadLnString}
```

The `while` loop reads each data character and stores it in the next element of `InString`, as determined by subscript `CurLength`. After loop exit, the statement

```
ReadLn (InFile);                      {Advance to next line}
```

advances to the next line of file `InFile`, skipping over any extra characters at the end of the current data line.

The end of a data string is indicated by `<eoln>`. If the data string length (`CurLength`) is less than `StrLength`, then a blank character should be stored in all array elements that did not receive data. This is called *padding a string with blanks* and is performed by the `for` statement in Fig. 10.20. If `CurLength` is equal to StrLength, the string is already filled with data, so the for loop body is not executed. If the length of the data string is greater than StrLength, only StrLength characters are stored and the extra characters at the end of the data string are not processed.

Table 10.7 shows the values returned through InString and CurLength for three calls to procedure ReadLnString when StrLength is 5. For the last call, only the uppercase letters are read; the lowercase letters are skipped. ■

Table 10.7 Results of Calls to ReadLnString

StrLength	Data String	InString	CurLength
5	ABC<eoln>	'ABC '	3
5	ABCDE<eoln>	'ABCDE'	5
5	ABCDEfg<eoln>	'ABCDE'	5

If you use Input as the first parameter in a call to ReadLnString, the data string is read from the keyboard. Because of differences in the way Pascal systems perform interactive input, ReadLnString may not always read data from the keyboard as expected.

Comparing Strings

Function SameArray in Fig. 10.11 determines whether two arrays of real numbers are identical. It is much easier to make this determination for strings because Pascal allows them to be operands of the relational operators. Assuming the declarations

```
type
   String3 = packed array [1..3] of Char;

var
   AlphaStr, BetaStr : String3;      {strings being compared}
   Same, Differ : Boolean;           {Boolean flags}
```

the statement

```
   Same := AlphaStr = BetaStr        {Are strings identical?}
```

assigns the value True to Same when AlphaStr and BetaStr contain the same string. The assignment statement

```
   Differ := AlphaStr <> BetaStr     {Are strings different?}
```

assigns the value True to Differ when AlphaStr and BetaStr contain different strings. Finally, the assignment statement

```
   Same := AlphaStr = 'Rob'
```

assigns the value True to Same when AlphaStr contains the string 'Rob'.

Using the relational operators <, <=, >, and >=, it is also possible to compare equal-length strings for *lexicographic*, or alphabetical, order. The result of such a comparison is based on the collating sequence (order of characters) for your computer.

For example, the condition

```
AlphaStr < BetaStr
```

is true if the string stored in AlphaStr is considered less than the string stored in BetaStr. This is determined by comparing corresponding characters in both strings starting with the first pair. If the characters are the same, the next pair is checked. If the characters in position i are the first different pair, then AlphaStr is less than BetaStr if AlphaStr[i] is less than BetaStr[i].

The conditions shown in Table 10.8 are true for all character codes shown in Appendix D. The reason each condition is true is explained in the last column.

Table 10.8 Some True String Comparisons

AlphaStr	**Operator**	BetaStr	**Reason Condition Is True**
'AAA'	<	'ZZZ'	'A' < 'Z'
'AZZ'	<	'ZZZ'	'A' < 'Z'
'ZAZ'	<	'ZZA'	'A' < 'Z'
'AZZ	<	'BAA'	'A' < 'B'
'B11'	>	'A99'	'B' > 'A'
'B11'	<	'B12'	'1' < '2'
'ACE'	<	'AID'	'C' < 'I'
'123'	>	'103'	'2' > '0'
'123'	>=	'123'	All characters equal
'30 '	>=	'123'	'3' > '1'

The last line of Table 10.8 shows the curious result that '30 ' >= '123' is true. It is true, because the condition result is based solely on the relationship between the first pair of different characters, '3' and '1'. To avoid these funny results, replace any blanks in numeric strings with zeros. The condition

```
'300' >= '123'
```

is true while the condition

```
'030' >= '123'
```

is false, as expected.

In summary, the following statements are true for string variables where AlphaStr is the string variable declared previously.

- A string literal can be assigned to a string variable of the same length (for example, AlphaStr := 'ABC').
- A string variable can be written without using a loop [for example, Write ('Alpha is ', AlphaStr)].
- A string variable can be compared to a string variable or a string literal of the same length (for example, AlphaStr <> 'ZZZ').

Exercises for Section 10.7

Self-Check

1. If an assignment statement is used to store a string into a packed array, what must be true about the length of the string? What can be done if this is not the case?
2. What is the difference in determining whether two arrays of real numbers are the same as opposed to determining if two packed arrays of characters are the same? What, if any, are the restrictions on the subscript types of the two packed arrays being compared?

Programming

1. Write a procedure that finds the working length of a string that is padded with blanks. Do not include the blank padding in the working length.
2. Write a procedure that stores the reverse of an input string parameter in its output parameter (for example, if the input string is `'happy    '`, the output string should be `'yppah    '`.) The actual length of the string being reversed (excluding blank padding) should also be an input parameter.
3. Write a program that uses the procedure in the preceding exercise to determine whether a string is a palindrome. (A palindrome is a string that reads the same way left to right as it does right to left, for example, `'level'`.)

 ## 10.8   Using Strings

Now that we have a way to store character strings in memory, we can improve our capability to manipulate textual data. Suppose that during the spring semester you begin thinking about a summer job. One thing you might want to do is write a program that prints form letters so you can do a mass mailing to inquire about summer job opportunities in a variety of fields.

● Case Study: Printing a Form Letter

Problem
You want a program that can help you write job application letters. Each letter will be sent to an output file for printing.

Design Overview
A letter consists of a heading, a salutation, the body, and a closing. The heading, salutation, and first line of the body will be different for each letter, but the body and the closing will be the same. First, you'll use an editor to create the letter body and closing and save it as a text file (BodyFile). To individualize each letter, you want to enter data for the first part of the letter at the keyboard

and then write the first part of the letter to the output file (Letter). Next, you can write the rest of the letter from file BodyFile to the output file.

An example of the data entry process for the first part of the letter follows. The information you'll enter is in color.

```
Today's date          > July 27, 1990
Employer name         > Peter Liacouras
Company name          > Temple University
Address               > Broad and Montgomery Streets
City, state, and zip> Philadelphia, PA 19122
```

This data would be inserted in the first several lines written to the output file, as shown in Fig. 10.21.

Figure 10.21 First Lines of File Letter

```
                                    July 27, 1990

Peter Liacouras
Temple University
Broad and Montgomery Streets
Philadelphia, PA  19122

Dear Peter Liacouras:

    I am interested in applying for a job at Temple University.
```

Data Requirements

Problem Inputs
The body of the letter (BodyFile : Text)
Today's date (Date : StringType)
Employer's name (Employer : StringType)
Company name (Company : StringType)
Company address (Address : StringType)
City, state, and zip (CityStZip : StringType)

Problem Outputs
The complete letter (Letter : Text)

Initial Algorithm
1. Read the preamble data from the keyboard and write it to Letter.
2. Copy the letter body to Letter.

Algorithm Refinement and Structure Chart
From the structure chart in Fig. 10.22, you can see that procedures Preamble and WriteBody perform steps 1 and 2, respectively.

Case Study: Printing a Form Letter, continued

Figure 10.22   Structure Chart for Form Letter Program

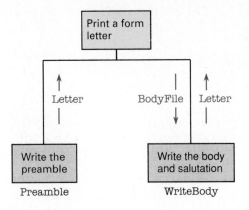

Coding the Main Program

The main program body, shown in Fig. 10.23, prepares both text files and calls procedures `Preamble` and `WriteBody`. Procedure `ReadLnString` (see Fig. 10.20) should be the first procedure declared in the main program, because it will be called by both `Preamble` and `WriteBody`. The main program displays a message before data entry begins and a message after the letter is completed.

Figure 10.23   Form Letter Writing Program

```
program FormLetter (Input, Output, BodyFile, Letter);
{
  Writes a job application letter to an output file. The data
  for the letter preamble is read from the keyboard; the letter
  body is copied from a data file to the output file.
}
  const
    StrLength = 40;

  type
    StringType = packed array [1..StrLength] of Char;

  var
    BodyFile,                      {input - body of letter}
    Letter    : Text;              {output - completed letter file}


  {Insert procedure ReadLnString here.}
  {Insert procedures Preamble and WriteBody here.}

begin {FormLetter}
  Reset (BodyFile);
  Rewrite (Letter);
  WriteLn (Output, 'Writing job application letter.');
  Preamble (Letter);
  WriteBody (BodyFile, Letter);
```

```
  WriteLn (Output, 'Letter copied to output file.')
end. {FormLetter}
```

Coding the Procedures

Procedure `Preamble` (see Fig. 10.24) reads, from the keyboard the strings needed for the letter heading and the salutation. After data entry, the strings read into `DateString`, `Employer`, `Company`, `Address`, `CityStZip` are written to file `Letter`.

Figure 10.24   Procedure Preamble

```
procedure Preamble (var Letter {output} : Text);
{
  Writes a preamble for a job application letter to an output file.
  Pre : The output file is opened.
  Post: Writes the heading, salutation, and first sentence of a
        job application letter using data entered at the keyboard.
  Uses: ReadLnString
}
  const
    PageWidth = 50;                      {padding for date}

  var
    DateString,                          {input - data strings}
    Employer, Company,                   {            "         }
    Address, CityStZip : StringType;     {            "         }
    DateLen,  EmpLen, CompLen,
    AddLen, CityLen    : Integer;        {length of each string}

begin {Preamble}
  {Enter all data}
  Write ('Today''s date        > ');
  ReadLnString (Input, StrLength, DateString, DateLen);
  Write ('Employer name       > ');
  ReadLnString (Input, StrLength, Employer, EmpLen);
  Write ('Company name        > ');
  ReadLnString (Input, StrLength, Company, CompLen);
  Write ('Address             > ');
  ReadLnString (Input, StrLength, Address, AddLen);
  Write ('City, state, and zip> ');
  ReadLnString (Input, StrLength, CityStZip, CityLen);

  {Write letter preamble.}
  WriteLn (Letter, ' ' :PageWidth, DateString :DateLen);
  WriteLn (Letter);
  WriteLn (Letter, Employer);
  WriteLn (Letter, Company);
  WriteLn (Letter, CityStZip);
  WriteLn (Letter);
  WriteLn (Letter, 'Dear ', Employer :EmpLen, ':');
  WriteLn (Letter);
  Write (Letter, '    I am interested in applying for a job at ');
  WriteLn (Letter, Company :CompLen, '.');
  WriteLn (Letter)
end; {Preamble}
```

Procedure `WriteBody` copies the body of the letter (not shown) from the input file to the output file. Procedure `WriteBody` is shown in Fig. 10.25. The `while` loop copies each line of the data file to the output file.

Figure 10.25   Procedure WriteBody

```
procedure WriteBody (var BodyFile {input},
                         Letter   {output} : Text);
{
    Copies the body of a job application letter from a data file
    to an output file.
    Pre : The input file and output file are opened.
    Post: Writes the letter body to the output file.
    Uses: ReadLnString
}
    var
       OneLine : StringType;          {next data line}
       LineLength : Integer;          {length of line read}

begin {WriteBody}
  {Copy each line until done}
  while not EOF(BodyFile) do
    begin
       ReadLnString (BodyFile, StrLength, OneLine, LineLength);
       WriteLn (Letter, OneLine :LineLength)
    end {while}
end; {WriteBody}
```

Testing

Test procedure `ReadLnString` using a driver program before you run the form letter program. Try to read strings from the keyboard as well as from a data file. See what happens when the data lines are longer than the length of the receiving string variable and when the data line is exactly the same length as the string variable. When you run the form letter program, try using an empty file `BodyFile`.

Exercises for Section 10.8

Self-Check

1. Procedure `Preamble` displays several character strings. What method is used so that the blank padding is not displayed?

Programming

1. Assume that the technique used in procedure `Preamble` to keep the blank padding from being displayed does not work on your computer. Write a procedure `WriteString` that displays characters 1 through `StrLen` of a string where the string and `StrLen` are passed as parameters.

10.9 Common Programming Errors

The most common error in the use of arrays is an index expression out of bounds run-time error. This error occurs when the subscript value is outside the allowable range for the array being processed. Most often, this error is caused by an incorrect subscript expression, a loop parameter error, or a non-terminating loop. Before you spend considerable time debugging, carefully check all suspect subscript calculations for out-of-range errors. You can do that most easily by inserting diagnostic output statements in your program to print subscript values that might be out of range.

If an out-of-range subscript occurs inside a loop, make sure the loop is terminating properly. If the loop-control variable is not being updated as expected, the loop may be repeated more often than required. This could happen, for example, if the update step comes after the loop end statement or if the loop begin and end are erroneously omitted.

Also doublecheck the subscript values at the loop boundaries. If these values are in range, it is likely that all other subscript references in the loop are in range as well.

As with all Pascal data types, make sure there are no type inconsistencies. The subscript type and element type used in all array references must correspond to the types specified in the array declaration.

Similarly, the types of two arrays used in an array copy statement or as corresponding parameters must be the same. Remember to use only identifiers without subscripts as formal array parameters and to specify the types of all array parameters using identifiers.

A variable of type packed array [1..N] of Char is a string variable of length N (a constant). A string variable of length N can be assigned a string value consisting of exactly N characters. An incompatible type syntax error is detected if a string value that is too short or too long is assigned to a string variable. If one string variable is assigned to another, they must both be the same length. If InString is a string variable, remember that InString[i] cannot correspond to a variable parameter of type Char.

Chapter Review

This chapter introduced a data structure called an array, which is a convenient facility for naming and referencing a collection of like items. We discussed how to declare an array type and how to reference an individual array element by placing a subscript in brackets following the array name.

The for statement enables us to easily reference the elements of an array in sequence. We can use for statements to initialize arrays, to read and print arrays, and to control the manipulation of individual array elements in sequence.

We also examined how to allocate storage for a string variable and how to store a string value in a string variable. You saw that operations such as comparison, assignment, and display are performed more easily on a string variable because the entire string can be processed as a unit rather than element by element.

New Pascal Constructs

Table 10.9 describes the new Pascal constructs introduced in this chapter.

Table 10.9 Summary of New Pascal Constructs

Construct	Effect

Array Declaration
`type`
`  IntArray = array [1..10] of Integer;`
 	
`var`
`  Cube, Count : IntArray;`
	The data type `IntArray` describes an array with 10 type `Integer` elements. `Cube` and `Count` are arrays with this structure.

Packed Array Declaration
`type`
`  String10 = packed array [1..10] of`
`Char;`
 	
`var`
`  Name : String10;`
	The data type `String10` describes a packed array of 10 characters. `Name` is a string variable of length 10.

Array References
`for I := 1 to 10 do`
`  Cube [I] := I * I * I`
	Saves I cubed in the Ith element of array `Cube`.

`if Cube[5] > 100 then`	Compares `Cube[5]` to 100.
`Write (Cube[1], Cube[2])`	Displays the first two cubes.
Array Copy `Count := Cube`	Copies contents of array `Cube` to array `Count`.
Operations on Strings `Name := 'R. Koffman'`	Saves `'R. Koffman'` in `Name`.
`WriteLn (Name)`	Displays `'R. Koffman'`.
`if Name > 'Daffy Duck' then`	Compares `Name` to `'Daffy Duck'`.

✓ Quick-Check Exercises

1. What is a data structure?
2. Which standard types cannot be array subscript types? Array element types?

3. Can values of different types be stored in an array?
4. If an array is declared to have ten elements, must the program use all ten?
5. When can the assignment operator be used with an array as its operands? Answer the same question for the equality operator.
6. The two methods of array access are _____ and _____.
7. The _____ loop allows us to access the elements of an array in _____ order.
8. Can the variable declared as follows be used to store a string of length five using an assignment statement? If not, why not?

```
var
   AString : packed array [6..10] of Char;
```

9. Explain why variable parameters are a more efficient use of memory when passing arrays to a procedure.
10. Declare variables First and Last that can be used to enter a person's first name and last name (maximum of twenty characters each) into separate strings. Under what circumstances can the Pascal Read procedure be used to read a data string into First or Last?

Answers to Quick-Check Exercises
1. A data structure is a grouping of related values in main memory.
2. Real and Integer; all can be element types.
3. No
4. No
5. If the arrays are the same type. If the arrays are packed arrays of characters with a subscript type of the form 1..N.
6. random and sequential
7. for, sequential
8. No, the subscript type must be the subrange type 1..5.
9. A local copy of each array used as a value parameter is made when a procedure is called.
10.
```
type
   AString = packed array [1..20] of Char;

var
   First, Last : AString;
```

No circumstances; a loop must always be used.

Review Questions

1. Identify the error in the following code segment. When will the error be detected?

```
program Test;
   type
      AnArray = array [1..8] of Integer;

   var
      X : AnArray;
      I : Integer;
```

```
begin {Test}
   for I := 1 to 9 do
      X[I] := I
end. {Test}
```

2. Declare an array of reals called Week that can be referenced by using any day of the week as a subscript, where Sunday is the first subscript.

3. Identify the error in the following segment of Pascal statements.

```
type
   AnArray = array [Char] of Real;

var
   X : AnArray;
   I : Integer;

begin
   I := 1;
   X[I] := 8.384
end.
```

4. Is the last statement in the following Pascal program segment a valid Pascal statement?

```
type
   RealArray = array [1..8] of Real;

var
   X : RealArray;
   I : Integer;

begin
   I := 1;
   X(I) := 8.384
end.
```

5. What are two common ways of selecting array elements for processing?

6. Write a Pascal program segment to print out the index of the smallest and the largest numbers in an array X of 20 integers with values from 0 to 100. Assume array X already has values assigned to each element.

7. The parameters for a procedure are two arrays (type RealArray) and an integer that represents the length of the arrays. The procedure copies the first array in the parameter list to the other array in reverse order using a loop structure. Write the procedure.

8. List three advantages to using packed character arrays.

9. What would be a valid reason for not passing an array that provides input to a procedure as a value parameter?

Programming Projects

1. Write a program to read N data items into two arrays X and Y of size 20. Store the product of corresponding elements of X and Y in a third array Z, also of size 20. Print a three-column table displaying the arrays X, Y, and Z. Then compute and print the square root of the sum of the items in Z. Make up your own data, with N less than 20.

2. Write a program for the following problem. You are given a collection of scores for the last exam in your computer course. You are to compute the average of these scores and then assign grades to each student according to the following rule.

If a student's score is within 10 points (above or below) of the average, assign a grade of Satisfactory. If the score is more than 10 points higher than the average, assign a grade of Outstanding. If the score is more than 10 points below the average, assign a grade of Unsatisfactory.

Hint: The output from your program should consist of a labeled three-column list containing the ID number, exam score, and grade of each student.

3. A number is prime if there is no smaller prime number other than 1 that divides it. Consequently, to determine whether N is prime, it is sufficient to check only the prime numbers less than N as possible divisors. Use this information to write a program that stores the first one hundred prime numbers in an array. Have your program print the array after it is done.

4. The results of a true-false exam given to a computer science class have been coded for input to a program. The information available for each student consists of a student identification number and the student's answers to ten true or false questions. The available data are as follows:

Student Identification	Answer String
0080	FTTFTFTTFT
0340	FTFTFTTTFF
0341	FTTFTTTTTT
0401	TTFFTFFTTT
0462	TTFTTTFFTF
0463	TTTTTTTTTT
0464	FTFFTFFTFT
0512	TFTFTFTFTF
0618	TTTFFTTFTF
0619	FFFFFFFFFF
0687	TFTTFTTFTF
0700	FTFFTTFFFT
0712	FTFTFTFTFT
0837	TFTFTTFTFT

Write a program that first reads in the answer string representing the ten correct answers (use FTFFTFFTFT as data). Next, read each student's data and compute and store the number of correct answers for each student in one array and store the student ID number in the corresponding element of another array. Determine the best score, Best. Then print a three-column table that displays the ID number, the score, and the grade for each student. The grade should be determined as follows: if the score is equal to Best or Best−1, give an A; if it is Best−2 or Best−3, give a C. Otherwise, give an F.

5. The results of a survey of the households in your township are available for public scrutiny. Each record contains data for one household, including a four-digit integer identification number, the annual income for the household, and the number of members of the household. Write a program to read the survey results into three arrays and perform the following analyses:

a. Count the number of households included in the survey and print a three-column table displaying the data read in. (Assume that no more than twenty-five households were surveyed.)

b. Calculate the average household income and list the identification number and income of each household that exceeds the average.

c. Determine the percentage of households that have incomes below the poverty level. Compute the poverty level income using the formula

$$p = \$6500.00 + \$750.00 * (m - 2)$$

where m is the number of members of each household. This formula shows that the poverty level depends on the number of family members, m, and the poverty level income increases as m gets larger.

Test your program on the following data.

Identification Number	Annual Income	Household Members
1041	12,180	4
1062	13,240	3
1327	19,800	2
1483	22,458	8
1900	17,000	2
2112	18,125	7
2345	15,623	2
3210	3,200	6
3600	6,500	5
3601	11,970	2
4725	8,900	3
6217	10,000	2
9280	6,200	1

6. Assume that a set of sentences is to be processed. Each sentence consists of a sequence of words, separated by one or more blank spaces. Write a program that will read these sentences and count the number of words with one letter, the number of words with two letters, and so on, up to ten letters.

7. Write an interactive program that plays the game of Hangman. Read the word to be guessed into string Word. The player must guess the letters belonging to Word. The program should terminate when either all letters have been guessed correctly (player wins) or a specified number of incorrect guesses have been made (computer wins). Hint: Use a string Solution to keep track of the solution so far. Initialize Solution to a string of symbols '*'. Each time a letter in Word is guessed, replace the corresponding '*' in Solution with that letter.

Records

11

The previous chapter introduced the array, a data structure that is fundamental to programming and included in almost every high-level programming language. This chapter examines another data structure, the record (available in Pascal but not in all other high-level languages). Records make it easier to organize and represent information in Pascal, a major reason for the popularity of the Pascal language.

Like an array, a record is a collection of related data items. Unlike an array, however, the individual components of a record can contain data of different types. We can use a record to store a variety of information about a person, such as the name, marital status, age, and date of birth. Each data item is stored in a separate record field; we can reference each data item stored in a record through its field name.

In this chapter, we also develop an abstract data type for complex arithmetic, consisting of a record type and associated operators.

 11.1   The Record Data Type

A *data base* is a collection of information stored in a computer memory or a disk file. A data base is subdivided into records, which normally contain information regarding particular data objects. For example, the description of a person, place, or thing would be stored as a record.

Record Type Declaration

Before a record can be created or saved, the record format must be specified through a record type declaration.

■ Example 11.1

The staff of our small software firm is growing rapidly. To keep the records more accessible and organized, we decide to store relevant data, such as the following descriptive information, in an employee data base.

```
ID  : 1234
Name: Caryn Jackson
Sex : Female
Number of Dependents: 3
Hourly Rate: 3.98
Taxable Salary (for 40 hour week): 130.40
```

We can declare a record type Employee to store this information. There must be six *fields* in the record type, one for each data item. We must specify the name of each field and the type of information stored in each field. We choose the names in the same way we choose all other identifiers: the names describe the nature of the information represented. The contents of each field determines the appropriate data type. For example, the employee's name should be stored in a string field.

The record type Employee has six distinct fields. One is a string type, two are type Real, one is type Integer, one is a subrange type, and one (Sex) is an enumerated type (Gender).

```
const
   StrLength = 20;

type
   IDRange = 1111..9999;
   StringType = packed array [1..StrLength] of Char;
   Gender = (Female, Male);

   Employee = record
               ID : IDRange;
               Name : StringType;
               Sex : Gender;
               NumDepend : Integer;
               Rate, TaxSal : Real
            end; {Employee}
```

The record type is a template that describes the format of each record and the name of each data element. A variable declaration is required to allocate storage space for a record. The record variables Clerk and Janitor are declared next.

```
var
   Clerk, Janitor : Employee;
```

The record variables Clerk and Janitor both have the structure specified in the declaration for record type Employee. Thus, the memory allocated for each consists of storage space for six distinct values. The record variable Clerk is pictured as follows, assuming the values shown earlier are stored in memory. ■

Record variable Clerk

ID	1234
Name	Caryn □Jackson□□□□□□□
Sex	Female
NumDepend	2
Rate	3.98
TaxSal	130.40

As illustrated in the type declaration for Employee, each field of a record can be a standard data type or a user-defined simple or structured data type. The record type declaration is described in the next display.

Record Type Declaration

Form: type
         rec type = record
                        id list$_1$: *type*$_1$;
                        id list$_2$: *type*$_2$;

> $\quad\quad\quad\quad\quad\quad$.
>
> $\quad\quad\quad\quad\quad\quad$.
>
> $\quad\quad\quad\quad\quad\quad$.
>
> $\quad\quad\quad\quad$ *id list*$_n$: *type*$_n$
>
> $\quad\quad\quad$ `end;`
>
> **Example:** `type`
>
> $\quad\quad\quad\quad$ `Complex = record`
>
> $\quad\quad\quad\quad\quad\quad\quad$ `RealPart, ImaginaryPart : Real`
>
> $\quad\quad\quad\quad\quad$ `end;`
>
> **Interpretation:** The identifier *rec type* is the name of the record structure being described. Each *id list*$_i$ is a list of one or more field names separated by commas; the data type of each field in *id list*$_i$ is specified by *type*$_i$.
>
> **Note:** *type*$_i$ can be any standard or user-defined data type, including a structured type. If *type*$_i$ is a user-defined data type, it can be defined either before the record or as part of the record description.

Manipulating Individual Fields of a Record

We can reference a record field by using a *field selector*, which consists of the record variable name followed by the field name. A period separates the field name and the record name.

■ Example 11.2

Figure 11.1 is an example of the record variable `Clerk`. The data shown earlier could be stored in `Clerk` through the sequence of assignment statements in the figure.

Figure 11.1 Record Variable Clerk

```
Clerk.ID := 1234;
Clerk.Name := 'Caryn Jackson       ';
Clerk.Sex := Female;
Clerk.NumDepend := 2;
Clerk.Rate := 3.98;
Clerk.TaxSal := Clerk.Rate * 40.0 - Clerk.NumDepend * 14.40
```

Once data are stored in a record, they can be manipulated the same as other data in memory. For example, the last assignment statement in Fig. 11.1 computes the clerk's taxable salary by deducting $14.40 for each dependent from the gross salary (`Clerk.Rate * 40.0`). The computed result is saved in the record field `Clerk.TaxSal`.

The statements

```
Write ('The clerk is ');
case Clerk.Sex of
  Female : Write ('Ms. ');
  Male   : Write ('Mr. ')
end; {case}
Write (Clerk.Name)
```

display the clerk's name after an appropriate title ('Ms.' or 'Mr.'); the output line follows.

```
The clerk is Ms. Caryn Jackson
```
■

Abstract Record

We can summarize what we have discussed about records in the following specification for an abstract record.

Specification for Abstract Records

Structure: A record is a collection of related data values of different types. Each data value is stored in a separate field of the record.

Operators: Two basic operators act on fields of a record: *store* and *retrieve*. The store operator inserts a value into the record field. If A is a record with a field named B, and C is an expression that is assignment compatible with the type of field B, the statement

```
A.B := C
```

stores the contents of C in field B of record A. If field B of record A is assignment compatible with the type of variable C, the statement

```
C := A.B
```

retrieves the value in field B of record A and copies it into C.

The assignment operator can also be used to copy the contents of one record to another record of the same type. If A and D are record variables of the same type, the statement

```
A := D
```

copies all values associated with record D to record A.

Exercises for Section 11.1

Self-Check

1. Each part in an inventory is represented by its part number, a descriptive name, the quantity on hand, and the price. Define a record type Part.
2. A catalog listing for a textbook consists of the author's name, the title, the publisher, and the year of publication. Declare a record type CatalogEntry

and variable Book and write assignment statements that store the relevant data for this textbook in Book.

 11.2 The with Statement

It is tedious to write the complete field selector each time you reference a field of a record. You can use the with statement to shorten the field selector.

```
with Clerk do
  begin
    Write ('The clerk is ');
    case Sex of
      Female : Write ('Ms. ');
      Male   : Write ('Mr. ')
    end;  {case}
    WriteLn (Name);

    TaxSal := 40.0 * Rate - 14.40 * NumDepend;
    WriteLn ('The clerk''s taxable salary is $', TaxSal :4:2)
  end; {with}
```

As you can see, you don't need to specify both the record variable and the field names inside a with statement. The record variable Clerk is identified in the with statement header; consequently, only the field name is needed, not the complete field selector (for example, Rate instead of Clerk.Rate). The with statement is particularly useful when you are manipulating several fields of the same record variable, as in this example.

SYNTAX
DISPLAY

---

with Statement

Form: with *record var* do
                statement

Example: with Clerk do
                if NumDepend > 3 then
                    Rate := 1.5 * Rate

Interpretation: *Statement* can be a single statement or a compound statement. *record var* is the name of a record variable. Anywhere within *statement*, you can reference a field of *record var* by specifying only its field name.

■ Example 11.3

The program in Fig. 11.2 computes the distance from an arbitrary point on the x-y plane to the origin (intersection of the x-axis and the y-axis). The values of the x-coordinate and the y-coordinate are entered as data and stored in the fields X and Y of the record variable Point1. The formula used to compute the distance, d, from the origin to an arbitrary point (X, Y) is

$$d = \sqrt{X^2 + Y^2}$$

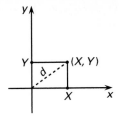

Because the record variable Point1 is specified in the with statement header, we need only the field names X and Y to reference the coordinates of the data point. Each coordinate is read separately, because it is illegal to use a record variable as a parameter of a ReadLn or WriteLn procedure (i.e., only individual fields of a record variable may be read or displayed at a terminal, not the entire record). ∎

Figure 11.2 Distance from Point to Origin

```
program DistOrigin (Input, Output);

{Finds the distance from a point to the origin.}

   type
      Point = record
                 X, Y : Real
              end;   {Point}

   var
      Point1 : Point;        {input - the data point}
      Distance : Real;       {output - its distance from the origin}

begin
   with Point1 do
      begin
         Write ('X> ');
         ReadLn (X);
         Write ('Y> ');
         ReadLn (Y);
         Distance := Sqrt(Sqr(X) + Sqr(Y));
         WriteLn ('Distance to origin is ', Distance :4:2)
      end {with}
end.

X> 3.00
Y> 4.00
Distance to origin is 5.00
```

PROGRAM
STYLE

A Word of Caution About the with Statement

Although the with statement is helpful in reducing the length of program statements that manipulate record components, it also can reduce the clarity of these statements. For example, in Fig. 11.2 it is not obvious that the statement

```
Distance := Sqrt(Sqr(X) + Sqr(Y));
```

is passing to the function Sqr two record fields (Point.X and Point.Y) and not two variables.

The possibility of confusion and error increases when you are manipulating two record variables (say, Point1 and Point2). In that case, if the field name X is referenced by itself, it is not apparent whether we mean Point1.X or Point2.X. Pascal uses the record variable specified in the closest with statement header.

Exercises for Section 11.2

Self-Check

1. Write the Pascal statements, using a with statement, required to print the values stored in Clerk in the form shown in Fig. 11.1.

Programming

1. Modify program DistOrigin to find the distance between two points. Use the formula

$$Distance = \sqrt{(X_1 - X_2)^2 + (Y_1 - Y_2)^2}$$

Store the points in two record variables of type Point.

11.3 Records as Operands and Parameters

Because arithmetic and logical operations can be performed only on individual memory cells, record variables cannot be used as the operands of arithmetic and relational operators. Arithmetic and logical operators must be used with individual fields of a record, as shown in the previous section. This is also true at this point for the standard procedures Read/ReadLn and Write/WriteLn. (Chapter 14 examines how to read and write entire record variables to certain types of files.)

Record Assignment

We can copy all the fields of one record variable to another record variable of the same type using a record copy (assignment) statement. If Clerk and Janitor are both record variables of type Employee, the statement

```
Clerk := Janitor      {copy Janitor to Clerk}
```

copies each field of Janitor into the corresponding field of Clerk.

Records as Parameters

A record can be passed as a parameter to a function or procedure, provided the actual parameter is the same type as its corresponding formal parameter. The use of records as parameters can shorten parameter lists considerably, because one parameter (the record variable) can be passed instead of several related parameters.

■ Example 11.4

In a grading program, the summary statistics for an exam might consist of the average score, the highest and lowest scores, and the standard deviation. In previous problems, we would have stored these data in separate variables; now, however, it makes sense to group them together as a record.

```
type
   ExamStats = record
                  Low, High : 0..100;
                  Average, StandardDev : Real;
               end;   {ExamStats}

var
   Exam : ExamStats;
```

A procedure that computes one of these results (for example, Average) could be passed a single record field (for example, Exam.Average). A procedure that manipulates more than one field could be passed the entire record. An example is procedure PrintStat, shown in Fig. 11.3. ■

Figure 11.3 Procedure PrintStat

```
procedure PrintStat (Exam {input} : ExamStats);
{
  Prints the exam statistics.
  Pre : The fields of record variable Exam are assigned values.
  Post: Each field of Exam is displayed.
}
begin {PrintStat}
  with Exam do
    begin
      WriteLn ('High score: ', High :1);
      WriteLn ('Low score: ', Low :1);
      WriteLn ('Average: ', Average :3:1);
      WriteLn ('Standard deviation: ', StandardDev :3:1)
    end  {with}
end;  {PrintStat}
```

■ Example 11.5

Before performing a potentially dangerous or costly experiment in the laboratory, we can often use a computer program to simulate the experiment. In computer simulations, we need to keep track of the time of day as the experiment progresses. Normally, the time of day is updated after a certain period has elapsed. The record type `Time` is declared as follows, assuming a twenty-four-hour clock.

```
type
  Time = record
    Hour : 0..23;
    Minute, Second : 0..59
  end;  {Time}
```

Procedure `ChangeTime` in Fig. 11.4 updates the time of day, `TimeOfDay` (type `Time`), after a time interval, `ElapsedTime`, which is expressed in seconds. Each statement that uses the `mod` operator updates a particular field of the record represented by `TimeOfDay`. The `mod` operator ensures that each updated value is within the required range; the `div` operator converts multiples of sixty seconds to minutes and multiples of sixty minutes to hours. ∎

Figure 11.4 Procedure ChangeTime

```
procedure ChangeTime (ElapsedTime {input} : Integer;
                      var TimeOfDay {input/output} : Time);
{
  Updates the time of day, TimeOfDay, assuming a 24-hour clock
  and an elapsed time of ElapsedTime in seconds.
  Pre : ElapsedTime and record TimeOfDay are assigned values.
  Post: TimeOfDay is incremented by ElapsedTime.
}

  var
    NewHour, NewMin, NewSec : Integer; {temporary values}

begin {ChangeTime}
  with TimeOfDay do
    begin
      NewSec := Second + ElapsedTime;          {total seconds}
      Second := NewSec mod 60;                 {seconds mod 60}
      NewMin := Minute + (NewSec div 60);      {total minutes}
      Minute := NewMin mod 60;                 {minutes mod 60}
      NewHour := Hour + (NewMin div 60);       {total hours}
      Hour := NewHour mod 24                   {hours mod 24}
    end {with}
end;  {ChangeTime}
```

Reading a Record

Normally, we use a procedure to read data into a record. Procedure Read-Employee in Fig. 11.5 could be used to read data into the first five fields of a record variable of type `Employee`. Because we are passing a record variable to ReadEmployee, only one parameter is needed, not five. The procedure call statement

```
ReadEmployee (Clerk)
```

causes the data read to be stored in record variable `Clerk`.

```
procedure ReadEmployee (var OneClerk {output} : Employee);
{
   Reads one employee record into OneClerk.
   Pre : None
   Post: Data are read into record OneClerk.
   Uses: procedure ReadLnString (see Fig. 10.20) and
         constant StrLength (value is 20).
}
   var
      SexChar : Char;              {letter indicating sex}
      NameLen : Integer;           {actual length of Name}

   {Insert procedure ReadLnString }
begin {ReadEmployee}
   with OneClerk do
      Write ('ID> ');
      ReadLn (ID);
      Write ('Name> ');
      ReadLnString (Input, StrLength, Name, NameLen);
      Write ('Sex (F or M)> ');
      Read (SexChar);
      case SexChar of
         'F', 'f' : Sex := Female;
         'M', 'm' : Sex := Male
      end; {case}

      Write ('Number of dependents> ');
      ReadLn (NumDepend);
      Write ('Hourly rate> ');
      ReadLn (Rate)
   end   {with}
end; {ReadEmployee}
```

The procedure call statement

```
ReadLnString (Input, StrLength, Name, NameLen);
```

calls procedure ReadLnString (see Fig. 10.20) to enter a data string. ReadLn–
String returns a character string (Name) and an integer value (NameLen) that
indicates the number of characters read into Name. The latter value is not saved
in the employee's record.

Exercises for Section 11.3

Self-Check

1. What does the following program segment do? Provide the declarations for
   variables Exam1 and Exam2.

```
PrintStat (Exam1);
Exam2 := Exam1;
Exam2.High := Exam2.High - 5.0;
PrintStat (Exam2)
```

2. If all fields of variable Now (type Time) are initially zero, how is Now changed by the execution of the following program segment?

```
ChangeTime (3600, Now);
ChangeTime (7125, Now)
```

Programming

1. Write a procedure that initializes all fields of a variable of type Time to zero.
2. Write a procedure to read in the data for a record variable of type CatalogEntry. (See exercise 2 at the end of Section 11.1).
3. Write a procedure that reads in the coordinates of a point (type Point) on the *x-y* plane.

11.4   Abstract Data Types Revisited

Abstraction is a powerful tool in programming. Procedural abstraction enables us to focus on the operations that we want to perform without having to provide immediately the details of how each operation will be implemented.

Data abstraction is the technique of focusing on the data and the operations to be performed without being concerned about how the data are actually represented in memory. Chapter 8 showed you how to implement an abstract data type (ADT) consisting of a data type and its relevant operators. An ADT can be saved as a separate file and inserted into a Pascal program as needed.

The program that uses an ADT is called the *client program*. A client program can declare and manipulate objects of this data type and use the data type's operators without knowing the details of the internal representation of the data type or the implementation of its operators; the details are hidden from the client program (called *information hiding*). In this way, we separate the use of the data and the operators (by the client program) from the representation and the implementation (by the ADT).

Data abstraction provides several advantages. It allows us to implement the client program and the ADT relatively independent of each other. If we decide to change the implementation of an operator (procedure) in the ADT, we can do so without affecting the client program. Finally, because the internal representation of a data type is hidden from its client program, we can even change the internal representation at a later time without modifying the client program.

● Case Study: Abstract Data Type for Complex Arithmetic

This section explains how to specify and implement an ADT for complex arithmetic.

Problem

An engineering professor wants us to write a set of procedures that can be used to perform arithmetic on complex numbers. A complex number is a number with a real part and an imaginary part. For example, the complex number $a +$ ib [also written as (a, b)] has a real part of a and an imaginary part of b, where the symbol i represents $\sqrt{-1}$. The professor wants us to provide a module for creating, defining, reading, and displaying a complex number. The module should also contain procedures for performing complex arithmetic (for example, addition, subtraction, multiplication, and division of complex numbers). There should also be operators for extracting real and imaginary parts and finding the absolute value (magnitude) of the complex number.

Design Overview

We will implement an ADT to represent the data structure for a complex number with operators for each of the tasks listed. The specification of the abstract data type `ComplexNumber` follows.

Specification of ComplexNumber

Structure: A complex number is an object of type `Complex` that consists of a pair of `Real` values.

Operators: In the following descriptions, assume these parameters:
A, B, and C represent complex numbers
X and Y represent type Real values

```
procedure InitialComplex (var C {output} : Complex);
{Creates a complex number C and initializes it to (0.0, 0.0).}

procedure SetComplex (X, Y {input} : Real;
                             var C {output} : Complex);
{Sets C to the complex number (X, Y).}

procedure ReadComplex (var C {output} : Complex);
{Reads a pair of values into complex number C.}

procedure WriteComplex (C {input} : Complex);
{Displays complex number C.}

procedure AddComplex (A, B {input}  : Complex;
                            var C {output} : Complex);
{Complex number C is the sum of complex numbers A and B.}

procedure SubtractComplex (A, B {input}  : Complex;
                                 var C {output} : Complex);
{Complex number C is the difference of complex numbers A and B.}

procedure MultiplyComplex (A, B {input}  : Complex;
                                 var C {output} : Complex);
{Complex number C is the product of complex numbers A and B.}

procedure DivideComplex (A, B {input}  : Complex;
                               var C {output} : Complex);
{Complex number C is the quotient of complex numbers A and B.}

function GetReal (A : Complex) : Real;
{Returns the real part of complex number A.}
```

```
function GetImaginary (A : Complex) : Real;
{Returns the imaginary part of complex number A.}

function AbsComplex (A : Complex) : Real;
{Returns the absolute value of complex number A.}
```

The first operator listed is `InitialComplex`, which initializes a variable of type `Complex` to (0.0, 0.0). The remaining operators are procedures that define the value of a complex number (`SetComplex` and `ReadComplex`), display a complex number (`WriteComplex`), perform complex arithmetic operations (`AddComplex`, etc.), extract the real and imaginary parts (`GetReal`, `GetImaginary`), and find the absolute value (`AbsComplex`).

After the specification is written, programmers can implement client programs that use the ADT `ComplexNumber`. If stubs are available for the operator procedures, the client programs can be compiled and executed to test the overall flow of control. Once the ADT is completed, the client programs can be executed in a meaningful way. Figure 11.6 is a partially completed implementation of the ADT.

Figure 11.6   ADT ComplexNumber

```
{
  Abstract data type Complex: contains declarations for record
  type Complex and procedures for manipulating complex numbers.

INTERFACE SECTION --

  EXPORTS:  Complex, InitialComplex, SetComplex, ReadComplex,
    WriteComplex, AddComplex, SubtractComplex, MultiplyComplex,
    DivideComplex, GetReal, GetImaginary, AbsComplex

  IMPORTS:  none

  DATA TYPE SPECIFICATION:
}

  type
    Complex = record
                RealPart, ImaginaryPart : Real
              end; {Complex}

{
  OPERATOR SPECIFICATION: See procedure documentation in
                          implementation section.

IMPLEMENTATION SECTION --
}

  procedure InitialComplex (var C {output} : Complex);
  {
    Initializes a complex number C to (0.0, 0.0).
    Pre : None
    Post: C is initialized to (0.0, 0.0)
```

```
  }
begin {CreateComplex}
  C.RealPart := 0.0;  C.ImaginaryPart := 0.0
end; {CreateComplex}


procedure SetComplex (X, Y {input} : Real;
                             var C {output} : Complex);
  {
  Sets the complex number C to (X, Y).
  Pre : None
  Post: C is the complex number (X, Y).
  }
begin {SetComplex}
  C.RealPart := X; C.ImaginaryPart := Y
end; {SetComplex}


procedure ReadComplex (var C {output} : Complex);
  {
  Reads a pair of values into complex number C.
  Pre : None
  Post: The first real number read is the real part of C;
        the second real number read is the imaginary part of C.
  }
begin {ReadComplex}
  Write ('Real part> ');
  ReadLn (C.RealPart);
  Write ('Imaginary part> ');
  ReadLn (C.ImaginaryPart)
end; {ReadComplex}


procedure WriteComplex (C {input} : Complex);
  {
  Displays complex number C.
  Pre : C is assigned a value.
  Post: Prints the real and imaginary parts of C.
  }
begin {WriteComplex}
  Write ('(', C.RealPart :4:2);
  WriteLn (', ', C.ImaginaryPart :4:2, ')')
end; {WriteComplex}


procedure AddComplex (A, B  {input}  : Complex;
                             var C {output} : Complex);
  {
  Complex number C is the sum of complex numbers A and B.
  Pre : A and B are assigned values.
  Post: C is the complex sum of A and B.
  }
begin {AddComplex}
  C.RealPart := A.RealPart + B.RealPart;
  C.ImaginaryPart := A.ImaginaryPart + B.ImaginaryPart
end; {AddComplex}


procedure SubtractComplex (A, B  {input}  : Complex;
                                 var C {output} : Complex);
```

```
{
  Complex number C is the difference of complex numbers A and B.
  Pre : A and B are assigned values.
  Post: C is the complex difference of A and B.
}
begin {SubtractComplex}
  C.RealPart := A.RealPart - B.RealPart;
  C.ImaginaryPart := A.ImaginaryPart - B.ImaginaryPart
end; {SubtractComplex}


procedure MultiplyComplex (A, B  {input}  : Complex;
                                var C {output} : Complex);
{
  Complex number C is the product of complex numbers A and B.
  Pre : A and B are assigned values.
  Post: C is the complex product of A and B.
}
begin {MultiplyComplex Stub}
  WriteLn ('Procedure MultiplyComplex called.')
end; {MultiplyComplex}


procedure DivideComplex (A, B  {input}  : Complex;
                              var C {output} : Complex);
{
  Complex number C is the quotient of complex numbers A and B.
  Pre : A and B are assigned values.
  Post: C is the complex quotient of A and B.
}
begin {DivideComplex Stub}
  WriteLn ('Procedure DivideComplex called.')
end; {DivideComplex}

function GetReal (A : Complex) : Real;
{
  Returns the real part of complex number A.
  Pre : A is assigned a value.
  Post: The real part of A is returned.
}
begin {GetReal}
  GetReal := A.RealPart
end; {GetReal}


function GetImaginary (A : Complex) : Real;
{
  Returns the imaginary part of complex number A.
  Pre : A is assigned a value.
  Post: The imaginary part of A is returned.
}
begin {GetImaginary}
  GetImaginary := A.ImaginaryPart
end; {GetImaginary}


function AbsComplex (A : Complex) : Real;
{
  Returns the absolute value of complex number A.
  Pre : A is assigned a value.
  Post: The absolute value of A is returned.
```

```
   }
 begin {AbsComplex}
   AbsComplex := Sqrt(A.RealPart * A.RealPart +
                      A.ImaginaryPart * A.ImaginaryPart)
 end; {AbsComplex}
```

The complex addition and subtraction operators are implemented as procedures `AddComplex` and `SubtractComplex`, respectively. From these procedures, we see that the sum (or difference) of two complex numbers is obtained by adding (or subtracting) the real and imaginary parts separately. Function `AbsComplex` computes the absolute value of a complex number according to the following formula (the multiply and divide procedures are left as an exercise).

$$|a + ib| = \sqrt{(a + ib) * (a - ib)} = \sqrt{a^2 + b^2}$$

The engineering professor can now execute client programs that use the ADT for complex arithmetic. The ADT must be inserted into each client program. It will be necessary to edit the completed program so that the declaration for data type `Complex` precedes the declaration of any complex objects (variables). Figure 11.7 is a client module that uses ADT `ComplexNumber`.

Figure 11.7 Using ADT ComplexNumber

```
program TestComplex (Input, Output);
{
   Reads two complex numbers and displays their sum and difference.
   Also displays the absolute value of one of the numbers.
   Uses the abstract data type ComplexNumber.
}

IMPORTS:  Complex, ReadComplex, AddComplex, SubtractComplex,
          WriteComplex, AbsComplex from ComplexNumber

   {Insert declaration for data type Complex here.}

   var
     A, B, C : Complex;                  {three complex numbers}

   {Insert operator procedures from ComplexNumber here.}

begin {TestComplex}
   {Read in complex numbers A and B.}
   WriteLn ('Enter the first complex number.');
   ReadComplex (A);
   WriteLn;
   WriteLn ('Enter the second complex number.');
   ReadComplex (B);

   AddComplex (A, B, C);                         {form the sum}
   Write ('The complex sum is ');
   WriteComplex (C);                             {display the sum}
```

```
      SubtractComplex (A, B, C);              {form the difference}
      Write ('The complex difference is ');
      WriteComplex (C);                       {display the difference}

      Write ('The absolute value of the first complex number is ');
      WriteLn (AbsComplex(A) :4:2)
end. {TestComplex}

Enter the first complex number.
Real part> 3.5
Imaginary part> 5.2

Enter the second complex number.
Real part> 2.5
Imaginary part> 1.2

The complex sum is (6.00, 6.40)
The complex difference is (1.00, 4.00)
The absolute value of the first complex number is 6.27
```

Figure 11.8 Module Dependency for TestComplex

Module `TestComplex` uses the data type `Complex` and five of its operators. The body of `TestComplex` begins by reading data into complex numbers A and B. Next, the sum and the difference of these complex numbers are saved in C and displayed. Finally, the absolute value of complex number A is displayed. Figure 11.8 shows the module dependency.

A client program that uses ADT `ComplexNumber` does not need to know the actual internal representation of data type `ComplexNumber` (that is, a record with two `Real` fields). The client program can call an operator procedure of ADT `ComplexNumber` to perform an operation (for example, complex addition) without having this knowledge. In fact, it is better to hide this information from the client program, to prevent the client from directly manipulating the individual fields of a complex variable.

PROGRAM
STYLE

Referencing a Data Structure Declared in an ADT

The client program in Fig. 11.7 could use the statements

```
AddComplex (A, B, C);       {form the sum}
Write ('The real part of the sum is ');
WriteLn (C.RealPart :4:2);
```

to display the real part only of the sum of A and B. This is a bad programming practice, however, because the field name C.RealPart is based on a particular internal representation (record with fields RealPart and ImaginaryPart) of the data type Complex. If we later decide to use a different internal representation (for example, an array of two elements) for data type Complex, the field name C.RealPart would no longer be correct, and the client program would have to be modified.

It would be much better to replace the last line with the line

```
WriteLn (GetReal(C) :4:2);
```

In this case, procedure GetReal (an operator of ComplexNumber) would extract the real part of complex number C before it is displayed. Now the client program will always be correct regardless of the internal representation used for data type Complex.

Exercises for Section 11.4

Self-Check

1. What does the program segment below display?

```
SetComplex (3.5, 5.0, A);
SetComplex (-5.0, 6.5, B);
SubtractComplex (A, B, C);
WriteComplex (C);
SetComplex (GetReal(A), -GetImaginary(A), C);
AddComplex (A, C, B);
WriteComplex (B);
WriteLn (AbsComplex(B) :4:2)
```

Programming

1. Write additional procedures MultiplyComplex and DivideComplex to implement the operations of multiplication and division of complex numbers defined as follows:

$$(a, b) \times (c, d) = (ac - bd, ad + bc)$$

$$(a, b) / (c, d) = \left(\frac{ac + bd}{c^2 + d^2}, \frac{bc - ad}{c^2 + d^2} \right)$$

 ## 11.5 Hierarchical Records

To solve any programming problem, we must select data structures that enable us to efficiently represent a variety of information. The selection of data structures is an important part of the problem-solving process. The data structures we use can profoundly affect the efficiency and the simplicity of the completed program.

The data-structuring facilities in Pascal are powerful and general. In the previous examples, all record fields were simple types or strings. It is possible to declare a record type with fields that are other structured types. We call a record type with one or more fields that are record types a *hierarchical record*.

We began our study of records by introducing the record type Employee. In this section, we modify that record by adding new fields for storage of the employee's address, starting date, and date of birth. The record type New-Employee is declared in Fig. 11.9, along with two additional record types, Date and Address.

Figure 11.9 Declaration of a Hierarchical Record

```pascal
const
  StrLength = 20;        {length of all strings except zipcode}
  ZipStringSize = 5;     {length of zipcode string}

type
  IDRange = 1111..9999;
  StringType = packed array [1..StrLength] of Char;
  ZipString = packed array [1..ZipStringSize] of '0'..'9';
  Month = (January, February, March, April, May, June,
           July, August, September, October, November, December);
  Gender = (Female, Male);

  Employee = record
               ID : IDRange;
               Name : StringType;
               Sex : Gender;
               NumDepend : Integer;
               Rate, TaxSal : Real
             end; {Employee}

  Address = record
              Street, City, State : StringType;
              ZipCode : ZipString
            end; {Address}

  Date = record
           ThisMonth : Month;
           Day : 1..31;
           Year : 1900..1999
         end;  {Date}

  NewEmployee = record
                  PayData : Employee;
                  Home : Address;
                  StartDate, BirthDate : Date
                end;  {NewEmployee}

var
  Programmer : NewEmployee;
```

Figure 11.10   Record Variable Programmer (Type NewEmployee)   **425**

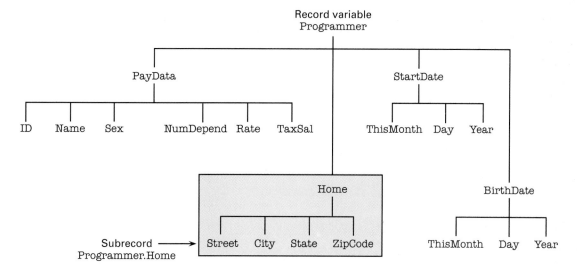

If `Programmer` is a record variable of type `NewEmployee`, the hierarchical structure of `Programmer` can be sketched as shown in Fig. 11.10. This diagram provides a graphic display of the record form.

The diagram in Fig. 11.10 shows that `Programmer` is a record with fields `PayData`, `Home`, `StartDate`, and `BirthDate`. Each of these fields is itself a record (called a *subrecord* of `Programmer`). The fields of each subrecord are indicated under that subrecord.

To reference a field in this diagram, we must trace a complete path to it starting from the top of the diagram. For example, the field selector

```
Programmer.StartDate
```

references the subrecord `StartDate` (type `Date`) of the variable `Programmer`. The field selector

```
Programmer.StartDate.Year
```

references the `Year` field of the subrecord `Programmer.StartDate`. The field selector

```
Programmer.Year
```

is incomplete (which `Year` field?) and would cause a syntax error.

The record copy statement

```
Programmer.StartDate := DayOfYear
```

is legal if `DayOfYear` is a record variable of type `Date`. This statement copies each field of `DayOfYear` into the corresponding field of the subrecord `Programmer.StartDate`.

In many situations, we can use the `with` statement to shorten the field selector. The statement

```
with Programmer.StartDate do
   WriteLn ('Year started: ', Year:4, ', day started: ', Day:1)
```

displays two fields of the subrecord `Programmer.StartDate`. The computation for taxable salary could be written as

```
with Programmer.PayData do
   TaxSal := Rate * 40.0 - NumDepend * 14.40
```

The `with` statement

```
with Programmer do
   WriteLn (PayData.Name, ' started work in ', StartDate.Year :4)
```

displays an output line of the form

```
Caryn Jackson        started work in 1976
```

It is also possible to nest `with` statements. The following nested `with` statement also displays the preceding output line.

```
with Programmer do
   with PayData do
      with StartDate do
         WriteLn (Name, ' started work in ', Year :4)
```

The record variable name (`Programmer`) must precede the subrecord names, as shown. The order of the field names `PayData` and `StartDate` is not important.

We can also use a list of record variable names and field names in a `with` statement. The statement

```
with Programmer, PayData, StartDate do
   WriteLn (Name, ' started work in ', Year :4)
```

is equivalent to the ones just discussed.

Procedure `ReadNewEmp` in Fig. 11.11 could be used to read in a record of type `NewEmployee`. It calls procedures `ReadEmployee` (see Fig. 11.5), `ReadAddress`, and `ReadDate` (see programming exercise).

Figure 11.11 Procedure ReadNewEmp

```
procedure ReadNewEmp (var NewEmp {output} : NewEmployee);
{
   Reads a record into record variable NewEmp.
   Pre : None
   Post: Reads data into all fields of record NewEmp.
   Uses: Procedures ReadEmployee (see Fig. 11.5),
         ReadAddress, and ReadDate (see exercises below)
}
begin {ReadNewEmp}
   with NewEmp do
      begin
         ReadEmployee (PayData);
         ReadAddress (Home);
         ReadDate (StartDate);
         ReadDate (BirthDate)

end; {ReadNewEmp}
```

Self-Check

1. What must be the type of NewAddress if the following statement is correct?

        Programmer.Home := NewAddress

2. Write the field selector needed to reference each of the following fields.
   a. the programmer's salary
   b. the programmer's street address
   c. the programmer's month of birth
   d. the month the programmer started working

Programming

1. Write procedures ReadAddress and ReadDate.

 # 11.6 Variant Records (Optional)

All record variables of type NewEmployee have the same form and structure. It is possible, however, to define record types that have some fields that are the same for all variables of that type (fixed part) and some fields that may be different (variant part).

For example, we might want to include additional information about an employee based on the employee's marital status. For all married employees, we might want to know the spouse's name and the number of children. For all divorced employees, we might want to know the date of the divorce. For all single employees, we might want to know whether the employee lives alone.

This new employee type, Executive, is declared in Fig. 11.12 and uses several data types declared earlier in Fig. 11.9.

Figure 11.12 Record Type Executive and Record Variable Boss

```
const
  StrLength = 20;        {length of all strings except zipcode}
  ZipStringSize = 5;     {length of zipcode string}

type
  IDRange = 1111..9999;
  StringType = packed array [1..StrLength] of Char;
  ZipString = packed array [1..ZipStringSize] of '0'..'9';
  Month = (January, February, March, April, May, June,
           July, August, September, October, November, December);

  Gender = (Female, Male);

  Employee = record
               ID : IDRange;
               Name : StringType;
               Sex : Gender;
               NumDepend : Integer;
               Rate, TaxSal : Real
             end; {Employee}
```

```
Address = record
           Street, City, State : StringType;
           ZipCode : ZipString
         end; {Address}

Date = record
         ThisMonth : Month;
         Day : 1..31;
         Year : 1900..1999
       end;  {Date}

NewEmployee = record
                PayData : Employee;
                Home : Address;
                StartDate, BirthDate : Date
              end;  {NewEmployee}

MaritalStatus = (Married, Divorced, Single);
Executive = record
              PayData : Employee;
              Home : Address;
              StartDate, BirthDate : Date;
              case MS : MaritalStatus of
              Married   : (SpouseName : StringType;
                         : NumberKids : Integer);
              Divorced : (DivorceDate : Date);
              Single    : (LivesAlone : Boolean)
            end; {Executive}

var
  Boss : Executive;
```

The fixed part of a record always precedes the variant part. The fixed part of record type `Executive` has the form of record type `NewEmployee`. The variant part begins with the *tag field*

```
case MS : MaritalStatus of
```

which defines a special field `MS`, of type `MaritalStatus`. The value of the tag field `MS` (`Married`, `Divorced`, or `Single`) indicates the form of the remainder of the record. If the value of the tag field is `Married`, there are two additional fields, `SpouseName` (type `StringType`) and `NumberKids` (type `Integer`); otherwise, there is only one additional field, `DivorceDate` (type `Date`) or `LivesAlone` (type `Boolean`).

Figure 11.13 shows three variants of record variable `Boss`, starting with the tag field. The fixed parts of all these records (not shown) have the same form.

For each variable of type `Executive`, the compiler allocates sufficient storage space to accommodate the largest of the record variants. However, only one variant is defined at any given time and that particular variant is determined by the tag field value.

The amount of storage required for each variant depends on how many bytes are used to store integer values and enumerated type values on a particular computer. The first variant in Fig. 11.13 requires more than twenty bytes of storage (one byte per character of the spouse's name) and should be the largest.

Boss.MS	Married
Boss.SpouseName	Elliot□Koffman□□□□□□
Boss.NumberKids	3

Boss.MS	Divorced
Boss.DivorceDate.ThisMonth	May
Boss.DivorceDate.Day	20
Boss.DivorceDate.Year	1989

Boss.MS	Single
Boss.LivesAlone	True

■ Example 11.6

If the value of Boss.MS is Married, then only the variant fields SpouseName and NumberKids can be correctly referenced; all other variant fields are undefined. Assuming the first variant shown in Fig. 11.14 is stored in record Boss, the program fragment

```
with Boss do
  begin
    WriteLn ('The spouse''s name is ', SpouseName, '.');
    WriteLn ('They have ', NumberKids :1, ' children.')
  end {with}
```

displays the line

```
The spouse's name is Elliot Koffman.
They have 3 children.
```

We must ensure that the variant fields that are referenced are consistent with the current tag field value. The compiler and run-time system do not normally check this. If the value of Boss.MS is not Married when the preceding fragment is executed, the information displayed will be meaningless. For that reason, a case statement is often used to process the variant part of a record. By using the tag field as the case selector, we can ensure that only the currently defined variant is manipulated. ■

■ Example 11.7

The fragment in Fig. 11.14 displays the data stored in the variant part of record Boss. The value of Boss.MS determines what information is displayed. ■

Figure 11.14 Displaying a Variant Record

```
{Display the variant part}
with Boss do
  case MS of
```

```
     Married :
        begin
           WriteLn ('The spouse''s name is ', SpouseName, ',');
           WriteLn ('. They have ', NumberKids :1, ' children.')
        end; {Married}
     Divorced :
        with DivorceDate do
           WriteLn ('Divorced on ', Ord(ThisMonth) + 1 :2,
                    '/', Day :2, '/', Year :4);
     Single :
        if LivesAlone then
           WriteLn ('Lives alone')
        else
           WriteLn ('Does not live alone')
end {case}
```

The syntax for a record with fixed and variant parts is described in the
following syntax display.

Record Type with Variant Part

Form: type

$rec\ type$ = record

   $id\ list_1$: $type_1$;

   $id\ list_2$: $type_2$;

      .

      .

      .

   $id\ list_n$: $type_n$; } *fixed part*

   case tag: $tag\ type$ of

   $label_1$: (*field list$_1$*);

   $label_2$: (*field list$_2$*);

      .

      .

      .

   $label_k$: (*field list$_k$*) } *variant part*

   end;

Example: type

   Face = record

      Eyes : Color;

      case Bald : Boolean of

         True : (WearsWig : Boolean);

         False : (HairColor : Color)

      end;

Interpretation: The *field list* for the fixed part is declared first. The
variant part starts with the reserved word case. The identifier *tag* is the

name of the tag field of the record; the tag field name is separated by a colon from its type (*tag type*), which must be type `Boolean`, an enumerated type, or a subrange of an ordinal type.

The case labels (*label₁*, *label₂* ,..., *label_k*) are lists of values of the tag field as defined by *tag type*. *Field list_i* describes the record fields associated with *label_i*. Each element of *field list_i* specifies a field name and its type; the elements in *field list_i* are separated by semicolons. *Field list_i* is enclosed in parentheses.

Note 1: All field names must be unique. The same field name may not appear in the fixed and variant parts or in two field lists of the variant part.

Note 2: An empty field list (no variant part for that `case` label) is indicated by an empty pair of parentheses, ( ).

Note 3: It is possible for a field list to also have a variant part. If it does, the variant part must follow the fixed part of the field list.

Note 4: There is only one `end` for the record type declaration; there is no separate `end` for the `case`.

When you initially store data in a record with a variant part, the tag field value should be read first. Once the value of the tag field is defined, data can be read into the variant fields associated with that value.

◼ Case Study: Areas and Perimeters of Different Figures

Problem
We want to write a program that determines the area and the perimeter for a variety of geometric figures.

Design Overview
To solve this problem, we will create an abstract data type that represents a geometric figure and contains operators for entering the figure's characteristics, computing its perimeter, computing its area, and displaying its characteristics. Because the characteristics for a figure are related, we want to save them in a record. However, the characteristics for each figure shape are different, so we must use a record with a variant part. The record declared next has two fixed fields for storing the figure's area and perimeter; the variant part is used for storing the figure's characteristics.

Data Requirements

Data Types

```
FigKind = (Circle, Rectangle, Square, Other);
```

```
Figure = record
          Area, Perimeter : Real;
       case Shape : FigKind of
          Circle     : (Radius : Real);
          Rectangle  : (Width, Height : Real);
          Square     : (Side : Real);
          Other      : ()
       end; {Figure}
```

Problem Inputs
A letter representing the kind of figure (FigChar : Char)
The relevant characteristics for the figure selected

Problem Outputs
The figure Area (Area : Real)
The figure perimeter (Perimeter : Real)

Initial Algorithm
1. Determine the type of the figure.
2. Read in the figure characteristics.
3. Compute the area of the figure.
4. Compute the perimeter of the figure.
5. Display the complete record for the figure.

Coding the Main Program
We will write a procedure to perform each algorithm step. The main program (Fig. 11.15) consists of a sequence of calls to these procedures.

Figure 11.15 Program Geometry

```
program Geometry (Input, Output);
{Finds perimeters and areas of various kinds of figures.}

  const
    Pi = 3.14159;

  type
    FigKind = (Circle, Rectangle, Square, Other);
    Figure = record
              Area, Perimeter : Real;
           case Shape : FigKind of
              Circle     : (Radius : Real);
              Rectangle  : (Width, Height : Real);
              Square     : (Side : Real);
              Other      : ()
           end; {Figure}

  var
    MyFig : Figure;                    {a figure}

  {
   Insert procedures GetFigureType, ReadFigure, DisplayFigure,
   ComputeArea, and ComputePerim.
  }
```

```
begin {Geometry}
  GetFigure (MyFig);
  ReadFigure (MyFig);
  ComputeArea (MyFig);
  ComputePerim (MyFig);
  DisplayFig (MyFig)
end. {Geometry}
```

```
Enter the object's shape.
Enter C (Circle), R (Rectangle), S (Square)> R
Enter width > 5.0
Enter height> 6.5

Figure shape is Rectangle
Width is 5.00
Height is 6.50
Area is 32.50
Perimeter is 23.00
```

Coding the Procedures

Procedure GetFigure reads in the character that denotes the kind of figure and saves the corresponding value of type FigKind in the tag field Shape. If the character entered is not one of the letters (C, R, or S), the value Other is stored in the tag field. ReadFigure must read the data required for the kind of figure indicated by the tag field. The other operator procedures are straightforward and are shown in Fig. 11.16.

Figure 11.16   Operator Procedures for Data Type Figure

```
procedure GetFigure (var OneFig {output} : Figure);
{
  Defines tag field of OneFig.
  Pre : None
  Post: The tag field value corresponds to the next data character.
}
  var
    FigChar : Char;        {input — data character for figure shape}

begin {GetFigure}
  WriteLn ('Enter the kind of object');
  Write ('Enter C (Circle), R (Rectangle), or S (Square)> ');
  Read (FigChar);
  if FigChar in ['c', 'C', 'r', 'R', 's', 'S'] then
    case FigChar of
      'c', 'C' : OneFig.Shape := Circle;
      'r', 'R' : OneFig.Shape := Rectangle;
      's', 'S' : OneFig.Shape := Square
    end {case}
  else
    OneFig.Shape := Other
end; {GetFigure}
```

```
procedure ReadFigure (var OneFig {input/output} : Figure);
{
   Enters data into OneFig.
   Pre : The tag field of OneFig is defined.
   Post: The characteristics of OneFig are defined.
}
begin  {ReadFigure}
  with OneFig do
    {Select the proper variant and read pertinent data}
    case Shape of
      Circle    : begin
                    Write ('Enter radius> ');
                    ReadLn (Radius)
                  end; {Circle}
      Rectangle : begin
                    Write ('Enter width > ');
                    ReadLn (Width);
                    Write ('Enter height> ');
                    ReadLn (Height)
                  end; {Rectangle}
      Square    : begin
                    Write ('Enter length of side> ');
                    ReadLn (Side)
                  end; {Square}
      Other     : WriteLn ('Characteristics are unknown')
    end {case}
end; {ReadFigure}


procedure ComputePerim (var OneFig {input/output} : Figure);
{
   Defines Perimeter field of OneFig.
   Pre : The tag field and characteristics of OneFig are defined.
   Post: Assigns value to Perimeter field.
}
begin {ComputePerim}
  with OneFig do
    case Shape of
      Circle    : Perimeter := 2.0 * Pi * Radius;
      Rectangle : Perimeter := 2.0 * (Width + Height);
      Square    : Perimeter := 4.0 * Side;
      Other     : Perimeter := 0.0
    end {case}
end; {ComputePerim}


procedure ComputeArea (var OneFig {input/output} : Figure);
{
   Defines Area field of OneFig.
   Pre : The tag field and characteristics of OneFig are defined.
   Post: Assigns value to Area field.
}
begin {ComputeArea}
  with OneFig do
    case Shape of
      Circle    : Area := Pi * Radius * Radius;
      Rectangle : Area := Width * Height;
      Square    : Area := Side * Side;
      Other     : Area := 0.0
    end {case}
end; {ComputeArea}
```

```
procedure DisplayFig (OneFig {input} : Figure);
{
  Displays the characteristics of OneFig.
  Pre : All fields of OneFig are defined.
  Post: Displays each field of OneFig.
}
begin {DisplayFig}
  with OneFig do
    {Display shape and characteristics}
    begin
      Write ('Figure shape is ');
      case FigShape of
        Circle    : begin
                      WriteLn ('Circle');
                      WriteLn ('Radius is ', Radius :4:2)
                    end; {Circle}
        Rectangle : begin
                      WriteLn ('Rectangle');
                      WriteLn ('Height is ', Height :4:2);
                      WriteLn ('Width is ', Width :4:2)
                    end; {Rectangle}
        Square    : begin
                      WriteLn ('Square');
                      WriteLn ('Side is ', Side :4:2)
                    end; {Square}
        Other     : WriteLn ('No characteristics for figure')
      end; {case}

    {Display area and perimeter}
    WriteLn ('Area is ', Area :4:2);
    WriteLn ('Perimeter is ', Perimeter :4:2)
  end {with}
end; {DisplayFig}
```

In each procedure, a case statement controls the processing of the data in the variant part. Procedures ComputePerim and ComputeArea define their respective fields in the data structure.

Exercises for Section 11.6

Self-Check

1. Determine how many bytes are needed to store each variant for a record of type Executive, assuming two bytes for an integer or an enumerated type value and one byte for a character or a Boolean value. Don't include the tag field in your calculations.
2. Write a statement that displays Boss.SpouseName if defined or the message Not married.

Programming

1. Write a procedure to display a record of type Face as declared in the syntax display in this section.

2. Add the variant

```
RightTriangle : (Base, Height : Real);
```

to Figure and modify the operator procedures to include triangles. Use the formulas

$area = \frac{1}{2} base \times height$

$hypotenuse = \sqrt{base^2 + height^2}$

where *base* and *height* are the two sides that form the right angle and *hypotenuse* is the side opposite the right angle.

 # 11.7   Common Programming Errors

When programmers use records, their most common error is incorrectly specifying the record field to be manipulated. The full field selector (record variable and field name) must be used unless the record reference is nested inside a with statement or the entire record is to be manipulated. So far, we have discussed the latter option only for record copy statements and for records passed as parameters. When reading or writing records at the terminal, you must process each field separately.

If a record variable name is listed in a with statement header, only the field name is required to reference fields of that record inside the with statement. You must still use the full field selector to reference fields of any other record variable.

For variant records, remember that the value of the tag field determines the form of the variant part that is currently defined. Manipulating any other variant will cause unpredictable results. You must ensure that the correct variant is being processed—the computer does not check this. So always manipulate a variant record in a case statement with the tag field as the case selector to ensure that the proper variant part is being manipulated.

 # Chapter Review

This chapter examined the record data structure. Records were shown to be useful for organizing a collection of related data items of different types. Using hierarchical records and variant records, we created some very general data structures to model our "real world" data organization.

In processing records, we discussed how to reference each individual component through the use of a field selector consisting of the record variable name and field name separated by a period. We introduced the with statement as a means of shortening the field selector. If a record variable name is specified in a with statement header, then the field name may be used by itself inside the with statement.

Each individual component of a record must be manipulated separately in an input or an output operation or in an arithmetic expression. However, it is permissible to assign one record variable to another record variable of the same type (record copy statement) or to pass a record as a parameter to a procedure or function.

New Pascal Constructs

The Pascal constructs introduced in this chapter are described in Table 11.1.

Table 11.1 Summary of New Pascal Constructs

Construct	Effect
Record Declaration	
| ```
type
  Part = record
          ID : [1111..9999];
          Quantity : Integer;
          Price : Real
        end; {Part}
var
  Nuts, Bolts : Part;
``` | A record type Part is declared with fields that can store two integers and a real number. Nuts and Bolts are record variables of type Part. |
| **Record Variant Declaration** | |
| ```
type
  ChildKind = (Girl, Boy);
  Child = record
           First, Last : Char;
           Age : Integer;
           case Sex : ChildKind of
           Girl : (Sugar, Spice :
                     Real):
           Boy : (Snakes, Snails,
                   Tails : Integer)
         end; {Child}
var
  Kid : Child;
``` | A record type with a variant part is declared. Each record variable can store two characters and an integer. One variant part can store two real numbers, and the other can store three integers. The record variable Kid is type Child. |
| **Record Reference** | |
| ```
TotalCost := Nuts.Quantity
             * Nuts.Price
``` | Multiplies two fields of Nuts. |
| ```
WriteLn (Bolts.ID :4)
``` | Prints ID field of Bolts. |
| **Record Copy** | |
| ```
Bolts := Nuts
``` | Copies record Nuts to Bolts. |
| **with Statement** | |
| ```
with Bolts do
  Write (ID :4, Price :8:2)
``` | Prints 2 fields of Bolts. |
| **Referencing a Record Variant** | |
| ```
with Kid do
  case Sex of
    Girl :
``` | Uses a case statement to read data into the variant part of record variable Kid. |
```

Table 11.1 *continued*

Construct	Effect

``
begin
   Write (Pounds of sugar> ');
   ReadLn (Sugar)
end; {Girl}
Boy :
   begin
      Write ('Number of snakes> ');
      ReadLn (Snakes)
   end {boy}
end; {case}
``
	If tag field Sex is Girl, reads a value into the field Sugar. If tag field Kind is Boy, reads a value into the field Snakes.

✓ *Quick-Check Exercises*

1. What is the primary difference between a record and an array? Which would you use to store the catalog description of a course? Which would you use to store the names of the students in the course?
2. What is a field selector?
3. Why do we use a with statement? What is a disadvantage of using the with statement?
4. If you use nested with statements to reference fields of a hierarchical record, what identifier should appear in the outermost with statement header?
5. When can you use the assignment operator with record operands? When can you use the equality operator?
6. For AStudent declared as follows, provide a statement that displays the initials of AStudent.

```
type
   StringType = packed array [1..StrLength] of Char;
   Student = record
               First, Last : StringType;
               Age, Score : Integer;
               Grade : Char
            end; {Student}

var
   AStudent : Student;
```

7. How many fields are there in a record of type Student?
8. If an Integer uses two bytes of storage, a character one, and StrLength is 20, how many bytes of storage are occupied by AStudent?
9. Write a procedure that displays a variable of type Student.
10. When should you use a record variant?

Answers to Quick-Check Exercises

1. The values stored in an array must all be the same type; the values stored in a record do not have to be the same type. Record for catalog item; array for list of names.
2. A field selector is used to select a particular record field for processing.
3. A with statement allows us to abbreviate field selectors. It is helpful when we must

reference several fields of the same record. Its disadvantage is that it makes the program less readable because it separates the record variable name from the field name. It is particularly confusing when there are multiple records of the same type or when a record has nested subrecords.

4. The record variable name.

5. When the records are the same type. Never.

6. `WriteLn (AStudent.First[1], AStudent.Last[1])`

7. Five.

8. Forty-five.

9.
```pascal
procedure WriteStudent (OneStu {input} : Student);
begin
    WriteLn ('Student is ', OneStu.FirstName,
             ' ', OneStu.LastName);
    WriteLn ('Age is ', OneStu.Age :1);
    WriteLn ('Score is ', OneStu.Score :1);
    WriteLn ('Grade is ', OneStu.Grade)
end;
```

10. When an object has some fields that are always the same and some fields that may be different.

Review Questions

1. Declare a record called `Subscriber` that contains the fields `Name`, `StreetAddress`, `MonthlyBill` (how much the subscriber owes), and which paper the subscriber receives (`Morning`, `Evening`, or `Both`).

2. Write a Pascal program to enter and then print out the data in record `Competition` declared as follows:

```pascal
const
   StrLength = 20;

type
   StringType = packed array [1..StrLength] of Char;
   OlympicEvent = record
                     Event,
                     Entrant,
                     Country : StringType;
                     Place : Integer
                  end; {OlympicEvent}

var
   Competition: OlympicEvent;
```

3. Explain the use of the `with` statement.

4. Identify and correct the errors in the following program.

```pascal
program Report (Input, Output);

   type
      String15 = packed array [1..15] of Char;
      SummerHelp = record
                      Name : String15;
                      StartDate : String15;
                      HoursWorked : Real
                   end; {SummerHelp}
```

```
var
   Operator : SummerHelp;
begin {Report}
   with SummerHelp do
      begin
         Name := 'Stoney Viceroy ';
         StartDate := 'June 1, 1984    ';
         HoursWorked := 29.3
      end; {with}
   WriteLn (Operator)
end.
```

5. Declare the proper data structure to store the following student data: GPA, Major, Address (consisting of StreetAddress, City, State, ZipCode), and ClassSchedule (consisting of up to six class records, each of which has Description, Time, and Days fields). Use whatever data types are most appropriate for each field.

6. Write the variant declaration for Supplies, which consists of Paper, Ribbon, or Labels. For Paper, the information needed is the number of sheets per box and the size of the paper. For Ribbon, the size, color, and kind (Carbon or Cloth) are needed. For Labels, the size and number per box are needed. For each supply, the cost, number on hand, and the reorder point must also be stored. Use whatever data types are appropriate for each field.

7. Write the declaration for Vehicle. If the vehicle is a Truck, then BedSize and CabSize are needed. If the vehicle is a wagon, then third seat or not is needed (Boolean). If the vehicle is a Sedan, then the information needed is TwoDoor or FourDoor. For all vehicles, you need to know whether the transmission is Manual or Automatic; if it has AirConditioning, PowerSteering, or PowerBrakes (all Boolean); and the Gas Mileage. Use whatever data types are appropriate for each field.

Programming Projects

1. Implement an abstract data type that consists of the data structure described in review question 5 and procedures for reading and displaying an object of that type.

2. Implement an abstract data type that consists of the data structure described in review question 6 and procedures for reading and displaying an object of that type.

3. Implement an abstract data type that consists of the data structure described in review question 7 and procedures for reading and displaying an object of that type.

4. A number expressed in scientific notation is represented by its mantissa (a fraction) and its exponent. Write a procedure that reads two character strings that represent numbers in Pascal scientific notation and stores each number in a record with two fields. Write a procedure that prints the contents of each record as a real value. Also write a procedure that computes the sum, the product, the difference, and the quotient of the two numbers. Hint: The string −0.1234E20 represents a number in scientific notation. The fraction −0.1234 is the mantissa and the number 20 is the exponent.

5. At a grocery store, the food has been categorized, and those categories are to be computerized. Write a procedure to read and store information into a variant record with appropriate data types.

   The first letter read will be M, F, or V (indicating meat, fruit, or vegetable, respectively). The second set of information (until a blank is encountered) will be the name of the food (maximum of twenty letters). The third item read will be the unit cost. The fourth item read will be the unit (O, for ounces, or P for pounds).

The last field read will be one character that indicates information based on the M, F, or V read earlier. For meat, the valid input values are R for red meat, P for poultry, and F for fish. For fruit, the valid input values are T for tropical and N for nontropical. For vegetables the valid input values are B for beans, P for potatoes, 0 for other.

The procedure should check that each data item is valid before assigning a value to the record parameter. Also write a procedure to print the data stored for a food object.

Arrays with Structured Elements

12

S o far, you have seen programs that use arrays with many different subscript and element types. All the arrays we have discussed to this point have had individual elements that were simple types. This chapter examines arrays whose elements are structured types.

We begin by examining arrays with elements that are themselves arrays. These arrays of arrays are called *multidimensional arrays* and are often used to store tables of data or to represent multidimensional objects.

We also examine arrays with elements that are records. Arrays of records are useful data structures that can represent many real-world objects. For example, it is convenient to use an array of records to represent a class of students or the members of a baseball team.

Finally, we show you how to perform some common operations on arrays of records. These operations include searching for a particular record in an array and ordering the array elements according to the values in a particular field (sorting the array).

 ## 12.1 Arrays of Arrays: Multidimensional Arrays

So far, we have used array elements to store single data values. But array elements can also be data structures. One application is an array whose elements are strings.

Arrays of Strings

In earlier examples, we wrote programs with enumerated types. One drawback to using enumerated types is that their values cannot be read or written directly. By using arrays of strings, we can simplify printing enumerated type values, as shown next.

■ Example 12.1

Procedure Initialize in Fig. 12.1 saves the names of the twelve months in an array, MonthName, declared as follows.

```
type
   Month = (January, February, March, April, May, June, July,
            August, September, October, November, December);
   String9 = packed array [1..9] of Char;
   MonthArray = array [Month] of String9;

var
   MonthName : MonthArray;       {array of strings}
```

The elements of array MonthName are strings. After procedure Initialize executes, each month name is stored as a string in its respective array element. Each string is right-justified, which means that it begins with leading blanks if necessary (for example, MonthName[January] is '   January').

```
procedure Initialize (var MonthName {output} : MonthArray);
{
   Initializes array MonthName.
   Pre : None
   Post: The name string for each month is stored right-justified
         in array MonthName.
}
begin {Initialize}
   MonthName[January]   := '  January';
   MonthName[February]  := ' February';
   MonthName[March]     := '    March';
   MonthName[April]     := '    April';
   MonthName[May]       := '      May';
   MonthName[June]      := '     June';
   MonthName[July]      := '     July';
   MonthName[August]    := '   August';
   MonthName[September] := 'September';
   MonthName[October]   := '  October';
   MonthName[November]  := ' November';
   MonthName[December]  := ' December'
end; {Initialize}


procedure WriteMonth (OneMonth {input} : Month);
{
   Displays the name string corresponding to OneMonth.
   Pre : Global array MonthName is initialized.
   Post: A string is displayed.
}
begin {WriteMonth}
   Write (MonthName[OneMonth])
end; {WriteMonth}


procedure ReadMonth (var OneMonth {output} : Month);
{
   Reads an integer from 1 to 12 and converts it to a month.
   Pre : None
   Post: Returns in OneMonth the month value corresponding
         to the integer value read.
   Uses: EnterInt
}
begin {ReadMonth stub}
   WriteLn ('Procedure ReadMonth entered');
   OneMonth := January
end; {ReadMonth}
```

Procedure `WriteMonth` in Fig. 12.1 displays the month name selected by its parameter. For example, the procedure call statement

```
WriteMonth (February)
```

displays the array element `MonthName[February]`, which contains the string `' February'`.

For the sake of completeness, Fig. 12.1 includes a stub for procedure, `ReadMonth`, which reads an integer from 1 to 12 and converts it to a month value. The three procedures in Fig. 12.1, together with data types Month and MonthArray, would form an abstract data type (ADT Month). The implementation of ReadMonth and ADT Month are left as programming exercises at the end of this section. ∎

Multidimensional Arrays

Because a string is an array of characters, the array type MonthArray is an array of arrays. Such a data structure is called a *two-dimensional array*. To make the two-dimensional nature of MonthArray more apparent, we could declare it in either of the following ways.

```
type
   MonthArray = array [Month] of packed array [1..9] of Char;
```

or

```
type
   MonthArray = packed array [Month, 1..9] of Char;
```

Either declaration could be substituted for the other.

∎ Example 12.2

A two-dimensional object we are all familiar with is a tic-tac-toe board. The declarations

```
type
   BoardRow = array [1..3] of Char;
   BoardArray = array [1..3] of BoardRow;

var
   TicTacToe : BoardArray;
```

allocate storage for the array TicTacToe. This array has nine storage cells arranged in three rows and three columns. A single character value can be stored in each cell.

In the preceding declarations, BoardRow is declared as an array type with three elements of type Char, and BoardArray is declared as an array type with three elements of type BoardRow. Consequently, the variable TicTacToe (type BoardArray) is an array of arrays, or a two-dimensional array, as pictured in Fig. 12.2. ∎

Figure 12.2 A Tic-Tac-Toe Board Stored as Array TicTacToe

It is generally clearer to use a single-type declaration to declare a multidimensional-array type. The declarations

```
type
   BoardArray = array [1..3, 1..3] of Char;

var
   TicTacToe : BoardArray;
```

are equivalent to the ones at the beginning of this example in that they allocate storage for a two-dimensional array (TicTacToe) with three rows and three columns. This array has nine elements, each of which must be referenced by specifying a row subscript (1, 2, or 3) and a column subscript (1, 2, or 3). Each array element contains a character value. The array element TicTacToe[2,3] (or TicTacToe[2][3]) pointed to in Fig. 12.2 is in row 2, column 3 of the array; it contains the character O. The diagonal line consisting of array elements TicTacToe[1,1], TicTacToe[2,2], and TicTacToe[3,3] represents a win for player X, because each cell contains the character X.

Array Type Declaration (Multidimensional)

Form:
```
type
    multidim = array [subscript₁] of array [subscript₂] ...
        of array [subscriptₙ] of element type;
```
or
```
type
    multidim =
        array [subscript₁, subscript₂, ... , subscriptₙ]
            of element type;
```

Example:
```
type
    YearByMonth = array [1900..1999, Month] of Real;
    Election = array [Candidate] of array [Precinct]
                of Integer;
```

Interpretation: *Subscript*ᵢ represents the subscript type of dimension *i* of array type *multidim*. The subscript type can be Boolean, Char, an enumerated type, or a subrange type with host type Integer or any other ordinal type. The *element type* can be any standard data type or a previously defined simple or structured data type.

Although we are focusing our discussion on arrays with two and three dimensions, there is no limit on the number of dimensions allowed in Pascal. There may, however, be a limit imposed by the particular compiler you are using. Be aware that the amount of memory space allocated for storage of a multidimensional array can be quite large. For this reason, avoid passing multidimensional arrays as value parameters.

■ **Example 12.3**

The array `Table` declared as

```
var
    Table : array [1..7, 1..5, 1..6] of Real;
```

consists of three dimensions: the first subscript can take on values from 1 to 7; the second, from 1 to 5; and the third, from 1 to 6. A total of 7 x 5 x 6, or 210, real numbers can be stored in the array `Table`. All three subscripts must be specified in each reference to array `Table` (for example, `Table[2,3,4]`). ■

Storage of Multidimensional Arrays

Most Pascal compilers store multidimensional arrays in adjacent memory cells to simplify accessing the individual elements. The elements of a two-dimensional array are normally stored in order by row (that is, first row 1, then row 2, and so on). This is called *row-major order*. To access a particular array element, the compiler computes the *offset* of that element from the first element stored. To perform this computation, the compiler must know the size of each element in bytes and the number of elements per row. Both values are available from the array type declaration.

For example, the array `TicTacToe` would be stored as shown in Fig. 12.3. There are three elements per row, and each element occupies one byte of storage. The offset for element `TicTacToe[i,j]` is computed from the formula

$$offset = (i-1) \times 3 + (j-1)$$

This formula gives a value of 0 as the offset for element `TicTacToe[1,1]` and a value of 5 as the offset for element `TicTacToe[2,3]`.

Manipulation of Two-Dimensional Arrays

We must specify a row subscript and a column subscript to reference an element of a two-dimensional array. The type of each subscript must be compatible with the corresponding subscript type specified in the array declaration.

Figure 12.3 Array TicTacToe in Memory

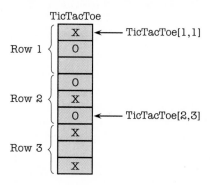

```
for I := 1 to 3 do
   Write (TicTacToe[1,I])
```

displays the first row of array TicTacToe (TicTacToe[1,1], TicTacToe[1,2], and TicTacToe[1,3]) on the current output line. The statement

```
for I := 1 to 3 do
   WriteLn (TicTacToe[I,2])
```

displays the second column of TicTacToe (TicTacToe[1,2], TicTacToe[2,2], and TicTacToe[3,2]) in a vertical line.

We can use nested loops to access all elements in a multidimensional array in a predetermined order. In the next three examples, the outer loop-control variable determines the row being accessed, and the inner loop-control variable selects each element in that row.

■ Example 12.4

Procedure PrintBoard in Fig. 12.4 displays the current status of a tic-tac-toe board. A sample output of this procedure is also shown.   ■

Figure 12.4   Procedure PrintBoard with Sample Output

```
procedure PrintBoard (TicTacToe {input} : BoardArray);
{
   Displays the status of a tic-tac-toe board.
   Pre : Array TicTacToe is defined.
   Post: Displays each element of array TicTacToe.
}
   var
     Row, Column : 1..3;

begin {PrintBoard}
   WriteLn ('--------');
   for Row := 1 to 3 do
     begin
       {Print all columns of current row}
       for Column := 1 to 3 do
         Write ('|', TicTacToe [Row,Column]);
       WriteLn ('|');
       WriteLn ('--------')
     end {Row}
end; {PrintBoard}


--------
|X|O| |
--------
|O|X|O|
--------
|X| |X|
```

■ Example 12.5

Function IsFilled in Fig. 12.5 returns a value of True if a tic-tac-toe board is all filled up; it returns a value of False if there is at least one cell that contains the constant Empty. Assume that all cells are initialized to Empty before the game begins. To move to a particular cell, a player replaces the constant Empty in that cell with an X or an O. A player can call function IsFilled before making a move to determine if there are any possible moves left. The if statement

```
if IsFilled(TicTacToe) then
   WriteLn ('Game is a draw!')
```

prints an appropriate message when there are no moves.

Figure 12.5 Function IsFilled

```
function IsFilled (TicTacToe : BoardArray) : Boolean;
{
  Tests whether the array TicTacToe is filled.
  Pre : All elements of array TicTacToe are assigned values.
  Post: Returns False if any cell contains the constant
        Empty; otherwise, returns True (array is filled).
}
  const
    Empty = ' ';

  var
    Row, Column : 1..3;    {row and column subscripts}

begin {IsFilled}
  IsFilled := True;                  {Assume the array is filled.}
  {Reset IsFilled to False if any cell is empty.}
  for Row := 1 to 3 do
    for Column := 1 to 3 do
      if TicTacToe[Row,Column] = Empty then
        IsFilled := False                  {array is not filled}
end; {IsFilled}
```

■ Example 12.6

Procedure EnterMove in Fig. 12.6 is used to enter a move into the array TicTacToe. EnterMove calls procedure EnterInt (see Fig. 7.17) twice to enter a pair of values into the move coordinates, MoveRow and MoveColumn. If the cell selected by these coordinates is empty, its value is reset to the character stored in Player (X or O).

Figure 12.6 Procedure EnterMove

```
procedure EnterMove (Player {input} : Char;
                     var TicTacToe {input/output} : BoardArray);
{
  Stores an X or O (identity of Player) in the array TicTacToe.
  Pre : Player is X or O and array TicTacToe has at least
        one empty cell.
  Post: The value of Player is stored in the empty cell of
        TicTacToe whose coordinates are read in; the rest
        of array TicTacToe is unchanged.
  Uses: Procedure EnterInt (see Fig. 7.17)
}
  const
    Empty = ' ';                    {contents of an empty cell}
```

```
     var
        MoveRow, MoveColumn : Integer;       {coordinates of
                                              selected cell}

     {Insert procedure EnterInt (see Fig. 7.17).}

     begin {EnterMove}
        repeat
          WriteLn ('Enter your move row and then the column');
          EnterInt (1, 3, MoveRow);
          EnterInt (1, 3, MoveColumn);
          if TicTacToe[MoveRow, MoveColumn] <> Empty then
            WriteLn ('Cell is occupied - try again')
        until TicTacToe[MoveRow, MoveColumn] = Empty;

        {assertion: A valid move is entered}
        TicTacToe[MoveRow, MoveColumn] := Player        {Define cell }
     end; {EnterMove}
```

Exercises for Section 12.1

Self-Check

1. Declare a three-dimensional array type in which the first subscript consists of letters from 'A' to 'F', the second subscript consists of integers from 1 to 10, and the third consists of the user-defined type Day. Real numbers will be stored in the array. How many elements can be stored in an array with this type?
2. Assuming the following declarations

   ```
   type
      MatrixType = array [1..5, 1..4] of Real;
   var
      Matrix : MatrixType,
   ```

   answer these questions:
   a. How many elements in array Matrix?
   b. Write a statement to display the element in row 3, column 4.
   c. What is the offset for this element?
   d. What formula is used to compute the offset for Matrix[i, j]?
   e. Write a loop that computes the sum of the elements in row 5.
   f. Write a loop that computes the sum of the elements in column 4.
   g. Write nested loops that compute the sum of all the array elements.
   h. Write nested loops that display the array elements in the following order: display column 4 as the first output line, column 3 as the second output line, and so on.

Programming

1. Write the ADT Month consisting of type declarations for Month and MonthArray and operators for reading and writing values of type Month. Procedure ReadMonth should use EnterInt to read in a value from 1 to 12 and then convert that integer to its corresponding month value.

2. Write a function that determines who has won a game of tic-tac-toe. The function should first check all rows to see if one player occupies all the cells in that row, then check all columns, and then check the two diagonals. The function should return a value from the enumerated type (NoWinner, XWins, OWins).

12.2 More Examples of Multidimensional Arrays

The subscript type for each dimension of the multidimensional array TicTacToe is a subrange of type Integer. It is not necessary for all the subscript types to have the same host type. The arrays in the next example have a different subscript type for each dimension.

■ Example 12.7

A university offers fifty courses at each of five campuses. The registrar's office can conveniently store the enrollments of these courses in the array Enroll, declared as follows:

```
const
  MaxCourse = 50;                        {maximum number of courses}

type
  Campus = (Main, Ambler, Center, Delaware, Montco);
  ClassArray = array [1..MaxCourse, Campus] of Integer;

var
  Enroll : ClassArray;
```

This array consists of 250 elements, as shown in Fig. 12.7. Enroll[1, Center] represents the number of students in course 1 at Center campus.

Figure 12.7 Two-Dimensional Array Enroll

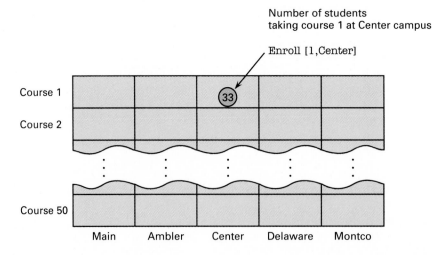

If the registrar wants to break down enrollment information according to student rank, it would require a three-dimensional array with 1,000 elements. This array is declared as follows and is shown in Fig. 12.8.

```
const
   MaxCourse = 50;              {maximum number of courses}

type
   Campus = (Main, Ambler, Center, Delaware, Montco);
   Rank = (Freshman, Sophomore, Junior, Senior);
   BigClassArray = array [1..MaxCourse, Campus, Rank] of Integer;

var
   ClassEnroll : BigClassArray;        {class enrollment}
   CurCampus : Campus;                 {current campus}
   ClassRank : Rank;                   {current rank}
   Total : Integer;                    {student totals}
```

The subscripted variable ClassEnroll[1, Center, Senior] represents the number of seniors taking course 1 at Center campus. ∎

■ Example 12.8

The program segment

```
Total :=  0;
for ClassRank := Freshman to Senior do
   Total := Total + ClassEnroll[1, Center, ClassRank]
```

computes the total number of students of all ranks in course 1 at Center campus.

Figure 12.8 Three-Dimensional Array ClassEnroll

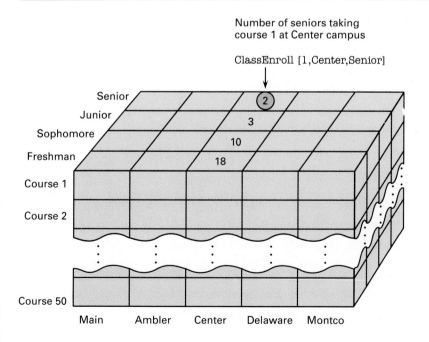

The program segment

```
Total := 0;
for CurCampus := Main to Montco do
  for ClassRank := Freshman to Senior do
    Total := Total + ClassEnroll[1, CurCampus, ClassRank]
```

computes the total number of students in course 1 (regardless of rank or campus). ■

Exercises for Section 12.2

Self-Check

1. Declare a three-dimensional array that can keep track of the number of students in the math classes (Math1, Algebra, Geometry, Algebra2, Trigo-nometry, Calculus) at your old high school according to the grade level and the sex of the students. How many elements are in this array?
2. Extend row-major order to three dimensions and show how the array ClassEnroll might be stored. What would be the offset for the array element ClassEnroll[1, Center, Senior] and the general formula for ClassEnroll[i, j, k]?

Programming

1. Redefine MaxCourse as 5 and write program segments that perform the following operations:
   a. Enter the enrollment data.
   b. Find the number of juniors in all classes at all campuses. Count students once for each course in which they are enrolled.
   c. Find the number of sophomores on all campuses who are enrolled in course 2.
   d. Compute and print the number of students at Main campus enrolled in each course and the total number of students at Main campus in all courses. Count students once for each course in which they are enrolled.
   e. Compute and print the number of upperclass students in all courses at each campus, as well as the total number of upperclass students enrolled. (Upperclass students are juniors and seniors.) Again, count students once for each course in which they are enrolled.

  12.3 Data Abstraction Illustrated

By this time, you have learned quite a lot about Pascal and programming. Your knowledge of arrays and records will enable you to write fairly sophisticated programs. This section develops a general program that might be used by a company to analyze sales figures. We will use data abstraction, focusing on the data structures and their operators, to solve this problem.

◆ Case Study: Analysis of Sales Trends

Problem

The HighRisk Software Company has employed us to develop a general sales analysis program that they can market to a number of different companies. This program will be used to enter and display sales figures in a variety of formats. The program will be *menu driven*, which means that users choose from a number of different options. The menu format is shown in Fig. 12.9.

Figure 12.9 Menu for Sales Analysis Program

```
Menu for Sales Analysis Program

 0. Get help.
 1. Enter sales data.
 2. Update sales data.
 3. Display sales data as a two-dimensional table.
 4. Compute annual sales totals.
 5. Tabulate monthly sales totals.
 6. Display annual sales totals.
 7. Display monthly sales totals.
 8. Display largest annual sales amount and year sold.
 9. Display largest monthly sales amount and month sold.
10. Graph annual sales data by year.
11. Graph monthly sales data by month.
12. Exit the program.
```

Design Overview

The operations to be performed are listed in the menu shown in Fig. 12.9. The main program will repeatedly display this menu and then perform the user's choice. The most difficult part of the problem is selecting the appropriate data structures and writing operators to perform each of the menu operations.

Data Requirements

Problem Inputs
The selected option (`Choice : Integer`)
The table of sales data (`Sales`)

Problem Outputs
The updated sales table displayed as a matrix (`Sales`)
The annual sales totals displayed in a table and as a bar graph
(`SumByYear`)
The monthly sales totals displayed in a table and as a bar graph
(`SumByMonth`)

There are three major data structures: a table of sales data organized by year and month, a collection of annual sales totals, and a collection of monthly sales totals. Menu choices 1 through 5 are performed on the complete table of sales data; menu choices 6, 8, and 10 are performed on the annual sales totals; and menu choices 7, 9, and 11 are performed on the monthly sales totals.

Data Type Specification

We can consider each data object and its associated operators as an abstract data type. We provide specifications for the sales table and annual sales totals next; the specification for monthly sales totals would be similar to the specification for annual sales totals.

Specification of Sales Table Abstract Data Type

Structure: The sales table, type `SalesRecord`, consists of a collection of `Real` values organized by year and month. There is one value for each month in the range of years covered. There are also two integer values that represent the starting year and the ending year.

Operators: Assume `Sales` is type `SalesRecord`.

`EnterSales (var Sales)`: Reads and saves the range of years covered and one sales amount for each month of the year.

`UpdateSales (var Sales)`: Modifies one or more entries in the sales table.

`DisplaySales (Sales)`: Displays the data in the sales table.

`TabYear (Sales, var SumByYear)`: Computes and stores the annual totals.

`TabMonth (Sales, var SumByMonth)`: Computes and stores the monthly totals.

Specification of Annual Sales Totals Abstract Data Type

Structure: The record for annual sales totals, type `YearSums`, consists of a collection of `Real` values, one for each year. There are also two integer values that represent the starting and the ending year.

Operators: Assume `SumByYear` is type `YearSums`.

`DisplayYear (SumByYear)`: Displays the annual sales total for each year of the range covered.

`MaxByYear (SumByYear, var LargeAmount, var LargeYear)`: Finds the largest annual sum (`LargeAmount`) and its year (`LargeYear`).

`GraphYear (SumByYear)`: Displays the annual sums in a bar graph.

The complete sales table stores a sales amount (type `Real`) for each month of a given year range (`MinYear..MaxYear`). The sales data can be stored in a two-dimensional array organized by year and month. This array will be part of a record, Sales, which also stores the first year (First) and the last year (Last) for which sales data are available (MinYear <= First <= Last <= MaxYear). Figure 12.10 shows the declarations for record Sales.

Figure 12.10   Declarations for Record Sales

```
const
  MinYear = 1985;
  MaxYear = 1999;

type
  YearRange = MinYear..MaxYear;
  SalesArray = array [YearRange, Month] of Real;
  SalesRecord = record
                  First, Last : YearRange;
                  Volume : SalesArray
                end; {SalesRecord}

var
  Sales : SalesRecord;
```

An object of type SalesRecord will accommodate sales data for the number of years in the subrange YearRange. For simplicity, we have chosen a rather small range.

Figure 12.11 shows a sketch of the memory area allocated to the record variable Sales. There is storage space for two Integer values (Sales.First and Sales.Last) and an array of 120 (10 rows by 12 columns) type Real values. As shown, array element Sales.Volume[1989,December] has the value 5549.00.

The collection of annual sales totals can be stored in a record SumByYear. This record has an array field, Sums, with type Real elements and subscript

Figure 12.11   Record Sales

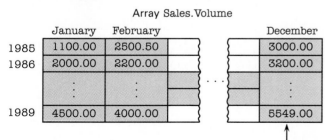

Sales.First `1985`
Sales.Last   `1989`

Array Sales.Volume

	January	February			December
1985	1100.00	2500.50			3000.00
1986	2000.00	2200.00			3200.00
⋮	⋮	⋮			⋮
1989	4500.00	4000.00			5549.00

Sales.Volume[1989, December]

type YearRange. For instance, SumByYear.Sums[1989] will contain the total of all sales in 1989. It also has two integer fields, First and Last, that specify the range of years covered (MinYear <= First <= Last <= MaxYear).

The collection of monthly sales totals can be stored in a one-dimensional array, SumByMonth, of type Real elements with subscript type Month. For instance, SumByMonth[January] will contain the total of all sales in January. Figure 12.12 shows the declarations and the memory layout for the record SumByYear; Fig. 12.13 shows the same for the array SumByMonth.

Figure 12.12 Record SumByYear

```
type
  YearArray = array [YearRange] of Real;
  YearSums = record
                First, Last : YearRange;
                Sums : YearArray
             end; {YearSums}

var
  SumByYear : YearSums;
```

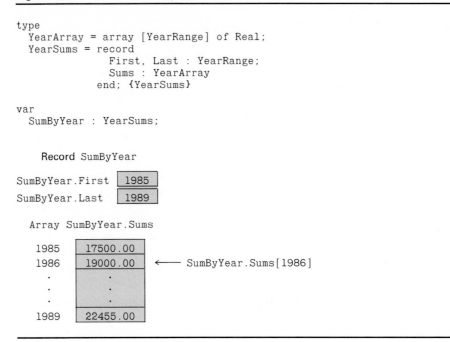

Figure 12.13 Array SumByMonth

```
type
  MonthSums = array [Month] of Real;

var
  SumByMonth : MonthSums;
```

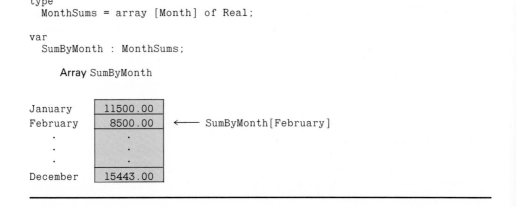

Design of Main Program

Now that we know the form of the major data objects and their operators, we can proceed with the design of the main program. The main program must allocate storage space for the data structures being manipulated, display the menu of choices, read each choice, and call the relevant operator procedure(s). Because certain operations must be performed before others, the main program must maintain the status of program flags that indicate which operations have been performed. If we use an array to store the month names, that array must also be declared in the main program. The additional data requirements for the main program follow.

> ### Program Variables
> A program flag indicating whether sales data are read
> (ReadDone : Boolean)
> A program flag indicating whether annual sums are computed
> (YearDone : Boolean)
> A program flag indicating whether monthly sums are computed
> (MonthDone : Boolean)
> An array of month names (MonthName : MonthArray)

Algorithm for Main Program

1. Initialize array MonthName.
2. Set status flags ReadDone, YearDone, and MonthDone to False.
3. repeat
   4. Display the menu.
   5. Read the user's choice.
   6. Perform the user's choice, updating Sales, SumByYear, SumByMonth, and the program flags.
   until user is done

Coding the Main Program

ReadDone, YearDone, and MonthDone (type Boolean) indicate whether the record Sales and arrays SumByYear and SumByMonth are defined. They are all initialized to False; ReadDone is set to True when Sales is defined, YearDone is set to True when SumByYear is defined, and MonthDone is set to True when SumByMonth is defined. The main program is shown in Fig. 12.14. The declarations in Fig. 12.10, Fig. 12.12, and Fig. 12.13 are inserted in the declaration part of the program.

Figure 12.14 Program SalesAnalysis

```
program SalesAnalysis (Input, Output);
{
  Analyzes data provided for a sales table organized by year
  and month. Tabulates, displays, and graphs sales totals
  by year and month as directed by the program user.
```

```
IMPORTS:  MonthArray, Month, Initialize, WriteMonth,
            ReadMonth from ADT Month (see Fig. 12.1)
          EnterInt (See Fig. 7.17)
          SalesRecord, YearRange, MinYear, MaxYear, EnterSales,
            UpdateSales, DisplaySales, TabYear, TabMonth from
            sales table ADT.
          YearSums, DisplayYear, MaxByYear, GraphYear from
            annual totals ADT.
          MonthSums, DisplayMonth, MaxByMonth, GraphMonth
            from monthly totals ADT.
}
  const
    MinYear = 1985;
    MaxYear = 1999;
    ExitChoice = 12;

  type
    Month = (January, February, March, April, May, June, July,
              August, September, October, November, December);
    MonthArray = array [Month] of packed array [1..9] of Char;

    YearRange = MinYear..MaxYear;
    SalesArray = array [YearRange, Month] of Real;
    SalesRecord = record
                    First, Last : YearRange;
                    Volume : SalesArray
                  end; {SalesRecord}

    YearArray = array [YearRange] of Real;
    YearSums = record
                    First, Last : YearRange;
                    Sums : YearArray
                  end; {YearSums}

    MonthSums = array [Month] of Real;

  var
    Sales : SalesRecord;                {table of sales data}
    SumByYear : YearSums;               {sales totals for each year}
    SumByMonth : MonthSums;             {sales totals for each month}
    ReadDone,                           {flag for Sales defined}
    YearDone,                           {flag for SumByYear defined}
    MonthDone : Boolean;                {flag for SumByMonth defined}
    MonthName : MonthArray;             {array of month names}
    Choice : Integer;                   {option selected}

{
  Insert EnterInt
  Insert Initialize, WriteMonth, and ReadMonth
  Insert EnterSales, UpdateSales, DisplaySales,
    TabYear, TabMonth
  Insert DisplayYear, MaxByYear, GraphYear
  Insert DisplayMonth, MaxByMonth, GraphMonth
  Insert DisplayHelp
  Insert DisplayMenu, DoChoice
}

begin {SalesAnalysis}
  {Initialize array MonthName and set program flags.}
  Initialize (MonthName);
```

```
  ReadDone := False;
  MonthDone := False;
  YearDone := False;

  {Perform user's choice until done}
  repeat
    DisplayMenu;
    EnterInt (0, ExitChoice, Choice);    WriteLn;
    DoChoice (Choice, Sales, SumByYear, SumByMonth,
              ReadDone, YearDone, MonthDone)
  until Choice = ExitChoice
end. {SalesAnalysis}
```

Figure 12.15 is the module dependency diagram for the sales analysis program. It shows the interaction between the various modules used in the program system. Each procedure must be declared before the modules that use it. For example, procedure `EnterInt` must be declared before the procedures in ADT `Month` or ADT `SalesTable`. The procedures in ADT `Month` must be declared before the procedures in ADT `SalesTable`, and so on.

Coding DisplayMenu and DoChoice

Procedure `DisplayMenu` consists of the collection of `WriteLn` statements needed to print the menu and is left as an exercise at the end of this section. Procedure

Figure 12.15 Module Dependency Diagram for Sales Analysis Program

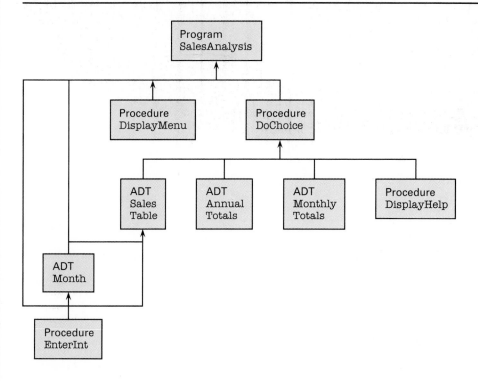

DoChoice (see Fig. 12.16) calls one or more of the operator procedures that are imported from the ADTs; the value of Choice determines which procedure(s) are called. If the preconditions are not met for a procedure, DoChoice displays an error message.

If the value of Choice is zero, DoChoice calls procedure DisplayHelp to print help messages to the user. DisplayHelp should provide information regarding any of the operations that the user wants clarified; DisplayHelp is also left as an exercise.

Figure 12.16 Procedure DoChoice

```
procedure DoChoice (var Choice {input/output} : Integer;
                    var Sales {input/output} : SalesRecord;
                    var SumByYear {input/output} : YearSums;
                    var SumByMonth {input/output} : MonthSums;
                    var ReadDone, YearDone,
                        MonthDone  {input/output} : Boolean);
{
   Performs the option selected by Choice.
   Pre : Choice, ReadDone, YearDone, and MonthDone are defined.
   Post: Performs operation selected by Choice on Sales,
         SumByYear, and SumByMonth and resets flags ReadDone,
         YearDone, and MonthDone as required.
   Uses: DisplayHelp, EnterSales, UpdateSales, DisplaySales,
         TabYear, TabMonth, DisplayYear, DisplayMonth, MaxByYear,
         MaxByMonth, GraphYear, GraphMonth
}
   var
      ExitChar : Char;        {used to validate exit request}
      LargeAmount : Real;     {the largest plotted value}
      LargeYear : Integer;    {year with largest annual amount}
      LargeMonth : Month;     {month with largest monthly amount}

begin {DoChoice}
   {
   Make sure that EnterSales is done first and that TabYear
   is performed before operations on SumByYear and that
   TabMonth is performed before operations on SumBymonth.
   }
   if (choice > 1) and (not ReadDone) then
     WriteLn ('Read sales data first - enter 1')
   else if (Choice in [6, 8, 10]) and (not YearDone) then
     WriteLn ('Tabulate annual sums first - enter 4')
   else if (Choice in [7, 9, 11]) and (not MonthDone) then
     WriteLn ('Tabulate monthly sums first - enter 5')
   else
     case Choice of
         0 :  DisplayHelp;
         1 :  begin
                 EnterSales (Sales);
                 ReadDone := True; YearDone := False; MonthDone := False
              end; {1}
         2 :  begin
                 UpdateSales (Sales);
                 YearDone := False;  MonthDone:= False
              end; {2}
         3 :  DisplaySales (Sales);
```

```
       4 :   begin
                 TabYear (Sales, SumByYear);
                 YearDone := True
              end; {4}
       5 :   begin
                 TabMonth (Sales, SumByMonth);
                 MonthDone := True
              end; {5}
       6 :   DisplayYear (SumByYear);
       7 :   DisplayMonth (SumByMonth);
       8 :   begin
                 MaxByYear (SumByYear, LargeAmount, LargeYear);
                 WriteLn ('Largest annual sum is $',
                         LargeAmount :4:2, ' in year ', LargeYear)
              end; {8}
       9 :   begin
                 MaxByMonth (SumByMonth, LargeAmount, LargeMonth);
                 WriteLn ('Largest monthly sum is $',
                         LargeAmount :4:2, ' in month ');
                 WriteMonth (LargeMonth))
              end; {9}
      10 :   GraphYear (SumByYear);
      11 :   GraphMonth (SumByMonth);
      12 :   begin
                 Write ('Exit program? Enter Y (Yes) or N (No) > ');
                 Read (ExitChar);
                 if (ExitChar = 'Y') or (ExitChar = 'y') then
                   WriteLn ('Sales analysis completed.')
                 else
                   Choice := 0          {cancel exit request}
              end {12}
     end {case}
end;   {DoChoice}
```

PROGRAM
STYLE

Verifying an Exit Request

The case statement in procedure DoChoice requires program users to verify that they want to exit the sales analysis program when Choice is ExitChoice (value is 12). Without this verification step, all data entry and analysis may have to be repeated if the program user selects the exit option by mistake.

Coding the Operators for the Sales Table ADT

Figure 12.17 shows the operators for the sales table ADT. Procedure Enter-Sales reads data into array Sales.Volume. EnterSales first calls EnterInt twice to read in the range of years covered. Next, a pair of nested for loops enters the sales data. Procedure WriteMonth displays the current month name as a prompt.

Procedure UpdateSales can be used to change an incorrect sales table value or to add new values at a later time. The program user must enter the year, month, and sales amount for each table entry being updated. ReadMonth enters an integer from 1 to 12 and converts it to a value of type Month.

Most screens are not wide enough to display the sales data for all twelve months of a year. Consequently, DisplaySales calls ShowHalf twice: first to print the sales figures for the first six months and then to print the figures for the last six months. ShowHalf begins by displaying six months as column headings. Next, a pair of nested for loops displays the sales figures for those six months of each year.

Procedure TabYear accumulates the sum of each row of the sales table and stores it in the appropriate element of array SumByYear. (Procedure TabMonth is left as an exercise at the end of this section.) Notice that record Sales is declared as a variable parameter in DisplaySales and TabYear even though it is used only for input. We have done this to save the time and memory that would be needed to make a local copy of this rather sizable record.

Figure 12.17 Operators for Sales Table ADT

```
procedure EnterSales (var Sales {output} : SalesRecord);
{
    Reads the sales data into the record Sales.
    Pre : None
    Post: The fields First and Last are defined and
          sales data are read into array Volume for each month of
          years First..Last.
    Uses: EnterInt and WriteMonth
}
    var
      CurMonth : Month;          {current month}
      CurYear : YearRange;       {current year}
      TempYear : Integer;        {holds data value for year}

begin {EnterSales}
   {Enter first and last years of sales data.}
   WriteLn ('Enter first year of sales data.');
   EnterInt (MinYear, MaxYear, TempYear);
   Sales.First := TempYear;
   WriteLn ('Enter last year of sales data.');
   EnterInt (Sales.First, MaxYear, TempYear);
   Sales.Last := TempYear;

   {Enter sales table data.}
   for CurYear := Sales.First to Sales.Last do
      begin
         WriteLn;
         Write ('For year ', CurYear :4);
         WriteLn (', enter sales amount for each month or 0.0');
         for CurMonth := January to December do
            begin
               WriteMonth (CurMonth);
               Write (' $');
               ReadLn (Sales.Volume[CurYear, CurMonth])
```

```
        end {for CurMonth}
      end {for CurYear}
end; {EnterSales}


procedure UpdateSales (var Sales {input/output} : SalesRecord);
{
  Changes one or more values in array Sales.Volume.
  Pre : Record Sales is defined.
  Post: Reads year, month, and value for each update
        and stores the new value in array Sales.Volume.
  Uses: EnterInt and ReadMonth
}
  var
    NewYear : Integer;        {Year of entry being updated.}
    NewMonth : Month;         {Month of entry being updated.}
    NewAmount : Real;         {Updated value}
    MoreChar : Char;          {More changes ('Y' or 'N')}

begin {UpdateSales}
  WriteLn ('Enter year, month, and amount for each update.');
  repeat
    Write ('For year - ');
    EnterInt (Sales.First, Sales.Last, NewYear);
    Write ('For month - ');
    ReadMonth (NewMonth);
    Write ('Enter amount $');
    ReadLn (NewAmount);
    Sales.Volume[NewYear, NewMonth] := NewAmount;
    Write ('Any more changes?  Enter Y (Yes) or N (No) > ');
    Read (MoreChar)
  until (MoreChar = 'N') or (MoreChar = 'n')
end; {UpdateSales}


procedure DisplaySales (var Sales {input} : SalesRecord);
{
  Displays the sales data.
  Pre : Record Sales is defined.
  Post: Displays a two-dimensional table of sales volume
        by month for years First..Last.
  Uses: ShowHalf to display table in chunks of 6 months.
}


  procedure ShowHalf (var Sales {input} : SalesRecord;
                      FirstMonth, LastMonth {input} : Month);
  {
    Displays the sales amounts by year for each of the months from
    FirstMonth to LastMonth.
    Pre : Record Sales and FirstMonth and LastMonth are defined.
    Post: Displays sales volumes in a table whose rows are
          Sales.First..Sales.Last and whose columns are
          FirstMonth..LastMonth.
    Uses: WriteMonth
  }
    var
      CurMonth : Month;              {loop-control variable}
      CurYear : YearRange;           {loop-control variable}
```

```
  begin {ShowHalf}
    {Print table heading for the months displayed.}
    Write ('Year');
    for CurMonth := FirstMonth to LastMonth do
      begin
        Write (' ');                        {Leave a space}
        WriteMonth (CurMonth)               {Print month name}
      end; {for}
    WriteLn;                                {End the heading}

    {Print sales figures for each month of each year.}
    for CurYear := Sales.First to Sales.Last do
      begin
        Write (CurYear :4);
        for CurMonth := FirstMonth to LastMonth do
          Write (Sales.Volume[CurYear, CurMonth] :10:2);
        WriteLn
      end {for CurYear}
  end; {ShowHalf}


begin {DisplaySales}
  {Display first 6 months and last 6 months of array Sales.}
  ShowHalf (Sales, January, June);    WriteLn;
  ShowHalf (Sales, July, December);   WriteLn
end; {DisplaySales}


procedure TabYear (var Sales {input} : SalesRecord;
                   var SumByYear {output} : YearSums);
{
   Tabulates sales totals by year. Sums are stored in
   array SumByYear.
   Pre : Record Sales is defined.
   Post: SumByYear.First  and  SumByYear.Last  are  defined and  elements
         SumByYear.Sums[First] through SumByYear.Sums[Last] are
         tabulated.
}
   var
      CurMonth : Month;                {loop-control variable}
      CurYear : YearRange;             {loop-control variable}
      Sum : Real;                      {sum for each year}

begin {TabYear}
  {Store range of years covered.}
  SumByYear.First := Sales.First;
  SumByYear.Last := Sales.Last;

  {Find each annual total.}
  for CurYear := Sales.First to Sales.Last do
    begin
      {Accumulate sum for 12 months}
      Sum := 0.0;
      for CurMonth := January to December do
        Sum := Sum + Sales.Volume[CurYear, CurMonth];
      SumByYear.Sums[CurYear] := Sum         {Store sales total}
    end; {for CurYear}
```

```
  WriteLn ('Annual sums tabulated')
end; {TabYear}
```

Coding the Operators for the Annual Totals ADT

Figure 12.18 shows the operators for the annual totals ADT. Procedure `DisplayYear` simply displays the values in array field `Sums` (a one-dimensional array) and is left as an exercise at the end of this section.

Procedure `MaxByYear` returns through `LargeAmount` the largest value in the array field `Sums`. It does this by saving the largest value found so far (starting with `Sums[SumByYear.First]`) in parameter `LargeAmount`. Each time an array element containing a larger value is found, its value is stored in `LargeAmount` and its subscript is stored in `LargeYear`.

Procedure `GraphYear` draws a bar chart of the values stored in array field `Sums`. First, `GraphYear` calls `MaxByYear` to determine the largest annual sales total. Next, it divides this value by the constant `ScreenWidth` (value is 50) to get the value represented by each point plotted. For each year being displayed, the `while` loop in `GraphYear` continues to plot points until the value plotted exceeds the sales total for that year. Hence, the largest value will be plotted as a bar of length `ScreenWidth`; all other bars will be smaller.

Figure 12.18 Operators for Annual Totals ADT

```
procedure MaxByYear (var SumByYear {input} : YearSums;
                     var LargeAmount {output} : Real;
                     var LargeYear {output} : Integer);
{
  Finds the largest value in array SumByYear.Sums
  Pre : Record SumByYear is defined.
  Post: Returns the largest value in array SumByYear.Sums
        through LargeAmount and its corresponding
        year through LargeYear.
}
  var
    CurYear : YearRange;        {loop control variable}

begin {MaxByYear}
  {First year's amount is largest so far.}
  with SumByYear do
    begin
      LargeYear := First;
      LargeAmount := Sums[First];

      {Find the largest value in array field Sums.}
      for CurYear := First + 1 to Last do
        {invariant:
          LargeAmount contains largest amount so far and
          Sums[LargeYear] is equal to LargeAmount.
        }
        if Sums[CurYear] > LargeAmount then
```

```
                    begin
                       {Save new largest amount so far.}
                       LargeAmount := Sums[CurYear];
                       LargeYear := CurYear
                    end {if}
            end {with}
end; {MaxByYear}


procedure GraphYear (var SumByYear {input} : YearSums);
{
  Displays a graph of array SumByYear.Sums.
  Pre : Record SumByYear is defined.
  Post: Displays a bar graph such that the size of the bar drawn for
        each element of array SumByYear.Sums is proportional to its
        value.
  Uses: MaxByYear
}
  const
     Star = '*';                  {symbol plotted}
     ScreenWidth = 50;            {longest bar length}

  var
     LargeAmount,                 {the largest value plotted}
     Increment,                   {the amount represented by each point}
     PlotVal : Real;              {the amount plotted so far}
     LargeYear : Integer;         {the year of largest annual amount}
     CurYear : YearRange          {loop control variable}

begin {GraphYear}
  {Define the scale for the horizontal axis.}
  MaxByYear (SumByYear, LargeAmount, LargeYear);
  Increment := Round(LargeAmount / ScreenWidth);

  {Plot the bar graph.}
  WriteLn;
  WriteLn ('Year|      Sales in Dollars');    {Print heading}
  {Print a bar for each element of array field SumByYear.Sums}
  with SumByYear do
     for CurYear := First to Last do
        begin
           Write (CurYear :4, '|');                    {Print the year}
           {Plot points until value plotted exceeds element value.}
           PlotVal := Increment;          {Initialize sum plotted}
           while PlotVal <= Sums[CurYear] do
              begin
                 Write (Star);                   {Plot a new point}
                 PlotVal := PlotVal + Increment  {Add to sum plotted}
              end {while}
        end; {for}

  {Draw horizontal scale}
  WriteLn ('0.00^          ^          ^          ^',
                  '          ^          ^', LargeAmount :4:2);
  WriteLn ('     Each point represents ', Increment :4:2);
end; {GraphYear}
```

Testing the Sales Analysis Program

A sample run of the sales analysis program is shown in Fig. 12.19. To save space, only part of the data entry process and only the first menu display are shown. The options selected are 1, 2, 4, 6, 8, 10, and 12.

To test this program completely, you should select options whose preconditions are not satisfied. For instance, selecting option 7, 9, or 11 should display the error message Tabulate monthly sums first – enter 5. You should also enter year values that are outside the expected range to make sure that they do not cause a fatal program error. Finally, provide the missing procedures and verify that they perform their intended operations.

Figure 12.19 Sample Run of the Sales Analysis Program

```
Menu for Sales Analysis Program

 0. Get help.
 1. Enter sales data.
 2. Update sales data.
 3. Display sales data as a two-dimensional table.
 4. Compute annual sales totals.
 5. Tabulate monthly sales totals.
 6. Display annual sales totals.
 7. Display monthly sales totals.
 8. Display largest annual sales amount and year sold.
 9. Display largest monthly sales amount and month sold.
10. Graph annual sales data by year.
11. Graph monthly sales data by month.
12. Exit the program.
Choose an option – Enter a number between 0 and 12> 1
Enter first year of sales data.
Enter a number between 1900 and 1999> 1987
Enter last year of sales data.
Enter a number between 1987 and 1999> 1988


For year 1987, enter sales amount for each month or 0.0
  January $1000.00
 February $0.00
    March $700.00
      .
      .
      .


For year 1988, enter sales amount for each month or 0.0
  January $500.00
 February $400.00
    March $400.00
      .
      .
      .


Choose an option – Enter a number between 0 and 12> 2
Enter year, month, and amount for each update.
For year – Enter a number between 1987 and 1988> 1987
```

Case Study: Analysis of Sales Trends, continued

```
For month - Enter a number between 1 and 12 > 2
Enter amount $600.00
Any more changes?  Enter Y (Yes) or N (No) > N

Choose an option - Enter a number between 0 and 12> 3
Table of Sales Volume by Year and Month

    Year   January   February   March    April      May     June
    1987   1000.00     600.00   700.00   800.00   950.00  1000.00
    1988    500.00     400.00   400.00   900.00  1000.00    55.00

    Year      July   August September   October November  December
    1987    500.00   500.00    900.00    600.00   950.50  1000.00
    1988    300.00   800.00    750.00    900.00   600.00   300.00

Choose an option - Enter a number between 0 and 12> 4
Annual sums tabulated.

Choose an option - Enter a number between 0 and 12> 6
Table of Sales Totals by Year

        Year     Sales
        1987   9500.50
        1988   6905.00

Choose an option - Enter a number between 0 and 12> 8
Largest annual sum is $9500.50 in year 1987
Choose an option - Enter a number between 0 and 12> 10
```

```
Year|     Sales in Dollars
1987|**************************************************
1988|************************************
0.00^        ^         ^         ^         ^          ^9500.50
      Each point represents    190.00
```

```
Choose an option - Enter a number between 0 and 12> 12
Exit program? Enter Y (Yes) or N (No) > Y
Sales analysis completed.
```

Exercises for Section 12.3

Self-Check

1. Explain why the variable TempYear is needed in procedure EnterSales.
2. Why is it necesary for DisplaySales to call ShowHalf twice?

Programming

1. Write procedures DisplayMenu, DisplayHelp, and DisplayYear.
2. Write procedures DisplayMonth, MaxByMonth, TabMonth, and GraphMonth for the monthly totals ADT.

Often a data collection contains items of different types. For example, the data that represent the performance of a class of students on an exam consist of the students' names, their exam scores, and their grades.

Parallel Arrays

One approach to organizing these data would be to declare separate arrays with identical subscript types for the names, scores, and grades, as follows:

```
const
  MaxClass = 200;
  StrLength = 20;

type
  ClassIndex = 1..MaxClass;
  StringType = packed array [1..StrLength] of Char;
  NameArray = array [ClassIndex] of StringType;
  ScoreArray = array [ClassIndex] of Integer;
  GradeArray = array [ClassIndex] of Char;

var
  Names  : NameArray;
  Scores : ScoreArray;
  Grades : GradeArray;
```

These three arrays are called *parallel arrays*, because all the data items with the same subscript (say, *i*) pertain to a particular student (the *i*th student). Related data items are in the same shade of color in Fig. 12.20. The data for the first student are stored in Names[1], Scores[1], and Grades[1]. A better way to organize the student data is shown next.

Declaring an Array of Student Records

A more natural and more convenient organization of the class performance data is to group all the information pertaining to a particular student in a record. The data structure declared next represents the class data as a single array of records named Class. A sample array Class is shown in Fig. 12.21.

```
const
  MaxClass = 200;
  StrLength = 20;

type
  ClassIndex = 1..MaxClass;
  StringType = packed array [1..StrLength] of Char;
  Student = record
              Name  : StringType;
              Score : Integer;
```

Figure 12.20 Three Parallel Arrays

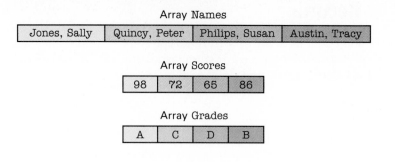

```
                     Grade : Char
                   end; {Student}
       StudentArray = array [ClassIndex] of Student;

     var
       Class : StudentArray;
```

In Fig. 12.21, the data for the first student are stored in record Class[1]. The individual data items are Class[1].Name, Class[1].Score, and Class[1].Grade. As shown, Class[1].Grade is A.

If procedure ReadOneStudent is available to read a single student record, the following for statement can be used to fill the entire array Class with data.

```
       for i := 1 to MaxClass do
         ReadOneStudent (Class[i]);
```

Each time ReadOneStudent is called, the record returned will be stored as the ith element (1 <= i <= MaxClass) of array Class. The following for statement can be used to display all the names read.

```
       for i := 1 to MaxClass do
         WriteLn (Class[i].Name)
```

Using the with Statement with an Array of Records

Be careful when you use a with statement to process an array of records. For example, the with statement that begins

Figure 12.21 Array of Records

Array Class

	Name	Score	Grade
Class[1]	Jones, Sally	98	A ◄——— Class[1].Grade
Class[2]	Quincy, Peter	72	C
Class[3]	Philips, Susan	65	D
Class[4]	Austin, Tracy	86	B

uses the subscripted variable Class[i] as its record variable. The particular array element referenced depends on the value of i. If i is undefined or is out of range, a run-time error will result.

If i is updated inside the with statement, the array element referenced will not change. For example, the following statements display the first student's name MaxClassSize times. Because i is 1 when the with statement is reached, Class[1] is the record referenced in the with statement body. Even though the for loop changes the value of i, Class[1] is still the record referenced, so Class[1].Name will be displayed repeatedly.

```
i := 1;
{incorrect attempt to display all student names}
with Class[i] do
  for i := 1 to MaxClass do
    WriteLn (Name)
```

The correct way to sequence these statements is shown next.

```
{Display all student names}
for i := 1 to MaxClass do
  with Class[i] do
    WriteLn (Name)
```

Now all student names will be printed, because i is changed by the for statement external to the with statement. Each time the with statement is reached, it references a new record. Whenever a for statement accesses an array of records in sequential order, the with statement should be nested inside the for statement and not vice versa.

Exercises for Section 12.4

Self-Check

1. For the array of records Class, what value is displayed by each of the following valid statements?

   a. WriteLn (Class[3].Name[4]);
   b. WriteLn (Class[3].Grade[4]);
   c. WriteLn (Class.Grade[3]);
   d. WriteLn (Class[4].Name);
   e. WriteLn (Class[4].Name[4].Grade)
   f. WriteLn (Class[3].Grade)
   g. WriteLn (Class[3]);
   h. WriteLn (Class.Name[4]);

2. Write a for loop that could be used to read data into the three parallel arrays declared in this section. Assume that the number of students, NumStu, is known before loop execution begins.

3. Does storage of an array of records require more or less memory space than storage of parallel arrays?

1. Write procedure ReadOneStudent. Read each student's name and score; leave the grade field undefined.

 ## 12.5 Processing an Array of Records

This problem illustrates the use of an array of records. It processes the array of students declared earlier.

● Case Study: Grading an Exam

Problem
Your computer science professor wants a program that will assist her in assigning grades for an exam. The program should read and display each student's name and exam score, compute and display all exam statistics (that is, the number of students who took the exam, the lowest score, the highest score, average score, median score, and standard deviation), and assign letter grades based on the class average and standard deviation.

Design Overview
Currently your professor stores the information for her classes in a gradebook. Each gradebook page lists the students on the left and has a column on the right for storing the exam scores and the corresponding letter grades. The exam statistics appear at the bottom of the page. A sample entry for one exam is shown in Fig. 12.22. The student names and numeric scores are provided as input data; the letter grades, the number of students, and the exam statistics are all undefined initially.

Figure 12.22 Sample Gradebook Entry

```
Name                     Score/Grade
Sally Adams               80    ?
Robert Baker              70    ?
Jane Cohen                60    ?
William Dooley            73    ?
        .
        .
        .

Number of Students        ?

Lowest Score              ?
Highest Score             ?
Median Score              ?
Average Score             ?
Standard Deviation        ?
```

Data Requirements

Problem Inputs
The name of each student taking the exam (a string)
The score of each student taking the exam (an integer)

Problem Outputs
Each student's name, score, and letter grade (a character)
The number of students taking the exam (an integer)
The exam statistics, including the lowest score, the highest score, and median score (integers) and the average and standard deviation (real numbers)

Data Type Specification
We can store the student data and exam statistics shown in Fig. 12.22 in two separate data structures. The first is a single record with two fields: an array of student records and the number of students. The second data structure is a record for storing the exam statistics. Figure 12.23 shows the declarations for these data structures; Fig. 12.24 sketches their layout in memory.

Specification of Gradebook Abstract Data Type

Structure: Consists of a record of data (a string, an integer, and a character) for each student who took the exam and a count of students (all stored in record Test). Also, consists of a collection of Real values that represent the exam statistics (stored in record Stats).

Operators: ReadStudents (var Test): Reads and saves the student names and exam scores. Also counts the number of students who took the exam.

DisplayStudents (Test): Displays the name, numeric score, and letter grade for each student who took the exam.

ComputeStats (Test, var Stats): Computes and stores the exam statistics.

DisplayStats (Stats): Displays the exam statistics.

AssignGrades (var Test, Stats): Assigns and stores the letter grade for each student.

Figure 12.23 Declarations for a Gradebook Entry

```
const
  StrLength = 20;              {length of each name string}
  MaxClass = 200;             {maximum number of students}
```

Case Study: Grading an Exam, continued

```
type
  StringType = packed array [1..StrLength] of Char;
  Student = record                              {one student record}
              Name : StringType;
              Score : Integer;
              Grade : Char
            end; {Student}

  ClassRange = 0..MaxClass;
  ClassIndex = 1..MaxClass;
  StudentArray = array [ClassIndex] of Student; {array of records}

  Exam = record
           Class : StudentArray;
           NumStu : ClassRange
         end; {Exam}

  Statistics = record
                 LowScore, HighScore,
                 Median : Integer;
                 Average,
                 StandardDev : Real
               end; {Statistics}
var
  Test  : Exam;            {the student data and count}
  Stats : Statistics;      {the exam statistics}
```

Figure 12.24 Records Test and Stats in Memory

Design of Main Program

The main program for the student grading program uses the operators in the gradebook entry ADT to process the data structures Test and Stats in the appropriate sequence. The main program algorithm is shown next.

Main Program Algorithm

1. Read the student data.
2. Compute the exam statistics.
3. Print the exam statistics.
4. Assign letter grades to each student.
5. Print each student's final record.

Coding the Main Program

The main program is shown in Fig. 12.25. The type and constant declarations from Fig. 12.23 are included in the declaration part. Figure 12.26 is the module dependency diagram.

Figure 12.25 Student Grading Program

```
program Grader (Input, Output);
{
  Computes and displays the exam statistics, assigns letter
  grades, and displays each student's record.

  IMPORTS:  MaxClass, Student, ClassRange, ClassIndex, StudentArray,
            Exam, Statistics, ReadStudents, DisplayStudents,
            ComputeStats, DisplayStats, AssignGrades from
            GradeBook ADT (see Fig. 12.27).
            ReadLnString (see Fig. 10.20)
}
  const
    StrLength = 20;                {length of each name string}
    MaxClass = 200;                {maximum number of students}

  type
    StringType = packed array [1..StrLength] of Char;
    Student = record                      {one student record}
                Name : StringType;
                Score : Integer;
                Grade : Char
              end; {Student}

    ClassRange = 0..MaxClass;
    ClassIndex = 1..MaxClass;
    StudentArray = array [ClassIndex] of Student; {array of records}

    Exam = record
             Class : StudentArray;
             NumStu : ClassRange
           end; {Exam}

    Statistics = record
                   LowScore, HighScore,
```

Case Study: Grading an Exam, continued

```
                              Median : Integer;
                              Average,
                              StandardDev : Real
                          end; {Statistics}

    var
      Test  : Exam;                {the student data and count}
      Stats : Statistics;          {the exam statistics}

  {
    Insert ReadLnString
    Insert ReadStudents, DisplayStudents, AssignGrade,
      ComputeStats, DisplayStats
  }

  begin {Grader}
    ReadStudents (Test);
    ComputeStats (Test, Stats);
    DisplayStats (Stats);
    AssignGrades (Test, Stats);
    DisplayStudents (Test)
  end. {Grader}
```

Coding the Operator Procedures

The operators for the gradebook ADT are shown in Fig. 12.27. Procedure `ReadStudents` calls procedure `ReadOneStudent` once for each student who took the exam. `ReadOneStudent` returns the next student's name and score through its parameter `NextStudent`. Entering a blank name (by pressing the Return key) indicates that there are no more students. If a nonblank name is read, the count of students processed (`i`) is incremented by one, and the statement

```
    Test.Class[i] := NextStudent
```

Figure 12.26 Module Dependency Diagram for Student Grading Program

copies the input data into the next element of the array Test.Class. The
number of students is stored in Test.NumStu and displayed just before the
procedure finishes.

Procedure DisplayStudents displays a table of student records, one student record per output line. The statements

```
for i := 1 to Test.NumStu do
  with Test.Class[i] do
    WriteLn (Name :20, Score :10, Grade :10)
```

display the next student record, Test.Class[i]. Because the with statement
is nested inside the for statement, a different student's record is printed on
each output line.

Procedure AssignGrades assigns a letter grade to each student. The grade
can be determined by comparing the student's score to the class average and
the standard deviation. Table 12.1 describes the desired grade assignments.

Table 12.1 Decision Table for Assigning Letter Grades

Score Range	Grade
>= Average + 1.5 * StandardDev	A
>= Average + 0.5 * StandardDev	B
>= Average − 0.5 * StandardDev	C
>= Average − 1.5 * StandardDev	D
< Average − 1.5 * StandardDev	F

The if statement in procedure AssignGrades implements the decision
table. The for loop causes the if statement to be repeated once for each
student. Because the if statement is also nested inside the with statement, the
fields Score and Grade reference fields of the record variable Test.Class[i]
(that is, the current student record).

Finally, procedure ComputeStats computes the exam statistics and stores
the results in the subrecord Test.Stats. ComputeStats calls a different function to compute each statistic. Function FindAverage returns the average score
and is shown in Fig. 12.27. Function FindStandardDev is discussed after the
figure, and function FindMedian is discussed in Section 12.7. The rest of the
statistical functions are left as exercises. Procedure DisplayStats displays the
contents of record Stats and is also left as an exercise.

Figure 12.27 Operators for Gradebook ADT

```
procedure ReadStudents (var Test {output} : Exam);
{
  Reads in the student records for one exam and counts the
  number of students who took the exam.
  Pre : None
  Post: Name and score of each student is stored in Test.Class and
        a count of students is displayed and stored in Test.NumStu.
```

```
    Uses: ReadOneStudent
  }

  const
    Sentinel = '                         ';     {sentinel name}

  var
    NextStudent : Student;                 {current student record}
    i : ClassRange;                  {loop control and array subscript}

  procedure ReadOneStudent (var NextStudent {output} : Student);
  {
    Enters the Name and Score for one student.
    Pre : None
    Post: A string is read into NextStudent.Name. If the string
          is not blank, an integer is read into NextStudent.Score.
    Uses: ReadLnString
  }
    var
      NameLength : Integer;                {length of name string}

  begin {ReadOneStudent}
    with NextStudent do
      begin
        WriteLn;  Write ('Name > ');
        ReadLnString (Input, StrLength, Name, NameLength);
        if NameLength <> 0 then
          begin
            Write ('Score> ');
            ReadLn (Score)
          end {if}
      end {with}
   end; {ReadOneStudent}

begin {ReadStudents}
  WriteLn ('Enter the data requested for each student.');
  WriteLn ('Press return (after prompt Name >) when done.');

  i := 0;                          {initial count of students}
  repeat
    {invariant:
       The sentinel name was not read and
       i < MaxClass
    }
    ReadOneStudent (NextStudent);     {Read next student}
    if NextStudent.Name <> Sentinel then
      begin
        i := i + 1;            {Increase count}
        Test.Class[i] := NextStudent   {Save the student's data}
      end {if}
  until (NextStudent.Name = Sentinel) or (i = MaxClass);

  {assert:  no more students or array is filled}
  Test.NumStu := i;
  WriteLn (i :1, ' student records were stored in memory.');
  if i = MaxClass then
    WriteLn ('Student array is completely filled.')
end; {ReadStudents}
```

```
procedure DisplayStudents (var Test {input} : Exam);
{
  Displays the student records.
  Pre : Record Test is defined.
  Post: Displays exam performance data for each student.
}
  var
    i : ClassIndex;              {loop-control variable}

begin {DisplayStudents}
  WriteLn;
  WriteLn ('The individual student data follow:');
  {Print heading}
  WriteLn ('Name', 'Score' :26, 'Grade' :10);

  {Print each student's data.}
  for i := 1 to Test.NumStu do
    with Test.Class[i] do
      WriteLn (Name :20, Score :10, Grade :10)
end; {DisplayStudents}


procedure AssignGrades (var Test {input/output} : Exam;
                            Stats {input} : Statistics);
{
  Assigns letter grade to each student based on the exam score,
  class average, and standard deviation.
  Pre : All exam scores are stored in Test.Class and Average and
        StandardDev are defined (part of record Stats).
  Post: The letter grade for each student is stored in
        Test.Class.
}
  var
    i : ClassIndex;              {loop control variable}

begin  {AssignGrades}
  with Test, Stats do
    for i := 1 to NumStu do
      with Class[i] do
        if Score >= Average + 1.5 * StandardDev then
          Grade := 'A'
        else if Score >= Average + 0.5 * StandardDev then
          Grade := 'B'
        else if Score >= Average - 0.5 * StandardDev then
          Grade := 'C'
        else if Score >= Average - 1.5 * StandardDev then
          Grade := 'D'
        else
          Grade := 'F'
end; {AssignGrades}


procedure ComputeStats (var Test {input}  : Exam;
                            var Stats {output} :Statistics);
{
  Computes all exam statistics.
  Pre : Student scores are read and record Test is defined.
  Post: Stores low, high, and median scores, and
        average and standard deviation in record Stats.
```

```
Uses: FindLow, FindHigh, FindMedian, FindAverage,
      and FindStandardDev
}

{Insert FindLow, FindHigh, FindMedian, FindStandardDev}

  function FindAverage (var Test : Exam) : Real;
  {
    Returns the average of the scores stored in array Test.Class.
    Pre : Student scores are stored in Test.Class.
    Post: Returns the average of the scores in Test.Class
  }
    var
      Sum : Real;            {the accumulating sum of scores}
      i : ClassIndex;       {loop control variable and subscript}

  begin {FindAverage}
    {Accumulate the sum of all scores}
    Sum := 0;
    for i := 1 to Test.NumStu do
      Sum := Sum + Test.Class[i].Score;

    {Return the average score or 0.0}
    if Test.NumStu <> 0 then
      FindAverage := Sum / Test.NumStu
    else
      FindAverage := 0.0
  end; {FindAverage}


begin {ComputeStats}
  with Stats do
    begin
      Average := FindAverage(Test);
      LowScore := FindLow(Test);
      HighScore := FindHigh(Test);
      Median := FindMedian(Test);
      StandardDev := FindStandardDev(Test, Average)
    end {with}
end; {ComputeStats}


procedure DisplayStats (Stats {input} : Statistics);
{Displays the statistics for an exam.}

begin {DisplayStats stub}
  WriteLn ('Procedure DisplayStats entered.')
end; {DisplayStats}
```

One of the functions called by ComputeStats is function FindStandardDev. This function implements the formula

$$\text{standard deviation} = \sqrt{\frac{\sum_{i=1}^{N} (score_i - average)^2}{N - 1}}$$

which is a measure of the spread, or dispersion, of the grades around the average grade. Statistical theory states that for a bell curve, 68.34 percent of the grades lie within one standard deviation of the average grade. Function FindStandardDev in Fig. 12.28 implements the formula for standard deviation.

Figure 12.28   Function FindStandardDev

```
function FindStandardDev (var Test {input} : Exam;
                              Average  {input} : Real) : Real;
{
  Returns the standard deviation of the scores in array
  Test.Class.
  Pre : The score fields are defined and Average was computed.
  Post: Returns the standard deviation if defined; otherwise,
        returns zero.
}
  var
    SumSquares : Real;        {Sum of squares}
    i : ClassIndex;           {loop control and subscript}

begin {FindStandardDev}
  SumSquares := 0;
  with Test do
    for i := 1 to NumStu do
      SumSquares := Sqr(Class[i].Score - Average)
                    + SumSquares;

  if Test.NumStu > 1 then
    FindStandardDev := Sqrt(SumSquares / (Test.NumStu - 1))
  else
    FindStandardDev := 0.0
end; {FindStandardDev}
```

Testing the Program

A sample run of the student grading program is shown in Fig. 12.29. We should verify that the program works correctly when the array Test.Class is completely filled (MaxClass students took the exam).

Figure 12.29   Sample Run of Student Grading Program

```
Enter the data requested for each student.
Press return (after prompt Name >) when done.

Name > Joe Costa
Score> 80

Name > Lee Hayes
Score> 70

Name > Bill Titcomb
Score> 60

Name >
3 student records were stored in memory.
```

Case Study: Grading an Exam, *continued*

```
Low    High   Median   Average   Standard deviation
 60     80       70      70.0          10.0
```

```
The individual student data follow:
Name                    Score     Grade
Joe Costa                 80         B
Lee Hayes                 70         C
Bill Titcomb              60         D
```

Exercises for Section 12.5

Self-Check

1. For the data in Fig. 12.29, what value is displayed by each of the following valid statements?
   a. WriteLn (Test.Class.NumStu);
   b. WriteLn (Exam.NumStu);
   c. with Test, Class[1] do
        WriteLn (Score, Grade, Name);
   d. WriteLn (Test.NumStu);
   e. WriteLn (Class.NumStu);
   f. WriteLn (Test.Class.Name[2]);
   g. WriteLn (Test[1].Class.Name[2]);
   h. WriteLn (Test.Class[1].Name[2]);
   i. WriteLn (Test.Class[1].Name);
   j. WriteLn (Statistics.Average);

Programming

1. Write procedure DisplayStats.
2. Write functions FindLow and FindHigh.

 ## 12.6   Searching an Array of Records

A common problem in processing arrays is *searching* an array to determine whether it contains a particular data item. If the array elements are records, then we must compare a particular field of each record, called the *record key*, to the data item we are seeking. Once we have located the item in question, we can display or modify the record. In this section, we will write a procedure that searches for a particular student's record.

■ Example 12.9

Function Search searches the array Test.Class for a record whose Name field matches the *target name*, StuName. If the target name is located, Search returns

the index of the student record with that name. Otherwise, it returns a value
of zero. For the array field Class shown in Fig. 12.24, the value returned would
be 2 for the target name 'Robert Baker   '; the value returned would
be 0 for the target name 'Bob Baker   '.

Figure 12.30   Function Search

```
function Search (var Test : Exam;
                 StuName : StringType) : Integer;
{
  Searches for StuName in the Name field of array Test.Class.
  Pre : Test is defined and 1 <= Test.NumStu <= MaxClass.
  Post: Returns the subscript of StuName if found;
        otherwise, returns zero.
}
  var
    CurStu : Integer;          {array subscript}

begin  {Search}
  {Compare the Name field of each record to StuName until done.}
  CurStu := 1;                 {Start with the first record}
  with Test do
    begin
      while (CurStu < NumStu) and (Class[CurStu].Name <> StuName) do
        {invariant:
            CurStu is <= NumStu and
            no prior Name field contains StuName
        }
        CurStu := CurStu + 1;                  {Check next record}

      {assertion: StuName is found or last element is reached.}
      {Define the function result.}
      if Class[CurStu].Name = StuName then
        Search := CurStu               {Return target subscript}
      else
        Search := 0                    {Return 0}
    end {with}
end; {Search}
```

The while condition compares the student name selected by CurStu to the
target name. If they are equal, loop exit occurs. If they are unequal and the
last record has not been reached, CurStu advances to the next student record.

Loop exit occurs when the target name is found or the last element is
reached. After loop exit, the if statement returns the location of the current
student (CurStu) if StuName was found; otherwise, it returns zero. ∎

∎ Example 12.10

Your computer science professor wants us to modify the grading program in
Fig. 12.25 so that it is menu driven. Besides the operators shown in Fig. 12.27,
she wants to be able to display a particular student's record and to change a
particular student's record.

Procedure DisplayOne in Fig. 12.31 performs the first of these two new
operations. It reads the target name, calls Search to locate the target name in
the array Test.Class, and then displays the complete student record. Proce-

dure ChangeRecord reads the target name, calls Search to locate the target name in the array Test.Class, and then reads and stores the new score and grade in the array. ∎

Figure 12.31 Procedures DisplayOne and ChangeRecord

```
procedure DisplayOne (var Test {input} : Exam);
{
  Displays a selected record of array Test.Class
  Pre : Test is defined.
  Post: Displays the record for the student whose name is read.
  Uses: Procedure ReadLnString and function Search
}
  var
    Target : StringType;       {data for record being updated}
    Index : ClassRange;        {subscript of target record or 0}
    TargetLen : Integer;       {length of target name}

begin {DisplayOne}
  Write ('Enter student name> ');
  ReadLnString (Input, StrLength, Target, TargetLen);
  Index := Search (Test, Target);        {Find Target}

  {Display record or error message.}
  if Index <> 0 then
    with Test.Class[Index] do
      WriteLn ('Score is ', Score :3, '; Grade is ', Grade)
  else
    WriteLn ('No record for student ', Target)
end; {DisplayOne}


procedure ChangeRecord (var Test {input/output} : Exam);
{
  Changes a selected record of array Test.Class
  Pre : Test is defined.
  Post: Changes the record for the student whose name is read.
  Uses: Procedure ReadLnString and function Search
}
  var
    Target : StringType;       {data for record being updated}
    Index : ClassRange;        {subscript of target record or 0}
    TargetLen : Integer;       {length of target name}

begin {ChangeRecord}
  {Enter and search for the target name.}
  Write ('Enter name of target student> ');
  ReadLnString (Input, StrLength, Target, TargetLen);
  Index := Search (Test, Target);

  {If target name is found, update the record.}
  if Index <> 0 then
    with Test.Class[Index] do
      begin
        Write ('New score> ');
        ReadLn (Score);
        Write ('New Grade> ');
        ReadLn (Grade)
      end {with}
```

```
        else
            WriteLn ('Student ', Target, ' did not take the exam. ')
end;   {ChangeRecord}
```

Exercises for Section 12.6

Self-Check

1. What happens in function Search if the last student name matches the target name? Why can't we use the condition CurStu <= NumStu in the while condition?
2. Another technique for searching an array is to introduce a program flag, say Found, that is initially False and that is set to True inside a search loop if the target value is found. Loop repetition continues as long as Found is False and all elements have not been tested. After loop exit, the value of Found determines whether the current subscript or zero is returned as the function result. Write the procedure body.

Programming

1. Write a procedure to count the number of students who scored a passing grade (D or higher) on an exam.
2. Rewrite the main program for the grading program as a menu-driven program. Provide as menu choices all the operations discussed in this section and Section 12.5.

 ## 12.7 Sorting an Array of Records

In Section 6.5 we discussed a simple sort operation that involved three numbers. We performed the sort by examining pairs of numbers and exchanging them if they were out of order. There are many times when we would like to sort the elements in an array, for example, to print a grade report in alphabetical order or in order by score.

This section discusses a fairly intuitive (but not very efficient) algorithm called the *selection sort*. To perform a selection sort of an array with N elements (subscripts 1..N), we locate the largest element in the array and then switch the largest element with the element at subscript N, thereby placing the largest element at position N. Then we locate the largest element remaining in the subarray with subscripts 1..N–1 and switch it with the element at subscript N–1, thereby placing the second largest element at position N–1. Then we locate the largest element remaining in subarray 1..N–2 and switch it with the element at subscript N–2, and so on.

Figure 12.32 traces the operation of the selection sort algorithm. The diagram on the left shows the original array. Each subsequent diagram shows the array after the next largest element is moved to its final position in the array. The subarray in the darker color represents the portion of the array that

Figure 12.32   Trace of Selection Sort

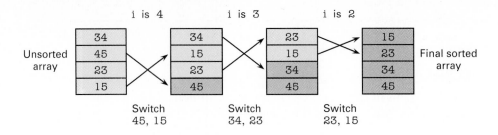

is sorted after each exchange occurs. Note that it requires at most N–1 exchanges to sort an array with N elements. The algorithm follows.

Selection Sort Algorithm

1. for i := N downto 2 do
   2. Find the largest element in subarray 1..i.
   3. if the largest element is not at subscript i then
       Switch the largest element with the one at subscript i.
   The refinement of step 2 also contains a for loop and is shown next.

Step 2 Refinement

2.1 Save i as the position of the largest so far in the subarray
2.2 for j := i–1 downto 1 do
     2.3 if the element at j is bigger than largest so far then
       Save j as the position of the largest so far.

Procedure SelectSort in Fig. 12.33 implements the selection sort algorithm for the array field Class of parameter Test. Local variable IndexOfMax holds the location of the largest exam score found so far in the current subarray. After each execution of the inner for loop, procedure Switch is called to exchange the elements with subscripts IndexOfMax and i, provided that the element at i is not the next largest element. After the execution of procedure SelectSort, the student records will be ordered by exam score (record with smallest score first).

Figure 12.33   Selection Sort Procedure

```
procedure SelectSort (var Test {input/output} : Exam);
{
  Orders the data in array Test.Class by exam score.
  Pre : Record Test is defined.
  Post: The records in array Test.Class are ordered by score.
}
  var
    i,                    {subscript of last element in subarray}
```

```
    j,                  {subscript of element being compared to max}
    IndexOfMax : ClassIndex;              {index of max so far}

  procedure Switch (var Stu1, Stu2 {input/output} : Student);

  {Switches records Stu1 and Stu2.}

      var
        TempStu : Student;          {temporary student record}

  begin  {Switch}
    TempStu := Stu1;  Stu1 := Stu2;  Stu2 := TempStu
  end; {Switch}

begin {SelectSort}
  with Test do
    {Order array Test.Class according to Score field.}
    for i := NumStu downto 2 do
      begin
        {Find the element in subarray 1..i with largest Score}
        IndexOfMax := i;
        for j := i-1 downto 1 do
          if Class[j].Score > Class[IndexOfMax].Score then
            IndexOfMax := j;

        {assert: element at IndexOfMax is largest in subarray}
        {Switch element at i with element at IndexOfMax}
        if IndexOfMax <> i then
          Switch (Class[i], Class[IndexOfMax])
      end {for i}
end; {SelectSort}
```

Analysis of Selection Sort

As mentioned earlier, at most N-1 exchanges are needed to sort an array of N elements. Each exchange occurs after exit from the inner for loop. An exchange is not performed, however, if the largest element is already at position i of subarray 1..i (that is, IndexOfMax = i).

For an array of N elements, there are N-1 comparisons of Score fields during the first execution of the inner loop, N-2 comparisons during the second execution, and so on. The number of Score field comparisons, therefore, is represented by the series

$$1 + 2 + 3 + \ldots + N{-}2 + N{-}1$$

The value of this series is expressed in the closed form

$$\frac{N \times (N-1)}{2}$$

Therefore, to sort an array of 10 elements requires 10 x 9/2, or 45, Score field comparisons and, at most, 9 exchanges.

Finally, there is an additional comparison after each exit from the inner for loop (i is compared to IndexOfMax). This comparison takes less time to perform because no array reference is required. We could eliminate these N-1 comparisons and always perform the exchange (even when the largest element was already at position i). However, this would be less efficient generally because it would take more time to perform an exchange of records than to do the comparisons. ∎

Coding Function FindMedian

Procedure ComputeStats (see Fig. 12.27) uses function FindMedian to compute the median score on an exam. It is relatively easy to determine the median score once the student records are in order by score. If there are an odd number of records, the median score is found in the middle element of array Test.Class where the subscript expression (NumStu div 2) + 1 selects the middle element. If there are an even number of records, the median score is the average of the two middle scores. As an example, for a sorted array with four scores, the median is the average of the second and third scores.

Function FindMedian is shown in Fig. 12.34. Notice that record Test is declared as a value parameter so that only the local copy of array Test.Class will be sorted, not the actual array.

Figure 12.34 Function FindMedian

```
function FindMedian (Test : Exam) : Integer;
{
  Returns the median score found in array Test.Class.
  Pre : Student scores are stored in Test.Class.
  Post: Returns the middle score if there are an odd number
        of scores; otherwise, returns the average of the
        middle two scores.
  Uses: SelectSort
}
  var
    Middle : Integer;         {index to middle element}

begin {FindMedian}
  SelectSort (Test);
  with Test do
    begin
      Middle := (NumStu div 2) + 1;
      if Odd(NumStu) then
        FindMedian := Class[Middle].Score
      else
        FindMedian := (Class[Middle - 1].Score +
                       Class[Middle].Score) div 2
    end {with}
end; {FindMedian}
```

Exercises for Section 12.7

Self-Check

1. Trace the execution of the selection sort on the following list of scores. Show the array after each exchange occurs. How many exchanges are required?

10 55 34 56 76 5

2. How could you get the scores in descending order (largest score first)? What changes would be needed to sort the array field Class by student name instead of by score?
3. Because we are ordering the array by Score field, we propose changing procedure Switch to exchange only the Score fields. Describe the effect of this proposal.
4. Trace function FindMedian for the list of scores in exercise 1.
5. When you are looking for the largest element in subarray 1..i-1, why it is more efficient to start the search with the last element (that is, IndexOfMax := i-1) rather than the first element?

Programming

1. Another method of performing the selection sort is to place the smallest element in position 1, the next smallest in position 2, and so on. Write this version.

 ## 12.8 Common Programming Errors

When you use multidimensional arrays, make sure the subscript for each dimension is consistent with its declared type. If any subscript value is out of range, a run-time error will be detected.

   If you use nested for loops to process the array elements, make sure that loop-control variables used as array subscripts are in the correct order. The order of the loop-control variables determines the sequence in which the array elements are processed.

   When an array of records is processed, the array name and the subscript must be included as part of the field selector (for example, X[i].Key references field Key of the ith record). If you use a for statement to process all array elements in sequence, then you must nest any with statement that references the array records inside the for statement, as shown next.

```
for i := 1 to N do
  with X[i] do
    . . .
```

As the loop-control variable i changes, the next array record is processed by the with statement. If the nesting order is reversed, as in

```
with X[i] do
  for i := 1 to N do
    . . .
```

then the same array record is processed N times. The record that is processed is determined by the value of i when the with statement is first reached. Changing the value of i inside the with statement has no effect.

Chapter Review

In this chapter, arrays of arrays, or multidimensional arrays, were used to represent tables of information and game boards. We used nested loops to manipulate the elements of a multidimensional array in a systematic way. The correspondence between the loop-control variables and the array subscripts determines the order in which the array elements are processed.

You also saw how to manipulate arrays of records. Arrays of records can be used to represent many real-world data collections. We also introduced a technique for searching and a technique for sorting arrays of records.

New Pascal Constructs

The Pascal constructs introduced in this chapter are described in Table 12.2.

Table 12.2 Summary of New Pascal Constructs

Construct	Effect
Declaring Multidimensional Arrays ```type Day = (Sunday,Monday,Tuesday,Wednesday, Thursday,Friday,Saturday); Matrix = array [1..52, Day] of Real; var Sales : Matrix;```	Matrix describes a two-dimensional array with 7 rows (days of the week) and 52 columns. Sales is an array of this type and can store 364 real numbers.
Array References `Write (Sales[3, Monday])`	Displays the element of Sales for Monday of week 3.
```for Week := 1 to 52 do for Today := Sunday to Saturday do Sales[Week, Today] := 0.0```	Initializes each element of Sales to zero.
`ReadLn (Sales[1, Sunday])`	Reads the value for the first Sunday into Sales.
Declaring Arrays of Records ```type AElement = record Data : Real; Key : Integer end; {AElement} DataArray= array [1..10] of AElement;```	DataArray is an array type with ten elements of type AElement (a record). Each element has fields named Data and Key.
```var MyData : DataArray```	MyData is a variable of type DataArray.

Table 12.2 *continued*

493

Chapter Review

Construct	Effect

Referencing an Array of Records
```
MyData[1].Data := 3.14159;
MyData[10].Key := 9999;
```

The real value 3.14159 is stored in the first Data field of array MyData; the value 9999 is stored in the last Key field.

✓ *Quick-Check Exercises*

1. In Pascal, how many subscripts can an array have?
2. What is the difference between row-major and column-major order? Which does Pascal use?
3. What does row-major order mean when an array has more than two subscripts?
4. What control structure is used to process all the elements in a multidimensional array?
5. Write a program segment to display the sum of the values (type Real) in each column of a two-dimensional array, Table, with data type array [1..5, 1..3] of Real. How many column sums will be displayed? How many elements are included in each sum?
6. Write the type declaration for an array that stores the batting averages by position (Catcher, Pitcher, FirstBase, etc.) for each of ten baseball teams in two leagues (American and National).
7. Write the type declaration for a data structure that stores a player's name, salary, position, batting average, fielding percentage, number of hits, runs, runs batted in, and errors.
8. Write the type declaration for a data structure that stores the information in exercise 7 for a team of twenty-five players.
9. If the array Team has the structure described in exercise 8, write a program segment that displays the first two categories of information for the first five players.

Answers to Quick-Check Exercises
1. There is no specific limit; however, the size of the array is limited by the memory space available, and multidimensional arrays can require considerable memory.
2. In row-major order, the first row of the array is placed at the beginning of the memory area allocated to the array. It is followed by the second row, and so on. In column-major order, the first column is placed at the beginning of the array memory area. Pascal uses row-major order.
3. If an array Table has N subscripts, the array elements are placed in memory in the order Table[1,1,...,1,1], Table[1,1,...,1,2], Table[1,1,...,1,3], and so on. Then the next-to-last subscript is changed and the elements Table[1,1,...,2,1], Table[1,1,...,2,2], Table[1,1,...,2,3] ... are placed. The first subscript will be the last one that changes.
4. Nested for loops
5.
```
   for Column := 1 to 3 do
     begin
       ColumnSum := 0.0;
```

```
      for Row := 1 to 5 do
        ColumnSum := ColumnSum + Table[Row,Column];
      WriteLn ('Sum for column ', Column :1, ' is ', ColumnSum)
    end {for Column}
```

Three column sums; five elements added per column

6. ```
   type
       Position = (Pitcher, Catcher, FirstBase, SecondBase, ThirdBase,
                   ShortStop, LeftField, CenterField, RightField);
       League = (American, National);
       BAArray = array [League, 1..10, Position] of Real;
   ```

7. ```
   type
       StringType = packed array [1..20] of Char;
       Player = record
                    Name : StringType;
                    Salary : Real;
                    Place : Position;
                    BatAve, FieldPct : Real;
                    Hits, Runs, RBIs, Errors : Integer
                end; {Player}
   ```

8. ```
   type
       StringType = ...
       Player = ...
       TeamArray = array [1..25] of Player;
   ```

9. ```
   for i := 1 to 5 do
       WriteLn (Team[i].Name, Team[i].Salary)
   ```

Review Questions

1. Define row-major order.
2. Declare an array that can be used to store each title of the Top40 hits for each week of the year given that the `TitleLength` will be twenty characters.
3. Write the declaration of the array `YearlyHours` to store the hours each of five employees works each day of the week, each week of the year.
4. Write the declarations for the array `CPUArray` that will hold twenty records of type `CPU`. The record `CPU` has the following fields: `IDNumber` (eleven characters in length), `Make` (five characters), `Location` (fifteen characters), and `Ports` (integer).
5. Use the following declarations for this exercise and exercises 6 through 9.

   ```
   const
      TotalEmployees = 20;

   type
      Employee = record
                    ID: Integer;
                    Rate,
                    Hours : Real
                 end; {Employee}
      EmpArray = array [1..TotalEmployees] of Employee;

   var
      Employees : EmpArray;
   ```

   Write the function `TotalGross` that will return the total gross pay given the data stored in array `Employees`.

6. Explain what is wrong with the following fragment and fix it.

   ```
   i := 1;
   with Employees[i] do
   ```

```
   while i <= TotalEmployees do
      begin
         WriteLn (Hours :12:2);
         i := i + 1
      end {while}
```

7. Explain what is wrong with the following fragment and fix it.

```
i := 1;
while (Employees[i].ID <> 999) and (i <= TotalEmployees) do
   i := i + 1
```

8. Write a fragment that displays the ID number of each employee who works between ten and twenty hours per week.
9. Write a fragment that displays the ID number of the employee who works the most hours.
10. How many exchanges are required to sort the following list of integers using selection sort? How many comparisons are performed?

   20 30 40 25 60 80

11. Procedure SelectSort in Figure 12.33 placed the elements of an array in order by Score field. Change the condition in the procedure so that records with the same Score value are ordered by name (smaller name first). The field Score is called the *primary key*, and the field Name is called the *secondary key*.

Programming Projects

1. Write a program that generates the Morse code for a sentence that ends with a period and contains no characters besides letters and blanks. First, read the Morse code for each letter of the alphabet and save it in an array of strings. Next, read each word and display its Morse equivalent on a separate line. The Morse code is as follows:
   A .-, B -..., C -.-., D -.., E ., F ..-., G --., H ...., I .., J .---, K -.-, L .-.., M --, N -., O ---, P .--., Q --.-, R .-., S ..., T -, U ..-, V ...-, W .--, X -..-, Y -.--, Z --..
2. Write a set of procedures to manipulate a pair of matrices. Provide procedures for addition, subtraction, and multiplication. Each procedure should validate its input parameters (that is, check all matrix dimensions) before performing the required data manipulation.
3. The results from the mayor's race have been reported by each precinct as follows:

Precinct	Candidate A	Candidate B	Candidate C	Candidate D
1	192	48	206	37
2	147	90	312	21
3	186	12	121	38
4	114	21	408	39
5	267	13	382	29

Write a program to do the following:
a. Print out the table with appropriate headings for the rows and columns.
b. Compute and print the total number of votes received by each candidate and the percent of the total votes cast.
c. If any one candidate received over 50 percent of the votes, the program should print a message declaring that candidate the winner.

    d. If no candidate received 50 percent of the votes, the program should print a message declaring a run-off between the two candidates who received the highest number of votes; the two candidates should be identified by their letter names.

    e. Run the program once with the preceding data and once with candidate C receiving only 108 votes in precinct 4.

4. Write a program that reads the five cards representing a poker hand into an array of records (first record field is suit, second record field is rank). Evaluate the poker hand by using procedures to determine if the hand is a flush (all one suit), a straight (five consecutive cards), a straight flush (five consecutive cards of one suit), four of a kind, a full house (three of one kind, two of another), three of a kind, two pairs, or one pair.

5. An array of records can contain descriptions of people, including name, height, weight, sex, color of hair, color of eyes, and religion. Write a program that reads and stores data into this array, sorts the array in alphabetical order by name, and prints its contents.

6. Write a program that searches an array of records of type `Employee` (see Section 11.1) to find and print the data stored for all employees who match a target description. The array of employee data should be read in first and then the target data. A blank target name indicates that the name field should be ignored during the matching process. Add a third category (`Unknown`) for the sex field. Enter a range of values for each numeric target field. A lower bound of -1 indicates that a particular numeric field should be ignored.

7. The inventory for a warehouse is stored on an inventory file and shipments into and from the warehouse (transactions) are to be processed. Each file line will contain an ID number (three digits), name (maximum of ten characters), initial quantity on hand, and cost per item. Write a procedure that will read and store the file data into an appropriate array of records. At that point, write the initial contents of the warehouse.

    Now process the transactions, which consist of the ID number for the item and the quantity of items shipped or received (if negative, the items were shipped; if positive, the items were received). Read each transaction from the keyboard.

    After transaction is processed, display a message indicating the item name, the quantity shipped or received, and the new quantity on hand. The program should check to make sure that more items are not shipped than are on hand and that the ID number requested for a transaction matches those in the warehouse.

    After all transactions are processed, print a list of all items in the warehouse. Show how many of each remain and the approximate total value of each item in the inventory.

    A sample inventory file might be

```
376    BOLTS      350    0.05
142    NUTS       425    0.03
261    HAMMERS    100    10.45
```

Sets and Strings

13

I n this chapter, we complete the study of the set data type. We first looked at sets in Chapter 9; since then, we have used sets and the set membership operator in to simplify conditions. In this chapter, you will learn how to perform the operations of set union, set intersection, and set difference in Pascal and how to test for subsets, supersets, and set equality. These operations make it easier to use sets in programming.

The string data type is the second topic covered in this chapter. Strings are used in programs that process textual data (for example, word processors, text editors, and business data-processing applications). The string data type is in many programming languages, but it is missing in standard Pascal. In standard Pascal, we store fixed-length strings in packed arrays of characters, and we only can display and compare strings.

A string data type, together with several string operators, is an extension found in many Pascal compilers. We will design and implement a string data type whose operators are based on those commonly found in Pascal compilers. If your version of Pascal supports the string data type, you may want to skip section 13.5, which implements the string operators.

 ## 13.1   Set Data Type

Chapter 7 discussed set values in conditional statements. Until now, we have used the set membership operator in only with set values. This section examines the other set operators and shows you how to declare and manipulate set variables.

■ Example 13.1

The following statements define a set type Digit and two set variables, Odds and Evens. Each set variable of type Digit can contain between zero and ten elements chosen from the integers in the subrange 0..9. The set variables Odds and Evens represent the set of odd digits and even digits in the range 0 through 9. ■

```
type
   Digit = set of 0..9;

var
   Odds, Evens : Digit;

begin
   Odds := [1, 3, 5, 7, 9];
   Evens := [0, 2, 4, 6, 8]
```

The set type declaration is described in the following display.

Set Type Declaration

Form: type
                set type = set of *base type*;

Example: `type`
`        Uppercase = set of 'A'..'Z';`
Interpretation: The identifier *set type* is defined over the values specified in *base type*. A variable declared to be of type *set type* is a set whose elements are chosen from the values in *base type*. The *base type* must be an ordinal type.
Notes: Most implementations impose a limit on the number of values in the *base type* of a set. In many implementations, this limit is the same as the number of values in the data type `Char` (64, 128, or 256). This allows you to declare `set of Char` as a set type. Given this limitation, you may not use the data type `Integer` as a *base type*; however, a suitable subrange of type `Integer` is allowed.

Set Assignment, Empty Set, and Universal Set

You can modify an existing set by using the set operators discussed in the next section. Before you can manipulate a set, however, you must define its initial elements with a set assignment statement, as shown in the next example.

■ Example 13.2

The following statements specify three set variables defined over the base type `Cars`.

```
type
   Cars = (Dodge, Ford, Lincoln, Cadillac, Fiesta, Pontiac,
           Corvette, Buick, Chevrolet, Mercury, Mustang);
   CarSet = set of Cars;

var
   Avis, Hertz, Merger : CarSet;

begin
   Avis := [Dodge, Lincoln, Fiesta];
   Hertz := [Dodge..Cadillac, Mercury];
```

Each assignment statement consists of a set variable on the left and a set value on the right. A pair of brackets and a list of values from the base type of the set being defined indicate a set value. As shown in the assignment statement for `Hertz`, a list of consecutive values can be denoted as a subrange (see Section 9.2). The set `Avis` consists of the three elements listed; the set `Hertz` consists of five elements (what are they?).

It is also possible to have a set variable on the right of the assignment statement, provided both set variables have compatible base types. The value of the set variable on the right would be assigned to the set variable on the left.

```
Merger := Hertz;
```

Often, we want to denote that a set is empty or has no elements. An *empty set* is indicated by an empty pair of brackets ([ ]).

```
Merger := []
```

A set variable must always be initialized before it can be used with any of the set operators. A set variable often is initialized to the empty set or to the *universal set*, which is the set that consists of all values of the base type. For instance, the universal set for a set of type `CarSet` would be denoted as `[Dodge..Mustang]`. ∎

The set-assignment statement is shown in the following display. As the display indicates, it is possible to write set expressions that involve set manipulation operators. These operators are described in the next section.

Set Assignment

Form: *set var* : = *set expression*

Example: `Uppercase := ['A'..'Z']` {set of uppercase letters}

Interpretation: The variable, *set var*, is defined as the set whose elements are determined by the value of *set expression*. The *set expression* may be a set value or another set variable. Alternatively, a *set expression* may specify the manipulation of two or more sets using the set operators. The base type of *set var* and *set expression* must be type compatible, and all the elements in *set expression* must be included in the base type of *set-var*.

Set Union, Intersection, and Difference

The set operators union, intersection, and difference require as operands two sets of the same type. The *union* of two sets (set operator +) is the set of elements that are contained in either set or both sets.

```
[1,3,4] + [1,2,4] is [1,2,3,4]
[1,3] + [2,4] is [1,2,3,4]
['A','C','F'] + ['B','C','D','F'] is ['A','B','C','D','F']
['A','C','F'] + ['A','C','D','F'] is ['A','C','D','F']
Avis + Hertz is [Dodge, Ford, Lincoln, Cadillac, Fiesta, Mercury];
```

The *intersection* of two sets (set operator *) is the set of all elements that are common to both sets.

```
[1,3,4] * [1,2,4] is [1,4]
[1,3] * [2,4] is []
['A','C','F'] * ['B','C','D','F'] is ['C','F']
['A','C','F'] * ['A','C','D','F'] is ['A','C','F']
Avis * Hertz is [Dodge, Lincoln]
```

The *difference* of set A and set B (set operator –) is the set of elements that are in set A but not in set B.

```
[1,3,4] – [1,2,4] is [3]
[1,3] – [2,4] is [1,3]
```

```
['A','C','F'] - ['B','C','D','F'] is ['A']
['A','C','F'] - ['A','C','D','F'] is []
['A','C','D','F'] - ['A','C','F'] is ['D']
Avis - Hertz is [Fiesta]
Hertz - Avis is [Ford, Cadillac, Mercury]
```

The set operator – is not *commutative*. This means that A – B and B – A can have different values. The set operators + and *, however, are commutative.

The operators +, *, and – are treated as set operators when their operands are sets. The compiler determines which operation is intended from its context (this is called *operator overloading*). You can use these operators to combine two sets to form a third set. If more than one set operator appears in an expression, the normal precedence rules for the operators +, *, and – apply (see Table 7.9). When in doubt, use parentheses to specify the intended order of evaluation.

Often, we need to insert a new element into an existing set. You perform the insertion by forming the union of the existing set and the *unit set*, which contains only the new element. The set [2], which follows, is a unit set.

```
[1,3,4,5] + [2] is [1,2,3,4,5]
```

It makes no difference how many times we insert an element into a set:

```
[1,2,3,4,5] + [2] is [1,2,3,4,5]
```

Avoid the common error of omitting the brackets around a unit set. For example, the expressions

```
[1,3,4,5] + 2
Avis + Cadillac
```

are invalid because one operand is a set and the other is a constant. The correct forms of these expressions follow.

```
[1,3,4,5] + [2]
Avis + [Cadillac]
```

Likewise, the expression

```
[Avis] + [Cadillac]
```

is invalid; the brackets around Avis are not needed because Avis is a set.

■ Example 13.3

Procedure BuildSets in Fig. 13.1 returns a set of odd numbers (Odds) and a set of even numbers (Evens) in the range 0 to MaxNum. Procedure BuildSets uses the set operators + (union) and – (difference). Given the declarations

```
const
   MaxNum = 60;

type
   IntSet = set of 0..MaxNum;

var
   OneSet, TwoSet : IntSet;
```

the procedure call statement

stores the set [1, 3, 5, ... , 57, 59] in OneSet and the set [0, 2, 4, 6, ... , 58, 60] in TwoSet. ∎

Figure 13.1 Procedure BuildSets

```
procedure BuildSets (var Odds, Evens {output} : IntSet);
{
  Builds a set of odd integers (Odds) and a set of even
  integers (Evens) in the range 0 to MaxNum.
  Pre : None
  Post: Odds contains the odd integers <= MaxNum and
        Evens contains the even integers <= MaxNum
}
  var
    I : Integer;                  {loop-control variable}

begin  {BuildSets}
  Odds := [];                {initialize Odds to the empty set}

  {Build a set of odd integers.}
  I := 1;                  {initialize I to first odd integer}
  while I <= MaxNum do
    {invariant:
       all prior values of I are <= MaxNum and
       Odds contains each prior value of I that is an odd number
    }
    begin
      Odds := Odds + [I];     {union next odd integer to Odds}
      I := I + 2              {get next odd integer}
    end; {while}

  {assertion:
     I is greater than MaxNum and Odds contains all
     odd numbers <= MaxNum
  }
  {Define set Evens.}
  Evens := [0..MaxNum] - Odds
end;  {BuildSets}
```

Set Relational Operators

You can also compare sets through the use of the relational operators $=$, $<>$, $<=$, and $>=$. Both operands of a set relational operator must have the same base type. The operators $=$ and $<>$ test whether two sets contain the same elements.

```
[1,3] = [1,3] is True    | [1,3] <> [1,3] is False
[1,3] = [2,4] is False   | [1,3] <> [2,4] is True
[1,3] = [3,1] is True    | [1,3] <> [3,1] is False
[]    = [1] is False     | []    <> [1] is True
```

As indicated by the next-to-last line, the order in which the elements of a set are listed is not important ([1,3] and [3,1] denote the same set). However, we normally list the elements of a set in increasing ordinal sequence.

- Set A is a *subset* of set B (A <= B) if every element of A is also an element of B.

```
[1,3]      <=[1,2,3,4] is True
[1,3]      <=[1,3]     is True
[1,2,3,4] <=[1,3]      is False
[1,3]      <=[]        is False
[]         <=[1,3]     is True
```

As indicated in the last line, the empty set, [ ], is a subset of every set.

- Set A is a *superset* of set B (A >= B) if every element of B is also an element of A.

```
[1,3]      >= [1,2,3,4] is False
[1,3]      >= [1,3]      is True
[1,2,3,4] >= [1,3]      is True
[1,3]      >= []         is True
[]         >= [1,3]      is False
```

The set relations A >= B and B <= A are equivalent for any two sets A and B.

The set operators are summarized in Table 13.1.

Table 13.1 Set Operators

Operator	Meaning	Example
+	Set union	['A'] + ['B'] is ['A', 'B']
–	Set difference	['A', 'B'] – ['A'] is ['B']
*	Set intersection	['A', 'B'] * ['A'] is ['A']
=	Set equality	['A', 'B'] = ['B', 'A'] is True
<>	Set inequality	['A', 'B'] <> ['A'] is True
<=	Subset	['A', 'B'] <= ['A'] is False
>=	Superset	['A', 'B'] >= ['B'] is True

Reading and Writing Sets

Like most other data structures, a set cannot be a parameter of the standard Read or Write procedures. Data items to be stored in a set must be read individually and inserted in an initially empty set using the set union operator.

■ Example 13.4

Procedure ReadSet in Fig. 13.2 reads a sequence of uppercase letters terminated by * and inserts them in the set represented by parameters Letters (set type LetterSet). Given the declarations

```
type
   LetterSet = set of 'A'..'Z';
```

```
var
   MyLetters : LetterSet;
```

you could use the procedure call statement

```
ReadSet (MyLetters)
```

to enter data in the set MyLetters.   ■

Figure 13.2   Procedure ReadSet

```
procedure ReadSet (var Letters {output} : LetterSet);
{
  Reads a set of uppercase letters terminated by *
  and stores them in Letters.
  Pre : None
  Post: Returns through Letters all the uppercase letters read
        before the character *.
}
  const
    Sentinel = '*';                          {sentinel character}

  var
    NextChar : Char;                         {next input character}

begin  {ReadSet}
  Letters := [];                       {initialize Letters}
  Write ('Enter a set of uppercase letters');
  WriteLn (' ending with the symbol ', Sentinel);
  Read (NextChar);                      {read first data item}
  while NextChar <> Sentinel do
    {invariant:
       No prior value of NextChar is the sentinel and
       Letters contains each uppercase letter read so far
    }
    begin
      if NextChar in ['A'..'Z'] then
        Letters := Letters + [NextChar];  {insert next letter}
      Read (NextChar)                      {read next character}
    end  {while}

  {assertion: last character read was the sentinel}
end;  {ReadSet}
```

To print a set, you need to test every value in the base type to see whether it is a set element. Only values that are set elements should be printed.

■ Example 13.5

Procedure PrintSet in Fig. 13.3 prints the uppercase letters in the set represented by its parameter Letters.   ■

Figure 13.3   Procedure PrintSet

```
procedure PrintSet (Letters {input} : LetterSet);
{
  Prints the uppercase letters in set Letters.
  Pre : Letters is defined.
```

```
    Post: Each uppercase letter in Letters is displayed.
}
    var
        NextLetter : 'A'..'Z';           {loop-control variable}

begin {PrintSet}
    for NextLetter := 'A' to 'Z' do
        if NextLetter in Letters then
            Write (NextLetter)            {print a set member}
end;  {PrintSet}
```

Exercises for Section 13.1

Self-Check

1. Given that A is the set [1,3,5,7], B is the set [2,4,6], and C is the set [1,2,3], evaluate the following set expressions.

    a. A + (B − C)   g. C + (A − C)
    b. A + (B * C)   h. C − (A − B)
    c. A + B + C   i. (C − A) − B
    d. (C − A) <= B   j. (B + C) = (A + C)
    e. [] <= A * B * C   k. A − C − [5,7] = []
    f. A + B <> [1..7]   l. A + B >= [1..7]

Programming

1. Modify PrintSet to print a set of type Digit.

 ## 13.2   Sets in Computer Graphics

In picture processing, we want to write programs that can find and analyze patterns of characters that appear in a picture that is displayed on a screen. Each screen position is called a *pixel*, or picture element. A pixel has a grey level associated with it that determines whether it is considered dark or light.

One approach to representing the screen is to store it as a two-dimensional array of pixel values; another approach is to store it as an array of sets. In the latter representation, each array element is the set of darkened pixels for a line, and there is one set for each line of the screen.

Figure 13.4 shows a section (called a *window*) of a monitor screen. There is a diagonal line on the left and a vertical bar on the right.

The type declarations for a picture displayed on a screen window consisting of ten rows and twenty columns follow.

```
    const
        ScreenHeight = 10;        {# of rows}
        ScreenWidth = 20;         {# of columns}

    type
        PixelValue = (Dark, Light);
        Line = set of 1..ScreenWidth;
        Screen = array [1..ScreenHeight] of Line;
```

Figure 13.4   Monitor Screen with Window

```
var
   Picture : Screen;
```

For the picture in Fig. 13.4, Picture[1] represents the set of darkened elements in the first line and is the set [1, 2, 18, 19, 20]. Picture[2] is the set [2, 3, 18, 19, 29], and Picture[3] is the set [3, 4, 18, 19, 20]. The intersection of these three sets is [18, 19, 20]. This implies that there is a vertical bar on the right. The union of these three sets is [1, 2, 3, 4, 18, 19, 20]. This implies that there is a diagonal bar on the left as well as a vertical bar on the right.

■ Example 13.6

Procedure SetPicture (Fig. 13.5) is called by a picture-processing program to define array Picture. For each pixel, the procedure reads an integer value that represents the grey level (darkness) of that pixel. If the grey level value is greater than Threshold (a parameter), that pixel is inserted in the appropriate set of darkened pixels. As an example, if the value passed to Threshold is 6, the dialogue that follows defines Picture[1] as [1, 2, 18, 19, 20].   ■

```
Enter the grey level (0 - 9) for row 1
Enter 20 values starting with column 1.
7 8 6 5 4 3 3 4 3 4 5 3 4 4 5 5 6 7 8 9
```

Figure 13.5   Procedure SetPicture

```
procedure SetPicture (Threshold {input} : Integer;
                      var Picture {output} : Screen);
{
  Defines the array Picture representing a computer image by
  reading in the grey level value for each pixel.
  Pre : Threshold is defined.
  Post: Picture[i] is the set of columns in row i with
        grey level value greater than Threshold
        (1 <= i <= ScreenHeight).
}
  var
    Row : 1..ScreenHeight;
    Column : 1..ScreenWidth;
    GreyLevel : 0..9;
```

```
begin {SetPicture}
  {Define array Picture.}
  for Row := 1 to ScreenHeight do
    begin
      WriteLn ('Enter the grey level (0 - 9) for row ', Row :1);
      Write ('Enter ', ScreenWidth :1);
      WriteLn (' values starting with column 1.');
      Picture[Row] := [];              {Initialize row set}
      for Column := 1 to ScreenWidth do
        begin
          Read (GreyLevel);
          if GreyLevel > Threshold then
              Picture[Row] := Picture[Row] + [Column]
        end; {for Column}
      ReadLn;
      WriteLn
    end {for Row}
end; {SetPicture}
```

Exercises for Section 13.2

Self-Check

1. What is the purpose of the ReadLn and WriteLn statements in procedure SetPicture?
2. Assuming MyPic is type Screen, what is the value of MyPic[1] for the procedure call statement

   ```
   SetPicture (5, MyPic)
   ```

   when the first data line is: 3 4 5 6 7 8 9 8 7 6 5 4 9 8 7 3 4 9 7 5?

Programming

1. Write procedure ShowPicture that displays the picture on a screen by writing the character @ in each pixel that is considered dark.

 ## 13.3 Variable-Length Strings

Many computer applications are concerned with the manipulation of character strings or textual data rather than numerical data. For example, a word processor was used in writing this text; computerized typesetters are used extensively in the publishing of books and newspapers; "personalized" junk mail is computer generated; and computers are used to analyze great works of literature. Basically, a Pascal program is a sequence of words and symbols that are interpreted by a compiler.

If you have ever used a word processor, you are familiar with the kinds of operations we might want to perform on string data. For example, we frequently want to insert one or more characters into an existing string, delete a portion of a string (called a *substring*), overwrite or replace one substring of a string with another, search for a target substring, or join two strings together to form a longer string.

Fixed-Length and Variable-Length Strings

An important characteristic of a string is its length. Standard Pascal allows us to store fixed-length strings in packed arrays of characters. If S is a variable whose type is packed array [1..n] of Char, there must always be exactly n characters stored in S. If we want to store a shorter string in S, we must pad it with blanks; those extra blank characters are treated as part of the string. This means that the blank characters will appear when we display a fixed-length string or when we join one fixed-length string to another.

To use strings effectively, the length of a string should be *variable* and should depend on its contents. This length must be between zero and some predefined maximum (the string *capacity*). A variable-length string type (String) is described next.

Specification for Abstract Data Type String

Structure: A string is a sequence of characters. The length of a string is variable and is based on its contents. This length must be between zero and some predefined maximum (string capacity). The assignment operator can be used with string operands.

Operators: Length (S): The function Length returns the length of its argument string.

MakeString (S1, var S2): Procedure MakeString initializes string S2 to string value S1, where S1 is a fixed-length string or a packed-character array whose length is the same as the capacity of S2. Trailing blanks at the end of string S1 are not considered part of the string stored in S2.

ReadLnStrVar (var F, var S): Procedure ReadLnStrVar reads characters from text file F into string S beginning with the character selected by the file position pointer for file F. If F is Input, the data is taken from the keyboard. Data entry stops when either an <eoln> is reached or the number of characters read equals the string capacity. In any event, the file-position pointer is advanced past the <eoln>. The length of S is defined as the number of characters read.

WriteString (var F, S): Procedure WriteString copies the characters stored in string S to file F. If F is Output, procedure WriteString displays string S on the screen.

GetChar (S, Index): Function GetChar retrieves the character at position Index in string S without changing string S.

PutChar (var S, Index, Ch): Procedure PutChar places character Ch into string S at position Index.

Copy (S1, Index, Size, var S2): Procedure Copy returns in string S2 the substring of string S1 that consists of Size characters and begins at position Index. If Index > Length(S1), the null string is stored in S2.

Concat (S1, S2, var S3): Procedure Concat returns in S3 the string formed by joining string S2 to the end of string S1. If the new string is too long, the extra characters at the end of string S2 are not stored.

Pos (S1, S2): If string S1 is a substring of string S2, function Pos returns the location in S2 of the first occurrence of string S1. The value returned is the position in S2 of the first character of S1. If string S1 is not found, function Pos returns zero. If string S1 is the null string, function Pos returns 1.

Delete (var S, Index, Size): Procedure Delete removes size characters from string S beginning at position Index. If Size is too big, all characters from Index to the end of string S are removed.

Insert (S1, var S2, Index): Procedure Insert inserts string S1 into string S2; the substring that formerly began at Index follows the string inserted. If the new string is too big, the extra characters at the right end are removed. If Index > Length(S2) is True before the insertion, string S1 is joined to the end of old string S2.

The specifications for procedures Copy and Pos refer to the null string. The *null string* is a string of length zero, that is, a string that contains no characters.

Internal Representation of Data Type String

From the preceding specification, we see that a variable-length string has two components: a sequence of characters (its contents) and the length of that sequence. Although it is not really necessary to settle on an internal representation at this time, it may help your understanding if we refer to a particular representation. The record shown in Fig. 13.6 is an obvious choice for representing and storing a string in memory. It consists of a packed array of characters (field Contents) and an Integer (field Len). The constant Capacity determines the number of characters that can be stored in field Contents.

Figure 13.6 Declarations for Data Type String

```
const
  Capacity = 20;        {predefined maximum length}

type
  StringType = packed array [1..Capacity] of Char;
  String = record
             Contents : StringType;
             Len : Integer
           end; {String}
```

The record SampleStr (type String) contains the string value 'xyz'. Because the string capacity is twenty characters, array SampleStr.Contents has seventeen elements that are undefined (indicated by ?).

SampleStr.Contents │ x │ y │ z │ ?{ ... }? │
SampleStr.Len   │   3   │

An operator for data type `String` processes the array field `Contents`, the integer field `Len`, or both. The operators are illustrated next and implemented in Section 13.5.

ReadLnStrVar, MakeString, Length, and WriteString

`ReadLnStrVar` and `MakeString` define a string's contents. `ReadLnStrVar` accomplishes this by reading data into a string. `ReadLnStrVar` reads and stores characters until it reaches an `<eoln>` or fills the string to its capacity. If you enter the data line

```
xyz<eoln>
```

when

```
ReadLnStrVar (Input, SampleStr)
```

executes, `SampleStr` will be defined as shown earlier.

`MakeString` assigns a fixed-length string to a variable-length string. In figuring the length of the variable-length string, any trailing blanks at the end of the fixed-length string are not counted. If `S1` is type `StringType`, the statements

```
S1 := 'xyz            ';
MakeString (S1, SampleStr);
```

also define `SampleStr` as shown earlier.

The function `Length` determines the current length of a string, which is variable and depends on the data stored in it (for example, `Length(SampleStr)` is 3).

Procedure `WriteString` displays a string. The number of characters displayed is determined by the string's length.

The statements

```
WriteString (Output, SampleStr);
WriteLn ('*')
```

display the output line

```
xyz*
```

■ Example 13.7

Assume that `Name` is a variable length string whose capacity is eleven characters. The statement

```
ReadLnStrVar (Input, Name);
```

reads up to eleven data characters from the keyboard and stores them in string `Name`. If the characters `Jane<eoln>` are typed at the keyboard, the string `'Jane '` is stored in `Name` and the length of `Name` is 5 (trailing blanks count when they are read by `ReadLnStrVar`). ■

For the string Name described above, the statements

```
MakeString ('abcde      ', Name);
Write ('Length of ');
WriteString (Output, Name);
Write (' is ', Length(Name) :1)
```

store 'abcde' in Name (length is 5) and display the output line

```
Length of abcde is 5
```

The statement

```
MakeString ('Leonardo   ', Name)
```

stores 'Leonardo' in Name (length is 8). (Notice that trailing blanks do not count when they are stored by MakeString.)   ■

GetChar and PutChar

Function GetChar and procedure PutChar are used to retrieve and insert individual characters of a string. Each call must specify the index in the string of the character being processed.

■ **Example 13.9**

The following statements use GetChar and PutChar to replace one character in a string with another.

```
Ch := GetChar(Expression, 1);
if Ch = '+' then
   PutChar (Expression, 1, '-')
```

The if statement tests whether the string Expression begins with a plus sign; if so, the plus sign in position one is replaced by a minus sign. If the contents of Expression are '+4*Y', the value of Ch is '+' and the new contents of Expression are '-4*Y'; the length of Expression is unchanged (value is 4).   ■

Substrings and Procedure Copy

It is often necessary to manipulate segments, or *substrings*, of a larger character string. For example, we might want to examine the three components (month, day, year) of the string 'Jun 25, 1986'. Procedure Copy can be used to do this, as shown next.

■ **Example 13.10**

Assume that a date string (stored in Date) always has the form 'MMM DD, YYYY', where the characters represented by MMM are the month name, DD the day of the month, and YYYY the year. Assuming Date, MonthStr, Day, and Year are variable-length strings, the procedure call statement

```
Copy (Date, 1, 3, MonthStr)
```

returns (in MonthStr) the substring of Name starting at position 1 and consisting of the first three characters. The procedure call statement

```
Copy (Date, 5, 2, Day)
```

returns (in Day) the two characters that represent the day of the month (positions five and six). Finally, the procedure call statement

```
Copy (Date, 9, 4, Year)
```

returns the four characters that represent the year (positions 9 through 12). If the contents of Date are 'Jun 25, 1986', the contents of the variable length strings MonthStr, Day, and Year become 'Jun', '25', and '1986', respectively. ∎

■ Example 13.11

Procedure PrintWords in Fig. 13.7 displays each word found in its parameter Sentence on a separate line. It assumes that there is always a single blank character between words.

The variable First always points to the start of the current word and is initialized to 1. During each execution of the for loop, the Boolean expression

```
GetChar(Sentence, Next) = WordSeparator
```

tests whether the next character is the symbol ' '. If so, the substring occupying positions First through Next−1 in Sentence is copied to Word and displayed on the next line by the statements

```
Copy (Sentence, First, Next–First, Word);   {get word}
WriteString (Output, Word);
WriteLn;
```

The values of First and Next are shown below just before the fourth word of a string stored in Sentence is displayed. The value of Next−First is 5, so the substring short is displayed.

After each word is printed, First is reset to Next + 1, the position of the first character of the next word. After loop exit, the statement

```
Copy (Sentence, First, Length(Sentence)–First+1, Word);
```

stores the last word of Sentence in Word. For the sentence above, the value of First is 17 and the value of the third parameter is 7 ($23 - 17 + 1$), so the last word displayed is example. ∎

Figure 13.7 Procedure PrintWords

513

13.3 Variable-Length
Strings

```
procedure PrintWords (Sentence {input} : String);
{
  Displays each word of a sentence on a separate line.
  Pre : Variable length string Sentence is defined.
  Post: Each word in sentence is displayed on a separate line.
  Uses: WriteString, Copy, and GetChar
}
  const
    WordSeparator = ' ';

  var
    Word : String;          {each word}
    First,                  {first character in each word}
    Next    : Integer;      {position of next character}

begin {PrintWords}
  {Display each word of Sentence on a separate line.}
  First := 1;               {first word starts at position 1}
  for Next := 1 to Length(Sentence) do
    begin
      if GetChar(Sentence, Next) = WordSeparator then
        begin
          Copy (Sentence, First, Next-First, Word);    {get word}
          WriteString (Output, Word);
          WriteLn;
          First := Next + 1
        end {if}
    end; {for}

  {Display last word.}
  Copy (Sentence, First, Length(Sentence)-First+1, Word);
  WriteString (Output, Word);
  WriteLn
end; {PrintWords}
```

Concatenating Strings

The `Copy` procedure is used to reference a substring of a longer string. You
can use the `Concat` procedure to combine two or more strings to form a new
string.

■ Example 13.12

The following statements join together, or *concatenate*, their string arguments.
The string result is stored in `Name`. For the string contents (the symbol □ denotes
a blank)

the statement

```
    Concat (Title, Last, Name);
```

stores the string value 'Ms. Peep' in Name. The statements

```
Concat (Title, First, Name);
Concat (Name, Last, Name)
```

store the string 'Ms. Bo Peep' in Name.   ■

String Search

In processing string data, we often need to locate a particular substring. For example, we might want to know if the string 'and ' appears in a sentence, and if so, where? If Target is a string of length 4 with contents 'and ', the statement

```
PosAnd := Pos(Target, Sentence)
```

assigns to PosAnd the starting position of the first occurrence of 'and ' in string Sentence. If the string 'Birds and bees fly all day' is stored in Sentence, the value assigned to PosAnd is 7. If the string 'and' is not in Sentence, the Pos function returns zero.

■ Example 13.13

A compiler can determine the form of many statements by checking whether the statement begins with a reserved word. If leading blanks are removed from Statement and if Target is a string of length four with contents 'for ', the condition

```
Pos(Target, Statement) = 1
```

is true when Statement is a for statement.

Another task of the compiler is to extract the syntactic elements of each statement. A for statement may have the syntactic form

for *counter* := *initial* to *final* do *statement*

The first two statements that follow use the Pos function to locate the strings 'for ' (contents of Target1) and ':=' (contents of Target2). The if statement copies the substring between these symbols into the string Counter.

```
PosFor := Pos(Target1, Statement);
PosAssign := Pos(Target2, Statement);
if (PosFor > 0) and (PosAssign > PosFor) then
   Copy(Statement, PosFor + 4, PosAssign - PosFor - 4, Counter)
```

Because the string 'for ' has four characters, the starting position of the *counter* is at position PosFor + 4. The number of characters in the *counter* is determined by the expression PosAssign − PosFor − 4. If the string 'for ID := 1 to N do X := X + 1' is stored in Statement, then PosFor gets 1, PosAssign gets 8, and the contents of Counter is the string 'ID ' (length is 8 − 1 − 4, or 3).

```
PosFor  PosAssign  Counter
┌─────┐   ┌─────┐   ┌──────┐
│  1  │   │  8  │   │  ID□ │
└─────┘   └─────┘   └──────┘
```

Procedures Delete and Insert

Besides the string-manipulation functions described so far, there are procedures to insert and delete substrings. They are illustrated next.

■ Example 13.14

Assume that Sentence contains the string 'This is the example.' before the first procedure call. The procedure call statement

```
Delete (Sentence, 1, 5);
```

deletes the first five characters from string Sentence. The new contents of Sentence become 'is the example'.

If Target is the string of length four with contents 'the ', the procedure call statement

```
Delete (Sentence, Pos(Target, Sentence), 4);
```

deletes the first occurrence of the string 'the ' from Sentence. The new contents of Sentence becomes 'is example'. Finally, the statements

```
PosTarg := Pos(Target, Sentence);
if PosTarg > 0 then
   Delete (Sentence, PosTarg, Length(Target))
```

delete the first occurrence of string Target from Sentence, provided Target is found. If Target is the string 'ex', the new contents of Sentence become 'is ample'.   ■

■ Example 13.15

Assume that the contents of Sentence is the string 'is the stuff?' and the contents of NewString is 'Where '. The procedure call statement

```
Insert (NewString, Sentence, 1)
```

inserts the string 'Where ' at the beginning of string Sentence, changing its contents to 'Where is the stuff?'.

If the contents of Target is 'stuff' and the contents of NewString is '*# %! ', the statements

```
PosStuff := Pos(Target, Sentence);
if PosStuff > 0 then
   Insert (NewString, Sentence, PosStuff)
```

insert the string '*#%! ' in front of the string 'stuff' in Sentence. The new contents of Sentence becomes 'Where is the *#%! stuff'.   ■

■ Example 13.16

Procedure Replace in Fig. 13.8 replaces a specified target string (Target) in a source string (Source) with a new string (Pattern). It uses function Pos to locate Target, Delete to delete it, and Insert to insert Pattern in place of Target. An error message is displayed if Target is not found.

Figure 13.8 Procedure Replace

```
procedure Replace (Target, Pattern : String;
                        var Source : String);
{
   Replaces first string Target in Source with Pattern if found.
   Pre : Target, Pattern, and Source are defined.
   Post: Source is modified.
   Uses: Pos, Length, Delete, Insert, and WriteString
}
   var
      PosTarg : Integer;                    {position of Target}

begin  {Replace}
   PosTarg := Pos(Target, Source);        {locate Target}
   if PosTarg > 0 then
      begin
         Delete (Source, PosTarg, Length(Target));
         Insert (Pattern, Source, PosTarg)
      end
   else
      begin
         Write ('No replacement -- string ');
         WriteString (Output, Target);
         WriteLn (' not found.')
      end {if}
end; {Replace}
```

Exercises for Section 13.3

Self-Check

1. Determine the results of the following procedure calls and function designators. Assume that all variables are type String with a capacity of twenty characters.

   a. MakeString ('Abra   ', Temp1);
   b. MakeString ('cadabra   ', Temp2);
   c. Concat (Temp1, Temp2, Magic)
   d. Length(Magic)
   e. Copy (Magic, 1, 8, HisMagic)
   f. Delete (HisMagic, 4, 3)
   g. Insert (Temp1, HisMagic, 3)
   h. Pos(Temp2, Magic)
   i. GetChar(Magic, 6)
   j. PutChar(Temp1, 1, 'a')
   k. Pos(Temp1, Magic)

2. Explain the difference between ReadLnString (see Fig. 10.20) and ReadLnStrVar, described in this section.

3. Source, Target, and Destin are three variables of type String with capacity 20. Assume that Source begins with a person's last name and has a comma and one space between the last and first names (that is, *last name, first name*). Use Pos and Copy to store the first name in Destin and the second name in Target.

Programming

1. Write a program that calls PrintWords to read in a sentence and then display each word on a separate line. Insert the necessary declarations and procedure calls.

 ## 13.4 String Processing Illustrated

You have been using a text editor to create and edit Pascal programs. This is probably a fairly sophisticated *screen-oriented* editor in which special commands move the cursor around the video screen and specify edit operations. Although you cannot develop such an editor yet, you can write a less sophisticated one.

 ## Case Study: Text Editor

Problem
We need an editor to perform some editing operations on a line of text. The editor should be able to locate a specified target string, delete a substring, insert a substring at a specified location, and replace one substring with another.

Design Overview
We can use the string manipulation functions and procedures in ADT String to perform the editing operations relatively easily. We will write a program that enters a string and then processes a series of edit commands for that string.

Data Requirements

Problem Inputs
The source string (Source : String)
Each edit command (Command : Char)

Problem Outputs
The modified source string (Source : String)

Initial Algorithm
1. Read the string to be edited into Source.
2. repeat
    3. Read an edit command
    4. Perform each edit operation.
   until done

Refinements and Program Structure
Step 4 is performed by procedure DoEdit. DoEdit is responsible for calling the appropriate string operators to read any data strings and to perform the required operations. A portion of the structure chart for the text editor is shown in Fig. 13.9; the local variables and algorithm for procedure DoEdit follow.

Figure 13.9   Structure Chart for Text Editor Program

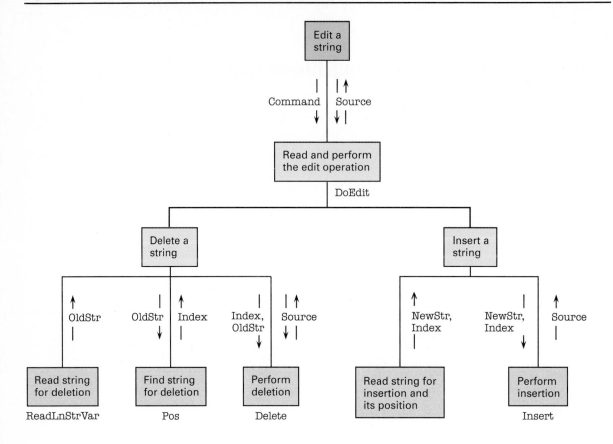

Local Variables

A substring to be found, replaced, or deleted
  (OldStr : String)
A substring to be inserted (NewStr : String)
An index to the string Source (Index : Integer)

Algorithm for DoEdit

1. case Command of
       'D': Read the substring to be deleted and delete it.
       'I': Read the substring to be inserted and its
            position and insert it.
       'F': Read substring to be found and print its position
            if found.
       'R': Read substring to be replaced and replace it.
     end {case}

The complete program is shown in Fig. 13.10, along with a sample run.

Figure 13.10   Text Editor Program and Sample Run

```
program TextEdit (Input, Output);
{
  Performs text editing operations on a source string.

  IMPORTS:  String, Insert, Delete, Pos, Length,
            ReadLnStrVar, WriteString from ADT String.
            Cap (see Fig. 9.19)
            Replace (see Fig. 13.8)
}
  const
    Sentinel = 'Q';        {sentinel command}
    Capacity = 80;         {predefined maximum length}

  type
    StringType = packed array [1..Capacity] of Char;
    String = record
               Contents : StringType;
               Len : Integer
             end; {String}

  var
    Source : String;           {the string being edited}
    Command : Char;            {each edit command}

  {
    Insert ReadLnStrVar, WriteString, Insert, Delete, Pos,
    Replace, Length, Cap
  }


procedure DoEdit (Command {input} : Char;
                  var Source : String);
{
  Performs the edit operation specified by Command.
  Pre : Command and Source are defined.
  Post: One or more data strings are read and
        Source is modified if Command is
        'D','I','F', or 'R'. If Command is 'Q',
        a message is displayed; otherwise, nothing
        is done.
}
  var
    NewStr, OldStr : String;     {work strings}
    Index : Integer;             {index to string Source}

  begin {DoEdit}
    {Perform the operation.}
    if Command in ['D', 'I', 'F', 'R', 'Q'] then
      case Command of
        'D' : begin {Delete}
              Write ('Delete what string? ');
              ReadLnStrVar (Input, OldStr);
              Index := Pos(OldStr, Source);
              if Index > 0 then
                Delete (Source, Index, Length(OldStr))
              else
                begin
                  WriteString (Output, OldStr);
```

```
                                WriteLn (' not found')
                              end {if}
                        end; {delete}
              'I' : begin {Insert}
                        Write ('Insert what string? ');
                        ReadLnStrVar (Input, NewStr);
                        Write ('At what position? ');
                        ReadLn (Index);
                        Insert (NewStr, Source, Index)
                      end; {Insert}
              'F' : begin {Find}
                        Write ('Find what string? ');
                        ReadLnStrVar (Input, OldStr);
                        Index := Pos(OldStr, Source);
                        if Index > 0 then
                          begin
                            WriteString (Output, OldStr);
                            WriteLn (' found at position ', Index :3)
                          end
                        else
                          begin
                            WriteString (Output, OldStr);
                            WriteLn (' not found')
                          end {if}
                      end; {Find}
              'R' : begin {Replace}
                        Write ('Replace old string? ');
                        ReadLnStrVar (Input, OldStr);
                        Write ('With new string? ');
                        ReadLnStrVar (Input, NewStr);
                        Replace (OldStr, NewStr, Source)
                      end; {Replace}
              'Q' : WriteLn ('Quitting text editor.')
          end {case}
        else
          WriteLn ('Invalid edit character')
    end; {DoEdit}

  begin {TextEdit}
    {Read in the string to be edited.}
    WriteLn ('Enter the source string:');
    ReadLnStrVar (Input, Source);

    {Perform each edit operation until done.}
    repeat
      {Get the operation symbol.}
      WriteLn;
      Write ('Enter D (Delete), I (Insert), ');
      Write ('F (Find), R (Replace), Q (Quit): ');
      ReadLn (Command);
      Command := Cap(Command);        {convert to uppercase}

      {Perform operation}
      DoEdit (Command, Source);

      {Display latest string}
      Write ('New source: ');
      WriteString (Output, Source);
      WriteLn
```

```
   until Command = Sentinel
end. {TextEdit}
```

```
Enter the source string:
Mary had a cute little lamb.

Enter D (Delete), I (Insert), F (Find), R (Replace), Q (Quit): f
Find what string? cute
cute   found at position 12
New source: Mary had a cute little lamb.

Enter D (Delete), I (Insert), F (Find), R (Replace), Q (Quit): i
Insert what string? very
At what position? 12
New source: Mary had a very cute little lamb.

Enter D (Delete), I (Insert), F (Find), R (Replace), Q (Quit): R
Replace old string? lamb
With new string? lamb chop
New source: Mary had a very cute little lamb chop.

Enter D (Delete), I (Insert), F (Find), R (Replace), Q (Quit): D
Delete what string? very cute little
New source: Mary had a lamb chop.

Enter D (Delete), I (Insert), F (Find), R (Replace), Q (Quit): q
Quitting text editor.
New source: Mary had a lamb chop.
```

Exercise for Section 13.4

Self-Check

1. Draw the program structure chart for finding a string and for replacing a
   string.

13.5   Implementing the String Operators

We showed one possible internal representation for a variable length string in
Fig. 13.6. This representation is repeated below.

```
{declarations for type String}
const
  Capacity = 20;        {predefined maximum length}
type
  StringType = packed array [1..Capacity] of Char;
  String = record
             Contents : StringType;
             Len : Integer
           end; {String}
```

As stated earlier, an operator for data type String processes the array field Contents, the integer field Len, or both. The operations on the array field involve searching an array or copying a portion of the array field that represents a substring. The string operators are implemented in the remainder of this section.

ReadLnStrVar, WriteString, Length, GetChar, and PutChar

Figure 13.11 shows four relatively simple operators in the specification for data type String. Procedure ReadLnStrVar is similar to procedure ReadLnString (see Fig. 10.20) except it does not pad the string read into InString.Contents with blanks.

Figure 13.11 ReadLnStrVar, WriteString, PutChar, and GetChar

```
procedure ReadLnStrVar (var InFile {input} : Text;
                        var InString {output} : String);
{
  Reads a variable length string from InFile into InString.
  Pre : File InFile has been prepared for input.
  Post: Reads up to Capacity characters from file InFile into
        InString and advances to the start of the next data
        line. Stops reading characters if the <eoln>
        character is reached before InString is filled. The
        length of InString is set to the number of characters
        read.
}
  const
    Pad = ' ';                       {character used for padding}

  var
    I : Integer;                     {loop-control variable}

begin {ReadLnStrVar}
  {Read each character and store it in the next array element.}
  with InString do
    begin
      Len := 0;                      {no characters read}
      while (not Eoln(InFile)) and (Len < Capacity) do
        {invariant:
            0 < Len <= Capacity and no character read
            is <eoln> and Len characters were read from
            InFile into InString.Contents [1..Len]
        }
        begin
          Len := Len + 1;                 {Increment subscript}
          Read (InFile, Contents[Len])    {Read next character}
        end;  {while}

      {assert: at end of line or string is filled}
      ReadLn (InFile)                      {Advance to next line}
    end  {with}
end; {ReadLnStrVar}


procedure WriteString (var OutFile {output} : Text;
                       OutString {input} : String);
```

```
{
    Writes the variable length string OutString to OutFile.
    Pre : File OutFile has been prepared for output
          and OutString is defined.
    Post: The characters stored in OutString are written
          to file OutFile.
}
begin {WriteString}
  if OutString.Len > 0 then
    Write (OutFile, OutString.Contents :OutString.Len)
end; {WriteString}


function Length (Str {input} : String) : Integer;
{
    Returns the length of string Str.
    Pre : Str is defined.
    Post: The current length of Str is returned as
          the function result.
}
begin {Length}
  Length := Str.Len
end; {Length}

procedure PutChar (var Str {input/output} : String;
                       Index : Integer;
                       Ch : Char);
{
    Stores Ch in Str at position Index.
    Pre : Str, Index, and Ch are defined.
    Post: Str.Contents[Index] gets Ch if 1 <= Index <= Str.Len.
}
begin
  if (Index < 1) or (Index > Str.Len) then
    WriteLn ('string index out of range')
  else
    Str.Contents[Index] := Ch
end; {PutChar}


function GetChar (Str : String;
                     Index : Integer) : Char;
{
    Retrieves the character at position Index of Str.
    Pre : Str and Index are defined.
    Post: Returns Str.Contents[Index] if 1 <= Index <= Str.Len.
}
begin {GetChar}
  if (Index < 1) or (Index > Str.Len) then
    WriteLn ('string index out of range')
  else
    GetChar := Str.Contents[Index]
end; {GetChar}
```

Procedure MakeString

We can use procedure ReadLnStrVar to read a string value into memory. We can also use the assignment operator to copy one string variable (type String) to another. It is not possible, however, to directly assign a string value to a string variable. Procedure MakeString accomplishes this task by storing the fixed-length string represented by its first parameter, S1, in the Contents field of its second parameter, S2.

Algorithm for MakeString

1. Assign the fixed length string S1 to S2.Contents
2. Set S2.Len to the actual length of string S2.Contents; ignore any blank padding at the right end of string S2.Contents.

The refinement of step 2 follows. Step 2 is a loop that searches for the first nonblank character in S2.Contents, starting at the right end of the string. Loop exit occurs after the character at position 1 is tested or after a nonblank character is reached. In procedure MakeString (Fig. 13.12), the Boolean variable In-Padding indicates whether the current character is part of the blank padding (InPadding is True).

Refinement of Step 2 of MakeString

2.1 Set S2.Len to Capacity and assume that the character
    at position S2. Len is part of the blank padding.
2.2 while still in the blank padding and S2.Len is > 0 do
        2.3 if the character at S2.Len is nonblank then
                Found first nonblank, so out of blank padding
            else
                Decrement S2.Len

Local Variables for MakeString

Flag indicating whether the current character is in the blank padding
    (InPadding : Boolean)

Figure 13.12 Procedure MakeString

```
procedure MakeString (S1 {input} : StringType;
                      var S2 {output} : String);
{ Stores the fixed length string S1 in the variable length
  string S2.
  Pre : S1 is defined.
  Post: The contents of S2 gets S1 and the length of S2 is
        the length of S1 not counting any trailing blanks.
}
  const
    Pad = ' ';                    {blank padding}

  var
    InPadding : Boolean;          {program flag}

begin {MakeString}
  S2.Contents := S1;             {store all of S1 in S2}

  {Set S2.Len to position of first nonblank at right end of S1.}
  S2.Len := Capacity;            {start at right end}
  InPadding := True;             {assume in blank padding}
```

```
while InPadding and (S2.Len > 0) do
   {invariant:
      Each prior value of S1[S2.Len] was the blank character
      and each prior value of S2.Len was greater than 0
   }
   if S1[S2.Len] <> Pad then
      InPadding := False          {out of blank padding}
   else
      S2.Len := S2.Len - 1        {move to the left}
end; {MakeString}
```

Procedure Copy

Procedure Copy (Fig. 13.13) copies a portion of its source string (S1) to its destination string (S2). The *substring* copied begins at position Index in the source string and begins at position 1 in the destination string. The parameter Size represents the length of the substring being copied. Assuming S1 contains the string

the procedure call statement

```
Copy (S1, 3, 2, S2)
```

copies the substring of S1 that starts at 3 and whose length is 2 to S2, as shown next.

Algorithm for Procedure Copy

1. if Size is <= 0 or Index is out of range then
    2. Store the null string in S2.
  else
    begin
       3. Define S2.Len.
       4. Copy S2.Len characters from S1 starting with
          the character at position Index.
    end

Step 3 defines S2.Len, the size of the substring copied to S2. S2.Len will be the same as Size unless the last character to be copied from S1, the character at Index + Size - 1, is beyond the end of string S1. In that case, S2.Len should be set to ensure that the character at S1.Len is the last character copied from S1.Contents. Step 4 is a loop that copies individual characters from S1 to S2.

Step 3 Refinement

3.1 if (Index + Size - 1) <= S1.Len then
        Set S2.Len to Size
     else
        Set S2.Len so that the character at position S1.Len
        is the last character copied.

Figure 13.13 Procedure Copy

```
procedure Copy (S1 {input} : String;
                Index, Size {input} : Integer;
                var S2 {output} : String);
{
 Copies a substring of S1 to S2. The substring copied
 starts at position Index of S1. The length of the substring
 to be copied is specified by Size.
 Pre : S1, Index, and Size are defined.
 Post: S2.Contents is the substring copied and S2.Len
       is the size of that substring. If Size is <= 0 or
       Index is out of range, the null string is copied.
       If Size is too big, the right end of string S1
       (through position S1.Len) is copied.
}
var
  I : Integer;                      {loop control variable}

begin {Copy}
   if (Size <= 0) or (Index < 1) or (Index > S1.Len) then
     S2.Len := 0                        {store the null string}
   else
     begin
       {Define S2.Len.}
       if (Index + Size - 1) <= S1.Len then
         S2.Len := Size                 {Size is O.K.}
       else
         S2.Len := S1.Len - Index + 1;  {Size is too big}

       {
        Copy S2.Len characters from S1 to S2 starting with
        S1.Contents[Index].
       }
       for I := 1 to S2.Len do
         S2.Contents[I] := S1.Contents[Index+I-1]
     end  {if}
end; {Copy}
```

Procedure Concat

Procedure Concat *concatenates,* or joins, its two source strings together. The destination string, S3, will contain the string in S1 followed by the string in S2. A result of the procedure call statement follows. A string of length 5 and a string of length 14 are joined together to make a string of length 19.

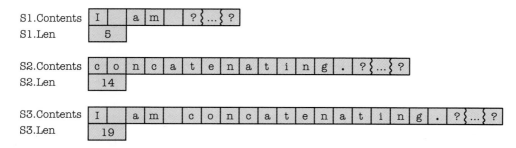

Algorithm for Procedure Concat

1. Store string S1 in S3.
2. Append each character in string S2.Contents to the end of the string being formed in S3.Contents, incrementing S3.Len as each new character is placed in S3.Contents.

Step 1 stores string S1 in string S3, initializing S3.Len to S1.Len. Step 2 is a loop that copies the next character from string S2.Contents to the end of string S3.Contents. In procedure Concat (Fig. 13.14), the variable S2Index selects the next character in string S2.Contents; the current length of string S3 (S3.Len) is incremented before each new character is inserted at S3.Contents[S3.Len].

Figure 13.14   Procedure Concat

```
procedure Concat (S1, S2 {input} : String;
                      var S3 {output} : String);
{
  Concatenates the strings in S1 and S2; the resulting
  string is stored in S3.
  Pre : S1 and S2 are defined.
  Post: S3 is string S1 followed by S2.
}
  var
    S2Index : 0..Capacity;    {subscript in S2.Contents}

begin  {Concat}
  S3 := S1;            {Store S1 in S3}

  {Copy S2 to S3 following S1}
  S2Index := 0;        {start at beginning of S2}
  while (S2Index < S2.Len) and (S3.Len < Capacity) do
    {invariant:
        S2Index <= S2.Len and S3.Len <= Capacity
        and S2Index character from S2 were copied to S3.
    }
    begin
      S2Index := S2Index + 1;
      S3.Len  := S3.Len + 1;
```

```
      {Copy next character from string S2 to string S3.}
      S3.Contents[S3.Len] := S2.Contents[S2Index]
   end; {while}

{assertion:
   S3.Contents is S1.Contents followed by
   as much of S2.Contents as will fit and S3.Len
   is the smaller of (S1.Len + S2.Len) and Capacity.
}
end; {Concat}
```

Function Pos

Finally, function Pos searches a source string for a specified target string. It does this by "sliding" the target string over the source string until each character in the target string matches the source string character under it. In Fig. 13.15, there is a match when the target string, S1.Contents, is over positions 3 and 4 of the source string, S2.Contents, so the function result should be 3.

Before searching for the target string, procedure Pos must first check for two special cases: a null target string and a target string that is longer than the source string. If the target string is null, Pos will return the value 1; if the target string is longer than the source string, Pos will return the value 0. The algorithm for Pos follows.

Algorithm for Pos

1. if S1 is the null string then
    2. Return 1
   else if S1.Len is greater than S2.Len then
    3. Return 0
   else
    4. Compare S1 to each substring in S2 until a match is found or there are no substrings left in S2.

The refinement of step 4 uses a repeat–until loop to perform the slide and match operations. Function Match, a local function in Pos (see Fig. 13.15), compares S1 to the current substring of S2 (step 4.4). Function Match returns False if a nonmatching pair of characters is found; function Match returns True if all pairs match. The Boolean variable Matched stores the result returned by function Match.

4.1 Initialize S2Index to 0
4.2 repeat
    4.3 Advance S2Index to the next substring in S2
    4.4 Compare S1 to the substring starting at S2Index
  until there is a match or there are no substrings left
4.5 if there is a match then
    4.6 Return S2Index
  else
    4.7 Return 0

Local Declaration in Pos

The index in S2.Contents of the current substring (S2Index : Integer)
A Boolean function that compares S1 to the current substring in S2 (function Match)
A flag that holds the result returned by Match (Matched : Boolean)

The algorithm for function Match follows. A repeat–until loop implements step 3 of Match.

Algorithm for Match

1. if S2 is too short then
    2. Return False
  else
    begin
      3. Compare corresponding characters in S1 and S2, starting with S1.Contents[1] and S2.Contents[S2Index], until an unequal pair is found or the end of S1 is reached.
      4. if an unequal pair is found then
          Return False
        else
          Return True
    end

Local Variables for Match

The index in S1.Contents of the next pair of characters being compared (S1Index : Integer)

Figure 13.15 Function Pos

```
function Pos (S1, S2 : String) : Integer;
{
  Returns the starting position in S2 of the first occurrence
  of the string S1. Returns 0 if S1 is not a substring of S2.
  Pre : S1 and S2 are defined.
```

```
          Post: Returns a value between 1 and S2.Len denoting the
                starting position of the first occurrence of S1 in S2.
                Returns 0 if S1 is not found.
          Uses: Match
        }
          var
            S2Index : 0..Capacity;     {subscript in S2.Contents}
            Matched : Boolean;         {program flag}


          function Match (S1, S2 : String;
                          S2Index : Integer) : Boolean;
          {
            Attempts to match string S1 with the substring of
            S2 beginning at position S2Index.
            Pre : S1, S2, and S2Index are defined and S1 is not null.
            Post: Returns True if match succeeds; otherwise,
                  returns False.
          }
            var
              S1Index : 0..Capacity;    {subscript in S1.Contents}

          begin {Match}
            if S1.Len > (S2.Len - S2Index + 1) then
              Match := False               {S2 is too short}
            else
              begin
                {
                  Compare corresponding characters in S1 and S2, starting
                  with S1.Contents[1] and S2.Contents[S2Index],
                  until an unequal pair is found or the end of S1 is reached.
                }
                S1Index := 0;                 {Start at beginning of S1}
                repeat
                  {invariant:
                     all prior pairs are equal
                     and S1Index <= S1.Len
                  }
                  S1Index := S1Index + 1       {Advance to next pair}
                until (S1.Contents[S1Index] <>
                  S2.Contents[S2Index+S1Index-1]) or (S1Index >= S1.Len);

                {assert: an unequal pair is found or at end of S1}
                {Define function result based on last pair tested.}
                Match := S1.Contents[S1Index] =
                         S2.Contents[S2Index+S1Index-1]
              end {if}
          end;   {Match}


        begin {Pos}
          if S1.Len > S2.Len then
            Pos := 0                     {S1 is longer than S2}
          else if S1.Len = 0 then
            Pos := 1                     {S1 is the null string}
          else
            begin {slide and match}
              {Search for S1 in S2}
              S2Index := 0;              {start at left end of S2}
              repeat
                {invariant:
                   No prior substring of S2 matches S1 and
                   no prior substring of S2 was the last substring
                }
```

```
      S2Index := S2Index + 1;      {slide to right in S2}
      Matched := Match(S1, S2, S2Index)
    until Matched or (S2Index > S2.Len - S1.Len);

    {assert:
       S1 found at S2.Contents[S2Index] or
       all substrings tested without success
    }
    {Define function result.}
    if Matched then
      Pos := S2Index                {S1 found at S2Index}
    else
      Pos := 0                      {S1 is not found}
  end {slide and match}
end; {Pos}
```

Procedures Delete and Insert

Rather than implement procedures Delete and Insert, we leave them as
exercises at the end of this section. Two methods for implementing these
procedures are described in those exercises.

String Comparison

Unfortunately, it is not easy to compare two variable-length strings because
records cannot be used as operands of the relational operators. We can use
relational operators to compare the contents of two strings (for example,
Str1.Contents <> Str2.Contents). The result of such a comparison, however,
is not always meaningful, because the Contents field may not be defined beyond
the string length. One approach would be to pad the Contents field of each
string with blanks before performing the comparison. Programming project 7
deals with the implementation of string-comparison operators.

Exercises for Section 13.5

Self-Check

1. What happens if you call Concat to join two strings whose combined length
   is larger than the string capacity? Is this flagged as an error?
2. Assume that the Write statement in procedure WriteString displays the
   entire string stored in OutString.Contents instead of the substring ending
   at position OutString.Contents[Len]. Show how you could use a loop in
   procedure WriteString to display the substring that is defined.
3. Replace the body of ReadLnStrVar with a call to ReadLnString.

Programming

1. Write a procedure Delete that can be used to delete a substring of a source
   string. The procedure parameters are the source string, the starting position
   of the substring to be deleted, and the length of the substring. The procedure
   should move each character that follows the substring being deleted to its
   new position in the source string.

2. Write a procedure to insert a new string into a source string. The parameters are the two strings and the position in the source string where the new string is to be inserted. First, move the part of the source string that will follow the new substring, to make room for the new string. Next, copy the new string into the space vacated. When you move the old substring, be sure to move the last character first (why?). Also, if the expanded source string is too long, don't move the extra characters at the right end.

3. Exercises 1 and 2 can be solved by using procedures Copy and Concat. Provide alternate solutions that utilize these procedures to extract and concatenate substrings. Hint: To delete, copy the substring following the one to be deleted to a local variable, shorten the original string by changing its length, and then concatenate the modified original string and the local string. To insert, copy the substring following the point of insertion to a local string, shorten the original string by changing its length, and then concatenate the modified original string, the new string, and the local string.

 ## 13.6 Strings in Pascal Extensions (Optional)

We have stated that many Pascal compilers provide variable-length strings as an extension. In those compilers, the declaration of a string type takes one of the following forms:

```
type                         type
  String10 = string[10];       String10 = string(10);
```

The variable declaration

```
var
  MyName, YourName : String10;
```

allocates storage for two variable-length strings (MyName and YourName) of capacity 10.

Many compilers provide functions and procedures similar to the ones discussed in the previous sections. They use the standard Pascal input/output procedures to enter and display strings instead of procedures like ReadLnStrVar and WriteString.

Instead of using GetChar and PutChar, we can reference a character in a variable-length string using normal subscript notation (for example, MyName[1] references the first character in string MyName). Instead of using procedure MakeString, we can assign a fixed-length string value to a string variable using the assignment operator. We can also use the relational operators to compare variable-length strings.

Operators Concat and Copy return a single string as their result; consequently, they are implemented as functions on most Pascal systems. For example, the statements

```
S2 := Copy (S1, 1, 7);     {replaces Copy (S1, 1, 7, S2)}
S3 := Concat (S2, S1)      {replaces Concat (S2, S1, S3)}
```

copy the first seven characters of string S1 to S2 and then store this substring of S1 followed by S1 itself in S3. If S1 is the string 'double trouble', S3 becomes the string 'double double trouble'. Because standard Pascal functions cannot return strings as values, we implemented these operators as procedures, using the last parameter to return the procedure result.

Finally, you have seen that the operator + might mean addition or set union depending on its operands. On most extended Pascal systems, it can also mean concatenation. This allows us to write the last line of the preceding example as

```
S3 := S2 + S1
```

Strings in Extended Pascal

In a version of Pascal called Extended Pascal, function Substr is used (instead of Copy) to copy a substring of one string to another string. The *substring variable* S1[3..5] denotes the substring of S1 found in positions 3 through 5, inclusive. A substring variable can be used just like a string variable. The statement

```
S1[3..5] := 'abc'
```

defines this substring of S1, and the statement

```
Write (S1[3..5])
```

displays this substring.

Function Index is used instead of function Pos to search for a substring and the function designator Pos(Target, Source) becomes Index(Source, Target). The function designator Trim(S1) removes any trailing blanks from the end of string S1 and redefines its length accordingly.

 ## 13.7 Common Programming Errors

Remember that a set variable, like any variable, must be initialized before it can be manipulated. It is tempting to assume that a set is empty and then to begin processing it without initializing it to the empty set, [ ], through an explicit assignment.

Many of the Pascal operators can be used with sets. The meaning of the operator is, of course, different when its operands are sets and not numbers. Remember to use a unit set (a set of one element) when you insert or delete a set element. The set union operation in the expression

```
['A','E','O','U'] + 'I'          {incorrect set union}
```

is incorrect and should be rewritten as

```
['A','E','O','U'] + ['I']        {correct set union}
```

It is not possible to use a set as an operand of the standard Read or Write procedure. You must read in the elements of a set individually and insert them into an initially empty set using the set union operator. To print a set, you must test each value in the base type of a set for set membership. Only those values that are in the set should be printed.

You can use the operators provided in ADT String or extensions to standard Pascal provided by your compiler. In either case, be careful not to mix fixed-length strings and variable-length strings. Fixed-length strings are stored in packed arrays of characters. Also, don't confuse the operators described in this chapter with similar operators provided in your Pascal system. Remember that operators such as Concat and Copy may be implemented as functions (and not procedures) in some versions of Pascal.

 # Chapter Review

The set data type can store a collection of elements of the same type (called the base type). Each value in the base type of a set is either a member of the set or it is not. Unlike an array, a value can be saved only once in a set, and there is no way to determine the sequence in which the values were stored in the set (for example, [1,5,2,4] is the same set as [1,2,4,5]).

String operators can simplify the processing of textual data. Because standard Pascal does not provide a variable-length string data type, we described and implemented ADT String in this chapter. Check with your instructor to find what string operators, if any, are provided in your Pascal system.

New Pascal Constructs

The Pascal constructs introduced in this chapter are described in Table 13.2.

Table 13.2 Summary of New Pascal Constructs

Construct	Effect
Set Type Declaration	
type	Declares a set type DigitSet
DigitSet = set of 0..9;	whose base type is the set
	of digits from 0 through 9.
var	Digits and Primes are set
Digits, Primes : DigitSet;	variables of type DigitSet.
Set Assignment	
Digits := [];	Digits is the empty set.
Primes := [2,3,5] + [7];	Primes is the set
	[2,3,5,7].
Digits := Digits + [1..3];	Digits is the set [1,2,3].

Table 13.2 *continued*   535

Chapter Review

Construct	Effect
`Digits := [0..9] - [1,3,5,7,9];` `Digits := [1,3,5,7,9] * Primes`	`Digits` is the set `[0,2,4,6,8]`. `Digits` is the set `[3,5,7]`.

Set Relations

`Primes <= Digits`	`True` if `Primes` is a subset of `Digits`.
`Primes >= []`	Always `True`.
`Primes <> []`	`True` if `Primes` contains any element.
`[1,2,3] = [3,2,1]`	`True` because order does not matter.

String Declaration

```
const Capacity = 10;
type StringType =
     packed array [1..Capacity] of Char;
   String = record
             Contents : StringType;
             Len : Integer
           end; {String}
var FirstName, LastName, TempName : String;
```

`FirstName`, `LastName`, and `TempName` are variable-length strings (string capacity is ten characters).

String Assignment

```
MakeString ('Daffy     ', FirstName);
MakeString ('Duck      ', LastName);
TempName := LastName;
```

Saves `'Daffy'` in `FirstName` and `'Duck'` in `LastName` and `TempName`.

String Length

```
Length(FirstName);
```

Returns the current length (5) of `FirstName`.

String Copy

```
Copy (FirstName, 1, 3, TempName);
```

Copies `'Daf'` to `TempName`.

String Concatenation

```
Concat (FirstName, LastName, TempName);
```

Stores `'DaffyDuck'` in `Temp-Name`.

String Search

```
Pos('Du', FirstName);
Pos('Du', LastName);
Pos('Du', TempName);
```

Returns 0 (`'Du'` not found).
Returns 1 (`'Du'` found at 1).
Returns 6 (`'Du'` found at 6).

String Deletion

```
Delete (TempName, 7, 2);
```

Changes `TempName` to `'DaffyDk'`.

String Insertion

```
Insert ('uc', TempName, 7);
```

Changes `TempName` to `'DaffyDuck`.

✓ *Quick-Check Exercises*

1. What is the universal set?
2. Which can have the most elements: a set union, an intersection, or a difference? Which of these operators is not commutative?
3. Can you have a set whose base type is Integer or Char? How about a subrange type with host type Integer or Char?
4. Does it make any difference in which order the elements of a set are inserted? Does it make any difference if an element is inserted more than once into the same set?
5. Given that Set1 is [1..3], what are the contents of the following sets?
   a. Set2 := Set1 + [4, 5, 6];
   b. Set3 := Set1 – Set2;
   c. Set4 := Set3 + [4, 7];
   d. Set5 := Set4 + [4, 6]
   e. Set6 := Set5 * Set2
6. What is the advantage of storing a string in a variable of type String instead of using a packed array of characters?
7. Is it easier to compare two strings stored in variables of type String or in packed arrays of characters? Explain your answer.
8. Assuming S1, S2, and S3 are type String, what is the effect of the following statements when Pos returns a nonzero value?
   a. Copy (S1, 1, 6, S3);
      Concat (S3, S2, S3);
   b. Copy (S2, 1, Pos(S1, S2) – 1, S3);
   c. Copy (S2, Pos(S1, S2), Length(S2), S3);
   d. Copy (S2, Pos(S1, S2), Length(S1), S3);
   e. Delete (S2, Pos(S1, S2), Length(S1));
   f. Insert (S2, Pos(S1, S2), Length(S1))
9. Answer exercise 8 when Pos returns 0.
10. Write procedure PadString that pads a variable-length string with blanks.

Answers to Quick-Check Exercises
1. The set containing all the values in the base type.
2. The union of two sets. Set difference (operator –) is not commutative.
3. You cannot use Integer as a base type, but you can probably use Char. A subrange of Integer or Char can be the base type.
4. No; no
5. a. [1..6] b. [] c. [4,7] d. [4,6,7] e. [4,6]
6. The actual length, excluding blank padding, is also stored. The operators in ADT String can be used to assist in processing the string data.
7. It is easier to compare two packed arrays because you can use the relational operators. The Contents fields of two variables of type String can be compared, but there may be some problems if the strings are not the same length and are not padded.
8. a. The substring consisting of the first six characters in S1 is concatentated with S2; the result is stored in S3.
   b. The substring of S2 that precedes the first occurrence of S1 in S2 is copied to S3.
   c. The substring of S2 starting at the first occurrence of S1 in S2 is copied to S3.
   d. The substring S1 is copied to S3.
   e. The first occurrence of S1 is deleted from S2.

f. The string S1 is inserted in S2 just before its first occurrence.
9. a. not affected
   b, c, d. The null string is stored in S3.
   e, f. S2 should not be changed.
10.

```
procedure PadString (var AString {input/output} : String);
  const
    Pad = ' ';
  var
    i : Integer;

begin {PadString}
  for i := AString.Len + 1 to Capacity do
    AString.Contents[i] := Pad
end; {PadString}
```

Review Questions

1. Why may we be unable to declare a set whose base type is Char?
2. Write the declarations for a set, Oysters, whose values are the months of the year (enumerated type Month). Initialize Oysters to the set of all months that contain the letter r in their name. Write an assignment statement that inserts the month May in this set and deletes the month September.
3. The following for loop prints each member of a set whose elements are values of enumerated type Day. Write the declaration for set TestSet. Rewrite the loop as a while loop whose repetition condition is TestSet <> []. Use the set operator – to delete each set element after it is displayed.

```
for Today := Sunday to Saturday do
  if Today in TestSet then
    WriteDay (Today)
```

4. Provide the declarations for the two sets below. What are the intersection and union of sets Vowel and Letter? What are the two set differences?

```
Vowel := ['Y','U','O','I'];
Letter := ['A'..'P'];
```

5. What is the difference between the current length of a string and the capacity of a string? Which does function Length return?
6. If MyString (type String) has capacity ten, store the string value 'Hello' in MyString using procedure MakeString. Next, write the assignment statements that would have the same effect.
7. Indicate whether each of the following identifiers is a procedure or function. Describe the type of result returned by each.

   Length, MakeString, Concat, Pos, Copy, Insert, Delete

8. Write the declarations and statements for a program segment that first reads a data line into a variable of type String and stores all of the symbols in the subrange '!'..'/' that appear in the string in a set Symbols1. Assume the ASCII character set and test each of the characters in this subrange using function Pos to determine whether it appears in the string. If so, insert it in the set Symbols1. Next, write a new

search loop that scans the string, testing each character in the string for membership in the set ['!'..'/']. Insert each character that qualifies in set Symbols2. When you are done, test whether Symbols1 and Symbols2 are identical sets.

Programming Projects

1. Write a program that removes all the blanks from a character string.
2. Write a program that reads in a sequence of lines and displays a count of the total number of words in those lines and counts of the number of words with one letter, two letters, and so on.
3. Write a program that reads in a sequence of lines and displays each line read with all four-letter words replaced with asterisks.
4. Write a program that reads in a sequence of lines and rewrites each line in a simplified form of "pig latin." If the word begins with a consonant, strip off the first letter and place it at the end of the word followed by the string 'ay'.
5. Write a procedure that reads in an array of cards and stores it in an array of sets, one set for each suit. Use an enumerated type for the suits and one for the card face values. The data for each card will be presented in the form of a character representing the suit and a character representing the card face value ('2'..'9', 'T', 'J', 'Q', 'K', 'A').
6. Consider a card of hands read in exercise 5 as a bridge hand and evaluate it. Award points for each card according to the following method:

Card Face Value	Points
two..ten	0
jack	1
queen	2
king	3
ace	4

Also add one point for each suit that has only two cards, two points for each suit that has only one card, and three points for each suit that is missing.
7. Provide a group of Boolean functions (LE, LT, EQ, NE, GE, GT) that can be used to compare two variable-length strings (for example, LE(S1, S2) returns True if string S1 is <= string S2). Two strings are equal only if they have the same contents and the same length. If one string is a substring of the other, the shorter string is considered less than the longer string.
8. Revise the text editor discussed in Section 13.4 so that it will edit a "page" of text. Store each line of the page in a separate element of an array of strings. Maintain a pointer (index) to the line currently being edited. In addition to the edit commands, include commands that move the index to the top of the page, the bottom of the page, and up or down a specified number of lines. Your program should also be able to delete an entire line, insert a new line preceding the current line, and replace the current line with another. The first two of these new operations will require moving a portion of the array of strings up or down by one element.
9. Write a program that will read 400 characters into a 20-by-20 array. Afterward, read in a character string of a maximum of ten characters that will be used to search the "table" of characters. Indicate how many times the second string occurs in the 20-by-20 array. This should include horizontal, vertical, and right-diagonal occurrences. (Right-diagonal means going down and to the right for the search.)
10. Write a program to scan a line of characters containing an equation and calculate

the result. Assume all operands are integers. Make tests to determine if the equation is valid.

Valid operations are +, –, /, *, and ^, where +, –, /, and * have their typical functions and ^ indicates the left value is raised to the power of the right operand (which must be positive).

Numbers may be negative. All operations are done in left-to-right order (no operator precedence). For example,

```
2 + 3 ^ 2 + 36 * 1
```

would be

```
5 ^ 2 + 36 * 1 = 25 + 36 * 1 = 61 * 1 = 61
```

Use sets to verify the equations' operations and ignore all blanks. Output should consist of an equal sign (=) and then the answer. If an equation is invalid, display the message ** INVALID **.

Files

14

Wͤ introduced files in Chapter 8. Like an array, a file is a collection of elements that are all the same type. Because files are located in secondary memory (that is, on a disk) rather than in main memory, they can be much larger than arrays. The elements of an array can be accessed in arbitrary, or *random order*; files in standard Pascal can be accessed only in *sequential order*. This means that file component 1, component 2, ..., component *n*-1 must be accessed before file component *n* can be accessed.

This chapter reviews text files. We also study other file types whose components are records. Finally, we discuss extensions to Pascal that allow a file to be accessed in random order, just like an array.

 ## 14.1   Review of Text Files

This section reviews what you learned about text files in Section 8.7. Files can store large quantities of data on disk. All components of a file are the same type. A text file is a file whose components are characters from the Pascal character set. A special character, the end-of-line mark, separates sequences of adjacent characters into lines. Associated with each file is a file-position pointer, which indicates the next file component to be processed.

You can use a file for input or for output, but not both simultaneously. If you're using a file for input, then its components can be read as data. If you're using a file for output, then new components can be written to the file.

If `InFile` is the name of a file, the statement

```
Reset (InFile)
```

calls the standard procedure `Reset` to prepare (*open*) file `InFile` for input. The file-position pointer is moved to the beginning of file `InFile`, so that the first file component is read by the next `Read` operation. The file-position pointer is automatically advanced after each `Read` operation.

If `OutFile` is the name of a file, the statement

```
Rewrite (OutFile)
```

calls the standard procedure `Rewrite` to prepare file `OutFile` for output. If `OutFile` is a new file, it is initialized to an empty file. If `OutFile` is an existing file in disk storage, its file-position pointer is returned to the beginning. In this way, `OutFile` becomes an empty file, and the data previously associated with the file are lost.

■ Example 14.1

Assume that `InFile` and `OutFile` are both text files. The statements

```
Reset (InFile);
Rewrite (OutFile);
```

open `InFile` for input and `OutFile` for output, as shown next. If file `OutFile` is non-empty, the `Rewrite` operation still returns the file-position pointer to the beginning, causing the existing file data to be lost.   ■

After Reset and Rewrite

File InFile

| A | C | E | { ... } | <eoln> | <eof> |

File-position pointer

File OutFile

<eof>

File-position pointer

Procedures Read and ReadLn can be used with system file Input (the keyboard) or any other text file that has been opened for input. Similarly, procedures Write and WriteLn can be used with system file Output (the screen) or any other text file that has been opened for output. The file to be processed is determined by the first parameter in a call to any of these procedures. If the first parameter is not a file variable, system file Input (for Read and ReadLn) or system file Output (for Write and WriteLn) is processed.

The EOF and EOLN functions test for the end of a file and the end of a line of a text file, respectively. The function parameter indicates which input file is being tested. If there is no parameter, system file Input is assumed. The function designator EOF(InFile) evaluates to True when the next character in file InFile is the <eof>. The function designator EOLN(InFile) evaluates to True when the next character in file InFile is an <eoln>.

The specification for the abstract data type text file follows.

Specification for Text File Abstract Data Type

Structure: A text file is an ordered collection of characters stored on disk. A special character, the end-of-line mark, segments the file into lines.

Operators:

Reset (F): Opens file F for input.

Rewrite (F): Opens file F for output.

Read (F, *input list*): Reads data from file F into the variables specified in *input list*. If F is missing, it reads data from system file Input.

ReadLn (F, *input list*): Same as Read except that it advances the file-position pointer for file F to the start of the next line after performing the data entry.

Write (F, *output list*): Writes data values in *output list* to file F. If F is missing, it writes data to system file Output.

WriteLn (F, *output list*): Same as Write except that it writes an <eoln> to file F after all data values.

EOF (F): Returns True if the <eof> is the next character in file F; otherwise, it returns False.

EOLN (F): Returns True if an <eoln> is the next character in file F; otherwise, it returns False.

■ Example 14.2

Procedure CopyFile in Fig. 14.1 reviews the use of the file operators. It copies each character of its input file to its output file. (Procedure CopyFile is based on an earlier program; see Fig. 8.9.) ■

Figure 14.1 Procedure CopyFile

```
procedure CopyFile (var InFile  {input},
                        OutFile {output} : Text);
{
  Copies file InFile to file OutFile.
  Pre : File InFile is defined.
  Post: File OutFile is a copy of InFile. The file-position
        pointers for both files are advanced to the <eof>
        character.
}
  var
    NextCh : Char;                {next character}

begin
  Reset (InFile);                 {prepare input file}
  Rewrite (OutFile);              {prepare output file}
  while not EOF(InFile) do
    begin
      While not EOLN(InFile) do
        begin
          Read  (InFile, NextCh);
          Write (OutFile, NextCh)  {copy character}
        end; {line}

      {assertion: <eoln> reached}
      ReadLn (InFile);            {skip <eoln>}
      WriteLn (OutFile)           {insert <eoln>}
    end {file}

  {assertion: <eof> reached}
end; {CopyFile}
```

Exercises for Section 14.1

Self-Check

1. Rewrite procedure CopyFile so that it uses procedure ReadLnString (see Fig. 10.20) to enter a data line instead of the inner while loop.
2. Answer exercise 1 for procedures ReadLnStrVar and WriteString.
3. What does the following program do? What happens if a data line does not contain enough characters to satisfy the input list?

```
program Mystery (InData, Output);
  var
    InData : Text;
    Ch1, Ch2, Ch3 : Char;
begin
  Reset (InData);
  while not EOF(InData) do
    begin
```

```
        ReadLn (InData, Ch1, Ch2, Ch3);
        WriteLn (Ch1, Ch2, Ch3)
      end {while}
    end. {Mystery}
```

Programming

1. Write procedure CompressFile that copies all nonblank characters in its input file to its output file.

 ## 14.2   File Processing Illustrated

In the game show called "Wheel of Fortune," three contestants attempt to guess a phrase. The contestants select consonants that they think are in the phrase. If a contestant picks a consonant that does occur in the phrase, the letter is inserted wherever it belongs. Contestants can also "buy" vowels; if the chosen vowel occurs in the phrase, it too is inserted.

 ## Case Study: Wheel of Fortune Problem

Problem

The game show producers want a computer program that can help them select phrases. Because the consonants are key, it would help the producers if the program can show them what the phrase looks like without vowels. The program should read a phrase entered at the keyboard, then display that phrase with a minus sign inserted in place of every vowel. A list of vowels and consonants occurring in the phrase should be printed underneath the phrase. For example, the phrase

```
THIS IS A SAMPLE
PHRASE WITH
VOWELS REMOVED
```

would generate the output

```
TH-S -S - S-MPL-
PHR-S- W-TH
V-W-LS R-M-V-D
The consonants are: DHLMPRSTVW
The vowels are: AEIO
```

Design Overview

We will read each line of the phrase, substitute a minus sign for each vowel, and write each converted line to a text file (Scratch). Each individual character in a line will be added to a set of consonants or vowels. After the phrase is completed, file Scratch will be echo printed.

Case Study: Wheel of Fortune Problem, continued

Data Requirements

Problem Inputs
Phrase to be processed (uppercase letters)

Problem Outputs
Phrase with vowels removed (Scratch : Text)
Set of consonants in the phrase (Consonants : set of 'A'..'Z')
Set of vowels in the phrase (Vowels : set of 'A'..'Z')

Initial Algorithm
1. Classify each character as a consonant or a vowel, substitute a minus sign for each vowel, and write the phrase to a scratch file.
2. Echo print the scratch file.
3. Print the set of consonants.
4. Print the set of vowels.

Program Structure
In the structure chart in Fig. 14.2, separate procedures accomplish steps 1 through 4. Step 1 is the only one that we have not yet solved; we will discuss procedure OutVowels later. Procedure CopyFile performs step 2, and procedure PrintSet (see Fig. 13.3) performs steps 3 and 4.

Coding the Main Program
The main program for the Wheel of Fortune problem appears in Fig. 14.3. A number of operators from ADT String are imported into the main program. They will be used by procedure OutVowels.

Figure 14.2   Structure Chart for Wheel of Fortune Problem

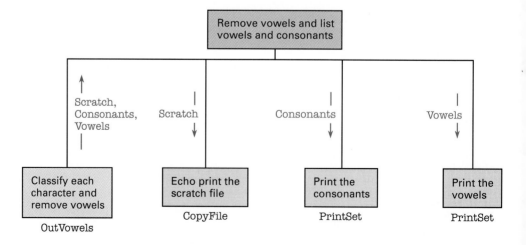

Figure 14.3 Main Program for Wheel of Fortune Problem

```
program Wheel (Input, Output);
{
  Displays a phrase with vowels removed. Also
  lists the consonants and vowels in the phrase.

  IMPORTS: String, Capacity, ReadLnStrVar, WriteString, Length
           PutChar, GetChar from ADT String (see Fig. 13.11)
           CopyFile (see Fig. 14.1)
           PrintSet (see Fig. 13.3)
           Cap (see Fig. 9.19)
}
  const
    Capacity = 80;             {string capacity}

  type
    StringType = packed array [1..Capacity] of Char;
    String = record
               Contents : StringType;
               Len : Integer
             end; {String}

    LetterSet = set of 'A'..'Z';       {set of letters}

  var
    Consonants,                        {set of consonants}
    Vowels      : LetterSet;           {set of vowels}
    Scratch : Text;                    {a scratch file}

  {
    Insert ReadLnStrVar, WriteString, GetChar,
    PutChar, Length, and Cap
  }

  {Insert OutVowels, CopyFile, PrintSet}

begin {Wheel}
  {
   Classify each character as a consonant or vowel, substitute
   - for each vowel, and write the scratch file.
  }
  OutVowels (Scratch, Consonants, Vowels);

  {Echo print the scratch file.}
  CopyFile (Scratch, Output);

  {Print the set of consonants.}
  Write ('The consonants are: ');
  PrintSet (Consonants);
  WriteLn;

  {Print the set of vowels.}
  Write ('The vowels are: ');
  PrintSet (Vowels)
end. {Wheel}
```

Case Study: Wheel of Fortune Problem, continued

Coding Procedure OutVowels

Procedure OutVowels creates the file Scratch and defines the sets Vowels and Consonants. The local variables and algorithm for OutVowels follow.

Local Variables for OutVowels
A line of the phrase (NextLine : String)

Algorithm for OutVowels
1. Prepare Scratch for output.
2. Initialize Consonants and Vowels to empty sets.
3. Read the first line of the phrase.
4. while there are more lines in the phrase do
    begin
      5. Replace each vowel in the current line with − and add the vowel to Vowels. Add each consonant to Consonants.
      6. Write the modified line to file Scratch.
      7. Read the next line of the phrase.
    end

Procedure ReadLnStrVar enters each line of the phrase into string variable NextLine. Procedure Classify performs step 5. The structure chart for OutVowels is shown in Fig. 14.4; procedure OutVowels is shown in Fig. 14.5.

Figure 14.4 Structure Chart for Procedure OutVowels

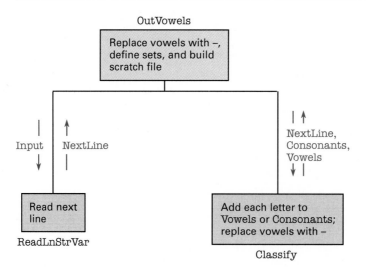

Figure 14.5   Procedure OutVowels

```
procedure OutVowels (var Scratch    {output} : Text;
                        var Consonants {output},
                            Vowels       {output} : LetterSet);
{
   Classifies each character as a consonant or vowel, substitutes
   - for each vowel, and writes the scratch file.
   Pre : None.
   Post: File Scratch is an echo of the input except each vowel
         is replaced by -, Consonants is the set of all consonants
         entered, and Vowels is the set of all vowels entered.
   Uses: ReadLnStrVar, WriteString, Length
}
   var
     NextLine : String;                {the next data line}


   procedure Classify (var NextLine  {input/output} : String;
                         var Consonants {input/output},
                             Vowels       {input/output} : LetterSet);
   {
     Adds each letter in NextLine to the set Consonants or Vowels.
     Replaces each vowel in NextLine with -.
     Pre : NextLine, Consonants, and Vowels are defined.
     Post: Each vowel in NextLine is inserted in set Vowels and
           each consonant in NextLine is inserted in Consonants.
     Uses: GetChar, PutChar, Length, Cap
   }
     const
       NewChar = '-';                    {replacement character}

     var
       AllVowels,                        {set of all vowels}
       AllConsonants : LetterSet;        {set of all consonants}
       NextChar : Char;                  {each character in the line}
       I : 1..Capacity;                  {loop-control variable}

   begin {Classify}
     {Initialize AllVowels and AllConsonants}
     AllVowels := ['A','E','I','O','U'];
     AllConsonants := ['A'..'Z'] - AllVowels;  {rest of alphabet}

     {Replace each vowel with -; update vowel and consonant sets.}
     for I := 1 to Length(NextLine) do
       begin
         NextChar := GetChar(NextLine, I);  {Get next character}
         NextChar := Cap(NextChar);
         if NextChar in AllVowels then
           begin  {vowel}
             Vowels := Vowels + [NextChar];       {insert vowel}
             PutChar (NextLine, I, NewChar)       {replace vowel}
           end  {vowel}
         else if NextChar in AllConsonants then
           Consonants := Consonants + [NextChar]   {add consonant}
       end  {for}
   end;  {Classify}
```

```
begin  {OutVowels}
   Rewrite (Scratch);                          {prepare Scratch for output}
   Consonants := [];   Vowels := [];                   {initialize sets}

   {Print user instructions.}
   WriteLn ('Enter each line of the text phrase.');
   WriteLn ('Press an extra return when done.');

   {Read each line, convert it, and write it to Scratch.}
   ReadLnStrVar (Input, NextLine);             {get the first line}
   while Length(NextLine) <> 0 do
      begin
         {Replace vowels with - and update Consonants and Vowels.}
         Classify (NextLine, Consonants, Vowels);

         {Write converted line to scratch file.}
         WriteString (Scratch, NextLine);
         WriteLn (Scratch);                     {insert <eoln>}
         ReadLnStrVar (Input, NextLine)         {get the next line}
      end  {while}
end;  {OutVowels}
```

The length of the input line controls repetition of the `while` loop in procedure `OutVowels`. A length of zero indicates that the Return key was pressed twice. Each line is written to file `Scratch` after it is processed by procedure `Classify`.

The sets `AllVowels` and `AllConsonants` are defined in `Classify` as the set of all vowels and consonants, respectively. The assignment statement

```
AllConsonants := ['A'..'Z'] - AllVowels;   {rest of alphabet}
```

defines `AllConsonants` properly when the letters are consecutive characters. If this is not the case on your system, you may want to rewrite the set `['A'..'Z']`. (For example, in the EBCDIC code, use `['A'..'I','J'..'R','S'..'Z']`).

In `Classify`, the statements

```
Vowels := Vowels + [NextChar];             {insert vowel}
PutChar (NextLine, I, Minus)               {replace vowel}
```

insert a letter (`NextChar`) that is a vowel in the set `Vowels` and replace that letter with a minus sign in the string `NextLine`. A letter that is a consonant is inserted into the set `Consonants` by the statement

```
Consonants := Consonants + [NextChar]      {add consonant}
```

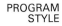

Use of Scratch Files

File `Scratch` is created by procedure `OutVowels` and echo printed by procedure `CopyFile`. Because it is completely processed during the execution of program Wheel, you don't need to retain file Scratch in second-ary storage after Wheel is finished. For this reason, the identifier Scratch was not listed as a file parameter in the program heading. Files that are defined only during the execution of a program are called *scratch*, or temporary, files. The space used by a scratch file on a disk can be reallo-cated after the program is finished.

It would have been just as easy to use an array of strings instead of a scratch file to store each line of the phrase being processed. We used a scratch file for two reasons: first, to demonstrate its use; second, because the number of lines in the input phrase is unknown. Because of limitations on available memory, it might be impossible to store a very long phrase in an array of strings; however, this is no problem if we use a scratch file.

Exercises for Section 14.2

Self-Check

1. In program Wheel, where are the vowels and consonants that are in the data phrase stored? How are they printed to the screen?
2. For program Wheel, discuss the changes that would be needed to save the phrase in an array of strings instead of a scratch file.

 ## 14.3 User-Defined File Types and Binary Files

In a text file, the individual components are characters from the Pascal character set. We can use the type constructor file to declare new file types whose components are any type, simple or structured, except for another file type.

■ Example 14.3

Program EchoFile in Fig. 14.6 creates and echo prints a file of integer values from 1 to 1000. The file type declaration

```
type
   NumberFile = file of Integer;
```

identifies NumberFile as a file type whose components are integer values. The file that is created, named Numbers, follows.

file Numbers

| 1 | 2 | 3 | 4 | 5 | 6 | ... | 999 | 1000 |

Figure 14.6 Program EchoFile

```
program EchoFile (Numbers, Output);

{Creates a file of integer values and echo prints it.}

  const
    NumInt = 1000;                    {number of integers in the file}

  type
    NumberFile = file of Integer;

  var
    Numbers : NumberFile; {file of integers}
    I,                        {loop control variable}
    NextInt : Integer;    {each integer read from file Numbers}
begin {EchoFile}
  {Create a file of integers.}
  Rewrite (Numbers);     {initialize Numbers to an empty file}
  for I := 1 to NumInt do
    Write (Numbers, I);  {write each integer to Numbers}

  {Echo print file Numbers.}
  Reset (Numbers);                        {prepare Numbers for input}
  while not EOF(Numbers) do
    begin
      Read (Numbers, NextInt); {read next integer into NextInt}
      WriteLn (Output, NextInt :4)              {display it}
    end  {while}
end. {EchoFile}
```

EchoFile begins by preparing file Numbers for output (the Rewrite statement). The for loop with loop-control variable I creates a file of integer values. The statement

```
    Write (Numbers, I);                  {write each integer to Numbers}
```

copies each value of I (1 to 1000) to file Numbers.

Next, file Numbers is prepared for input (the Reset statement). The while loop echo prints each value stored in Numbers until the end of file Numbers is reached (EOF(Numbers) is True). Within the loop, the statement

```
    Read (Numbers, NextInt);   {read next integer into NextInt}
```

reads the next file component (an integer value) into variable NextInt. The statement

```
    WriteLn (Output, NextInt :4)                      {display it}
```

displays this value on a separate line of the screen (system file Output). ∎

Comparison of Binary Files and Text Files

File Numbers is called a binary file. A *binary file* is a file that is created by the execution of a program and in which the internal representation of each component is stored directly. It is faster to process a binary file than a text file. For example, if the variable NextInt has the value 244, the statement

```
Write (Numbers, NextInt)
```

copies the internal binary representation of NextInt from memory to file Numbers. If your computer uses two bytes to store an integer value, the byte that stores the highest-order bits would contain all zeros and the byte that stores the lowest-order bits would contain the binary string 11110100 (244 = 128 + 64 + 32 + 16 + 4). Both bytes would be written to disk as the next file component.

Assuming OutFile is a text file, the statement

```
Write (OutFile, NextInt :4)
```

writes the value of NextInt to OutFile using four characters (four bytes). To do this, the computer must first convert the binary number in NextInt to the character string ' 244' and then write the binary code for the characters blank, 2, 4, and 4 to file OutFile. Obviously, it takes more time to do the conversion and copy each character than it does to copy the internal binary representation to disk. It also requires twice as much disk space to store four characters as it does to store the internal binary representation of the integer value (four bytes versus two).

There is another advantage to a binary file. Each time we write a Real value to a text file, the computer must convert this value to a character string, whose precision is determined by the format specification. This may result in a loss of accuracy.

As shown in Fig. 14.4, you can use the standard procedures Read and Write with binary files. The file name must be the first parameter. For the Read procedure, all variables in the input list must be the same type as the file components. For the Write procedure, each output expression must be the same type as the file components.

The Pascal system uses an <eof> to denote the end of a binary file; however, we will not show this indicator when we sketch a binary file. We can use the EOF function to test for the end of a binary file in the same way that it tests for the end of a text file. The file name must be passed as a parameter to the EOF function (for example, EOF(Numbers)).

Unlike text files, binary files cannot be segmented into lines. Consequently, the standard procedures ReadLn, WriteLn, and EOLN cannot be used with binary files.

In the next section, you will see that complete data structures (that is, records and arrays) can be read from binary files and written to binary files with a single Read or Write operation. This simplifies input/output considerably and makes it much more efficient. This, of course, is not possible with text files;

each array element or record field must be read or written separately. The only exception for text files is writing a packed array of characters.

File Type Declaration

Form: type *file type* = file of *component type*;

Example: type
```
        Item = record
                   ID : Integer;
                   Salary : Real
               end; {Item}
        ItemFile = file of Item;
```
Interpretation: A new type *file type* is declared whose components must be type *component type*. Any standard or previously declared data type, except for another file type or a structured type with a file type as one of its constituents, can be the component type.

Read Procedure (for Binary Files)

Form: Read (*infile*, *input list*)

Example: Read (NumberFile, NextInt)

Interpretation: The Read procedure reads one component of file *infile* into each variable in *input list* and then advances the file-position pointer to the next unread file component. The type of each variable must correspond to the component type for *infile*. The value of EOF (*infile*) must be False before the Read operation occurs.

Write Procedure (for Binary Files)

Form: Write (*outfile*, *output list*)

Example: Write (Numbers, NextInt, 500)

Interpretation: The Write procedure appends the value of each expression in *output list* to file *outfile*. The type of each expression must correspond to the component type for *outfile*.

Exercises for Section 14.3

Self-Check

1. Assume your computer uses four bytes to store a type Real value in memory. How many bytes would be required to store six Real numbers in a binary file? Answer the same question for a text file in which each number is written using the format specification :4:2. Are there any circumstances under which either of your answers might change?

2. Complete the following program. What does it do?

```
program Mystery (_____, _____, _____);
  type
    NumberType = file of _____;

  var
    Data : _____;
    OutData : _____;
    Next : Integer;

begin
  _____ (Data);
  _____ (OutData);
  while not EOF (_____) do
    begin
      Read (_____, Next);
      if Next < 50 then
        begin
          Write (_____, Next);
          WriteLn (_____, Next :2, ' Failed')
        end {if}
    end {while}
end. {Mystery}
```

 # 14.4   Files of Records

The components of a binary file can be any type, simple or structured, except for another file type. Often, the components of a binary file are records. This section looks at ways to create a binary file of records.

Creating a Binary File

Unlike a text file, a binary file cannot be created using an editor program. To create a binary file, we must write and run a program that repeats the following steps until the binary file is completed.

1. Read the data for the next file component from a text file (or the keyboard) and save it in memory.
2. Copy the internal binary representation from memory to the binary file.

After the program executes, the binary file is stored on disk and is available for further processing.

The process of creating a binary file with two records is illustrated in Fig. 14.7. The text file InData is read by program MakeBinary (see Fig. 14.8) which creates the binary file Employee. The data for each employee consisting of an ID number, hourly rate, and hours worked, appears on two lines of file InData. After MakeBinary reads an employee's data from InData into record OneEmp, the statement

```
Write (Employee, OneEmp);
```

Figure 14.7 Creating a Binary File with Two Records

File InData (text file)

1234<eoln>
3.50 50<eoln>
2335<eoln>
4.35 40<eoln><eof>

File Employee (binary file)

writes the resulting record to file Employee. Because InData is type Text, it has 26 components (all characters) and terminates with an <eof> (not counted). File Employee has only two components; each component is a record with three fields.

Figure 14.8 Program MakeBinary

```
program MakeBinary (InData, Employee);

{Creates a binary file of records.}

   type
     Item = record
              ID : Integer;
              Rate : Real;
              Hours : Integer
            end; {Item}
     ItemFile = file of Item;

   var
     InData : Text;          {input - text file}
     Employee : ItemFile;    {output - binary file}
     OneEmp : Item;          {each record}

begin
  Reset (InData);
  Rewrite (Employee);
  while not EOF(InData) do
```

```
      begin
        {Read next record}
        with OneEmp do
          begin
            ReadLn (InData, ID);
            ReadLn (InData, Rate, Hours)
          end; {with}
        Write (Employee, OneEmp)        {Write it to Employee}
      end  {while}
end. {MakeBinary}
```

■ Example 14.4

The program in Fig. 14.9 creates a binary file, Inventory, that represents the inventory of a bookstore. Each file component is a record of type Book, because Inventory is declared as type BookFile (file of Book). The information saved in each component consists of a four-digit stock number, the book's author and title (strings), the price, and the quantity on hand. The program also computes and prints the total value of the inventory.

   The main program calls procedure ReadBook to enter the data for each book from the terminal into record variable OneBook. ReadBook first reads the book's stock number. If the stock number is not the sentinel, ReadBook calls procedure ReadLnString (see Fig. 10.20) to read the author and title strings. After OneBook is defined, the statements

```
    Write (Inventory, OneBook);    {Copy the book to Inventory}
    InvValue := InvValue + OneBook.Price * OneBook.Quantity;
```

copy the internal, binary form of the entire record OneBook to file Inventory and update the inventory value.   ■

Figure 14.9   Creating a Bookstore Inventory File

```
program BookInventory (Inventory, Input, Output);
{
 Creates an inventory file, Inventory, from data entered at the
 terminal. Also computes and prints the total inventory value.
}
  const
    StrLength = 20;                     {size of each string}
    Sentinel = 9999;                    {sentinel stock number}

  type
    StockRange = 1111..9999;            {range of stock numbers}
    StringType = packed array [1..StrLength] of Char;
    Book = record
             StockNum : StockRange;
             Author,
             Title    : String20;
             Price : Real;
             Quantity : Integer
           end;  {Book}
    BookFile = file of Book;

  var
    Inventory : BookFile;                {the new inventory file}
```

```
OneBook : Book;                          {each book}
InvValue : Real;                         {value of inventory}


procedure ReadBook (var OneBook {output} : Book);
{
   Reads a book from the keyboard into OneBook.
   Pre : None
   Post: Data are read from the keyboard into each field of the
         record represented by parameter OneBook.
   Uses: ReadLnString
}
   var
      CurLength: Integer;                {length of a data string}

   {Insert procedure ReadLnString}

begin  {ReadBook}
   with OneBook do
      begin
         Write ('Stock number> ');    ReadLn (StockNum);
         if StockNum <> Sentinel then
            begin
               Write ('Author> ');
               ReadLnString (Input, StrLength, Author, CurLength);
               Write ('Title> ');
               ReadLnString (Input, StrLength, Title, CurLength);
               Write ('Price $');
               ReadLn (Price);
               Write ('Quantity> ');
               ReadLn (Quantity)
            end {if}
      end; {with}
   WriteLn
end;   {ReadBook}



begin   {BookInventory}
   Rewrite (Inventory);         {Prepare Inventory for output}
   InvValue := 0.0;             {Initialize inventory value}

   {Read and copy each book until done.}
   WriteLn ('Enter the data requested for each book.');
   WriteLn ('Enter a stock number of 9999 when done.');
   ReadBook (OneBook);                          {Read first book}
   while OneBook.StockNum <> Sentinel do
      begin
         Write (Inventory, OneBook);   {Copy the book to Inventory}
         InvValue := InvValue + OneBook.Price * OneBook.Quantity;
         ReadBook (OneBook)                      {Read next book}
      end;   {while}

   OneBook.StockNum := Sentinel;   {write sentinel record to file}
   Write (Inventory, OneBook);

   {Print inventory value.}
   WriteLn ('Inventory value is $', InvValue :4:2)
end. {BookInventory}

Enter the data requested for each book.
Enter a stock number of 9999 when done.
Stock Number> 1234
```

```
Author> Robert Ludlum
Title> The Parsifal Mosaic
Price $17.95
Quantity> 10

Stock Number> 7654
Author> Blaise Pascal
Title> Pascal Made Easy
Price $50.00
Quantity> 1

Stock Number> 9999

Inventory value is $229.50
```

The binary file created when the program in Fig. 14.9 is run is shown next. The last record serves as a sentinel. The StockNum field (value is 9999) is the only field of the sentinel record that has its value defined.

File Inventory

1234	7654	9999
Robert Ludlum	Blaise Pascal	?
The Parsifal Mosaic	Pascal Made Easy	?
17.95	50.00	?
10	1	?

Exercises for Section 14.4

Self-Check

1. Assume a real number uses four bytes and an integer uses two bytes. How many bytes are processed when a component of file Inventory is read or written? Answer the same question for file Employee in Fig. 14.7.
2. Why does it not matter that some of the fields of the sentinel record are not defined? Under what circumstances might this present a problem?
3. Write all the declarations necessary for a file whose components are student records, where each record consists of a student ID number and an array of five scores. Write a loop that reads each student's record from the file and displays the student's ID number and first score.
4. Redo exercise 3 assuming that there are ten students and each student record is an element of the array Class, which is stored as the only component of a binary file.

Programming

1. Write a procedure that resets file Inventory and displays each inventory record on the screen. Call procedure WriteOneRecord to display each record.
2. Write procedure WriteOneRecord.

14.5   File Merge Illustrated

Like most data structures, a file frequently needs to be modified or updated after it has been created. You may want to modify one or more fields of an existing record, delete a record, insert a new record, or simply display the current field values for a record.

Unlike a text file, a binary file cannot be modified with an editor. Instead, we must create a new file whose records are based on the original file. To do this, we must read each existing record, perhaps modify it, and then write it to the new file.

One kind of update operation is a *file merge*. In a file merge, we combine two files of the same type into a third file. If the records in the two original files are ordered according to a key field, the records in the new file must also be in order by key field.

 ## Case Study: Merging Files

Problem

Whenever our bookstore receives a new shipment of books, a file (Update) is prepared that describes the new shipment. To keep our inventory file (Inventory) up to date, we need a program to combine or merge the information on these two files, assuming the records on both files are the same type (Book).

Design Overview

Merging two files is a common data-processing operation. To perform this task efficiently (and most other tasks involving sequential files), we assume that the records on both files are in order by stock number. We also reserve the largest stock number (9999) as a special sentinel record always found at the end of each file.

Our task is to create a third file (NewInven) that contains all data appearing on the two existing files. If a stock number appears on only one of the files, then its corresponding record will be copied directly to NewInven. If a stock number appears on both files, then the data from file Update will be copied to NewInven, because that is the most recent information; however, the Quantity field of the record written to NewInven must be the sum of both Quantity fields (the quantity shipped plus the quantity on hand). The records on the new file must be in order by stock number.

Figure 14.10 illustrates the result of merging two small sample files. For simplicity, only the Stock and Quantity fields of all three files are shown. The only stock numbers appearing on all three files are 4234 and the sentinel stock number (9999). The original inventory file (Inventory) and the update file (Update) each contains four records (including the sentinel); the new inventory file (NewInven) contains six records (including the sentinel), in order by stock number. Records 1111 and 8955 are copied directly from file Inventory; rec-

Figure 14.10   Sample File Merge Operation

ords 6345 and 7789 are copied directly from file `Update`; and record 4234 is a combination of the data on files `Inventory` and `Update`.

The data requirements and algorithm for a `Merge` procedure are described next. Because we are writing a procedure, the type declarations, which should appear in the main program, would be similar to those in Fig. 14.9.

Data Requirements

Problem Inputs
The current inventory file (`Inventory : BookFile`)
The file of new books received (`Update : BookFile`)

Problem Outputs
The new inventory file (`NewInven : BookFile`)

Local Variables
The current record from `Inventory` (`InvenBook : Book`)
The current record from `Update` (`UpdateBook : Book`)

Initial Algorithm

1. Prepare files `Inventory` and `Update` for input and file `NewInven` for output.
2. Read the first record from `Inventory` into `InvenBook` and from `Update` into `UpdateBook`.
3. Copy all records that appear on only one input file to `NewInven`. If a record appears on both input files, sum both `Quantity` values before copying record `UpdateBook` to `NewInven`.

Refinements and Program Structure

Step 3 compares each pair of records stored in `InvenBook` and `UpdateBook`. Because the records on file `NewInven` must be in order by stock number, the record with the smaller stock number is written to `NewInven`. Another record is then read from the file containing the record just written, and the comparison process is repeated. If the stock numbers of `UpdateBook` and `InvenBook` are

Case Study: Merging Files, continued

the same (a record appears on both files), the new value of Update-Book.Quantity is computed, the modified record is written to NewInven, and the next records are read from both input files.

Step 3 Refinement

3.1 **while** there are more records to copy **do**
    3.2 **if** InvenBook.StockNum < UpdateBook.StockNum **then**
        3.3 Write InvenBook to NewInven and read the next
            record of Inventory into InvenBook.
      else if InvenBook.StockNum > UpdateBook.StockNum **then**
        3.4 Write UpdateBook to NewInven and read the next
            record of Update into UpdateBook.
      else
        3.5 Modify the Quantity field of UpdateBook, write
            UpdateBook to NewInven, and read the next record
            from Inventory and Update.
3.6 Write the sentinel record to NewInven.

Let's trace this step assuming InvenBook and UpdateBook initially contain the first file records.

Because 1111 is less than 4234, record InvenBook is copied to file NewInven (step 3.3) and the next record is read into InvenBook.

Now the stock numbers are equal, so the quantity fields are summed (step 3.5), the new record with stock number 4234 is written to file NewInven, and the next records are read into InvenBook and UpdateBook.

This time the record in UpdateBook is copied to NewInven (step 3.4), the next record is read into UpdateBook, and the merge continues.

What happens when the end of one input file is reached? The stock number for the current record of that file will be 9999 (the maximum), so each record read from the other input file will be copied directly to file NewInven. When the ends of both input files are reached, the while loop is exited and the sentinel record is written to file NewInven (step 3.6).

Figure 14.11 Structure Chart for Procedure Merge

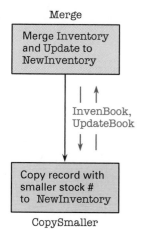

Procedure `CopySmaller` implements step 3.2 above. The structure chart for the `Merge` procedure is shown in Fig. 14.11.

Coding Procedure Merge

Procedure `Merge` is shown in Fig. 14.12. The only output displayed on the screen as a result of executing procedure `Merge` is the message `File merge completed`. After the procedure's execution, you may want to echo print file `NewInven`. You could do this by resetting file `NewInven` and then writing individual fields of each record to the screen. Once you are certain file `NewInven` is correct, you can use an operating system command to rename it `Inventory`. You could then use `Inventory` as the input inventory file and merge it with another `Update` file at a later time.

Figure 14.12 Procedure Merge

```
procedure Merge (var Inventory, Update {input} : BookFile;
                 var NewInven {output} : BookFile);
{
   Merges the data on files Inventory and Update to file NewInven.
   Pre : Files Inventory and Update are existing files ordered by
         stock number and ending with a sentinel stock number.
   Post: Each record appearing in only Inventory or Update
         is copied to NewInventory. If a stock number appears in
         both files, the Quantity fields are summed and the
         remaining fields are copied from Update. File NewInven
         is in order by stock number and ends with the sentinel.
}
   var
      InvenBook,               {current record of file Inventory}
```

```
    UpdateBook : Book;          {current record of file Update}

procedure CopySmaller (var InvenBook,
                           UpdateBook {input/output} : Book;
                       var Inventory, Update, {input}
                           NewInventory {output} : BookFile);
{
 Writes the next record to file NewInven using data in
 InvenBook and UpdateBook. Also reads a new record from
 Inventory into InvenBook or from Update into UpdateBook or both
 to replace the record(s) that were written.
 Pre : InvenBook and UpdateBook are defined, and files
       Inventory and Update are opened for input and file
       NewInven is opened for output.
 Post: The record with the smaller StockNum field is written to
       NewInven and new data are read into that record. If both
       records have the same StockNum value, the Quantity fields
       are summed in UpdateBook, the modified record is written,
       and new records are read from both input files.
}
begin   {CopySmaller}
   if InvenBook.StockNum < UpdateBook.StockNum then
      begin {<}
         Write (NewInven, InvenBook);        {copy InvenBook}
         Read (Inventory, InvenBook)
      end   {<}
    else if InvenBook.StockNum > UpdateBook.StockNum then
      begin {>}
         Write (NewInven, UpdateBook);       {copy UpdateBook}
         Read (Update, UpdateBook)
      end {>}
    else
      begin {=}
         UpdateBook.Quantity := UpdateBook.Quantity +
                                  InvenBook.Quantity;
         Write (NewInven, UpdateBook);        {copy new UpdateBook}
         Read (Inventory, InvenBook);         {read both records}
         Read (Update, UpdateBook)
      end   {=}
  end;   {CopySmaller}


begin {Merge}
   {Prepare Inventory and Update for input, NewInven for output.}
   Reset (Inventory);  Reset (Update);  Rewrite (NewInven);

   {Read the first record from Inventory and Update.}
   Read (Inventory, InvenBook);  Read(Update, UpdateBook);

   {Copy all records from file Inventory and Update to NewInven.}
   while not EOF(Update) or not EOF(Inventory) do
      CopySmaller (InvenBook, UpdateBook, Inventory,
                   Update, NewInven);

   {Write the sentinel record to NewInven.}
   Write (NewInven, InvenBook);
   WriteLn ('File merge completed')
end;   {Merge}
```

You can adapt the merge procedure to perform other update operations. For example, you could merge a file that represents the daily sales of all books (file `Sales`) with file `Inventory` to generate an updated inventory file at the end of each day. If the quantity field of each record in file `Sales` is subtracted from the quantity field of the corresponding record in file `Inventory`, the difference would represent the quantity remaining in stock. You could even delete records whose quantity fields became negative or zero by simply not copying such records to `NewInven`.

Analysis of the Merge Procedure

A number of questions arise about the merge procedure shown in Fig. 14.12. For example, what happens if an input file is empty or contains only the sentinel record? Because procedure `Merge` always reads at least one record, an execution error will occur if either input file is empty. If a file contains only the sentinel record, then only the sentinel record will be read from that file, and all the records in the other file will be copied directly to file `NewInven`. If both input files contain only the sentinel record, the `while` loop will be exited immediately, and only the sentinel record will be copied to file `NewInven` after loop exit.

Finally, we must ask about the efficiency of the merge procedure when the end of one file is reached much sooner than the other. This imbalance would result in the stock number 9999 being repeatedly compared to the stock numbers on the file that is not yet finished. It would be more efficient to exit the `while` loop when the end of one file is reached, then copy all remaining records on the other file directly to file `NewInven`. This modification is left as an exercise at the end of this section.

Testing

To test the merge procedure, provide files that contain only the sentinel record as well as files with one or more actual records. Make sure that the merge procedure works properly regardless of which of the two input files has all its records processed first. Also make sure that there is exactly one sentinel record on the merged file.

Exercises for Section 14.5

Self-Check

1. In procedure `Merge`, what three important assumptions are made about the two files that are merged? Must the two input files have the same number of records?
2. What happens if a record from one input file has the same stock number as

a record from the other input file? What happens if one input file has two consecutive records with the same stock number?

Programming

1. Modify procedure `Merge` assuming that its input files do not contain a sentinel record. In this case, there should not be a sentinel record on the merged file. Exit from the merge loop when the end of either file is reached and then copy the remaining records from the unfinished file.

 14.6   Searching a Data Base

Computerized matching of data against a file of records is becoming a common practice. For example, many real estate companies maintain a large file of property listings; a realtor can process the file to locate desirable properties for a client. Similarly, computerized dating services maintain a file of clients from which compatible matches can be made.

These large files of data are called *data bases*. In this section we will write a program that searches a data base to find all records that match a proposed set of requirements.

 Case Study: Data Base Inquiry

Problem

One reason for storing the bookstore inventory as a computer file is to facilitate answering questions regarding that data base. Some questions of interest might be

- What books by Robert Ludlum are in stock?
- What books in the price range $5.95 to $8.00 are in stock?
- What is the stock number of the book *Pascal Made Easy* and how many copies are in stock?
- What books costing more than $25 are in stock in quantities greater than 10?

These questions and others can be answered if we know the correct way to ask them.

Design Overview

A data base inquiry program has two phases: setting the search parameters and searching for records that satisfy the parameters. In our program, we will assume that all the record fields can be involved in the search. The program user must enter low and high bounds for each field. Let's illustrate how we might set the search parameters to answer this question:

What are the books by Tennyson that cost less than $11 and for which two or more copies are in stock?

Assuming that there are never more than 5,000 copies of a book in stock and that the price of any book does not exceed $1,000, we can use this sample dialogue to set the search parameters.

```
Enter the low bound for stock number or 1111: 1111
Enter the high bound for stock number or 9999: 9999
Enter the low bound for author name or AAA: Tennyson
Enter the high bound for author name or zzz: Tennyson
Enter the low bound for title or AAA: AAA
Enter the high bound for title or zzz: zzz
Enter the low bound for price or $0: $0
Enter the high bound for price or $1000: $10.99
Enter the low bound for quantity or 0: 2
Enter the high bound for quantity or 5000: 5000
```

Data Requirements

Problem Inputs
The search parameter bounds (`Params : SearchParams`)
The inventory file (`Inventory : BookFile`)

Problem Outputs
All books that satisfy the search parameters

Initial Algorithm
1. Prepare file `Inventory` for input.
2. Enter the search parameters.
3. Display all books that match the parameters.

Refinements and Program Structure
To simplify parameter passing between the procedures that implement steps 1 and 2, we store the search parameters in record variable `Params` (type `SearchParams`). The structure chart for the data base inquiry problem is shown in Fig. 14.13.

Figure 14.13 Structure Chart for Data Base Inquiry Problem

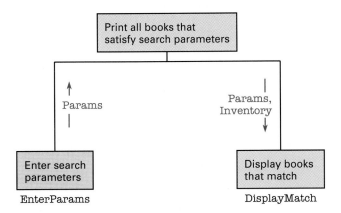

Params

Params,
Inventory

EnterParams

DisplayMatch

Case Study: Data Base Inquiry, continued

Coding the Main Program
The main program is shown in Fig. 14.14.

Figure 14.14 Main Program for Data Base Inquiry Problem

```
program Inquire (Inventory, Input, Output);
{
  Prints all books that satisfy the search parameters specified
  by the program user.
}

  const
    StrLength = 20;                      {size of each string}
    MaxQuantity = 5000;                  {maximum quantity}
    MaxPrice = 1000.00;                  {maximum book price}
    MinStock = 1111;                     {minimum stock number}
    MaxStock = 9999;                     {maximum stock number}

  type
    StringType = packed array [1..StrLength] of Char;
    StockRange = MinStock..MaxStock;
    Book = record
             StockNum : StockRange;      {four digit stock number}
             Author,
             Title   : StringType;
             Price : Real;
             Quantity : Integer
           end;  {Book}

    BookFile = file of Book;

    SearchParams = record               {search parameter bounds}
                     LowStock, HighStock : StockRange;
                     LowAuthor, HighAuthor,
                     LowTitle, HighTitle   : StringType;
                     LowPrice, HighPrice : Real;
                     LowQuant, HighQuant : Integer
                   end; {SearchParams}
  var
    Inventory : BookFile;                {the inventory file}
    Params : SearchParams;               {the search parameters}


  procedure EnterParams (var Params {output} : SearchParams);
  {
   Enters the search parameters and validates them.
   Pre : None
   Post: Returns the low bound and high bound for each search
         parameter though Params. The low bound for a parameter
         must be <= the high bound and both bounds must be in
         range.
   Uses: ReadLnString (see Fig. 10.20)
  }
  begin  {EnterParams stub}
    WriteLn ('Procedure EnterParams entered.')
  end;  {EnterParams}
```

```
procedure DisplayMatch (var Inventory {input} : BookFile;
                            Params {input} : SearchParams);
  {
  Displays all records of Inventory that satisfy search
  parameters.
  Pre : File Inventory is opened for input and Params is defined.
  Post: An inventory record is displayed if its field values are
        within the bounds specified by record Params.
  }
  begin  {DisplayMatch}
    WriteLn ('Procedure DisplayMatch entered.')
  end;  {DisplayMatch}


begin  {Inquire}
  {Prepare Inventory for input.}
  Reset (Inventory);

  {Enter the search parameters.}
  EnterParams (Params);

  {Display all books that match the search parameters.}
  DisplayMatch (Inventory, Params)
end. {Inquire}
```

Coding the Procedures

Procedure `EnterParams` is left as an exercise at the end of this section. Procedure `DisplayMatch` must examine each file record with a stock number between the low and high bounds for stock numbers. If a record satisfies the search parameters, it is displayed. `DisplayMatch` should also print a message if no matches are found. The local variables and algorithm for procedure `DisplayMatch` follow.

Local Variables for DisplayMatch
The current book (`NextBook : Book`)
A program flag indicating whether or not there are any matches
(`NoMatches : Boolean`)

Algorithm for DisplayMatch
1. Advance to the first record whose stock number is within range.
2. Initialize `NoMatches` to `True`.
3. `while` the current stock number is still in range `do`
     `begin`
         4. `If` the search parameters match `then`
         5. Display the book and set `NoMatches` to `False`.
         6. Read the next book record.
     `end`
7. `if` there are no matches `then`
     8. Print a `no books available` message

Case Study: Data Base Inquiry, continued

Figure 14.15   Structure Chart for DisplayMatch

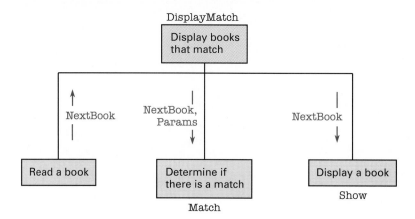

The structure chart for `DisplayMatch` is shown in Fig. 14.15. The Boolean function `Match` implements step 3; procedure `Show` implements step 4. The program is shown in Fig. 14.16.

Figure 14.16   Procedure DisplayMatch

```
procedure DisplayMatch (var Inventory {input} : BookFile;
                            Params {input} : SearchParams);
{
  Displays all records of Inventory that satisfy search
  parameters.
  Pre : File Inventory is opened for input and Params is defined.
  Post: An inventory record is displayed if its field values are
        within the bounds specified by record Params.
}
  var
    NextBook : Book;       {the current record}
    NoMatches : Boolean;   {indicates if there were any matches}


  function Match (NextBook : Book;
                  Params : SearchParams) : Boolean;
  {
   Determines whether record NextBook satisfies all search
   parameters.
   Pre : NextBook and Params are defined.
   Post: Returns True if all parameters are matched; otherwise,
         returns False.
  }
    var
      Matched : Boolean;                          {local Boolean flag}

  begin  {Match}
    with Params do
      begin
        Matched := (LowAuthor <= NextBook.Author)
                   and (NextBook.Author <= HighAuthor);
```

```
              Matched := Matched and (LowTitle <= NextBook.Title)
                          and (NextBook.Title <= HighTitle);
              Matched := Matched and (LowPrice <= NextBook.Price)
                          and (NextBook.Price <= HighPrice);
              Matched := Matched and (LowQuant <= NextBook.Quantity)
                          and (NextBook.Quantity <= HighQuant)
        end;  {with}

     {Define function result.}
     Match := Matched
   end;  {Match}

   procedure Show (var NextBook {input} : Book);
   {
     Displays each field of NextBook at the terminal. Leaves a
     line space after each book.
     Pre : NextBook is defined.
     Post: All fields of NextBook are displayed.
   }
   begin  {Show stub}
     WriteLn ('Procedure Show entered.');
     WriteLn ('Stock number is ', NextBook.StockNum :1)
   end;  {Show}


begin  {DisplayMatch}
   {
    Advance to first record with a stock number greater than
    or equal to the lower bound.
   }
   Read (Inventory, NextBook);
   while not EOF(Inventory) and
         (Params.LowStock > NextBook.StockNum) do
     Read (Inventory, NextBook);

   {assert: end of file reached or NextBook.StockNum in range}
   {Display each book that satisfies the search parameters.}
   NoMatches := True;              {assume no matches to start}
   WriteLn ('Books that satisfy the search parameters follow.');
   while (NextBook.StockNum <= Params.HighStock)
             and not EOF(Inventory) do
     {invariant:
         each record that matches the parameters is displayed and
         no record with stock number > Params.HighStock was
         processed and the file position pointer has not passed
         the end of file.
     }
     begin
       if Match(NextBook, Params) then
         begin
           NoMatches := False;        {signal a match}
           Show (NextBook)            {print matched record}
         end; {if}
       Read (Inventory, NextBook)     {read the next record}
     end; {while}

   {assert: all records in range searched or at end of file}
   if NoMatches then
     WriteLn ('Sorry, no books are available.')
end;  {DisplayMatch}
```

In function `Match`, a local Boolean variable, `Matched`, indicates whether or not each search parameter is satisfied. Four assignment statements—one for each parameter except stock number—assign a value to `Matched`. If a search parameter is not satisfied, its corresponding assignment statement sets `Matched` to `False`. Because `Matched` is "anded" with the result of each parameter test, once `Matched` is set to `False`, it remains `False`. Consequently, for the function result to be `True`, `NextBook` must satisfy all search parameters.

Testing

Before you can test the data base program, you have to create a binary file using program `BookInventory` (see Fig. 14.9). Make sure you provide search requests that are not satisfied by any file records as well as requests that are. If you specify the maximum range for each search parameter, the program should display all records of the binary file. After a request is satisfied, verify that you can eliminate one or more of the records displayed by narrowing the search parameters.

Exercises for Section 14.6

Self-Check

1. Write the search parameters needed to answer the questions listed at the beginning of this section.
2. Which procedure or function determines whether a particular record matches the search parameters? What procedure or function displays each record that matches the search parameters?
3. How does Boolean variable `Matched` work in function `Match`? Why is it not necessary to test field `StockNum` in function `Match`?

Programming

1. Write procedures `EnterParams` and `Show` described in the data base inquiry problem.

 ## 14.7 File Buffer Variable

Unlike other Pascal data structures, a file is located in secondary storage rather than main memory. For this reason, it is less convenient to access data stored in a file. The file component must first be transferred into main memory (by a `Read` operation) before the data in that component can be manipulated.

To simplify file access, Pascal allocates within main memory a *file-buffer variable* for each file declared in a program. The buffer variable acts as a "window" through which file data can be accessed. The buffer variable for a data file contains a copy of the file component currently selected by the file-position pointer. During a file read, as the file-position pointer moves, the file-buffer variable is automatically updated.

We can access a file's records through its buffer variable. Using the buffer variable is more efficient because it eliminates the need to allocate memory space for a record variable that stores the current file record (for example, record NextBook in Fig. 14.16). It also saves the processing time required to copy the current file record into that record variable.

We denote the file buffer variable by writing the file name followed by an arrow (↑) or a caret (^), depending on the Pascal system. Therefore, Inventory↑ and Inventory^ represent the file-buffer variable for file Inventory. The field selector Inventory^.Author may look strange, but it correctly references the Author field of the file-buffer variable. The with statement

```
with Inventory^ do
   begin
      WriteLn ('Stock number of book sold is ', StockNum :4);
      Quantity := Quantity - 1;
      SalesTotal := SalesTotal + Price
   end
```

manipulates the StockNum, Price, and Quantity fields of the record currently in the file-buffer variable for file Inventory.

Get and Reset

The Reset operator moves the file-position pointer to the beginning of a file. It also initializes the file-buffer variable for that file. The effect of the statement

```
Reset (Inventory)
```

follows:

As indicated, the Reset operation moves the file-position pointer to the first file record and copies the data in that record to the file-buffer variable Inventory^. The statement

```
Get (Inventory)
```

advances the file-position pointer to the next file component and automatically updates the file-buffer variable, as shown next.

File-position pointer

When the file-position pointer is at the last file component, the next Get operation causes the buffer variable to become undefined, and EOF(Inventory) becomes True.

SYNTAX
DISPLAY

> ### Reset Procedure (Effect on File Buffer Variable)
> **Form:**   Reset (*infile*)
> **Example:** Reset (Inventory)
> **Interpretation:** The file-position pointer for file *infile* is moved to the beginning of file *infile*. The first file component is stored in the file-buffer variable *infile^*.
> **Note:** The Reset operation is automatically performed on system file Input, so Reset (Input) is not needed and may cause an error on some Pascal systems.

SYNTAX
DISPLAY

> ### Get Operator
> **Form:** Get (*infile*)
> **Interpretation:** The file-position pointer for file *infile* is advanced, and the next file component is stored in the file-buffer variable *infile^*.
> **Note:** The effect of the Get operation is undefined if EOF(*infile*) is True before or after the Get is executed. The first Get must be preceded by a Reset operation (except for system file Input).

Put and Rewrite

We write a file in Pascal by appending data to the end of the file. Data stored in a file-buffer variable can be appended using the Put operator. Whenever the statement

    Put (*outfile*)

is executed, the current contents of the file-buffer variable *outfile^* are appended to the end of file *outfile*. The data to be transferred must be stored in the file-buffer variable *outfile^* before the Put is executed. The statement

    Rewrite (*outfile*)

must be executed before the first Put operation.

■ **Example 14.5**
Procedure `BuildSmall` in Fig. 14.17 creates an abbreviated inventory file,
`SmallInv`, that consists only of the stock number and quantity of every record
in file `Inventory`. You must declare file types `BookFile` and `SmallBookFile` in
the calling program. There is no need to declare record variables for storing
the current record of each of these files.

Figure 14.17   Procedure BuildSmall

```
procedure BuildSmall (var Inventory {input} : BookFile;
                          var SmallInv {output} : SmallBookFile);
{
  Creates a new inventory file (SmallInv) containing only stock
  numbers and quantities of the records in Inventory.
  Pre : Inventory is defined.
  Post: SmallInv contains a smaller version of each record in
        Inventory.
}
begin {BuildSmall}
  {Initialize buffer variable for Inventory and open SmallInv.}
  Reset (Inventory);
  Rewrite (SmallInv);

  {Copy stock number and quantity from Inventory to SmallInv.}
  while not EOF(Inventory) do
    begin
      {Define buffer variable SmallInv^.}
      SmallInv^.StockNum := Inventory^.StockNum;
      SmallInv^.Quantity := Inventory^.Quantity;
      Put (SmallInv);                {Append data to SmallInv}
      Get (Inventory)                {Access next record}
    end  {while}
end;  {BuildSmall}
```

Each assignment statement

```
SmallInv^.StockNum := Inventory^.StockNum;
SmallInv^.Quantity := Inventory^.Quantity;
```

copies one field from the file-buffer variable for `Inventory` to the file-buffer
variable for `SmallInv`. The statement

```
Put (SmallInv);                {Append data to SmallInv}
```

appends the data just copied to file `SmallInv`; the statement

```
Get (Inventory);                {Access next record}
```

updates the file-buffer variable for `Inventory` so that it contains the next
record. ■

Rewrite Procedure (Effect on File Buffer Variable)

Form: Rewrite (*outfile*)
Example: Rewrite (SmallInv)

Interpretation: The file-position pointer for file *outfile* is returned to the beginning of file *outfile*, thereby erasing any data that might be stored on the file. The file-buffer variable *outfile^* becomes undefined. The Rewrite operation is automatically performed on system file Output, so it is not needed, and Rewrite (Output) may cause an error on some Pascal systems.

Put Operator

Form: Put (*outfile*)
Example: (Put (SmallInv)
Interpretation: The contents of the file-buffer variable *outfile^* are appended to the end of file *outfile*. The file-buffer variable must be defined before the Put operation; it becomes undefined after the Put operation.
Note: The first Put operation must be preceded by a Rewrite operation (except for system file Output).

Get and Put versus Read and Write

Get and Read both can access data stored in a file. The Read procedure enters the current file component into a local variable of the same type. The statement

```
Read (Inventory, NextBook)
```

stores the next component of file Inventory in the variable NextBook and advances the file-position pointer for Inventory.

A local variable is not needed with Get because the data in the file-buffer variable can be accessed directly. However, you can still use Get to store data in a local variable. The statements

```
NextBook := Inventory^;
Get (Inventory)
```

have the same effect as the preceding Read statement; the current file component (stored in Inventory^) is copied into NextBook, and the file-position pointer is advanced.

The statement

```
Write (NewInven, NextBook)
```

writes the data stored in variable NextBook to file NewInven. This can also be accomplished using the statements

```
NewInven^ := NextBook;
Put (NewInven)
```

The assignment statement defines the file-buffer variable NewInven^; the Put operation appends these data to the end of file NewInven.

Self-Check

1. Complete the following program segment. What does it do?

```
program Mystery (_____, _____);
  type
    NumberFile = file of Integer;

  var
    Next : Integer;
    InFile, OutFile : _____;

begin
  Reset (_____);
  Rewrite (_____);
  while not EOF(_____) do
    begin
      _____^ := 2 * _____^;
      Put (_____);
      Get (_____)
    end {while}
end. {Mystery}
```

2. How would you modify procedures Merge and CopySmaller (see Fig. 14.12) to use Get and Put instead of Read and Write? Manipulate the file-buffer variables directly instead of local variables UpdateBook and InvenBook.

Programming

1. Rewrite procedure BuildSmall to copy every other record of file Inventory to file SmallInv.

 # 14.8 Direct-Access Files (Optional)

The files processed so far in this chapter have been sequential files. This means that each operation is performed on every file record and that the records are processed in order, starting with the first one. Sequential files are perfectly adequate whenever a file-processing operation involves most of the records in a file. However, if we want to modify only a few records in a large file, it is wasteful and time-consuming to have to process every record in the file.

For this reason, several extended versions of Pascal provide operators that enable *direct access* or *random access* to a file. Direct access means that a program can access any file record at any time. A direct-access file is analogous to a large array stored on disk in that the records can be accessed in either sequential order or arbitrary order. With direct access, we can intermix read and write operations on the same file. With sequential access, we can either read all the records of a file or write all its records.

We cannot use an editor program to create a direct-access file. We must write a program that reads the data for a direct-access file from a text file (or the keyboard), stores this data in a record, and copies the record to the direct-access file. To access a particular file component, we must first move the file-position pointer to that component. Once the file-position pointer has been moved, a read or write operation can be performed.

The next few sections detail specifics of direct-access file processing in Turbo Pascal and Extended Pascal. You should read only the sections that pertain to the Pascal system you are using. If your Pascal system does not support direct-access files, skip these sections.

Direct-Access Files in Turbo Pascal

In Turbo Pascal, direct access is supported for any binary file but not for text files. If binary file Inventory (see Fig. 14.9) has been opened for input, the procedure call statement

```
Seek (Inventory, 9);
```

advances the file-position pointer for Inventory to record number 9. This is actually the tenth record, because the first record has record number 0. Function FileSize returns the number of records in a binary file. If there are twenty records in file Inventory (record numbers 0 through 19), the function designator FileSize(Inventory) returns 20.

■ Example 14.6

Procedure UpdateBook in Fig. 14.18 updates the record of file Inventory selected by parameter RecNum. The condition

```
(RecNum >= 0) and (RecNum < FileSize(Inventory))
```

is true if RecNum is in range. The statement

```
Seek (Inventory, RecNum);
```

moves the file-position pointer to record number RecNum just before the Read operation and just before the Write operation. It is necessary to execute this statement twice because the Read operation advances the file-position pointer to record RecNum + 1. ■

Figure 14.18   Procedure UpdateBook in Turbo Pascal

```
procedure UpdateBook (var Inventory {input/output} : BookFile;
                          RecNum,
                          Sales {input} : Integer);
{
  Updates record RecNum of file Inventory by subtracting the
  amount sold (Sales) from the Quantity field.
  Pre : Inventory is opened for input (using Reset)
        and RecNum and Sales are defined.
  Post: Quantity field of record RecNum is decremented by Sales.
}
  var
    OneBook : Book;        {record being updated}

begin {UpdateBook}
  if (RecNum >= 0) and (RecNum < FileSize(Inventory)) then
```

```
  begin
    Seek (Inventory, RecNum);          {Move to record RecNum}
    Read (Inventory, OneBook);
    OneBook.Quantity := OneBook.Quantity - Sales;   {Update}
    Seek (Inventory, RecNum);       {Return to record RecNum}
    Write (Inventory, OneBook)         {Write updated record}
  end
  else
    WriteLn ('Record number is out of range.')
end; {UpdateBook}
```

> **Seek Procedure**
>
> **Form:**   Seek (*iofile*, *recnum*)
> **Example:** Seek (Inventory, 10)
> **Interpretation:** The file-position pointer for binary file *iofile* is moved to record number *recnum*, where the first record has record number 0. Unpredictable results will occur if the value of *recnum* is less than 0 or greater than *n* for a file of *n* records. It is not advisable to perform two Seek operations without an intervening Read or Write.

> **FileSize Function**
>
> **Form:**   FileSize(*iofile*)
> **Example:** FileSize(Inventory)
> **Interpretation:** The FileSize function returns the number of records in binary file *iofile*.

Appending a Record in Turbo Pascal

In Turbo Pascal, the function designator FileSize(Inventory) returns the number of records in file Inventory. The statements

```
Seek (Inventory, FileSize(Inventory));
Write (Inventory, NewBook)
```

can be used to append a new record, NewBook, to the end of file Inventory. If there are *n* records in file Inventory, function FileSize returns *n*. Procedure Seek advances the file-position pointer to record number *n* or just past the last record (record number $n - 1$) in the current file. Procedure Write then writes NewBook to the end of the file.

Direct-Access Files in Extended Pascal

In extended Pascal, the file-type declaration for a direct-access file must include an index type. For example, the declarations

```
type
  Book = record
           ....
         end; {Book}

  DABookFile = file [1..100] of Book;

var
  DAInventory : DABookFile;
```

declare a direct-access file type `DABookFile`. A file of this type can have up to 100 records, indexed by the integers 1 through 100. Any ordinal type can be used as an index type.

You can process the records of file `DAInventory` in sequential order using any of the standard Pascal procedures and functions discussed earlier. Direct access of selected records of file `DAInventory` is also permitted with procedure `SeekUpdate`, which is part of extended Pascal. The procedure call statement

```
SeekUpdate (DAInventory, 10)
```

advances the file-position pointer for file `DAInventory` to record number 10 (the tenth record) and stores the contents of this record in the file-buffer variable `DAInventory^`. In extended Pascal, function `LastPosition` returns the number of records currently in direct-access file `DAInventory`.

■ Example 14.7

Procedure `UpdateBook` in Fig. 14.19 updates the record of direct-access file `DAInventory` selected by parameter `RecNum`. The condition

```
(RecNum >= 1) and (RecNum <= LastPosition(DAInventory))
```

is true if `RecNum` is in range. The statement

```
SeekUpdate (DAInventory, RecNum);
```

moves the file-position pointer to record number `RecNum` and copies that record to the file-buffer variable. After the file-buffer variable is modified, the `Put` statement replaces record number `RecNum` with the new contents of the file-buffer variable.   ■

Figure 14.19 Procedure UpdateBook in Extended Pascal

```
procedure UpdateBook (var DAInventory {input/output} : DABookFile;
                          RecNum {input} : Integer;
                          Sales {input} : Integer);
{
  Updates record RecNum of direct access file DAInventory by
  subtracting the amount sold (Sales) from the Quantity field.
  Pre : DAInventory is opened for input and RecNum and Sales
        are defined.
  Post: Quantity field of record RecNum is decremented by Sales.
}
begin {UpdateBook}
  if (RecNum >= 1) and (RecNum <= LastPosition(DAInventory)) then
    begin
      SeekUpdate (DAInventory, RecNum);
      {Modify the file buffer variable.}
```

```
      DAInventory^.Quantity := DAInventory^.Quantity - Sales;
      Put (DAInventory)                    {Replace record}
    end
  else
    WriteLn ('Record number is out of range.')
end; {UpdateBook}
```

Direct-Access-File Type Declaration

Form: type *dafile* = file *index type* of *component type*;
Example: type DAInventory = file [1..MaxSize] of Book;
Interpretation: The identifier *dafile* is associated with a direct-access file type. Each component of a file of type *dafile* has type *component type*. One file record corresponds to each value in *index type*. The first file record corresponds to the minimum value of *index type*; the last file record corresponds to the maximum value of *index type*.

SeekUpdate Procedure

Form: SeekUpdate (*iofile, recnum*)
Example: SeekUpdate (DAInventory, 10)
Interpretation: The file-position pointer for direct-access file *iofile* is moved to record number *recnum*, where *recnum* is an expression that is assignment compatible with the index type of file *iofile*. The first record in the file is selected when *recnum* takes on the smallest value in its range. Unpredictable results occur if the value of *recnum* is less than its minimum value or greater than its maximum value. The contents of record *recnum* are copied to the file buffer variable *iofile*^.

LastPosition Function

Form: LastPosition(*iofile*)
Example: LastPosition(DAInventory)
Interpretation: The LastPosition function returns the number of records currently stored in direct-access file *iofile*.

Appending a New Record to the End of a File in Extended Pascal

Use the procedure call statements

```
Extend (Inventory);
Write (Inventory, NewBook)
```

to append a new record, NewBook, to the end of file Inventory.

14.9   Common Programming Errors

File processing in any programming language tends to be difficult to master, and Pascal is no exception. Remember to declare a file variable for each file you process (except `Input` or `Output`). If the file is a permanent file that exists on disk or will be saved on disk, its file variable must appear in the program heading. All file types (except `Text`) must be declared as well.

Do not forget to prepare a file for input or output using the `Reset` or `Rewrite` procedure (except for system files `Input` and `Output`). If you rewrite an existing file, the data on that file may be lost. Make sure you do not inadvertently place the `Reset` or `Rewrite` statement in a loop. If you do, a `Read` operation in the loop will repeatedly read the first file component; a `Write` operation in the loop will repeatedly write the first file component.

You can use the `Read` or `ReadLn` procedure only after you have prepared a file for input. Similarly, you can use the `Write` or `WriteLn` procedure only after you have prepared a file for output. Be sure to specify the file name as the first procedure parameter; otherwise, the system file `Input` or `Output` is assumed. An attempt to read beyond end of file error occurs if a `Read` operation is performed when the file-position pointer for a file has passed the last file component. When you are using the `EOF` function to control a loop that is reading data from a file, don't forget to pass the file name to function `EOF`.

You can perform a number of operations with text files that you cannot perform with binary files, because binary files are not segmented into lines. You cannot use the `EOLN` function and `ReadLn` and `WriteLn` procedures with binary files. Also, you cannot create or modify a binary file using an editor program. A binary file must be created by running a program before it can be used.

You can access the current file component through the file-buffer variable. Avoid the common error of writing the operators that manipulate the file-buffer variable as Get (*infile*^) or Put (*outfile*^). The caret should be deleted and the operators written as Get (*infile*^) or Put (*outfile*^).

Chapter Review

The components of a file can be any simple or structured type except for another file type. The file type `Text` is predefined. Its components are the Pascal characters and a special character, `<eoln>`. The `EOLN` function can test for an `<eoln>`, and the `WriteLn` statement places one in a text file. If an `<eoln>` is read into a type `Char` variable, it is stored as a blank character.

When you process text files, sequences of characters are transferred between main memory and disk storage. The data type of a variable in an input list must be `Char`, `Integer`, `Real`, or a subrange of `Char` or `Integer`. The data type of an expression in an output list must be `Char`, `Integer`, `Real`, `Boolean`, a character string, or a subrange of

Char or Integer. Structured variables cannot appear in an input list or an output list for a text file.

In this chapter, you learned how to declare and manipulate binary files whose components may be any simple or structured type (except for another file type). We created a file of records and merged two files of records into a third file. We also searched a data base to retrieve file records that matched a specified set of search parameters.

Binary files do have an advantage in that an entire record can be transferred between a binary file and a variable in main memory. The variable involved in the data transfer must be the same type as the components of the binary file. Accessing the current file component through the file buffer variable eliminates the need for a separate variable in main memory. The operators Reset and Rewrite initialize the file-buffer variable. The operator Get retrieves the next file component and the operator Put appends the contents of the file-buffer variable to the end of its file.

Finally, we reviewed extensions to Pascal that permit direct access to files. We also showed you how to append a record to the end of a file.

New Pascal Constructs

The Pascal constructs introduced in this chapter are summarized in Table 14.1.

Table 14.1   Summary of New Pascal Constructs

Construct	Effect
File-Type Declaration	

`type`
`  DigitFile = file of Integer;`
 	
`var`
`  MoreDigits : DigitFile;`
`  MoreChars : Text;`
`  I : Integer;`
`  NextCh : Char;`
	Declares a file type `DigitFile` whose components are integers.
	`MoreDigits` is a file of type `DigitFile`.
	`MoreChars` is a file of type `Text`.

Reset and Rewrite Procedures	
`Reset (MoreDigits);` `Rewrite (MoreChars);`	`MoreDigits` is prepared for input. `MoreChars` is prepared for output.
Read and Write Procedures	
`Read (MoreDigits, I);` `WriteLn (MoreChars, 'number: ', I)`	The next integer is read from file `MoreDigits` into variable `I` (type `Integer`). A sequence of characters representing a string and the value of `I` are written to file `MoreChars`.
EOF Function	

`while not EOF(MoreDigits) do`
`  begin`
`    Read (MoreDigits, I);`
`    WriteLn (MoreChars, I)`
`  end  {while}`
	Every integer value on file `MoreDigits` is written as a sequence of characters on a separate line of file `MoreChars`.

Table 14.1 *continued*

Construct	Effect
EOLN Function	
```Reset (MoreChars);```	File MoreChars is prepared for input.
```while not EOLN(MoreChars) do```	Each character on the current line of file
``` begin```	MoreChars is read into NextCh and
``` Read (MoreChars, NextCh);```	displayed on the screen.
``` Write (NextCh)```	
``` end {while}```	
Get Operator	
```Reset (MoreDigits);```	The first integer in file MoreDigits is
```I := MoreDigits^```	placed in the file buffer variable and
```Get (MoreDigits);```	assigned to variable I. The second in-
```Write (MoreDigits^)```	teger is displayed.
Put Operator	
```Rewrite (MoreDigits);```	A new file MoreDigits is created whose
```MoreDigits^ := 99;```	first component is 99.
```Put (MoreDigits)```	

✓ *Quick-Check Exercises*

1. What data types can be read or written to a text file?
2. What data types can be read or written to a binary file?
3. Under what circumstances can a file variable not appear in the program heading? Under what circumstances can a file variable not appear in the variable declarations? Under what circumstances can a file type not appear in the type declarations?
4. When is it appropriate to pass a file as a value parameter to a procedure?
5. Comment on the correctness of this statement: It is more efficient to use a text file because the computer knows that each component is a single character that can be copied into a single byte of main memory; with a binary file, however, the size of the components may vary.
6. What limits the number of records that can be written to a file?
7. What limits the number of records that can be read from a file? How do you know when you have read them all?
8. What happens if the Reset operation is performed on a file that has just been created in a program? What happens if the Rewrite operation is performed on the same file?
9. How does the Pascal compiler know how big to make the file-buffer variable for a file?
10. The _____ operator stores the first file record in the _____ _____. The _____ operator stores the record pointed to by the _____ _____ _____ in the _____ _____ _____ and advances the _____ _____. The _____ operator copies the record in the _____ _____ _____ to the file and advances the _____ _____ _____.

1. Any of the standard data types (or a subrange thereof) except type Boolean can be read; any of the standard data types (or a subrange thereof) or a string can be written.

2. The file's component type, which is any simple or structured type that does not have a file type as one of its constituents.

3. When a file that is being written will not be retained as a permanent file after program execution. When the file is system file `Input` or `Output`. When the file type is type `Text`.

4. Never

5. The statement is not correct. It is true that two binary files may have components of different sizes, but the components of a particular file must all be the same data type and the same size. This size can be determined from the type declarations. Because no data conversions are necessary when you use binary files, binary files are more efficient than text files.

6. The only limit is the available space on disk.

7. The number of records that were written to the file when it was created. Use the `EOF` function to test for the end-of-file marker.

8. `Reset` prepares the file for input so we can echo print it if we want to check the records that were written. `Rewrite` wipes the file out.

9. The file-buffer variable is the same size as the file components, which can be determined from the type declarations.

10. The `Reset` operator stores the first file record in the file-buffer variable. The `Get` operator stores the record pointed to by the file-position pointer in the file-buffer variable and advances the file-position pointer. The `Put` operator copies the record in the file-buffer variable to the file and advances the file-position pointer.

Review Questions

1. What are three advantages to using files for input and output as opposed to the standard input (keyboard) and output (screen)?

2. Where are files stored?

3. Modify procedure `CopyFile` to write data to both the file `OutFile` and the system file `Output`.

4. Consider an `EmpStat` file (type `Text`) that contains records for up to fifteen employees. The data for each employee consist of the employee's name (maximum length, twenty characters), social security number (maximum length, eleven characters), gross pay for the week (real), taxes deducted (real), and the net pay (real) for the week. Each data item is on a separate line of file `EmpStat`. Write a program called `PayReport`, which will create a text file `ReportFile` with the heading line

```
NAME            SOC.SEC.NUM         GROSS      TAXES      NET
```

followed by two blank lines, then the pertinent information under each column heading. `ReportFile` should contain up to eighteen lines of information after `PayReport` is executed.

5. What is a scratch file?

6. What are the characteristics of a binary file?

7. Imagine for a moment that you are a college professor who uses a computerized system to maintain student records. Write the type and variable declaration for a file that will consist of multiple records of type `StudentStats`. The statistics kept on

each student are the GPA, Major, Address (consisting of Name, StreetAddress, City, State, and ZipCode), and ClassSchedule (consisting of up to six records of Class, each containing Description, Time, and Days fields). Use whatever variable types are appropriate for each field.

8. Explain the use and manipulation of a file-buffer variable.

9. What Pascal procedures advance the file-position pointer in a file being used for input?

10. Write a procedure PlaceLastName that will accept a file of names of the form *Lastname. Firstname* (example: Drend, Jane) and Put only the last name in the file LastOnly. Use ADT String (see Section 13.3) and its operators, two files whose components are type String, and process their file buffer variables.

Programming Projects

1. Assume you have a file of records, each containing a person's last name, first name, birth date, and sex. Create a new file of records containing only first names and sex. Also print out the complete name of every person whose last name begins with the letter A, C, F, or P through Z and who was born in a month beginning with the letter J.

2. Create separate files of saleswomen and salesmen in your furniture store. For each employee on these files, include an employee number (four digits), a name, and a salary. Each file should be in order by employee number. Merge these two files into a third file that also has a gender field containing one of the values in the type (Female, Male). After the file merge operation, find the average salary for all employees. Then search the new file and print a list of all female employees earning more than the average salary and a separate list of all male employees earning more than the average. Hint: You will have to search the new file once for each list.

3. Write a procedure that will merge the contents of three sorted files by ID number and write the merged data to an output file. The parameters to the procedure will be the three input files and the one output file. Data will be of the form

```
Data = record
        ID : Integer;
        Name : String;
        Length : Integer;
        Salary : Real
      end;
```

Assume there is no sentinel record and use procedures Get and Put. Test your procedure with some sample data.

4. Cooking recipes can be stored on a computer and, with the use of files, can be quickly referenced.

   a. Write a procedure that will create a text file of recipes from information entered at the terminal. The format of the data to be stored is

   (1) recipe type (Dessert, Meat, etc.)
   (2) subtype (for Dessert, use Cake, Pie, or Brownies)
   (3) name (for cake, German Chocolate)
   (4) number of lines in the recipe to follow
   (5) the actual recipe

   Items 1, 2, 3, and 4 should be on separate lines.

b. Write a procedure that will accept as parameters a file and a record of search parameters that will cause all recipes of a type, all recipes of a subtype, or a specific recipe to be written.

5. College football teams need a service to keep track of records and vital statistics. Write a program that will maintain this information on a file. An update file will be "posted" weekly against the master file of all team statistics to date, and all the records will be updated. All of the information in both files will be stored in order by ID number. Each master record will contain the team's ID number; team name; number of games won, lost, and tied; total yards gained by the team's offense; total yards gained by the other teams against this one; total points scored by this team; and total points scored by the other teams against this one.

   For this program, use the master file `Teams` and update `Teams` from file `Weekly`. Write the updated information to a file called `NewTeams`. In addition, each record of the weekly file should be echo printed. At the completion of processing the files, write a message indicating the number of weekly scores processed, the team that scored the most points, and the team with the most offensive yardage for this week.

6. Write a program that takes a master file of college football information and prints out teams that match a specified set of search parameters. The bounds on the search parameters could be presented in the format described in Section 14.6. Some information you might want to print: all teams with a won/lost percentage in a certain range; all teams within a certain range of points scored or scored upon; all teams with a certain range of yardage gained or given up; all teams with a certain number of games won, tied, or lost. (Note: The won/lost percentage is calculated by dividing number of games won by total games played; ties count as half a game won.)

7. Write a program that updates a file of type `Inventory` (see Section 14.4). Your program should be able to modify an existing record, insert a new record, and delete an existing record. Assume that the update requests are in order by stock number and that they have the form

```
type
   ChangeKind = (Delete, Insert, Modify);
   UpdateReq = record
                 case Change : ChangeKind of
                   Delete : (StockNumber : StockRange);
                   Insert : (NewBook : Book);
                   Modify : (ModBook : Book)
               end; {UpdateReq}
```

   Each update request should be read from a binary file. Only the stock number appears in an update request for a deletion. The new book record is supplied for a request to insert a record or to modify an existing record. Your program should also print an error message for invalid requests, such as an attempt to delete a record that does not exist, an attempt to insert a new record with the same stock number as an existing record, or an attempt to modify a record that does not exist.

Recursion

15

A recursive procedure or function is one that calls itself. This ability enables a recursive procedure to be repeated with different parameter values. You can use recursion as an alternative to iteration (looping). Generally, a recursive solution is less efficient, in terms of computer time, than an iterative one because of the overhead for the extra procedure calls. In many instances, however, the use of recursion enables us to specify a natural, simple solution to a problem that would otherwise be difficult to solve. For this reason, recursion is an important and powerful tool in problem solving and programming.

 ## 15.1 The Nature of Recursion

Problems that lend themselves to a recursive solution have the following characteristics:

- One or more simple cases of the problem (called *stopping cases*) have a simple, nonrecursive solution.
- The other cases of the problem can be reduced (using recursion) to problems that are closer to stopping cases.
- Eventually the problem can be reduced to stopping cases only, which are relatively easy to solve.

The recursive algorithms that we write generally consist of an `if` statement with this form:

> if the stopping case is reached then
>   Solve it
> else
>   Reduce the problem using recursion

Figure 15.1 illustrates this approach. Let's assume that for a particular problem of size N, we can split the problem into a problem of size 1, which we can solve (a stopping case), and a problem of size $N-1$. We can split the problem of size $N-1$ into another problem of size 1 and a problem of size $N-2$, which we can split further. If we split the problem N times, we end up with N problems of size 1, all of which we can solve.

■ Example 15.1

Consider how we might solve the problem of multiplying 6 by 3, assuming that we know the addition tables but not the multiplication tables. The problem of multiplying 6 by 3 can be split into the two problems:

1. Multiply 6 by 2.
2. Add 6 to the result of problem 1.

Because we know the addition tables, we can solve problem 2 but not problem 1. Problem 1, however, is simpler than the original problem. We can split it into two problems, 1.1 and 1.2, leaving us three problems to solve, two of which are additions.

Figure 15.1 Splitting a Problem into Smaller Problems

591

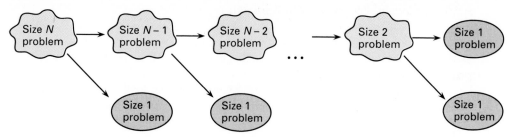

1.1 Multiply 6 by 1.
1.2 Add 6 to the result.

Even though we don't know the multiplication tables, we are familiar with the simple rule that, for any M, $M \times 1$ is M. By solving problem 1.1 (the answer is 6) and problem 1.2, we get the solution to problem 1 (the answer is 12). Solving problem 2 gives us the final answer, 18.

Figure 15.2 implements this approach to doing multiplication as the recursive Pascal function `Multiply` which returns the product, `M × N`, of its two arguments. The body of function `Multiply` implements the general form of a recursive algorithm shown earlier. The stopping case is reached when the condition `N = 1` is true. In this case, the statement

```
Multiply := M                    {stopping case}
```

ex .utes, so the answer is `M`. If `N` is greater than 1, the statement

```
Multiply := M + Multiply(M, N-1)   {recursive step}
```

executes, splitting the original problem into the two simpler problems:

1. Multiply `M` by `N-1`.
2. Add `M` to the result.

The first of these problems is solved by calling `Multiply` again with `N-1` as its second argument. If the new second argument is greater than 1, there will be additional calls to function `Multiply`.

Figure 15.2 Recursive Function Multiply

```
function Multiply (M, N : Integer) : Integer;
{
   Performs multiplication using + operator.
   Pre : M and N are defined and N > 0.
   Post: Returns M * N
}
begin {Multiply}
   if N = 1 then
      Multiply := M                        {stopping case}
   else
      Multiply := M + Multiply(M, N-1)     {recursive step}
end; {Multiply}
```

Note the two different uses of the identifier `Multiply` in the recursive step in Fig. 15.2. The first one assigns a value to `Multiply` representing the function result, while the second calls the function recursively. ∎

For now, you will have to take our word that function `Multiply` performs as desired. We will see how to trace the execution of a recursive function or procedure in the next section.

The next example illustrates how we might solve a difficult problem just by splitting it into smaller problems. You will see how to solve this problem after you have more experience using recursion.

∎ Example 15.2

The Towers of Hanoi problem involves moving a specified number of disks that are all different sizes from one tower (or peg) to another. Legend has it that the world will come to an end when the problem is solved for sixty-four disks. In the version of the problem shown in Fig. 15.3, there are five disks (numbered 1 through 5) and three towers or pegs (lettered A, B, and C). The goal is to move the five disks from peg A to peg C subject to the following rules:

1. Only one disk may be moved at a time, and this disk must be the top disk on a peg.
2. A larger disk can never be placed on top of a smaller disk.

The stopping cases of the problem involve moving only one disk (for example, "move disk 2 from peg A to peg C"). Simpler problems than the original would be to move four disks subject to the conditions above, to move three disks, and so on. Therefore, we want to split the original five-disk problem into one or more problems involving fewer disks. Let's consider splitting the original problem into three problems:

1. Move four disks from peg A to peg B.
2. Move disk 5 from peg A to peg C.
3. Move four disks from peg B to peg C.

Step 1 moves all disks but the largest to tower B, an auxiliary tower not mentioned in the original problem. Step 2 moves the largest disk to the goal tower, tower C. Step 3 then moves the remaining disks from B to the goal tower, where they will be placed on top of the largest disk. Let's assume that we can perform step 1 and step 2 (a stopping case); Fig. 15.4 shows the status of the

Figure 15.3 Towers of Hanoi

three towers after completion of these steps. At this point, it should be clear that we can solve the original five-disk problem if we can complete step 3.

Unfortunately, we still don't know how to perform step 1 or step 3. Both steps, however, involve four disks instead of five, so they are easier than the original problem. We should be able to split them into even simpler problems. Step 3 involves moving four disks from tower B to tower C, so we can split it into two three-disk problems and one one-disk problem:

3.1 Move three disks from peg B to peg A.
3.2 Move disk 4 from peg B to peg C.
3.3 Move three disks from peg A to peg C.

Figure 15.5 shows the towers after completion of steps 3.1 and 3.2. The two largest disks are now on peg C. Once we complete step 3.3, all five disks will be on peg C.

By splitting each N-disk problem into two problems involving N-1 disks and a one-disk problem, we eventually reach the point where all the cases involve only one disk, cases that we know how to solve. Later, we will write a Pascal program that solves the Towers of Hanoi problem. ∎

Exercises for Section 15.1

Self-Check

1. Show the problems that are generated by the function designator `Multiply(5, 4)`. Use a diagram similar to Fig. 15.1.
2. Show the problems that are generated when you attempt to solve the problem "Move two disks from peg A to peg C." Answer the same question for the problem "Move three disks from peg A to peg C." Draw a diagram similar to Fig. 15.1.

Figure 15.5 Towers of Hanoi after Steps 1, 2, 3.1, and 3.2

15.2 Tracing a Recursive Procedure or Function

Hand-tracing an algorithm's execution provides us with valuable insight as to how that algorithm works. We can also trace the execution of a recursive procedure or function. We illustrate how to do this with a recursive function and procedure.

Tracing a Recursive Function

In the last section, we wrote the recursive function `Multiply`. We can trace the execution of the function designator `Multiply(6, 3)` by drawing an *activation frame* that corresponds to each call of the function. An activation frame shows the parameter values for each call and summarizes its execution.

The three activation frames generated to solve the problem of multiplying 6 by 3 are shown in Fig. 15.6. The part of each activation frame that executes before the next recursive call is in color; the part that executes after the return from the next call is in gray. The darker the color of an activation frame, the greater the depth of recursion.

The value returned from each call is shown alongside each black arrow. The return arrow from each function call points to the operator **+**, because the addition is performed just after the return.

Figure 15.6 Trace of Function Multiply

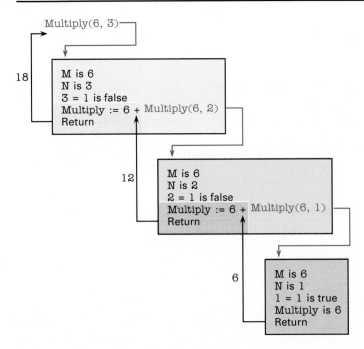

The figure shows that there are three calls to function `Multiply`. Parameter M has the value 6 for all three calls; parameter N has the values 3, 2, and finally 1. Because N is 1 in the third call, the value of M (6) is returned as the result of the third and last call. After the return to the second activation frame, the value of M is added to this result, and the sum (12) is returned as the result of the second call. After the return to the first activation frame, the value of M is added to this result, and the sum (18) is returned as the result of the original call to function `Multiply`.

Tracing a Recursive Procedure

▪ Example 15.3

Procedure `Palindrome` in Fig. 15.7 is a recursive procedure that reads in a string of length N and prints it out backward. (A *palindrome* is a string of characters that reads the same backward and forward.) If the procedure call statement

        Palindrome (5)

is executed, the five characters entered at the screen are printed in reverse order. If the characters abcde are entered when this procedure is called, the line

        abcdeedcba

appears on the screen. The letters in color are entered as data and the letters in black are printed. If the procedure call statement

        Palindrome (3)

is executed instead, only three characters are read, and the line

        abccba

appears on the screen.

Figure 15.7   Procedure Palindrome

```
procedure Palindrome (N : Integer);
{
  Displays a string of length N in
  reverse of the order in which it is entered.
  Pre : N is greater than or equal to one.
  Post: Displays N characters.
}
  var
    Next : Char;     {next data character}

begin {Palindrome}
  if N <= 1 then
    begin {stopping case}
      Read (Next);
      Write (Next)
    end {stopping case}
```

```
        else
          begin {recursion}
            Read (Next);
            Palindrome (N-1);
            Write (Next)
          end {recursion}
end; {Palindrome}
```

Like most recursive procedures, the body of procedure `Palindrome` consists of an `if` statement that evaluates a *terminating condition*, N <= 1. When the terminating condition is true, the problem has reached a stopping case: a data string of length 1. If N <= 1 is true, the `Read` and `Write` statements are executed.

If the terminating condition is false (N > 1), the recursive step (following `else`) is executed. The `Read` statement enters the next data character. The procedure call statement

```
        Palindrome (N-1);
```

calls the procedure recursively, with the parameter value decreased by one. The character just read is not displayed until later. This is because the `Write` statement comes after the recursive procedure call; consequently, the `Write` statement cannot be performed until after the procedure execution is completed and control is returned back to the `Write` statement. For example, the character that is read when N is 3 is not displayed until after the procedure execution for N equal to 2 is done. Hence, this character is displayed after the characters that are read when N is 2 and N is 1.

To fully understand this, trace the execution of the procedure call statement

```
        Palindrome (3)
```

The trace shown in Fig. 15.8 assumes the letters abc have been entered as data.

The trace shows three separate activation frames for procedure Palindrome. Each activation frame begins with a list of the initial values of N and Next for that frame. The value of N is passed into the procedure when it is called, because N is a value parameter; the value of Next is initially undefined, because Next is a local variable.

Figure 15.8   Trace of Palindrome (3)

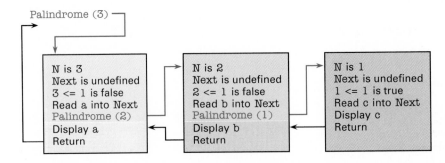

The statements that are executed for each frame are shown next. The statements in color are recursive procedure calls and result in a new activation frame, as indicated by the colored arrows. A procedure return occurs when the procedure end statement is reached. This is indicated by the word Return and a black arrow that points to the statement in the calling frame to which the procedure returns. Tracing the colored arrows and then the black arrows in Fig. 15.8 gives us the sequence of events listed in Fig. 15.9. To help you understand this list, all the statements for a particular activation frame are indented to the same column.

Figure 15.9   Sequence of Events for Trace of Palindrome (3)

Call Palindrome with N equal to 3.
   Read the first character (a) into Next.
   Call Palindrome with N equal to 2.
      Read the second character (b) into Next.
      Call Palindrome with N equal to 1.
         Read the third character (c) into Next.
         Display the third character (c).
         Return from third call.
      Display the second character (b).
      Return from second call.
   Display the first character (a).
   Return from original call.

As shown, there are three calls to procedure Palindrome, each with a different parameter value. The procedure returns always occur in the reverse order of the procedure calls; that is, we return from the last call first, then we return from the next to last call, and so on. After we return from a particular execution of the procedure, we display the character that was read into Next just prior to that procedure call. ■

Parameter and Local Variable Stacks

You may be wondering how Pascal keeps track of the values of N and Next at any given point. Pascal uses a special data structure called a *stack*, which is analogous to a stack of dishes or trays. Think of the countless times you have stood in line in a cafeteria. Recall that clean dishes are always placed on top of a stack of dishes. When we need a dish, we always remove the one most recently placed on the stack. This causes the next to last dish placed on the stack to move to the top of the stack. (The stack data structure is discussed further in Chapter 16.)

Similarly, whenever a new procedure call occurs, the parameter value associated with that call is placed on the top of the parameter stack. Also, a new cell whose value is initially undefined is placed on top of the stack that is maintained for the local variable Next. Whenever N or Next is referenced, the value at the top of the corresponding stack is always used. When a procedure return occurs, the value currently at the top of each stack is removed, and the value just below it moves to the top.

As an example, let's look at the two stacks right after the first call to Palindrome. There is one cell on each stack, as follows.

After first call to Palindrome

```
N          Next
| 3 |      | ? |
```

The letter a is read into Next just before the second call to Palindrome.

```
N          Next
| 3 |      | a |
```

After the second call to Palindrome, the number 2 is placed on top of the stack for N, and the top of the stack for Next becomes undefined again, as shown next. The value in color is at the top of each stack.

After second call to Palindrome

```
N          Next
| 2 |      | ? |
| 3 |      | a |
```

The letter b is read into Next just before the third call to Palindrome.

```
N          Next
| 2 |      | b |
| 3 |      | a |
```

However, Next becomes undefined again right after the third call.

After third call to Palindrome

```
N          Next
| 1 |      | ? |
| 2 |      | b |
| 3 |      | a |
```

During this execution of the procedure, the letter c is read into Next, and c is echo printed immediately because N is 1 (the stopping case).

```
N          Next
| 1 |      | c |
| 2 |      | b |
| 3 |      | a |
```

The procedure return causes the values at the top of the stack to be removed, as shown next.

```
  N         Next
 ┌───┐     ┌───┐
 │ 2 │     │ b │
 │ 3 │     │ a │
 └───┘     └───┘
```

Because control is returned to a `Write` statement, the value of `Next` (b) at the top of the stack is then displayed. Another return occurs, causing the values currently at the top of the stack to be removed.

After second return

```
  N         Next
 ┌───┐     ┌───┐
 │ 3 │     │ a │
 └───┘     └───┘
```

Again, control is returned to a `Write` statement, and the value of `Next` (a) at the top of the stack is displayed. The third and last return removes the last pair of values from the stack, and N and `Next` both become undefined.

After third return

```
  N         Next
 ┌───┐     ┌───┐
 │ ? │     │ ? │
 └───┘     └───┘
```

Chapter 16 shows you how to declare and manipulate stacks yourself. Because these steps are all done automatically by Pascal, we can write recursive procedures without worrying about the stacks.

Implementation of Parameter Stacks in Pascal

For illustrative purposes, we have used separate stacks for N and `Next` in our discussion; the compiler, however, actually maintains a single stack. Each time a call to a procedure or function occurs, all its parameters and local variables are pushed onto the stack along with the memory address of the calling statement. The latter gives the computer the return point after execution of the procedure or function. Although multiple copies of a procedure's parameters may be saved on the stack, only one copy of the procedure body is in memory.

Exercises for Section 15.2

Self-Check

1. Why is N a value parameter in Fig. 15.7?
2. Assume the characters `*+-/` are entered for the procedure call statement

   ```
   Palindrome (4)
   ```

   What output line would appear on the screen? Show the contents of the stacks immediately after each procedure call and return.

3. Trace the execution of `Multiply(5, 4)` and show the stacks after each recursive call.

 ## 15.3   Recursive Mathematical Functions

Many mathematical functions are defined recursively. An example is the factorial of a number n ($n!$).

- $0!$ is 1
- $n!$ is $n \times (n-1)!$, for $n > 0$

Thus, $4! = 4 \times 3! = 4 \times 3 \times 2!$, and so on. It is easy to implement this definition as a recursive function in Pascal.

■ Example 15.4

Function `Factor` in Fig. 15.10 computes the factorial of its argument `N`. The recursive step

```
Factor := N * Factor(N-1)
```

implements the second line of the factorial definition. This means that the result of the current call (argument `N`) is determined by multiplying the result of the next call (argument `N–1`) by `N`.

Figure 15.10   Recursive Function Factor

```
function Factor (N : Integer) : Integer;
{
  Computes the factorial of N (N!).
  Pre : N is defined and N >= 0.
  Post: Returns N!
}
begin {Factor}
  if N = 0 then
    Factor := 1
  else
    Factor := N * Factor(N-1)
end;  {Factor}
```

A trace of

```
Fact := Factor(3)
```

is shown in Fig. 15.11. The value returned from the original call, `Factor(3)`, is 6, and this value is assigned to `Fact`. Be careful when you use the factorial function; its value increases rapidly and could lead to an integer-overflow error (for example, `10!` is `24320`). ■

Although the recursive implementation of function `Factor` follows naturally from its definition, this function can be implemented easily using iteration. The iterative version is shown in Fig. 15.12.

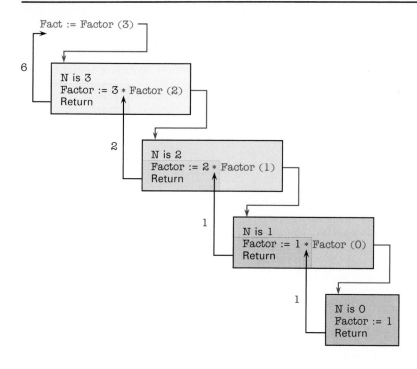

Figure 15.12   Iterative Function Factor

```
function Factor (N : Integer) : Integer;
{
   Computes the factorial of N (N!).
   Pre : N is defined and N >= 0.
   Post: Returns N!
}
   var
     i,                        {loop-control variable}
     Factorial : Integer;      {storage for accumulating product}

begin {Factor}
   Factorial := 1;
   for i := 2 to N do
     Factorial := Factorial * i;

   Factor := Factorial        {Define result}
end; {Factor}
```

Notice that the iterative version contains a loop as its major control structure, whereas the recursive version contains an `if` statement. Also, a local
variable, `Factorial`, is needed in the iterative version to hold the accumulating
product.

■ **Example 15.5**

The Fibonacci numbers are a sequence of numbers that have many varied uses. They were originally intended to model the growth of a rabbit colony. We will not go into details of the model here, but you can see that the Fibonacci sequence 1, 1, 2, 3, 5, 8, 13, 21, 34, ... increases rapidly. The fifteenth number in the sequence is 610 (that's a lot of rabbits!). The Fibonacci sequence is defined as follows:

- Fib_1 is 1.
- Fib_2 is 1.
- Fib_n is $Fib_{n-2} + Fib_{n-1}$, for $n > 2$.

Verify for yourself that the sequence of numbers shown in the preceding paragraph is correct.

A recursive function that computes the Nth Fibonacci number is shown in Fig. 15.13. Although easy to write, the Fibonacci function is not very efficient, because each recursive step generates two calls to function Fibonacci. ■

Figure 15.13 Recursive Function Fibonacci

```
function Fibonacci (N : Integer) : Integer;
{
  Computes the Nth Fibonacci number.
  Pre : N is defined and N > 0
  Post: Returns the Nth Fibonacci number.
}
begin  {Fibonacci}
  if (N = 1) or (N = 2) then
    Fibonacci := 1
  else
    Fibonacci := Fibonacci(N-2) + Fibonacci(N-1)
end;  {Fibonacci}
```

■ **Example 15.6**

Euclid's algorithm for finding the greatest common divisor (GCD) of two positive integers, (M and N), is defined recursively as follows. The *greatest common divisor* of two integers is the largest integer that divides them both.

- GCD(M,N) is N if N <= M and N divides M
- GCD(M,N) is GCD(N,M) if M < N
- GCD(M,N) is GCD(N, remainder of M divided by N)

This algorithm states that the GCD is N if N is the smaller number and N divides M. If M is the smaller number, then the GCD determination should be performed with the arguments transposed. If N does not divide M, the answer is obtained by finding the GCD of N and the remainder of M divided by N. The declaration and use of the Pascal function GCD is shown in Fig. 15.14. ■

Figure 15.14 Function GCD

603

15.3 Recursive
Mathematical
Functions

```
program FindGCD (Input, Output);

{Prints the greatest common divisor of two integers.}
  var
    M, N : Integer;                  {two input items}

  function GCD (M, N : Integer) : Integer;
  {
    Finds the greatest common divisor of M and N.
    Pre : M and N are defined and both are > 0.
    Post: Returns the greatest common divisor of M and N.
  }
  begin {GCD}
    if (N <= M) and (M mod N = 0) then
      GCD := N
    else if M < N then
      GCD := GCD(N, M)
    else
      GCD := GCD(N, M mod N)
    end; {GCD}

begin {FindGCD}
  Write ('Enter two positive integers separated by a space: ');
  ReadLn (M, N);
  WriteLn ('Their greatest common divisor is ', GCD (M, N) :1)
end. {FindGCD}


Enter two positive integers separated by a space: 24 84
Their greatest common divisor is 12
```

Exercises for Section 15.3

Self-Check

1. Complete the following recursive function, which calculates the value of a
   number (Base) raised to a power (Power). Assume that Power is positive.

```
function PowerRaiser (Base, Power : Integer) : Integer;
begin
  if Power = _____ then
    PowerRaiser := _____
  else
    PowerRaiser := _____ * _____
end;
```

2. What is the output of the following program? What does function Strange
   compute?

```
program TestStrange (Output);

  function Strange (N : Integer) : Integer;
  begin
    if N = 1 then
      Strange := 0
```

```
          else
            Strange := 1 + Strange (N div 2)
          end;  {Strange}

      begin {Strange}
        WriteLn (Strange(8))
      end. {TestStrange}
```

3. What would happen if the terminating condition for function `Fibonacci` is just (N = 1)?

Programming

1. Write a recursive function, `FindSum`, that calculates the sum of successive integers starting at 1 and ending at N (for example, `FindSum(N) = 1 + 2 + ... + (N-1) + N`).
2. Write an iterative version of the Fibonacci function.
3. Write an iterative function for the greatest common divisor.

 ## 15.4   Recursive Procedures with Array Parameters

This section examines three familiar problems and implements recursive procedures to solve them. All three problems involve processing an array.

● Case Study: Printing an Array Backward

Problem
Provide a recursive solution to the problem of printing the elements of an array in reverse order.

Design Overview
If the array X has elements with subscripts 1..N, then the element values should be printed in the sequence X[N], X[N-1], X[N-2], ..., X[2], X[1]. The stopping case is printing an array with one element (N is 1); the solution is to print that element. For larger arrays, the recursive step is to print the last array element (X[N]) and then print the subarray with subscripts 1..N-1 backward.

Data Requirements

Problem Inputs
An array of integer values (X : IntArray)
The number of elements in the array (N : Integer)

Problem Outputs
The array values in reverse order (X[N], X[N-1], ... , X[2], X[1])

Initial Algorithm

```
1. if N is 1 then
      2. Print X[1]
   else
     begin
        3. Print X[N]
        4. Print the subarray with subscripts 1..N-1
     end
```

Coding

Procedure `PrintBack` in Fig. 15.15 implements the recursive algorithm.

Figure 15.15 Procedure PrintBack

```
procedure PrintBack (var X {input} : IntArray;
                         N {input} : Integer);
{
  Prints an array of integers (X) with subscripts 1..N.
  Pre : Array X and N are defined and N > 0.
  Post: Displays X[N], X[N-1], ... , X[2], X[1]
}
begin {PrintBack }
  if N = 1 then
    WriteLn (X[1])                    {stopping case}
  else
    begin {recursive step}
      WriteLn (X[N]);
      PrintBack (X, N-1)
    end {recursive step}
end; {PrintBack }
```

Testing

Given the declarations

```
type
   IntArray = array [1..20] of Integer;

var
   Test : IntArray;
```

and the procedure call statement

```
PrintBack (Test, 3)
```

three `WriteLn` statements will be executed in the following order, and the elements of `Test` will be printed backward.

```
WriteLn (Test[3]);
WriteLn (Test[2]);
WriteLn (Test[1])
```

Case Study: Printing an Array Backward, continued

Figure 15.16 Trace of PrintBack (Test, 3)

To verify this, in Fig. 15.16 we trace the execution of the original call to PrintBack. Tracing the colored arrows and then the black arrows leads to the sequence of events listed in Fig. 15.17.

Figure 15.17 Sequence of Events for Trace of PrintBack (Test, 3)

Call PrintBack with parameters Test and 3.
   Print Test[3].
   Call PrintBack with parameters Test and 2.
      Print Test[2].
      Call PrintBack with parameters Test and 1.
         Print Test[1].
         Return from third call.
      Return from second call.
   Return from original call.

As shown in Fig. 15.17, there are three calls to procedure PrintBack, each with different parameters. This time, there are no statements left to execute after the returns, because the recursive call

```
PrintBack (X, N-1)
```

occurs at the end of the recursive step.

◖ Case Study: Printing an Array in Normal Order

Problem
Provide a recursive procedure that prints the elements of an array in normal order.

Design Overview

We can use the approach we just followed in the preceding problem to print
the elements of an array in normal order. Again, the stopping case is an array
with just one element.

Data Requirements

Problem Inputs
An array of integer values (X : IntArray)
The number of elements in the array (N : Integer)

Problem Outputs
The array values in normal order (X[1], X[2], ... , X[N–1], X[N])

Initial Algorithm

1. if N is 1 then
        2. Print X[1]
    else
        begin
            3. Print the subarray with subscripts 1..N–1
            4. Print X[N]
        end

The only difference between this algorithm and the one shown earlier is
that steps 3 and 4 are transposed.

Coding

Procedure PrintNormal is shown in Fig. 15.18.

Figure 15.18 Procedure PrintNormal

```
procedure PrintNormal (var X {input} : IntArray;
                           N {input} : Integer);
{
  Prints an array of integers (X) with subscripts 1..N.
  Pre : Array X and N are defined and N > 0.
  Post: Displays X[1], ... , X[N–1], X[N]
}
begin {PrintNormal }
  if N = 1 then
    WriteLn (X[1])                       {stopping case}
  else
    begin {recursive step}
       PrintNormal (X, N–1);
       WriteLn (X[N])
    end  {recursive step}
end;  {PrintNormal}
```

Case Study: Printing an Array in Normal Order, continued

Figure 15.19 Trace of PrintNormal (Test, 3)

Testing

The trace of PrintNormal (Test, 3) is shown in Fig. 15.19. Following the colored arrows and then the black arrows results in the sequence of events listed in Fig. 15.20. This time, there are no statements that precede the recursive calls; a display operation is performed after each return.

Figure 15.20 Sequence of Events for Trace of PrintNormal (Test, 3)

Call PrintNormal with parameters Test and 3.
　　Call PrintNormal with parameters Test and 2.
　　　　Call PrintNormal with parameters Test and 1.
　　　　　　Print Test[1].
　　　　　　Return from third call.
　　　　Print Test[2].
　　　　Return from second call.
　　Print Test[3].
　　Return from original call.

PROGRAM
STYLE

Avoiding Value Array Parameters in Recursive Procedures

X is declared as a variable parameter in procedures PrintBack and PrintNormal, even though it is used for input only. If X was a value parameter instead, each recursive call would generate a local copy of the actual array corresponding to X in each activation frame. This could result in a tremendous waste of time and memory space. For example, if X corresponds to an array with ten elements and we want to print the entire array (N is 10), there will be 10 activation frames and storage space will be needed for 100 integer values. If N is 100, then storage space will be needed for 100 x 100, or 10,000, integer values.

609

15.4 Recursive
Procedures with
Array Parameters

● Case Study: Recursive Selection Sort

Problem

We have discussed selection sort and implemented an iterative selection sort procedure. Because the selection sort first finds the largest element in an array and places it where it belongs, then finds and places the next largest element, and so on, it is a good candidate for a recursive solution.

Design Overview

The selection sort algorithm follows from the preceding description. The stopping case is an array of length 1, which is sorted by definition. Review Fig. 12.33 to see how the elements of an array are placed in their final positions by a selection sort.

Recursive Algorithm for Selection Sort

1. if N is 1 then
    2. The array is sorted.
   else
     begin
        3. Place the largest array element in X[N].
        4. Sort the subarray with subscripts 1..N-1.
     end

Coding

The algorithm is implemented as a recursive procedure at the end of Fig. 15.21. Procedure PlaceLargest performs step 3 of the algorithm. The recursive procedure SelectSort is simpler to understand than the one shown in Fig. 12.33 because it contains a single if statement instead of nested for loops. The recursive procedure executes more slowly, however, because of the extra overhead due to the recursive procedure calls.

Figure 15.21 PlaceLargest and Recursive SelectSort

```
procedure PlaceLargest (var X {input/output} : IntArray;
                        N {input} : Integer);
{
  Finds the largest element in array X[1]..X[N] and exchanges
  it with the element at X[N].
  Pre : Array X and N are defined and N > 0.
  Post: X[N] contains the largest value.
}
  var
    Temp : Integer;        {temporary copy for exchange}
    j,                     {array subscript and loop control}
    MaxIndex : Integer;    {index of largest so far}
```

```
begin {PlaceLargest}
  {Save subscript of largest element in MaxIndex}
  MaxIndex := N;                    {assume X[N] is largest}
  for j := N-1 downto 1 do
    if X[j] > X[MaxIndex] then
      MaxIndex := j;                {X[j] is largest so far}

  {assertion: MaxIndex is subscript of largest element}
  if MaxIndex <> N then
    begin {exchange X[N] and X[MaxIndex]}
      Temp := X[N];  X[N] := X[MaxIndex];  X[MaxIndex] := Temp
    end {if}
  end; {PlaceLargest}


procedure SelectSort (var X {input} : IntArray;
                          N {input} : Integer);
{
  Sorts an array of integers (X) with subscripts 1..N.
  Pre : Array X and N are defined and N > 0.
  Post: The array elements are in numerical order.
}
begin {SelectSort}
  if N > 1 then
    begin {recursive step}
      {Place largest value in X[N] and sort subarray 1..N-1.}
      PlaceLargest (X, N);
      SelectSort (X, N-1)
    end {recursive step}
end; {SelectSort}
```

If N = 1, procedure SelectSort returns without doing anything. This behavior is correct because a one-element array is always sorted.

Exercises for Section 15.4

Self-Check

1. Trace the execution of SelectSort on an array that has the integers 5, 8, 10, and 1 stored in consecutive elements.
2. For the array in exercise 1, trace the execution of PrintNormal and PrintBack.

Programming

1. Provide an iterative procedure that is equivalent to PrintBack in Fig. 15.15.
2. Write a recursive procedure that reverses the elements in an array X[1..N]. The recursive step should shift the subarray X[2..N] down one element into the subarray X[1..N-1] (for example, X[1] gets X[2], X[2] gets X[3], ... X[N-1] gets X[N]), store the old X[1] in X[N], and then reverse the subarray X[1..N-1].

15.5   Problem Solving with Recursion

The next case study is considerably more complicated than the preceding ones. It leads to a recursive procedure that solves the Towers of Hanoi problem you encountered in Section 15.1.

⬡ Case Study: Towers of Hanoi Problem

Problem
Solve the Towers of Hanoi problem for N disks, where N is a parameter.

Design Overview
The solution to the Towers of Hanoi problem consists of a printed list of individual disk moves. We need a recursive procedure that can be used to move any number of disks from one peg to another, using the third peg as an auxiliary.

Data Requirements

Problem Inputs
The number of disks to be moved (N : Integer)
The *from* peg (FromPeg : 'A'..'C')
The *to* peg (ToPeg : 'A'..'C')
The *auxiliary* peg (AuxPeg : 'A'..'C')

Problem Outputs
A list of individual disk moves

Initial Algorithm
1. if N is 1 then
      2. Move disk 1 from the *from* peg to the *to* peg
   else
     begin
        3. Move N–1 disks from the *from* peg to the *auxiliary* peg using the *to* peg.
        4. Move disk N from the *from* peg to the *to* peg.
        5. Move N–1 disks from the *auxiliary* peg to the *to* peg using the *from* peg.
     end

If N is 1, a stopping case is reached. If N is greater than 1, the recursive step (following else) splits the original problem into three smaller subproblems, one of which is a stopping case. Each stopping case displays a move instruction. Verify that the recursive step generates the three problems listed before Fig. 15.3 when N is 5, the *from* peg is A, and the *to* peg is C.

Case Study: Towers of Hanoi Problem, continued

The implementation of this algorithm is shown as procedure Tower in Fig. 15.22. Procedure Tower has four parameters. The procedure call statement

```
Tower ('A', 'C', 'B', 5)
```

solves the problem posed earlier of moving five disks from tower A to tower C using B as an auxiliary.

In Fig. 15.22, the stopping case (move disk 1) is implemented as a call to procedure WriteLn. Each recursive step consists of two recursive calls to Tower, with a call to WriteLn sandwiched between them. The first recursive call solves the problem of moving N–1 disks to the *auxiliary* peg. The call to WriteLn displays a message to move disk N to the *to* peg. The second recursive call solves the problem of moving the N–1 disks back from the *auxiliary* peg to the *to* peg.

Figure 15.22 Recursive Procedure Tower

```
procedure Tower (FromPeg,
                 ToPeg,
                 AuxPeg {input} : Char;
                 N       {input} : Integer);
{
  Moves N disks from FromPeg to ToPeg
  using AuxPeg as an auxiliary.
  Pre : FromPeg, ToPeg, AuxPeg, and N are defined.
  Post: Displays a list of move instructions that transfer
        the disks.
}
begin  {Tower}
  if N = 1 then
    WriteLn ('Move disk 1 from peg ', FromPeg,
             ' to peg ', ToPeg)
  else
    begin {recursive step}
      Tower (FromPeg, AuxPeg, ToPeg, N-1);
      WriteLn ('Move disk ', N :1, ' from peg ', FromPeg,
               ' to peg ', ToPeg);
      Tower (AuxPeg, ToPeg, FromPeg, N-1)
    end {recursive step}
end;  {Tower}
```

Testing

The procedure call statement

```
Tower ('A', 'C', 'B', 3)
```

solves a simpler three-disk problem: move three disks from peg A to peg C. Its execution is traced in Fig. 15.23; the output generated is shown in Fig. 15.24. Verify for yourself that this list of steps does indeed solve the three-disk problem.

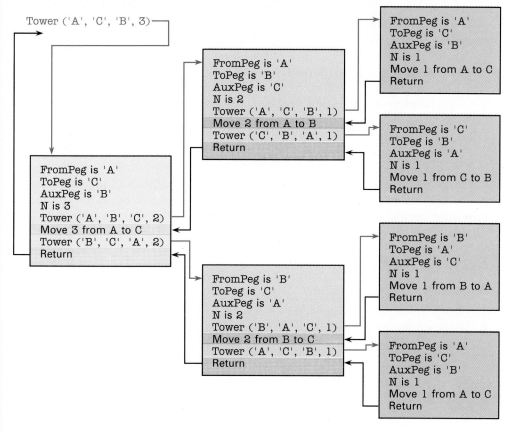

Figure 15.24   Output Generated by Tower ('A', 'C', 'B', 3)

| Move disk 1 from A to C |
| Move disk 2 from A to B |
| Move disk 1 from C to B |
| Move disk 3 from A to C |
| Move disk 1 from B to A |
| Move disk 2 from B to C |
| Move disk 1 from A to C |

Comparison of Iteration and Recursive Procedures

It is interesting to consider that procedure Tower in Fig. 15.22 will solve the Towers of Hanoi problem for any number of disks. The three-disk problem results in a total of seven calls to procedure Tower and is solved by seven disk moves. The five-disk problem would result in a total of thirty-one calls to procedure Tower and is solved in thirty-one moves. In general, the number of moves required to solve the n-disk problem is $2^n - 1$. Because each procedure call requires the allocation and initialization of a local data area in memory, the computer time increases exponentially with the problem size. For this reason, be careful about running the program with a value of N larger than 10.

The dramatic increase in processing time for larger towers is a function of the problem, not of recursion. In general, however, if there are recursive and iterative solutions to the same problem, the recursive solution requires more time and space because of the extra procedure calls. We discuss algorithm efficiency later.

Although recursion was not really needed to solve the simpler problems in this section, it was extremely useful in formulating an algorithm for the Towers of Hanoi. For certain problems, recursion leads naturally to solutions that are much easier to read and understand than their iterative counterparts. In those cases, the benefits gained from increased clarity far outweigh the extra cost in time and memory of running a recursive program.

Exercises for Section 15.5

Self-Check

1. How many moves are needed to solve the six-disk problem?
2. Write a main program that reads in a data value for N (the number of disks) and calls procedure Tower to move N disks from A to B.

 ## 15.6 Recursive Functions with Array Parameters

We can follow the process described in the previous sections to write recursive functions with array parameters. That process involves identifying the stopping cases of a problem. For other cases, we must be able to reduce the problem to one that is closer to a stopping case.

● Case Study: Summing the Values in an Array

Problem

We want to write a recursive function that finds the sum of the values in an array X with subscripts 1..N.

Design Overview

The stopping case occurs when N is 1, that is, the sum is X[1]. If N is not 1, then we must add X[N] to the sum we get when we add the values in the subarray with subscripts 1..N-1.

Data Requirements

Problem Inputs
An array of integer values (X : IntArray)
The number of elements in the array (N : Integer)

Problem Outputs
The sum of the array values

Initial Algorithm
1. if N is 1 then
     2. The sum is X[1]
   else
     begin
       3. Add X[N] to the sum of values in the subarray with
          subscripts 1..N-1
     end

Coding
Function FindSum in Fig. 15.25 implements this algorithm. The result of calling
FindSum for a small array (N is 3) is also shown.

Figure 15.25   Using Recursive Function FindSum

```
program TestFindSum (Input, Output);

{Tests function FindSum.}

  type
    IntArray = array [1..20] of Integer;

  var
    N : Integer;
    X : IntArray;


  function FindSum (var X : IntArray;
                        N : Integer) : Integer;
  {
    Finds the sum of the values in elements 1..N of array X.
    Pre : Array X and N are defined and N > 0.
    Post: Returns sum of first N elements of X.
  }
  begin {FindSum}
    if N = 1 then
       FindSum := X[1]

    else
       FindSum := X[N] + FindSum(X, N-1)
  end;  {FindSum}
```

Case Study: Summing the Values in an Array, continued

```
begin {TestFindSum}
  N := 3;
  X[1] := 5;  X[2] := 10;  X[3] := -7;
  WriteLn ('The array sum is ', FindSum(X, 3) :3)
end. {TestFindSum}
```

```
The array sum is 8
```

Testing

Figure 15.26 shows a trace of the function call FindSum(X, 3). As before, the colored part of each activation frame executes before the next recursive function call, and each colored arrow points to a new activation frame. The gray part of each activation frame executes after the return from a recursive call, and each black arrow indicates the return point (the operator +) after a function execution. The value returned is indicated alongside the arrow. The value returned for the original call, FindSum(X, 3), is 8, which is printed.

Functions that return Boolean values (True or False) can also be written recursively. These functions do not perform a computation; however, the function result is still determined by evaluating an expression (type Boolean) con-

Figure 15.26 Trace of FindSum(X, 3)

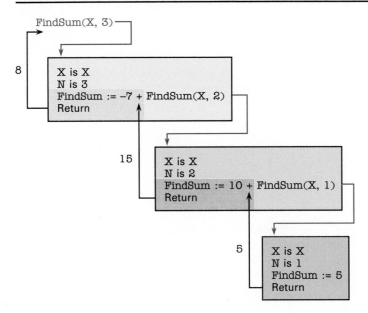

taining a recursive call. We will write recursive functions that search an array and compare two arrays.

■ Example 15.7

The Boolean function `Member` in Fig. 15.27 returns the value `True` if the argument `Target` is in the array `X` with subscripts `1..N`; otherwise, it returns the value `False`. If `N` is `1` (the stopping case), the result is determined by comparing `X[1]` and `Target`. If `N` is not `1` (the recursive step), then the result is true if either `X[N]` is `Target` or `Target` occurs in the subarray with subscripts `1..N-1`. The recursive step is implemented as the assignment statement

```
Member := (X[N] = Target) or Member(X, Target, N-1)
```

in Fig. 15.27.

Figure 15.27   Recursive Function Member

```
function Member (var X : IntArray;
                     Target,
                     N        : Integer) : Boolean;
{
  Searches for Target in array X with subscripts 1..N.
  Pre : Target, N and array X are defined and N > 0.
  Post: Returns True if Target is located in array X; otherwise,
        returns False.
}
begin {Member}
  if N = 1 then
    Member := (X[1] = Target)
  else
    Member := (X[N] = Target) or Member(X, Target, N-1)
end; {Member}
```

The function designator `Member(X, 10, 3)` is traced in Fig. 15.28 for the array `X` defined in Fig. 15.25. The value returned is `True`, because the expression `X[N] = Target` is `True` when `N` is `2` (the second activation frame).   ■

■ Example 15.8

The Boolean function `Equal` returns the value `True` if two arrays, say `X` and `Y`, of `N` elements are the same (for example, `X[1] = Y[1]`, `X[2] = Y[2]`,..., `X[N] = Y[N]`). This function (see Fig. 15.29) looks similar to function `Member`. For the stopping case, single-element arrays, the function result depends on whether or not `X[1] = Y[1]`. For larger arrays, the result is `True` if `X[N] = Y[N]` and the subarrays with subscripts `1..N-1` are equal.   ■

Figure 15.28 Trace of Function Member

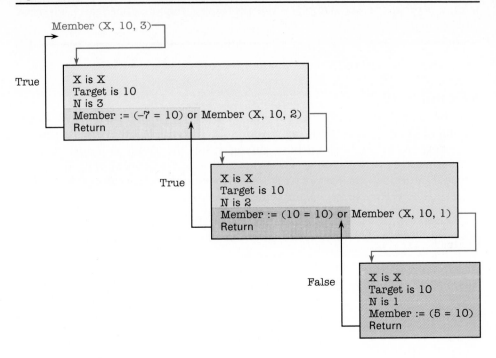

Figure 15.29 Recursive Function Equal

```
function Equal (var X, Y : IntArray;
               N : Integer) : Boolean;
{
  Compares arrays X and Y with elements 1..N.
  Pre : Arrays X and Y are defined and N > 0.
  Post: Returns True if arrays X and Y are equal; otherwise,
        returns False.
}
begin {Equal}
  if N = 1 then
    Equal := X[1] = Y[1]
  else
    Equal := (X[N] = Y[N]) and Equal(X, Y, N-1)
end;   {Equal}
```

Comparison of Iterative and Recursive Functions

Consider the iterative version of function Member shown in Fig. 15.30. A for loop is needed to examine each array element. Without recursion, it is not possible to use the function name in an expression, so a local variable, Found, is needed to represent the result so far. Before returning from the function, the final value of Found is assigned as the function result.

```
function Member (var X : IntArray;
                 Target,
                 N       : Integer) : Boolean;
{
  Compares arrays X and Y with elements 1..N.
  Pre : Arrays X and Y are defined and N > 0.
  Post: Returns True if arrays X and Y are equal; otherwise,
        returns False.
}
var
  Found : Boolean;              {local flag}
  I : Integer;                  {loop-control variable}

begin {Member}
  Found := False;              {assume Target not found}
  {Search array X for Target.}
  for I := 1 to N do
    Found := Found or (X[I] = Target);

  Member := Found                        {define result}
end;   {Member}
```

This is a little different from the iterative array search shown in Chapter 12 (see Fig. 12.30). We could make it more efficient by using a while loop and exiting from the loop when Found becomes True; however, the version shown in Fig. 15.30 would still execute faster than the recursive version.

Many programmers would argue that the recursive version is esthetically more pleasing. It is certainly more compact (a single if statement) and requires no local variables. Once you are accustomed to thinking recursively, the recursive form is somewhat easier to read and understand than the iterative form.

Some programmers like to use recursion as a conceptual tool. Once they have written the recursive form of a function or procedure, they can always translate it into an iterative version if run-time efficiency is a major concern.

Exercises for Section 15.6

Self-Check

1. Trace the execution of recursive function Equal for the three-element arrays X (element values 1, 15, 10) and Y (element values 1, 5, 7). Write out completely in one equivalent Boolean expression the values that function Equal is assigned through all three recursive calls for array X. Spell out all the values that are being compared.
2. Answer exercise 1 for the recursive function Member and array X.
3. What does the following recursive function do? Trace its execution on array X in exercise 1.

```
function Mystery (X : IntArray;
                  N : Integer) : Integer;
   var
     Temp : Integer;
```

```
begin
  if N = 1 then
    Mystery := X[1]
  else
    begin
      Temp := Mystery(X, N-1);
      if X[N] > Temp then
        Mystery := X[N]
      else
        Mystery := Temp
    end {if}
end; {Mystery}
```

Programming

1. Write a recursive function that finds the product of the elements in an array X of N elements.
2. Write a recursive function that finds the index of the smallest element in an array.

 ## 15.7 Picture Processing with Recursion

◗ Case Study: Counting Cells in a Blob

This problem illustrates the power of recursion. The problem would be much more difficult without using recursion, but its solution is relatively easy to write recursively.

Problem

We have a two-dimensional grid of cells, each of which may be empty or filled. The filled cells that are connected form a blob. There may be several blobs on the grid. We want a function that accepts as input the coordinates of a particular cell and returns the size of the blob containing that cell.

There are three blobs in the sample grid in Fig. 15.31. If the function parameters represent the X and Y coordinates of a cell, the result of Blob-Count(3, 4) is 5; the result of BlobCount(1, 2) is 2; the result of BlobCount(5, 5) is 0; the result of BlobCount(5, 1) is 4.

Design Overview

Function BlobCount must test the cell specified by its arguments to see if it is filled. There are two stopping cases: the cell (X, Y) is not on the grid, or the cell (X, Y) is empty; in either case, the value returned by BlobCount is 0. If the cell is on the grid and is filled, the value returned is 1 plus the size of the blobs containing each of its neighbors. To avoid counting a filled cell more than once, we mark it as empty once we have visited it.

Figure 15.31   Grid with Three Blobs

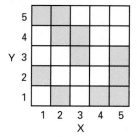

Data Requirements

Problem Inputs
The grid (Grid : BlobArray)
The X and Y coordinates of the point being visited
  (X, Y : Integer)

Problem Outputs
The number of the cells in the blob containing point (X, Y)

Initial Algorithm
1. if cell (X, Y) is not in the array then
      2. Return a count of 0
   else if cell (X, Y) is empty then
      3. Return a count of 0
   else
     begin
         4. Mark cell (X, Y) as empty
         5. Add 1 and see whether the blob contains any of
             the 8 neighbors of cell (X, Y)
     end

Coding
Function BlobCount is shown in Fig. 15.32. The array type BlobArray has
element values Filled or Empty. The constants MaxX and MaxY represent the
largest X and Y coordinate, respectively.

Figure 15.32   Function BlobCount

```
const
  MaxX = 100;
  MaxY = 100;

type
  BlobArray = array [1..MaxX, 1..MaxY] of (Filled, Empty);
```

```
function BlobCount (Grid : BlobArray;
                    X, Y : Integer) : Integer;
{
   Counts the number of filled cells in the blob containing
   point (X, Y).
   Pre : Array Grid and point (X, Y) are defined.
   Post: Returns the size of the blob containing the point (X, Y).
   Uses: Blob to perform the counting operation.
}


   function Blob (var Grid {input/output} : BlobArray;
                 X, Y : Integer) : Integer;
   {
    Performs counting operation for BlobCount.
    Pre : Array Grid and point (X, Y) are defined.
    Post: Returns the size of the blob containing the point (X, Y).
        Resets the status of each cell in the blob to Empty.
   }
   begin {Blob}
     if (X < 1) or (X > MaxX) or (Y < 1) or (Y > MaxY) then
        Blob := 0                    {cell not in grid}
     else if Grid[X, Y] = Empty then
        Blob := 0                    {cell is empty}
     else {cell is filled}
       begin {recursive step}
         Grid[X, Y] := Empty;
         Blob := 1 + Blob(Grid, X-1, Y+1) + Blob(Grid, X, Y+1) +
                 Blob(Grid, X+1, Y+1) + Blob(Grid, X+1, Y) +
                 Blob(Grid, X+1, Y-1) + Blob(Grid, X, Y-1) +
                 Blob(Grid, X-1, Y-1) + Blob(Grid, X-1, Y)
       end {recursive step}
   end; {Blob}


begin {BlobCount}
  {Call Blob and return its result.}
  BlobCount := Blob(Grid, X, Y)
end; {BlobCount}
```

Function Blob in Fig. 15.32 implements the counting algorithm; function BlobCount simply calls the recursive function Blob, passes on its arguments, and returns the count computed by function Blob as its own result. The reason we use two functions instead of one is to protect the actual array from being modified when filled cells are reset to empty by function Blob. We will come back to this point shortly.

If the cell being visited is off the grid or is empty, a value of zero is returned immediately. Otherwise, the recursive step executes, causing function Blob to call itself eight times; each time, a different neighbor of the current cell is visited. The cells are visited in a clockwise manner, starting with the neighbor above and to the left. The function result is the sum of all values returned from these recursive calls plus 1 (for the current cell).

The sequence of operations performed in function Blob is important. The if statement tests whether the cell (X, Y) is on the grid before testing whether

(X, Y) is empty. If the order was reversed, an index out of bounds run-time error would occur whenever (X, Y) was off the grid.

Also, the recursive step resets Grid[X, Y] to Empty before visiting the neighbors of point (X, Y). If this was not done first, then cell (X, Y) would be counted more than once, because it is a neighbor of all its neighbors. A worse problem is that the recursion would not terminate. When each neighbor of the current cell is visited, Blob is called again with the coordinates of the current cell as arguments. If the current cell is Empty, an immediate return occurs. If the current cell was still Filled, the recursive step would be executed erroneously. Eventually the program would run out of time or memory space (the latter is often indicated by a stack overflow run-time error).

A side effect of the execution of function Blob is that all cells that are part of the blob being processed are reset to Empty. This is the reason for using two functions. Because the array is passed as a value parameter to function Blob–Count, a local copy is saved when BlobCount is first called. Only this local array, not the actual array, is changed by function Blob. If the counting operation was performed in function BlobCount instead of function Blob, eight copies of this array would be made each time the recursive step was executed, and we would soon run out of memory.

Exercise for Section 15.7

Self-Check

1. Trace the execution of function BlobCount for the coordinate pairs (1, 1) and (1, 2) in the sample grid.
2. Is the order of the two tests performed in function Blob critical? What happens if we reverse them or combine them into a single condition?

Programming

1. Write the recursive function FindMin that finds the smallest value in an integer array X with subscripts 1..N.

 # 15.8 Common Programming Errors

The most common problem with a recursive procedure is that it may not terminate properly. For example, if the terminating condition is not correct or is incomplete, then the procedure may call itself indefinitely or until all available memory is used up. Normally, a stack overflow run-time error indicates that a recursive procedure is not terminating. Make sure you identify all stopping cases and provide a terminating condition for each one. Also be sure that each recursive step leads to a situation that is closer to a stopping case and that repeated recursive calls eventually lead to stopping cases only.

The use of large arrays or other data structures as value parameters can quickly consume all available memory. Unless absolutely essential for data protection, arrays should be passed as variable parameters. Any expression such as N–1 must be passed as a value parameter.

Sometimes it is difficult to observe the result of a recursive procedure execution. If each recursive call generates a large number of output lines and there are many recursive calls, the output will scroll down the screen more quickly than you can read it. On most systems, it is possible to stop the screen temporarily by pressing a control character sequence (for example, control-S). If this cannot be done on your system, you can cause your output to stop temporarily by printing a prompting message followed by a Read (NextChar) operation. Your program then resumes execution when you enter a data character.

 # Chapter Review

This chapter provides several examples of recursive procedures and functions. Studying them should give you some appreciation of the power of recursion as a problem-solving and programming tool and provide you with valuable insight regarding its use. It may take you some time to feel comfortable thinking in this new way, but it is certainly worth the effort.

✓ *Quick-Check Exercises*

1. Explain the use of a stack in recursion.
2. Which is generally more efficient, recursion or iteration?
3. Which control statement is always in a recursive procedure or function?
4. What are the two uses of the function name in a recursive function?
5. How many times does the function name appear in a recursive function? In a recursive procedure?
6. Why would a programmer use recursion to conceptualize a problem solution but use iteration to implement it?
7. What is the problem with value array parameters in recursion?
8. In a recursive problem involving N items, why must N be a value parameter?
9. What causes a stack overflow error?
10. What can you say about a recursive algorithm that has the following form?
    if *condition* then
       Perform recursive step.

Answers to Quick-Check Exercises
1. The stack is used to hold all parameter and local variable values and the return point for each execution of a recursive procedure.

2. Iteration
3. `if` statement
4. To assign a value to the function and to call it recursively
5. At least three or more times in a function: once to assign a value for the stopping case, once to assign a value for the recursive step, and once to call the function recursively. There may be more than one recursive call, as in function `Fibonacci`. At least once in a procedure.
6. When its solution is much easier to conceptualize using recursion but its implementation would be too inefficient.
7. A copy of the array must be pushed onto the stack each time a call occurs. All available stack memory could be exhausted.
8. If N was a variable parameter, it would not be possible to use the expression N–1 as an actual parameter in a recursive call.
9. Too many recursive calls.
10. Nothing is done when the stopping case is reached.

Review Questions

1. Explain the nature of a recursive problem.
2. Discuss the efficiency of recursive procedures.
3. Differentiate between stopping cases and a terminating condition.
4. Write a recursive procedure that prints the accumulating sum of ordinal values corresponding to each character in a packed array. For example, if the string value is 'a boy', the first value printed would be the ordinal number of a, then the sum of ordinals for a and the space character, then the sum of ordinals for a, space, b, and so on.
5. Write a recursive function that returns the sum of ordinal values corresponding to the string stored in a packed array of characters; however, this time exclude any space characters from the sum.
6. Convert the following program from an iterative process to a recursive function that calculates an approximate value for e, the base of the natural logarithms, by summing the series

    $$1 + 1/1! + 1/2! + ...1/N!$$

    until additional terms do not affect the approximation.

```
program ELog (Output);

   var
     ENL, Delta, Fact : Real;
     N : Integer;

begin {ELog}
   ENL  := 1.0;
   N  := 1;
   Fact := 1.0;
   Delta := 1.0;
   repeat
     ENL  := ENL + Delta;
     N  := N + 1;
     Fact := Fact * N;
     Delta := 1 / Fact;
```

```
        until ENL = (ENL + Delta);
        Write ('The value of e is ', E :18:15)
      end. {ELog}
```

7. Write a recursive function that returns the actual length of a character string stored left-justified in a packed array. Exclude any blank padding from the length returned.

Programming Projects

1. Write a procedure that reads each row of an array as a string and converts it to a row of Grid (see Fig.15.31). The first character of row 1 corresponds to Grid[1,1], the second character to Grid[1,2], and so on. Set the element value to Empty if the character is blank; otherwise, set it to Filled. The number of rows in the array should be read first. Use this procedure in a program that reads in cell coordinates and prints the number of cells in the blob containing each coordinate pair.

2. The expression for computing $C(n,r)$, the number of combinations of n items taken r at a time is

$$c(n,r) = \frac{n!}{r!(n-r)!}$$

Write and test a function for computing $c(n,r)$, given that $n!$ is the factorial of n.

3. A palindrome is a word that is spelled exactly the same when the letters are reversed, for example, level, deed, and mom. Write a recursive function that returns the Boolean value True if a word, passed as a parameter, is a palindrome.

4. Write a recursive function that returns the value of the following recursive definition:

```
F(X,Y) = X - Y, if X or Y < 0
F(X,Y) = F(X-1,Y) + F(X,Y-1), otherwise
```

5. Write a recursive procedure that lists all the pairs of subsets for a given set of letters. For example:

```
['A', 'C', 'E', 'G'] => ['A', 'C'], ['A', 'E'], ['A', 'G'],
                        ['C', 'E'], ['C', 'G'], ['E', 'G']
```

6. Write a procedure that accepts an 8-by-8 array of characters that represents a maze. Each position can contain either an 'X' or a blank. Starting at position [1,1], list any path through the maze to get to location [8,8]. Only horizontal and vertical moves are allowed (no diagonal moves). If no path exists, write a message indicating such.

   Moves can be made only to locations that contain a blank. If an 'X' is encountered, that path is blocked and another must be chosen. Use recursion.

7. One method of solving a continuous numerical function for a root is the *bisection method* described next. Given a numerical function, defined as f(X), and two values of X that are known to bracket one of the roots, an approximation to this root can be determined through a method of repeated division of this bracket.

   For a set of values of X to bracket a root, the value of the function for one X must be negative and the other must be positive. This is illustrated in the diagram, which plots f(X) for values of X between X1 and X2.

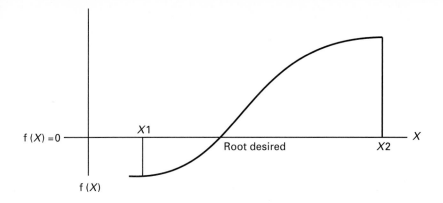

The algorithm requires that the midpoint between the left X and the right X be evaluated in the function. If the midpoint equals zero, the root is found; otherwise, the left X ($X1$) or the right X ($X2$) is set to this midpoint. To determine whether to replace $X1$ or $X2$, the sign of the midpoint is compared against the signs of the values of $f(X1)$ and $f(X2)$. The midpoint replaces the X ($X1$ or $X2$) whose function value has the same sign as the function value at the midpoint.

This routine can be written recursively. The terminating conditions are true when either the midpoint evaluated in the function is zero or the absolute value of the left X minus the right X is less than some small predetermined value (for example, 0.0005). If the second condition occurs, the root is said to be approximately equal to the midpoint of the last set of left and right Xs.

8. We can use a merge technique to sort two arrays. The *mergesort* begins by taking adjacent pairs of array values and ordering the values in each pair. It then forms groups of four elements by merging adjacent pairs (first pair with second pair, third pair with fourth pair, etc.) into another array. It then takes adjacent groups of four elements from this new array and merges them back into the original array as groups of eight, etcetera. The process terminates when a single group is formed that has the same number of elements as the array. The following illustration is of a mergesort for an array with eight elements. Write a `MergeSort` procedure.

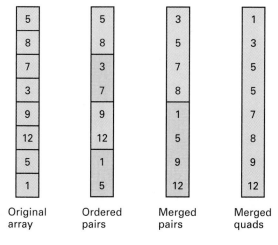

Original array · Ordered pairs · Merged pairs · Merged quads

Stacks and Queues

16

Chapter 15 introduced the stack as a useful data structure for storing the actual parameters passed in each call to a recursive procedure or function. A stack is a convenient mechanism for storing information (or dishes in a cafeteria); we can access only the top item in a stack. The first part of this chapter illustrates how to use a stack and how to implement an abstract data type for a stack.

The rest of the chapter discusses a related data structure, the queue. The British people don't "wait in line," they "queue up." We will use a queue to represent a list of airline passengers waiting to see a ticket agent. We will also implement an abstract data type for a queue.

 # 16.1   The Stack Abstract Data Type

In this section, we discuss a data abstraction, the stack, that is useful in computer science applications such as writing compilers. A stack is characterized by the property that at any one time only the top element of the stack is accessible. Some of the operations that we might want to perform on a stack are summarized in the following specification.

Specification of Abstract Data Type Stack

Elements: A stack consists of a collection of elements that are all the same data type.

Structure: The elements of a stack are ordered according to when they were placed on the stack. Only the element that was last inserted onto the stack can be removed or examined. New elements are inserted at the top of the stack.

Operators: The following descriptions assume these parameters:

> S represents the stack.
> X has the same data type as the stack elements.
> Success is type Boolean and indicates whether or not the operation succeeds.

CreateStack (var S): Creates an empty stack.

Push (var S, X, var Success): If stack S is not full, the value in X is placed on the top of the stack and Success is set to True. Otherwise, the top of the stack is not changed and Success is set to False.

Pop (var S, var X, var Success): If stack S is not empty, the value at the top of the stack is removed, its value is placed in X, and Success is set to True. If the stack is empty, X is not defined and Success is set to False.

Retrieve (S, var X, var Success): If stack S is not empty, the value at the top of the stack is copied into X, and Success is set to True. If the

---

stack is empty, X is not defined and Success is set to False. In either case, the stack is not changed.

IsEmpty(S): Returns True if stack S is empty; otherwise, returns False.

IsFull(S): Returns True if stack S is full; otherwise, returns False.

We can illustrate how these operators work and use them in a client program without worrying about the details of how the stack is represented in memory. We discuss an internal representation for a stack (ADT Stack) and implement the stack operators in Section 16.4. Because we want to be able to manipulate different types of data objects using a stack, we use the identifier StackElement to represent the type of each stack element. Each client program must import data types StackElement and Stack from ADT Stack.

A client program can allocate multiple stacks by declaring several variables of type Stack. Because StackElement can only be declared once in a program, all stacks used in a particular program must have the same type of element.

Procedure CreateStack must be called before a stack can be processed. CreateStack creates a stack that is initially empty. If S is declared as type Stack, the statements

```
CreateStack (S);
if IsEmpty(S) then
   WriteLn ('Stack is empty')
```

display the message Stack is empty.

■ Example 16.1

A stack S of character elements is shown in Fig. 16.1. The stack has four elements; the first element placed on the stack was '2', and the last element placed on the stack was '*'.

For stack S in Fig. 16.1, the value of IsEmpty(S) is False. The value of IsFull(S) is False if stack S can store more than four elements; otherwise, the value of IsFull(S) is True. The procedure call statement

```
Retrieve (S, X, Success)
```

stores '*' in X (type Char) without changing S. The procedure call statement

```
Pop (S, X, Success)
```

Figure 16.1 Stack S

```
 ___
| * |
| C |
| + |
| 2 |
 ‾‾‾
  S
```

Figure 16.2 Stack S after Pop Operation

```
C
+
2
```
S

removes '*' from S and stores it in X. The new stack S contains three elements and is shown in Fig. 16.2.

The procedure call statement

```
Push (S, '/', Success)
```

pushes '/' onto the stack; the new stack S contains four elements and is shown in Fig. 16.3. The value of Success (type Boolean) after each of the operations should be True. ∎

Exercise for Section 16.1

Self-Check

1. Assume that the stack S is defined as in Fig. 16.3. Perform the following sequence of operations. Indicate the result of each operation and the new stack if it is changed. Rather than draw the stack each time, use the notation |2+C/ to represent the stack in Fig. 16.3 where the last symbol on the right (/) is at the top of the stack.

```
Push (S, '$', Success);
Push (S, '-', Success);
Pop (S, NextCh, Success);
Retrieve (S, NextCh, Success);
IsEmpty (S);
IsFull (S)
```

 16.2 Stack Applications

This section examines some client programs that use stacks. These programs should give you some idea of the importance of the stack data type.

Figure 16.3 Stack S after Push Operation

```
/
C
+
2
```
S

● Case Study: Displaying a String in Reverse Order

Program

A reading instructor is studying dyslexia and wants a program that displays a word or a sentence in reverse order.

Design Overview

A stack of characters is a good data structure for such a program. If we first push each data character onto a stack and then pop each character and display it, the characters will be displayed in reverse order. The sequence of characters is displayed in reverse order because the last character pushed onto the stack is the first one popped. For example, the diagram in Fig. 16.4 shows the stack S after the letters in the string 'house' are processed. The first letter popped and displayed is e, the next letter is s, and so on.

Data Requirements

Problem Inputs
Each data character

Problem Outputs
Each character on the stack

Program Variables
The stack of characters (S : Stack)

Algorithm

1. Create an empty stack of characters.
2. Push each data character onto a stack.
3. Pop each character and display it.
4. Indicate whether the stack is empty or full.

Program Structure

The structure chart (Fig. 16.5) shows that procedure CreateStack performs step 1, procedure FillStack performs step 2, and procedure DisplayStack performs step 3. FillStack and DisplayStack call procedures Push and Pop

Figure 16.4 Pushing 'house' onto a Stack

```
  e
  s
  u
  o
  h
S
```

Figure 16.5 Structure Chart for PrintReverse

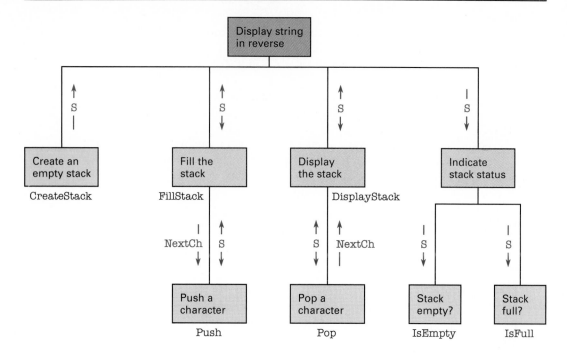

from ADT Stack. Functions IsEmpty and IsFull (from ADT Stack) are called to perform step 4.

Coding the Main Program

The main program and its procedures are shown in Fig. 16.6. The type declarations for StackElement (type is Char) and Stack must be imported from ADT Stack, along with the stack operators. Procedures FillStack and DisplayStack are described after the program.

Figure 16.6 Program PrintReverse

```
program PrintReverse (Input, Output);
{
  Reads a sequence of characters and displays it in reverse
  order.

  IMPORT: Stack, StackElement, CreateStack, Push, Pop,
          IsFull, IsEmpty from ADT Stack (see Section 16.4)
}

  {Insert type declaration for StackElement}
  {Insert type declaration for Stack}
```

```
var
   S : Stack;                    {the stack of characters}

{Insert CreateStack, Push, Pop, IsFull, IsEmpty}

{Insert FillStack and DisplayStack}


begin {PrintReverse}
   CreateStack (S);              {start with an empty stack}

   {Fill the stack.}
   FillStack (S);

   {Display the characters in reverse order.}
   DisplayStack (S);

   {Display status of stack S.}
   if IsEmpty(S) then
      WriteLn ('Stack is empty - operation succeeds')
   else if IsFull(S) then
      WriteLn ('Stack is full - reversal failed')
end. {PrintReverse}


Enter a string of one or more characters.
Press return when done.
This is a short string.
.gnirts trohs a si sihT
Stack is empty - operation succeeds
```

Coding the Procedures

The repeat-until loop in procedure `FillStack` (Fig. 16.7) reads each data character (at least one) into `NextCh` and pushes it onto the stack. The `if` statement displays an error message when the input string is too long (if the user enters more characters than the stack capacity before pressing the return key).

Figure 16.7 Procedure FillStack

```
procedure FillStack (var S {in/out} : Stack);
{
   Reads data characters and pushes them onto the stack.
   Pre : S is a stack.
   Post: Each data character read is pushed onto stack S.
   Uses: Push
}
   var
      NextCh : Char;             {the next character}
      Success : Boolean;         {flag}

begin {FillStack}
   WriteLn ('Enter a string of one or more characters.');
   WriteLn ('Press return when done.');
```

```
repeat
  Read (NextCh);                      {read next character}
  Push (S, NextCh, Success)           {push it onto stack}
until Eoln(Input) or not Success;

{Print an error if stack overflows.}
if not Success then
  WriteLn ('Stack overflow error - string too long')
end; {FillStack}
```

The while loop in procedure `DisplayStack` (Fig. 16.8) pops each character from the stack into `NextCh` and then displays it. The loop is repeated as long as there are characters remaining on the stack (`Success` is `True`). After `DisplayStack` is finished, the stack should be empty.

Figure 16.8 Procedure DisplayStack

```
procedure DisplayStack (var S {in/out} : Stack);
{
  Pops each stack character and displays it.
  Pre : Stack S is defined.
  Post: Each character is displayed and S is empty.
  Uses: Pop
}

  var
    NextCh : Char;                    {the next character}
    Success : Boolean;                {flag}

begin {DisplayStack}
  Pop (S, NextCh, Success);
  while Success do
    begin
      Write (NextCh);
      Pop (S, NextCh, Success)
    end; {while}
  WriteLn
end; {DisplayStack}
```

Testing

It is a good idea to see what happens when the stack overflows. This can be done by setting `MaxStack` to a small value (for example, `10`).

Case Study: Checking for Balanced Parentheses

One application of a stack is to determine whether an expression is balanced with respect to parentheses. For example, the expression

```
(a + b * (c / (d − e))) + (d / e)
1          2    3    321   1     1
```

is balanced. We can solve this problem without using a stack by ignoring all characters except the symbols (and). We add 1 to a counter for each open parenthesis that follows another open parenthesis and subtract 1 for each close parenthesis that follows another close parenthesis. Because we are ignoring all other symbols, the parentheses being considered do not have to be consecutive characters. Assuming the initial count is 1, for a balanced expression the count ends at 1, and is never less than one.

This task becomes more difficult if we use different types of enclosure symbols as parentheses. For example, the expression

```
(a + b * {c / [d − e]}) + (d / e)
```

is balanced, but the expression

```
(a + b * {c / [d − e}]) + (d / e)
```

is not because the subexpression [d − e} is incorrect.

Problem
The set of open parentheses includes {, [, (. An expression is balanced if each subexpression that starts with the symbol { ends with the symbol }; the same is true for the symbol pairs [,] and (,). Another way of saying this is that the unmatched open parenthesis that is nearest to each close parenthesis must have the correct shape (for example, if } is the close parenthesis in question, the symbol { must be the nearest unmatched open parenthesis.)

Design Overview
Without stacks it would be fairly difficult to solve this problem, but with stacks it becomes easy. First, we scan the expression from left to right, ignoring all characters except for parentheses. Then we push each open parenthesis onto a stack of characters. When we reach a close parenthesis, we see if it matches the symbol on the top of the stack. If the characters don't match or the stack is empty, there is an error in the expression. If they do match, we continue the scan.

Data Requirements

Problem Inputs
The expression to be checked for balanced parentheses
(Expression : String)

Problem Outputs
The function result indicating whether the parentheses in Expression are balanced

Case Study: Checking for Balanced Parentheses, continued

Program Variables
The stack of open parentheses (ParenStack : Stack)
A flag indicating whether parentheses are balanced
(Balanced : Boolean)
The next character in Expression (NextCh : Char)
The index of the next character (Index : Integer)
The open parenthesis at the top of the stack (Open : Char)
The close parenthesis being matched (Close : Char)

Algorithm

1. Create an empty stack of characters.
2. Assume that the expression is balanced (Balanced is True).
3. while the expression is balanced and still in the string do
     begin
        4. Get the next character in the data string.
        5. if the next character is an open parenthesis then
              6. Push it onto the stack
          else if the next character is a close parenthesis then
            begin
                7. Pop the top of the stack
                8. if stack was empty or its top was incorrect then
                      Set Balanced to False.
            end
     end
9. if the expression is balanced then
        10. There is an error if the stack is not empty.

The if statement at step 5 tests each character in the expression, ignoring all characters except for open and close parentheses. If the next character is an open parenthesis, it is pushed onto the stack. If the next character is a close parenthesis, the nearest unmatched open parenthesis is retrieved (by popping the stack) and compared to the close parenthesis (steps 7 and 8).

Coding
Figure 16.9 shows a function that determines whether its input parameter (an expression) is balanced. The if statement in the while loop tests for open and close parentheses. Each open parenthesis is pushed onto stack ParenStack. For each close parenthesis, procedure Pop retrieves the nearest unmatched open parenthesis from the stack. If the stack was empty, Pop sets Balanced to False, causing the while loop exit. Otherwise, the case statement sets Balanced to indicate whether the character popped matches the current close parenthesis. After loop exit occurs, the function result is defined. It is true only when the expression is balanced and the stack is empty.

Figure 16.9   Function IsBalanced

```
function IsBalanced (Expression {input} : String) : Boolean;
{
  Determines whether Expression is balanced with respect
  to parentheses.
  Pre : Expression is defined.
  Post: Returns True if Expression is balanced; otherwise,
        returns False.
  Uses: String, Length, and GetChar from ADT String
        (see Fig. 13.12)
        Stack, Push, Pop and IsEmpty from ADT Stack.
}
  var
    ParenStack : Stack;         {the stack of open parentheses}
    NextCh,                     {the next character in Expression}
    Close,                      {close parenthesis to be matched}
    Open : Char;                {open parenthesis at top of stack}
    Index : Integer;            {index to Expression}
    Balanced : Boolean;         {program flag}

begin {IsBalanced}
  CreateStack (ParenStack);            {Create an empty stack}
  Balanced := True;
  Index := 1;
  while Balanced and (Index <= Length(Expression)) do
    {invariant:
        All closing parentheses so far were matched and
        Index <= Length(Expression) + 1
    }
    begin
      NextCh := GetChar(Expression, Index);     {access next
                                                 character}
      if NextCh in ['(', '[', '{'] then
        Push (ParenStack, NextCh, Balanced) {stack parenthesis}
      else if NextCh in [')', ']', '}'] then
        begin {close paren}
          Close := NextCh;
          {Get nearest unmatched open parenthesis}
          Pop (ParenStack, Open, Balanced);
          if Balanced then
            {Check for matching parentheses.}
            case Close of
              ')' : Balanced := Open = '(';
              ']' : Balanced := Open = '[';
              '}' : Balanced := Open = '{'
            end {case}
        end; {close paren}
      Index := Index + 1      {access next character}
    end; {while}

  {Define function result}
  if Balanced then
    IsBalanced := IsEmpty(ParenStack)
  else
    IsBalanced := False
end; {IsBalanced}
```

Case Study: Checking for Balanced Parentheses, continued

Testing

You have to write a driver program to test function IsBalanced. The driver program has to import type declaration String (from ADT String) and the type declarations for StackElement (type is Char) and Stack (from ADT Stack). It also has to import the stack operators and string operators that are called by IsBalanced and ReadLnStrVar to read in the string being tested. Make sure you use a variety of balanced and unbalanced expressions to test IsBalanced, as well as an expression without parentheses.

Exercises for Section 16.2

Self-Check

1. Trace the execution of function IsBalanced for each of the following expressions. Your trace should show the stack after each Push or Pop operation. Also show the values of Balanced, Open, and Close after each close parenthesis is processed.

    ```
    (a + b * {c / [d - e]}) + (d / e)
    (a + b * {c / [d - e}}) + (d / e)
    ```

Programming

1. Write a main program to test function IsBalanced.

 ## 16.3   Evaluating Expressions

One task of a compiler is to evaluate arithmetic expressions. This section discusses one approach to expression evaluation.

Some of you may use calculators that evaluate postfix expressions. A *postfix expression* is an expression in which each operator follows its operands. We discuss postfix expressions further in Chapter 18; for the time being, however, you can get a pretty good idea of what a postfix epression is by studying the examples in Table 16.1. The grouping marks under each expression should

Table 16.1   Table of Postfix Expressions

Example	Infix Expression	Value
5 6 *	5 * 6	30
5 6 1 + *	5 * (6 + 1)	35
5 6 * 10 -	(5 * 6) - 10	20
4 5 6 * 3 / +	4 + ((5 * 6) / 3)	14

help you visualize the operands for each operator. The more familiar *infix expression* corresponding to each postfix expression is also shown.

The advantage of postfix form is that there is no need to group subexpressions in parentheses or to consider operator precedence. The grouping marks in Table 16.1 are only for our convenience and are not required. Next, we write a program that evaluates a postfix expression.

● Case Study: Evaluating Postfix Expressions

Problem
Simulate the operation of a calculator by reading an expression in postfix form and displaying its result. Each data character will be a blank, a digit character, or one of the operator characters from the set [+, -, *, /].

Design Overview
Using a stack of integer values makes it easy to evaluate the expression. Our program will push each integer operand onto the stack. When an operator is read, the top two operands are popped, the operation is performed on its operands, and the result is pushed back onto the stack. The final result should be the only value remaining on the stack when the end of the expression is reached.

Data Requirements

Problem Inputs
The expression to evaluate (Expression)

Problem Outputs
The expression value (Result : Integer)

Program Variables
The stack of integer operands (OpStack : Stack)
Program flag indicating result of a stack operation
(Success : Boolean)
The next character in Expression (NextCh : Char)
The index to the next character (Index : Integer)
The next integer value in Expression (NewOp : Integer)
The two operands of an operator (Op1, Op2 : Integer)

Algorithm
 1. Read the expression string.
 2. Create an empty stack of integers.
 3. Set Success to True.
 4. while Success is True and not at the end of the expression do
    begin
      5. Get the next character.

Case Study: Evaluating Postfix Expressions, continued

6. if the character is a digit then
   begin
       7. Get the integer that starts with this digit.
       8. Push the integer onto the stack.
   end
  else if the character is an operator then
    begin
       9. Pop the top two operands.
      10. Evaluate the operation.
      11. Push the result onto the stack.
    end

  end
12. Display the result

Table 16.2 shows the evaluation of the third expression in Table 16.1 using this algorithm. The arrow under the expression points to the character being processed; the stack diagram shows the stack after this character is processed.

Table 16.2 Evaluating a Postfix Expression

Expression	Action	Stack
5 6 * 10 − ↑	Push 5.	5
5 6 * 10 − ↑	Push 6.	6 5
5 6 * 10 − ↑	Pop 6 and 5; evaluate 5 * 6; push 30.	30
5 6 * 10 − ↑	Push 10.	10 30
5 6 * 10 − ↑	Pop 10 and 30; evaluate 30 − 10, push 20.	20
5 6 * 10 − ↑	Pop 20; stack is empty; result is 20.	

Refinements and Program Structure

The stack operators perform algorithm steps 2, 8, 9, 11, and 12. Steps 1 and 5 are performed by procedure ReadLnStrVar and function GetChar (imported from ADT String). Steps 7 and 10 are the only algorithm steps that require refinement. Step 7 is performed by procedure GetInteger and step 10 by function Eval. The structure chart in Fig. 16.10 shows the data flow between these two subprograms and the main program.

Figure 16.10 Structure Chart for Program PostFix

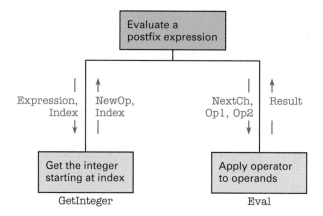

GetInteger   Eval

Coding the Main Program

The main program is shown in Fig. 16.11. Besides the operators mentioned earlier, data types StackElement (type is Integer), Stack, and String must all be imported into the main program.

Each time stack S is manipulated, the Boolean flag Success is set to indicate the success or failure of that operation. If Success is False, the program displays an error message and terminates the expression evaluation. If the final value of Success is True and the stack is empty, the result is displayed.

Figure 16.11 Program PostFix and Sample Run

```
program PostFix (Input, Output);
{
  Evaluates a postfix expression.

  IMPORT: Stack, StackElement, CreateStack, Pop, Push,
          IsEmpty from ADT Stack (see Section 16.4)
          String, Length, GetChar, RdLnStrVar from ADT String
          (see Section 13.5)
}
  {Insert type declaration for StackElement}
  {Insert type declaration for Stack}
  {Insert type declaration for String}

  var
    OpStack : Stack;              {a stack of integers}
    Expression : String;          {expression to be evaluated}
    NextCh : Char;                {the next data character}
    Index : Integer;              {index of next character}
    Op1, Op2,                     {operand values from stack}
    NewOp,                        {new operand for the stack}
    Result : Integer;             {result of operator evaluation}
    Success : Boolean;            {flag for stack operation}

  {Insert CreateStack, Push, Pop, IsEmpty}
  {Insert ReadLnStrVar, Length, and GetChar}
```

```
                    {Insert GetInteger and Eval}

        begin {Postfix}
          Write ('Enter your expression> ');
          ReadLnStrVar (Input, Expression);

          CreateStack (OpStack);                        {Create an empty stack}
          Index := 1;
          Success := True;
          while Success and (Index <= Length(Expression)) do
            {invariant:
                OpStack contains all unprocessed operands and results and
                Index <= Length(Expression) + 1
            }
            begin
              NextCh := GetChar(Expression, Index);    {Get the next character}
              if NextCh in ['0'..'9'] then
                begin {digit}
                  GetInteger(Expression, Index, NewOp);    {Get integer value}
                  Push (OpStack, NewOp, Success);          {Push integer value}
                  if not Success then
                    WriteLn ('Stack overflow error')
                end {digit}
              else if NextCh in ['+','-','*','/'] then
                begin {operator}
                  Pop (OpStack, Op2, Success);          {Get last operand}
                  Pop (OpStack, Op1, Success);          {Get first operand}
                  if not Success then
                    WriteLn ('Invalid expression')
                  else
                    begin {evaluate operator}
                      Result := Eval(NextCh, Op1, Op2);
                      Push (OpStack, Result, Success);       {Push result}
                      if not Success then
                        WriteLn ('Stack overflow')
                    end {evaluate operator}
                end; {operator}
              Index := Index + 1                        {Go to next character}
            end; {while}

          if Success then
            Pop (OpStack, Result, Success);             {Get the result}
          if Success and IsEmpty(OpStack) then
            WriteLn ('Expression value is ', Result :1)    {Print it}
          else
            WriteLn ('Invalid expression')
        end. {Postfix}

        Enter your expression> 5 6 * 10 -

        Expression value is 20
```

Coding the Subprograms

Procedure GetInteger (Fig. 16.12) accumulates the integer value of a string of consecutive digit characters and returns this value through parameter NewOp. The assignment statement

```
NewOp := (10 * NewOp) + Ord(NextCh) - Ord('0');
```

adds the numeric value of the digit character in NextCh to the numeric value being accumulated in NewOp. For example, if the current value of NewOp is 15 and NextCh is '3', NewOp gets the value 153. When GetInteger returns to the main program, Index points to the last digit of the number just processed.

Figure 16.12 Procedure GetInteger

```
procedure GetInteger (Expression {input} : String;
                      var Index {input/output},
                      NewOp {output} : Integer);
{
  Returns in NewOp the integer whose first digit is at position
  Index.
  Pre : Expression and Index are defined and the character at Index
        is a digit.
  Post: Index points to the last digit of the number whose first digit
        is pointed to by the initial value of Index.
        NewOp is the value of that number.
  Uses: Length and GetChar from ADT String
}
begin {GetInteger}
  NewOp := 0;
  NextCh := GetChar(Expression, Index);
  while (NextCh in ['0'..'9']) and (Index <= Length(Expression)) do
    {invariant:
       Prior character in NextCh was a digit and
       Index <= Length(Expression) + 1 and
       NewOp is the numerical value of all digits processed so far
    }
    begin
      NewOp := (10 * NewOp) + Ord(NextCh) - Ord('0');
      Index := Index + 1;
      NextCh := GetChar(Expression, Index)
    end; {while}

  {assert:
    NewOp is the numerical value of the substring processed and
    Index is at the end of the substring or just past it.
  }
  if not (NextCh in ['0'..'9']) then
    Index := Index - 1                   {point to the last digit}
end; {GetInteger}
```

Whenever an operator is encountered, the main program pops its two operands off the stack and calls function Eval (Fig. 16.13) to compute the result of applying the operator (passed through NextCh) to its operands (passed through Op1, Op2). The case statement in function Eval selects the appropriate operation and performs it.

Case Study: Evaluating Postfix Expressions, continued

Figure 16.13   Function Eval

```
function Eval (NextCh : Char;
               Op1, Op2 : Integer) : Integer;
{
  Applies operator NextCh to operands Op1, Op2.
  Pre : NextCh is an operator and Op1, Op2 are defined.
  Post: If NextCh is '+', returns Op1 + Op2, and so on.
}
begin {Eval}
  if NextCh in ['+', '-', '*', '/'] then
    case NextCh of
      '+' : Eval := Op1 + Op2;
      '-' : Eval := Op1 - Op2;
      '*' : Eval := Op1 * Op2;
      '/' : Eval := Op1 div Op2      {integer division}
    end {case}
  else
    WriteLn ('Error in operator symbol')
end; {Eval}
```

Testing

You have to import the necessary data types and procedures to test program PostFix. See what happens when the expression is not a valid postfix expression or when it contains characters other than those expected.

Exercises for Section 16.3

Self-Check

1. Trace the evaluation of the last expression in Table 16.1. Show the stack each time it is modified and how the values of NewOp and Result change as the program executes.

Programming

1. Modify program PostFix to handle the exponentiation operator, indicated by the symbol ^. Assume that the first operand is raised to the power indicated by the second operand.

 # 16.4   Implementing ADT Stack

This section discusses how we might implement a stack in Pascal. We begin with the internal representation for a stack.

Declaration for Type Stack

The data type `Stack` declared in the interface section for ADT `Stack` (Fig. 16.14) has two fields, `Top` and `Items`. The array field `Items` provides storage for the stack elements. `Top` is an index to this array and selects the element at the top of the stack. We can store up to `MaxStack` (value is `100`) elements in an object of type `Stack`.

Figure 16.14 Interface Section for ADT Stack

```
{
 Abstract data type Stack: contains declarations for record
 type Stack and operator procedures for an object of type Stack.

INTERFACE SECTION —

  EXPORTS: Stack, StackElement, CreateStack, Push, Pop,
           Retrieve, IsEmpty, IsFull

  DATA TYPE SPECIFICATION:
}
    const
       MaxStack = 100;

    type
       {Insert declaration for StackElement}

    Stack = record
               Top : 0..MaxStack;
               Items : array [1..MaxStack] of StackElement
            end; {Stack}
```

The comment

```
{Insert declaration for StackElement}
```

reminds us that we must declare data type `StackElement` before we can declare record type `Stack`. If we use the declaration

```
StackElement = Char;
```

a variable of type `Stack` will be able to store up to 100 characters.

As always, storage is not allocated until a variable of type `Stack` is declared. Assuming `StackElement` is type `Char`, the variable declaration

```
var
  S : Stack;
```

allocates storage for a stack, `S`, of up to 100 characters. Notice that the storage space for the entire stack is allocated at one time, even though there will not be any items on the stack initially.

The following abstract stack `S` (on the left) would be represented in memory by the record shown on the right. `S.Top` is 3, and the stack consists of the subarray `S.Items[1..3]`; the subarray `S.Items[4..100]` is currently undefined.

The array element `S.Items[S.Top]` contains the character value `'{'`, which is the value at the top of the stack.

We can change the capacity of a stack by redefining the constant `MaxStack`. Also, we can change the stack elements to another simple type or a structured type by changing the declaration for `StackElement`. If we use the declaration

```
StackElement = Integer;
```

a variable of type `Stack` will be able to store up to 100 integer values.

■ Example 16.2

Figure 16.15 shows the effect of the statement

```
Push (S, '(', Success)
```

where the initial stack S is shown on the left. Before `Push` is executed, `S.Top` is 3, so `S.Items[3]` is the element at the top of the stack. Procedure `Push` must increment `S.Top` to 4 so the new item (`'('`) will be stored in `S.Items[4]`, as shown on the right of the figure.   ■

Stack Operators

The stack operators manipulate the array field `Items` using the `Integer` field `Top` as an index to the array. Their implementation is fairly straightforward. You should have little difficulty in reading and understanding the stack operators shown in the implementation section of ADT `Stack` (Fig. 16.16).

Figure 16.15 Pushing '(' onto Stack S

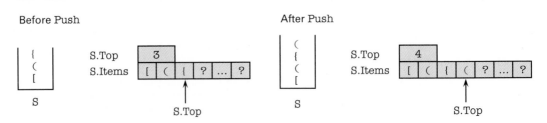

```
{
IMPLEMENTATION SECTION —

  OPERATORS:
}
  procedure CreateStack (var S {output} : Stack);
  {
    Creates an empty stack.
    Pre : None
    Post: S is an empty stack.
  }
  begin {CreateStack}
    S.Top := 0               {stack is empty}
  end; {CreateStack}


  procedure Push (var S {in/out} : Stack;
                  X {in} : StackElement;
                  var Success {out} : Boolean);
  {
    Pushes X onto stack S.
    Pre : X is defined and S is a stack that has been created.
    Post: Sets Success to indicate success (True) or failure (False)
          of push operation.
  }
  begin {Push}
    if S.Top >= MaxStack then
      Success := False       {no room on stack}
    else
      begin
        S.Top := S.Top + 1;      {increment top of stack pointer}
        S.Items[S.Top] := X;     {push X onto stack}
        Success := True
      end {if}
  end; {Push}


  procedure Pop (var S {in/out} : Stack;
                 var X {out} : StackElement;
                 var Success {out} : Boolean);
  {
    Pops the top of stack S into X.
    Pre : S is a stack that has been created.
    Post: Contents of X is character at top of stack S which is then
          removed from S. Sets Success to indicate success (True)
          or failure (False) of pop operation.
  }
  begin {Pop}
    if S.Top <= 0 then
      Success := False
    else
      begin
        X := S.Items[S.Top];     {pop top of stack into X}
        S.Top := S.Top - 1;      {decrement top of stack pointer}
        Success := True
      end {if}
  end; {Pop}
```

```
procedure Retrieve (S {in} : Stack;
                    var X {out} : StackElement;
                    var Success {out} : Boolean);
{ Copies the value at the top of the stack into X.
  Pre : S is a stack.
  Post: Contents of X is character at top of stack S; S is
        unchanged. Sets Success to indicate success (True) or
        failure (False).
}
begin {Retrieve}
  if S.Top <= 0 then
    Success := False
  else
    begin
      X := S.Items[S.Top];        {copy top of stack into X}
      Success := True
    end {if}
end; {Retrieve}


function IsEmpty (S : Stack) : Boolean;
{
  Pre : S is a stack.
  Post: Returns True if stack S is empty;
        otherwise, returns False.
}
begin {IsEmpty}
  IsEmpty := S.Top <= 0
end; {IsEmpty}


function IsFull (S : Stack) : Boolean;
{
  Pre : S is a stack.
  Post: Returns True if stack S is full;
        otherwise, returns False. }
begin {IsFull}
  IsFull := S.Top >= MaxStack
end; {IsFull}
```

Procedure `CreateStack` must be called before the stack can be manipulated. In `CreateStack`, the statement

```
S.Top := 0                    {stack is empty}
```

initializes a stack by setting its top-of-stack pointer to zero.

Procedure `Push` increments the top-of-stack pointer before it pushes a new value onto the stack. Procedure `Pop` copies the value at the top of the stack (denoted by `S.Items[S.Top]`) into `X` before decrementing the top-of-stack pointer. Procedure `Retrieve` copies the value at the top of the stack into `X` without changing the top-of-stack pointer. Functions `IsFull` and `IsEmpty` test the top-of-stack pointer to determine the stack status.

PROGRAM
STYLE

Efficiency versus Readability

Procedure `Push` in Fig. 16.16 uses the condition `S.Top >= MaxStack` to determine whether the stack represented by `S` is full. It would be more readable, but less efficient, to use the function designator IsFull(S) to test whether stack S is full. You should use the function designator Is-Full(S) for this purpose in any client program that manipulates the stack, because the stack's internal representation may be hidden from a client program. It is perfectly reasonable, however, for another stack operator to directly manipulate internal fields of a stack.

Exercises for Section 16.4

Self-Check

1. Declare a stack of fifty student records, where each record consists of a student's name (packed array of twenty characters), an exam score, and a letter grade. Can you use the stack operators to manipulate this stack?

Programming

1. Write an operator SizeOfStack that returns the number of elements currently on the stack.

 ## 16.5 The Queue Abstract Data Type

A *queue* is a data abstraction that can be used, for example, to model a line of customers waiting at a checkout counter or a stream of jobs waiting to be printed by a printer in a computer center. A queue differs from a stack in that new elements are inserted at one end (the rear of the queue) and existing elements are removed from the other end (the front of the queue). In this way, the element that has been waiting longest is removed first. In contrast, stack elements are inserted and removed from the same end (the top of the stack). A queue is called a *first-in, first-out* structure (FIFO), while a stack is called a *last-in, first-out* (LIFO) structure.

A queue of three passengers waiting to see an airline ticket agent is shown in Fig. 16.17. The name of the passenger who has been waiting the longest is

Figure 16.17 A Passenger Queue

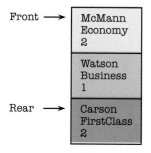

McMann (pointed to by Front); the name of the most recent arrival is Carson (pointed to by Rear). Passenger McMann will be the first one removed from the queue when an agent becomes available, and pointer Front will be moved to passenger Watson. Any new passengers will follow passenger Carson in the queue, and pointer Rear will be adjusted accordingly.

The specification for the abstract data type Queue follows; compare it with the earlier specification for an abstract stack.

Specification of Abstract Data Type Queue

Elements: A queue consists of a collection of elements that are all the same data type.

Structure: The elements of a queue are ordered according to time of arrival. The element that was first inserted into the queue is the only one that may be removed or examined. Elements are removed from the front of the queue and inserted at the rear of the queue.

Operators: The following descriptions assume these parameters:

Q represents the queue.
El (pronounced el) has the same data type as the queue elements.
Success is type Boolean and indicates whether the operation succeeds.

CreateQueue (var Q): Creates an empty queue Q.

Insert (var Q, El, var Success): If queue Q is not full, the value in El is inserted at the rear of the queue, and Success is set to True. Otherwise, the queue is not changed, and Success is set to False.

Remove (var Q, var El, var Success): If queue Q is not empty, the element at the front of the queue is removed and copied to El, and Success is set to True. If the queue is empty, El is not changed, and Success is set to False.

Retrieve (Q, var El, var Success): If queue Q is not empty, the element at the front of the queue is copied into El, and Success is set to True. If the queue is empty, El is not defined, and Success is set to False. In either case, the queue is not changed.

IsEmpty(Q): Returns True if queue Q is empty; otherwise, returns False.

IsFull(Q): Returns True if queue Q is full; otherwise, returns False.

SizeOfQueue(Q): Returns the number of elements in the queue.

We implement ADT Queue in the next section. As before, we assume that the identifier QueueElement represents the type of each queue element. Each client program must declare type QueueElement and import the type declaration for Queue.

Self-Check

1. Draw the queue in Fig. 16.17 after the insertion of first-class passenger Harris (3 seats reserved) and the removal of one passenger from the queue. Which passenger is removed? How many passengers are left?

 16.6   Queue Application

Our application is a program that processes a queue of airline passengers.

● Case Study: Maintaining a Queue of Passengers

Problem
Write a menu-driven program that maintains a queue of passengers waiting to see a ticket agent. The program user should be able to insert a new passenger at the rear of the queue, display the passenger at the front of the queue, and remove the passenger at the front of the queue. Just before it terminates, the program should display the number of passengers left in the queue.

Design Overview
We can use the queue abstract data type and operators Insert, Retrieve, and Remove to process the queue. We can simplify the program by using an abstract data type, Passenger, that contains type declarations for an airline passenger and provides its input/output operators (ReadPass and WritePass). We will implement this abstract data type later.

Data Requirements

Problem Inputs
The operation to be performed (Choice : Char)
The next passenger's data (NextPass : Passenger)

Problem Outputs
The passenger at the front of the queue (FirstPass : Passenger)

Program Variables
The queue of passengers (PassQueue : Queue)
A flag for storing the result of a queue operation
(Success : Boolean)

Algorithm
1. Initialize the queue.

Case Study: Maintaining a Queue of Passengers, continued

2. repeat
> 3. Display the menu.
> 4. Read the operation selected.
> 5. Perform the operation selected.

until user is done or a queue operation fails

6. Display the number of passengers left in the queue.

Coding the Main Program

The main program (Fig. 16.18) imports the type declarations for Passenger (from ADT Passenger) and for QueueElement and Queue (both from ADT Queue). Procedure CreateQueue (from ADT Queue) initializes the passenger queue to an empty queue. In the main program body, the statement

```
Write ('Enter I(nsert), R(emove), D(isplay), or Q(uit)> ');
```

displays the menu of choices (step 3). After the selection is read into Choice, the main program calls procedure ModifyQueue to perform step 5. Procedure ModifyQueue is discussed next.

Figure 16.18 Program UseQueue

```
program UseQueue (Input, Output);
{
  Manipulates a queue of airline passengers.

  IMPORT: Passenger, ReadPass, WritePass from ADT Passenger
          (see Fig. 16.21)
          Queue, QueueElement, CreateQueue, Insert,
          Remove, and Retrieve from ADT Queue (see Section 16.5).


  Insert type declaration for Passenger
  Insert type declaration for QueueElement
  Insert type declaration for Queue
}
  var
    PassQueue : Queue;        {a passenger queue}
    Choice : Char;            {operation request}
    Success : Boolean;        {program flag}
  {
    Insert ReadPass, WritePass
    Insert CreateQueue, Insert, Remove, Retrieve, SizeOfQueue

    Insert ModifyQueue (see Fig. 16.19)
  }

begin {UseQue}
  CreateQueue (PassQueue);              {start with an empty queue}

  {Process all requests until done.}
  repeat
    Write ('Enter I(nsert), R(emove), D(isplay), or Q(uit)> ');
    ReadLn (Choice);
```

```
      {Process current request.}
      ModifyQueue (PassQueue, Choice, Success);
      WriteLn
   until (Choice = 'Q') or (not Success)
end. {UseQueue}
```

Coding ModifyQueue

For each selection, procedure ModifyQueue (Fig. 16.19) calls the operators
required to manipulate the Queue (from ADT Queue) and the operators needed
to read or display a passenger record (from ADT Passenger). The main control
structure is a case statement that determines which operators are called.

Figure 16.19 Procedure ModifyQueue

```
procedure ModifyQueue (var Q {in/out} : Queue;
                           Choice {input} : Char;
                           var Success {output} : Boolean);
{
  Performs the operation indicated by Choice on the queue Q.
  Pre : Q has been created.
  Post: Q is modified based on Choice and Success indicates
        whether requested operation was performed.
  Uses: ReadPass, WritePass, Insert, Remove, Retrieve
}
  var
    NextPass,                   {new passenger}
    FirstPass : Passenger;      {passenger at front of queue}

begin {ModifyQueue}
  if Choice in ['I', 'R', 'D', 'Q'] then
    case Choice of
      'I' : begin {insert}
              WriteLn ('Enter passenger data.');
              ReadPass (NextPass);
              Insert (Q, NextPass, Success);
              if not Success then
                 WriteLn ('Queue is full - no insertion');
            end; {insert}
      'R' : begin {remove}
              Remove (Q, FirstPass, Success);
              if Success then
                begin
                  WriteLn ('Passenger removed from queue follows.');
                  WritePass (FirstPass)
                end
              else
                 WriteLn ('Queue is empty - no deletion')
            end; {remove}
      'D' : begin {display}
              Retrieve (Q, FirstPass, Success);
              if Success then
                begin
                  WriteLn ('Passenger at head of queue follows.');
                  WritePass (FirstPass)
                end
```

```
               else
                  WriteLn ('Queue is empty - no passenger')
               end; {display}
        'Q' : begin
                  WriteLn ('Leaving passenger queue.');
                  WriteLn ('Number of passengers in the queue is ',
                           SizeOfQueue(Q) :1)
               end {quit}
      end {case}
   else
      WriteLn ('Incorrect choice - try again.')
end; {ModifyQueue}
```

Testing

Before you can run program UseQueue, you must insert all the necessary type declarations and procedures imported from ADTs Passenger and Queue. If these ADTs import other data types and/or procedures, they also must be inserted in program UseQueue (because ADT Passenger includes operators that read and display strings, this is highly likely). We examine ADT Passenger next.

You can store the initial passenger list by selecting a sequence of insert operations. In the sample run of program UseQueue, shown in Fig. 16.20, passenger Brown is inserted first, followed by passenger Watson. After passenger Brown is removed from the queue, the new passenger at the front of the queue (Watson) is displayed.

To test the program thoroughly, you have to try to display or remove a passenger after the queue is empty. Either attempt should cause the error message Queue is empty – to be displayed before the program terminates. To check that there is no insertion after the queue is full, it is necessary to redefine the queue capacity (part of the declaration for type Queue) so that the message Queue is full – no insertion appears after a small number of passenger insertions takes place.

Figure 16.20   Sample Run of Program UseQueue

```
Enter I(nsert), R(emove), D(isplay), or Q(uit)> I
Enter passenger data.
Passenger Name> Brown
Class (F, B, E, S)> E
Number of seats - Enter an integer between 1 and 30> 2

Enter I(nsert), R(emove), D(isplay), or Q(uit)> I
Enter passenger data.
Passenger Name> Watson
Class (F, B, E, S)> B
Number of Seats - Enter an integer between 1 and 30> 1

Enter I(nsert), R(emove), D(isplay), or Q(uit)> I
Enter passenger data.
Passenger Name> Dietz
```

```
Class (F, B, E, S)> E
Number of Seats — Enter an integer between 1 and 30> 3

Enter I(nsert), R(emove), D(isplay), or Q(uit)> R
Passenger removed from queue follows.
Brown
Economy Class
  2 Seats

Enter I(nsert), R(emove), D(isplay), or Q(uit)> D
Passenger at head of queue follows.
Watson
Business Class
  1 Seat

Enter I(nsert), R(emove), D(isplay), or Q(uit)> Q
Leaving passenger queue.
Number of passengers in the queue is 2
```

Coding the Abstract Data Type Passenger

Figure 16.21 shows an ADT that contains a declaration for record type Passenger. Because the Name field is a packed array of characters (type String-
Type), procedure ReadLnString is needed to read a passenger's name. Procedure ReadPass and WritePass read and write a single passenger's record. (The
completion of WritePass is left as an exercise.)

Figure 16.21   ADT Passenger

```
{
  Abstract data type Passenger: contains declarations for record
  type Passenger and procedures for reading and displaying values of
  type Passenger.

INTERFACE SECTION —

  EXPORT: Passenger, ReadPass, WritePass

  IMPORT: ReadLnString (see Fig. 10.20)
          EnterInt (see Fig. 7.7)

  DATA TYPE SPECIFICATION:
}
  const
    MaxSeats = 30;
    StringSize = 20;

  type
    ClassType = (FirstClass, Business, Economy, StandBy, Undesignated);
    StringType = packed array [1..StringSize] of Char;
    Passenger = record
                  Name : StringType;
                  Class : ClassType;
                  NumSeats : Integer
                end; {Passenger}
```

```
{
IMPLEMENTATION SECTION —

  OPERATORS:
}

  {Insert EnterInt and ReadLnString}


  procedure ReadPass (var OnePass {output} : Passenger);
  {
    Reads one record of type Passenger.
    Pre : None
    Post: Data are read into all fields of OnePass
    Uses : ReadLnString
  }
    var
       ClassCh : Char;          {input — character for class type}
       NameLen : Integer;       {input — length of Name}

    function ClassConvert (ClassCh : Char) : ClassType;
    {
      Converts a character to a class type.
    }
    begin {ClassConvert stub}
      ClassConvert := Economy
    end; {ClassConvert}

  begin {ReadPass}
    with OnePass do
      begin
        Write ('Passenger name> ');
        ReadLnString (Input, StringSize, Name, NameLen);
        Write ('Class (F, B, E, S)> ');
        ReadLn (ClassCh);
        Class := ClassConvert(ClassCh);
        Write ('Number of Seats — ');
        EnterInt (1, 30, NumSeats)
      end {with}
  end; {ReadPass}


  procedure WritePass (OnePass : Passenger);
  {
    Displays one record of type Passenger.
  }
  begin {WritePass stub}
    Write ('Name: ');
    WriteLn (OnePass.Name)
  end; {WritePass stub}
```

At this point, we can draw the module-dependency diagram for program UseQueue (Fig. 16.22). The type declaration for Passenger should appear first in UseQueue, followed by the type declaration for QueueElement (QueueElement = Passenger) and Queue. The first procedures declared should be EnterInt

Figure 16.22   Module-Dependency Diagram for UseQueue

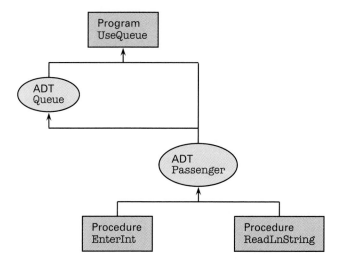

`EnterInt` and `ReadLnString`, followed by the operators for `Passenger` and the operators for `Queue` (implemented next).

Exercises for Section 16.6

Self-Check

1. Draw the queue after the completion of the sample run in Fig. 16.20.

Programming

1. Complete procedure `WritePass`.
2. Complete function `ClassConvert` (in procedure `ReadPass`).

16.7   Implementing ADT Queue

To represent a queue, we will use a record structure that consists of three `Integer` fields (`Front`, `Rear`, `NumItems`) and an array field, `Items`, that provides storage for the queue elements. The declarations for a queue whose capacity is 100 elements is shown in the interface section for `QueueADT` (Fig. 16.23).

Figure 16.23   Interface Section for ADT Queue

```
{
   Abstract data type Queue: contains declarations for record
   type Queue and operator procedures for an object of type Queue.
```

```
INTERFACE SECTION —

   EXPORTS: Queue, QueueElement, CreateQueue, Insert, Remove,
            Retrieve, IsEmpty, IsFull, SizeOfQueue

   SPECIFICATION:
}
   const
     MaxQueue = 100;

   type
     {insert declaration for QueueElement}

     QueueRange = 1..MaxQueue;
     Queue = record
               Front, Rear : QueueRange;
               NumItems : 0..MaxQueue;
               Items : array [QueueRange] of QueueElement
             end; {Queue}
```

The Integer fields Front and Rear are pointers to the queue elements at the front and the rear of the queue, respectively. The Integer field NumItems keeps track of the actual number of items in the queue and allows us to easily determine if the queue is Empty (NumItems is 0) or Full (NumItems is MaxQueue). The comment

```
{insert declaration for QueueElement}
```

reminds us that we must declare data type QueueElement before we can declare record type Queue.

If we use the type declaration

```
type
   QueueElement = Char;
```

a variable of type Queue can store up to 100 characters. If we import data type Passenger (from ADT Passenger) and use the declaration

```
type
   QueueElement = Passenger;
```

a variable of type Queue can store up to 100 airline passengers.

It makes sense to store the first queue record in element 1, the second queue record in element 2, and so on. After a queue is filled with data, Front has a value of 1 and Rear points to the last record inserted in the queue (Rear <= MaxQueue). Fig. 16.24 shows a queue, Q, that is filled to its capacity (NumItems is MaxQueue). The queue contains the symbols &, *, +, /, − in that order.

Because Q is filled to capacity, we cannot insert a new character. We can remove a queue element by decrementing NumItems and incrementing Front to 2, thereby removing Q.Items[1] (the symbol &). However, we still cannot insert a new character, because Rear is at its maximum value. One way to solve this problem is to represent the array field Items as a circular array. In a *circular array*, the elements wrap around so that the first element actually follows the

Figure 16.24   A Queue Filled with Characters

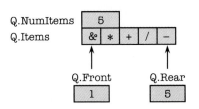

Figure 16.25   A Queue as a Circular Array

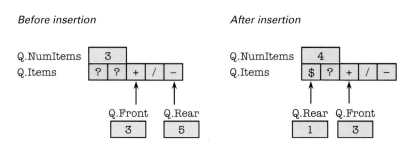

last. This allows us to "increment" `Rear` to 1 and store a new character in
`Q.Items[1]`.

■ Example 16.3

Figure 16.25 shows the effect of inserting a new element in the queue just
described. As shown on the left of the figure, three characters are currently in
this queue (stored in `Q.Items[3..5]`). The question marks in `Q.Items[1..2]`
indicate that the values stored in these elements have been removed from the
queue. The two elements that are currently unused are shown in gray.

The right side of Fig. 16.25 shows the queue after insertion of a new
character (`'$'`). The value of `Rear` is "incremented" to 1, and the next element
is inserted in `Q.Items[1]`. This queue element follows the character `'-'` in
`Q.Items[5]`. The value of `Q.Front` is still 3 because the character `'+'` at
`Q.Items[3]` has been in the queue the longest. `Q.Items[2]` is now the only
queue element that is unused. The new queue contains the symbols +, /, −, $
in that order.

Figure 16.26 shows the operators for the queue abstract data type.   ■

Figure 16.26   Operators for ADT Queue

```
{
IMPLEMENTATION SECTION −

  OPERATORS:
}
```

```
procedure CreateQueue (var Q {output} : Queue);
{
   Creates an empty queue.
   Pre : None
   Post: Q is initialized to a queue of zero elements.
}
begin {CreateQueue}
   Q.NumItems := 0;              {queue is empty}
   Q.Front := 1;
   Q.Rear := MaxQueue            {queue is circular}
end; {CreateQueue}


procedure Insert (var Q {in/out} : Queue;
                      El {in} : QueueElement;
                      var Success {out} : Boolean);
{
   Inserts El in queue Q.
   Pre : Q has been created.
   Post: If Q is not full, increments Rear and inserts El.
         Sets Success to indicate success or failure.
}
begin {Insert}
   if Q.NumItems = MaxQueue then
     Success := False         {queue is full}
   else
     begin {insert El}
       Q.Rear := (Q.Rear mod MaxQueue) + 1;     {increment Rear}
       Q.Items[Q.Rear] := El;
       Q.NumItems := Q.NumItems + 1;
       Success := True
     end {insert El}
end; {Insert}


procedure Remove (var Q {in/out} : Queue;
                      var El {out} : QueueElement;
                      var Success {out} : Boolean);
{
   Removes the element at the front of queue Q and copies it into
   El.
   Pre : Q has been created.
   Post: Front is decremented,
         If Q is not empty, El contains its first element,
         and Success indicates success or failure.
}
begin {Remove}
   if Q.NumItems = 0 then
     Success := False          {queue is empty}
   else
     begin
       {Remove the element at the front of the queue.}
       El := Q.Items[Q.Front];
       Q.Front := (Q.Front mod MaxQueue) + 1; {increment Front}
       Q.NumItems := Q.NumItems - 1;
       Success := True
     end {if}
end; {Remove}


procedure Retrieve (Q {in} : Queue;
```

```
              var El {out} : QueueElement;
              var Success {out} : Boolean);
{
  Copies the value at the front of queue Q into El without
  removing it.
  Pre : Q has been created.
  Post: If Q is not empty, El contains its first element
        and Success indicates success or failure.
}
begin {Retrieve}
  if Q.NumItems = 0 then
    Success := False            {queue is empty}
  else
    begin
      {Retrieve the item at the front of the queue.}
      El := Q.Items[Q.Front];
      Success := True
    end {if}
end; {Retrieve}

function IsEmpty (Q : Queue) : Boolean;
{
    Tests for an empty queue.
    Pre : Q has been created.
    Post: Returns True if queue Q is empty; otherwise, returns False.
}
begin {IsEmpty}
  IsEmpty := Q.NumItems = 0
end; {IsEmpty}

function IsFull (Q : Queue) : Boolean;
{
    Test for a full queue.
    Pre : Q has been created.
    Post: Returns True if queue Q is full; otherwise, returns False.
}
begin {IsFull}
  IsFull := Q.NumItems = MaxQueue
end; {IsFull}

function SizeOfQueue (Q : Queue) : Integer;
{
    Finds the number of elements in a queue.
    Pre : Q has been created.
    Post: Returns the number of elements in the queue.
}
begin {SizeOfQueue}
  SizeOfQueue := Q.NumItems
end; {SizeOfQueue}
```

Procedure CreateQueue must be called before any of the other operators. CreateQueue sets Q.NumItems to 0 and Q.Front to 1, because array element Q.Items[1] is considered the front of the empty queue. Q.Rear is initialized to MaxQueue because the queue is circular.

In procedure Insert, the statement

```
    Q.Rear := (Q.Rear mod MaxQueue) + 1;        {increment Rear}
```

is used to increment the value of Q.Rear. When Q.Rear is less than MaxQueue, this statement simply increments its value by 1. But when Q.Rear is equal to MaxQueue, this statement sets Q.Rear to 1 (MaxQueue mod MaxQueue is 0), thereby wrapping the last element of the queue around to the first element. Because CreateQueue initializes Q.Rear to MaxQueue, the first queue element will be placed in Items[1], as desired.

In procedure Remove, the element currently stored in Items[Front] is copied into El before Q.Front is incremented. In procedure Retrieve, the element at Items[Front] is copied into El, but Q.Front is not changed.

The number of elements in the queue is changed by procedures Insert and Remove, so Q.NumItems must be incremented by 1 in Insert and decremented by 1 in Remove. The value of Q.NumItems is tested in both IsFull and IsEmpty to determine the status of the queue. Function SizeOfQueue simply returns the value of Q.NumItems.

Exercises for Section 16.7.

Self-Check

1. What are the final values of Q.Front, Q.Rear, and the Name fields of Q.Items[1..3] after the sample run of UseQueue in Fig. 16.20?
2. Provide the algorithm for the operator in programming exercise 1, which follows. If program UseQueue calls this operator, how does it affect the module dependency diagram in Fig. 16.22?

Programming

1. Write an operator that displays the entire queue contents, from Front to Rear, inclusive.

 ## 16.8 Common Programming Errors

In this chapter, we used an array field to store the contents of a stack or a queue. Consequently, all stack and queue operators manipulated an array subscript. The errors you are likely to encounter are the same errors discussed at the end of Chapter 10. The most common error when using arrays is an out-of-range subscript.

The client programs in this chapter all used one or more abstract data types. Make sure that the abstract data types are available in your procedure library and that all necessary type declarations and procedure declarations are inserted where they belong in the client program. Take advantage of any compiler directives provided by your Pascal compiler to perform this insertion automatically. Otherwise, you will have to use an editor to do the insertions yourself.

This chapter introduced two data structures, stacks and queues. Stacks are used to implement recursion and expression translation. A stack is a last-in, first-out data structure. This means that the last item inserted is the first one removed. In contrast, a queue is a first-in, first-out data structure. Queues are used to implement waiting lists.

We showed how to use these abstractions to perform many useful operations. In particular, we used stacks to check for balanced parentheses and to evaluate arithmetic expressions. We also showed how to implement stacks and queues using arrays.

✓ Quick-Check Exercises

1. A stack is a _____ data structure; a queue is a _____ data structure.
2. Would a compiler use a stack or a queue in a program that converts regular arithmetic expressions to postfix form?
3. Would a time-sharing system use a stack or a queue in a program that determines which job should be executed next?
4. Would a compiler use a stack or a queue to keep track of return addresses for procedure calls?
5. Draw the array representation of the following stack. What is S.Items[1]? What is the value of S.Top? What is the value of S.Items[S.Top-1]?

```
   ┌─────┐
   │  $  │
   │  *  │
   │  &  │
   └─────┘
      S
```

6. Why should the statement S.Top := S.Top – 1 not appear in a client program of ADT Stack?
7. Write a program segment that removes the element just below the top of the stack from the stack. Use the stack operators.
8. Write a stack operator called PopNextTop that performs the operation in exercise 7. Do not use the stack operators.
9. Assume that a circular queue Q of capacity 6 contains the five characters +, *, –, &, #, where + is stored in the front of the queue. In the array representation, what is the value of Q.Front? What is the value of Q.Rear? What is the value of Q.Items[Q.Rear-1]?
10. Delete the character at the front of the queue in exercise 9 and insert the character \ and then %. Draw the new queue. What is the value of Q.Front? What is the value of Q.Rear? What is the value of Q.Items[Q.Rear-1]?
11. Can you have two stacks of real numbers in the same client program? Can you have a stack of integers and a stack of characters in the same client program?

Answers to Quick-Check Exercises
1. Last-in, first-out; first-in, first-out
2. Stack
3. Queue—give priority to the job waiting the longest to execute.

4. Stack
5. &, S.Top is 3, *

S.Top   `3`

S.Items   `&` `*` `$`

6. The client program should not be aware of the internal representation of the stack.
7. Pop (S, X, Success);
   Pop (S, Y, Success);
   Push (S, X, Success)
8. ```
procedure PopNextTop (var S {input/output} : Stack;
                      var Ch {output} : Char;
                      var Success {output} : Boolean);
begin
  S.Items[Top-1] := S.Items[S.Top];
  S.Top := S.Top - 1
end; {PopNextTop}
```
9. Q.Front is 1; Q.Rear is 5; &
10. Q.Front is 2; Q.Rear is 1; \

Q.Items   `%` `*` `−` `&` `#` `\`

      ↑   ↑

   Q.Rear   Q.Front

11. Yes; no

# Review Questions

1. Show the effect of each of the following operations on stack S. Assume that Y (type Char) contains the character '&'. What are the final values of X and Success (type Boolean) and the contents of stack S? Ignore any statements with syntax errors.

```
CreateStack (S);
Push (S, '+', Success);
Pop (S, X, Success);
Pop (S, X, Success);
Push (S, '(', Success);
Push (S, Y, Success);
Pop (S, '&', Success)
```

2. Assuming stack S is implemented in an array, answer exercise 1 by showing the values of integer field Top and array field Items after each operation.
3. Write a stack operator called PopTwo that removes the top two stack elements and returns them as procedure results. Use procedure Pop.
4. Answer exercise 3 without using Pop.
5. Answer exercise 1 for a queue Q of characters. Replace CreateStack with CreateQueue, Push with Insert, and Pop with Remove.
6. Assuming queue Q is implemented in an array with five elements, answer exercise 2 by showing the values of integer fields Front and Rear and array field Items after each operation.
```

7. Write a queue operator called `MoveToRear` that moves the element currently at the front of the queue to the rear of the queue. The element that was second in line will be at the front of the queue. Do this using `Insert` and `Remove` operators.

8. Answer exercise 7 without using `Insert` and `Remove` operators. Manipulate the internal queue fields directly.

9. Write a queue operator called `MoveToFront` that moves the element at the rear of the queue to the front of the queue. Do this using `Insert` and `Remove`.

10. Answer exercise 9 without using `Insert` and `Remove`.

Programming Projects

1. Extend the queue abstract data type to include an operator that displays a queue. Change `QueueElement` to represent a customer at a bank. Store the customer's name, transaction type, and amount in the customer record. Write a client module that simulates a typical session for a bank teller. After every five customers are processed, display the size of the queue and the names of the customers who are waiting.

2. Carry out project 1 using a stack instead of a queue.

3. Write a program to monitor the flow of an item into and out of a warehouse. The warehouse will have numerous deliveries and shipments for this item (a widget) during the time period covered. A shipment out is billed at a profit of 50 percent over the cost of a widget. Unfortunately, each shipment received may have a different cost associated with it. The accountants for the firm have instituted a first-in, first-out system for filling orders. This means that the newest widgets are the first ones sent out to fill an order. This method of inventory can be represented using a stack. The `Push` procedure will insert a shipment received. The `Pop` procedure will delete a shipment out. Each data record will consist of

   S or O: shipment received or an order to be sent
   #: quantity received or shipped out
   Cost: cost per widget (for a shipment received only)
   Vendor: character string that names company sent to or
           received from

   Write the necessary procedures to store the shipments received and to process orders. The output for an order will consist of the quantity and the total cost for all the widgets in the order. Hint: Each widget price is 50 percent higher than its cost. The widgets used to fill an order may come from multiple shipments with different costs.

4. Redo project 3 assuming the widgets are shipped using a first-in, first-out strategy. Use a queue to store the widget orders.

5. Write a client program for the stack abstract data type that can be used to compile a simple arithmetic expression without parentheses. For example, the expression

   ```
   A + B * C - D
   ```

   should be compiled as the table

Operation	Operand1	Operand2	Result
*	B	C	Z
+	A	Z	Y
−	Y	D	X

The table shows the order in which the operations are performed (*, +, –) and the operands for each operator. The result column gives the name of an identifier (working backward from Z) chosen to hold each result. Assume the operands are the letters A through F and the operators are (+, –, *, /).

Your program should read each character and process it as follows. If the character is a blank, ignore it. If it is an operand, push it onto the operand stack. If the character is not an operator, display an error message and terminate the program. If it is an operator, compare its precedence with that of the operator on top of the stack (* and / have higher precedence than + and –). If the new operator has higher precedence than the one currently on top (or if the stack is empty), it should be pushed onto the stack.

If the new operator has the same or lower precedence, the operator on the top of the stack must be evaluated next. This is done by popping it off the operator stack along with a pair of operands from the operand stack and writing a new line of the output table. The character selected to hold the result should then be pushed onto the operand stack. Next, the new operator should be compared to the new top of the operator stack. Continue to generate output table lines until the top of the operator stack has lower precedence than the new operator or the stack is empty. At this point, push the new operator onto the top of the stack and examine the next character in the data string. When the end of the string is reached, pop any remaining operators along with its operand pair as just described. Remember to push the result character onto the operand stack after each table line is generated.

Dynamic Data Structures

17

T his chapter discusses how Pascal can be used to create *dynamic data struc-tures*. Dynamic data structures are data structures that expand and contract as a program executes. A dynamic data structure is a collection of elements (called *nodes*) that are records. Unlike an array, which always contains storage for a fixed number of elements, the number of records stored in a dynamic data structure changes as the program executes.

Dynamic data structures are extremely flexible. It is relatively easy to add new information by creating a new node and inserting it between two existing nodes. It is also relatively easy to delete a node.

In this chapter, we examine several examples of dynamic data structures. These include lists, stacks, queues, and circular lists. You will learn how to store information in these data structures and how to process that information.

17.1 Pointers and the New Statement

Before discussing dynamic data structures, we will introduce the pointer data type. We can declare variables (called *pointer variables*) whose types are pointer types. We can store the memory address of a data object in a pointer variable and, in this way, reference or access the data object through the pointer variable that points to it.

For example, the type declaration

```
type
   RealPointer = ^Real;

var
   P : RealPointer;
```

identifies `RealPointer` as the name of a data type. Read `^Real` as "pointer to Real." The variable declaration specifies that `P` is a pointer variable of type `RealPointer`. This means that we can store the memory address of a type `Real` variable in `P`.

The statement

```
New (P);
```

calls the Pascal procedure `New`, which allocates storage for a type `Real` value and places the address of this memory cell in pointer variable P. Once storage is allocated for the type `Real` value pointed to by P, we can store a value in that memory cell and manipulate it. The exact location in memory of this particular cell is immaterial.

We can represent the value of a pointer variable by an arrow drawn to a memory cell. The diagram

shows that pointer variable P points to a memory cell whose contents are un-known. This is the situation that exists just after `New(P)` is executed.

Notice that the two memory cells shown in the diagram are allocated storage at different times. Storage is allocated for the cell on the left during compilation when the variable declaration is reached. Storage is allocated for the cell on the right during run-time when the New statement is executed.

The symbol P^ or P↑ references the memory cell pointed to by pointer variable P. The ^ (caret) or ↑ (uparrow) is called the *dereferencing operator.* (Don't confuse the symbol ↑ with a cursor movement key.) The assignment statement

```
P^ := 15.0
```

stores the Real value 15.0 in memory cell P^ (the cell pointed to by P), as shown next.

P

The statement

```
Write (P^ :12:1)
```

displays the value (15.0) stored in memory cell P^. The statements

```
P := 15.0;          {invalid assignment}
Write (P :12:1)     {invalid address display}
```

are both invalid because we cannot store a type Real value in pointer variable P nor can we display the value (an address) of a pointer variable.

We are introducing pointer variables and pointer types now because they are used to create and access dynamic data structures. Later in this chapter, you will see how to use a pointer variable to reference a dynamic data structure and how to use pointer fields to connect the nodes of a dynamic data structure.

Pointer Type Declaration

SYNTAX DIAGRAM

Form: type *ptype* = ^*dtype;*
Example: type RealPointer =^Real;
Interpretation: Pointer type *ptype* is a data type whose values are memory cell addresses. A data object whose address is stored in a variable of type *ptype* must be type *dtype*.

New Procedure

SYNTAX DIAGRAM

Form: New (*pvar*)
Example: New (P)
Interpretation: Storage for a new data object is allocated, and the address of this data object is stored in pointer variable *pvar*. If *pvar* is type *ptype*, the internal representation and size of the new data object is determined from the declaration for *ptype*. *pvar*^ (or *pvar*↑) references this data object.

Records with Pointer Fields

Because we don't know beforehand how many nodes will be in a dynamic data structure, we cannot allocate storage for a dynamic data structure in the conventional way, that is, through a variable declaration. Instead, we must allocate storage for each node as needed and, somehow, join that node to the rest of the structure.

We can connect two nodes if we include a pointer field in each node. The declarations

```
type
  NodePointer = ^Node;
  Node = record
            Current : packed array [1..2] of Char;
            Volts : Integer;
            Link : NodePointer
         end; {Node}

var
  P, Q, R : NodePointer;
```

identify `NodePointer` as a pointer type. A pointer variable of type `NodePointer` points to a record of type `Node` with three fields: `Current`, `Volts`, and `Link`. The `Link` field is also type `NodePointer`. We can use this field to point to the "next" node in a dynamic data structure. We illustrate how to connect two nodes in the next section.

Notice that the type declaration for `NodePointer` makes reference to the identifier `Node`, which is not yet declared. The declaration of a pointer type is the only situation in which Pascal allows us to reference an undeclared identifier.

Variables `P`, `Q`, and `R` are pointer variables and can be used to reference records of type `Node` (denoted by `P^`, `Q^`, and `R^`). An address can be stored in a pointer variable in one of two ways. The statements

```
New (P);  New (Q);
```

allocate storage for two records of type `Node`. The memory address of the first of these records is stored in `P`, and the memory address of the second of these records is stored in `Q`. All three fields of these two nodes are initially undefined.

The assignment statements

```
P^.Current := 'AC';  P^.Volts := 115;
Q^.Current := 'DC';  Q^.Volts := 12;
```

define two fields of these nodes, as shown in Fig. 17.1. The `Link` fields are still undefined. It makes no difference where the arrow representing the value of a pointer variable touches its node.

Besides using a `New` statement, we can also use an assignment statement to store an address in a pointer variable. The *pointer assignment statement*

```
R := P;
```

copies the value of pointer variable `P` into pointer variable `R`. This means that pointers `P` and `R` contain the same memory address and, therefore, point to the same node, as shown in Fig. 17.2.

Figure 17.1 Nodes P^ and Q^

673

17.1 Pointers and the
New Statement

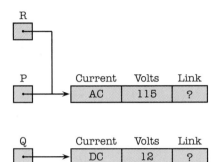

Figure 17.2 Nodes (R^, P^) and Q

We can compare two pointer variables using the relational operators = and
<>. The following conditions are all true for pointer variables P, Q, and R above.
We cannot use any of the other relational operators with pointer variables.

```
P = R
P <> Q
R <> Q
```

The pointer assignment statements

```
P := Q;   Q := R;
```

would have the effect of exchanging the nodes pointed to by P and Q, as shown
in Fig. 17.3.

Figure 17.3 Nodes (R^, Q^) and P^

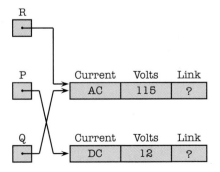

The statement

```
WriteLn (Q^.Current, P^.Current);
```

displays the Current fields of the records pointed to by Q and P. For the situation depicted in Fig. 17.3, the line

```
ACDC
```

would be displayed.

The statement

```
New (Q)
```

changes the value of Q to the address of a new node, thereby disconnecting Q from its previous node. The new values of pointer variables P, Q, and R are shown in Fig. 17.4. The data fields of the new node pointed to by Q are initially undefined.

Pointers P, Q, and R are analogous to subscripts in that they select a particular node, or element, of a data structure. Unlike subscripts, however, their range of values is not declared and their values (memory cell addresses) cannot be printed.

It is important that you understand the difference between using P and P^ in a program. P is a pointer variable (type NodePointer) and is used to store the address of a data structure of type Node. P can be assigned a new value through a pointer assignment or execution of a New statement. P^ is the name of the record pointed to by P and can be manipulated like any other record in Pascal. The field selectors P^.Current and P^.Volts can be used to reference data (a string and an integer) stored in this record.

Connecting Nodes

One purpose of dynamically allocated nodes is to enable us to grow data structures of varying size. We accomplish this by connecting individual nodes. If you look at the nodes allocated in the last section, you will see that their Link fields

Figure 17.4 Nodes R^, P^, and Q^

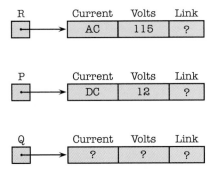

Figure 17.5 Connecting Nodes

675

17.1 Pointers and the
New Statement

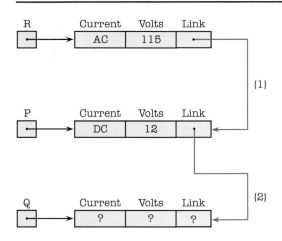

are undefined. Because the Link fields are type NodePointer, they can be used
to store a memory cell address. The pointer assignment statement

    {1} R^.Link := P;

copies the address stored in P into the Link field of Node R^, thereby connecting
node R^ to Node P^. Similarly, the pointer assignment statement

    {2} P^.Link := Q

copies the address stored in pointer variable Q into the Link field of node P^,
thereby connecting node P^ to node Q^. The situation after execution of these
two assignment statements is shown in Fig. 17.5. The arrows that represent the
new values of R^.Link and P^.Link are shown in color. The label next to the
arrow denotes one of the pointer assignments.

   The data structure pointed to by R has now grown to include all three
nodes. The first node is referenced by R^. The second node can be referenced
by P^ or R^.Link^. Finally, the third node can be referenced by Q^, P^.Link^,
or even R^.Link^.Link^.

Exercises for Section 17.1

Self-Check

1. For Fig. 17.5, explain the effect of each of the following legal assignment
   statements:
   a. R^.Current := 'CA'   e. R^.Link^.Volts := 0
   b. P^ := R^   f. P := R
   c. P.Current := 'HT'   g. R^.Link^.Link^.Current := 'XY'
   d. P := 54   h. Q^.Volts := R^.Volts

2. The assignment statements

       R := P;   P := Q;   Q := R

exchange the values of pointer variables P and Q (type NodePointer). What do the following assignment statements do?

```
R^.Current := P^.Current;
P^.Current := Q^.Current;
Q^.Current := R^.Current
```

Programming

1. Write a program segment that creates a collection of nodes and stores the musical scale (do, re, mi, fa, so, la, ti, do) in those nodes. Connect the nodes so that do is stored in the first node, re in the second, and so on. Leave the Volts field undefined.

 ## 17.2 Manipulating the Heap

In the last section, you saw that a new record is created whenever the New procedure is executed. You may be wondering where in memory the new record is stored. Pascal maintains a storage pool of available memory cells called a *heap*; memory cells from this pool are allocated whenever procedure New is executed.

Effect of the New Statement on the Heap

If P is a pointer variable of type NodePointer (declared in the last section), the statement

```
New (P)
```

allocates memory space for the storage of two characters, an integer variable, and an address. These cells are originally undefined (they retain whatever data was last stored in them) and the memory address of the first cell allocated is stored in P. Allocated cells are no longer considered part of the heap. The only way to reference allocated cells is through pointer variable P (for example, P^.Current, P^.Volts, or P^.Link).

Figure 17.6 shows the pointer variable P and the heap before and after the execution of New (P). The *before* diagram shows pointer variable P as undefined

Figure 17.6 Heap before and after New (P)

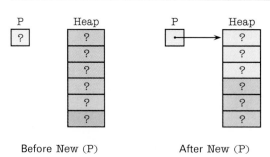

before the execution of New (P). The *after* diagram shows P pointing to the first of three memory cells allocated for the new record (assuming that three memory cells can accommodate a record of type Node). The cells still considered part of the heap are in the darker color.

For example, if the memory cells with addresses 1000 through 1005 were originally in the heap, after the execution of New (P) only the memory cells with addresses 1003 through 1005 would be considered still part of the heap. The address 1000 would be stored in pointer variable P, and that cell would be named P^.Current; memory cells 1001 and 1002 would be named P^.Volts and P^.Link, respectively.

Returning Cells to the Heap

The procedure call statement

```
Dispose (P)
```

returns the memory cells pointed to by P to the heap. The value of pointer variable P becomes undefined, and the data formerly associated with P^ are no longer accessible. The three cells that are returned to the heap can be reused later when another New statement is executed.

Often, more than one pointer points to the same record. For this reason, you must be careful when you return the storage occupied by a record to the heap. If cells are reallocated after they are returned, errors may result if they are later referenced by another pointer that still points to them. Make sure you have no need for a particular record before you return the storage occupied by it.

SYNTAX DISPLAY

The Dispose Procedure

Form: Dispose (*pvar*)
Example: Dispose (P)
Interpretation: The memory cells that make up the record whose address is stored in pointer *pvar* are returned to the heap. These cells can be reallocated when procedure New is called.

 # 17.3   Linked Lists

This section introduces an important data structure called a *linked list* or, simply, *list*. You will see how to build and manipulate lists in Pascal.

Abstract Lists

An abstract list is a sequence of nodes in which each node is linked or connected to the node following it. An abstract list with three nodes follows.

Each node in the list has two fields: the first field contains data; the second field is a pointer (represented by an arrow) to the next list element. A pointer variable (Head) points to the first list element, or *list head*. The last list element always has a diagonal line in its pointer field to indicate the end of the list.

Lists are an important data structure because they can be modified easily. For example, a new node containing the string 'Bye' can be inserted between the strings 'Boy' and 'Cat' by changing only one pointer value (the one from 'Boy') and setting the pointer from the new node to point to 'Cat'. This is true regardless of how many elements are in the list. The list shown next is after the insertion; the new pointer values are shown in color.

Similarly, it is quite easy to delete a list element. Only one pointer value has to be changed, the pointer that currently points to the element being deleted. The linked list is redrawn as follows after the string 'Boy' is deleted, by changing the pointer from the node 'Ace'. The node containing the string 'Boy' is effectively disconnected from the list and can be returned to the heap. The new list consists of the strings 'Ace', 'Bye', 'Cat'.

Representing Linked Lists Using Pointers

The preceding abstract list is relatively easy to create in Pascal using pointers and dynamic allocation. In Section 17.1, you saw how to connect three nodes with pointer fields. Although you didn't know it at the time, the data structure shown in Fig. 17.5 could be considered a list of three nodes with pointer variable R as the pointer to its head.

In Pascal, the reserved word nil is a predefined value that can be assigned to any pointer variable. It indicates that the pointer variable does not point to any memory cells on the heap. If Head is a pointer variable, we can use the assignment statement

```
Head := nil
```

to indicate that Head points to an *empty list*, a list with zero nodes.

The pointer value `nil` is drawn as a diagonal line.

Normally, we assign the value `nil` to the pointer field of the last node in a list. After the assignment statement

```
Q^.Link := nil
```

is executed, the data structure in Fig. 17.5 implements the following linked list. Each node has two data fields (`Current` and `Volts`) and one pointer field (`Link`).

Representing Linked Lists Using Arrays

You can also represent a linked list as an array of records in which an `Integer` field stores the index of the next list element. Figure 17.7 shows the previous abstract list stored in an array (`Nodes`) whose elements are records (type `Node`). The last field of each record contains the index (subscript) of the next element. The variable `R` contains the subscript of the first list element. The three list nodes happen to be stored in array elements 2, 4, and 1, in that order, although any three elements could be used. Element 1 has a link field of 0, which indicates the end of the list.

PROGRAM STYLE

Storage Considerations for List Representations

Lists stored in arrays are just as easy to modify as lists that are created using pointer variables. To insert or delete a list element, it is necessary only to change one or more subscript values. The disadvantage, however, is that memory space for the entire array must be allocated at one time. If you create a list using pointer variables and dynamic allocation, the size of the list in memory will grow and shrink as needed, and the storage allocated to it will change accordingly. For this reason, we recommend using pointers to implement lists.

Exercises for Section 17.3

Self-Check

1. For the array `Nodes` shown in Fig. 17.7, trace the execution of the following program fragment. What is printed?

Figure 17.7 Array Representation of a Linked List

```
R := 2;
while R <> 0 do
  begin
    WriteLn (Nodes[R].Current, Nodes[R].Volts);
    R := Nodes[R].Link
  end; {while}
```

Programming

1. Solve programming exercise 1 from Section 17.1, assuming that array Nodes
   is used to store the scale.

17.4 Linked-List Operators

This section and the ones that follow consider some common list-processing
operations and show how to implement them using pointer variables. We assume
that the structure of each list node corresponds to type ListNode, declared as
follows. Pointer variable Head points to the list head.

```
const
  StringSize = 3;

type
  StringType = packed array [1..StringSize] of Char;
  ListPointer = ^ListNode;
  ListNode = record
               Word : StringType;
               Link : ListPointer;
             end; {ListNode}

var
  Head : ListPointer;              {pointer to list head}
```

Traversing a List

In many list-processing operations, we must process each node in the list in
sequence; this is called *traversing* a list. To traverse a list, we must start at the
list head and follow the list pointers.

One operation that we must perform on any data structure is displaying
its contents. To display the contents of a list, we traverse the list and display

only the values of the information fields, not the link fields. Procedure PrintList in Fig. 17.8 displays the Word field of each node (type ListNode) in the existing list whose list head is passed as a parameter (type ListPointer). If Head points to the list

Head

```
 ___      _____      _____      _____
|_|_|--->| Hat |_|--->| Boy |_|--->| Cat |/|
```

the procedure call statement

```
      PrintList (Head)
```

displays the output lines

```
      Hat
      Boy
      Cat
```

Figure 17.8 Procedure PrintList

```
procedure PrintList (Head {input} : ListPointer);
{
   Displays the list pointed to by Head.
   Pre : Head points to a list whose last node has a pointer
         field of nil.
   Post: The Word field of each list node is displayed and
         the last value of Head is nil.
}
begin {PrintList}
   {Traverse the list until the end is reached.}
   while Head <> nil do
     {invariant:
         No prior value of Head was nil.
     }
     begin
       WriteLn (Head^.Word);
       Head := Head^.Link                {advance to next node}
     end {while}
end; {PrintList}
```

The while condition

```
      Head <> nil
```

is very common in loops that process lists. If the list to be printed is an empty list, this condition is true initially and the loop body is skipped.

If the list is not empty, the loop body executes and the statement

```
      Head := Head^.Link        {advance to next node}
```

advances the pointer Head to the next list element, which is pointed to by the Link field of the current list element. After the last value in the list is printed, the value nil is assigned to Head and the while loop is exited.

Because Head is a value parameter, a local copy of the pointer to the first list element is established when the procedure is entered. This local pointer is advanced, but the corresponding pointer in the calling program remains unchanged. What would happen to our list if Head was a variable parameter?

Warning About Variable Parameters for Pointers

The last line in the preceding paragraph asks you to consider the effect of parameter Head being a variable parameter instead of a value parameter. We know that this would allow the procedure to change the corresponding actual parameter, regardless of our intentions. In PrintList and many similar procedures, the last value assigned to the pointer parameter is nil. If Head is a variable parameter, the corresponding actual parameter would be set to nil, thereby disconnecting it from the list that it pointed to before the procedure call.

Creating a List

Procedure CreateList in Fig. 17.9 creates a linked list by reading in a sequence of data strings that end with a sentinel ('***') and storing each string in a list. If the data lines

```
Hat
Boy
Cat
***
```

are entered, the list shown in the preceding section is created. Notice that the sentinel string is not stored in the list.

Figure 17.9 Procedure CreateList

```
procedure CreateList (var Head {output} : ListPointer);
{
  Creates a linked list of strings pointed to by Head.
  Each new string is appended to the end of the list so the
  strings will be stored in the order in which they were read.
  Pre : None
  Post: Head points to the first string entered. Head is
        set to nil if the sentinel string is the first string.
  Uses: ReadLnString
}
  const
    Sentinel = '***';

  var
    FirstWord : StringType;      {first data word}
    FirstLen : Integer;          {its length}


  procedure FillRest (Last {input} : ListPointer);
  {
    Appends new nodes to the end of a list.
```

```
      Pre : Last points to the last node in a list of length n.
      Post: Last points to the last node in a list of length >= n.
            Each data string is stored in a new node in the order
            in which it was read. The last node contains the data
            string just before the sentinel.
      Uses: ReadLnString
   }
      var
        NextWord : StringType;      {next data word}
        NextLen : Integer;          {its length}

   begin {FillRest}
   ReadLnString (Input, StringSize, NextWord, NextLen);
   while NextWord <> Sentinel do
      {invariant:
         Last points to the last node in a list and
         the last string read is stored in node Last^ and
         no prior data string was the Sentinel
      }
        begin
          New (Last^.Link);           {attach a new node to Last^}
          Last := Last^.Link;         {reset Last to new list end}
          Last^.Word := NextWord;         {store current word}
          ReadLnString (Input, StringSize, NextWord, NextLen)
        end; {while}

      {assertion: The last string read was the Sentinel}
      Last^.Link := nil                  {mark end of list}
   end; {FillRest}


begin {CreateList}
   {Display instructions to user.}
   WriteLn ('Enter each data string on a line.');
   WriteLn ('Enter ', Sentinel, ' when done.');

   {Create and fill the list head with the first word.}
   ReadLnString (Input, StringSize, FirstWord, FirstLen);
   if FirstWord = Sentinel then
      Head := nil                                 {empty list}
   else
      begin {build list}
        New (Head);                        {create the list head}
        Head^.Word := FirstWord;      {store FirstWord in list head}
        FillRest (Head)                      {fill rest of list}
      end {build list}
end; {CreateList}
```

Procedure `CreateList` first displays the user's instructions and then reads the first data word into `FirstWord`. If `FirstWord` is the sentinel, `Head` is set to `nil` to indicate an empty list. If `FirstWord` is not the sentinel, the statements

```
   New (Head);                    {create the list head}
   Head^.Word := FirstWord;       {store data in list head}
```

allocate a new node `Head^`, into which `FirstWord` (string `'Hat'`) is copied. The procedure call statement

```
   FillRest (Head)                        {fill rest of list}
```

Figure 17.10 List after Call to FillRest

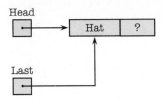

calls procedure `FillRest` to grow the rest of the list. The value of `Head` is passed into `FillRest` as the initial value of parameter `Last`. Figure 17.10 shows the partial list right after `FillRest` is called.

The `while` loop in `FillRest` is repeated until the sentinel is read. Each time the loop is repeated, the statements

```
{1} New (Last^.Link);          {attach a new node to Last^}
{2} Last := Last^.Link;         {reset Last to new list end}
    Last^.Word := NextWord;     {store last word read}
```

attach a new node to the current end of the list, reset `Last` to point to the new end of the list, and then store the data word in node `Last^`. The list after the first execution of the loop body is shown in Fig. 17.11. Each new pointer value is shown in color, along with the label of the statement that defines it; the initial value of `Last` is shown in gray.

After loop exit, the statement

```
Last^.Link := nil                         {mark end of list}
```

marks the end of the list. If the sentinel string followed `'Boy'`, the `Link` field of the second node in Fig. 17.11 would be set to `nil`.

Searching a List for a Target

Another common operation is searching for a target value in a list. A list search is similar to an array search in that we must examine the list elements in sequence until we find the value we are seeking or we examine all list elements without success. The latter is indicated by reaching the list node whose pointer field is `nil`.

Function `Search` in Fig. 17.12 returns a pointer to the first list node that contains the target value. If the target value is missing, `Search` returns a value

Figure 17.11 List after First Execution of while Loop

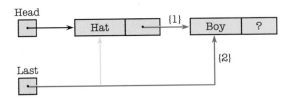

of nil. Search uses the Boolean flag Found to indicate whether the target value was found. The `if` statement in the `while` loop sets Found to True if the current list node contains the target value. The `while` loop exit occurs right after Found is set to True or the last list node is tested.

Figure 17.12 Function Search

```
function Search (Head : ListPointer;
                 Target : StringType) : ListPointer;
{
  Searches a list for a specified Target string.
  Pre : Head points to a list and Target is defined.
  Post: Returns a pointer to Target if found;
        otherwise, returns nil if Target is not found.
}
  var
    Found : Boolean;        {flag indicating Target found}

begin {Search}
  Found := False;           {Target not found}
  while not Found and (Head <> nil) do
    {invariant:
       no prior list node contained Target and
       no prior value of Head was nil
    }
    if Head^.Word = Target then
      Found := True
    else
      Head := Head^.Link;     {move down the list}

  {assertion: Target was found or end of list was reached.}
  if Found then
    Search := Head           {success}
  else
    Search := nil            {failure}
end; {Search}
```

PROGRAM STYLE

Avoiding Falling off the End of a List

It is tempting to eliminate the Boolean flag in Fig. 17.12 and to rewrite the `while` loop as

```
while (Head <> nil) and (Head^.Word <> Target) do
  Head := Head^.Link;
```

The `while` loop exit occurs if all list elements test without success (Head is nil) or the current node contains the target value. We can then return the value of Head as the search result. If your compiler uses short-circuit evaluation, the `while` loop will execute as expected. However, if it doesn't use short-circuit evaluation, a run-time error will occur whenever the target value is missing because the condition

```
Head^.Word <> Target
```

is undefined when Head is nil.

Exercises for Section 17.4

Self-Check

1. Trace the execution of function Search for the list that contains the three strings 'Hat', 'Boy', 'Cat'. Show the value of pointer Head after each execution of the while loop. Do this for the target strings 'Boy', 'Cap', and 'Dog'.

Programming

1. Write a function that finds the length of a list.
2. Write a recursive version of function Search. Your function should implement the following recursive algorithm:

```
if the list is empty then
    Target is missing - return nil
else if Target is in the list head then
    Return a pointer to the list head
else
    Search the rest of the list
```

17.5   Linked-List Representation of a Stack

Chapter 16 introduced stack and queue abstract data types and showed you how to implement them using an array for storage of the individual elements of a stack or queue. Because the number of elements in a stack or queue varies, it makes good sense to implement these data structures as linked lists.

Think of a stack as a linked list in which all insertions and deletions are performed at the list head. A list representation of a stack S is shown on the left of Fig. 17.13. The pointer S.Top points to the top of stack S. If a new node is pushed onto the stack, it should be inserted in front of the node currently

Figure 17.13   Physical Stack S (left) and Abstract Stack (right)

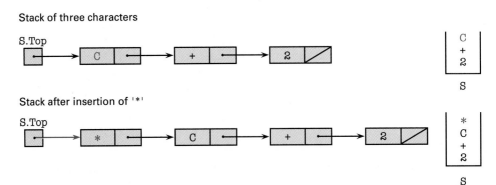

pointed to by S.Top. Stack S after the insertion of the symbol '*' is shown at the bottom of the figure.

Each element of a stack can be stored in a node with a data field (type StackElement) and a pointer field (type StackNext) that points to the next stack node (type StackNode). These data types are declared as follows:

```
type
   {Insert declaration for StackElement}

   StackNext = ^StackNode;
   StackNode = record
                 Item : StackElement;
                 Next : StackNext
               end; {StackNode}
```

The stack S can be represented by a record variable with a single pointer field, Top, that points to the top of the stack. The declarations for type Stack and record variable S (type Stack) follow.

```
type
   Stack = record
             Top : StackNext          {top of stack pointer}
           end; {stack}

var
   S : Stack;
   NextCh : Char;
   Success : Boolean;
```

■ Example 17.1

If data type StackElement is the same as Char, the assignment statement

```
S.Top := nil;
```

initializes stack S to the empty stack, as shown next.

Assuming procedure Push (see Fig. 16.16) has been modified to handle the new stack declaration, the statements

```
Push (S, '+', Success);
Push (S, 'A', Success);
```

should redefine stack S, as shown next.

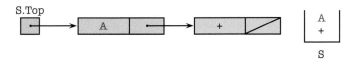

Two new nodes must be allocated to create stack S. Assuming Pop has also been modified, the statement

```
Pop (S, NextCh, Success);
```

should return the character value 'A' to NextCh (type Char) and redefine stack S as shown next. ∎

Stack Operators

Each of the stack operators first shown in Fig. 16.16 is rewritten in this section assuming the previous type declaration for Stack. We begin with CreateStack, shown in Fig. 17.14. CreateStack must be called first; it creates an empty stack by intializing the top of stack pointer to nil.

Figure 17.14 Procedure CreateStack

```
procedure CreateStack (var S {out} : Stack);
{
  Creates an empty stack.
  Pre : None
  Post: S is an empty stack.
}
begin {CreateStack}
  S.Top := nil            {set top of stack pointer to nil}
end; {CreateStack}
```

Procedure Push (Fig. 17.15) must allocate a new node for storing the data item being pushed onto the stack. The node just allocated becomes the new top of the stack.

Figure 17.15 Procedure Push

```
procedure Push (var S {in/out} : Stack;
                X {in} : Char;
                var Success {out} : Boolean);
{
  Pushes X onto stack S.
  Pre : X is defined and S is a stack.
  Post: Sets Success to indicate success (True) or failure (False)
        of push operation.
}
  var OldTop : StackNext;        {pointer to old top of stack}

begin {Push}
  if IsFull(S) then
   'Success := False
  else
    begin
      OldTop := S.Top;          {save old top of stack}
      New (S.Top);              {allocate new node at top of stack}
      S.Top^.Next := OldTop;    {link new node to old stack}
```

```
        S.Top^.Item := X;              {store X in new node}
        Success := True
      end {if}
end; {Push}
```

Figure 17.16 Pushing 'A' onto a Stack

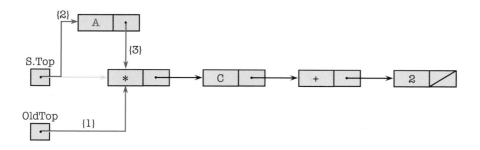

Each call to procedure Push places a new node on the stack. The statements

```
{1} OldTop := S.Top;           {save old top of stack}
{2} New (S.Top);               {allocate new node at top of stack}
{3} S.Top^.Next := OldTop;     {link new node to old stack}
```

allocate a new node (pointed to by S.Top) and connect this node to the former
top of the stack (pointed to by OldTop). Figure 17.16 shows a stack before and
after the letter 'A' is pushed onto it. The original value of S.Top is shown in
gray, and the new value is shown in color.

Procedure Pop (Fig. 17.17) retrieves the value at the top of the stack and
returns the node in which it is stored to the heap. The node that follows the
one just popped becomes the new top of the stack.

Figure 17.17 Procedure Pop

```
procedure Pop (var S {in/out} : Stack;
               var X {out} : Char;
               var Success {out} : Boolean);
{
  Pops the top of stack S into X.
  Pre : S is a stack.
  Post: Contents of X is character at top of stack S which is then
        removed from S. Sets Success to indicate success (True)
        or failure (False) of pop operation.
}
  var
    OldTop : StackNext;          {pointer to old top of stack}

begin {Pop}
  if S.Top = nil then
    Success := False
  else
    begin
      X := S.Top^.Item;          {copy top of stack into X}
      OldTop := S.Top;           {save old top of stack}
```

```
        S.Top := S.Top^.Next;        {reset top of stack}
        Dispose (OldTop);            {return top node to the heap}
        Success := True
      end {if}
  end; {Pop}
```

Figure 17.18 Popping the Stack

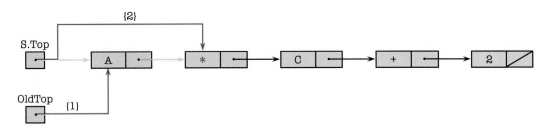

Procedure Pop first copies the value at the top of the stack into X. Next, the statement with label {2}

```
{1} OldTop := S.Top;          {save old top of stack}
{2} S.Top := S.Top^.Next;     {reset top of stack}
{3} Dispose (OldTop);         {return top node to he heap}
```

resets S.Top to point to the node following the current top node. The statement with label {3} returns the former top node to the heap so its memory cells can be reallocated. The effect of popping 'A' from the stack is shown in Fig. 17.18.

Procedure Retrieve accesses the value at the top of the stack but does not pop it off the stack. (Retrieve is left as an exercise at the end of the next section.)

Function IsEmpty tests whether the stack is empty, and function IsFull tests whether the stack is full. The stack is considered full when there are no storage cells left on the heap that can be allocated to the stack. Unfortunately, standard Pascal does not allow us to test the availability of cells on the heap, so we assume that there is always space for one more stack element and that IsFull will always return False. This may eventually lead to a stack overflow error. Functions IsEmpty and IsFull are shown in Fig. 17.19.

Figure 17.19 Functions IsEmpty and IsFull

```
function IsEmpty (S : Stack) : Boolean;
{
  Pre : S is a stack.
  Post: Returns True if stack S is empty; otherwise, returns False.
}
begin {IsEmpty}
  IsEmpty := S.Top = nil
end; {IsEmpty}
```

```
function IsFull (S : Stack) : Boolean;
{
  Pre : S is a stack.
  Post: Returns True if stack S is full; otherwise, returns False.
}
begin {IsFull}
  IsFull := False          {assume unlimited heap storage}
end; {IsFull}
```

Time and Space Tradeoffs for Stack Implementations

The advantage of using pointer types to implement a stack is that we can increase the size of the stack when we push on a new element and decrease its size when we pop off an element. In this way, the storage space allocated to the stack expands and contracts as needed. In the array implementation shown earlier, the entire array is allocated at once whether or not it is all needed.

This apparent saving of memory is not without cost. Each stack element requires an additional pointer field that is used for storage of the address of the next stack element. An array implementation does not require this extra field, because the elements of an array are implicitly linked together.

With respect to time, it is usually more costly for a compiler to access elements of a stack stored in an array. This is because the compiler must compute the actual memory address corresponding to a subscript value that represents the top of the stack. If the top of the stack is stored in a pointer field, no computation is required because the address of the first stack node is stored directly.

Exercises for Section 17.5

Self-Check

1. Explain why the field NumItems is not needed in the type declaration for Stack. What changes would be required to the type declaration and the stack operators if field NumItems was included?
2. Provide the algorithm for operator CopyStack that makes a copy of an existing stack.
3. What changes would have to be made to program PrintReverse (Fig. 16.6) to use the new stack data type and its operators?

Programming

1. Implement CopyStack.

17.6 Linked-List Representation of a Queue

We can also implement a queue as a linked list that grows and shrinks as elements are inserted and deleted. We declare queue Q using the following declarations.

```
type
    {Insert declaration for QueueElement}

    QueueNext = ^QueueNode;
    QueueNode = record
                    Item : QueueElement;
                    Next : QueueNext
                end; {QueueNode}

    Queue = record
                Front, Rear : QueueNext;
                NumItems : Integer
            end; {Queue}

  var
    Q : Queue;
    NextPass : QueueElement;
    Temp : QueueNext;
```

The declaration for variable Q allocates storage for a record with two pointer fields, Front and Rear, and one integer field, NumItems. As shown in Fig. 17.20, Front points to the first record inserted in the queue, Rear points to the last record, and NumItems is a count of records. Each node of the queue (type QueueNode) contains storage for a queue element (type QueueElement) and a pointer to the next queue node (type QueueNext).

In a linked-list representation of a queue, the queue expands and contracts as queue elements are inserted and removed during program execution. If we store the queue elements in an array, we must allocate storage for the entire queue at compile-time.

The statements

```
{1} Temp := Q.Front;
    NextPass := Q.Front^.Item;
{2} Q.Front := Q.Front^.Next;
    Q.NumItems := Q.NumItems - 1;
    Dispose (Temp);
```

remove the first passenger from the front of the queue, storing the passenger data in NextPass (type QueueElement). The effect of these statements on the queue above is shown in Fig. 17.21. The Dispose statement returns node Temp^ to the storage heap.

The statements

```
{1} New (Q.Rear^.Next);              {Attach a new node at end of queue}
{2} Q.Rear := Q.Rear^.Next;              {Reset Rear to new node}
    Q.Rear^.Item := NextPass;          {Define new passenger data}
    Q.NumItems := Q.NumItems + 1;
```

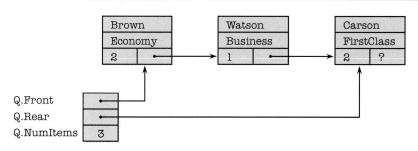

Figure 17.21   Removing a Queue Element with Passenger Brown

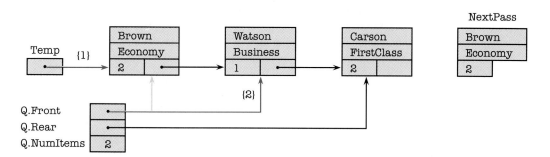

allocate a new node at the rear of the queue and insert passenger data from
NextPass into the queue. The effect of these statements is shown in Fig. 17.22
for variable NextPass and the queue in Fig. 7.21. By executing both of the
preceding program fragments, we shift the element originally at the front of
the queue to the rear of the queue.

Queue as a Circular List

Section 16.7 demonstrated that a circular array was a convenient data structure
for storing the elements of a queue. In this section we will see how to represent
and manipulate a queue using a circular list.

Figure 17.22   Inserting a Queue Element with Passenger Brown

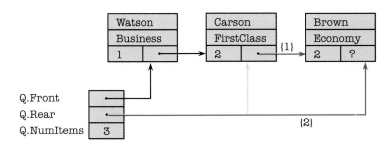

Figure 17.23   A Queue as a Circular List

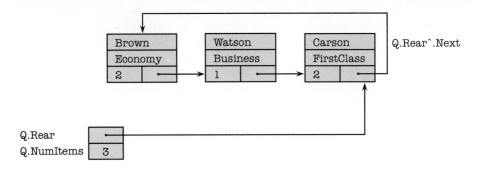

Figure 17.23 shows a queue, Q, of three elements represented as a circular list. This is called a *circular list* because the pointer field of the last list element (passenger Carson) is not nil; instead, it points back to the first list element (passenger Brown). Only the pointer Q.Rear is required to access the queue because the pointer Q.Rear^.Next points to the first record in the queue (passenger Brown).

This enables us to eliminate the pointer field Front from the record type Queue.

The statements

```
{1} New (Temp);
{2} Temp^.Next := Q.Rear^.Next;
    Temp^.Item := NextPass;
{3} Q.Rear^.Next := Temp;
{4} Q.Rear := Temp;
```

insert a new node in a circular queue. Statement {1} allocates a new node, and statements {2} and {3}insert the new node at the rear of the queue. Statement {4} resets Q.Rear to point to the new node. The effect of these statements is shown in Fig. 17.24 assuming the data for passenger McMann are stored in NextPass.

Figure 17.24   Inserting Passenger McMann in a Queue

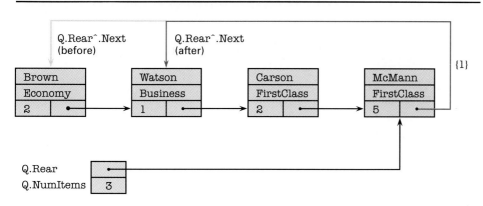

To remove a node, the pointer Q.Rear^.Next should be reset to point to the node following the one that is currently at the front of the queue. The statements

```
     NextPass := Q.Rear^.Next^.Item;
{1} Q.Rear^.Next := Q.Rear^.Next^.Next;
```

store the data for passenger Brown in NextPass and remove the first queue element. Figure 17.25 shows the effect of statement {1} on the queue above.

The implementation of a queue as a circular list is left as a programming project at the end of this chapter.

Exercises for Section 17.6

Self-Check

1. What does the following segment do to queue Q shown in Fig. 17.20?

```
New (Q.Rear^.Next);
Q.Rear := Q.Rear^.Next;
Q.Rear^.Name := 'Johnson
Q.Rear^.Class := Econony;
Q.Rear^.NumSeats := 5;
Q.NumItems := Q.NumItems + 1
```

2. What does the following statement do to queue Q shown in Fig. 17.23?

```
Q.Rear := Q.Rear^.Next;
```

3. Insert passenger Billingsly, Business class, 2 seats in the queue of Fig. 17.23.

Programming

1. Write function SizeOfQueue for both a listed-list queue and a queue as a circular list.
2. Write procedure Retrieve for both a linked-list queue and a queue as a circular list.

17.7 Common Programming Errors

Syntax Errors

Make sure you use the dereferencing operator ^ (or ↑) where it is needed. If P is a pointer variable, P^.X should be used to reference field X of the record pointed to by P.

The New and Dispose procedures allocate and deallocate storage, respectively. Both procedures require a parameter that is a pointer variable. New (P) is correct, while New (P^) is incorrect.

Run-Time Errors

Many run-time errors occur when you are traversing linked data structures. For example, if Next is supposed to point to each node in the linked list, the statement

```
while Next <> nil do
  Write (Next^.Word);
  Next := Next^.Link;
```

executes forever. That happens because the pointer assignment statement is not included in the loop body, so Next is not advanced down the list.

A run-time error can occur when the pointer Next is advanced too far down the list and Next takes on the value nil, indicating the end of the list. If pointer Next has the value nil, the while condition

```
while (Next <> nil) and (Next^.ID <> 9999) do
```

causes a run-time error on some systems because Next^.ID is undefined when Next is nil. The while condition should be rewritten as

```
while (Next^.Link <> nil) and (Next^.ID <> 9999) do
```

Finally, if pointer Next is a procedure parameter that corresponds to a list head pointer, make sure it is a value parameter. Otherwise, the last value assigned to Next will be returned as a procedure result. This may cause you to lose some of the elements originally in the linked list.

Problems with heap management can also cause run-time errors. If your program gets stuck in an infinite loop while you are creating a dynamic data structure, it is possible for your program to consume all memory cells on the storage heap. This situation will lead to a heap overflow or stack overflow run-time error.

Make sure your program does not attempt to reference a list node after the node is returned to the heap. All pointers to a node being returned should be assigned new values so that the node can never be accessed unless it is reallocated.

Debugging Tips

Because the value of a pointer variable cannot be printed, it is difficult to debug programs that manipulate pointers. You have to trace the execution of such a program by printing an information field that uniquely identifies the list element being processed instead of the pointer value itself.

When you are writing driver programs to test and debug list operators, it is often helpful to create a sample linked structure using the technique shown in Section 17.1. You can use assignment statements to define the data and pointer fields of the structure.

 # Chapter Review

This chapter introduced several dynamic data structures. We discussed the use of pointers to reference and connect elements of a dynamic data structure. The procedure New was used to allocate additional elements, or nodes, of a dynamic data structure; the procedure Dispose returns memory cells to the storage heap.

We also covered many different aspects of manipulating linked lists. We showed how to build or create a linked list, how to traverse a linked list, and how to insert and delete elements of a linked list.

We revisited stacks and queues and showed you how to implement them as linked data structures. And we wrote new stack operators for the representation of a stack using a linked list.

New Pascal Constructs

The Pascal constructs introduced in this chapter are described in Table 17.1.

Table 17.1 New Pascal Constructs

Construct	Effect
Pointer Type Declaration	

`type`
  `Pointer = ^Node:`
  `Node = record`
        `Info : Integer;`
        `Link : Pointer`
     `end; {Node}`
	The identifer `Pointer` is declared as a pointer to a record of type `Node`, where `Node` is a record type containing a field (`Link`) of type `Pointer`.

`var` `Head : Pointer;`	`Head` is a pointer variable of type `Pointer`.
New Procedure	
`New (Head)`	A new record of type `Node` is allocated. This record is pointed to by `Head` and is referenced by `Head^`.

Table 17.1 *continued*

Construct	Effect
Dispose Procedure `Dispose (Head)`	The memory space occupied by the record `Head^` is returned to the storage pool.
Pointer Assignment `Head := Head^.Link`	The pointer `Head` is advanced to the next node in the dynamic data structure pointed to by `Head`.

✓ *Quick-Check Exercises*

1. Procedure _____ allocates storage space for a data object that is referenced through a _____; procedure _____ returns the storage space to the _____.
2. What is the major advantage of using pointer representations of linked lists instead of array representations?
3. It is just as easy to modify a linked list that is represented as an array as one that is represented using pointers. True or false?
4. When an element is deleted from a linked list represented using pointers, it is automatically returned to the heap. True or false?
5. All pointers to a node that is returned to the heap are automatically reset to `nil` so they cannot reference the node returned to the heap. True or false?
6. Why do you need to be wary of passing a list pointer as a variable parameter to a procedure?
7. If a linked list contains three elements with values `'Him'`, `'Her'`, and `'Its'` and H is a pointer to the list head, what is the effect of the following statements? Assume the data field is `Pronoun`, the link field is `Next`, and N and P are pointer variables?

```
N := H^.Next;
N^.Pronoun := 'She';
```

8. Answer exercise 7 for the following segment.

```
P := H^.Next;
N := P^.Next;
P^.Next := N^.Next;
Dispose (N);
```

9. Answer exercise 7 for the following segment.

```
N := H;
New (H);
H^.Pronoun := 'His';
H^.Next := N;
```

10. Write a single statement that will place the value `nil` in the last node of the three-element list in exercise 7.

1. New; pointer; Dispose; heap
2. Storage space is allocated as needed and not all at once.
3. True
4. False; Dispose must be called.
5. False
6. The actual parameter may be advanced down a list, and in this way part of the list will be lost.
7. Replaces 'Her' with 'She'
8. Deletes the third list element
9. Inserts a new list with value 'His' at the front of the list
10. H^.Next^.Next^.Next := nil;

Review Questions

1. Differentiate between dynamic and nondynamic data structures.
2. Define a simple linked list. Indicate how the pointers are utilized to establish a link between nodes. Also indicate any other variables that would be needed to reference the linked list.
3. Give the missing type declarations and show the effect of each of the following statements. What does it do?

```
New (P);
P^.Word := 'ABC';
New (P^.Next);
Q  := P^.Next;
Q^.Word := 'abc';
Q^.Next := nil;
```

4. Assume the following type declarations for questions 4 through 9.

```
type
   StringType = packed array [1..10] of Char;
   ListPointer = ^Node;
   Node = record
             Name : StringType;
             Link : ListPointer
          end;

   HeadNode = record
                 Head : ListPointer;
                 NumItems : Integer
              end;

   var
      List : HeadNode;
```

Write a program segment that places the names Washington, Roosevelt, and Kennedy in successive elements of the linked list referenced by record List. Define List.NumItems accordingly.

5. Write a program segment to insert the name Eisenhower between Roosevelt and Kennedy.
6. Write an operator called DeleteLast that removes the last element from any list referenced by record List.

7. Write a procedure called PlaceFirst that places its second parameter value as the first node of the linked list referenced by record List.
8. Write a procedure called CopyList that creates a linked list with new nodes that contain the same data as the linked list referenced by List.
9. Write a procedure to delete all nodes with Name field Smith from a linked list referenced by record List.

Programming Projects

1. Rewrite the queue operators shown in Section 16.7 for a queue represented as a linked list.
2. Rewrite the queue operators shown in Section 16.7 for a queue represented as a circular list.
3. Do programming project 1 at the end of Chapter 16 using the queue operators from programming project 1 or 2 of this chapter.
4. Do programming project 3 at the end of Chapter 16 using the stack operators implemented in this chapter.
5. Do programming project 4 at the end of Chapter 16 using the queue operators from programming project 1 or 2 of this chapter.
6. A polynomial can be represented as a linked list, where each node contains the coefficient and the exponent of a term of the polynomial. The polynomial $4x^3 + 3x^2 - 5$ would be represented as the following linked list:

Write an abstract data type Polynomial that has operators for creating a polynomial, reading a polynomial, and adding and subtracting a pair of polynomials. Hint: To add or subtract two polynomials, traverse both lists. If a particular exponent value is present in either one, it should also be present in the result polynomial unless its coefficient is zero.

7. Each student in the university takes a different number of courses, so the registrar has decided to use a linked list to store each student's class schedule and an array of records to represent the whole student body. A portion of this data structure follows.

The records show that the first student (ID is 1111) is taking section 1 of CIS120 for 3 credits and section 2 of HIS001 for 4 credits; the second student (ID is 1234) is not enrolled, and so on. Write an abstract data type for this data structure. Provide operators for creating the original array of student ID numbers, inserting a student's initial class schedule, adding a course, and dropping a course. Write a menu-driven program that uses this abstract data type.

Ordered Lists and Trees

18

Chapter 17 introduced dynamic data structures, including pointers, linked lists, and linked-list implementations of stacks and queues. This chapter discusses dynamic data structures that provide improved search behavior, including ordered lists and binary search trees. An ordered list is a list in which each node's position is determined by the value of its key field, so that the key values form an increasing sequence as we advance down the list. This is different from a stack or a queue, in which a node's position is determined by when it was inserted in the list.

Each list node you have seen so far has had a single pointer field connecting it to the next node. This chapter introduces data structures that have two pointer fields, which enable each node to be connected to two others. The binary tree, as one such data structure, has wide application in computer science. This chapter shows you how to use binary trees to represent expressions. We discuss traversing a tree and its relationship to expression evaluation. We also show you how to store information in a binary search tree and how to retrieve that information in an efficient manner.

 # 18.1 The Ordered List Abstract Data Type

This section considers the problem of maintaining an ordered list. We want to be able to insert an element and know that the list will still be in order after the insertion. Similarly, after a list element is deleted, the remaining elements should still be in order. As long as we maintain the order of the list elements as we perform each insertion, we will never have to sort the list. It is also easier to search for a particular list element if the elements are in order.

The specification of an abstract data type for an ordered list (type OrderList) and its operators follows.

Specification of Ordered List Abstract Data Type

Structure: An ordered list is a collection of elements such that each element includes among its data fields a special field that is considered the key field. The key-field values in an ordered list form an increasing sequence. For simplicity, assume that there are no duplicate keys.

Operators: For the following descriptions, assume these parameters:

List represents the ordered list.
El (pronounced el) has the same data type as the list elements.
Target is a possible key-field value.
Success is a Boolean flag indicating success (True) or failure (False) of an operation.

CreateList (var List): Creates an empty ordered list; must be called before any other operators.

SizeOfList(List): Returns the number of elements currently in the ordered list.

Search (List, Target, var Success): Searches a list to find the key Target. If Target is found, sets Success to True; otherwise, sets Success to False.

Insert (var List, El, var Success): Inserts item El into the list, maintaining the list order, and sets Success to True. If there is already an element with the same key value as El, Success is set to False and no insertion is performed.

Delete (var List, Target, var Success): Deletes the element whose key value is Target, maintaining the list order, and sets Success to True. If Target is not located, sets Success to False.

Retrieve (List, Target, var El, var Success): Copies the element whose key is Target into El and sets Success to True. If there is no element with key Target, El is not defined and Success is False.

Replace (var List, El, var Success): Replaces the element whose key value is the same as the key value of El and sets Success to True. If there is no element whose key value matches the key value of El, sets Success to False.

DisplayList (List): Displays the list elements in sequential order by key.

As before, we can illustrate how these operators work and use them in a client program without worrying about the details of how the list is represented in memory. In Section 18.3, we discuss one internal representation for an ordered list and implement the ordered list operators. Because we want to be able to manipulate different types of data objects stored in an ordered list, we use the identifier ListElement to represent the type of each list element and KeyType to indicate the type of the record key. We also need two constants, MinKey and MaxKey (both type KeyType), that bracket the range of allowable values for the key field. Each client program must import constants MinKey and MaxKey and data types ListElement, KeyType, and OrderList from ADT OrderList.

Examples of Ordered Lists

The top of Fig. 18.1 shows an ordered list that contains three four-digit integer values (1234, 2222, and 5669). The list head (variable MyList) contains a pointer field that points to a *dummy list node* with key field 999 (value of MinKey). This node and the dummy list node with key field 10000 (value of MaxKey) are not considered part of the ordered list; they serve as sentinels and are used to simplify writing the list operators (discussed in Section 18.3). Record variable MyList also contains an integer field that indicates the number of actual nodes (3) in the list (the dummy nodes are not counted). The bottom of the figure shows the same list after insertion of a new node with key field 4000.

In Fig. 18.2, record variable PassList represents an ordered list of airline

Figure 18.1 Insertion into an Ordered List

Figure 18.2 Ordered List of Airline Passengers

passengers. In this list, the key field is the passenger name, so the records are in order by passenger name. The first and last nodes are dummy nodes and are not included in the count (2) of list elements.

 # 18.2   Using an Ordered List

As you might expect, we can use the ordered list abstract data type to maintain an ordered list of integers, real numbers, or airline passengers. We can modify the menu-driven program in Fig. 16.18 to maintain an ordered list of airline passengers instead of placing the passengers in a queue. As shown in Fig. 18.2, the key field for each passenger record would be the passenger's name. The advantage of using an ordered list is that we can remove or delete any passenger from the list, whereas in a queue only the passenger at the front can be removed. Also, we can easily display the passengers in an ordered list in sequence by key field. Programming project 1 at the end of this chapter asks you to modify the menu-driven program to use an ordered list of passenger data. We solve a simpler problem next.

● Case Study: Building an Ordered List of Integers

Problem
To illustrate the ordered list operators, we will write a short client program that builds and displays an ordered list of integer values.

Design Overview

The client program must import all necessary constants and data types from ADT OrderList. The program begins by creating an empty list. Next, it reads a group of integer values and inserts them in the ordered list. After the ordered list is formed, it displays the ordered list. Then it performs a list search, a list deletion, and displays the final ordered list.

Data Requirements

Problem Inputs
Each record key (NextKey : KeyType)

Problem Outputs
The ordered list (MyList : OrderList)

Program Variables
Each list node (NextNode : ListElement)
A flag indicating the result of a list operation (Success : Boolean)

Algorithm

1. Create an empty ordered list.
2. Read the first key value.
3. while the sentinel is not read do
     begin
         4. Insert the next key in the ordered list.
         5. Read a new key value
     end
6. Display the ordered list and its size.
7. Perform a search operation.
8. Perform a delete operation.
9. Display the ordered list and its size.

Coding

The client program is shown in Fig. 18.3. The constants MinKey and MaxKey and data types KeyType and ListElement for an ordered list of integers are already in the program. We must import data type OrderList and the operators that manipulate the ordered list from ADT OrderList.

Figure 18.3   Program UseOrderList

```
program UseOrderList (Input, Output);
{
  Builds and displays an ordered list using data type OrderList.
```

```
   IMPORT: MinKey, MaxKey, OrderList, KeyType, ListElement,
           CreateList, Insert, Delete, DisplayList, SizeOfList,
           Search from ADT OrderList (see Section 18.3)
}
  const
    MinKey = 999;
    MaxKey = 10000;
    Sentinel = MaxKey;

  type
    KeyType = Integer;
    ListElement = KeyType;

    {Insert type declaration for OrderList}

  var
    MyList : OrderList;              {ordered list}
    NextNode : ListElement;          {each list node}
    Target : KeyType;                {target key}
    Success : Boolean;               {program flag}


    {Insert CreateList, Insert, Delete, Search, DisplayList, SizeOfList}

begin {UseOrderList}
  {Initialize the list}
  CreateList (MyList);

  {Read and insert the keys in the ordered list.}
  WriteLn ('Enter ', Sentinel :1, ' to stop.');
  Write ('Enter next key value or ', Sentinel :1, '> ');
  ReadLn (NextNode);
  while NextNode <> Sentinel do
    {invariant:
        all prior values of NextNode that are not duplicates were
          inserted in MyList and
        no prior value of NextNode was the sentinel
    }
    begin
      Insert (MyList, NextNode, Success);
      if Success then
        WriteLn (NextNode :1, ' inserted.')
      else
        WriteLn ('Out-of-range or duplicate key - no insertion.');
      Write ('Enter next key value or ', Sentinel :1, '> ');
      ReadLn (NextNode)
    end; {while}

  {assert: Ordered list completed.}
  {Display the ordered list and its size.}
  WriteLn;  WriteLn ('The ordered list follows.');
  DisplayList (MyList);
  Write ('The number of nodes in the list is ');
  WriteLn (SizeOfList(MyList) :1);  WriteLn;

  {Perform Search operation.}
  Write ('Find record with key> ');
  ReadLn (Target);
  Search (MyList, Target, Success);
```

```
  if Success then
    WriteLn (Target, ' found.')
  else
    WriteLn ('Not in the list.');

  {Perform Delete operation.}
  Write ('Delete record with key> ');
  ReadLn (Target);
  Delete (MyList, Target, Success);
  if Success then
    WriteLn (Target :1, ' deleted.')
  else
    WriteLn ('Key not found - no deletion.');
  WriteLn;

  {Display the ordered list and its size.}
  WriteLn ('The ordered list follows.');
  DisplayList (MyList);
  Write ('The number of nodes in the list is ');
  WriteLn (SizeOfList(MyList) :1)
end. {UseOrderList}
```

The client program begins by calling operator CreateList to create an empty ordered list. Next, the while loop reads each key value into NextNode and calls operator Insert to place the new key value in the ordered list. If ListElement were a structured type instead of a simple type, we would need to import an operator to read all record data. After loop exit, the program calls other list operators and displays the result of each operation on the ordered list.

Testing

Before you can run program UseOrderList, it is necessary to insert the missing type and procedure declarations that are imported from ADT OrderList. When testing the program, make sure that the final list is in order by record key, that there are no duplicate keys in the list, and that the nodes with key values MinKey and MaxKey are not displayed or counted. You should test the program using record keys that are outside the range of allowable values and using duplicate keys. Also try to delete an element that is not in the list. A sample run is shown in Fig. 18.4.

Figure 18.4 Sample Run of OrderList

```
Enter 10000 to stop.
Enter next key value or 10000> 2345
2345 inserted.
Enter next key value or 10000> 3456
3456 inserted.
Enter next key value or 10000> 1111
1111 inserted.
Enter next key value or 10000> 2345
```

```
Out-of-range or duplicate key - no insertion.
Enter next key value or 10000> 10000

The ordered list follows.
1111
2345
3456
The number of nodes in the list is 3

Find record with key> 2345
2345 found.
Delete record with key> 1111
1111 deleted.

The ordered list follows.
2345
3456
The number of nodes in the list is 2
```

Exercises for Section 18.2

Self-Check

1. Replace the body of Fig. 18.3 with the following program fragment. What is the effect? What is displayed?

```
begin
  CreateList (MyList);
  Insert (MyList, 3000, Success);
  Insert (MyList, 5000, Success);
  Insert (MyList, 4000, Success);
  Insert (MyList, 4000, Success);
  Delete (MyList, 4000, Success);
  if Success then
    WriteLn ('O.K.')
  else
    WriteLn ('Error');
  DisplayList (MyList);
  WriteLn ('Number of elements is ', SizeOfList(MyList) :1)
end.
```

2. Indicate what changes would be necessary to the program in Fig. 18.3 to process an ordered list of passengers instead of integers.

 # 18.3 Implementing ADT OrderList

In Chapter 17, you saw many advantages to using pointer variables and dynamic allocation to implement linked lists. We have repeatedly emphasized the ease with which insertions and deletions can be performed on such a list. For these reasons, we will represent each node of an ordered list by a record with a pointer field.

The interface section for ADT OrderList is shown in Fig. 18.5. Each node in an ordered list contains a data field, Item, and a pointer field, Link, which connects it to the next node in the list. The data field (type ListElement) must include a record key (type KeyType) and can be a simple type or a structured type. Data types ListElement and KeyType must be declared where shown or imported into ADT OrderList if they are declared elsewhere.

The record type OrderList is also declared. A variable of type OrderList repesents a header node for an ordered list. The header node contains a pointer to the first node in the list (field Head) and a count of list items (field NumItems).

Figure 18.5 Interface Section for ADT OrderList

```
{
  Abstract data type OrderList: contains declaration for data
  type OrderList and operator procedures for an object of type
  OrderList.

INTERFACE SECTION --

  EXPORT:   MinKey, MaxKey, OrderList, KeyType, ListElement,
            CreateList, SizeOfList, Search, Insert, Delete,
            Retrieve, Replace, DisplayList

  IMPORT:   InsertKey, ExtractKey, DisplayOne

  DATA TYPE SPECIFICATION:
}
     const
       {Insert declaration for MinKey}
       {Insert declaration for MaxKey}

     type
       {Insert declaration for KeyType}
       {Insert declaration for ListElement}

     NodePointer = ^ListNode;
     ListNode = record
                  Item : ListElement;          {Includes a key field}
                  Link : NodePointer
                end; {ListNode}

     OrderList = record
                   Head : NodePointer;
                   NumItems : Integer
                 end; {OrderList}
```

Several declarations must be inserted into the interface section shown in Fig. 18.5. The constants MinKey and MaxKey must be defined as well as data types ListElement and KeyType. For the ordered list of integers discussed in the previous section, these declarations were as follows.

```
const
  MinKey = 999;
  MaxKey = 10000;

type
  ListElement = Integer;
  KeyType = Integer;
```

For an ordered list of airline passenger records, we would use the following declarations.

```
const
  MinKey = 'AAAAAAAAAAAAAAAAAAAA';
  MaxKey = 'ZZZZZZZZZZZZZZZZZZZZ';

type
  ListElement = Passenger;
  KeyType = StringType;
```

We also would have to import data types StringType and Passenger from ADT Passenger.

Procedures InsertKey and ExtractKey

We implement the ordered list operators starting with CreateList in the next section. But first, we will examine two procedures, InsertKey and ExtractKey, that must be imported into ADT OrderList because they are called by the list operators. They are used to store (InsertKey) and retrieve (ExtractKey) key field values. Figure 18.6 shows the form of these procedures for an ordered list of integers.

Figure 18.6 InsertKey and ExtractKey for a List of Integers

```
procedure InsertKey (var El {output} : ListElement;
                         Key {input} : KeyType);
{
  Stores Key in the key field of El.
  Pre : Key is defined and El is an ordered list element.
  Post: The key field of El becomes Key.
}
begin {InsertKey}
  El := Key
end; {InsertKey}


procedure ExtractKey (El {input} : ListElement;
                      var Key {output} : KeyType);
{
  Retrieves the key field of El.
  Pre : El is an ordered list element.
  Post: Key gets the key field of El.
}
begin {ExtractKey}
  Key := El
end; {ExtractKey}
```

The procedure bodies depend on the structure of ListElement. If ListElement is type Passenger, its key field is Name (type StringType). In this case, the body of InsertKey would be the assignment statement

```
El.Name := Key
```

and the body of ExtractKey would be the assignment statement

```
Key := El.Name
```

Procedure CreateList

To simplify the list-processing operations, we assume that an ordered list always begins and ends with a dummy node. The dummy node at the head of the list should have a key value (MinKey) that is smaller than all the list keys; the dummy node at the end of the list should have a key value (MaxKey) that is larger than all the list keys.

The dummy nodes are analogous to sentinels. The presence of the first dummy node means that we never have to change the pointer to the list head (field Head) when a new node is inserted. The presence of the second dummy node keeps us from "falling off" the end of the list when we are searching for a target key. If MyList is type OrderList, the procedure call statement

```
CreateList (MyList)
```

builds the empty list shown in Fig. 18.7, which contains the two dummy nodes. Procedure CreateList is shown in Fig. 18.8; CreateList and all the other operators discussed in this section belong in the implementation section of ADT OrderList.

Figure 18.7   An Empty Ordered List

MyList.Head
MyList.NumItems   0

Figure 18.8   Procedure CreateList

```
procedure CreateList (var List {output} : OrderList);
{
   Creates an ordered list containing two dummy nodes whose keys
   are the constants MinKey and MaxKey.
   Pre : None
   Post: List points to the header node for an ordered list.
   Uses: MinKey, MaxKey, InsertKey
}
begin {CreateList}
   New (List.Head);                  {allocate first dummy node}
   New (List.Head.Link);             {allocate second dummy node}
   InsertKey (List.Head^.Item, MinKey);
   InsertKey (List.Head^.Link^.Item, MaxKey);
```

```
      List.Head^.Link^.Link := nil;    {second node is last node}
      List.NumItems := 0               {dummy nodes don't count}
   end; {CreateList}
```

Each call to procedure New allocates storage for a dummy node. The pointer List.Head points to the first dummy node; the pointer from the first dummy node, List.Head^.Link, points to the second dummy node. Procedure InsertKey stores the key values MinKey and MaxKey in the two dummy nodes. The Link field of the second dummy node is set to nil. The field List.NumItems is set to zero because the dummy nodes are not counted as actual list nodes.

Procedure Locate

Before we can insert an element into an ordered list, we must locate the list nodes that bracket the element we want to insert. For example, if we want to insert the key 2345, we must advance the pointer Next to the first node with a key larger than 2345 and pointer Previous to the node just before that one, as shown in Fig. 18.9. Then we can execute the statements

```
   {1} New (Previous^.Link);           {join new node to Previous^}
   {2} Previous^.Link^.Link := Next;   {join new node to Next^}
```

The effect of these statements is shown in Fig. 18.10. The new pointer values are in color; the original pointer value is in gray.

Similarly, before we can delete a list element, we must locate the list node that contains that element and the previous node. For example, if we want to delete the key 3456, we must advance pointer Next to the node with key 3456 and pointer Previous to the node just before it. For the original list shown in Fig. 18.9, pointers Previous and Next should be positioned as shown. Once Next and Previous are positioned as required, we can execute the statement

```
   Previous^.Link := Next^.Link;    {disconnect node Next^}
```

This statement joins node Previous^ to the node that follows node Next^ (the second dummy node), thereby disconnecting node Next^.

The two pointers Next and Previous appear in each ordered-list operator

Figure 18.9 Previous and Next after Search for 2345 or 3456

Figure 18.10 Inserting 2345

713

18.3 Implementing
ADT OrderList

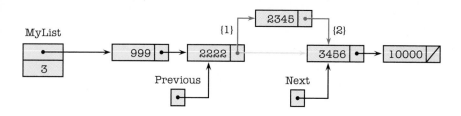

that we write. Each operator calls procedure Locate to position these pointers as required. Procedure Locate (Fig. 18.11) advances pointer Next to the first list node whose key value is greater than or equal to the Target key. Locate advances pointer Previous to the node preceding node Next^.

Figure 18.11 Procedure Locate

```
procedure Locate (Target {input} : KeyType;
                  var Previous, {input/output}
                      Next        {output} : NodePointer;
                  var SearchSuccess {output} : Boolean);
{
  Attempts to locate a node with key value Target in the
  list whose first node is pointed to by Previous.
  Pre : Target is defined; Previous points to the first dummy node.
  Post: If Target is located, SearchSuccess is set to True;
        otherwise, SearchSuccess is set to False.
        Previous points to the last list node with key < Target;
        Next points to the first list node with key >= Target.
  Uses: ExtractKey
}
  var
    NextKey : KeyType;                    {key of node Next^}

begin {Locate}
  {Search for first node with key >= Target.}
  Next := Previous^.Link;               {Start at first actual node}
  ExtractKey (Next^.Item, NextKey);              {Get first key}
  while Target > NextKey do
    {invariant:
        Target > key of each node pointed to by Next so far.
    }
    begin
      Previous := Next;                  {Advance Previous}
      Next := Next^.Link;                {Advance Next}
      ExtractKey (Next^.Item, NextKey)   {Get next key}
    end; {while}

  {assert: Target is located or NextKey is larger than Target.}
  {Set flag to indicate search results.}
  SearchSuccess := not (NextKey > Target)
end; {Locate}
```

The precondition for Locate states that pointer Previous must point to the first dummy node when Locate is called. Locate initializes pointer Next to the first actual list node. The statement

```
ExtractKey (Next^.Item, NextKey);
```

calls procedure ExtractKey to store the key of node Next^ in NextKey. The while loop moves Next and Previous to their desired positions in the normal way. Loop exit occurs when Next advances to a node whose key is greater than or equal to Target. After loop exit, the Boolean variable SearchSuccess is set to True if NextKey is equal to the Target key.

Procedure Search

Procedure Search (Fig. 18.12) determines whether a particular target key is in the list. Search initializes Previous to point to the first dummy node, calls procedure Locate to perform the actual search, and returns the search result.

Figure 18.12   Procedure Search

```
procedure Search (List {input} : OrderList;
                  Target {input} : KeyType;
                  var Success {output} : Boolean);
{
  Searches an ordered List for Target.
  Pre : List points to the header node for an ordered list.
  Post: Success is True if Target is found; otherwise,
        Success is False.
}
  var
    Previous,                     {pointer to previous node}
    Next       : NodePointer;  {pointer to current node}

begin {Search}
  {Start search at first dummy node.}
  Previous := List.Head;
  {Perform search and define Success}
  Locate (Target, Previous, Next, Success)
end; {Search}
```

Procedure Insert

Procedure Insert inserts a node into an ordered list. It first calls Locate to search for the key value of the new record and, in this way, determines where the new record should be inserted. If there is already a node with the same key value as the new record, the insertion is not performed. Procedure Insert is shown in Fig. 18.13.

Figure 18.13   Procedure Insert

```
procedure Insert (var List {input/output} : OrderList;
                  El {input} : ListElement;
                  var Success {input/output} : Boolean);
```

```
{
    Inserts item El into an ordered list.
    Pre : List points to the header node for an ordered list.
    Post: Success is True if insertion is performed; Success is False
          if insertion is not performed because there is already
          an element with the same key as El.
    Uses: ExtractKey
}
    var
      Previous,              {pointer to node preceding El}
      Next : NodePointer;    {pointer to node following El}
      SearchSuccess : Boolean;             {search result}
      ElKey : KeyType;                   {key of record El}

begin {Insert}
  {Validate ElKey and search for a valid key.}
  ExtractKey (El, ElKey);
  if (MinKey > ElKey) or (ElKey > MaxKey) then
    Success := False                      {ElKey is out of range}
  else
    begin
      {Is ElKey already in the list?}
      Previous := List.Head;              {Start at first dummy node}
      Locate (ElKey, Previous, Next, SearchSuccess);
      Success := not SearchSuccess     {ElKey is new if search fails}
    end; {if}

  {Insert if ElKey is in range and is a new key}
  if Success then
    begin
      New (Previous^.Link);              {Join new node to Previous^}
      Previous^.Link^.Link := Next;      {Join new node to Next^}
      Previous^.Link^.Item := El;        {Store El in new node}
      List.NumItems := List.NumItems + 1
    end {if}
end; {Insert}
```

Procedure `Insert` begins by extracting `ElKey` from `El` and validating it. If `ElKey` is not in the range `MinKey` to `MaxKey`, the Boolean flag `Success` is set to `False`. If `ElKey` is within the allowable range, function `Locate` is called to find `ElKey`, and `Success` is set to `True` if `ElKey` is a new key and is not found. The last `if` statement inserts the new record `El` into the list if its key value is not already there.

Procedure Delete

Procedure `Delete` (Fig. 18.14) calls `Locate` to find the node that contains the `Target` key. If present, this node is deleted and the statement

```
    Dispose (Temp);                       {Deallocate storage}
```

returns its storage cells to the heap.

Figure 18.14   Procedure Delete

```
procedure Delete (var List {input/output} : OrderList;
                      Target {input} : KeyType;
                      var Success {input/output} : Boolean);
{
  Deletes the element with key Target from an ordered list.
  Pre : List points to the header node for an ordered list.
  Post: Success is True if deletion is performed; Success is False
        if deletion is not performed because there is no element
        whose key is Target.
}
  var
    Previous,              {pointer to last list key < ElKey}
    Next,                  {pointer to first list key >= ElKey}
    Temp : NodePointer;    {temporary variable}

begin {Delete}
  {Search the list for the key Target.}
  Previous := List.Head;              {start at first dummy node}
  Locate (Target, Previous, Next, Success);

  {If Target is found, delete it.}
  if Success then
    begin
      Temp := Next;           {Point Temp to the node being deleted}
      Previous^.Link := Next^.Link;       {Disconnect node Next^}
      Dispose (Temp);                       {Deallocate storage}
      List.NumItems := List.NumItems - 1
    end {if}
end; {Delete}
```

Procedures `Retrieve` and `Replace` are similar to `Delete` and are left as an exercise at the end of this section, along with function `SizeOfList`.

Procedure DisplayList

Procedure `DisplayList` traverses the ordered list, displaying each actual node, but not the dummy nodes. Procedure `DisplayList` calls procedure `DisplayOne` to display each list element. Procedure `DisplayOne` must also be imported into ADT `ListOrder`. Procedure `DisplayList` is shown in Fig. 18.15.

Figure 18.15   Procedure DisplayList

```
procedure DisplayList (List {input} : OrderList);
{
  Repeatedly calls procedure DisplayOne to display each
  element of an ordered list.
  Pre : List points to the header node of an ordered list.
  Post: The data fields of each actual element are displayed.
  Uses: ExtractKey and DisplayOne
}
  var
    Next : NodePointer;      {pointer to each list node}
    NextKey : KeyType;       {key of node Next^}
```

```
begin {DisplayList}
   Next := List.Head^.Link;              {Start with first actual node}
   ExtractKey (Next^.Item, NextKey);                  {Get node key}
   while MaxKey > NextKey do
      {invariant:
         MaxKey > key of each prior node pointed to by Next
      }
      begin
         DisplayOne (Next^.Item);        {Display node data}
         Next := Next^.Link;                 {Advance Next}
         ExtractKey (Next^.Item, NextKey)
      end {while}
end; {DisplayList}
```

If we are processing an ordered list of integers, procedure `DisplayOne` displays just one value and would have the form shown in Fig. 18.16. If we are processing an ordered list of passengers, procedure `DisplayOne` would be the same as procedure `WritePass` (see Fig. 16.21).

Figure 18.16   Procedure DisplayOne for a List of Integers

```
procedure DisplayOne (El {input} : ListElement);
{
  Displays element El.
  Pre : El is defined.
  Post: Displays each data field of El.
}
begin {DisplayOne}
  WriteLn (El :1)
end; {DisplayOne}
```

More on InsertKey, ExtractKey, and DisplayOne

Three procedures were imported into abstract data type `ListOrder`. These procedures manipulate one or more data fields of a list node. If the data type `ListElement` is a structured type, these procedures could be part of an abstract data type for that structured type. An example would be an ordered list of passenger data. In this case, we could add new procedures `InsertKey` and `ExtractKey` to ADT `Passenger`, shown in Fig. 16.21, and rename procedure `WritePass` as `DisplayOne`.

Analysis of Operations on an Ordered List

We have gone through considerable effort to maintain our linked list in ascending order by key value; however, the improvement in search efficiency that results is relatively modest. If we assume that a target key is equally likely to be at the front of a list as at the end of a list, then on the average, we have to examine half of the list elements to find it. This is the same whether or not the target key is in the list. If a list is not ordered, we have to examine all of its elements to determine that a key is not in the list, but only half of its elements, on the average, to find a key that is in the list.

It actually takes longer to insert an item into an ordered list than into an unordered list. In an unordered list, we can arbitrarily insert a new element at the list head. In an ordered list, we must first search for the appropriate position of the new element before we insert it.

The main advantage to using ordered lists occurs when we display the list contents. If the list is unordered, we must find some way to sort it before we can display it. We can always display the elements of an ordered list in ascending order by key without sorting the list.

Exercises for Section 18.3

Self-Check

1. In specifying the ordered list ADT, we assumed that there would be no insertion if the key of a new record was already present in the list. If we decide to allow insertion of duplicate keys, what change to `Insert` would be required? Would the new record be inserted before or after the existing record with the same key?
2. Two dummy records were placed in the initial list to ensure that there would be no need to insert a record into an empty list or in front of the first list node (that is, all valid keys follow the key `MinKey` in the first dummy node). How would `CreateList`, `Locate`, `Insert`, and `Delete` be modified if these nodes were not present?

Programming

1. Write function `SizeOfList`.
2. Write procedure `Retrieve`.
3. Write procedure `Replace`.

 ## 18.4 Multiple-Linked Lists and Trees

All the examples you have seen so far have involved elements or nodes with a single pointer field. It is possible to have a list of elements with more than one pointer field. For example, each element in the following list has a forward pointer that points to the next list element and a backward pointer that points to the previous list element. This allows us to traverse the list in the left or the right direction.

This structure is called a *doubly linked list*. The following declarations describe a general node of such a list.

```
type
  MultiLink = ^MultiNode;
```

```
MultiNode = record
          . . . . .
          . . . . .  } Data Fields
          . . . . .
      Left, Right : MultiLink
    end; {MultiNode}
```

Introduction to Trees

A special kind of multiple-linked list that has wide applicability in computer science is a data structure called a *tree*. A sample tree is drawn in Fig. 18.17.

Trees in computer science actually grow from the top down rather than from the ground up. The topmost element is called the *root of the tree*. The pointer variable Root (type Branch) points to the root of the tree in Fig. 18.17. Each tree node has a single data field and two pointer fields called the *left branch* and the *right branch*.

Genealogical terminology is also used to describe computer science trees. The node that contains the string 'HEN' is the *parent* of the nodes that contain the strings 'HAT' and 'HOG'. Similarly, the nodes 'HAT' and 'HOG' are *siblings*, because they are both *children* of the same parent node. The root of the tree is an *ancestor* of all other nodes in the tree, and they, in turn, are *descendants* of the root node.

Think of each node in a tree as the root node of its own *subtree*. Because each node has two branches, it spawns two more subtrees, a *left subtree* and a *right subtree*. One or both of these subtrees can be empty (denoted by a branch value of nil). A node with two empty subtrees is called a *leaf node*. The *left (right) child* of a node is the root node of its left (right) subtree. The *depth* of a tree is the length of the longest path from the root node to a leaf node.

The following statements describe the form of a tree node in Fig. 18.17. Because each node can have at most two children, such a tree is called a *binary tree*.

Figure 18.17 Tree

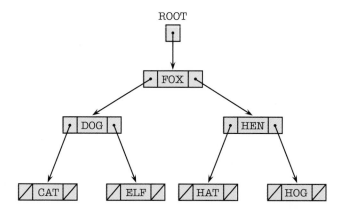

Figure 18.18 Expression Stored in a Tree

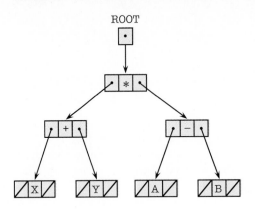

```
const
    StringSize = 3;

type
    StringType = packed array [1..3] of Char;
    Branch = ^TreeNode;
    TreeNode = record
                    Info : StringType;
                    Left, Right : Branch
                end; {TreeNode}
```

Field `Info` contains the data associated with the tree node, a string of three characters.

Trees can be used to represent expressions in memory. For example, the expression

```
(X + Y) * (A - B)
```

could be represented as the tree drawn in Fig. 18.18. This tree has the same shape as the one in Fig. 18.17.

The root node contains the operator (*) that is evaluated last in the expression. Each subtree is also an expression and contains either the subexpression operator (+ or –) in its root or a variable (X, Y, A, or B). There are subtrees for the subexpressions (X + Y) and (A – B).

Exercises for Section 18.4

Self-Check

1. For the tree in Fig. 18.17, what statement can be made about the relationship between the word in a node and its left child and right child? What statement can be made regarding the relationship between the word in a node and the words in its left subtree? What about the words in its right subtree?
2. What expression is stored in the following tree?

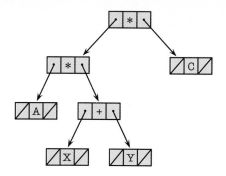

3. Draw the binary-tree representation of the following expressions. Assume the normal rules of expression evaluation.

```
X * Y / (A + B) * C
X * Y / A + B * C
```

 # 18.5 Traversing a Tree

To process the data stored in a tree, we need to be able to traverse the tree, or visit each node in a systematic way. The first approach we illustrate is called an *inorder traversal*. The algorithm for an inorder traversal follows.

Algorithm for Inorder Traversal

1. Traverse the left subtree.
2. Visit the root node.
3. Traverse the right subtree.

You will recall that the left subtree of any node is the part of the tree whose root is the left child of that node. The inorder traversal for the tree shown in Fig. 18.17 would visit the nodes in the sequence

```
'CAT' 'DOG' 'ELF' 'FOX' 'HAT' 'HEN' 'HOG'
```

If we assume that data of each node are printed when it is visited, the strings are printed in alphabetical order, as shown.

In Fig. 18.19, a numbered circle is drawn around each subtree. The subtrees are numbered in the order that they are traversed. Subtree 1 is the left subtree of the root node. Its left subtree (numbered 2) has no left subtree (or right subtree); thus, the string 'CAT' would be printed first. The root node for subtree 1 would then be visited and 'DOG' would be printed. Its right subtree consists of the leaf node containing the string 'ELF' (number 3). After 'ELF' is printed, the root node for the complete tree is visited ('FOX' is printed) and the right subtree of the root node (number 4) is traversed in a like manner.

Procedure Traverse in Fig. 18.20 is a recursive procedure that performs an inorder traversal of a tree and displays each node's data. The parameter

Figure 18.19 Subtrees of a Tree

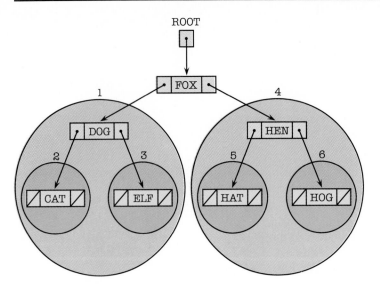

Root represents the pointer to the root node of the tree being traversed. If the tree is empty (Root = nil), an immediate return occurs. Procedure Traverse, like most procedures that process trees, can be written much more simply with recursion than without it.

Figure 18.20 Procedure Traverse

```
procedure Traverse (Root {input} : Branch);
{
   Performs an inorder traversal of a binary tree.
   Pre : Root points to a binary tree or is nil.
   Post: Displays each node visited.
}
begin {Traverse}
   if Root <> nil then
      begin {recursive step}
         Traverse (Root^.Left);        {traverse left subtree}
         WriteLn (Root^.Info);            {print root value}
         Traverse (Root^.Right)    {traverse right subtree}
      end {recursive step}
end; {Traverse}
```

The if statement in Fig. 18.20 differs from the if statements shown in earlier recursive algorithms. Those if statements had the form

    if a stopping case is reached then
        Perform stopping step
    else
        Perform recursive step

In a tree traversal, there is nothing to do when a stopping case is reached except unwind from the recursion. Thus, the if statement in Fig. 18.20 has the form

> if a stopping case is not reached then
>   Perform recursive step

As you saw earlier, an inorder traversal of the tree shown in Fig. 18.17 would visit the nodes in alphabetical sequence. If we performed an inorder traversal of the expression tree in Fig. 18.18, the nodes would be visited in the sequence

```
X + Y * A - B
```

Except for the absence of parentheses, this is the form in which we would normally write the expression. The expression is called an *infix* expression, because each operator is between its operands.

Switching the sequence of the three statements in the if statement shown in Fig. 18.20 produces rather different results. The sequence

```
Traverse (Root^.Left);      {traverse left subtree}
Traverse (Root^.Right);     {traverse right subtree}
WriteLn (Root^.Info)          {print root value}
```

displays the root node after traversing each of its subtrees; consequently, each root value will be printed after all the values in its subtrees. This is called a *postorder* traversal. The nodes in Fig. 18.17 would be visited in the sequence

```
CAT    ELF    DOG    HAT    HOG    HEN    FOX
```

The nodes in the expression tree in Fig. 18.18 would be visited in the sequence

```
X Y + A B - *
```

The preceding expression is called a postfix expression (see Chapter 16), because each operator follows its operands. The operands of + are X and Y; the operands of − are A and B; the operands of * are the two triples X Y + and A B −.

Finally, the sequence

```
WriteLn (Root^.Info);        {print root value}
Traverse (Root^.Left);       {traverse left subtree}
Traverse (Root^.Right)       {traverse right subtree}
```

displays the root node before traversing its subtrees; consequently, the data field of the root node will be displayed before the data fields of its subtrees. This is called a *preorder* traversal. The nodes in Fig. 18.17 would be visited in the sequence

```
FOX    DOG    CAT    ELF    HEN    HAT    HOG
```

The nodes in the expression tree in Fig. 18.18 would be visited in the sequence

```
* + X Y - A B
```

Figure 18.21   Outlining the Contour of a Tree

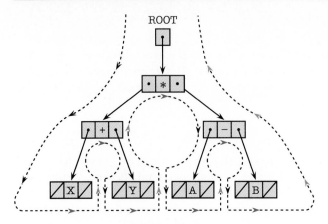

The preceding expression is called a *prefix* expression, because each operator precedes its operands. The operands of **+** are X and Y; the operands of **–** are A and B; the operands of ***** are the two triples **+ X Y** and **– A B**.

Tracing the Contour of a Tree

An easy way to determine the order in which the nodes of a tree are visited is to outline the contour of the tree, following all indentations as shown in Fig. 18.21. Move your finger along the tree contour, starting to the left of the root node. As your finger passes under a node (indicated by a colored arrow head), that node is visited in an inorder traversal.

   As your finger passes to the right of a node (indicated by a gray arrow head), that node is visited in a postorder traversal. Your finger should be moving in an upward direction when a node is visited in a postorder traversal. As your finger passes to the left of a node (indicated by a black arrow head), that node is visited in a preorder traversal. Your finger should be moving in a downward direction when a node is visited in a preorder traversal.

Exercises for Section 18.5

Self-Check

1. Rewrite the expressions shown in exercise 3 for Section 18.4 in prefix and postfix forms.
2. What would be printed by the inorder, preorder, and postorder traversals of the tree in exercise 2 for Section 18.4?
3. What would be printed by the inorder, preorder, and postorder traversals of the tree that follows?

18.6   The Binary Search Tree Abstract Data Type

Trees are also used to organize related data items to facilitate efficient search for and retrieval of an item. For example, the *binary search tree* shown in Fig. 18.17 is arranged so that the left child of each node alphabetically precedes its parent and the right child alphabetically follows its parent.

A binary search tree has the property that for any node all key values less than that node's key value are in its left subtree and all key values greater than that node's key value are in its right subtree. For this reason, searching a binary search tree is a relatively efficient process. To find a particular item (the target key) at any level of the tree, we compare the target key to the key in the subtree root. If the target key is less than the key of the root node, we can eliminate the right subtree and search only the left subtree, thereby cutting the number of nodes to be searched in half. We analyze this process in more detail in Section 18.9.

Binary Search Tree Specification

The binary search tree abstract data type must include operators similar to those provided in the ordered-list abstract data type discussed earlier. The following operations must be performed: create an empty tree, search for a target key, insert a node, delete a node, retrieve a node, replace a node, display the tree, and return its size. The specification for a binary search tree and its operators follows.

Specification of Binary Search Tree Abstract Data Type

Structure: A binary search tree is a collection of elements such that each element includes among its data fields a special field called the key field. Each element of a binary tree has zero, one, or two subtrees connected to it. The key field of each element in a binary search tree is larger than all keys in its left subtree and smaller than all keys in its right subtree.

Operators: For the following descriptions, assume these parameters:

`Tree` represents the binary search tree.
`El` (pronounced el) has the same data type as the tree elements.
`Target` is a possible key field value.
`Success` is a Boolean flag indicating success (`True`) or failure (`False`) of an operation.

`CreateTree (var Tree):` Creates an empty binary search tree; must be called before any other operators.

`SizeOfTree(Tree):` Returns the number of elements currently in the binary search tree.

`TreeSearch (Tree, Target, var Success):` Searches a tree to find the key `Target`. If `Target` is found, sets `Success` to `True`; otherwise, sets `Success` to `False`.

`TreeInsert (var Tree, El, var Success):` Inserts item `El` into the binary search tree and sets `Success` to `True`. If there is already an element with the same key value as `El`, `Success` is set to `False` and no insertion is performed.

`TreeDelete (var Tree, Target, var Success):` Deletes the element whose key value is `Target` and sets `Success` to `True`. If `Target` is not located, sets `Success` to `False`.

`TreeRetrieve (Tree, Target, var El, var Success):` Copies the element whose key is `Target` into `El` and sets `Success` to `True`. If there is no element with key `Target`, `El` is not defined and `Success` is `False`.

`TreeReplace (var Tree, El, var Success):` Replaces the element whose key value is the same as the key value of `El` and sets `Success` to `True`. If there is no element whose key value matches the key value of `El`, sets `Success` to `False`.

`DisplayTree (Tree):` Displays the tree elements in sequential order by key.

Space prevents us from covering the binary search tree abstract data type with the same thoroughness as we covered the ordered list. We show how to use the binary search tree next; in Section 18.8, we implement operators `CreateTree`, `TreeInsert`, `TreeSearch`, and `DisplayTree`.

18.7 Using a Binary Search Tree

We can use the binary search tree operators in a manner analogous to the way we use the ordered list operators. The program in Fig. 18.22 stores a collection of integer data values in a binary search tree. It does this by repeatedly calling procedure `TreeInsert` to insert the node just read at its correct position in the tree. After the tree is completed, it performs a search for a target key. Finally, the program displays the keys in sequential order and displays the tree size. Compare it with program `UseOrderList` in Fig. 18.3.

Figure 18.22   Using a Binary Search Tree

```
program UseSearchTree (Input, Output);
{
  Builds and displays a binary search tree using ADT SearchTree.

  IMPORT: SearchTree, TreeElement, KeyType,
          CreateTree, TreeInsert, TreeSearch, DisplayTree,
          SizeOfTree from ADT SearchTree
}
  const
    Sentinel = -1;

  type
    KeyType = Integer;
    TreeElement = Integer;

    {Insert type declaration for SearchTree}

  var
    MyTree : SearchTree;        {binary search tree}
    NextNode : TreeElement;     {each tree element}
    Target : KeyType;           {target key}
    Success : Boolean;          {program flag}


    {Insert CreateTree, TreeInsert, TreeSearch, DisplayTree, SizeOfTree}

begin {UseSearchTree}
  {Initialize the tree}
  CreateTree (MyTree);

  {Read and insert the keys in the tree.}
  WriteLn ('Enter ', Sentinel :1, ' to stop.');
  Write ('Enter next key value or ', Sentinel :1, '> ');
  ReadLn (NextNode);
  while NextNode <> Sentinel do
    {invariant:
        all prior values of NextNode that are not duplicates were
        inserted in MyTree and
        no prior value of NextNode was the sentinel
    }
    begin
      TreeInsert (MyTree, NextNode, Success);
      if Success then
        WriteLn (NextNode :1, ' inserted.')
      else
        WriteLn ('Duplicate key - no insertion.');
      Write ('Enter next key value or ', Sentinel :1, '> ');
      ReadLn (NextNode)
    end; {while}

  {assert: binary search tree completed.}
```

```
{Perform Search operation.}
WriteLn;
Write ('Find record with key> ');
ReadLn (Target);
TreeSearch (MyTree, Target, Success);
if Success then
  WriteLn (Target, ' found.')
else
  WriteLn ('Not in the tree.');
WriteLn;

{Display the binary search tree and its size.}
WriteLn ('The binary search tree follows.');
DisplayTree (MyTree);
Write ('The number of nodes in the tree is ');
WriteLn (SizeOfTree(MyTree) :1)
end. {UseSearchTree}
```

Building a Binary Search Tree

Figure 18.23 shows a sample run of program UseSearchTree that builds a binary tree of seven elements with integer-valued keys. The keys are inserted in the order 4000, 2000, 1000, 5000, 6500, 4500, 3000.

Figure 18.23 Sample Run of Program UseSearchTree

```
Enter -1 to stop.
Enter next key value or -1> 4000
4000 inserted.
Enter next key value or -1> 2000
2000 inserted.
Enter next key value or -1> 1000
1000 inserted.
Enter next key value or -1> 4000
Duplicate key - no insertion
Enter next key value or -1> 5000
5000 inserted.
Enter next key value or -1> 6500
6500 inserted.
Enter next key value or -1> 4500
4500 inserted.
Enter next key value or -1> 3000
3000 inserted.
Enter next key value or -1> -1

Find record with key> 2000
2000 found.

The binary search tree follows.
1000
2000
3000
4000
4500
```

5000
6500
The number of nodes in the tree is 7

729

18.7 Using a Binary
Search Tree

The keys are inserted one at a time, and each insertion increases the size of the binary tree. To find the insertion point for each new key, compare each new key to the key in the root. If the new key is smaller than the root key, then compare it to the key in the left subtree root; otherwise, compare it to the key in the right subtree root. In this way, move down the tree, branching left or right, until you reach a `nil` pointer. Attach a new node to the `nil` pointer and insert the new key in this node.

Figure 18.24 shows the seven partial trees formed by inserting each element. We show the branches followed for each key insertion in color. For example, to insert the integer 4500, we first compare 4500 to 4000; 4500 is bigger, so we follow the right branch. Next, we compare 4500 to 5000; 4500 is smaller, so we follow the left branch. Because the left branch from the node with key 5000 is `nil`, we attach a new node with key 4500 to that pointer. We provide a recursive insertion algorithm in the next section.

The order in which data items are stored in a binary tree has a profound effect on the shape of the binary search tree and, as you will see later, on the efficiency of the search process. The last tree shown in Fig. 18.24 is called a *balanced binary tree*, because the left subtree and the right subtree from each node are the same depth. A tree is also considered balanced if the depth of each node's subtrees differ by at most one.

An entirely different search tree results when the data values arrive in increasing sequence (for example, 1000, 2000, 3000, ...). This unbalanced tree (Fig. 18.25) actually looks more like an ordered list than a tree. Because procedure `DisplayTree` displays the tree elements in ascending order by key, the program output is the same regardless of the shape of the tree being displayed.

Exercises for Section 18.7

Self-Check

1. Explain the effect of the following program segment. Draw the tree. Is it balanced or unbalanced? If unbalanced, when does it first become unbalanced? What would be displayed by the preorder and postorder tree traversals?

```
begin
  CreateTree (MyTree);
  Insert (MyTree, 3000);
  Insert (MyTree, 2000);
  Insert (MyTree, 4000);
  Insert (MyTree, 5000);
  Insert (MyTree, 2500);
  Insert (MyTree, 6000);
  DisplayTree (MyTree);
  WriteLn ('Number of nodes is ', SizeOfTree(MyTree) :1)
end.
```

Insert 4000
MyTree

Insert 2000
MyTree

Insert 1000
MyTree

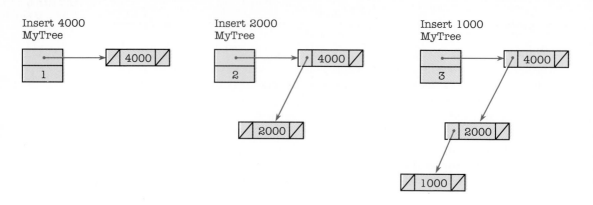

Insert 5000
MyTree

Insert 6500
MyTree

Insert 4500
MyTree

Insert 3000
MyTree

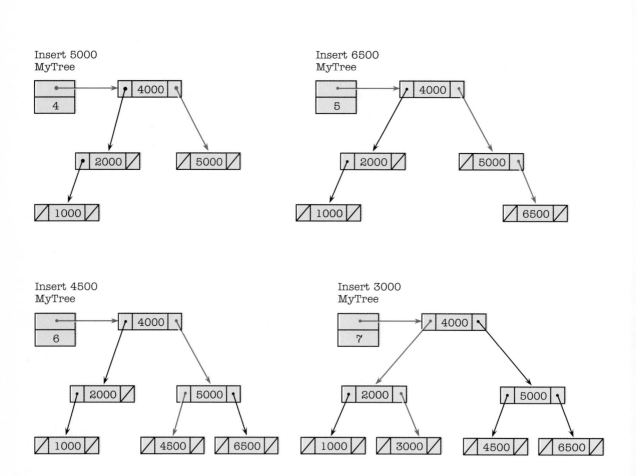

Figure 18.25 Unbalanced Binary Tree

731

18.8 Implementing
ADT SearchTree

18.8   Implementing ADT SearchTree

The interface section for ADT SearchTree is shown in Fig. 18.26. Each node in a binary search tree contains a data field, Item, and two pointers, Left and Right, that connect it to its children. The data field (type TreeElement) must include a record key (type KeyType) and can be a simple type or a structured type. Data types TreeElement and KeyType must be declared where shown or, if they are declared elsewhere, imported into ADT SearchTree.

The record type SearchTree is also declared. A variable of type Search-Tree represents a header node for a binary tree. The header node contains a pointer to the root of the tree (field Root) and a count of tree items (field NumItems).

Figure 18.26   Interface Section for ADT SearchTree

```
{
  Abstract data type SearchTree: contains declaration for data
  type SearchTree and operator procedures for an object of type
  SearchTree.

INTERFACE SECTION --

   EXPORT:   SearchTree, TreeElement, KeyType,
             CreateTree, SizeOfTree, TreeSearch, TreeInsert,
             TreeDelete, TreeRetrieve, TreeReplace, DisplayTree

   IMPORT:   InsertKey, ExtractKey, DisplayOne

   DATA TYPE SPECIFICATION:
}
```

```
type
  {Insert declaration for KeyType}
  {Insert declaration for TreeElement}

  Branch = ^TreeNode;
  TreeNode = record
               Item : TreeElement;        {Includes a key field}
               Left, Right : Branch
             end; {TreeNode}

  SearchTree = record
                 Root : Branch;
                 NumItems : Integer
               end; {SearchTree}
```

We implement all the operators called in program `UseSearchTree` in the remainder of this section except for `SizeOfTree`, which is left as a programming exercise. These operators call procedures `InsertKey`, `ExtractKey`, and `DisplayOne`, which were discussed earlier. To use these procedures, change the formal parameter data type `ListElement` to `TreeElement` wherever it appears.

Procedure CreateTree

Procedure `CreateTree` is shown in Fig. 18.27. It simply creates a record of type `Tree` with a `Root` field of `nil` and a count field (`NumItems`) of zero. Assuming `MyTree` is a variable of type `SearchTree`, the tree formed by

        CreateTree (MyTree)

is shown next.

MyTree.Root

MyTree.NumItems   0

Figure 18.27   Procedure CreateTree

```
procedure CreateTree (var Tree {output} : SearchTree);
{
  Creates an empty tree. Must be called first.
  Pre : None
  Post: Tree is the header node for a binary tree.
}
begin {CreateTree}
  Tree.Root := nil;
  Tree.NumItems := 0
end; {CreateTree}
```

Procedure TreeSearch

It is much easier to write a recursive search algorithm than an iterative one. The recursive algorithm for searching a binary tree is shown next.

Algorithm for Binary Tree Search

1. `if` the tree is empty `then`
   2. The target key is not in the tree.
   `else if` the target key matches the root key `then`
   3. The target key is found in the root node.
   `else if` the target key is larger than the root key `then`
   4. Search the right subtree.
   `else`
   5. Search the left subtree.

Step 2 is an unsuccessful stopping step; step 3 is a successful stopping step. Steps 4 and 5 continue to search the right subtree and the left subtree, respectively.

Procedure `TreeSearch` is shown in Fig. 18.28. It starts the search at the tree root by calling `DoSearch` with a parameter of `Tree.Root`. `DoSearch` implements the preceding recursive search algorithm. In `DoSearch`, we assume that the key field is type `KeyType` and that procedure `ExtractKey` is used to extract keys.

Figure 18.28 Procedure TreeSearch

```
procedure TreeSearch (Tree {input} : SearchTree;
                      Target {input} : KeyType;
                      var Success {output} : Boolean);
{
  Searches for Target in a binary search tree.
  Pre : Tree is the header node of a binary search tree.
  Post: If Target is located, Success is True;
        otherwise, Success is False.
}

  procedure DoSearch (Parent {input} : Branch;
                      Target {input} : KeyType;
                      var Success {output} : Boolean);
  {
    Searches the subtree pointed to by Parent.
    Pre : Target and Parent are defined.
    Post: If Target is not found, Success is False; otherwise,
          Success is True.
    Uses: ExtractKey
  }
    var
      NextKey : KeyType;          {key of node Parent^}

  begin {DoSearch}
    if Parent = nil then
      Success := False                    {tree is empty}
    else
      begin
        ExtractKey (Parent^.Item, NextKey);
        if Target = NextKey then
          Success := True                 {Target is found}
        else if Target > NextKey then
          DoSearch (Parent^.Right, Target, Success)
        else
```

```
                    DoSearch (Parent^.Left, Target, Success)
          end {if}
  end; {DoSearch}


begin {TreeSearch}
  DoSearch (Tree.Root, Target, Success)
end; {TreeSearch}
```

Procedure TreeInsert

Procedure `TreeInsert` is shown in Fig. 18.29. It stores a tree element (parameter `El`) in the tree whose header is passed as parameter `Tree`. It begins by storing the key of `El` in `ElKey`. Then it calls `DoInsert` to perform a recursive search for `ElKey`, starting at the tree root. We discussed the insertion process earlier; a recursive insertion algorithm follows.

Algorithm for DoInsert

1. `if` the pointer from the last node tested is `nil` `then`
    2. Attach a new node to that pointer, store `El` in this node, and set `Success` to True.
   `else` `if` the key of the current node is `ElKey` `then`
    3. Duplicate key; set `Success` to False.
   `else` `if` `ElKey` is greater than the key of the parent node `then`
    4. Insert the node with key `ElKey` in the left subtree of the parent node.
   `else`
    5. Insert the node with key `ElKey` in the right subtree of the parent node.

There are two stopping states in the algorithm. If `DoInsert` is passed a pointer with value `nil` (step 1), it replaces `nil` with the address of a new node, stores `El` in the new node, and sets `Success` to `True` before returning from the recursion (step 2). If `DoInsert` finds `ElKey` in the tree, it sets `Success` to `False` and returns (step 3). Otherwise, `DoInsert` calls itself recursively to process the left subtree or the right subtree of its current tree. After the return from the original call to `DoInsert`, procedure `TreeInsert` increments the count of tree nodes if the insertion was performed.

Figure 18.29 Procedure TreeInsert

```
procedure TreeInsert (var Tree {in/out} : SearchTree;
                      El {input} : TreeElement;
                      var Success {in/out} : Boolean);
{
  Inserts item El into a binary tree.
  Pre : El is defined and Tree is the header node of a binary tree.
  Post: Success is True if the insertion is performed. If there is
        a node with the same key value as El, Success is False.
  Uses: ExtractKey
}
```

```
var
   ElKey : KeyType;                    {key of record El}

procedure DoInsert (var Parent {in/out} : Branch;
                    El {input} : TreeElement;
                    ElKey {input} : KeyType;
                    var Success {in/out} : Boolean);
{
   Inserts item El in the subtree with root Parent.
   Pre : Parent, El, and ElKey are defined.
   Post: If a node with key ElKey is found, sets Success to False.
         If a nil pointer is reached, attaches a new node
         containing El to this pointer and sets Success to True.
   Uses: ExtractKey and InsertKey
}
   var
      NextKey : KeyType;           {key of Parent}

begin {DoInsert}
   {Check for empty tree.}
   if Parent = nil then
      begin {Attach new node containing El to Parent}
         New (Parent);                   {connect Parent to new node}
         Parent^.Left := nil;                 {make new node a leaf}
         Parent^.Right := nil;
         InsertKey (Parent^.Item, El);  {insert El in node Parent^}
         Success := True
      end {attach}
   else
      begin
         ExtractKey (Parent^.Item, NextKey);
         if ElKey = NextKey then
            Success := False                {ElKey is in tree}
         else if ElKey > NextKey then
            DoInsert (Parent^.Right, El, ElKey, Success)
         else
            DoInsert (Parent^.Left, El, ElKey, Success)
      end {if}
   end; {DoInsert}

begin {TreeInsert}
   ExtractKey (El, ElKey);                  {Get key}
   DoInsert (Tree.Root, El, ElKey, Success);
   if Success then
      Tree.NumItems := Tree.NumItems + 1    {new node is in tree}
end; {TreeInsert}
```

Procedure DisplayTree

Procedure DisplayTree (Fig. 18.30) calls procedure Traverse to perform an inorder tree traversal. Traverse then calls procedure DisplayOne to display each tree node.

Figure 18.30   Procedure DisplayTree

```
procedure DisplayTree (Tree {input} : SearchTree);
{
   Displays the elements of a binary search tree.
```

```
        Pre : Tree is the header node of a binary search tree.
        Post: Each element of the tree is displayed. The elements
              are displayed in ascending order by key.
      }

    procedure Traverse (Root {input} : Branch);
     {
       Performs an inorder traversal of a binary tree.
       Pre : Root points to a binary tree or is nil.
       Post: Displays each node visited.
       Uses: DisplayOne
     }
    begin {Traverse}
      if Root <> nil then
        begin {recursive step}
          Traverse (Root^.Left);           {traverse left subtree}
          DisplayOne (Root^.Item);         {print root value}
          Traverse (Root^.Right)           {traverse right subtree}
        end {recursive step}
    end; {Traverse}


begin {DisplayTree}
  Traverse (Tree.Root)
end; {DisplayTree}
```

Exercises for Section 18.8

Self-Check

1. Procedure `TreeDelete` should search for the target key and then delete the node containing it from the tree. Write a recursive algorithm for `Tree-Delete`, assuming that procedure `DeleteNode` performs the deletion of the node. `DeleteNode` has one parameter, which is the pointer from its parent to the node being deleted. Why is `DeleteNode` a difficult procedure to write?

Programming

1. Write function `SizeOfTree`
2. Write procedures `Retrieve` and `Replace` for the search tree abstract data type.

18.9   Analysis of Algorithms: Big-O Notation

This chapter has discussed two techniques for storing data in a systematic way to facilitate searching for a target item and displaying the data in order by key field. The first approach is to store the data in sequence by key field in an ordered list. The second approach is to store the data in a binary search tree. This section discusses the relative merits of each method.

Big-O Notation

It is difficult to get a precise measure of the performance of an algorithm or a program. For this reason, we normally try to approximate the effect on an algorithm of a change in the number of items, N, that it processes. In this way, we can see how an algorithm's execution time increases with N, so we can compare two algorithms by examining their growth rates.

For example, if we determine that the expression

$2N^2 + N - 5$

expresses the relationship between processing time and N, we say that the algorithm is an $O(N^2)$ algorithm, where O stands for *order of magnitude*. This notation is called *Big-O Notation*. The reason that this is an $O(N^2)$ algorithm instead of an $O(2N^2)$ or an $O(N^2 + N - 5)$ algorithm is that we are interested only in the fastest-growing term (the one with the largest exponent) and we ignore constants.

Earlier we showed that we would have to examine $N/2$ items on average to locate an item in an ordered list or to determine that the item is not in the list. Consequently, searching for a data item in an ordered list is an $O(N)$ process, so the growth rate is linear.

Searching a binary search tree is more difficult to analyze. If the tree is balanced, each probe into the tree eliminates ½ of the items. Consequently, we first search a tree with N nodes, then $N/2$ nodes, then $N/4$ nodes, and so on. For example, if N is 1024 it requires searching ten more trees (sizes 512, 256, 128, 64, 32, 16, 8, 4, 2, and 1) to determine that a target is missing. It should require fewer than eleven probes to find a target in the tree. Because 1024 happens to be a power of 2 (1024 is 2 raised to the power 10), the numbers in the preceding list are all powers of 2. Therefore, searching a balanced binary search tree is an $O(\log_2 N)$ process ($\log_2 1024$ is 10). Keep in mind that a binary search tree is not always balanced, so this is really a *best-case analysis*.

What difference does it make whether an algorithm is an $O(N)$ process or an $O(\log_2 N)$ process? Table 18.1 evaluates $\log_2 N$ for different values of N. A doubling of N causes $\log_2 N$ to increase by only 1. Because $\log_2 N$ increases much more slowly with N, the performance of an $O(\log_2 N)$ algorithm is not as adversely affected by an increase in N.

Table 18.1 Table of Values of $\log_2 N$

N	$\log_2 N$
32	5
64	6
128	7
256	8
512	9
1,024	10

Both storage techniques enable us to easily display the data items in sequence by key field. In an ordered list, we simply advance a pointer down the list and display the data fields of the node selected by the pointer. Therefore, displaying the data in an ordered list is an $O(N)$ process.

To display the data in a binary search tree, we must perform an inorder traversal of the tree, displaying the data stored in each node as we visit it. The tree-traversal algorithm is recursive, and the number of procedure calls depends on the size of the tree. The left and the right subtrees of each tree must be traversed, so for a tree of N nodes, there are $2N$ procedure calls. Therefore, a binary search tree display is also an $O(N)$ process. Even though both algorithms are $O(N)$, it takes more time to display a binary search tree, because calling a procedure takes more time than advancing a list pointer.

Another question is the effect on memory of using an ordered list versus a binary search tree. One additional pointer field is needed for each node of a binary search tree, so the storage requirements for a tree versus a list increase linearly with N.

The memory requirements for the algorithms to search and display an ordered list are not affected by N. However, the algorithms to search and display a binary search tree are recursive, so their memory requirements increase with the depth of the tree. If the tree is balanced, its depth is related to $\log_2 N$. The worst case for an inorder traversal occurs for an unbalanced tree with all its nodes in the left subtree (why?). This tree has a depth of N.

 ## 18.10   Common Programming Errors

The procedures in this chapter manipulate pointer fields, so review the errors described in Section 17.7. The first and last nodes of an ordered list must be treated as special cases unless you provide dummy or sentinel nodes. Make sure all recursive procedures do, in fact, terminate. Also, be careful when using pointers to list heads as procedure parameters. If the pointer is passed as a variable parameter and is moved down the list, you may disconnect the list head from its list. The same warning applies when using pointers to tree roots.

 # Chapter Review

This chapter discussed techniques for maintaining an ordered collection of records and examined two data structures for this purpose. We implemented an abstract data type for an ordered list and one for a binary search tree. These ADTs included operators to search, insert, and delete records.

We also discussed binary trees in general and showed how they can be used to represent expressions in memory. We discussed inorder, preorder, and postorder traversal and related these three methods to infix, prefix, and postfix expressions.

1. Is it more or less efficient to search an ordered list or an unordered list? Is it more or less efficient to insert a new element in an ordered list or in an unordered list?
2. What is the purpose of the dummy nodes in the ordered lists shown in this chapter?
3. Is an ordered list a last-in, last-out structure, a first-in, first-out structure, or neither?
4. In what direction do computer science trees grow?
5. Name the three traversal methods and relate them to the three forms of arithmetic expressions.
6. A node in a Pascal tree can have a maximum of two children. True or false?
7. A node in a binary search tree can have a maximum of two children. True or False?
8. What is the relationship between the left child and the right child of a binary search tree? Between the left child and the parent? Between the right child and the parent?
9. When is searching a binary search tree more efficient than searching an ordered list? When isn't it?
10. How do we know if a binary tree is balanced?
11. Traverse the following tree three ways. Is this tree a binary search tree? Is it balanced or unbalanced? If it is unbalanced, why?

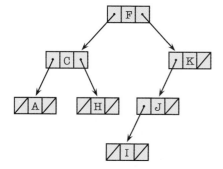

Answers to Quick-Check Exercises

1. Search of an ordered list is more efficient; insertion into an ordered list is less efficient.
2. As sentinel values, they eliminate the need to insert an element at the beginning of a list or to delete the last list element and also help prevent us from searching beyond the last list element.
3. Neither
4. From the top down
5. Inorder (infix), preorder (prefix), postorder (postfix)
6. False
7. True
8. Left child < parent < right child
9. When tree is balanced; when tree is badly unbalanced
10. The depth of the subtrees from every node differ by at most one.
11. Inorder:　　　A C H F I J K
    Preorder:　　　F C A HKJ I
    Postorder:　　　A HC I J KF

    It is not a binary search tree, because H is in the wrong subtree of the root. It is not balanced, because the left subtree of K has depth 2, and the right subtree of K has depth zero.

Review Questions

1. Write a procedure to link a node into an existing ordered list. The procedure parameters will be a pointer to the first dummy node and a pointer to the node to be inserted. Assume that dummy sentinel records exist at the beginning and the end of the list and that there are no duplicate records.

   Given the following declarations, insert the new element, preserving ID order:

   ```
   const
     StringLen = 20;

   type
     StringType = packed array [1..StringLen] of Char;
     Ptr = ^Node;
     Node = record
               ID : Integer;
               Name : StringType;
               GPA : Real;
               Link : Ptr
            end; {Node}
   ```

2. Write a procedure to delete a node (parameter `TargetID`) from an ordered list that does not contain a dummy record at the beginning. Assume the declarations above. Let the parameter `Head` (type `Ptr`) point to the first actual list node. Return a Boolean flag.

3. Write a procedure that creates a list of nodes with a GPA of 3.5 or better by copying all qualified records from one linked list into another linked list. The original list is ordered by ID number; the new list should be ordered by GPA. Assume the list nodes are type `Node` as described in exercise 1. The parameters will be a pointer to the head of the existing list and a pointer to the head of the new linked list (`GPAHead`). Don't remove nodes from the original list, just copy their data.

4. Declare a node for a two-way, or doubly linked, list; indicate how a traversal would be made in reverse order (from the last list element to the list head). Include any variables or fields that are necessary.

5. Discuss the differences between a simple linked list and a binary tree. Consider such things as number of pointer fields per node, search technique, and insertion algorithm.

6. How can you determine if a node is a leaf?

7. Traverse the following tree in inorder, preorder, and postorder.

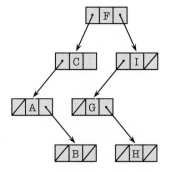

Provide one data sequence that would create this ordered binary tree. Are there any letters that must occur before other letters?

8. Discuss how you might delete a node from a binary tree. Consider nodes with 0 or 1 child first.

Programming Projects

1. Use an ordered list to maintain an airline passenger list. The main program should be menu driven and allow the user to display the data for a particular passenger, display the entire list, create a list, insert a node, delete a node, and replace the data for a particular passenger.

2. Redo project 1 using a binary search tree for storage of the airline passenger list. When deleting a node, simply change the number of seats assigned to zero and leave the passenger's node in the tree.

3. The set capability is limited in the number of elements that can be stored in a set. A more universal system can be implemented using an ordered list to store a set.

   Write the necessary operators needed to insert and delete integer values from a set. Also write the operators necessary to implement the set difference, intersection, and union operations. To verify the results, display the contents of the sets before and after each operation.

4. In preparing mailing lists, it is often useful to be able to reference the information by using either the person's name or zip code. This can be done if each list node has a pointer to the next node by name and a pointer to the next node by zip code. The nodes representing each person's data should be linked together in both name and zip code order; there should be only one copy of the data for each person. Provide a header node that has pointers to the first element in each of the two lists.

   Write a program that reads a record containing first name, last name, street address, city, state, and zip code and connects each new record to the appropriate nodes of both lists. After all the information has been entered, display a list of the information in name order and a second list in zip code order.

5. In this chapter, we wrote recursive procedures to perform preorder, inorder, and postorder tree traversals. A tree traversal can be written without using recursion. In that case, it is necessary to push the address of a tree node that is reached during the traversal onto a stack. The node will be popped off later when it is time to traverse the subtree rooted at this node. For example, the algorithm for a nonrecursive preorder traversal follows.

   1. Push nil onto the stack.
   2. Assign the root node as the current node.
   3. while the current node is not nil do
       begin
         4. Print the current node.
         5. if the current node has a right subtree then
                 Push the right subtree root onto the stack.
         6. if the current node has a left subtree then
                 Make it the current node.
             else
                 Pop the stack and make the node removed the current node.
       end

In this algorithm, each right subtree pointer that is not `nil` is pushed onto the stack; the stack is popped when the current left subtree pointer is `nil`.

Implement and test a nonrecursive procedure for preorder traversal. Write a nonrecursive algorithm for inorder traversal and implement and test it as well.

6. If an arithmetic expression is written in prefix or postfix notation, there is no need to use parentheses to specify the order of operator evaluation. For this reason, some compilers translate infix expressions to postfix notation first and then evaluate the postfix string.

Write a procedure that simulates the operation of a calculator. The input will consist of an expression in postfix notation. The operands will all be single-digit numbers. Your program·should print the expression value. For example, if the input string is '54+3/', the result printed should be ((5 + 4) / 3), or 3.

To accomplish this, examine each character in the string in left- to-right order. If the character is a digit, push its numeric value onto a stack. If the character is an operator, pop the top two operands, apply the operator to them, and push the result onto the stack. After the string has been competely scanned, there should be only one number on the stack, and that should be the expression value. Besides the operators +, −, *, and /, use ^ to indicate exponentiation.

7. Save each word appearing in a block of text in a binary search tree. Also save the number of occurrences of each word and the line number for each occurrence. Use a stack for the line numbers. After all words have been processed, display each word in alphabetical order. Along with each word, display the number of occurrences and the line number for each occurrence.

8. Store the Morse code (see programming project 1 for Chapter 12) in a binary tree, as shown. A dot should cause a branch to the left, and a dash should cause a branch to the right. Each node should contain the letter represented by the code symbol formed by tracing a path from the root to that node. For example, following two left branches gives us two dots, which repesents the letter I. The first two levels of the Morse-code tree are shown next.

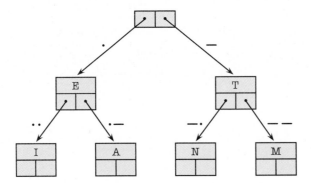

First, build an empty Morse-code tree by constructing a tree of four levels. Then read each letter, followed by its code from a data line, and insert it where it belongs in the tree. Use ADT `String` for processing the data line. After the tree is filled, read in a coded message using a space between each letter of the message and a double space between words. Translate the message into English.

Searching and Sorting

19

Chapter 12 introduced one technique for searching an array for a target key and one technique for sorting an array. Chapter 18 considered other methods of data storage (that is, using ordered lists and binary search trees) that facilitate searching for a target key and eliminate the need for sorting.

Even though alternative methods are available, arrays are frequently used for data storage. Computer scientists have also spent much time and effort to devise efficient algorithms for searching and sorting arrays. This chapter discusses two techniques for searching an array and several techniques for sorting an array and compares these algorithms with respect to their efficiency.

 ## 19.1   Binary Search of an Array

We discussed one technique for searching an array in Section 12.6 and wrote a function that returned the index of a target key in an array or the value 0 if the target was not present. To do this, we had to compare array element keys to the target key, starting with the first array element. The comparison process is terminated when the target key is found or the end of the array is reached. We must make N comparisons to determine that a target key is not in an array of N elements. On the average, we must make $N/2$ comparisons to locate a target key that is in the array. Because the constant 2 is ignored, array search is an $O(N)$ process.

Often, we want to search an array whose elements are arranged in order by key field (analogous to an ordered list). We can take advantage of the fact that the array keys are in increasing order and terminate the search when an array key greater than or equal to the target key is reached. There is no need to look any further in the array; all other keys will be larger than the target key.

Both these search techniques are called *sequential search* because we examine the array elements in sequence. The modified algorithm just discussed is a sequential search of an ordered array. On the average, a sequential search of an ordered array requires $N/2$ comparisons either to locate the target key or to determine that it is not in the array; so we still have an $O(N)$ process.

● Case Study: Binary Search

The array searches described here are considered *linear searches*, because their execution time increases linearly with the number of array elements. This can be a problem when we are searching very large arrays (for example, N > 1000). Consequently, we often use the *binary-search algorithm* for large sorted arrays.

Problem
Your employer has a directory of customers that she keeps in alphabetical order. Because business has been very good, this list is now too large to search effi-

ciently using a linear search. Write an improved search algorithm that takes advantage of the fact that the array is sorted.

Design Overview

The *binary-search algorithm*, like a binary-tree search, takes advantage of the fact that the array is ordered to eliminate half of the array elements with each probe into the array. Consequently, if the array has 1,000 elements, it either locates the target value or eliminates 500 elements with its first probe, 250 elements with its second probe, 125 elements with its third probe, and so on. Therefore, a binary search of an ordered array is an $O(\log_2 N)$ process. You can use the binary search algorithm to find a name in a large metropolitan telephone directory using thirty or fewer probes, so this algorithm should be suitable for your employer.

Because the array is ordered, all we have to do is compare the target value with the middle element of the subarray we are searching. If their values are the same, we are done. If the middle value is larger than the target, we should search the left half of the array next; otherwise, we should search the right half of the array.

The subarray to be searched has subscripts `First..Last`. The variable `Middle` is the subscript of the middle element in this range. The right half of the array (subscripts `Middle..Last`) is eliminated by the first probe, as shown in Fig. 19.1.

`Last` should be reset to `Middle − 1` to define the new subarray to be searched, and `Middle` should be redefined, as shown in Fig. 19.2. The target value, 35, would be found on this probe.

The binary-search algorithm can be stated clearly using recursion. The stopping cases are

- The array bounds are improper (`First > Last`).
- The middle value is the target value.

Figure 19.1 First Probe of Binary Search

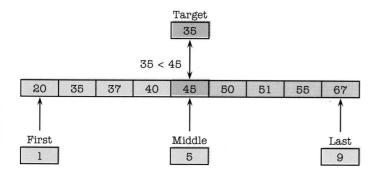

Case Study: Binary Search, continued

Figure 19.2 Second Probe of Binary Search

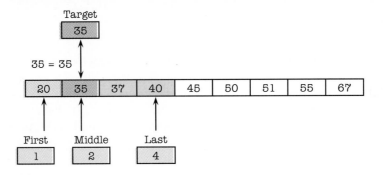

In the first case, the function result is zero; in the second case, the function result is Middle. The recursive step is to search the appropriate subarray.

Data Requirements

Problem Inputs
Array to be searched (Table : SearchArray)
Target being searched for (Target : KeyType)
The first subscript in the subarray (First : Integer)
The last subscript in the subarray (Last : Integer)

Problem Outputs
The location of the Target value or 0 if not found

Binary Search Algorithm
1. Compute the subscript of the middle element
2. if the array bounds are improper then
     3. Return a result of 0
   else if the target is the middle value then
     4. Return the subscript of the middle element
   else if the target is less than the middle value then
     5. Search the subarray with subscripts First..Middle−1
   else
     6. Search the subarray with subscripts Middle+1..Last

For each of the recursive steps (steps 5 and 6), the bounds of the new subarray must be listed as actual parameters in the recursive call. The actual parameters define the search limits for the next probe into the array.

Coding Binary Search

In the initial call to the recursive procedure, First and Last should be defined as the first and last elements of the entire array, respectively. For example, you could use the function designator

```
BinSearch(X, 35, 1, 9)
```

to search an array X with subscripts 1..9 for the target value 35 (assuming X has type SearchArray and KeyType is Integer). Function BinSearch is shown in Fig. 19.3.

Figure 19.3   Recursive Binary Search Function

```
function BinSearch (var Table : SearchArray;
                        Target : KeyType;
                        First, Last : Integer) : Integer;
{
  Performs a recursive binary search of an ordered array
  with subscripts First..Last.
  Pre : The elements of Table are in increasing order by
        key field and First and Last are defined.
  Post: Returns the subscript of Target if found in array Table;
        otherwise, returns a value of 0.
}
  var
    Middle : Integer;      {the subscript of the middle element}

begin {BinSearch}
  Middle := (First + Last) div 2;

  {Determine if Target is found or missing or redefine subarray.}
  if First > Last then
    BinSearch := 0                        {Target missing}
  else if Target = Table[Middle] then
    BinSearch := Middle                   {Target found}
  else if Target < Table[Middle] then
    BinSearch := BinSearch(Table, Target, First, Middle-1)
  else
    BinSearch := BinSearch(Table, Target, Middle+1, Last)
end;   {BinSearch}
```

The assignment statement

```
Middle := (First + Last) div 2;
```

computes the subscript of the middle element by finding the average of First and Last. This value has no meaning when First is greater than Last, but it does no harm to compute it.

An iterative version of the binary search function is shown in Fig. 19.4. A Boolean flag, Found, controls repetition of a search loop. Found is set to False before the while loop is reached. The while loop executes until the Target is found (Found is True) or the search array is reduced to an array of zero elements

Case Study: Binary Search, continued

(a *null array*). The if statement in the loop either sets Found to True (Target
= Table[Middle]) or resets index First or index Last. The if statement after
the loop defines the function result.

Figure 19.4 Iterative Binary Search Function

```
function BinarySearch (var Table : SearchArray;
                           Target : KeyType;
                           First, Last : Integer) : Integer;
{
  Performs an iterative binary search of an ordered array
  with subscripts First..Last.
  Pre : The elements of Table are in ascending order by key field
        and First and Last are defined.
  Post: Returns the subscript of Target if found in array Table;
        otherwise, returns a value of 0.
}
  var
    Middle : Integer;     {the subscript of the middle element}
    Found : Boolean;      {program flag}

begin   {BinarySearch}
  Found := False;                             {Target not found}
  while (First <= Last) and (not Found) do
    {invariant:
        Last subarray searched was not null and
        Target <> Table[Middle] for all prior values of Middle
    }
    begin
      Middle := (First + Last) div 2;
      if Target = Table[Middle] then
        Found := True
      else if Target < Table[Middle] then
        Last := Middle - 1                    {search left subarray}
      else if Target > Table[Middle] then
        First := Middle + 1                   {search right subarray}
    end; {while}

  {Assert: Target is found or search subarray is null.}
  if Found then
    BinarySearch := Middle                    {Target is found}
  else
    BinarySearch := 0                         {Target not found}
end;   {BinarySearch}
```

Testing

You should test both versions of the binary search function carefully. Besides
verifying that they locate target values present in the array, verify that they also
determine when a target value is missing. Use target values within the range of
values stored in the array, a target value less than the smallest value in the array,
and a target value greater than the largest value in the array. Make sure the
binary-search function terminates regardless of whether the target is missing
or, if it is not missing, where it is located.

The result returned by the binary-search function is inconclusive if 0 is included in the subrange First..Last. For example, if the array being searched has subscript type [−5..5], First is −5 and Last is 5. In this case, it would be better to convert the binary-search function to a procedure with two output parameters: the index of the target if found and a program flag indicating whether the target was found. This modification is left as an exercise.

Exercises for Section 19.1

Self-Check

1. Trace the search of the array Table for a Target of 40. Specify the values of First, Middle, and Last during each recursive call.
2. Provide the algorithm for a recursive procedure that performs binary search and returns a flag as its second output parameter that indicates whether the search was successful.

Programming

1. Write the procedure for exercise 2.

 ## 19.2 Searching by Hashing

So far, we have discussed the advantages of using the binary-search technique to retrieve information stored in a large array. Binary search can be used only when the contents of the array are ordered.

Another technique for storing data in an array so that it can be retrieved in an efficient manner is called *hashing*. Hashing consists of implementing a *hash function*, which accepts as its input a designated field of a record (called the *record key*) and returns as its output an integer *hash index*. The hash index selects the particular array element that stores the new data. To retrieve the item later, you need only to recompute the hash index and access the item in that array location. This process is illustrated in the following diagram, where the hash index is 3.

For example, let's assume that we have to maintain a collection of student records. Each record (type Student) has a Name field that is a packed array of characters, an exam score, and a grade. The student data can be stored in an array with subscripts 1..MaxSlots. For reasons that will be discussed later, MaxSlots should be a prime number that is at least 20 percent larger than the number of records in the collection. Record types Student and HashArray are declared next.

```
const
   StringLen = 20;                      {length of each name string}
   BlankString = '                  ';        {string of blanks}
   MaxSlots = 97;                         {size of hash table}

type
   StringType = packed array [1..StringLen] of Char;
   Student = record                      {one student record}
                Name : StringType;
                Score : Integer;
                Grade : Char
             end; {Student}

   HashArray = array [1..MaxSlots] of Student;
```

We can use the student's name as the record key. One possible hash function would simply add up the ordinal values of each nonblank character in the student's name, then use the mod function to convert this sum to an integer in the range 1 to MaxSlots. Such a function is shown in Fig. 19.5.

Figure 19.5 Function Hash

```
function Hash (Key {input} : StringType;
               MaxSlots {input} : Integer) : Integer;
{
  Computes an integer value between 1 and MaxSlots.
  Pre : Key, MaxSlots, and StringLen are defined.
  Post: Returns an integer value between 1 and MaxSlots
        based on the nonblank characters in Key.
}
const
  Pad = ' ';                  {pad character}

var
   I,                         {loop-control variable}
   HashIndex : Integer;       {accumulated hash value}

begin {Hash}
   HashIndex := 0;                        {initialize hash sum}
   {Add ordinal values for all nonblank characters in Key.}
   for I := 1 to StringLen do
     if Key[I] <> Pad then
       HashIndex := HashIndex + Ord(Key[I]);

   {Assert:
     HashIndex is the sum of ordinal values for all
     nonblank characters in Key
   }
   Hash := (HashIndex mod MaxSlots) + 1     {define result}
end; {Hash}
```

Inserting a student record then becomes a matter of passing its key to function Hash and storing the record in the array element selected by Hash. After all records are stored in the array, we can retrieve a particular student's record by passing the student's name to function Hash and accessing the array element selected by Hash. The nice thing about all of this is that it usually takes only one probe into the array to get the record we are seeking. (Sometimes it does take more than one probe, as explained in the next subsection.)

A good hash function disperses the records arbitrarily throughout the hash table. If we display the records starting with the record in position 1 of the table, their keys follow no special order. Empty slots are intermixed with slots that contain actual records. For this reason, do not use hashing when it is important to display frequently the student records in order by key field.

Effect of Collisions

The hashing technique just described works fine as long as Hash never returns the same hash index for two different keys. However, the names 'SILLY SAM' and 'SALLY SIM' would both yield the same hash index because they contain the same letters. It would be an easy matter to improve the hash function so that this does not happen for these two names (see exercise 2 at the end of this section); however, regardless of the hash function used, it is always possible that two different keys will hash to the same index. Such an occurrence is called a *collision*.

One simple way to handle collisions is to insert a new record into the element selected by function Hash only if that slot is currently empty. If that slot is filled, advance to the next empty slot in the array and place the record in that location. The record keys can all be initialized to blank strings to indicate that they are initially empty.

Function LocateSlot (Fig. 19.6) uses this approach to find a desired key, Target, or to determine where in the array a new record with key Target should be placed. To indicate that there is neither a record with key Target nor an empty slot, the function returns zero. Function Locate uses the constant BlankString, a string of all blanks, which should be declared earlier.

Algorithm for LocateSlot

1. Start at element selected by Hash function.
2. Initialize number of probes to 1.
3. while Target key not found and
   empty slot not found and
   all elements not examined do
   begin
      4. Advance to next slot.
      5. Increment count of probes.
   end
6. if all table entries were examined without success then
   7. Return 0.

else
8. Return position of Target or first empty slot.

Figure 19.6 Function LocateSlot

```
function LocateSlot (var Class : HashArray;
                         MaxSlots : Integer;
                         Target : StringType) : Integer;
{
   Searches array Class for the student with key field Target.
   Pre : Class, MaxSlots, and Key are defined.
   Post: Returns the index of the student whose name field is
         Target. Returns the location where Target should be
         inserted if missing. Returns MaxSlots + 1 if there
         are no empty slots.
   Uses: Hash
}
   var
     Index,                                  {index to array}
     Probe : Integer;                        {probe counter}

begin {LocateSlot}
   {Search for student whose name is Target.}
   Index := Hash(Target, MaxSlots); {starting point for search}
   Probe := 1;
   while(Class[Index].Name <> Target) and
        (Class[Index].Name <> BlankString) and
        (Probe <= MaxSlots) do
     {invariant:
        No prior record key matched Target and
        no prior array element was empty and
        number of probes <= MaxSlots + 1
     }
     begin
       Index := (Index mod MaxSlots) + 1;    {get next element}
       Probe := Probe + 1
     end; {while}

   {assert: Target found or empty slot found or array is full}
   if Probe > MaxSlots then
     LocateSlot := 0                         {Target not found}
   else
     LocateSlot := Index           {Target or empty slot found}
end; {LocateSlot}
```

The assignment statement

```
Index := (Index mod MaxSlots) + 1;   {get next element}
```

increments the value of Index. If the current value of Index is MaxSlots, the new value will be 1; otherwise, the new value will be one more than the current value.

The local variable Probe counts the number of probes into the array. If Target is missing and the array is completely filled, it would be possible to search forever for an empty slot. The `while` condition (`Probe <= MaxSlots`) prevents this from happening.

We can write procedures to insert and retrieve records in a hash table. Procedure `InsertHash` (Fig. 19.7) inserts a student record into a hash table. The procedure call statement

```
InsertHash (Class, MaxSlots, NextStu, Success)
```

calls `InsertHash` to store record `NextStu` in array `Class`. `InsertHash` uses `LocateSlot` to find the correct slot for the record. If an empty slot is found, the record is inserted and the Boolean flag is set to `True`. If there are no empty slots or there is already a student with the same name in the table, the Boolean flag is set to `False`.

Figure 19.7   Procedure InsertHash

```
procedure InsertHash (var Class {input/output} : HashArray;
                          MaxSlots {input} : Integer;
                          NextStu {input} : Student;
                          var Inserted {output} : Boolean);
{
   Inserts a new student record (NextStu) in the array of
   student records Class using hashing.
   Pre : Class, MaxSlots, and NextStu are defined. An empty slot
         in Class is indicated by a record with a blank Key field.
   Post: If there is no existing record with the same key as
         NextStu, NextStu is inserted in the first empty array
         element that is nearest to the one selected by Hash.
         Inserted is set to True if the insertion was performed;
         otherwise, Inserted is set to False.
   Uses: LocateSlot
}
   var
     NewIndex : Integer;                     {insertion point}

begin {InsertHash}
   {Locate first empty slot or NextStu.}
   NewIndex := LocateSlot (Class, MaxSlots, NextStu.Name);

   {Perform insertion if slot is empty}
   if NewIndex = 0 then
     Inserted := False                          {table is full}
   else if Class[NewIndex].Name = BlankString then
     begin
       Class[NewIndex] := NextStu;           {insert new student}
       Inserted := True
     end
   else
     Inserted := False                         {duplicate entry}
end;   {InsertHash}
```

Procedure `RetrieveHash` (Fig. 19.8) is similar to `InsertHash`. If the target key is in the hash table, the procedure returns the record with that key through its fourth parameter. The procedure returns a Boolean value indicating success or failure through its last parameter.

Figure 19.8 Procedure RetrieveHash

```
procedure RetrieveHash (Class {input/output} : HashArray;
                        MaxSlots {input} : Integer;
                        Target {input} : StringType;
                        var NextStu {output} : Student;
                        var Retrieved {output} : Boolean);
{
  Retrieves the record with key target from the array Class.
  Pre : Class, MaxSlots, and Target are defined. An empty slot
        in Class is indicated by a record with a blank Key field.
  Post: Returns in NextStu the record with key Target.
        Retrieved is set to True if Target is present;
        otherwise, Retrieved is set to false.
  Uses: LocateSlot
}
  var
    NewIndex : Integer;                    {insertion point}

begin {RetrieveHash}
    {Locate first empty slot or NextStu.}
    NewIndex := LocateSlot (Class, MaxSlots, Target);

    {Retrieve record or display error message.}
    if NewIndex <> 0 then
      begin
        NextStu := Class[NewIndex];
        Retrieved := True
      end
    else
      Retrieved := False
end;   {RetrieveHash}
```

Analysis of Hashing

In the best case, it requires just one probe into the hash table to locate a target key or to insert a new record. The more records that are in the array, the greater the chance of one or more collisions and additional probes. To reduce the likelihood of collisions, it is a good idea to leave at least 20 percent extra capacity in the hash table. We can also reduce the chance of multiple collisions by providing better algorithms for resolving a collision than by using the simple approach of advancing to the next slot in the array. Experience shows that the latter approach causes records to be placed in adjacent slots of the hash table, which leads to bands of filled slots and increases the likelihood of multiple collisions.

The hash function should also be constructed so that it distributes the records throughout the hash table. However, we do not want a hash function that is overly complicated, which would require too much computer time to compute the initial hash index. Best results are obtained when the number of table slots is a prime number.

Self-Check

1. Assume that the ordinal number for the letter A is 1, B is 2, and so on; MaxSlots is 10 (array Class has ten elements). Compute the hash values for the following names and indicate where each name would be stored in the array: 'SAL', 'BIL', 'JILL', 'LIB', 'HAL', 'ROB'

2. A modification to function Hash is proposed in which the ordinal value for each letter is multiplied by its position in the string (for example, for 'SAL', multiply Ord('S') by 1, Ord('A') by 2, and Ord('L') by 3). Why is this a better hash function?

3. An improved way of handling collisions is called quadratic hashing, where 1 is added to the hash index after probe 1, 4 (2^2) is added after probe 2, 9 (3^2) is added after probe 3, and so on. Modify LocateSlot to use this technique.

 # 19.3 Selection Sort Revisited

So far, we have examined a technique, the selection sort, for sorting an array. Sorting has been widely studied by computer scientists, and many other techniques are available. The remainder of this chapter introduces several sorting algorithms and compares their performance. For each sorting algorithm, we want to see how the array size (N) affects the number of record key comparisons and the number of exchanges performed.

Analysis of Selection Sort

The following selection sort algorithm and its refinement first appeared in Section 12.7.

Selection Sort Algorithm

1. for i := N downto 2 do
   begin
       2. Find the largest element in subarray 1..i.
       3. if the largest element is not at subscript i then
           Switch the largest element with the one at subscript i.
   end

Step 2 Refinement

2.1 Save i as the position of the largest so far in the subarray.
2.2 for j := i-1 downto 1 do
       2.3 if the element at j is bigger than largest so far then
           Save j as the position of the largest so far.

Step 3 is performed $N - 1$ times and involves both a comparison of record keys and a possible exchange of records. Step 2.3 involves a comparison of record keys and is performed $i - 1$ times for each value of i. Because i takes on all values between 2 and N, the following sum computes the number of executions of step 2.3.

$$1 + 2 + 3 + ... + (N - 1)$$

This sum is equivalent to

$$\frac{N \times (N - 1)}{2} = N^2/2 - N/2$$

Therefore, the total number of record key comparisons is

$$N^2/2 + N/2 - 1$$

and the maximum number of record exchanges is

$$N - 1$$

For very large N, we can ignore all but the most significant term in an expression, so the number of comparisons is $O(N^2)$ and the number of exchanges is $O(N)$. Because the number of comparisons increases with the square of N, the selection sort is called a *quadratic sort*.

 ## 19.4   Bubble Sort

This section discusses a fairly simple (but not very efficient) algorithm called the *bubble sort*. The bubble sort compares adjacent array elements and exchanges their values if they are out of order. In this way, the smaller values "bubble" up to the top of the array (toward the first element), while the larger values sink to the bottom of the array. The bubble sort algorithm follows.

Algorithm for Bubble Sort

1. repeat
    2. for each pair of adjacent array elements do
    3. if the values in a pair are out of order then
          Exchange the values
   until the array is sorted

For example, let's trace through one execution of step 2, or one *pass* through an array being sorted. By scanning the diagrams in Fig. 19.9 from left to right, we can see the effect of each comparison. The pair of array elements being compared is shown in a darker color in each diagram. The first pair of values (M[1] is 60, M[2] is 42) is out of order, so the values are exchanged. The next pair of values (M[2] is now 60, M[3] is 75) is compared in the second array; this pair is in order, and so is the next pair (M[3] is 75, M[4] is 83). The last pair (M[4] is 83, M[5] is 27) is out of order, so the values are exchanged.

Figure 19.9   One Pass of Bubble Sort of Array M

757

19.4 Bubble Sort

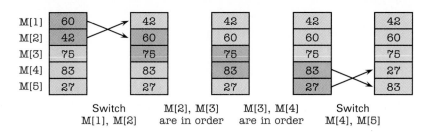

| | | Switch
M[1], M[2] | M[2], M[3]
are in order | M[3], M[4]
are in order | Switch
M[4], M[5] |

The last array shown in Fig. 19.9 is closer to being sorted than is the original. The only value out of order is the number 27 in M[4]. Unfortunately, it is necessary to complete three more passes through the entire array before this value bubbles up to the top of the array. In each pass, only one pair of values is out of order, so only one exchange is made. The contents of array M after the completion of each pass are shown in Fig. 19.10; the portion that is sorted is shown in the darker color.

We can tell by looking at the contents of the array at the end of pass 4 that the array is now sorted; however, the computer can recognize this only by making one additional pass without doing any exchanges. If no exchanges are made, then all pairs must be in order. This is the reason for the extra pass shown in Fig. 19.10 and for the Boolean flag NoExchanges, described next.

Local Variables for Bubble Sort

Flag to indicate whether or not any exchanges were made in a pass (NoExchanges : Boolean)
Loop-control variable and subscript (First : Integer)
Number of the current pass starting with 1 (Pass : Integer)

Refinement of Step 2 of Bubble Sort

2.1 Initialize NoExchanges to True
2.2 for each pair of adjacent array elements do

Figure 19.10   Array M after Completion of Each Pass

| | End of
pass 1 | End of
pass 2 | End of
pass 3 | End of
pass 4 | End of
pass 5 |

        2.3 if the values in a pair are out of order then
             begin
                2.4 Exchange the values
                2.5 Set NoExchanges to False
             end

Step 2.2 is the header of a for statement. The for loop-control variable, First, is also the subscript of the first element in each pair; consequently, First+1 is the subscript of the second element in each pair. During each pass, the initial value of First is 1. The final value of First must be less than the number of array elements so that First+1 will be in range.

For an array of N elements, the final value of First can be N–Pass, where Pass is the number of the current pass, starting with 1 for the first pass. The reason for this is that at the end of pass 1 the last array element must be in its correct place, at the end of pass 2 the last two array elements must be in their correct places, and so on. There is no need to examine array elements that are already in place.

Procedure BubbleSort in Fig. 19.11 performs a bubble sort on an array of student records, Class. Each record is type Student as declared in Section 19.2. The array Class has type StudentArray:

```
type
   StudentArray = array [1..MaxSize] of Student;
```

MaxSize is a constant that determines the maximum number of student records that can be stored, and ClassSize is a variable that specifies the number of records actually stored (1 <= ClassSize <= MaxSize).

The array is being sorted on the Name field, so Class[First].Name is compared to Class[First+1].Name. If the student names are out of order, the statement

```
Switch (Class[First], Class[First+1]);   {Switch data}
```

calls procedure Switch to exchange the records of the two array elements listed as actual parameters. Notice that the entire records are switched, not just the names. When BubbleSort is done, the array of records will be in alphabetical order by student name.

Figure 19.11 Procedure BubbleSort

```
procedure BubbleSort (var Class {input/output} : StudentArray;
                          ClassSize {input} : Integer);
{
  Sorts the data in array Class by student name.
  Pre : Class and ClassSize are defined
          (1 <= ClassSize <= MaxSize).
  Post: Array Class is sorted.
}
  var
    NoExchanges : Boolean;      {any exchanges in current pass?}
    First,                      {first element of a pair}
    Pass    : Integer;          {number of current pass}
```

```
procedure Switch (var Stul, Stu2 {input/output} : Student);

{Switches records Stul and Stu2.}
var
   TempStu : Student;                   {temporary student record}

begin  {Switch}
   TempStu := Stul;  Stul := Stu2;  Stu2 := TempStu
end;  {Switch}


begin  {BubbleSort}
   Pass := 1;                              {Start with pass 1}
   repeat
      {invariant:
         No prior array was sorted and
         elements following Class[N-Pass+1] are in place
      }
      NoExchanges := True;                {no exchanges yet}

      {Compare student names in each pair of adjacent elements}
      for First := 1 to ClassSize - Pass do
         if Class[First].Name > Class[First+1].Name then
            begin  {exchange}
               Switch (Class[First], Class[First+1]);  {Switch data}
               NoExchanges := False                    {Reset flag}
            end;  {exchange}

      Pass := Pass + 1                   {Increment pass number}
   until NoExchanges

   {assert: array is sorted}
end; {BubbleSort}
```

Analysis of Bubble Sort

Because the actual number of comparisons and exchanges performed depends on the array being sorted, the bubble-sort algorithm provides excellent performance in some cases and horrible performance in other cases. It works best when an array is nearly sorted to begin with.

Because all adjacent pairs of elements are compared in each pass, the number of comparisons is represented by the series

$$(N - 1) + (N - 2) + ... 3 + 2 + 1$$

However, if the array becomes sorted early, the later passes and comparisons are not performed. In the worst case, the number of comparisons is $O(N^2)$; in the best case, the number of comparisons is $O(N)$.

Unfortunately, each comparison can lead to an exchange if the array is badly out of order. The worst case occurs when the array is *inverted* (that is, the array elements are in descending order by key) and the number of exchanges is $O(N^2)$. In the best case, only one exchange is made during each pass [($O(N)$ exchanges)], so the number of exchanges also lies between $O(N)$ and $O(N^2)$.

When estimating the performance of a sorting algorithm on a large array whose initial element values are determined arbitrarily, it is best to be pessimistic.

For this reason, bubble sort is considered a quadratic sort; its performance is usually worse than selection sort, because the number of exchanges can be $O(N^2)$.

Exercises for Section 19.4

Self-Check

1. How would you modify procedure BubbleSort to arrange student records in decreasing sequence by exam score? How about in increasing sequence by letter grade and then alphabetically by name (that is, all A students should be first, listed in alphabetical order; next all B students in alphabetical order; and so on).
2. How many passes of a bubble sort are needed to sort the following array of integers? How many comparisons are performed? How many exchanges? Show the array after each pass.

   40   35   80   75   60   90   70   75

 ## 19.5   Insertion Sort

The next sorting algorithm is based on the technique used by a card player to arrange a hand of cards. The player keeps the cards picked up so far in sorted order. After picking up a new card, the player makes room for the new card and inserts it in its proper place in the hand.

The top diagram in Fig. 19.12 shows a hand of cards (ignoring suits) after three cards have been picked up. If the next card is an 8, it should be inserted between the 6 and the 10, maintaining the numerical order. If the card after that is a 7, it should be inserted between the 6 and the 8, as shown in the bottom diagram of the figure. This is also the technique we use to insert new elements into an ordered list.

To adapt this *insertion algorithm* to an array that has been filled with data, we start with a sorted subarray consisting of only the first element. We then insert the second element either before or after the first element, and the sorted subarray has two elements. Next, we insert the third element where it belongs, and the sorted subarray has three elements, and so on. Figure 19.13 illustrates an insertion sort for a five-element array; the sorted portion of the array after each pass is in color.

Figure 19.12   Picking Up a Hand of Cards

Hand of 3 cards	3	6	10		
Hand of 4 cards	3	6	8	10	
Hand of 5 cards	3	6	7	8	10

Figure 19.13   Insertion Sort

761

19.5 Insertion Sort

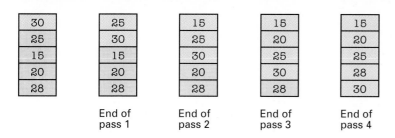

Algorithm for Insertion Sort

1. for each array element after the first do
      begin
         2. Save the value of this element in NextVal.
         3. Make room for NextVal by shifting all larger
            values down one position.
         4. Insert NextVal in place of the last value moved.
      end

Steps 3 and 4 are illustrated in Fig. 19.14. For the array shown on the left of the figure, the subarray with subscripts 1..3 is sorted, and we want to insert the next element, 20, into its proper place. Because 30 and 25 are greater than 20, both values are shifted down one place. After the shift occurs (middle column), there are temporarily two copies of the value 25 in the array. The first of these is erased when 20 is moved into its correct position, element 2 of the four-element sorted subarray on the right. The shift and insert operations should then be repeated to insert the new next value (28) where it belongs.

Procedure InsertSort is shown in Fig. 19.15, where IntArray is an array of Integer values. Procedure ShiftBigger is called to perform the shift operation and to determine the correct position for the array element currently being inserted (NextVal).

Figure 19.14   Inserting the Fourth Array Element

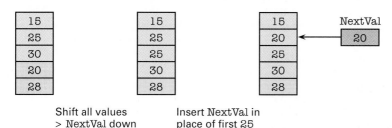

Figure 19.15   Procedure InsertSort

```
procedure InsertSort (var Table {input/output} : IntArray;
                          N {input} : Integer);
{
  Performs an insertion sort on array Table with subscripts 1..N.
  Pre : Table and N are defined.
  Post: Table is sorted.
}
  var
    NextPos,     {subscript of the next element to be inserted}
    NewPos,         {subscript of this element after insertion}
    NextVal : Integer;    {temporary storage for next element}

  {Insert ShiftBigger here.}
begin  {InsertSort}
  for NextPos := 2 to N do
    begin
      {invariant: subarray Table[1..NextPos-1] is sorted}
      NextVal := Table[NextPos];       {get next element to insert}

      {Shift all values > NextVal down one element.}
      ShiftBigger (Table, NextPos, NextVal, NewPos);

      {Insert NextVal in location NewPos.}
      Table[NewPos] := NextVal
    end  {for}
end;  {InsertSort}
```

Coding Procedure ShiftBigger

Procedure ShiftBigger must move all array element values larger than NextVal, starting with the array element at position NextPos-1. If NextVal is the smallest value so far, the shift operation terminates after all array elements are moved. If NextVal is not the smallest value so far, the shift operation terminates when a value less than or equal to NextVal is reached. NextVal should be inserted into the position formerly occupied by the last value that was moved. The algorithm for ShiftBigger follows; the procedure is shown in Fig. 19.16.

Algorithm for ShiftBigger

1. Start with the element in position NextPos-1.
2. while first element not moved and element value > NextVal do
   begin
      3. Move element value down one position.
      4. Check next smaller element value.
5. Define NewPos as original position of last value moved.
   end

Figure 19.16   Procedure ShiftBigger

763

19.5 Insertion Sort

```
procedure ShiftBigger (var Table {input/output} : IntArray;
                           NextPos, NextVal {input} : Integer;
                           var NewPos {output} : Integer);
{
  Makes room for NextVal in the subarray Table[1..NextPos]
  and sets NewPos as an index to the correct position of NextVal.
  Pre : Table, NextPos, and NextVal are defined.
  Post: Shifts values in subarray Table[1..NextPos-1] > NextVal
        by one position and sets NewPos to subscript of last
        element moved.
}
     var Done : Boolean;                {flag}

begin  {ShiftBigger}
  {Shift all values > NextVal. Start with element at NextPos - 1.}
  Done := False;
  while (NextPos > 1) and (not Done) do
    {invariant:
        NextVal <= each element moved so far and
        NextPos >= 1
    }
    if (Table[NextPos-1] > NextVal) then
      begin
        Table[NextPos] := Table[NextPos-1];    {shift value down}
        NextPos := NextPos - 1                  {try next element}
      end {if and while}
    else
      Done := True;

  {assert: position of NextVal is found}
  NewPos := NextPos
end;  {ShiftBigger}
```

The while statement in Fig. 19.16 compares and shifts all values greater than NextVal in the subarray Table[1..NextPos-1]. We could attempt to eliminate the if statement by using the compound condition

```
(NextPos > 1) and (Table[NextPos-1] > NextVal)
```

as the while condition. However, the second part of this condition causes an index out of bounds error when NextPos = 1 (NextPos − 1 = 0).

Analysis of Insertion Sort

Procedure ShiftBigger is called $N - 1$ times. In the worst case, ShiftBigger compares all elements in the subarray being processed to NextVal, so the maximum number of record key comparisons is represented by the series

$$1 + 2 + 3 + \dots + (N - 1)$$

which is $O(N^2)$. In the best case, only one comparison is required for each call to ShiftBigger [$O(N)$]. The number of record exchanges performed by

ShiftBigger is one less than the number of comparisons or, when the new value is the smallest so far, the same as the number of comparisons. Also, each new record is copied into NextVal before the call to ShiftBigger, and NextVal is placed in the array after the return from ShiftBigger (2 more exchanges). An "exchange" in insertion sort requires the movement of only one record, whereas in bubble sort or selection sort, an exchange involves a temporary record and requires the movement of three records.

Exercises for Section 19.5

Self-Check

1. Use an insertion sort to sort the following array. How many passes are needed? How many comparisons are performed? How many exchanges? Show the array after each pass.

   40   35   80   75   60   90   70   75

2. Explain how you would modify the insertion sort procedure to sort an array of student records. What changes would be needed to order the array elements as described in exercise 1 of Section 19.4?

 # 19.6   Comparison of Quadratic Sorts

Table 19.1 summarizes the performance of the three quadratic sorts. To give you some idea of what these numbers mean, Table 19.2 shows some values of N and N^2. If N is small (say 20 or less), it really does not matter which sorting algorithm you use. However, if N is large, avoid using bubble sort unless you are certain that all arrays are nearly sorted to begin with. For most arrays, insertion sort provides better performance than selection sort. Remember that an exchange in insertion sort requires only one record assignment instead of three records assignments, as in the other sorts.

Table 19.1   Comparison of Quadratic Sorts

	Number of Comparisons		Number of Exchanges	
	Best	Worst	Best	Worst
Selection sort	$O(N^2)$	$O(N^2)$	$O(N)$	$O(N)$
Bubble sort	$O(N)$	$O(N^2)$	$O(N)$	$O(N^2)$
Insertion sort	$O(N)$	$O(N^2)$	$O(N)$	$O(N^2)$

Because the time required to sort an array of N elements is proportional to N^2, none of these algorithms is particularly good for large arrays (that is, N

>= 100). The sorting algorithms discussed next provide $N \times \log_2 N$ behavior and are considerably faster for large arrays. You can get a feel for the difference in behavior by comparing the last column of Table 19.2 with the middle column.

Table 19.2 Comparison of Rates of Growth

N	N^2	$N \times \log_2 N$
8	64	24
16	256	64
32	1,024	160
64	4,096	384
128	16,384	896
256	65,536	2,048
512	262,144	4,608

Exercise for Section 19.6

Self-Check

1. Indicate the best method to sort each of the following arrays in ascending order. Explain your choices.

   a. 10 20 30 50 60 80 70
   b. 90 80 70 60 50 40 30
   c. 20 30 40 50 60 70 10
   d. 30 50 10 40 80 90 60

 19.7 MergeSort

The next algorithm we consider is called MergeSort. Section 14.5 showed you how to merge two ordered files to generate a third ordered file. MergeSort works in a similar way. The idea is to split the array into two halves, sort each half, and then merge the halves together to get a new sorted array.

We should get an overall improvement in performance, because merging is an $O(N)$ process, and Table 19.1 shows that sorting two smaller arrays takes less effort than sorting one large array. For example, even if we use a quadratic sort to sort each half of the original array, the effort required to sort and merge would be

$$(N/2)^2 + (N/2)^2 + N$$

compared to N^2 to sort the entire array at once. For $N = 100$, the preceding equation evaluates to 5,100, while N^2 is 10,000. You will see that the improvement in performance is even more dramatic. The MergeSort algorithm follows.

Algorithm for MergeSort

1. Split the array into two halves.
2. Sort the left half.

Figure 19.17   Merging Two Sorted Subarrays

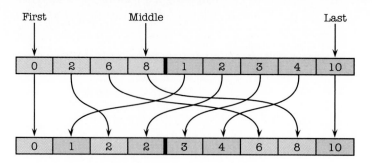

3. Sort the right half.
4. Merge the two arrays together.

   Figure 19.17 illustrates this process. An array with subscript type
`First..Last` has been split into a left and a right subarray, both of which are
sorted. `Middle` is the index of the last element in the left subarray. The two
subarrays are merged to form a sorted array.

   We can reformulate this algorithm using recursion. The stopping case is
an array with one element. Because an array with one element is sorted by
definition, we do nothing when the stopping condition (`First = Last`) is `True`.
If the array has more than one element (`First < Last`), we want to sort subarray
`Table[First..Middle]` and then sort subarray `Table[Middle+1..Last]` using
`MergeSort`. Next, we merge the sorted subarrays together.

Procedure Inputs

   The original subarray (`Table : IntArray`)
   The leftmost subscript (`First : Integer`)
   The rightmost subscript (`Last : Integer`)

Procedure Outputs

   The sorted array (`Table : IntArray`)

Local Variables

   Index of the last element in right subarray (`Middle : Integer`)

Recursive MergeSort Algorithm

1. if First < Last then
      begin
         2. Set `Middle` to (First + Last) div 2
         3. MergeSort Table[First..Middle].
         4. MergeSort Table[Middle+1..Last]

5. Merge Table[First..Middle] with Table[Middle+1..Last].
   end

Procedure MergeSort is shown in Fig. 19.18. When the recursive step executes, MergeSort calls itself first to sort the left subarray and then to sort the right subarray. Next, it calls procedure Merge (discussed next) to merge the two sorted subarrays together. Use the procedure call statement

```
MergeSort (Table, 1, N)
```

to sort the array Table (type IntArray) with subscripts 1..N.

Figure 19.18 Procedure MergeSort

```
procedure MergeSort (var Table {input/output} : IntArray;
                         First, Last {input} : Integer);
{
  Recursive procedure to sort the subarray Table[First..Last].
  Pre : Table, First, and Last are defined.
  Post: Array Table is sorted.
}
  var
    Middle : Integer;   {index of last element in right subarray}

  {Insert procedure Merge.}


begin {MergeSort}
  if First < Last then
    begin
      Middle := (First + Last) div 2;
      MergeSort (Table, First, Middle);
      MergeSort (Table, Middle+1, Last);
      Merge (Table, First, Middle, Last)
    end {if}
end; {MergeSort}
```

The two recursive calls to MergeSort in Fig. 19.18 cause the MergeSort procedure to be applied to two smaller subarrays. If any subarray contains just one element, an immediate return occurs.

Coding Procedure Merge

At the end of MergeSort, the statement

```
Merge (Table, First, Middle, Last)
```

calls procedure Merge to merge the two sorted subarrays. We stated earlier that merging two arrays is analogous to merging two files. In a file merge, two ordered files are merged to form a third file. Procedure Merge must merge two ordered subarrays that are split at Middle into a third array (Temp). The contents of array Temp are copied back into the original array (Table) after the merge. The algorithm for procedure Merge follows.

Local Variables for Merge

The result of the merge (`Temp : IntArray`)
The index to the left subarray (`NextLeft : Integer`)
The index to the right subarray (`NextRight : Integer`)

Algorithm for Merge

1. Start with the first element of each subarray.
2. `while` not finished with either subarray `do`
   3. `if` the current element of the left subarray `<`
      the current element of the right subarray `then`
      4. Copy the current element of the left subarray to the
         merged array and advance to the next element in the
         left subarray and the merged array.
   `else`
      5. Copy the current element of the right subarray to the
         merged array and advance to the next element in the
         right subarray and the merged array.
6. Copy the remaining elements from the unfinished array to the
   merged array.
7. Copy the merged array back to the original array.

Procedure `Merge` is shown in Fig. 19.19. The variables `NextLeft` and
`NextRight` are indexes to the two subarrays being merged; the variable `Index`
is the index to the merged array, `Temp`. `NextLeft` and `Index` are initialized to
`First`; `NextRight` is initialized to `Middle + 1`, which is the first element in the
right subarray.

Figure 19.19 Procedure Merge

```
procedure Merge (var Table {input/output} : IntArray;
                 First, Middle, Last {input} : Integer);
{
  Merges Table[First..Middle] with Table[Middle+1..Last].
  Pre : Table is defined and First <= Last and
        Middle = (First + Last) div 2
  Post: Array Table is sorted.
}
  var
    Temp     : IntArray;      {merger of left and right arrays}
    NextLeft,                 {next element in left subarray}
    NextRight,                {next element in right subarray}
    Index : Integer;          {index to array Temp}

begin {Merge}
  {Start with first element of all three arrays.}
  NextLeft := First;
  NextRight := Middle + 1;
  Index := First;

  {Perform the merge until one subarray is finished.}
  while (NextLeft <= Middle) and (NextRight <= Last) do
```

```
        if Table[NextLeft] < Table[NextRight] then
          begin {copy left element}
            Temp[Index] := Table[NextLeft];
            NextLeft := NextLeft + 1;
            Index := Index + 1
          end  {copy left element}
        else
          begin {copy right element}
            Temp[Index] := Table[NextRight];
            NextRight := NextRight + 1;
            Index := Index + 1
          end;  {copy right element}

    {Copy any remaining elements in the left subarray.}
    while NextLeft <= Middle do
      begin
        Temp[Index] := Table[NextLeft];
        NextLeft := NextLeft + 1;
        Index := Index + 1
      end; {while}

    {Copy any remaining elements in the right subarray.}
    while NextRight <= Last do
      begin
        Temp[Index] := Table[NextRight];
        NextRight := NextRight + 1;
        Index := Index + 1
      end; {while}

    {Copy the merged array back into Table.}
    for Index := First to Last do
      Table[Index] := Temp[Index]
end;   {Merge}
```

Analysis of MergeSort

Our preliminary analysis indicated that MergeSort would be more efficient than a quadratic sort, but how much better is it? Procedure Merge copies data into two N-element arrays (array Temp and then Table). Each array copy is an $O(N)$ process, so procedure Merge is also an $O(N)$ process (remember, we drop the 2 from $2N$.)

The remaining question is how many times procedure Merge is called. The answer is that Merge is called once for each execution of the recursive step in MergeSort. The recursive step splits the array into half each time it executes. From earlier splitting processes (for example, binary search), we know that it requires $\log_2 N$ splits to reach the stopping state (N one-element subarrays). Therefore, MergeSort appears to be an $O(N \times \log_2 N)$ process.

Table 19.2 shows that MergeSort provides significant improvement over a quadratic sort for a large array. Bear in mind that this analysis does not provide the whole picture. There is quite a bit of overhead for each recursive call to Merge. Also, MergeSort requires an additional auxiliary array with the same number of elements as the original array. If the array being sorted is truly a very large array, the memory requirements of MergeSort could become a burden. Next, we discuss an $O(N \times \log_2 N)$ sort that moves elements around in the original array and does not require an auxiliary array.

Exercises for Section 19.7

Self-Check

1. Explain why array `Temp` is needed in `Merge`.
2. Trace the execution of `MergeSort` on the following array. Show the values of `First`, `Last`, and `Middle` for each recursive call and the array elements after returning from each call to `Merge`. How many times is `MergeSort` called? How many times is `Merge` called?

   55 50 10 40 80 90 60 100 70 80 20

 # 19.8   QuickSort

The last algorithm we will study is called QuickSort, which works in the following way. Given an array with subscripts `First..Last` to sort, QuickSort rearranges the array so that all element values smaller than a selected *pivot value* are first, followed by the pivot value, followed by all element values larger than the pivot value. After this rearrangement (called a *partition*), the pivot value is in its proper place. All element values smaller than the pivot value are closer to where they belong, because they precede the pivot value. All element values larger than the pivot value are closer to where they belong, because they follow the pivot value.

An example of this process follows. We assume that the first array element is arbitrarily selected as the pivot. A possible result of the partitioning process is shown beneath the original array.

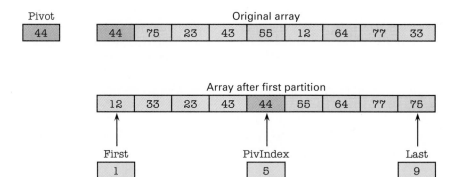

After the partitioning process, `PivIndex` is 5 and the fifth array element contains the pivot value, 44. All values less than 44 are in the left subarray (color background); all values greater than 44 are in the right subarray (gray background). The next step would be to apply QuickSort recursively to the two subarrays on either side of the pivot value. The algorithm for QuickSort follows. We describe how to do the partitioning later.

Procedure Inputs

The array being sorted (`Table : IntArray`)
The first subscript (`First : Integer`)
The last subscript (`Last : Integer`)

Procedure Outputs

The sorted array (`Table : IntArray`)

Local Variables

The subscript of the pivot value after partitioning
(`PivIndex : Integer`)

Algorithm for QuickSort

1. if `First < Last` then
   begin
      2. Partition the elements in the subarray `First..Last` so
         that the pivot value is in place (subscript is `PivIndex`)
      3. Apply QuickSort to the subarray `First..PivIndex−1`.
      4. Apply QuickSort to the subarray `PivIndex+1..Last`.
   end

A stopping case for QuickSort is an array of one element (`First = Last`) that is sorted by definition, so nothing is done. If `First > Last` is true, then the array bounds are improper (also a stopping case). If the array has more than one element, we partition it into two subarrays and sort the subarrays using QuickSort.

The implementation of procedure `QuickSort` is shown in Fig. 19.20. Use the procedure call statement

```
QuickSort (Table, 1, N)
```

to sort the array `Table` (type `IntArray`) with subscripts `1..N`.

Figure 19.20   Procedure QuickSort

```
procedure QuickSort (var Table {input/output} : IntArray;
                        First, Last {input} : Integer);
{
  Recursive procedure to sort the subarray Table[First..Last].
  Pre : First, Last, and array Table are defined.
  Post: Table is sorted.
}
  var
    PivIndex : Integer;              {subscript of pivot value --
                                       returned by Partition}
```

```
                    {Insert Partition here.}

begin  {QuickSort}
  if First < Last then
    begin
      {Split into two subarrays separated by value at PivIndex}
      Partition (Table, First, Last, PivIndex);
      QuickSort (Table, First, PivIndex-1);
      QuickSort (Table, PivIndex+1, Last)
    end  {if}
end;  {QuickSort}
```

The two recursive calls to QuickSort in Fig. 19.20 cause the QuickSort procedure to be applied to the subarrays that are separated by the value at PivIndex. If any subarray contains just one element (or zero elements), an immediate return occurs.

Coding Procedure Partition

Procedure Partition selects the pivot and performs the partitioning operation. If the arrays are randomly ordered to begin with, it does not really matter which element we choose to be the pivot value. For simplicity, we have selected the element with subscript First. We search for the first value at the left end of the subarray that is greater than the pivot value. When we find it, we search for the first value at the right end of the subarray that is less than or equal to the pivot value. These two values are exchanged, and we repeat the search and exchange operations. This is illustrated next, with Up pointing to the first value greater than the pivot and Down pointing to the first value less than or equal to the pivot value.

75 is the first value at the left end of the array larger than 44; 33 is the first value at the right end less than or equal to 44, so these two values are exchanged. The pointers Up and Down are then advanced from their current positions to the positions shown next.

55 is the next value at the left end larger than 44; 12 is the next value at the right end less than or equal to 44, so these two values are exchanged, and Up and Down are advanced again.

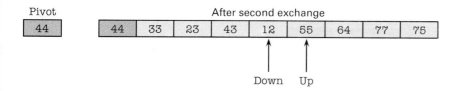

After the second exchange, the first five array elements contain the pivot value and all values less than or equal to the pivot; the last four elements contain all values larger than the pivot. 55 is selected once again by Up as the next element larger than the pivot; 12 is selected by Down as the next element less than or equal to the pivot. Because Up has now "passed" Down, these values are not exchanged. Instead, the pivot value (subscript is First) and the value at position Down are exchanged. This puts the pivot value in its proper position (new subscript is Down), as shown next.

The partitioning process is now complete, and the value of Down is returned as the pivot index (PivIndex). QuickSort is called recursively to sort the left subarray and the right subarray. The algorithm for Partition follows and is implemented in Fig. 19.21.

Local Variables for Partition

The pivot value (Pivot : Integer)
Index to array elements larger than Pivot (Up : Integer)
Index to array elements less than or equal to Pivot
(Down : Integer)

Algorithm for Partition

1. Define the pivot value as the contents of Table[First].
2. Initialize Up to First and Down to Last.
3. repeat
    4. Increment Up until Up selects the first element greater than the pivot value.
    5. Decrement Down until Down selects the first element less than or equal to the pivot value.
    6. if Up < Down then

7. Exchange their values.
until Up meets or passes Down
8. Exchange Table[First] and Table[Down].
9. Define PivIndex as Down.

Figure 19.21 Procedure Partition

```
procedure Partition (var Table {input/output} : IntArray;
                         First, Last {input} : Integer;
                         var PivIndex {output} : Integer);
{
  Partitions the subarray of Table with subscripts First..Last
  into two subarrays.
  Pre : First, Last, and array Table are defined.
  Post: PivIndex is defined such that all values
        less than or equal to Table[PivIndex] have
        subscripts <= PivIndex; all values
        greater than Table[PivIndex] have subscripts > PivIndex.
}
var
    Pivot,                       {the pivot value}
    Up,                          {index to values > Pivot}
    Down : Integer;              {index to values <= Pivot}


  procedure Exchange (var X, Y {input/output} : Integer);

  {Switches the values in X and Y.}

      var
        Temp : Integer;                {temporary cell for exchange}

  begin {Exchange}
    Temp := X;        X := Y;        Y := Temp
  end;  {Exchange}


begin  {Partition}
  Pivot := Table[First];   {define leftmost element as the pivot}

  {Find and exchange values that are out of place.}
  Up := First;             {set Up to point to leftmost element}
  Down := Last;            {set Down to point to rightmost element}
  repeat
    {Move Up to the next value larger than Pivot.}
    while (Table[Up] <= Pivot) and (Up < Last) do
      Up := Up + 1;

    {assertion: Table[Up] > Pivot or Up is equal to Last}
    {Move Down to the next value less than or equal to Pivot.}
    while Table[Down] > Pivot do
      Down := Down - 1;

    {assertion: Table[Down] <= Pivot}
    {Exchange out of order values.}
    if Up < Down then
      Exchange (Table[Up], Table[Down])
  until Up >= Down;               {until Up meets or passes Down}
  {assertion: values <= Pivot have subscripts <= Down and
              values > Pivot have subscripts > Down}
```

```
{Put pivot value where it belongs and define PivIndex.}
    Exchange (Table[First], Table[Down]);
    PivIndex := Down
end;  {Partition}
```

The two `while` loops in Fig. 19.21 advance pointers `Up` and `Down` to the left and the right, respectively. Because `Table[First]` is equal to `Pivot`, the second loop stops if `Down` happens to reach the left end of the array (`Down` is `First`). The extra condition (`Up < Last`) is added to the first `while` loop to ensure that it also stops if `Up` happens to reach the right end of the array.

Analysis of QuickSort

The QuickSort procedure works better for some arrays than for others. It works best when the partitioning process splits each subarray into two subarrays of almost the same size. The worst behavior results when one of the subarrays has zero elements and the other has all the other elements except for the pivot value. Ironically, this worst-case behavior results when QuickSort is applied to an array that is already sorted. The pivot value remains in position `First`, and the rest of the elements are in the subarray with subscripts `First+1..Last`.

Procedure `Partition` compares each array element to the pivot value (an $O(N)$ process). If the array splits are relatively even, the number of calls to partition is $O(\log_2 N)$. Therefore, QuickSort is an $O(N \times \log_2 N)$ process in the best case. In the worst case, there are N calls to `Partition` and QuickSort degenerates to an $O(N^2)$ process.

Because data values are normally distributed in random order in an array, QuickSort as presented will work quite well. A possible improvement would be to use the average of two or more array elements as the pivot value. This requires more computation time and also a modification to the algorithm, because the pivot value is no longer an array element value.

Exercises for Section 19.8

Self-Check

1. Complete the trace of `QuickSort` for the subarrays remaining after the first partition.
2. If an array contains some values that are the same, in which subarray (left or right) will all values that are equal to the pivot value be placed?
3. Trace the execution of `QuickSort` on the following array. Show the values of `First` and `Last` for each recursive call and the array elements after returning from each call. Also, show the value of `Pivot` during each call and the value returned through `PivIndex`. How many times is `QuickSort` called? How many times is `Partition` called?

   55   50   10   40   80   90   60   100   70   80   20

   Which provides better performance: MergeSort or QuickSort? How would insertion sort do compared to these two?

19.9 Common Programming Errors

One problem with search and sort procedures is the possibility of going beyond the bounds of a subarray. Make sure your Pascal system checks for subscript-range errors. On some systems, the programmer must activate this important check; otherwise, subscript range violations are not detected. If this is the case on your system, make sure you activate this feature when you are debugging any program that manipulates arrays, particularly a search or sort.

When you are debugging a search or sort procedure, it is best to use relatively small arrays (ten elements or fewer). Make sure you print the new contents of the array after each pass through a sort procedure.

 # Chapter Review

This chapter discussed the binary-search technique, which provides significant improvement over linear search when you are searching large arrays. A linear search is an $O(N)$ process, while binary search is an $O(\log_2 N)$ process. This means that the time required to perform a binary search increases very slowly. For example, it takes only about twice as long to perform a binary search on an array with 256 elements ($\log_2 256$ is 8) as it takes to perform a binary search on an array with 16 elements ($\log_2 16$ is 4).

We also discussed using a hash table to provide quick access to data stored in an array. The record key is passed to the hash function, which computes an index to the array. In most cases, only one probe is required to access the desired record. If there are collisions (multiple keys with same index value), the array elements following the one selected by the index are examined until the desired key is found or an empty table slot is reached.

We also analyzed several sorting algorithms. Three of these, selection sort, bubble sort, and insertion sort, are $O(N^2)$ or quadratic sorts. Two of these, MergeSort and QuickSort, are $O(N \times \log_2 N)$. For small arrays, either insertion sort or selection sort should generally be used; bubble sort is a good choice only when the array is likely to be nearly sorted. For large arrays, use MergeSort or QuickSort. Avoid MergeSort when storage space is likely to be limited. Avoid QuickSort when the array is nearly sorted.

✓ Quick-Check Exercises

1. What are three techniques for searching an array?
2. What are two techniques for searching an array whose elements are in order by key field?
3. Rate the three search algorithms in terms of time efficiency for a large array.
4. Rate the three search algorithms in terms of space efficiency for a large array.
5. Define a collision in hashing. What is one technique of resolving collisions?
6. Name three quadratic sorts.
7. Name two sorts with $N \times \log_2 N$ behavior.
8. Which algorithm is particularly good for an array that is already sorted? Which is particularly bad? Explain.

9. What determines whether you should use a quadratic sort or a logarithmic sort?
10. Which quadratic sort's performance is least affected by the ordering of the array elements? Which is most affected?

Answers to Quick-Check Exercises
1. Sequential search, binary search, hashing
2. Sequential search of an ordered array, binary search
3. Hashing, binary search, sequential search
4. Sequential search and binary search followed by hashing
5. A collision occurs when two keys have the same hash value. Linear resolution involves scanning consecutive table entries until an empty slot is found or the target is located.
6. Selection, insertion, bubble
7. MergeSort, QuickSort
8. Bubble sort and insertion sort: both require $N - 1$ comparisons with no exchanges. QuickSort is bad because the partitioning process always creates one subarray with a single element.
9. Array size
10. Selection sort; bubble sort

Review Questions

1. Show how the following keys would be stored in a hash table with five slots, assuming the linear method for resolving collisions discussed in the text. The value returned by function Hash is shown after each key.
   'Ace' 3, 'Boy' 4, 'Cat' 5, 'Dog' 3, 'Bye' 1
2. When does quicksort work best? When does it work worst?
3. Write a function that will recursively search a packed array of thirty characters and return the position of the first comma in the string. If the string does not contain a comma, the function should return 0.
4. What is the purpose of the pivot value in quicksort? How did we select it in the text? What is wrong with that approach for choosing a pivot value?
5. For the array

   30 40 20 15 60 80 75 4 20

   show the new array after each pass of insertion sort and bubble sort. How many comparisons and exchanges are performed by each?
6. For the array in exercise 5, trace the execution of mergesort and quicksort.
7. The shaker sort is an adaptation of the bubble sort that alternates the direction in which the array elements are scanned during each pass. The first pass starts its scan with the first element, moving the larger element in each pair down the array. The second pass starts its scan with the next-to-last element, moving the smaller element in each pair up the array, and so on. Indicate what the advantage of the shaker sort might be. Show how it would sort the array in exercise 5.

Programming Projects

1. Write an abstract data type called HashTable that consists of a declaration for a hash table and the operators in Section 19.2. Write a menu-driven program that maintains

a list of passenger records in a hash table (see programming project 1 of Chapter 18). Import the necessary data types and operators.

2. Do programming project 7 in Chapter 18 using ADT HashTable described in project 1 of this chapter.

3. If your Pascal system has a random-number function, use it to store a list of 1,000 random integer values in an array. Apply each of the sort procedures described in this chapter to the array and determine how long it takes each procedure to sort the array. Make sure the same array is passed to each procedure. Your Pascal system may contain a function that displays the current time or the elapsed time for a program.

4. One technique for handling collisions in a hash table is to place all records with keys that hash to the same value in a linked list (called a *bucket*). One slot in the hash table is allocated for each hash value, and each slot consists of space for one record and a single pointer field (initially nil). The first record with a particular hash value is placed directly in the hash table. When a second key is encountered with that same hash value, that record is linked to the first record in the table via the pointer field. The third record with that hash value is linked to the second, and so on. Rewrite the operators in ADT HashTable, assuming this technique is used to resolve collisions.

5. The Shell sort is a sorting technique that applies insertion sort to chains of elements in an array where the elements in the chain are chosen by adding an increment value. The increment value decreases with each pass. For example, if an array has fifteen elements and the initial increment value is 5, the five chains of elements listed next would be sorted in the "first pass." Each chain would be sorted using insertion sort.

```
X[1], X[6],  X[11]
X[2], X[7],  X[12]
X[3], X[8],  X[13]
X[4], X[9],  X[14]
X[5], X[10], X[15]
```

If the next increment is 3, the following three chains would be sorted. Notice that the chains increase in size as the increment shrinks.

```
X[1], X[4], X[7], X[10], X[13]
X[2], X[5], X[8], X[11], X[14]
X[3], X[6], X[9], X[12], X[15]
```

When the increment shrinks to 1, the whole array is sorted using insertion sort.

The initial insertion sorts involve short chains, so the sorts should be relatively quick. Normally, the performance of insertion sort degrades quickly as the length of the array being sorted increases. However, because the longer chains have had their elements presorted during earlier passes, insertion sort should be able to handle the longer chains more efficiently than would be the case without presorting.

Implement the Shell sort algorithm. Read the increment values for each pass into an array Increments before reading in the elements of the array to be sorted.

Appendix A
Reserved Words, Standard Identifiers, Operators, Functions, and Procedures

Reserved Words

and	end	nil	set
array	file	not	then
begin	for	of	to
case	function	or	type
const	goto	packed	until
div	if	procedure	var
do	in	program	while
downto	label	record	with
else	mod	repeat	

Standard Identifiers

Constants:

False, True, MaxInt

Types:

Integer, Boolean, Real, Char, Text

Program parameters:

Input, Output

Functions:

Abs, ArcTan, Chr, Cos, EOF, EOLN, Exp, Ln, Odd, Ord,
Pred, Round, Sin, Sqr, Sqrt, Succ, Trunc

Procedures:

Get, New, Pack, Page, Put, Read, ReadLn, Reset,
Rewrite, Unpack, Write, WriteLn

Table A.1 Table of Operators

Operator	Operation	Type of Operand(s)	Result Type
:=	assignment	any type except file types	—
Arithmetic			
+ (unary)	identity	integer or real	same as operand
– (unary)	sign inversion		
+	addition	integer or real	integer or real
–	subtraction		
*	multiplication		
div	integer division	integer	integer
/	real division	integer or real	real
mod	modulus	integer	integer
Relational			
=	equality	ordinal, real, string, set, or pointer	Boolean
<>	inequality		
<	less than	ordinal, real, or string	Boolean
>	greater than		
<=	less than or equal	ordinal, real, or string	Boolean
	-or-		
	subset	set	
>=	greater than or equal	ordinal, real, or string	Boolean
	-or-		
	superset	set	
in	set membership	first operand is any ordinal, the second is its set type	Boolean
Logical			
not	negation		
or	disjunction	Boolean	Boolean
and	conjunction		
Set			
+	union		
–	set difference	any set type	same as operand
*	intersection		

Table A.2 Standard Functions

Name	Description of Computation	Argument	Result
Abs	The absolute value of the argument	real/integer	same as argument
Exp	The value of e (2.71828) raised to the power of the argument	real/integer	real
Ln	The logarithm (to the base e) of the argument	real/integer (positive)	real
Sqr	The square of the argument	real/integer	same as
Sqrt	The positive square root of the argument	real/integer (positive)	argument
Round	The closest integer value to the argument	real	integer
Trunc	The integral part of the argument	real	integer
ArcTan	The arc tangent of the argument	real/integer (radians)	real
Cos	The cosine of the argument	real/integer (radians)	real
Sin	The sine of the argument	real/integer (radians)	real
Chr	Returns the character whose ordinal number is its argument	integer	Char
Odd	Returns True if its argument is an odd number; otherwise returns False	integer	Boolean
Ord	Returns the ordinal number of its argument	ordinal	integer
Pred	Returns the predecessor of its argument	ordinal	ordinal
Succ	Returns the successor of its argument	ordinal	ordinal

Table A.3   Table of Standard Procedures

Procedure Call	Description
Dispose (P)	Returns the record pointed to by pointer variable P to free storage.
Get (F)	Advances the file position pointer for file F to its next component and assigns the value of the component to F^.
New (P)	Creates a record of the type pointed to by pointer P and saves its address in P.
Pack (U, I, P)	Copies the elements in unpacked array U, starting with U[I], to packed array P, starting with the first element.
Page (F)	Advances the printer to a new page before printing the next line of file F.
Put (F)	Appends the current contents of F^ to file F.
Read (F, *variables*)	Reads data from file F to satisfy the list of *variables*. If F is not specified, file Input is read.
ReadLn (F, *variables*)	Reads data from text file F to satisfy the list of *variables*. Skips any characters at the end of the last line read.
Reset (F)	Resets the file position pointer for file F to the beginning. File F may then be read.
Rewrite (F)	Resets the file position pointer for file F to the beginning; any prior contents are lost. File F may then be written.
Unpack (P, U, I)	Copies the elements in packed array P, starting with the first element, to unpacked array U, starting with U[I].
Write (F, *outputs*)	Writes the data in the order specified by *outputs* to file F. If F is not specified, the data are written to file Output.
WriteLn (F, *outputs*)	Writes the data in the order specified by *outputs* to text file F. Writes an end-of-line mark after the data.

Appendix B
Pascal Syntax Diagrams

program

program parameters

body

declaration part

label declaration

constant definition

type definition

variable declaration

statement label

constant

unsigned constant

identifier

function declaration

procedure declaration

formal parameter list

type

enumerated type

subrange type

pointer type

array type

record type

field list

variant

file type

set type

compound statement

statement

assignment statement

procedure call statement

if statement

while statement

for statement

case statement

case label

repeat statement

with statement

goto statement

actual parameter

expression

simple expression

term

factor

function designator

set value

variable

unsigned number

integer

real

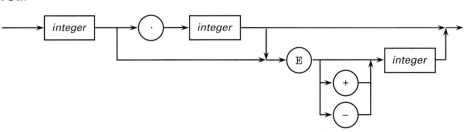

Appendix C
Compiler Error Messages

The following error codes and messages are representative of those displayed by a compiler when it detects a syntax error. The actual code and/or message may be different for your compiler. If you don't understand an error message displayed by your compiler, you should check the compiler reference manual to determine its meaning.

```
 1: error in simple type
 2: identifier expected
 3: 'program' expected
 4: ')' expected
 5: ':' expected
 6: illegal symbol
 7: error in parameter list
 8: 'of' expected
 9: '(' expected
10: error in type
11: '[' expected
12: ']' expected
13: 'end' expected
14: ';' expected
15: integer expected
16: '=' expected
17: 'begin' expected
18: error in declaration part
19: error in field-list
20: ',' expected
21: '*' expected

50: error in constant
51: ':=' expected
52: 'then' expected
53: 'until' expected
54: 'do' expected
55: 'to'/'downto' expected
56: 'if' expected
57: 'file' expected
58: error in factor
59: error in variable
60: identifier not declared
```

101: identifier declared twice
102: low bound exceeds high bound
103: identifier is not of appropriate class
104: identifier not declared
105: sign not allowed
106: number expected
107: incompatible subrange types
108: file not allowed here
109: type must not be real
110: tagfield type must be scalar or subrange
111: incompatible with tagfield type
112: index type must not be real
113: index type must be scalar or subrange
114: base type must not be real
115: base type must be scalar or subrange
116: error in type of standard procedure parameter
117: unsatisfied forward reference
118: forward reference type identifier in variable declaration
119: forward declared; repetition of parameter list not allowed
120: function result type must be scalar, subrange or pointer
121: file value parameter not allowed
122: forward declared function; repetition of result type not allowed
123: missing result type in function declaration
124: F-format for real only
125: error in type of standard function parameter
126: number of parameters does not agree with declaration
127: illegal parameter substitution
128: result type of parameter function does not agree with declaration
129: type conflict of operands
130: expression is not of set type
131: tests on equality allowed only
132: strict inclusion not allowed
133: file comparison not allowed
134: illegal type of operand(s)
135: type of operand must be Boolean
136: set element type must be scalar or subrange
137: set element types not compatible
138: type of variable is not array
139: index type is not compatible with declaration
140: type of variable is not record
141: type of variable must be file or pointer
142: illegal parameter substitution
143: illegal type of loop control variable
144: illegal type of expression
145: type conflict
146: assignment of files not allowed
147: label type incompatible with selecting expression
148: subrange bounds must be scalar
149: index type must not be integer
150: assignment to standard function is not allowed
151: assignment to formal function is not allowed

152: no such field in this record
153: type error in read
154: actual parameter must be a variable
155: control variable must neither be formal nor nonlocal
156: multidefined case label
157: too many cases in case statement
158: missing corresponding variant declaration
159: real or string tagfields not allowed
160: previous declaration was not forward
161: again forward declared
162: parameter size must be constant
163: missing variant in declaration
164: substitution of standard proc/func not allowed
165: multidefined label
166: multideclared label
167: undeclared label
168: undefined label
169: error in base set
170: value parameter expected
171: standard file was redeclared
172: undeclared external file
173: Fortran procedure or function expected
174: Pascal procedure or function expected
175: missing file "input" in program heading
176: missing file "output" in program heading

201: error in real constant: digit expected
202: string constant must not exceed source line
203: integer constant exceeds range
204: 8 or 9 in octal number

250: too many nested scopes of identifiers
251: too many nested procedures and/or functions
252: too many forward references of procedure entries
253: procedure too long
254: too many long constants in this procedure
255: too many errors on this source line
256: too many external references
257: too many externals
258: too many local files
259: expression too complicated

300: division by zero
301: no case provided for this value
302: index expression out of bounds
303: value to be assigned is out of bounds
304: element expression out of range

398: implementation restriction
399: feature not implemented

Appendix D
Character Sets

The following charts show the character sets: ASCII (American Standard Code for Information Interchange), EBCDIC (Extended Binary Coded Decimal Interchange Code), and CDC* Scientific. Only printable characters are shown. The ordinal number for each character is shown in decimal. For example in ASCII, the ordinal number for 'A' is 65 and the ordinal number for 'z' is 122. The blank character is denoted by a "□".

Left Digit(s) \ Right Digit	0	1	2	3	4	5	6	7	8	9
							ASCII			
3			□	!	"	#	$	%	&	'
4	(	)	*	+	,	−	.	/	0	1
5	2	3	4	5	6	7	8	9	:	;
6	<	=	>	?	@	A	B	C	D	E
7	F	G	H	I	J	K	L	M	N	O
8	P	Q	R	S	T	U	V	W	X	Y
9	Z	[	/	]	^	−	`	a	b	c
10	d	e	f	g	h	i	j	k	l	m
11	n	o	p	q	r	s	t	u	v	w
12	x	y	z	{	|	}	~			

Codes 00-31 and 127 are nonprintable control characters.

---

*CDC is a trademark of Control Data Corporation

EBCDIC

Left Digit(s) \ Right Digit	0	1	2	3	4	5	6	7	8	9
6					□					
7					¢	.	<	(	+	|
8	&									
9	!	$	*	)	;	¬	–	/		
10							^	,	%	—
11	>	?								
12			:	#	@	'	=	"		a
13	b	c	d	e	f	g	h	i		
14						j	k	l	m	n
15	o	p	q	r						
16			s	t	u	v	w	x	y	z
17								\	{	}
18	[	]								
19				A	B	C	D	E	F	G
20	H	I								J
21	K	L	M	N	O	P	Q	R		
22							S	T	U	V
23	W	X	Y	Z						
24	0	1	2	3	4	5	6	7	8	9

Codes 00-63 and 250-255 are nonprintable control characters.

CDC

Left Digit(s) \ Right Digit	0	1	2	3	4	5	6	7	8	9
0	:	A	B	C	D	E	F	G	H	I
1	J	K	L	M	N	O	P	Q	R	S
2	T	U	V	W	X	Y	Z	0	1	2
3	3	4	5	6	7	8	9	+	−	*
4	/	(	)	$	=	□	,	.	≡	[
5	]	%	≠	↱	∨	∧	↑	↓	<	>
6	≤	≥	¬	;						

Appendix E
Additional Pascal Features

This appendix describes additional features of Pascal not covered in the text.

Functions and Procedures as Parameters

A procedure or function may be passed as a parameter to another procedure or function. As an example, we may wish to compute the sum below for the integers 1 through N where f represents a function that is applied to each integer.

$$f(1) + f(2) + f(3) + ... + f(N)$$

If f is the function Sqr (square), then we wish to compute the sum

a) $1 + 2^2 + 3^2 + ... + N^2$

If f is the function Sqrt (square root), then we wish to compute the sum

b) $\sqrt{1} + \sqrt{2} + \sqrt{3} + ... + \sqrt{N}$

In function SumInt below, the function F is declared as a function parameter. The function designator

```
SumInt(Sqr, 10)
```

computes sum a) above for N = 10; the function designator

```
SumInt(Sqrt, 10)
```

computes sum b) above for N = 10.

```
function SumInt (function F(X : Integer) : Real;
                 N : Integer) : Real;
{Computes F(1) + F(2) + . . . + F(N).}
  var
    Sum : Real;                         {the partial sum}
    I : Integer;                        {loop control variable}
begin {SumInt}
  Sum := 0.0;                           {initialize Sum}

  for I := 1 to N do
    Sum := Sum + F(I);

    SumInt := Sum                       {define result}
end; {SumInt}
```

The parameter of function F is represented by X (type Integer) in the heading for function SumInt; any identifier may be used. F can also represent a user-defined function with one type Integer parameter.

goto Statements and Labels

The goto statement is used to transfer control from one program statement to another. The label (a positive integer) is used to indicate the statement to which control is transferred. Labels must be declared in label declaration statements at the beginning of a block. In function SameArray below, the goto statement is used to exit a for loop before the specified number of repetitions (N) are performed.

```
function SAMEARRAY (A, B : RealArray;
                    N : Integer) : Boolean;
{Returns True if arrays A[1..N] and B[1..N] are the same array.}

   label 100;

   var
     I : Integer;              {loop control variable}

begin {SameArray}
   SameArray := False;         {assume arrays are not the same}

   {Compare elements 1..N until an unequal pair is found.}
   for I := 1 to N do
     if A[I] <> B[I] then
        goto 100;

   {assert: arrays A and B are equal.}
   SameArray := True;

100: {return from function}
end; {SameArray}
```

The function result is initialized to False and corresponding array elements are compared in the for loop. If an unequal pair of elements is found, the loop is exited via an immediate transfer of control to label 100. If all pairs are equal, the loop is exited after the Nth pair is tested and the function result is set to True. This function can easily be implemented without using the goto; computer scientists generally avoid using the goto except when absolutely necessary.

Pack and Unpack

The standard procedures Pack and Unpack are used to transfer data between packed and unpacked arrays. Given the declarations

```
var
  PA : packed array [1..N] of Char;
  UA : array [1..M] of Char;
  I : Integer
```

the procedure call statement

```
Pack (UA, I, PA)
```

copies elements from unpacked array UA (starting with UA[I]) to packed array PA (starting with PA[1]). The procedure (call) statement

```
Unpack (PA, UA, I)
```

copies elements from packed array PA (starting with PA[1]) to unpacked array UA (starting with UA[I]). Arrays PA and UA do not have to be the same size.

Conformant Array Parameters

One of the principal frustrations in using earlier versions of Pascal is that a function or procedure that manipulates an array of one type cannot also manipulate an array of a similar type. For example, a procedure that manipulates array Name declared below cannot manipulate array Flower because the arrays have different types.

```
type
    String1 = packed array [1..20] of Char;
    String2 = packed array [1..8] of Char;

var
    Name : String1;
    Flower : String2;
```

Even though the only difference between these two arrays is their size (number of elements), separate procedures would have to be written to read data into them.

In later versions of Pascal, the *conformant array schema*

```
packed array [U..V : Integer] of Char
```

describes a packed array of characters whose subscript type is a subrange of type Integer. The use of this schema in the procedure header below enables procedure ReadString to read data into a packed array of characters (represented by InString) of any size (represented by Size).

```
procedure ReadString (Size {input : INTEGER;
    var InString {output} : packed array [U..V : Integer] of CHAR);
```

The procedure call statement

```
ReadString (20, Name)
```

could be used to read up to twenty characters into array Name; the procedure call statement

```
ReadString (8, FLOWER)
```

could be used to read up to eight characters into array Flower.

Any identifiers can be used in the declaration of the index-type specification [U..V : Integer] for InString. The data type listed (Integer) must be an ordinal type.

Conformant array schemas can be used with packed and unpacked arrays of any element type, not just Char. Conformant array schemas can also be used with multidimensional arrays. The two-dimensional conformant array schema below is valid if Month is declared as an enumerated type.

```
array [U..V : Integer; J..K : Month] of Real;
```

The corresponding actual parameter must be a two dimensional array of type Real values. The first subscript type must be a subrange of the integers; the second subscript type must be a subrange of type Month.

Answers to Selected Self-Check Exercises

Chapter 1

Section 1.2

1. Contents: −27.2, 75.62.
   Memory cells: 998, 2.

Section 1.4

1. Add A, B, and C. Store the result in X.
   Divide Y by Z. Store the result in X.
   Subtract B from C and then add A. Store the result in D.
3. Assembly language; machine language

Section 1.5

1. A compiler attempts to translate a source file into machine language. If there are syntax errors, the compiler generates error messages. If there are no errors, it creates an object file. Syntax errors occur when statements do not follow exactly the syntax rules of the language. They are found in the source file.

Chapter 2

Section 2.1

1. It is not a good idea to use a standard identifier as the name of a memory cell because the identifier then cannot be used for its intended purpose.
   The compiler does not allow the use of reserved words as memory cell names.

Section 2.2

1. Because Pi never changes, it should be stored as a constant.
3. MyProgram and prog2 are valid Pascal identifiers.

Section 2.3

1. 0.0103   1234500.0   123450.0
3. Enter two integers:
   M = 10
   N = 21

Section 2.4

1. | Identifier | Before Execution | After Execution |
   | --- | --- | --- |
   | CentPerInch | 2.54 | 2.54 |
   | Inches | ? | 30.00 |
   | Cent | ? | 76.20 |

Section 2.5

1. `WriteLn` statements used to display prompts are placed before the `ReadLn` statements and are used in interactive programs. `WriteLn` statements that echo data are placed after the `ReadLn` statements and are used in batch programs.

Section 2.6

1. `WriteLn` causes the cursor to be advanced to the next line after the output is printed. If `Write` is used, the cursor remains positioned immediately after the last character printed. You would use `WriteLn` without an output list if you wanted to print a blank line or to advance the cursor to the start of the next line.

3. ```
   -15.5640
    -15.564
     -15.56
      -15.6
        -16
   -1.6E+01
   ```

Section 2.7

1. | 15 | , Integer | 'XYZ' | , Invalid | '*' | , Char |
   | --- | --- | --- | --- | --- | --- |
   | $ | , Invalid | 25.123 | , Real | 15. | , Invalid |
   | -999 | , Integer | .123 | , Invalid | 'x' | , Char |
   | ''x'' | , Invalid | '9' | , Char | Invalid | , Char |
   | True | , Boolean | 'True' | , Char | | |

Chapter 3

Section 3.1

1. Algorithm
   1. Put the baby's milk in the bottle.
   2. Put the bottle in a pan of water and heat on stove.
   3. Test the milk to see if it is the right temperature.
   4. Remove bottle from stove when it is the correct temperature.

   Step 3 Refinement
   3.1. Repeat step 3.2 until the milk is the right temperature.
      3.2 If it is too cold, put it back on the stove for a few minutes; if it is too warm, take it off the stove to cool for a few minutes.

Section 3.2

1. Problem Input
   Hours worked (Hours : Real)
   Hourly rate (Rate : Real)
   ```

Problem Outputs
    Gross salary (Salary : Real)

Algorithm
1. Enter hours worked and hourly rate.
2. Compute gross salary (Salary).
3. Print gross salary (Salary).

Section 3.3

1. The brackets are mismatched in the first example. The second example has an embedded comment, which is not allowed in Pascal.

Section 3.4

1.

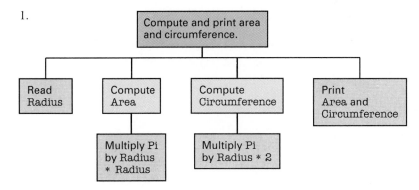

Section 3.6

1. Executing this program would display the message OH HIM vertically with three blank lines between words.

Chapter 4

Section 4.1

1. True, false, true, true

Section 4.2

1. a. 12.5
  b. 30.0

Section 4.3

1.
Case 1 (Both conditions are True. Data: MUD)

Program Statement	Ch1 ?	Ch2 ?	Ch3 ?	AlphaFirst ?	Effect
Write ('Enter three . . .')					Prints prompt.
ReadLn (Ch1, Ch2, Ch3)	M	U	D		Reads data.
if Ch1 < Ch2 then					Is 'M' < 'U'?
					Value is True.
AlphaFirst := Ch1				M	'M' is first so far.
if Ch3 < AlphaFirst then					Is 'D' < 'M' ?
					Value is True.
AlphaFirst := Ch3				D	'D' is first.
WriteLn (AlphaFirst . . .)					Prints D is the first letter . . ..

Case 2 (First condition is True, second is False. Data: COT)

Program Statement	Ch1 ?	Ch2 ?	Ch3 ?	AlphaFirst ?	Effect
Write ('Enter three . . .')					Prints prompt.
ReadLn (Ch1, Ch2, Ch3)	C	O	T		Reads data.
if Ch1 < Ch2 then					Is 'C' < 'O'?
					Value is True.
AlphaFirst := Ch1				C	'C' is first so far.
if Ch3 < AlphaFirst then					Is 'T' < 'C'?
					Value is False
WriteLn (AlphaFirst . . .					Prints C is the first letter . . ..

Case 3 (Both conditions are False. Data: TOP)

Program Statement	Ch1 ?	Ch2 ?	Ch3 ?	AlphaFirst ?	Effect
Write ('Enter three . . .')					Prints prompt.
ReadLn (Ch1, Ch2, Ch3)	T	O	P		Reads data.
if Ch1 < Ch2 then					Is 'T' < 'O'?
					Value is False.
AlphaFirst := Ch2				O	'O' is first so far.
if Ch3 < AlphaFirst then					Is 'P' < 'O'?
					Value is False.
WriteLn (AlphaFirst . . .					Prints O is the first letter . . ..

Both conditions evaluate to False if all three letters are the same.

Section 4.4

1. Initial Algorithm
   1. Display user instructions.
   2. Enter hours worked and hourly rate.
   3. Compute gross salary (including overtime pay).
   4. Compute net salary.
   5. Print gross salary and net salary.

   Step 3 Refinement

```
3.1 if Hours > MaxHours then
        begin
            3.2  Compute overtime pay
            3.3  Add overtime pay to base pay
        end
    else
            3.4 Compute gross salary
```

Section 4.5

1. A23B, Alc

Section 4.6

```
1. if X > Y then
     begin
       X := X + 10.0;
       WriteLn ('X Bigger')
     end
   else
       WriteLn ('X Smaller');
   WriteLn ('Y is ', Y);
```
3. Y would be printed only when X is not greater than Y.
5. The if statement, expression, simple expression, term, factor, variable, statement and assignment statement syntax diagrams would be used to validate this if statement. The syntax diagrams that describe elements of this statement are the expression and statement diagrams.

Section 4.7

1.

Statement Part	Salary	Tax	Effect
	13500.00	?	
if Salary < 0.0			13500.00 < 0.00 is False.
else if Salary < 1500.00			13500.00 < 1500.00 is False.
else if Salary < 3000.00			13500.00 < 3000.00 is False.
else if Salary < 5000.00			13500.00 < 5000.00 is False.
else if Salary < 8000.00			13500.00 < 8000.00 is False.

Statement Part	Salary	Tax	Effect
else if Salary <= 15000.00			13500.00 <= 15000.00 is True.
Tax := (Salary - 8000.00)			Evaluates to 5500.00.
* 0.25			Evaluates to 1375.00.
+ 1425.00		2800.00	Tax is 2800.00.

Chapter 5

Section 5.1

1. The loop body will be repeated three times.
   Output: 9
   ```
         81
         6561
   ```
3. The loop will execute forever (infinite loop) if the last statement in the loop body is omitted.

Section 5.2

1. The WriteLn prints a blank line between each employee's data.
3. 25
   125
   625
   3125

Section 5.3

1. 0
3. Output with data value of 9.45:

   ```
   Enter initial distance between worm and apple: 9.45
   The distance is 9.45
   The distance is 4.72
   The distance is 2.36
   The distance is 1.18
   The distance is 0.59

   Final distance between the worm and apple is 0.30
   The worm enters the apple.
   ```

   Output with data value of 9.45 and order of statements in loop body reversed:

   ```
   Enter initial distance between worm and apple: 9.45
   The distance is 4.72
   The distance is 2.36
   The distance is 1.18
   The distance is 0.59
   The distance is 0.30

   Final distance between the worm and apple is 0.30
   The worm enters the apple.
   ```

Section 5.4

1. a. `CountEmp` must be 0 just before the loop is entered.
   b. `CountEmp` must be 1 more during pass i than it was during pass i−1 (for i > 1).
   c. `CountEmp` must be between 1 and `NumberEmp` just after loop exit.

Section 5.5

1. ```
   {invariant:
        t during pass i is equal to DeltaT * (i-1) (for i > 1) and
        Height is equal to Tower - 0.5 * g * t * t}

   {assert:
        Height <= 0.0}
   ```

Section 5.6

1. The `else` condition will always be executed if the user enters something other than an F or a V. You can correct this problem by using a `while` loop that continually prompts the user for a letter until either an F or a V is entered.

Chapter 6

Section 6.1

1. Parameters make procedures versatile by enabling them to manipulate different data each time they are called.
3. Output: `5 cubed is 125`
   M would still have the value of 5 after procedure `Cube` executed. It should be declared as an integer in the calling program or procedure.

Section 6.2

1.

X	Y	Z
5	3	8
5	3	8
11	3	8
16	3	8
16	6	8

Section 6.3

1.

Actual Parameter	Formal Parameter	Description
M	A	Integer, value
MaxInt	B	Integer, value
Y	C	Real, variable
X	D	Real, variable
Next	E	Char, variable
35	A	Integer, value
M * 10	B	Integer, value
   ```

Actual Parameter	Formal Parameter	Description
Y	C	Real, variable
X	D	Real, variable
Next	E	Char, variable

3. a. Type Real of Z does not correspond to type Integer of formal parameter X.
   b. Procedure call is correct.
   c. Procedure call is correct.
   d. Type Integer of M does not correspond to type Real of formal parameter A.
   e. 25.0 and 15.0 cannot correspond to variable parameters.
   f. Procedure call is correct.
   g. Parameter names A and B have not been declared in the main program.
   h. Procedure call is correct.
   i. Expressions (X + Y) and (Y – Z) may not correspond to a variable parameter.
   j. Type Real of actual parameter X does not correspond with type Integer of formal parameter X.
   k. Four actual parameters are one too many for three formal parameters.
   l. Procedure call is correct.

Section 6.4

1. The if statement in FindTax is preferable because it allows FindTax to be highly cohesive. That is, FindTax performs only one function and passes on the result to the calling program that handles the error condition.

Section 6.5

1.

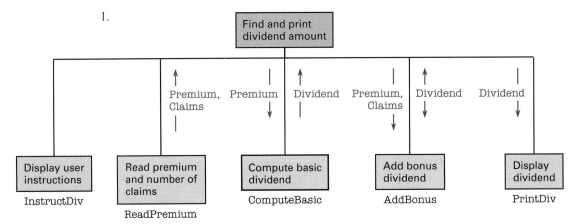

```
procedure ReadPremium (var Premium, Claims {output} : Real);

{Read number of premiums and Claims}

begin {ReadPremium}
  {Enter Premium and Claims}
  Write ('Premium amount > $');
```

```
    ReadLn (Premium);
    Write ('Number of claims> ');
    ReadLn (Claims)
  end; {ReadPremium}


  procedure ComputeBasic (Premium {input} : Real;
                          var Dividend {output} : Real);

  {Compute basic dividend}

  begin {ComputeBasic}
    Dividend := Premium * FixedRate
  end; {ComputeBasic}


  procedure AddBonus (Premium, Claims {input} : Real;
                      var Dividend {input/output} : Real);

  {Add bonus dividend for zero claims}

  begin {AddBonus}
    if Claims = 0.0 then
      Dividend := Dividend + (Premium * BonusRate)
  end; {AddBonus}


  procedure PrintDiv (Dividend {input} : Real);

  {Print dividend value}

  begin {PrintDiv}
    WriteLn ('Total dividend is $', Dividend :12:2)
  end; {PrintDiv}
```

3.
Case 1 (Num1 = 8.0, Num2 = 10.0, Num3 = 6.0)

Statement	X	Y	Temp	Effect
Order (Num3, Num2) if X > Y	6.0	10.0	?	Call procedure Order. Is 6.0 > 10.0? Value is False.
Order (Num3, Num1) if X > Y	6.0	8.0	?	Call procedure Order. Is 6.0 > 8.0? Value is False.
Order (Num2, Num1) if X > Y	10.0	8.0	?	Call procedure Order. Is 10.0 > 8.0? Value is True.
Temp := X			10.0	Set Temp to 10.0.
X := Y	8.0			Set X to 8.0.
Y := Temp		10.0		Set Y to 10.0.

Result: Num1 = 10.0, Num2 = 8.0, Num3 = 6.0

Section 6.6

1. The scope of variable N declared in Outer is procedure Outer. The main program body and procedure Too are not included in the scope of N. Inner is excluded because N is declared as a local variable in Inner.

3. For Outer: Parameter X is set to 5.5; global variable Y is set to 6.6; local variables M and N are set to 2 and 3, respectively; identifier O is undeclared.
   For Too and Nested: Global variables X and Y are set to 5.5 and 6.6, respectively; identifiers M, N, and O are undeclared.

5. If X is the actual parameter, the values of W, X, and Y are 5.5, 6.0 and 4.0, respectively. If Y is the actual parameter, the values of W, X, and Y are 5.5, 2.0, and 7.0, respectively. If the formal parameter is a value parameter, the values of W, X, and Y are 5.5, 2.0, and 4.0, respectively.

Chapter 7

Section 7.1

1. Valid constants: MinInt = -MaxInt;
                       MaxLetter = 'Z';
                       MaxSize = 50;

Section 7.2

1. If Base is 2 instead of base 10, a binary number is printed in reverse. When Base is 2, PrintDigits(23) displays the binary digits 1, 1, 1, 0, 1 (the binary number 10111 has the decimal value 23); PrintDigits(64) displays the binary digits 0, 0, 0, 0, 0, 0, 1 (the binary number 1000000 has the decimal value 64).
   When Base is 8, PrintDigits(23) displays 7, 2 (the octal number 27 has the decimal value 23); PrintDigits(64) displays 0, 0, 1 (the octal number 100 has the decimal value 64).

3. a. 3 b. -3 c. invalid, Real operand for mod d. -3.14159 e. invalid use of Integer division operator with Real operands f. 0.75 g. invalid assignment of Integer expression to Real variable h. invalid, division by 0 i. invalid, negative divisor for mod j. 3 k. -3.0 l. invalid assignment of Real expression to Integer variable m. invalid Real operand for div operator n. 0; o. 1 p. invalid, division by 0 q. 3

5. a. White is 1.6666... b. Green is 0.6666... c. Orange is 0 d. Blue is +3.0 e. Lime is 2 f. Purple is 0.666...

Section 7.3

1. a. Sqrt (U + V) * Sqr (W)
   b. Ln (X * Y)
   c. Sqrt (Sqr (X - Y))
   d. Abs ((X * Y) - (W / Z))

Section 7.4

1. True   4.0   2.0   3.0   2.0
   not (Flag or ((Y + Z) >= (X - Z)))

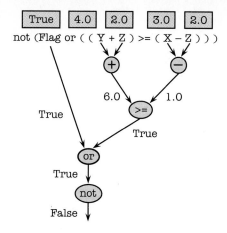

not (Flag or ((Y + Z) >= (X − Z)))

Section 7.5

1. a. 1   b. False   c. True   d. 1

Section 7.7

1. Invalid subranges: f, g, h, i, j

Section 7.8

1. a. No constraints b. No way to avoid the error c. No constraints d. J > 0 e. Not valid
   - Real result f. J >= 0 g. Not valid; expression is Real

Chapter 8

Section 8.1

1. The five phases of the software life cycle are (1) requirements specification, (2) design,
   (3) coding and debugging, (4) testing, and (5) operation and maintenance.
   The last phase, operation and maintenance, extends for the longest time.

Section 8.4

1. a. 1 b. 4 c. False d. Thursday e. Thursday f. Friday g. Wednesday h. True i. undefined
   j. 2
3.
```
type
   Month = (January, February, March, April, May, June, July,
            August, September, October, November, December);

var
   CurMonth : Month;

   . . .

   if CurMonth = January then
      WriteLn ('Happy new year')
   else if CurMonth = June then
      WriteLn ('Summer begins')
```

```
      else if CurMonth = September then
        WriteLn ('Back to school')
      else if CurMonth = December then
        WriteLn ('Happy Holidays');
```

Section 8.5

1. Specifications for data type `integer`
   Elements: The elements are integer numbers whose range depends on the number of bits used for storage. The standard identifier `MaxInt` can be used to determine this range on any system: it will always be between $-MaxInt - 1$ and `MaxInt`, inclusive.
   Operators: The assignment operator is `:=`. The logical operators, not, and, and or, take Boolean operands. The relational operators are =, <>, <, >, <=, and >=. The functions `Ord`, `Pred`, and `Succ` can be used with type `Boolean` arguments. Also, type `Integer` arguments. Also, procedures `Read`, `ReadLn`, `Write`, and `WriteLn` can be called with type `Integer` parameters.

   Specifications for data type `Char`
   Elements: The elements are any single-character values enclosed in single quotation marks (e.g., `'A'`) when written in a Pascal statement; quotation marks are not used, however, when type `Char` data are entered at a terminal or from an input file.
   Also, procedures `Read`, `ReadLn`, `Write`, and `WriteLn` can be called with type `Char` parameters.

   Specifications for data type `Boolean`
   Elements: Only two values are associated with this data type, `True` and `False`.
   Operators: The assignment operator is `:=`. The logical operators, not, and, and or, functions `Ord`, `Pred`, and `Succ` can be used with type `Boolean` arguments. Also, procedures `Write` and `WriteLn` can be called with type `Boolean` parameters.

Section 8.7

1.
X	N	C
a. 3.145	123	'3'
b. 3.145	123	' '
c. 3.145	123	'X'
d. ?	123	'3'
e. 123.0	5	'3'
f. 3.145	23	'3'
g. 3.145	35	'3'
h. 3.145	35	'Z'
i. 3.145	123	'Z'

Chapter 9

Section 9.1

```
1. if X > Y then
     WriteLn ('X' greater')
   else
     WriteLn ('Y greater or equal');
```

Section 9.2

1. a. Valid; 1, 2, 3, 4, 5
   b. Valid; '1', '2', '3', '4', '5'
   c. Invalid; mixed types
   d. Valid; '1', '3', 'A', 'B', 'C'

Section 9.3

1.
a.

Program Statement	i ?	J ?	Effect
J := 10		10	Set J to 10.

for i := 1 to 5 do
  WriteLn (i, J)
  J := J - 2
	1	8	Initialize i to 1.
			Display 1 and 10.
			Assign 10 - 2 to J.

increment and test i
  WriteLn (i, J)
  J := J - 2
	2	6	2 <= 5 is True.
			Display 2 and 8.
			Assign 8 - 2 to J.

increment and test i
  WriteLn (i, J)
  J := J - 2
	3	4	3 <= 5 is True.
			Display 3 and 6.
			Assign 6 - 2 to J.

increment and test i
  WriteLn (i, J)
  J := J - 2
	4	2	4 <= 5 is True.
			Display 4 and 4.
			Assign 4 - 2 to J.

increment and test i
  WriteLn (i, J)
  J := J - 2
	5	0	5 <= 5 is True.
			Display 5 and 2.
			Assign 2 - 2 to J.

increment and test i	?		Exit loop.

Section 9.4

1. a. (X > Y) or (X = 15)
   b. ((X > Y) or (X = 15)) and (Z <> 7.5)
   c. (X = 15) and ((Z <> 7.5) or (X > Y))
   d. not Flag and (X = 15.7)
   e. Flag or not (NextCh in ['A' .. 'H'])

Section 9.5

1. a.
```
*
**
***
****
*****
```

   b.
```
***
***
***
***
***
```

Section 9.6

1. This function will not return any value to the function name and has the side effect of changing X and Y to the absolute values of X and Y. There is no need for the parameter Result, because a function always returns a single value. The function declaration should be

   ```
   function MyTest (X, Y : Real) : Real;
   ```
   and the second-to-last line should be
   ```
   MyTest := Sqrt(X) + Sqrt (Y)
   ```

Section 9.7

1.
```
Tens := TwoDigitNum div 10;
Units := TwoDigitNum mod 10;
```

```
Ex:   TwoDigitNum = 87
      Tens = 87 div 10 = 8
      Units = 87 mod 10 = 7
Ex:   TwoDigitNum = 20
      Tens = 20 div 10 = 2
      Units = 20 mod 10 = 0
```

```
CheckPennies := Round(CentsPerDollar * Amount);
Dollars := CheckPennies div CentsPerDollar;
Cents := CheckPennies mod CentsPerDollar;
```

```
Ex:   Amount = 36.92
      CheckPennies = Round(100 * 36.92) = Round(3692.00) = 3692
      Dollars = 3692 div 100 = 36
      Cents = 3692 mod 100 = 92
```

```
Ex:   Amount = 94.13
      CheckPennies = Round(100 * 94.13) = Round(9413.00) = 9413
      Dollars = 9413 div 100 = 94
      Cents = 9413 mod 100 = 13
```

Chapter 10

Section 10.1

1. X3 is a simple variable, whereas X[3] refers to the third element of the array named X.

3. a. ```
   type
       RealArray = array [Boolean] of Real;

   var
       N : RealArray;
   ```

   b. ```
   type
       IntArray = array ['A'..'F'] of Integer;

   var
       N : IntArray;
   ```

   c. ```
   type
       BoolArray = array [Char] of Boolean;

   var
       Flags : BoolArray;
   ```

   d. Invalid array

   e. ```
   type
       RealArray = array [Char] of Real;

   var
       X : RealArray;
   ```

   f. Invalid array

   g. ```
   type
       Day = (Sun, Mon, Tues, Wed, Thurs, Fri, Sat);
       RealArray = array [Day] of Real;

   var
       Y : RealArray;
   ```

# Section 10.2

1. No
3. a. ```
   X[3] := 7.0;
   ```
   b. ```
   X[1] := X[5];
   ```
   c. ```
   X[5] := X[4] - X[1];
   ```
   d. ```
   X[6] := X[6] + 2;
   ```
   e. ```
   Sum := 0;
   for I := 1 to 5 do
     Sum := Sum + X[I];
   ```

   f. ```
   for I := 1 to 6 do
     AnswerArray[I] := X[I] * 2;
   ```

   g. ```
   I := 2;
   while I <= 8 do
     begin
       Write (X[I] :8);
       I := I + 2
     end; {while}
   ```

Section 10.3

1. The user will be continually prompted to choose a category until a valid one is entered.

Section 10.4

1. It is better to pass the entire array of data rather than individual elements if several elements of the array are being manipulated by a procedure.
3. I is equal to MaxSize if both arrays are the same; I is equal to 3 if the third elements do not match.

Section 10.5

1. The while loop that calls EnterInt is exited when MaxSize is reached.
3. repeat
```
  {invariant:
      No prior value read is Sentinel and
      ClassSize <= MaxSize
  }
  EnterInt (Sentinel, MaxScore, TempScore);
  if TempScore <> Sentinel then
    begin
      ClassSize := ClassSize + 1;        {Increment ClassSize}
      Scores[ClassSize] := TempScore     {Save the score}
    end {if}
until (TempScore = Sentinel) or (ClassSize = MaxSize);
```

The repeat-until loop necessitates that you check twice to see whether the sentinel value has been entered, whereas it is necessary to check only once with the while loop. A for loop cannot be used in this situation because we do not know in advance how many data items are going to be entered.

Section 10.6

1. a. An array of characters with twenty elements and subscripts of one to twenty
   b. An array of Boolean type values with ten elements and subscripts of the digit characters '0' to '9'
   c. An array of real numbers with eleven elements and subscripts of the integers –5 to 5
   d. An array of characters with two elements and subscripts of False and True
3. Program Cryptogram checks to see that a letter is in the set ['A' .. 'Z'] before encoding it. Because commas and blanks are not members of this set, they are not encoded.

Section 10.7

1. The length of the string must be the same as the length of the packed array to be assignment compatible. The string can be padded out with blanks if it is too short.

Section 10.8

1. The number of characters used to display each string is determined by its length (e.g., Company :CompLen); consequently, only the characters actually read in are displayed, not the blank padding.

Chapter 11

Section 11.1

```
1. const
     StrLength = 20;

   type
     StringType = packed array [1..StrLength] of Char;
     Part = record
                PartNum : Integer;
                Name : StringType;
                Quantity : Integer;
                Price : Real
            end; {Part}
```

Section 11.2

```
1. with Clerk do
     begin
       WriteLn ('ID: ', ID);
       WriteLn ('Name: ', Name);
       Write ('Sex: ');
       case Sex of
         Female : WriteLn ('Female');
         Male   : WriteLn ('Male')
       end; {case}
       WriteLn ('Number of Dependents: ', NumDepend);
       WriteLn ('Hourly Rate: ', Rate :4:2);
       WriteLn ('Taxable Salary: ', TaxSal :4:2)
     end; {with}
```

Section 11.3

```
1. type
     ExamStats = record
                    Low, High : 0..100;
                    Average, StandardDev : Real
                 end; {ExamStats}

   var
     Exam1, Exam2 : ExamStats;
```

This program segment prints the statistics for Exam1, copies Exam1 into Exam2, modifies the High field of Exam2, and finally prints new statistics for Exam2.

Section 11.4

```
1. (8.50, −1.50)
   (7.00, 10.00)
   12.21
```

Section 11.5

1. NewAddress must be type Address.

Section 11.6

1. Married: 22 bytes
   Divorced: 6 bytes
   Single: 1 byte

Section 11.7

1.
```
program Geometry (Input, Output);

{Finds perimeters and areas of various kinds of figures.}

    type
       FigKind = (Circle, Rectangle, Square, Triangle, Other);
       Figure = record
                   Area, Perimeter : Real;
                case Shape : FigKind of
                   Circle    : (Radius : Real);
                   Rectangle : (Width, Height : Real);
                   Square    : (Side : Real);
                   Triangle  : (Sidel, Side2, Angle : Real);
                   Other     : ()
                end; {Figure}
     var
        MyFig : Figure;                          {a figure}
  begin {Geometry}
    GetFigure (MyFig);
    ReadFigure (MyFig);
    ComputeArea (MyFig);
    ComputePerim (MyFig);
    DisplayFig (MyFig)
  end. {Geometry}
```

The case label `Triangle` should be added to the `case` statement in each procedure
of the operator procedures. The computations for the area and the perimeter of a
triangle should be added alongside this `case` label where appropriate.

Chapter 12

Section 12.1

1.
```
type
   Day = (Sun, Mon, Tues, Wed, Thurs, Fri, Sat);
   AnArray = array ['A'..'F', 1..10, Day] of Real;
```
An array of this type can hold 420 elements (6 * 10 * 7).

Section 12.2

1.
```
type
   Class = (Mathl, Algebra, Geometry, Algebra2,
             Trigonometry, Calculus);
   Sex = (Male, Female);
   MathClassArray = array [Class, 10..12, Sex] of Integer;
var
   MathInfo : MathClassArray;
```

This array would have thirty-six elements (6 * 3 * 2).

Section 12.3

1. TempYear is needed in EnterSales to enable use of procedure EnterInt. This is because EnterInt has an Integer as its formal variable argument and Sales.First is type YearRange. A compilation error would result from trying to read Sales.First directly.

Section 12.4

1. a. 1
   d. Austin, Tracy
   f. D

3. It takes the same amount of space to store an array of records as it does to store parallel arrays.

Section 12.5

1. c. 80AJoe Costa
   d. 3
   h. o
   i. Joe Costa

Section 12.6

1. After exiting the loop, the if statement would return the location of the last element if the last student matches the target name. Using the condition CurStu <= NumStu causes an array out of bound error if the condition Class[CurStu].Name <> Stuname is evaluated when CurStu is equal to MaxClass + 1.

Section 12.7

1.

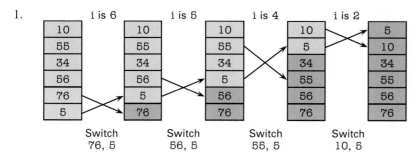

Fifteen comparisons and four exchanges were made.

3. Only switching the score fields would destroy the data. A student's name would be associated with an arbitrary score rather than with his or her own score.

5. If the last value in the subarray is also the largest value in the subarray, no exchange is performed when we start the scan at the last element. If we start the scan at the first element and there is a duplicate of the last value in the array, an exchange is performed.

Chapter 13

Section 13.1

1. a. [1,3,4,5,6,7] b. [1,2,3,5,7] c. [1,2,3,4,5,6,7] d. True e. True f. False g.
[1,2,3,5,7] h. [2] i. [] j. False k. True l. True

Section 13.2

1. The ReadLn advances to the start of the next data line after all the values for one
picture row have been read. The WriteLn advances the cursor to the next screen
line.

Section 13.3

1. a. Store 'Abra' in Templ; current length is 4.
    b. Store 'cadabra' in Temp2; current length is 7.
    c. Store 'Abracadabra' in Magic; current length is 11.
    d. Return 11.
    e. Store 'Abracada' in HisMagic; current length is 8.
    f. Change HisMagic to 'Abrda'; current length is 5.
    g. Change HisMagic to 'AbAbrarda'; current length is 9.
    h. Return 5.
    i. Return 'a'.
    j. Change Templ to 'abra'
    k. Return 8.
3. Comma := MakeString (',   ');
    PosComma := Pos (Comma, Source);
    Copy (Source, 1, PosComma-1, Target);
    Copy (Source, PosComma+2, Capacity-PosComma-1, Destin);

Section 13.5

1. Concat copies as many characters as will fit in the new string. It is not flagged as an
error.
3. ReadLnString (InFile, Capacity, InString.Contents, InString.Len);

Chapter 14

Section 14.1

1. Change the while loop body as follows:

```
while not EOF(InData) do
   begin
      ReadLnString (InFile, StrLength, InString, Len);
      WriteLn (OutFile, InString :Len)
   end; {while}
```

InString is type StringType (maximum length of StrLength), and Len is a type
Integer variable.
3. It reads in the first three characters of each line of file InData and displays them on
a separate output line. If a line contains fewer than three characters, it reads the

<eoln> at the end of the line and displays it as a blank. It then skips the next line of data.

Section 14.2

1. Vowels and consonants are stored in sets named Vowels and Consonants. The main program calls PrintSet to display them.

Section 14.3

1. It requires 24 bytes to store six numbers in a binary file and 24 bytes in a text file using format specification :4:2. Each number that is larger than 9.99, requires more than four bytes and increases the storage requirements for the text file.

Section 14.4

1. Forty-eight bytes for each record of type Book. 8 bytes for an Employee record.

3.
```
type
    ScoreArray = array [1..5] of Integer;
    Student = record
                ID : Integer;
                Scores : ScoreArray
              end;
    StudentFile = File of Student;

  var
    StuFile : StudentFile;
    NextStu : Student;

begin
  Reset (StuFile);
  while not EOF(StuFile) do
    begin
      Read (StuFile, NextStu);
      WriteLn (Output, NextStu.ID, NextStu.Scores[1])
    end; {while}
```

Section 14.5

1. The file types are the same, all records are in order by stock number in each file, and both files have a sentinel record at the end. They do not need to have the same number of records.

Section 14.6

1.

Question	Stock	Author	Title	Price	Quantity
2	1111..9999	'AAA'..'zzz'	'AAA'...'zzz'	5.95–8.0	1..5000
3	1111..9999	'AAA'..'zzz'	'Pascal ...'	0–1000.00	0..5000
4	1111..9999	'AAA'..'zzz'	'AAA'...'zzz'	25–1000.0	11..5000

3. Only books whose stock numbers qualify are passed to function Match. The Boolean variable Matched has the value of the expression

```
Matched := (LowAuthor <= Author) and (Author <= HighAuthor) and
           (LowTitle <= Title) and (Title <= HighTitle) and ...
```

Chapter 15

Section 15.1

1.

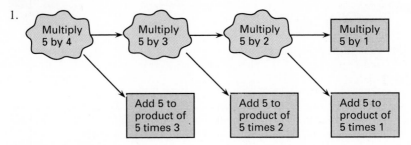

Section 15.2

1. The actual parameter in the recursive call Palindrome (N–1) is an expression and must, therefore, correspond to a formal parameter that is a value parameter.

3.

	M		N		Result
Multiply (5, 4)	M	5	N	4	?
Multiply (5, 3)	M	5,5	N	4,3	?
Multiply (5, 2)	M	5,5,5	N	4,3,2	?
Multiply (5, 1)	M	5,5,5,5	N	4,3,2,1	?
return from (5, 1)	M	5,5,5	N	4,3,2	5
return from (5, 2)	M	5,5	N	4,3	10
return from (5, 3)	M	5	N	4	15
return from (5, 4)	M		N		20

Section 15.3

1.

```
function PowerRaiser (Base, Power : Integer) : Integer;
begin
  if Power = 1 then
    PowerRaiser := Base
  else
    PowerRaiser := Power * PowerRaiser (Base, Power–1)
end; {PowerRaiser}
```

3. The recursion would go on forever. When N is 2, a recursive call to Fibonacci(0) results. This causes calls to Fibonacci(–1), Fibonacci(–2), and so on.

Section 15.4

1.

X is 5, 8, 10, 1.	→	X is 5, 8, 1, 10.	→	X is 5, 1, 8, 10.
N is 4.		N is 3.		N is 2.
X becomes 5, 8, 1, 10.		X becomes 5, 1, 8, 10.		X becomes 1, 5, 8, 10.
SelectSort(X, 3)		SelectSort(X, 2)		SelectSort(X, 1)

For the last frame (not shown) N is 1, so an immediate return occurs.

Section 15.5

1. $2^6 - 1$, or 63

1.

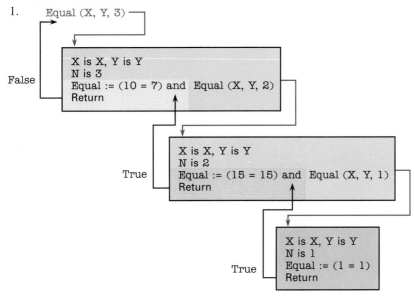

$$\text{Equal} := (X[3] = Y[3]) \text{ and } (X[2] = Y[2]) \text{ and } (X[1] = Y[1])$$

Section 15.7

1.

BlobCount(1,1); Grid[X,Y] is empty so 0 is returned.

BlobCount(1,2) has the value of the expression:
1 + BlobCount(0,3) + BlobCount(1,3) + BlobCount(2,3) +
   BlobCount(2,2) + BlobCount(2,1) + BlobCount(1,1) +
   BlobCount(0,1) + BlobCount(0,2)

An immediate return occurs with a value of 0 for all function designators except
BlobCount(2,1).

BlobCount(2,1) has the value of the expression:
1 + BlobCount(1,2) + BlobCount(2,2) + BlobCount(3,2) +
   BlobCount(3,1) + BlobCount(3,0) + BlobCount(2,0) +
   BlobCount(1,0) + BlobCount(1,1)

An immediate return with a value of 0 occurs for each function designator, so
BlobCount(2,1) returns 1 and BlobCount(1,2) returns 1 + 1, or 2.

Chapter 16

Section 16.1

1.
2+C/$	Success is True.
2+C/$-	Success is True.
2+C/$	NextCh is '-'; Success is True.
2+C/$	NextCh is '$'; Success is True.

```
IsEmpty returns False.
IsFull returns False.
```

Section 16.2

1. First expression:

```
| ({
| ({[
| ({        Open is '[', Close is ']', Balanced is True
| (         Open is '{', Close is '}', Balanced is True
|           Open is '(', Close is ')', Balanced is True
|
| (
|           Open is '(', Close is ')', Balanced is True
```

Second expression:

```
| . . .
| ({[
| ({        Open is '[', Close is '}', Balanced is False
```

Section 16.3

1.

Expression	OpStack	NextCh	NewOp	Result
4 5 6 * 3 / + ^	|4	'4'	4	
4 5 6 * 3 / + ^	|4 5	'5'	5	
4 5 6 * 3 / + ^	|4 5 6	'6'	6	
4 5 6 * 3 / + ^	|4 30	'*'		30
4 5 6 * 3 / + ^	|4 30 3	'3'	3	
4 5 6 * 3 / + ^	|4 10	'/'		10
4 5 6 * 3 / + ^	|14	'+'		14

Section 16.4

```
1. const
     MaxStack = 50;
     StringLen = 20;

   type
     StringType = packed array [1..20] of Char;
     Student = record
                 Name : StringType;
                 Score : Integer;
                 Grade : Char
               end; {Student}

   StackElement = Student;
```
Yes, the stack operators can be used.

1.

Watson	Dietz
Business	Economy
1	3

   ↑   ↑

  Front   Rear

Section 16.6

1. `Q.Front` is 2, `Q.Rear` is 3, and `Q.Items[1..3]` are `'Brown'`, `'Watson'`, `'Dietz'`, respectively.

Chapter 17

Section 17.1

1. a. The string `'CA'` is stored in the `Current` field of the record pointed to by R.
   b. The record pointed to by R is copied into the record pointed to by P.
   c. Illegal; `P.Current` should be written as `P^.Current`.
   d. Illegal; P cannot be assigned an integer value.
   e. The integer 0 is stored in the `Volts` field of the record pointed to by the `Link` field of the record pointed to by R.
   f. Pointer P is reset to point to the same record as pointer R.
   g. The string `'XY'` is stored in the `Current` field of the third record, where the first record is pointed to by R. This is equivalent to `Q^.Current := 'XY'`.
   h. The `Volts` field of the record pointed to by R is copied into the `Volts` field of the record pointed to by Q.

Section 17.3

1. AC   115
   DC   12

Section 17.4

1. When `Target` is `'Boy'`, `Head` points to nodes containing `'Hat'` and `'Boy'`, `Found` is set to `True`, and pointer to `'Boy'` is returned. When `Target` is `'Cap'` or `'Dog'`, `Head` points to nodes containing `'Hat'`, `'Boy'`, `'Cat'`; final value of `Head` is `nil`. This value is returned.

Section 17.5

1. Heap management is performed by the Pascal system. It determines when there are no cells available on the heap.
3. We should not have to change a client program just because the stack internal representation has changed. These details are hidden from a client program.

Section 17.6

1. It inserts a new stack element (Johnson, Economy class, 5) at the rear of the queue.
3. Because the queue is a circular queue, it "moves" the element formerly at the front of the queue to the rear of the queue. The second element placed in the queue moves to the front of the queue.

Chapter 18

Section 18.2

1. The first three calls to Insert would build the ordered list of integers, 3000, 4000, 5000, pointed to by MyList. The second request to insert 4000 returns False in Success. The call to Delete changes MyList to the 2-element list 3000, 5000. The program output is as follows:

```
O.K.
3000
5000
Number of elements is 2
```

Section 18.3

1. We could eliminate the call to Locate which searches for ElKey and simply insert ElKey as long as it was in range.
   The node with the duplicate key would be inserted before the first existing list node with that key.

Section 18.4

1.
   Word in left child < word in tree root < word in right child.
   All words in the left subtree are less than the word in the root, and all words in the right subtree are greater.
3. Inserting parentheses according to the algebraic rules for expression evaluation gives us the following two expressions and trees.

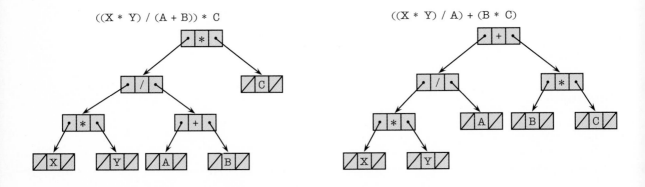

$((X * Y) / (A + B)) * C$

$((X * Y) / A) + (B * C)$

1. The three forms follow. The parentheses would not appear in the infix forms.

Infix	Prefix	Postfix
X * Y / (A + B) * C	* / * X Y + A B C	X Y * A B + / C *
X * Y / A + B * C	+ / * X Y A * B C	X Y * A / B C * +

3. Inorder: BDCA–X+Y
   Preorder: ABCD–+XY
   Postorder: DCBXY+–A

Chapter 19

Section 19.1

1.

First Call			Second Call			Third Call			Fourth Call		
First	Last	Middle	First	Last	Middle	First	Last	Middle	First	Last	Middle
1	9	5	1	4	2	3	4	3	4	4	4

The result is 4.

Section 19.2

1.
```
'SAL', Hash is (32 mod 10) + 1 = 3, stored at Class[3]
'BIL', Hash is (23 mod 10) + 1 = 4, stored at Class[4]
'JIL', Hash is (31 mod 10) + 1 = 2, stored at Class[2]
'LIB', Hash is (23 mod 10) + 1 = 4, stored at Class[5]
'HAL', Hash is (21 mod 10) + 1 = 2, stored at Class[6]
'ROB', Hash is (35 mod 10) + 1 = 6, stored at Class[7]
```
3. Change the first statement in the while loop body to

   Index := (Index + Sqr(Probe)) mod MaxSlots

Section 19.4

1. Change the if statement to
```
if Class[First].Score < Class[First+1].Score then
  begin {exchange}
```
Change the if statement to
```
if (Class[First].Grade > Class[First+1].Grade)
   or ((Class[First].Grade = Class[First+1].Grade) and
      (Class[First].Name > Class[First+1].Name)) then
      begin {exchange}
```

1. 40	35	80	75	60	90	70	75	Pass	Comparison	Exchange
35	40	75	60	80	70	75	90	1	7	5
35	40	60	75	70	75	80	90	2	6	3
35	40	60	70	75	75	80	90	3	5	1
35	40	60	70	75	75	80	90	4	4	0
								Total	22	9

Section 19.5

1. 40	35	80	75	60	90	70	75	Pass	Comparison	Exchange
35	40							1	1	2
35	40	80						2	1	1
35	40	75	80					3	2	2
35	40	60	75	80				4	3	3
35	40	60	75	80	90			5	1	1
35	40	60	70	75	80	90		6	4	4
35	40	60	70	75	75	80	90	7	3	3
								Total	15	16

Section 19.6

1. a. Bubble sort; would be sorted in one pass.
   b. Selection sort; array is inverted.
   c. Insertion sort; all elements except the last would be placed with one comparison.
   d. Insertion sort or selection sort; relatively random order.

Section 19.7

1. When doing a merge on two files or two arrays, you need a third file or a third array to store the result.

Index

Reference Guide to Pascal Constructs

(continued from inside front cover)

Construct	Page	Example of Use
function declaration	331	`function Member (NextCh : Char;`
formal parameters	164	`                    TestSet : GradeSet) : Boolean;`
		`{Returns True only if NextCh in TestSet}`
		`begin {Member}`
Boolean assignment	230	`  Member := NextCh in TestSet`
set operator in	309	
		`end; {Member}`
procedure declaration	162	`procedure PrintSet (InSet : GradeSet);`
		`{Displays set InSet}`
local variable	73	`  var`
		`    NextCh : Char; {loop control variable}`
		`begin {PrintSet}`
for statement	314	`  for NextCh := 'A' to 'Z'do`
if statement	87	`    if Member(NextCh, InSet) then`
function designator	332	
Write procedure	44	`      Write (NextCh);`
WriteLn procedure	34	`  WriteLn`
end of procedure	74	`end; {PrintSet}`
program body	36	`begin {Guide}`
WriteLn procedure	34	`  WriteLn ('Registration for ', School);`
assignment	30	`    CountProb := 0;                          {initialize counter}`
with statement	410	`  with CurStu do`
compound statement	103	`    begin                              {define fields of CurStu}`
string assignment	389	`      Name := 'Jackson, Michael Bad';`
display prompt	34	`      Write ('Enter GPA> ');`
ReadLn procedure	33	`      ReadLn (GPA);`
enumerated assign	268	`      InCollege := Arts;`
pointer assign	672	`      NextStu := nil`
		`    end; {with}`
case statement with	306	`case CurStu.InCollege of`
field selector as	408	`   Business : WriteLn ('Business major');`
case selector		`   Arts     : WriteLn ('Arts major');`
		`   Science  : WriteLn ('Science major');`
		`   General  : WriteLn ('General major')`
		`end; {case}`
nested if	106	`if CurStu.GPA > DeansList then`
embedded apostrophe	53	`   WriteLn ('  On the Dean''s List')`
		`else if CurStu.GPA > Probation then`
		`   WriteLn ('Satisfactory progress')`
		`else`
		`   begin`
format a string	47	`     WriteLn ('On Probation' :21);`
increment counter	119	`     CountProb := CountProb + 1`
		`   end; {nested if}`